Study Guide

West Federal Taxation
Comprehensive Volume
2007 EDITION

Eugene Willis, Ph.D., CPA

University of Illinois, Urbana-Champaign

William H. Hoffman, Jr., J.D., Ph.D., CPA

University of Houston

David M. Maloney, Ph.D., CPA

University of Virginia

William A. Raabe, Ph.D., CPA

The Ohio State University

Prepared by

David M. Maloney, Ph.D., CPA
University of Virginia

William A. Raabe, Ph.D., CPA
The Ohio State University

THOMSON
SOUTH-WESTERN

Australia · Brazil · Canada · Mexico · Singapore · Spain · United Kingdom · United States

THOMSON

SOUTH-WESTERN

Study Guide for
West Federal Taxation: Comprehensive Volume, 2007 Edition
Eugene Willis, William H. Hoffman, Jr., David M. Maloney, William A. Raabe

Prepared by David M. Maloney and William A. Raabe

VP/Editorial Director
Jack W. Calhoun

Publisher
Rob Dewey

Acquisitions Editor
Daniel Jones

Senior Developmental Editor
Craig Avery

Marketing Manager
Chris McNamee

Senior Production Project Manager
Tim Bailey

Manager of Technology, Editorial
Vicky True

Technology Project Editor
Kelly Reid

Ancillary Coordinator
Erin M. Donohoe

Manufacturing Coordinator
Doug Wilke

Art Director
Michelle Kunkler

Cover Images
© Getty Images, Inc.

Production Artist
Patti Hudepohl

Printer
Globus Printing
Minster, OH

For more information about our products, contact us at:

Thomson Learning Academic Resource Center

1-800-423-0563

Thomson Higher Education
5191 Natorp Boulevard
Mason, OH 45040
USA

CONTENTS

PREFACE

This *Study Guide* accompanies the 2007 edition of *West Federal Taxation: Comprehensive Volume.* The textbook is designed for a thorough one- or two-semester undergraduate or graduate course in federal taxation. Thus, because the scope of the text is quite broad, you will be required to digest a large amount of fairly complex information in a short period of time.

In recognition of the difficulty of such a task, this *Study Guide* was created. It offers you an additional review of the content of the text chapters in outline form, to allow a rapid perusal. Moreover, additional problems and exercises are contained in the *Study Guide* for review. These exercises are presented in a self-evaluation format, with the suggested solutions directly following the problem statements, so that you can receive immediate feedback as to the accuracy of your answers. In addition, to aid further study, the reference is provided for each solution to the appropriate section within the text where the relevant material is discussed. These problems take a number of different formats, including true and false, fill-in-the-blank, multiple choice, and short answers. We believe that this arrangement will maximize your understanding of the text material in a reasonable period of time.

It is important that you use this *Study Guide* as an *aid* to mastering the material in the textbook, and *not* as a replacement for it. We suggest that you incorporate the *Study Guide* into your regular study routine, perhaps by reviewing the Chapter Highlights after reading the text, and then working the *Study Guide* problems before attempting those assigned in the text.

We wish you the best of luck in your study of federal taxation and hope that this *Study Guide* will prove beneficial!

David M. Maloney
William A. Raabe
March 2006

Chapter 1

An Introduction to Taxation

CHAPTER HIGHLIGHTS

A proper analysis of the US tax system begins with an examination of historical principles that guide the development of the system, and with an investigation of the various motivations that underlie existing provisions of the tax law. This chapter also introduces the reader to important tax terminology.

I. History of US Taxation [p. 1-3]
    A. An income tax on individuals was used to provide financing for the Civil War. When the war ended, the tax was repealed. In 1894, a new individual income tax was enacted, but the Supreme Court held the tax to be unconstitutional. After a constitutional challenge to the taxation of income, the Sixteenth Amendment, which sanctioned both the federal individual and corporate income taxes, was ratified in 1913. The present income tax on individuals was enacted in 1913. A corporate income tax was adopted in 1909.

B. Revenue Acts, which rewrote completely the federal tax provisions, were enacted every year or two between 1913 and 1939. These provisions were reorganized and included, in a more permanent form, in the Internal Revenue Code of 1939. Thereafter, tax laws were changed when Congress adopted amendments to the 1939 Code; i.e., a complete rewriting of the laws was unnecessary. A revised Internal Revenue Code was adopted in 1954. The 1954 Code was the controlling body of the tax law until 1986. In 1986, Congress enacted the most comprehensive overhaul of the Internal Revenue Code in over thirty years. As a result of the massive changes contained in the new law, the federal tax code was renamed the Internal Revenue Code of 1986. Nevertheless, many of the provisions of the 1954 Code were carried over to the 1986 Code.

C.   In an effort to close various loopholes and to reduce a recurring budget deficit, changes in the tax law have been enacted nearly every year since 1986.

D.   One trend that has caused considerable concern is the increased complexity of the federal income tax laws, which imposes substantial taxpayer compliance costs. Congress has added to this complexity through frequent changes in the tax laws.

E.   Income tax collections from individuals and corporations constitute about half of all federal tax receipts. The FICA (Social Security) tax now constitutes over one-third of all federal tax receipts, while corporate income tax receipts have fallen drastically since the 1940s.

II.   Tax Terminology [The Tax Structure p. 1-5]

A.   Tax rates can be structured to yield a
1.   Proportional tax: The rate of tax remains constant over the tax base;
2.   Progressive tax: Tax rates increase as the tax base grows larger; or,
3.   Regressive tax: Tax rates decrease as the tax base grows larger.

B.   Taxes should be designed with
1.   Equality of tax treatment among taxpayers in similar circumstances;
2.   Convenience of collection, computation, and administration;
3.   Certainty in application, so that tax planning can occur; and,
4.   Economical administration, which requires only nominal collection costs by the government and involves minimal compliance costs on the part of the taxpayer.

C.   Types of taxes observed in recent history include
1.   *Ad valorem* taxes are taxes on wealth or capital. For instance, these taxes include the existing real property taxes and personal property taxes, presently favored by state and local governments. The real property tax features a high degree of taxpayer compliance, political manipulation of the assessment process, and

> **KEY TERMS**
>
> - Progressive/Regressive/ Proportional Tax Rates
> - Economic, Social, Equity, Political Motivations
> - IRS, Treasury Department
> - Income, Wealth, Excise, Employment Taxes

assessments based on appraisals, capitalization of attendant income, and actual purchase or construction costs. However, there is inconsistent taxpayer compliance relative to personal property taxes.

2.   Transaction taxes are levied on the transfer of property among taxpayers. Examples of transaction taxes include: excise taxes, sales and use taxes; death and gift taxes; severance taxes, and the value added tax (VAT). Excise taxes are levied by federal and state governments on the exchange of specified commodities, e.g., certain "luxury" items, oil, alcohol, and tobacco. Excise taxes are effective when consumers demonstrate a price-inelastic demand for the commodity.

Sales and use taxes, which are applied by state and local governments cover a multitude of transactions. Debate relative to this tax centers on the appropriate items, the sale of which will be subject to the tax. Death and gift taxes are levied by federal and state governments on lifetime or testamentary transfers of property to others. Severance taxes are imposed by some states on the extraction of natural resources. In the Common Market countries of Western Europe, the VAT has gained acceptance as a major source of revenue.

      3.   Income taxes are levied chiefly by federal and state governments on the annual incremental change in the taxpayer's wealth. Specific definitions relative to includible income, and allowable deductions, vary greatly among those governments that impose the tax. Most taxing jurisdictions attempt to ensure the collection of income taxes by requiring certain pay-as-you-go procedures.

      4.   Employment taxes include unemployment taxes, which finance state and federal unemployment compensation benefits, and retirement taxes, e.g., the federal FICA tax. These taxes are levied upon or collected by employers, and they provide some income security for employees. The FICA tax is paid equally by employer and employee; the FUTA tax is paid by only the employer. Debate relative to these taxes includes the proper definition of "employer" and "employee," and the desirable employment tax bases and rates.

      5.   Other taxes that are part of the U.S. tax system include federal custom duties and miscellaneous state and local taxes, e.g., franchise taxes, occupational taxes or license fees.

   D.   The responsibility for administering the federal tax laws rests with the Treasury Department.

      1.   The Internal Revenue Service (IRS) is part of the Treasury Department and is responsible for enforcing the tax law.

      2.   The IRS utilizes mathematical formulas and statistical sampling techniques to select tax returns for audit. However, due to budget constraints, the IRS audits only a small minority of returns.

      3.   A statute of limitations provides both parties to a tax a defense against "stale" claims. Generally, the IRS may assess additional tax liabilities against the taxpayer within three years of the filing of an income tax return. This three year time period is extended to six years for omissions of gross income in excess of 25% of that reported. NO statute of limitations protection is available with respect to fraudulent tax return positions

In a typical survey, taxpayers respond that about fifteen to twenty percent of all tax returns are audited. Actually, the rate is under one percent, although high-income, cash-business, and previously audited taxpayers certainly are subject to a higher rate. This looks like a good application of stratified sampling, but the IRS clearly has a public relations problem!

III.   Motivations Underlying Specific Tax Provisions [Understanding the Federal Tax Law p. 1-24]

   A.   Although the major objective of the federal tax law is to raise revenue, economic, social, equity, and political considerations play a significant role in the design of specific tax provisions.

B.   Economic considerations, including a stimulation or temperance of the national economy, and encouragement or discouragement of specific activities or industries, have led to a large number of recent amendments to the Code. Examples of such economic considerations include:

      1.   ACRS depreciation, to encourage expenditures on long-lived productive assets, such as machinery and equipment. However, subsequent law changes modified the cost recovery system, on the grounds that these provisions favored capital-intensive, rather than labor-intensive, industries, and to reduce the growing federal budget deficit.

      2.   Lower individual and corporate income nominal tax rates. Such measures can stimulate the general economy, by increasing disposable income.

      3.   Special tax treatment of technological development, including favorable treatment allowed research and development expenditures and patents, and tax credits for certain research and energy expenditures.

      4.   Support for farmers, thrift institutions, and small business owners. Such taxpayers can claim immediate deductions for expenditures for farm feed and fertilizers, exemption from the uniform capitalization rules for certain farmers, and the "flow-through" of the operating losses of certain small business corporations to their shareholders.

      5.   Concern over the growing federal budget deficit has led to a reduction in many of the incentives that had been enacted to stimulate the economy.

C.   Social considerations also affect tax legislation. Tax-favored treatment concerning certain employer-provided life and health insurance policies, contributions to retirement plans and charitable organizations, and expenditures for child care services are a response to various social goals. On the other hand, tax laws discourage expenditures contrary to public policy, such as bribes and fines.

D.   Equity considerations with respect to the tax law attempt to maintain a sensitivity in the law toward taxpayers in various circumstances. Of course, definitions of equity often produce heated debate among interested parties. Nevertheless, the tax law offers:

      1.   relief from multiple taxation through dividend income deductions;

      2.   deferral of tax liability is available until the taxpayer has funds available with which to pay a tax;

      3.   several provisions, such as the installment sales method, and loss carryovers, that offer relief from hardships that may be created by the annual accounting period concept; and,

      4.   relief from the eroding results of inflation is provided through indexation of tax brackets, standard deductions, and exemptions.

E.   Political considerations are evident in the tax law, as might be expected with respect to provisions that are forged in a legislative process. The effects of political considerations on the tax law largely are a result of special interest legislation, political expediency situations, and state and local government influences.

      For instance, special interest legislation has been created in response to lobbying activities by wealthy taxpayers, while various provisions attempt to ensure that those wealthy taxpayers do pay some "fair" share of tax. Examples of such provisions include the alternative minimum tax, the imputed interest rules, the passive loss rules, and the limitation on deductible investment interest expense.

F.   Tax administrators and the courts also have contributed to the system by imposing or encouraging alterations in specific provisions in the tax law. In its capacity as the protector of the national revenue, the IRS has been instrumental in securing passage of legislation designed to curtail flagrant tax avoidance practices and to ease administration of the tax laws.

In addition to interpreting statutory provisions and the administrative pronouncements issued by the IRS, the federal courts have influenced tax law by formulating certain judicial concepts that serve as guides in the application of various tax provisions and by making decisions that have been of such consequence that changes in the Internal Revenue Code were enacted by Congress specifically to incorporate the decision in the Code, or to provide tax provisions that are *contrary* to the decision.

TEST FOR SELF-EVALUATION - CHAPTER 1

True or False

Indicate which of the following statements are true or false by circling the correct answer.

T   F   1.   The federal government raises a large portion of its revenue through the property tax.

T   F   2.   A value added tax resembles a national sales tax.

T   F   3.   Current tax law is based on the "Internal Revenue Code of 2005."

T   F   4.   Property taxes are a form of *ad valorem* tax.

T   F   5.   Transaction taxes are most effective when consumers demonstrate a price-elastic demand for the commodity.

T   F   6.   If tax rates increase as the tax base grows larger, the tax is regressive.

T   F   7.   A severance tax is a tax on the use, consumption, or storage of tangible property.

T   F   8.   The primary purpose of some tax laws is to simplify the task of the IRS in collecting the revenue and administering the law.

T   F   9.   State governments use the sales tax as one of their primary sources of tax revenues.

T   F   10.   If tax rates decrease as the tax base grows larger, the tax is progressive.

Fill-in-the-Blanks

Complete the following statements with the appropriate word(s) or amount(s).

1.   The _____ Amendment, ratified in _____, authorized the federal income tax on individuals.

2.   _____ _____ taxes are taxes on capital or wealth.

3.   The research and development tax credit is an example of the effect of _____ considerations in the development of the tax law.

4.   The "minimum tax" on wealthy taxpayers is an example of the effect of _____ considerations in the development of the tax law.

5.   The deduction for charitable contributions is an example of the effect of _____ considerations in the development of the tax law.

6.   Adam Smith believed that a "good" tax would include provisions to assure its _____,
       _____, _____, and _____.

7.   With respect to employment taxes, the _____ tax is paid equally by the employer and
       employee, while only the employer pays _____ taxes.

8.   The _____-_____-_____-_____ feature of the income tax system compels employers to
       withhold a specific portion of an employee's wages for taxes.

9.   _____ taxes are levied on an activity or event, or the exercise of a specific right in
       property or on a privilege granted.

10.   _____, _____, and _____ taxes are levied on the transfer of property and
       normally are determined by a percentage rate multiplied by the value involved.

11.   A(n) _____ tax is a tax on the right to receive property from a decedent.

12.   The purpose of the _____ system is to provide funds that the states can use to
       provide unemployment benefits.

13.   A _____ _____ _____ establishes the maximum time during which the IRS
       can assess additional tax and the taxpayer can claim a refund.

Multiple Choice

Choose the best answer for each of the following questions.

_____ 1.   When the tax base is $10,000, the tax liability is $3,000; When the tax base is
             $100,000, the tax liability is $20,000. This tax has a rate structure that is:
             a.   Progressive.
             b.   Regressive.
             c.   Proportional.
             d.   *Ad Valorem.*

_____ 2.   When the tax base is $10,000, the tax liability is $3,000; When the tax base is
             $100,000, the tax liability is $35,000. This tax has a rate structure that is:
             a.   Progressive.
             b.   Regressive.
             c.   Proportional.
             d.   *Ad Valorem.*

_____ 3.   When the tax base is $10,000, the tax liability is $3,000; When the tax base is
             $100,000, the tax liability is $30,000. This tax has a rate structure that is:
             a.   Progressive.
             b.   Regressive.
             c.   Proportional.
             d.   *Ad Valorem.*

_____ 4.   The federal gift and estate taxes are:
             a.   regressive taxes.

b.   proportional taxes.
c.   progressive taxes.
d.   the gift tax is regressive and the estate tax is progressive.

_____ 5.   The concept that recognizes the inequity of taxing a transaction when the taxpayer lacks the means with which to pay the tax is:
a.   double taxation.
b.   pay-as-you-go.
c.   revenue neutrality.
d.   wherewithal to pay.

_____ 6.   There are a number of provisions in the Internal Revenue Code that favor small business. They include: (More than one answer may be correct)
a.   the corporate minimum tax.
b.   the environmental tax.
c.   the tax rates applicable to corporations.
d.   the dividends-received deduction.

_____ 7.   Examples of social considerations that have affected tax legislation include:
a.   the alternative minimum tax.
b.   deductions for contributions to retirement plans.
c.   the investment tax credit.
d.   the installment sales method.

_____ 8.   The concept of equity appears in tax provisions to:
a.   alleviate the effect of multiple taxation.
b.   postpone the recognition of gain when the taxpayer lacks the ability or wherewithal to pay the tax.
c.   mitigate the effect of the application of the annual accounting period concept.
d.   all of the above.

_____ 9.   The last major reorganization of the Internal Revenue Code was enacted in:
a.   1954.
b.   1986.
c.   1998.
d.   2005.

_____ 10.   In addition to interpreting statutory provisions and administrative pronouncements issued by the IRS, the Federal courts have influenced tax law by:
a.   formulating certain judicial concepts that serve as guides in the application of various tax provisions.
b.   changing Congressional intent as to the application of Federal tax law.
c.   making key decisions that have led to changes in the Internal Revenue Code.
d.   Both a and c.

_____ 11.   The federal income tax rate structure for individuals is becoming:
a.   less regressive.
b.   more regressive.
c.   less progressive.
d.   more progressive.

_____ 12.   Which of the following states do not impose an income tax on individuals? More than one choice may be correct.
        a.   Alabama.
        b.   Georgia.
        c.   South Carolina.
        d.   Texas.
        e.   All of the above states impose an income tax.

_____ 13.   Special tax-reduction provisions supporting the owners of small businesses can be justified on the following grounds. More than one answer may be correct.
        a.   Economic expansion
        b.   Political expediency
        c.   Social justice
        d.   Equity among taxpayers
        e.   All of the above

_____ 14.   Over time, the Internal Revenue Service has worked to
        a.   Make the federal tax system more complex.
        b.   Make the federal tax system less complex.
        c.   Keep the federal tax system at a constant level of complexity.
        d.   Both a. and b.
        e.   None of the above

SOLUTIONS TO CHAPTER 1 QUESTIONS

True or False

1.   F   Property taxes are imposed by state and local governments. [Property Taxes p.1-6]
2.   T   Both are transaction taxes. [General Sales Tax p. 1-10]
3.   F   Current tax law includes the Internal Revenue Code of 1986. [Revenue Acts p. 1-3]
4.   T   Such taxes are based on the value of the taxed property. [Property Taxes p. 1-6]
5.   F   Transaction taxes are effective when consumers demonstrate a price-inelastic demand for the commodity. [General Sales Taxes, p. 1-10]
6.   F   The tax is progressive. [Tax Rates, p. 1-6]
7.   F   The tax described is the use tax. [Use Tax, p. 1-10]
8.   T   This practice reduces compliance costs. [Criteria Used in the Selection of a Tax Structure, p. 1-4]
9.   T   Sales and use taxes are key revenue sources for the states. [General Sales Taxes, p. 1-10]
10. F   The tax is regressive. [Tax Rates, p. 1-6]

Fill-in-the-Blanks

1.   16th, 1913 [Early Periods, p. 1-3]
2.   *ad valorem* [Property Taxes, p. 1-6]
3.   economic [Encouragement of Certain Activities, p. 1-25]
4.   political [Political Expediency Situations, p. 1-30]
5.   social [Social Considerations, p. 1-27]
6.   equality, convenience, certainty, economy [Criteria Used in the Selection of a Tax Structure, p. 1-4]
7.   FICA, unemployment [Employment Taxes, p. 1-15]
8.   pay-as-you-go [Income Taxes, p. 1-14]
9.   Excise [Federal Excise Taxes, p. 1-9]
10. Excise, sales, severance [Transaction Taxes, p. 1-9]
11. Inheritance [Death Taxes, p. 1-11]
12. FUTA [FUTA Taxes, p. 1-16]
13. statute of limitations [Statute of Limitations p. 1-21]

Multiple Choice

1.   b   On a tax base of $10,000 the effective tax rate was 30% and, as the tax base increased to $100,000, the effective tax rate decreased to 20%. [Tax Rates p. 1-5]
2.   a   On a tax base of $10,000 the effective tax rate was 30% and, as the tax base increased to $100,000, the effective rate increased to 35%. [Tax Rates p. 1-5]
3.   c   On a tax base of $10,000 the effective tax rate was 30% and, as the tax base increased to $100,000, the effective tax rate remained 30%. [Tax Rates p. 1-5]
4.   c   Both taxes' rates increase as the value of the transferred property increases. [Death Taxes p. 1-11]
5.   d   This concept is embodied in the installment method of income recognition. [The Wherewithal to Pay Concept p. 1-27]
6.   a,b,c The graduated tax rates and the $40,000 AMT exemption favor small businesses.

The environmental tax also favors small businesses since the tax is not imposed unless a corporation's alternative minimum taxable income exceeds $2,000,000. [Encouragement of Small Business p. 1-25]

7.　b　These provisions stabilize the need for government support of retirees. [Social Considerations p. 1-27]

8.　d　Equity reflects fairness among taxpayers and across income levels. [Equity Considerations p. 1-27]

9.　b　Several amendments to the 1986 Code have been adopted since then. [Revenue Acts p. 1-3]

10.　d　Courts cannot change congressional intent as to the tax law. [Influence of the Courts p. 1-31]

11.　c　In 1986 there were 15 rates ranging from 0 to 50%; the current tax structure includes rates of 0, 10, 15, 27, 30, 33, and 35%. [Incidence of Taxation p. 1-6]

12.　d　Fewer than ten states do not impose a broad income tax. [State Income Taxes p. 1-15]

13.　a,b,c　Small business generally draws the favor of congress. [Understanding the Federal Tax Law p. 1-24]

14.　d　The federal income tax law seldom gets *less* complex. [Understanding the Federal Tax Law p. 1-24]

Chapter 2
Working with the Tax Law

CHAPTER HIGHLIGHTS

There are three primary sources of federal tax law: statutory, administrative, and judicial. Each of these sources contributes significantly to the development and evolution of tax law. Therefore, each of these influences must be considered and understood when working with the tax law. Numerous resources are available to assist an individual when studying the tax law or when a tax problem is being investigated. If a thorough research effort is to be performed, it is important that the researcher consider all aspects of the law's development and status, from its origin up to the very day that the research is being conducted.

I.   Tax Sources -- The three sources of federal tax law are *statutory*, *administrative,* and *judicial*.

    A.   Statutory Sources of the Tax Law

        1.   The statutory provisions comprising the tax law are contained in the *Internal Revenue Code of 1986*, which was redesignated as such by the Tax Reform Act of 1986. Subsequent statutory amendments to the tax law have been integrated into the 1986 Code. Prior to the 1986 Code, the body of tax law was contained in the *Internal Revenue Code of 1954*.

        2.   The 1954 Code was preceded by the *Internal Revenue Code of 1939,* which was the initial attempt to codify all of the tax law provisions in a logical sequence in a separate part of the federal statutes.

        3.   The legislative process generally originates in the *House Ways and Means Committee*. The Senate Finance Committee also considers tax bills. However, in order for legislation to become law, differences between the House and Senate versions must be resolved, the final version must be approved by Congress, and finally, the President must sign the legislation.

        4.   The Code is arranged by subtitles, chapters, subchapters, parts, sections, subsections, paragraphs and subparagraphs.

2-2   2007 Annual Edition   COMPREHENSIVE VOLUME

B.   Administrative Sources of the Tax Law -- The source of administrative pronouncements is either the US Treasury Department or the IRS. These pronouncements come in the form of Treasury Department Regulations, Revenue Rulings, Revenue Procedures, and various other administrative pronouncements. These different sources possess varying degrees of authority.

C.   Judicial Sources of the Tax Law

    1.   If no satisfactory remedy to a dispute is achieved administratively within the IRS, a taxpayer may take the dispute to one of *four* federal courts. These four trial courts (courts of original jurisdiction) are: a *Federal District Court*, the *US Court of Federal Claims*, the *US Tax Court*, and the *Small Cases Division of the US Tax Court*.

    2.   Some of the differences between the four trial courts follow.

        a.   There is only one US Court of Federal Claims and one Tax Court, but there are many Federal District Courts.

        b.   The number of judges who will hear a taxpayer's case may vary, depending on the court involved.

        c.   The US Court of Federal Claims meets most often in Washington, D.C., whereas the other courts will hear cases at specified times and places throughout the country.

KEY TERMS

- Sources of the Tax Law
  - Statutory
  - Administrative
  - Judicial
- Tax Research
- Tax Planning (Avoidance)
- Tax Evasion

---

        d.   The US Court of Federal Claims has jurisdiction in judgment over any claim against the United States that is based on the Constitution, any Act of Congress, or any Regulation of an executive department.

        e.   The Tax Court hears only tax cases; whereas, the US Court of Federal Claims and the Federal District Courts hear nontax litigation as well as tax litigation. For this reason, some people suggest that the US Tax Court has more expertise in tax matters than the other courts.

        f.   The Federal District Court is the only court in which a taxpayer can obtain a jury trial.

        g.   A taxpayer may go to the Tax Court without first paying the disputed tax deficiency; whereas, with the US Court of Federal Claims and the Federal District Courts, the taxpayer must first pay the tax deficiency and then sue for a refund. A taxpayer who selects the Tax Court may deposit a cash bond to stop the running of interest.

        h.   Appeals from the Tax Court and the Federal District Court are taken to the US Court of Appeals. However, appeals from the US Court of Federal Claims are taken to the US Court of Appeals for the Federal Circuit.

    3.   There are 13 circuits in the US Court of Appeals, including the Washington, D.C. Circuit and the Federal Circuit. Each circuit, except for the District of Columbia Circuit and the Federal Circuit, has several states within its jurisdiction.

        4.   The Supreme Court will not hear an appeal from a lower court automatically, but instead, it will hear only those cases that it feels are of particular importance (e.g., to resolve a conflict between various US Courts of Appeals). If the Supreme Court accepts jurisdiction, it will grant a *Writ of Certiorari*.

        5.   The Tax Court (formerly the Board of Tax Appeals) issues two types of decisions: *regular* and *memorandum* decisions. The regular decisions are published by the government in a series designated *Tax Court of the United States Reports*. The memorandum decisions are published by Commerce Clearing House in *CCH Tax Court Memorandum Decisions*, by Research Institute of America (RIA) in *RIA T.C. Memorandum Decisions,* and at the Tax Court's website.

        6.   Tax cases heard before the other courts are also printed by Commerce Clearing House (*US Tax Cases* or *USTC*) and by Research Institute of America (*American Federal Tax Reports* or *AFTR* series).

        7.   West Publishing Company publishes all Federal District Court decisions (tax and nontax) in their *Federal Supplement Series*. They publish decisions from the US Court of Federal Claims and the US Court of Appeals in their reporters--designated *Federal Second Series* and *Federal Third Series*. West's *Supreme Court Reporter* contains all of the Supreme Court decisions.

        8.   The US Government Printing Office also publishes the Supreme Court decisions in the *United States Supreme Court Reports*.

    D.   Other Sources of the Tax Law

        1.   Tax treaties serve as another source of tax law. Tax treaties with foreign countries have been established with the intent of assisting tax enforcement and mitigating double taxation. Neither a tax law nor a tax treaty automatically takes precedence.

        2.   Relevant tax periodicals also may be useful resources to tax professionals in the tax research process.

II.   Working with the Tax Law -- Locating Tax Sources

    A.   Electronic versus Paper Tax Research

        1.   Computerized tax research tools have largely replaced paper resources in most tax practices.

        2.   The two fundamental ways to conduct tax research using computer resources involve:

            a.   Online and CD-ROM subscription services.

            b.   Free online Internet sites.

        3.   Using electronic resources to conduct tax research offers a number of advantages. However, they cannot take away the need to maintain a thorough knowledge of the tax law, which is necessary to logically and analytically review open tax issues.

    B.   Tax Services -- Several commercial publishers offer useful tax services.

        1.   RIA publishes *U.S. Tax Reporter* and *Federal Tax Coordinator 2d*.

        2.   CCH publishes *Standard Federal Tax Reporter.*

    C.   Electronic Services

        1.   Tax law is typically found using one of the following strategies: search, link, and browse.

        2.   Vast libraries can be provided through CD-ROM services, which are offered on one or more discs.

3.   Online research systems allow for almost instantaneous access to tax law sources.

4.   The Internet provides a wide array of tax resources, sometimes at no direct cost to the researcher.

III.   Working With the Tax Law -- Tax Research

    A.   Tax research involves the following procedures.

        1.   Identifying and refining the problem.

        2.   Locating the appropriate tax law sources.

        3.   Assessing the validity of the tax law sources.

        4.   Arriving at the solution or alternative solutions with due consideration given to nontax factors.

        5.   Effectively communicating the solution(s) to the taxpayer or the taxpayer's representative.

        6.   Following up on the solution(s) where appropriate in light of new developments.

    B.   In locating the appropriate tax law sources, a tax researcher should use one or more of the major tax services as well as reviewing tax periodicals for articles relating to a particular problem. In addition, the researcher will likely utilize electronic resources.

    C.   After the sources of tax law have been located, their validity must be assessed based on the facts and circumstances at hand.

    D.   The researcher should communicate the results of the tax research after the problem has been adequately examined. This communication is often accomplished by a memo and/or a letter that should tell the taxpayer the following.

        1.   What was researched.

        2.   The results of the research.

        3.   The justification for the recommendation made.

Tax research typically is conducted, not with stacks of case books and legal pads, but with CD-ROM and online resources, as the publishers of primary and secondary source materials have converted the content of their services to electronic form. Researchers can, by using electronic tax research materials, make certain that the most current law sources are available to them, and optimize the use of existing computer equipment, including laser printers, communication devices, and high-speed processing chips.

IV.   Working With the Tax Law -- Tax Planning

    A.   A primary purpose of tax planning is to minimize a taxpayer's total tax liability. However, nontax considerations should be taken into account as well as tax considerations when a taxpayer considers alternative business activities and goals.

    B.   A distinction exists between legal tax planning -- *tax avoidance*, and illegal tax procedures -- *tax evasion*.

TEST FOR SELF-EVALUATION -- CHAPTER 2

True or False

Indicate which of the following statements are true or false by circling the correct answer.

T   F   1.   The codification of tax law that is used today is known as the *Internal Revenue Code of 1986*.

T   F   2.   The Joint Conference Committee is called on to resolve differences between the House Ways and Means Committee version and the full House version of tax legislation.

T   F   3.   Revenue Rulings are issued by the Ways and Means Committee.

T   F   4.   A distinction exists between Temporary Regulations and Proposed Regulations.

T   F   5.   Appeals may be made directly from the US Court of Federal Claims to the Supreme Court.

T   F   6.   In tax cases, the taxpayer has a choice between one of only three trial courts: the Federal District Court, the US Tax Court, and the US Court of Federal Claims.

T   F   7.   No appeal is available for cases heard in the Small Cases Division of the US Tax Court.

T   F   8.   A jury trial is available in both a Federal District Court and in the US Court of Federal Claims.

T   F   9.   Tax evasion and tax avoidance are two terms that have essentially the same meaning.

T   F   10. Tax research is a process that begins with identifying and refining the problem.

T   F   11. Income Tax Regulations are issued by the IRS.

T   F   12. Final Regulations are issued as Treasury Decisions.

T   F   13. Revenue Rulings carry the same legal force and effect as Regulations.

T   F   14. For the US Court of Federal Claims or a Federal District Court to have jurisdiction, the taxpayer must pay the tax deficiency assessed by the IRS and sue for a refund.

T   F   15. Tax Court Memorandum decisions are not published by the US Government.

Fill-in-the-Blanks

Complete the following statements with the appropriate word(s) or amount(s).

1. Federal tax legislation generally originates in the _____ where it is first considered by the _____ Committee.

2. The _____ is the committee in the Senate that considers tax legislation.

3. _____, which may be legislative, interpretive, or procedural by nature, are issued by the US Treasury Department under authority granted by Congress.

4. _____ are issued by the IRS and are interpretive in nature, but do not carry the same legal force as Regulations.

5. The Internal Revenue Bulletins are reorganized and published semi-annually in bound volumes called _____.

6. Appeals from the US Tax Court or the Federal District Courts are taken to the _____.

7. The _____ hears only tax cases, while the _____ and the _____ hear nontax litigation as well as tax litigation.

8. For the _____ or _____ to have jurisdiction, the taxpayer must first pay any tax deficiency assessed by the IRS and then sue for a refund.

9. The _____ and _____ must abide by the precedents set by the US Court of Appeals of jurisdiction.

10. Before 1943, the US Tax Court was called the _____.

11. A tax dispute may be heard before the Small Cases Division of the US Tax Court if the amount involved does not exceed _____.

12. When the Senate version of a tax bill differs from that passed by the House, the _____ is called on to resolve these differences.

13. Proposed, final, and temporary Regulations are published in the _____.

14. An _____ by the IRS indicates that it agrees with a decision reached by a court.

15. The role of appellate courts is limited to a review of the record of trial compiled by the _____.

Multiple Choice

Choose the best answer for each of the following questions.

_____ 1. Which of the following is not an available major tax service?
a.   *Standard Federal Tax Reporter* (Commerce Clearing House).

      b.   *United States Tax Reporter* (Research Institute of America).
      c.   *Federal Tax Coordinator 2d* (Research Institute of America).
      d.   *Tax Management Portfolios* (Bureau of National Affairs).
      e.   All of these choices are major tax services.

_____ 2. The Internal Revenue Code is not organized by which of the following categories?
      a.   Subtitles.
      b.   Paragraph.
      c.   Section.
      d.   Listing.
      e.   Chapter.

_____ 3. Which of the following is not an administrative source of the federal tax law?
      a.   Treasury Department Regulations.
      b.   Board of Tax Appeals rulings.
      c.   Revenue Rulings.
      d.   Revenue Procedures.
      e.   Treasury Decisions.

_____ 4. Which of the following is not printed in the *Internal Revenue Bulletin*?
      a.   Code Sections.
      b.   Revenue Rulings.
      c.   Revenue Procedures.
      d.   Announcements.
      e.   Treasury Decisions.

_____ 5. Which of the following is not a court of original jurisdiction?
      a.   US Tax Court.
      b.   Small Cases Division of the US Tax Court.
      c.   Federal District Court.
      d.   US Court of Federal Claims.
      e.   All of these choices are courts of original jurisdiction.

_____ 6. Which of the following courts normally meets only in Washington, D.C.?
      a.   US Court of Federal Claims.
      b.   US Tax Court.
      c.   Federal District Court.
      d.   US Court of Appeals.
      e.   Both US Court of Federal Claims and US Tax Court.

_____ 7. Which courts hear only tax litigation?
      a.   US Court of Federal Claims.
      b.   US Tax Court.
      c.   US Court of Tax Appeals.
      d.   US Court of Appeals.
      e.   Both US Tax Court and US Court of Tax Appeals.

_____ 8. Appeal to the Supreme Court is made by:
      a.   A *Writ of Certiorari*.
      b.   Having a conflict in the districts.
      c.   Having a conflict between two or more US Courts of Appeal.

    d.   Having the Commissioner of the IRS petition the Chief Justice of the Supreme Court.

    e.   None of these choices.

___ 9.   The following citation is associated with which of the volumes listed below: Walter H. Johnson, 34 TCM 1056.

    a.   *CCH Tax Court Memorandum Decisions.*

    b.   *RIA T.C. Memorandum Decisions.*

    c.   *Tax Court of the United States Reports.*

    d.   *BNA Daily Tax Reporter.*

    e.   None of these choices.

___ 10.   The court cases heard in the Federal District Court, the US Court of Federal Claims, and the US Court of Appeals are reported by:

    a.   Commerce Clearing House.

    b.   Research Institute of America.

    c.   West Publishing Company.

    d.   Commerce Clearing House and Research Institute of America.

    e.   Commerce Clearing House, Research Institute of America, and West Publishing Company.

___ 11.   If the prefix 1 precedes a Regulation, that designation indicates that it is what type of Regulation?

    a.   Income tax.

    b.   Gift tax.

    c.   Estate tax.

    d.   Employment tax.

    e.   None of these choices.

___ 12.   Appeals from the US Court of Federal Claims are heard by what court?

    a.   Federal District Court.

    b.   US Tax Court.

    c.   US Court of Tax Appeals.

    d.   US Court of Appeals for the Federal Circuit.

    e.   None of these choices.

___ 13.   Which of the following could *not* be the result of an appeal?

    a.   Affirm.

    b.   Reverse.

    c.   Remand.

    d.   Any of the above could be a possibility.

    e.   None of these choices.

___ 14.   Which of the following is *not* a computer-based (i.e., tax CD service, on-line service) tax research system?

    a.   ALLTAX.

    b.   RIA Checkpoint.

    c.   Westlaw.

    d.   LEXIS/NEXIS.

    e.   CCH ACCESS.

    f.   All of these choices are computer-based tax research systems.

_____ 15. If a taxpayer loses a case taken to the Small Cases Division of the US Tax Court, an appeal could be heard by which court?

  a. US Tax Court.
  b. US Court of Appeals.
  c. US Court of Federal Claims.
  d. Supreme Court.
  e. None of these choices.

SOLUTIONS TO CHAPTER 2 QUESTIONS

True or False

1.   T   Statutory amendments to the tax law are integrated into the existing Code, the *Internal Revenue Code of 1986*. [Origin of the Internal Revenue Code p. 2-2]
2.   F   The committee is used to resolve differences between the House version and Senate version of a tax bill. [The Legislative Process p. 2-3]
3.   F   Revenue Rulings are official pronouncements of the National Office of the IRS. [Revenue Rulings and Revenue Procedures p. 2-8]
4.   T   Temporary Regulations are issued on matters where immediate guidance is important. These Regulations are issued without the comment period required for Proposed Regulations. [Treasury Department Regulations p. 2-7]
5.   F   Appeals from the US Court of Federal Claims are made to the US Court of Appeals for the Federal Circuit. [Appellate Courts p. 2-14]
6.   F   Four trial courts are available, including the Small Cases Division of the US Tax Court. [Trial Courts p. 2-12]
7.   T   This is the only trial court from which an appeal is not allowed. [The Judicial Process in General p. 2-11]
8.   F   A jury trial is available only in a Federal District Court. [Trial Courts p. 2-12]
9.   F   Tax avoidance is legal and tax evasion is illegal. [Tax Evasion and Tax Avoidance p. 2-34]
10. T   Identifying the tax problem or issue typically is the first critical step in the tax research process. [Working with the Tax Law—Tax Research p. 2-27]
11. F   Regulations are issued by the US Treasury Department. [Treasury Department Regulations p. 2-7]
12. T   Final Regulations are issued by the government as Treasury Decisions (TDs). [Treasury Department Regulations p. 2-7]
13. F   Revenue Rulings do not carry the same legal force and effect as Regulations and usually deal with more restricted problems. [Revenue Rulings and Revenue Procedures p. 2-8]
14. T   Before the Court of Federal Claims or a District Court can have jurisdiction, the taxpayer must pay the tax deficiency assessed by the IRS and then sue for a refund. Jurisdiction in the Tax Court, however, is usually obtained without first paying the assessed tax deficiency. [Trial Courts p. 2-12]
15. T   Tax Court Memorandum decisions are not officially published, while regular Tax Court decisions are published by the US Government in the series called *Tax Court of the United States Reports*. [Judicial Citations—The U.S. Tax Court p. 2-16]

Fill-in-the-Blanks

1.   House of Representatives, Ways and Means [The Legislative Process p. 2-3]
2.   Senate Finance Committee [The Legislative Process p. 2-3]
3.   Treasury Department Regulations [Treasury Department Regulations p. 2-7]
4.   Revenue Rulings [Revenue Rulings and Revenue Procedures p. 2-8]
5.   Cumulative Bulletins [Revenue Rulings and Revenue Procedures p. 2-8]
6.   US Court of Appeals (i.e., of a regional circuit and not the Federal Circuit) [Appellate Courts p. 2-14]

7.   US Tax Court, Federal District Courts, US Court of Federal Claims [Trial Courts p. 2-12]
8.   US Court of Federal Claims, Federal District Courts [Trial Courts p. 2-12]
9.   Federal District Courts, US Tax Court [Appellate Courts p. 2-14]
10.   Board of Tax Appeals [Judicial Citations—The U.S. Tax Court p. 2-16]
11. $50,000 [The Judicial Process in General p. 2-11]
12.   Joint Conference Committee [The Legislative Process p. 2-3]
13.   Federal Register [Treasury Department Regulations p. 2-7]
14.   acquiescence [Judicial Citations—The U.S. Tax Court p. 2-16]
15.   trial courts [Appellate Courts p. 2-14]

Multiple Choice

1.   e   Each choice provided is a major tax service. [Locating the Appropriate Tax Law Sources p. 2-29]
2.   d   A listing is not a means by which the *Internal Revenue Code* is organized. [Arrangement of the Code p. 2-5]
3.   b   The Board of Tax Appeals, the predecessor to the current Tax Court, is a judicial source of tax law. [Judicial Citations—The U.S. Tax Court p. 2-16]
4.   a   The statutory language found in the *Internal Revenue Code* is promulgated by Congress, not the Internal Revenue Service, and, as a result, is not included in the IRS's *Internal Revenue Bulletin*. [Other Administrative Pronouncements p. 2-10]
5.   e   Each court is a trial court or a court of original jurisdiction. [The Judicial Process in General p. 2-11]
6.   a   The Court of Federal Claims meets most often in Washington, D.C. The Tax Court is officially based in Washington, D.C., but the various judges travel to different parts of the country and hear cases at predetermined locations and dates. [Trial Courts p. 2-12]
7.   b   The Tax Court hears only tax cases, while the other courts hear a wide variety of cases. [Judicial Sources of the Tax Law p. 2-11]
8.   a   The Supreme Court must agree to hear the case, and if it does so, it grants the *Writ of Certiorari*. [Appellate Courts p. 2-14]
9.   a   This reflects the format followed by Commerce Clearing House in its volumes containing the Tax Court Memorandum decisions. [Judicial Citations—The U.S. Tax Court p. 2-16]
10.   e   Each of the companies listed publishes these tax decisions. [Judicial Citations—The U.S. District Court, Court of Federal Claims, and Courts of Appeals p. 2-18]
11.   a   The prefix 1 designates the Regulations under the income tax law. [Treasury Department Regulations p. 2-7]
12.   d   Appeals from the Court of Federal Claims go to the Court of Appeals for the Federal Circuit. [Trial Courts p. 2-12]
13.   d   Any of the results listed could occur on appeal. [Appellate Courts p. 2-14]
14.   a   ALLTAX is not a computer-based tax research system. [Electronic Services p. 2-23]
15.   e   No appeal is available for cases heard in the Small Cases Division of the US Tax Court. [The Judicial Process in General p. 2-11]

Chapter 3
Tax Determination; Personal and Dependency Exemptions; An Overview of Property Transactions

CHAPTER HIGHLIGHTS

This chapter describes the general scheme of the federal income taxation of individuals, which involves the computation of the amount referred to as *taxable income*. Generally, all realized income is included in the computation, unless specifically excluded. Conversely, deductions from income are not allowed unless Congress includes them in the law. Special deductions, such as the standard deduction and personal exemptions, are available to individual taxpayers except in certain situations. In essence, these deductions exempt a taxpayer's income from taxation up to specified amounts. After taxable income is determined, the tax liability is computed by reference to tax tables or tax rate schedules. Finally, tax prepayments and credits are subtracted from the gross tax liability to determine a taxpayer's net tax payable (or refund due). In addition to the discussion relating to the computation of the income tax liability, this chapter introduces the basic concepts of property transactions and their effect on the computation of taxable income.

I. Tax Formula
    A. The federal individual income tax liability is based on the concept known as *taxable income*. Taxable income is determined using the formula shown in Exhibit 3-1.
    B. Components of the Tax Formula
        1. Income (broadly conceived) includes all income, both taxable and nontaxable. For this purpose, income is *not* equivalent to gross receipts.
        2. A number of exclusions from income have been specifically provided in the law by Congress. Congress has chosen to exclude various items from the tax base for equity, social, economic, and other reasons. Certain other items have been excluded by administrative action of the IRS.
        3. Gross income is broadly defined in the Internal Revenue Code as "except as otherwise provided . . . all income from whatever source derived." The phrase "except as otherwise provided" refers to exclusions. Gross income includes only *realized* gains.

Exhibit 3-1
TAX FORMULA

> *Income (broadly conceived)*
> *Less:*   *Exclusions*
> *Equals:*   *Gross income*
> *Less:*   *Deductions <u>for</u> adjusted gross income*
> *Equals:*   *Adjusted gross income*
> *Less:*   *The greater of total itemized deductions, or*
>   *the standard deduction*
> *Less:*   *Personal and dependency exemptions*
> *Equals:*   *Taxable income*
> *Tax on taxable income (see Tax Tables or Tax Rate*
>   *Schedules)*
> *Less:*   *Tax credits (including income taxes withheld*
>   *and prepaid*
> *Equals:*   *Tax due (or refund)*

4.   Two categories of deductions apply to individual taxpayers.
   a.   Deductions *for* adjusted gross income (sometimes referred to as above-the-line deductions).
   b.   Deductions *from* adjusted gross income.
5.   Expenses deductible *for* adjusted gross income include the following.
   a.   Ordinary and necessary expenses incurred in a trade or business.
   b.   One-half of self employment tax paid.
   c.   Alimony paid.
   d.   Certain payments to traditional Individual Retirement Accounts and Health Savings Accounts.
   e.   Moving expenses.
   f.   Forfeited interest for premature withdrawal of time deposits.
   g.   Capital loss deductions.
   h.   Deductions attributable to rents and royalties.
6.   Adjusted gross income (AGI) is an important subtotal that serves as the basis for computing percentage limitations on certain deductions, such as medical expenses, charitable contributions, and certain casualty losses.
7.   Itemized deductions, which generally are personal or nonbusiness in nature, are deductions *from* adjusted gross income. The actual amount of itemized deductions is claimed if the total exceeds the standard deduction. Otherwise, the appropriate standard deduction is claimed by a taxpayer.
8.   Certain itemized deductions that have been specified by Congress include medical expenses, certain taxes, certain interest expenses, and charitable contributions. In addition, taxpayers are allowed to itemize expenses related to the following.
   a.   The production or collection of income.
   b.   The management of property held for the production of income.
   c.   The determination, collection, or refund of any tax.

9.   The standard deduction, which is set by Congress, is used to exempt a taxpayer's income from federal income taxes up to a certain amount. The *basic* standard deduction amounts, which are dependent on a taxpayer's filing status, are shown in Exhibit 3-2.

10.   The standard deduction amounts are adjusted for inflation annually.

11.   Certain taxpayers are not allowed to claim the standard deduction, and the standard deduction is limited for others.

 Each year, the tax system is adjusted to remove the effects of inflation on the computation of taxable income and a taxpayer's tax liability. This process, known as indexing, applies to the tax rate structure, the standard deduction, and other provisions in the tax code. Over the years, more and more elements of taxation have been indexed for inflation. Now the IRS has to do nearly 100 different computations each year to bring the tax tables, deductions, exemptions, and exclusions up to date.

12.   An *additional* standard deduction amount is allowed for a taxpayer who is either elderly (age 65 or over) or blind.

   a.   For a single taxpayer or a taxpayer qualifying for the head of household status, in 2006 an additional $1,250 ($1,250 in 2005) standard deduction is allowed ($2,500 in 2006 if both elderly *and* blind).

   b.   For a married taxpayer filing jointly or separately, and for a surviving spouse, in 2006 an additional $1,000 ($1,000 in 2005) standard deduction is allowed ($4,000 in 2006 if the taxpayer *and* spouse are both elderly *and* blind).

   c.   The additional standard deduction may not be claimed for dependents.

Exhibit 3-2
BASIC STANDARD DEDUCTION AMOUNTS: 2006 AND 2005

Filing Status	Standard Deduction 2006	2005
Single	$5,150	$5,000
Married, filing jointly	10,300	10,000
Surviving spouse	10,300	10,000
Head of household	7,550	7,300
Married, filing separately	5,150	5,000

13. Taxpayers whose itemized deductions are less than the standard deduction amount will calculate their taxable income using the standard deduction rather than their itemized deductions. In this situation, taxable income will be equal to adjusted gross income minus the sum of the standard deduction and the personal and dependency exemptions.

14. Taxpayers are allowed to deduct personal and dependency exemptions of $3,300 each in 2006 ($3,200 in 2005) in arriving at taxable income. An exemption normally may be claimed for the taxpayer and the taxpayer's spouse, as well as for each dependent of the taxpayer.

15. In some situations, taxpayers may *not* use the standard deduction amount. The following individual taxpayers must itemize their deductions.

   a. A married individual who files a separate income tax return when either spouse itemizes deductions.

   b. A nonresident alien.

   c. An individual making a return for a period of less than 12 months because of a change in annual accounting period.

16. If a taxpayer may be claimed as a dependent on another taxpayer's income tax return, the dependent's basic standard deduction for 2006 is limited to the following.

   a. The *greater* of $850 ($800 in 2005) *or* the sum of the dependent's earned income plus $300 ($250 in 2005).

   b. In no case may the basic standard deduction exceed the amount shown in Exhibit 3-2 (i.e., $5,150 in 2006 assuming the dependent is single).

17. A taxpayer (e.g., minor child) claimed as a dependent on another's (e.g., his parents') income tax return may *not* claim a personal exemption on his or her own income tax return.

II. Personal Exemptions

   A. A personal exemption of $3,300 (in 2006) is allowed for the taxpayer and for the taxpayer's spouse. The number of personal exemptions available is based on marital status as of the end of the year, except when a spouse dies during the year.

   B. A personal exemption is not allowed, however, if the taxpayer is claimed as a dependent on another taxpayer's income tax return.

> ## KEY TERMS
>
> - Adjusted Gross Income (AGI)
> - Standard Deduction
> - Personal and Dependency Exemptions
> - Filing Status
> - Recognized Gain or Loss

III. Dependency Exemptions -- A dependency exemption is available for one who is either a qualifying child or a qualifying relative. The qualifying child definition is also used to determine eligibility for other tax benefits (e.g., child tax credit, head of household filing status).

   A. Qualifying Child -- A qualifying child must meet the relationship, abode, age, and support tests.

      1. Relationship -- The child must be the taxpayer's son, daughter, adopted child, stepchild, eligible foster child, brother, sister, stepbrother, stepsister, half brother, half sister, or a descendant of any of these parties.

        2.   Abode -- The child must live with the taxpayer for more than half of the year. Temporary absences are disregarded.

        3.   Age -- The child must be under age 19 (or under age 24 in the case of a full-time student).

        4.   Support -- To be a qualifying child, the individual must not be self-supporting (i.e., provide more than one-half of his or her own support).

        5.   Tie-breaker rules specify the person who claims the dependency exemption if the child is a qualifying child for more than one person.

B.   Qualifying Relative -- A qualifying relative must meet the relationship, gross income, and support tests.

        1.   Relationship -- The relationship test for a qualifying relative is more expansive than for a qualifying child and includes other relations, including unrelated individuals who are members of the taxpayer's household.

        2.   Gross income -- The dependent's gross income must be less than the exemption amount ($3,300 in 2006). Gross income is determined by the income that is taxable.

        3.   Support -- Over one-half of the support of the individual must be furnished by the taxpayer. Support includes expenditures for food, shelter, clothing, medical and dental care, and education, but not scholarships.

            a.   Special rules apply where more than one taxpayer provides support to another person but where no one taxpayer can meet the support test.

            b.   Another special rule applies when parents with children are divorced or separated under a decree of separate maintenance. Typically, the rule grants the dependency exemption to the noncustodial parent if the divorce decree so specifies or if the custodial parent issues a waiver.

C.   Other Rules for Dependency Exemptions -- In addition to coming within either the qualifying child or qualifying relative categories, a dependent must meet the joint return and citizenship or residency tests.

        1.   If a dependent is married, in order to meet the joint return test, the individual may not file a joint income tax return with his or her spouse unless he or she is filing a joint income tax return in order to receive a refund of tax withheld, no tax liability would exist for either spouse on separate income tax returns, and neither spouse is required to file an income tax return.

        2.   The citizenship or residency test requires that to be a dependent, an individual must be either a US citizen or resident, or a resident of Canada or Mexico for some part of the calendar year.

D.   Comparison of Categories for Dependency Exemption

        1.   The relationship test is considerably more expansive for the qualifying relative category.

        2.   The support tests are entirely different. For a qualifying child category, the child cannot be self-supporting.

        3.   The gross income test is inapplicable in the case of a qualifying child, while there is no age restriction for a qualifying relative.

        4.   Exhibit 3-3 summarizes the fundamental tests involved in the two dependency exemption categories.

2007 Annual Edition COMPREHENSIVE VOLUME

Exhibit 3-3
TESTS FOR DEPENDENCY EXEMPTION:
QUALIFYING CHILD VERSUS QUALIFYING RELATIVE

Qualifying Child	Qualifying Relative
Relationship	*Support*
Abode	*Relationship or member of household*
Age	*Gross income*
Support	*Joint return*
Joint return	*Citizenship or residency*
Citizenship or residency	

E. Phaseout of Exemptions
1. Personal and dependency exemptions are phased out as AGI exceeds specified threshold amounts. The threshold amounts (which are indexed for inflation) at which the phase-out begins are shown in Exhibit 3-4.
2. Exemptions are phased out by two percent for each $2,500 or fraction thereof by which the taxpayer's AGI exceeds the threshold amounts. For married taxpayers filing separately, the phaseout is calculated at the rate of two percent for each $1,250 or fraction thereof. The amount of the phaseout is then multiplied by 2/3 for tax years 2006 and 2007.

Exhibit 3-4
PHASEOUT OF EXEMPTIONS: THRESHOLD AMOUNTS

	2006	2005
Single	$150,500	$145,950
Head of household	188,150	182,450
Married, filing jointly	225,750	218,950
Surviving spouse	225,750	218,950
Married, filing separately	112,875	109,475

F.   Child Tax Credit -- In addition to providing a dependency exemption, a child of the taxpayer may also generate a tax credit. Called the child tax credit, the amount allowed is $1,000 for each qualifying child under the age of 17.

IV.   Tax Determination
    A.   Tax Table Method --Taxpayers who are eligible *must* use the Tax Table to compute their tax liability. However, the following taxpayers may not use this method.
        1.   An individual who files a short period return.
        2.   Individuals whose taxable income exceeds the maximum amount in the Tax Table (i.e., $100,000 for Form 1040).
        3.   An estate or trust.
    B.   Tax Rate Schedule Method
        1.   There are six rate brackets for 2006 (i.e., 10%, 15%, 25%, 28%, 33%, and 35%) for each filing status. The rate schedules are indexed for inflation each year.
        2.   Several terms are often used to describe tax rates.
            a.   *Statutory* (or *nominal*) *rates* -- the rates in the tax rate schedules.
            b.   *Marginal rate* -- the highest rate that is applied in the tax computation for a particular taxpayer.
            c.   *Average rate* -- the rate that equals the tax liability divided by taxable income.
        3.   A special computation limits the income tax on long-term capital gains (see Chapter 14 for a complete discussion).
    C.   Computation of Net Taxes Payable or Refund Due -- The total tax determined by reference to the appropriate Tax Table or Tax Rate Schedule is reduced by income taxes withheld by employers on compensation paid to employees, estimated tax payments made, and various other tax credits (e.g., child tax credit, credit for child and dependent care expenses, foreign tax credit) to derive net taxes payable or refund due.

An interest-free loan to the government? That's what happens if too much has been withheld from an individual's salary followed by a big tax refund at the end of the year. Changing the number of allowances claimed on a Form W-4 will increase the take-home pay and reduce or eliminate the year-end refund.

    D.   Unearned Income of Children under Age 14 Taxed at Parents' Rate
        1.   If a child reports a positive amount of *net unearned income*, it is taxed at the parents' marginal tax rate. This provision is commonly referred to as the *kiddie tax*.
        2.   A *child* for this purpose is defined as an individual who possesses the following attributes.
            a.   Has not reached age 14 by the close of the taxable year.
            b.   Has at least one living parent.
            c.   Has net unearned income for the year (i.e., unearned income of more than $1,700).
        3.   Net unearned income for 2006 is computed as provided in Exhibit 3-5.

4.   Any amount of net unearned income is taxed at the parents' marginal tax rate. The tax is computed as though the income was included on the parents' income tax return, and allocated to the child (defined as *allocable parental tax*).

Exhibit 3-5
COMPUTATION OF NET UNEARNED INCOME

> *Unearned income*
> *Less: $850*
> *Less: The <u>greater</u> of --*
> - *$850 of the standard deduction.*
> - *The amount of allowable itemized deductions directly connected with the production of the unearned income.*
>
> *Equals: Net unearned income*

5.   A parent whose child is under 14 may elect to report the child's unearned income that exceeds $1,700 on the parent's own income tax return if the following requirements are met.
   a.   Gross income is from interest and dividends only.
   b.   Gross income is more than $850 but less than $8,500.
   c.   No estimated tax has been paid in the name and Social Security number of the child.
   d.   The child is not subject to the backup withholding rules.
   If the election is made, the child need not file an income tax return because the child is treated as having no gross income. It is not wise in every case to make the parental election: calculations must be made both *with* the parental election and *without* the election to determine the best choice.
6.   In the case of divorced parents, the income of the custodial parent is used to determine the allocable parental tax. If a married couple files separately, the parent with the greater taxable income is the applicable parent.

For tax planning purposes, one always should know the marginal tax rate of the taxpayer, as this measures the incremental change in exemptions and itemized deductions, as well as the potential for kiddie tax and alternative minimum tax amounts. The marginal tax rate can be very difficult to determine.

V.   Filing Considerations
      A.   Filing Requirements
           1.   An individual must file an income tax return annually if certain minimum amounts of gross income have been received. These filing requirements

generally are based on the sum of the basic standard deduction amount, the additional standard deduction amount for the elderly (but not for blindness), and the allowable personal exemptions.

2.   A self-employed individual with net earnings from a business or profession of $400 or more must file an income tax return regardless of the amount of gross income.

3.   An individual who can be claimed as a dependent by another taxpayer must file an income tax return if *any* of the following applies.

    a.   Has earned income only and gross income that is more than the total standard deduction.

    b.   Has unearned income only and gross income of more than $850 plus any additional standard deduction that the individual is allowed for the year.

    c.   Has both earned and unearned income and gross income of more than the larger of $850 or the sum of earned income plus $300 (but limited to the applicable basic standard deduction), plus any additional standard deduction that the individual is allowed for the year.

4.   Individual taxpayers file an income tax return on either Form 1040, Form 1040A, or Form 1040EZ, depending, in general, on the complexity of the taxpayer's financial situation. For a calendar year taxpayer, the appropriate form is due by April 15 of the following year.

5.   In addition to traditional paper returns, the e-file program is an increasingly popular alternative. Here, the required tax information is transmitted to the IRS electronically. This approach can be advantageous because errors that otherwise may occur are reduced and the time required for processing a refund is shortened.

B.   Filing Status

1.   The amount of tax on a given amount of taxable income will vary depending on the filing status of the taxpayer. A taxpayer will file as either single; married, filing jointly; married, filing separately; or head of household.

2.   Head of household rates may be used by an unmarried taxpayer who maintains a household for a dependent. Further, if a married taxpayer meets the *abandoned spouse rules*, then the head of household rates may be used.

3.   The joint return rates also apply to a surviving spouse for two years following the death of the spouse providing that the taxpayer maintains a household for a dependent child.

VI.   Gains and Losses from Property Transactions -- In General

A.   Gain or loss *may* be recognized for income tax purposes on the sale or other disposition of property to the extent of gain or loss realized. All gain is *recognized* to the extent *realized* unless a specific provision in the law provides otherwise. Realized losses may or may not be recognized, depending on the circumstances involved.

B.   The concept of realized gain or loss can be expressed as follows.

Amount realized from the sale or other disposition
Minus: Adjusted basis of property
Equals: Realized gain (or loss)

---

1. The amount realized from the sale of property is its selling price less any costs of disposition.
2. Adjusted basis is determined as follows.

> Cost (or other original basis) at date of acquisition
> Plus: Capital additions
> Minus: Depreciation (if appropriate) and other capital recoveries
> Equals: Adjusted basis at date of sale or other disposition

C. After determining that gain or loss must be recognized on a sale or other disposition, then the gain or loss must be classified as to its nature (e.g., ordinary, capital).

VII. Gains and Losses from Property Transactions -- Capital Gains and Losses
A. Special characterization is required on the sale or exchange of capital assets. While capital gains may be taxed at preferential income tax rates for individual taxpayers, capital losses may be only partially deductible in the year incurred. Any unused capital losses may be carried forward and deducted in later years. See Chapter 14 for an in-depth treatment of this topic.
B. Definition of a Capital Asset
1. The Code defines a capital asset as any property held by a taxpayer *other than* property listed in § 1221. This list includes inventory, accounts receivable, and depreciable or real property used in a business.
2. The principal capital assets held by individuals include assets held for personal use such as automobiles or personal residences, and assets held for investment, such as corporate securities and land. Collectibles are also capital assets, but they are subject to somewhat unique tax treatment.
C. Taxation of Net Capital Gain
1. Currently, capital gains are subject to the following maximum rates:
   a. Short-term gains (held for one year or less) – 35%.
   b. Long-term gains (held for *more than* one year).
      (1) Collectibles – 28%.
      (2) Certain depreciable real property used in a trade or business (unrecaptured § 1250 gain discussed in Chapter 14) – 25%.
      (3) All other long-term capital gains – 15% or 5%.
2. The special tax rate applicable to long-term capital gains is called the *alternative tax* computation.
3. In no event will the capital gain be taxed at a rate higher than the regular bracket for the year.
4. If a taxpayer has a long-term capital gain and his or her regular income tax bracket for the year is 10% or 15%, the long-term capital gains rate is reduced from 15% to 5%.
D. Determination of Net Capital Gain -- Capital losses must be taken into account in order to arrive at a net capital gain. The capital losses are aggregated by holding

period (short-term and long-term) and applied against the gains in that category. If excess losses result, they are then shifted to the category carrying the *highest* tax rate. A net capital gain will occur if the net long-term capital gains exceed the net short-term capital losses.

E.   Treatment of Net Capital Loss

    1.   For individual taxpayers, net capital loss can be used to offset ordinary income (*for* adjusted gross income) up to $3,000. The short-term category is used first if the taxpayer has both short- and long-term capital losses.

    2.   Any remaining net capital loss is carried over indefinitely until exhausted. When carried over, the excess capital loss retains its classification as either short- or long-term.

TEST FOR SELF-EVALUATION -- CHAPTER 3

True or False

Indicate which of the following statements are true or false by circling the correct answer.

T   F   1.   Income broadly conceived for tax purposes only includes income that is taxable.

T   F   2.   An additional standard deduction amount is allowed if either the taxpayer or a dependent of the taxpayer is blind or over age 65.

T   F   3.   The Tax Table and the Tax Rate Schedule are basically the same and taxpayers have a choice between the two when calculating their tax.

T   F   4.   The standard deduction amount in 2006 is limited for an individual who may be claimed as a dependent on his or her parents' income tax return to the greater of $850 or the sum of the dependent's earned income plus $300 up to the basic standard deduction amount.

T   F   5.   Except in situations when a spouse dies during the year, the determination of marital status is made at the end of the taxable year.

T   F   6.   A self-employed individual taxpayer with net earnings from a business or profession of less than $400 would never be required to file an income tax return.

T   F   7.   A taxpayer who can be claimed as a dependent on another taxpayer's income tax return is not allowed a personal exemption.

T   F   8.   All realized gains are recognized for income tax purposes.

T   F   9.   Under current tax provisions, individual taxpayers lose the benefit of the personal exemption after their adjusted gross income exceeds a certain level.

T   F   10.   Individuals may carry forward unused capital losses for an indefinite period until they are finally utilized.

T   F   11.   The dependency exemption for children of divorced parents must always be claimed by the custodial parent, regardless of the amount of support provided by the noncustodial parent.

T   F   12.   To qualify for the head of household status, an unmarried taxpayer must pay more than half of the cost of maintaining a household as his or her home and the household must be the principal home of a dependent.

T   F   13.   For the abandoned spouse rules to apply, an abandoned spouse must provide over half of the cost of maintaining a household and must share the household with a child for more than one-half of the tax year.

T   F   14.   A residence and an automobile owned by an individual taxpayer and held for personal use are both classified as capital assets.

T   F   15.   Alicia purchased a painting in 2005 for $5,000 and sold it in 2006 for $7,500. Her gross income from the sale is $7,500.

T   F   16.   One of the most common types of expenditures that is deductible *for* adjusted gross income is medical expenses.

T   F   17.   Greta is a dependent of her parents. During 2006, she earned wages of $1,000 and received interest income of $450. Her standard deduction is $1,300.

T   F   18.   Gail is a dependent of her parents. During 2006, she received interest income of $450. Her standard deduction is $850.

T   F   19.   Capital transactions are classified as being either short term or long term.

T   F   20.   Individual taxpayers who incur capital losses may never deduct those losses against ordinary income.

T   F   21.   A qualifying child must meet the tests of relationship, abode, age, and support.

Fill-in-the-Blanks

Complete the following statements with the appropriate word(s) or amount(s).

1.   There are two categories of deductions for individual taxpayers: deductions _____ adjusted gross income and deductions _____ adjusted gross income.

2.   Assuming the abandoned spouse rules do not apply, the filing status of a married taxpayer may either be _____ or _____.

3.   The standard deduction amounts in 2006 for single taxpayers and married taxpayers filing jointly who are neither 65 years old nor blind are _____ and _____, respectively.

4.   To be considered a qualifying relative for purposes of the dependency exemption rules, the following tests must be met: _____, relationship, _____, joint return, and citizenship or residency.

5.   To meet the support test under the qualifying relative dependency exemption category, over _____ of the support of a dependent must be furnished by the taxpayer.

6.   A qualified surviving spouse who is 65 years of age or older and who has a dependent child must file an income tax return in 2006 if his/her gross income is _____ or more.

7.   The tax rate schedules must be used to compute an individual taxpayer's income tax liability if taxable income is more than _____.

8.   In determining the realized gain or loss from a sale, the property's _____ must be subtracted from the amount realized from the sale.

9.   Once it has been determined that the disposition of property results in recognizable gain or loss, the next step is to classify such gain or loss as _____ or _____.

10.   If an individual has net capital losses, they are deductible _____ adjusted gross income, up to a maximum of _____ per year.

11.   In 2006, the total standard deduction for a single taxpayer who is blind and 66 years old is _____.

12.   In computing taxable income, taxpayers are allowed to deduct the greater of allowable _____ or the _____.

13.   In order for a taxpayer to claim a relative as a dependent under a multiple support agreement, the taxpayer must contribute more than _____ percent of the relative's support.

14.   The *kiddie tax* does not apply after a dependent child reaches _____ years of age.

15.   In order for the *kiddie tax* to apply for 2006, the child must have unearned income in excess of _____.

16.   A dependent is one who is either a qualifying _____ or a qualifying _____.

Multiple Choice

Choose the best answer for each of the following questions.

_____   1.   Which of the following are *not* deductible as itemized deductions?
              a.   Expenses related to the production or collection of income.
              b.   Expenses related to the management of investment property.
              c.   Unreimbursed travel expenses related to employment.
              d.   Expenses related to the determination, collection, or refund of any tax.
              e.   All of these choices are deductible as itemized deductions.

_____   2.   The basic standard deduction in 2006 for a taxpayer filing under the single filing status is the following amount.
              a. $3,200.
              b. $3,300.
              c. $5,100.
              d. $5,150.
              e. $7,550.

_____ 3. Mr. and Mrs. Keller file a joint income tax return for the year. Mr. Keller is 65 and Mrs. Keller is 64. Their eldest son lives in their home. The son generates no income, is legally disabled, blind, single, and 29 years of age, and is totally supported by the Kellers. How many exemptions may the Kellers claim on their income tax return?

     a.   2.
     b.   3.
     c.   4.
     d.   5.
     e.   6.

_____ 4. The McCoys, who are both age 42, are married taxpayers and have a sixteen-year-old daughter who attends a boarding school. The McCoys' adjusted gross income is $43,750 and their total itemized deductions are $9,500. Assuming they file a joint income tax return, calculate their taxable income for 2006.

     a. $23,550.
     b. $23,900.
     c. $26,600.
     d. $31,050.
     e.   None of these choices.

_____ 5. Mrs. Stooge is supported by her sons, Moe, Larry, and Curly and an old, dear friend to the following extent.

Moe	35%
Larry	30%
Curly	10%
Friend	25%

Assuming a multiple support agreement is filed, who may claim Mrs. Stooge as a dependent?

     a.   Moe or Larry.
     b.   Moe, Larry, or Curly.
     c.   Moe, Larry, Curly or Friend.
     d.   Moe, Larry, or Friend.
     e.   Only Moe, since he contributed the most.

_____ 6. Louise qualifies to file her income tax return in 2006 using the head of household status. The amount of the basic standard deduction available is the following amount.

     a. $5,100.
     b. $5,150.
     c. $7,300.
     d. $7,550.
     e.   Some other amount.

_____ 7. Doug has the following transactions during the current year: sale of his personal residence at a loss of $3,200; sale of his antique automobile at a gain of $300; and sale of Skyview Corporation stock at a gain of $2,800. What amount of gain or loss does Doug recognize for the year?

     a. $100 loss.
     b. $3,100 gain.

    c. $2,800 gain.

    d.   No gain or loss is recognized because the assets are all personal use assets.

    e.   None of these choices.

_____ 8.   Margaret had taxable income of $15,000 for the current year not including capital asset transactions. Her recognized gains and losses from sales of capital assets follow.

Short-term gains	$1,000
Short-term losses	2,000
Long-term gains	0
Long-term losses	3,000

Calculate Margaret's taxable income after consideration of the above capital asset transactions.

    a. $11,000.

    b. $12,000.

    c. $13,000.

    d. $14,000.

    e.   None of these choices.

_____ 9.   Donny and Jeanna furnished over one-half of the total support of the following individuals during 2006.

- Daughter, age 23, with gross income of $900 who is a full-time college student.

- Their neighbor's son, age 17, who has lived with them since March (while his parents are in France) and who has no gross income.

- Jeanna's brother, age 33, a full-time student with gross income of $4,600.

Donny and Jeanna are married and file a joint income tax return for the year. How many *dependency* exemptions may they claim?

    a.   5.

    b.   4.

    c.   3.

    d.   2.

    e.   1.

_____ 10.   Sally, a single, full-time college student, was claimed by her parents as their dependent in 2006. In 2006, Sally earned $1,400 from a summer job, she received $103 in dividends from stock of a domestic corporation she inherited from her grandmother, and she received $1,350 in interest from a savings account funded by her parents and transferred to Sally several years ago. Sally's itemized deductions for 2006 totaled $600. What is Sally's taxable income for the year?

    a.   ($1,647).

    b. $603.

    c. $103.

    d. $2,803.

    e.   None of these choices.

_____ 11.   Juan and Connie, both age 37, have been legally separated since late 2005. Juan and Connie have five children, ages 15, 12, 9, 6, and 3. Juan's and Connie's separation agreement is silent as to which spouse may claim the dependency exemptions. Connie has always had custody of the two oldest children. During 2006, Connie has received no support from Juan. Connie, however, gave Juan a check for $3,300 in 2006 specifically for use in supporting the three children in Juan's custody. Given the current arrangement, what is the maximum number of personal and dependency exemptions Connie may claim in 2006?

    a.   7.

    b.   6.

    c.   5.

    d.   4.

    e.   3.

_____ 12.   During the year, Sylvia Henderson had taxable income from salary of $78,000. In addition, she sustained a short-term capital loss of $1,000 and a long-term capital loss of $2,800. By what amount will these losses reduce taxable income for the year?

    a. $0.

    b. $1,000.

    c. $2,800.

    d. $3,000.

    e.   None of these choices.

_____ 13.   Mr. and Mrs. Westphal, who are both over 65, file a joint income tax return that reflects the following.

Salary	$10,000
Long-term capital gain	8,000
Short-term capital loss	2,000
Rental receipts	19,000
Expenses attributed to the rental property (all are deductible)	8,000

From the above information, how much gross income do the Westphals have?

    a. $19,400.

    b. $23,400.

    c. $31,400.

    d. $35,000.

    e.   None of these choices.

_____ 14.   Mrs. Walker's husband died on June 5 of this year. She maintains a household for herself and her unmarried son, Artie. Artie qualifies as a dependent. What is Mrs. Walker's filing status?

	This Year	*Next year*
a.	Married Filing Jointly	Surviving Spouse
b.	Surviving Spouse	Head of Household

c.   Single   Single
d.   Married Filing Jointly   Head of Household
e.   Head of Household   Head of Household
f.   None of these choices

_____ 15.   Bill is single and has a $47,500 salary as his sole source of income. Bill also
             sustains a long-term capital loss of $10,000. What is Bill's capital loss
             carryforward to future years?
             a. $0.
             b. $3,000.
             c. $4,000.
             d. $7,000.
             e.   None of these choices.

_____ 16.   Gene is a single, self-employed automatic washer and dryer repairman. From the
             following data, indicate if Gene needs to file an income tax return.

	This year	Next year
Interest Income	$ 500	$ 600
Receipts from business	20,000	22,000
Deductible business expenses	19,800	22,400

	This year	Next year
a.	Yes	Yes
b.	Yes	No
c.	No	Yes
d.	No	No

_____ 17.   Don had the following items of income and expense during the year.

Salary	$28,000
Dividends	1,500
Short-term capital gain	1,000
Long-term capital loss	1,300

             Additionally, Don fulfilled the pledge of $1,600 that he made to his church. What
             amount should Don report as his adjusted gross income for the year?
             a. $28,000.
             b. $29,200.
             c. $29,500.
             d. $30,500.
             e.   None of these choices.

_____ 18.   Bill, age 25, is a single, self-employed accountant. His only income is from his
             sole proprietorship. Bill must file an income tax return for 2006 if his net earnings
             from self-employment are at least what amount?
             a. $400.
             b. $3,200.
             c. $3,300.
             d. $5,150.
             e.   Some other amount.

_____ 19.   Jim owns the following assets used in his business.

	Adjusted Basis
Land on which his office was built	$ 5,000
Office and equipment	10,000

The adjusted basis of the *capital assets* used by Jim in his business total what amount?

a. $0.
b. $5,000.
c. $10,000.
d. $15,000.
e.   Some other amount.

_____ 20.   Darron's wife died in 2003. Darron has not remarried, and continues to maintain a home for himself and his dependent seven year old child during 2004, 2005, and 2006, providing full support for himself and his child during these three years. For 2003, Darron properly filed a joint income tax return. Determine Darron's filing status for 2006.

a.   Single.
b.   Married filing joint return.
c.   Head of household.
d.   Qualifying widower with dependent child.
e.   Surviving spouse.

_____ 21.   Marilou was widowed five years ago and has lived alone at her current address since her husband's death. She had no income during the year but was supported in full by the following persons.

	Amount of Support	Percent of Total
Paul (an unrelated friend)	$3,010	43
Hortense (Marilou's sister)	3,430	49
Dave (Marilou's adopted son)	560	8
	$7,000	100

Under a multiple support agreement, who can claim a dependency exemption for Marilou?

a.   No one.
b.   Paul.
c.   Hortense.
d.   Dave.
e.   Hortense and Dave.

_____ 22.   Ameldo, a calendar-year taxpayer, filed her 2006 income tax return on April 1, 2007, and included a check for the balance of tax due as shown on the return. However, Ameldo discovered on June 30, 2007 that she had failed to include as an itemized deduction $2,500 of interest expense paid on her home mortgage. In order for Ameldo to recover the tax that she would have saved by claiming the $2,500 deduction, by what date must she file an amended return?

a.   December 31, 2009.

  b. April 1, 2010.
  c. April 15, 2010.
  d. June 30, 2010.
  e. Some other date.

_____ 23. Marta received the following during the year.

Salary	$40,000
Gifts from parents	5,000
Royalties	1,000
Prize winnings	6,000
Child support payments	6,000
Alimony from ex-husband	10,000

  What receipts from the above list must Marta include in the computation of taxable income?
  a. $52,000.
  b. $57,000.
  c. $58,000.
  d. $68,000.
  e. None of these choices.

_____ 24. Which of the following is an itemized deduction?
  a. Alimony payment.
  b. Charitable contributions.
  c. Ordinary and necessary expenses incurred in a trade or business.
  d. All of these choices are itemized deductions.
  e. None of these choices is an itemized deduction.

_____ 25. Which of the following is *not* deductible *from* adjusted gross income?
  a. Interest on a home mortgage.
  b. Charitable contributions.
  c. State and local income taxes.
  d. Certain payments to a traditional Individual Retirement Account.
  e. All of these choices are deductible *from* adjusted gross income.

_____ 26. Bruce and Jane, who have 3 dependent children, file a joint income tax return in 2006. They have gross income of $69,450 and itemized deductions of $10,000. Calculate their taxable income for the year.
  a. $42,650.
  b. $42,950.
  c. $43,150.
  d. $59,450.
  e. None of these choices.

_____ 27. Under the qualifying relative category for the dependency exemption, individuals must satisfy the following test.
  a. Support.
  b. Relationship or member of household.
  c. Gross income.
  d. Joint return.

e.   Citizenship or residency.
f.   All of these choices.

_____ 28.   Under the qualifying child category for the dependency exemption, which test below need not be satisfied?
a.   Relationship.
b.   Abode.
c.   Age.
d.   Support.
e.   Joint return.
f.   Citizenship or residency.
g.   All of these choices must be met.

Code Section Recognition

Several important sections of the Internal Revenue Code are described below. Indicate, by number, the appropriate Code section.

1.   _____   Gross income is defined as "except as otherwise provided . . . all income from whatever source derived."

2.   _____   The principal section of the Code in which the definition of a capital asset is given.

3.   _____   Taxable income is defined in this section of the Code.

Short Answer

1.   Sam and Sue are married and have 2 dependent children and a pet rabbit. Sam and Sue's earnings from their jobs total $50,000. Their other income consists of the following.

Interest income from savings account	$1,000
Dividends	500
Municipal bond interest	600
State lottery winnings	400

They also sustain a short-term capital loss of $2,000 on the disposition of Blue Corporation stock. Their itemized deductions during the year are $10,000. Calculate their taxable income for 2006.

2.   During the year, Leroy has the following capital transactions.

LTCG	$6,000
LTCL	2,000
STCG	2,000
STCL	4,000

How are these transactions treated?

SOLUTIONS TO CHAPTER 3 QUESTIONS

True or False

1.   F   Income broadly conceived includes all income of the taxpayer, both taxable and nontaxable. [Income (Broadly Conceived) p. 3-3]

2.   F   This additional standard deduction ($1,000 for each married taxpayer and $1,250 for single taxpayers) is allowed only for the taxpayer and the taxpayer's spouse. [Standard Deduction p. 3-6]

3.   F   Although many taxpayers use the Tax Tables, there are certain situations when the Tax Rate Schedules *must* be used. [Tax Table Method p. 3-19]

4.   T   A dependent's basic standard deduction is limited to:
   - The *greater* of:
     $850; or
     The sum of the dependent's earned income plus $300
   - However, the amount may not exceed the basic standard deduction for a single taxpayer ($5,150)

   [Special Limitations for Individuals Who Can Be Claimed as Dependents p. 3-9]

5.   T   For the year of death, the surviving spouse is treated as being married. [Rates for Married Individuals p. 3-28]

6.   F   An income tax return would be required if certain minimum amounts of *gross income* have been received. [Filing Requirements p. 3-24]

7.   T   A taxpayer who claims an individual as a dependent is allowed to claim an exemption for the dependent; however, the dependent cannot claim a personal exemption on his or her own return. [Special Limitations for Individuals Who Can Be Claimed as Dependents p. 3-9]

8.   F   The tax law provides exceptions in certain situations when realized gains and losses are not recognized. [Gains and Losses from Property Transactions—In General p. 3-31]

9.   T   This is one of the provisions of the tax law that is intended to increase the tax liability of more affluent taxpayers who might otherwise enjoy some benefit from having their taxable income subject to the lower income tax brackets. [Phaseout of Exemptions p. 3-17]

10.   T   The net capital losses may be carried forward by individual taxpayers until they are exhausted. [Treatment of Net Capital Loss p. 3-34]

11.   F   The noncustodial parent may claim the dependency exemption if the custodial parent agrees in writing to forgo the exemption. [Support Test p. 3-14]

12.   T   An unmarried individual who maintains a household for a dependent (or dependents) is entitled to use the head-of-household rates. [Rates for Heads of Household p. 3-30]

13.   T   These requirements, among others, must be met in order to use the abandoned spouse rules. [Abandoned Spouse Rules p. 3-31]

14.   T   These are examples of capital assets commonly held by individuals. [Definition of a Capital Asset p. 3-32]

15.   F   The gross income is computed after consideration of the $5,000 nontaxable return of capital invested in the painting. [Gains and Losses from Property Transactions—In General p. 3-31]

16.   F   Medical expenses are deductible *from* adjusted gross income. [Itemized Deductions p. 3-6]

17.   T   A dependent's basic standard deduction is limited to the *lesser* of:

- The basic standard deduction for a single taxpayer ($5,150)
- The *greater* of:
  $850; or
  The sum of the dependent's earned income plus $300

Therefore, Greta's standard deduction is $1,300 ($1,000 + $300).
[Special Limitations for Individuals Who Can Be Claimed as Dependents p. 3-9]

18.   T   The taxpayer's standard deduction is $850 because she has no earned income.
[Special Limitations for Individuals Who Can Be Claimed as Dependents p. 3-9]

19.   T   Capital gains or losses are classified as either short term or long term. [Taxation of Net Capital Gain p. 3-33]

20.   F   Net capital losses may offset up to $3,000 of ordinary income each year. [Treatment of Net Capital Loss p. 3-34]

21.   T   [Qualifying Child p. 3-11]

Fill-in-the-Blanks

1.   for, from [Deductions for Adjusted Gross Income p. 3-5]
2.   married, filing jointly; married, filing separately [Rates for Married Individuals p. 3-28]
3. $5,150, $10,300 [Standard Deduction p. 3-6]
4.   support, gross income [Qualifying Relative p. 3-13]
5.   one-half [Support Test p. 3-14]
6. $14,600 ($14,600 = $10,300 + $3,300 + $1,000) [Filing Requirements p. 3-25]
7. $100,000 [Tax Table Method p. 3-19]
8.   adjusted basis [Gains and Losses from Property Transactions—In General p. 3-31]
9.   capital, ordinary [Gains and Losses from Property Transactions—In General p. 3-31]
10.   for, $3,000 [Treatment of Net Capital Loss p. 3-34]
11. $7,650 ($7,650 = $5,150 + $1,250 + $1,250) [Filing Requirements p. 3-25]
12.   itemized deductions, standard deduction [Standard Deduction p. 3-6]
13.   10 [Support Test p. 3-14]
14.   14 [Unearned Income of Children Under Age 14 Taxed at Parents' Rate p. 3-22]
15. $1,700 [Unearned Income of Children Under Age 14 Taxed at Parents' Rate p. 3-22]
16.   child, relative [Dependency Exemptions p. 3-11]

Multiple Choice

1.   e   Each of the items listed may be deducted as an itemized deduction. [Itemized Deductions p. 3-6]

2.   d   The standard deduction amounts are adjusted for inflation every year. [Standard Deduction p. 3-6]

3.   b   Mr. Keller, Mrs. Keller, and their son [Dependency Exemptions p. 3-11]

4.   a

Adjusted gross income	$43,750
Less: Itemized deductions: $9,500 (Use the standard deduction)	(10,300)
Personal and dependency exemptions ($3,300 X 3)	(9,900)
Taxable income	$23,550

[Application of the Tax Formula p. 3-8]

5.   a   A multiple support agreement may be made if no one individual meets the support test. [Support Test p. 3-14]

6.   d   The standard deduction amounts are adjusted for inflation every year. [Standard Deduction p. 3-6]

7.   b $3,100 = $300 + $2,800. The loss from the sale of the personal residence is not deductible. [Gains and Losses from Property Transactions—Capital Gains and Losses p. 3-32]

8.   b $12,000 = $15,000 - $3,000 (net capital losses allowed--limited to $3,000 per year) [Gains and Losses from Property Transactions—Capital Gains and Losses p. 3-32]

9.   d   A *dependency* exemption may be claimed for the daughter and the neighbor's son. [Dependency Exemptions p. 3-11]

10.   e

AGI ($1,400 + $103 + $1,350)	$2,853
Less: Greater of basic standard deduction ($850) or earned income + $300 ($1,400 + $300), limited to $5,150	(1,700)
Less: Personal exemption	(0)
Taxable income	$1,153

[Application of the Tax Formula p. 3-8]

11.   e   Connie plus the two children in her custody. [Support Test p. 3-14]

12.   d   Up to $3,000 of net capital losses may be deducted by individuals per year. [Treatment of Net Capital Loss p. 3-34]

13.   d $35,000 = $10,000 + ($8,000 - $2,000) + $19,000--the rental expenses are deducted from gross income in arriving at adjusted gross income. [Gross Income p. 3-3]

14.   a   Because Artie qualifies as a dependent, Mrs. Walker may file using the joint return rates as a surviving spouse in the year following her husband's death. [Rates for Married Individuals p. 3-28]

15.   d   Of the $10,000 loss incurred, $3,000 is used currently and $7,000 is carried forward to future years. [Treatment of Net Capital Loss p. 3-34]

16.   a   In each year, Gene's gross income ($20,500 and $22,600) exceeds the sum of the standard deduction plus the personal exemption. Therefore, in each year an income tax return must be filed. [Filing Requirements p. 3-25]

17.   b $29,200 = $28,000 + $1,500 + $1,000 - $1,300 [Adjusted Gross Income (AGI) p. 3-5]

18.   a   Regardless of the amount of gross income, a self-employed individual with net earnings of $400 or more from a business or profession must file a tax return. [Filing Requirements p. 3-25]

19.   a   The land, office, and equipment are assets used in a trade or business, not capital assets. [Definition of a Capital Asset p. 3-32]

20.   c   A taxpayer may continue to use the joint return rates for two years following the death of one spouse if the surviving spouse maintains a household for a dependent child. Afterwards, the head-of-household rates may apply if a home is maintained for a dependent (or dependents). [Rates for Heads of Household p. 3-30]

21.   c   Paul would not qualify to receive the exemption because he and Marilou are not related. Dave would not qualify because his support does not exceed 10 percent of the total. [Support Test p. 3-14]

22.   c   If a taxpayer needs to file an amended return, it generally must be filed within three years of the filing date of the original return or within two years from the time the tax was paid, whichever is later. [When and Where to File p. 3-27]

23.   b $57,000 = $40,000 (salary) + $1,000 (royalties) + $6,000 (prize winnings) + $10,000 (alimony received) [Gross Income p. 3-3]

24.   b   A charitable contribution is one type of personal expenditure that may be claimed as an itemized deduction. [Itemized Deductions p. 3-6]

25.   d   Contributions to a traditional IRA are deductible *for* AGI. [Deductions for Adjusted

Gross Income p. 3-5; Itemized Deductions p. 3-6]

26.   a   Gross income $69,450

Gross income	$69,450
Less: Itemized deductions: $10,000 (Use the standard deduction)	(10,300)
Personal and dependency exemptions ($3,300 X 5)	(16,500)
Taxable income	$42,650

[Application of the Tax Formula p. 3-8]

27.   f   [Qualifying Relative p. 3-13]

28.   g   [Qualifying Child p. 3-11]

Code Section Recognition

1.   61 [Gross Income p. 3-3]

2.   1221 [Definition of a Capital Asset p. 3-32]

3.   63 [Standard Deduction p. 3-6]

Short Answer

1.   Gross income:

Gross income:		
Salary		$50,000
Interest income		1,000
Dividends		500
State lottery winnings		400
Total gross income		$51,900
Less: Deduction *for* AGI –		
Capital loss		(2,000)
Adjusted gross income		$49,900
Less: The greater of --		
Itemized deductions	$10,000	
Standard deduction	10,300	(10,300)
Less: Personal and dependency exemptions ($3,300 X 4)		(13,200)
Taxable income		$26,400

[Application of the Tax Formula p. 3-8]

2.   The $4,000 NLTCG is offset by the $2,000 NSTCL. A $2,000 net capital gain results. [Gains and Losses from Property Transactions—Capital Gains and Losses p. 3-32]

Chapter 4
Gross Income: Concepts and Inclusions

CHAPTER HIGHLIGHTS

Gross income is a key component of the base used in calculating a taxpayer's income tax liability. The Internal Revenue Code provides an *all-inclusive* definition of gross income. However, a number of exclusions from gross income have evolved over time because of legislative, judicial, or administrative action. The method of accounting adopted by a taxpayer is important because it generally determines the period in which income is recognized. However, special rules apply in certain situations with various types of income that affect the time of recognition. Finally, another important issue involves deciding who or what entity should recognize any income that is subject to tax. Fundamentally, however, all realized income must be recognized for income tax purposes unless a provision in the law specifically exempts the item from taxation.

I.   Gross Income -- What Is It?
    A.   Definition -- Section 61 provides an *all-inclusive* definition of gross income: "gross income means all income from whatever source derived."
    B.   Economic and Accounting Concepts -- An *economist's concept of income* differs from an *accountant's concept of income*. Economic income reflects consumption of goods and services during a period plus the net change in the fair market value of a taxpayer's net assets during the period. Accounting income, however, is based on the realization principle. The IRS, Congress, and the courts have rejected the economist's concept of income as impractical for tax purposes.
    C.   Comparison of the Accounting and Tax Concepts of Income -- Differences exist between income tax rules and financial accounting measurement concepts because the goals of each concept differ.
    D.   Form of Receipt -- Income may include any increase in wealth that is received in the form of money, property, or services.
    E.   Recovery of Capital Doctrine -- *Gross receipts* (i.e., selling price) must be reduced by the amount of the capital invested (plus or minus appropriate

adjustments such as capital improvements and cost recovery allowances) in determining the amount of *gross income* subject to tax.

II.   Year of Inclusion
    A.   Taxable Year
        1.   The annual accounting period or tax year is a basic component of our tax system. Generally, an entity uses the *calendar year* to report income. However, those taxpayers that keep adequate books and records may elect to use a *fiscal year* to report income. The fiscal year option generally is not available to partnerships, S corporations, and personal service corporations.
        2.   Determining the annual accounting period is important in its impact on the taxpayer's tax liability because of the following reasons.
            a.   Congress may change the tax rate schedule.
            b.   The entity's income may fluctuate from year to year, which means that if income is shifted from one year to another, it may be taxed at a different marginal rate.
            c.   The form or status of the entity may change and a different tax rate schedule may apply.
    B.   Accounting Methods
        1.   The year an item of income is reported often depends on the method of accounting a taxpayer uses.
        2.   Taxpayers generally will use either the *cash receipts and disbursements method*, the *accrual method*, or a *hybrid method* in reporting income.
        3.   Except for certain small businesses, the accrual method *must* be used in determining income from the purchase and sale of inventory.
        4.   The IRS may prescribe the method of accounting if a taxpayer has not adopted a method or if the taxpayer's method does not *clearly reflect income*.
        5.   Cash Receipts Method
            a.   Property or services are included in gross income in the year of actual or constructive receipt. The income need not be reduced to cash; rather, all that is necessary for income recognition is that the property or services received must have a fair market value or a cash equivalent.
            b.   A primary tax advantage of using the cash receipts method is the control that the taxpayer may have over the timing of recognition of income and expense.
        6.   Accrual Method
            a.   Gross income is recognized in the year in which it is earned, regardless of when the income is collected.
            b.   The income is earned when all events have occurred that fix the right to receive such income (the *all events test*) and its amount can be determined with reasonable accuracy.
            c.   The measure of the amount of accrual basis income is generally the amount the taxpayer has the right to receive, and not necessarily the fair market value of the receivable.
        7.   Hybrid Method -- The hybrid method is a combination of the accrual method and the cash method.
    C.   Exceptions Applicable to Cash Basis Taxpayers
        1.   The *doctrine of constructive receipt* limits the ability of a taxpayer to shift

income arbitrarily from one year to another. If a taxpayer is entitled to receive income and it is made available to him or her, and the actual receipt is not subject to *substantial limitations* or *restrictions*, the income is considered to have been constructively received and it must be included in income.

2. *Original issue discount*, which is the difference between the amount due at maturity and the amount of an original loan, must be reported as income or expense by the lender and borrower when it accrues, regardless of the taxpayer's method of accounting.

3. Series E and Series EE Bonds -- A taxpayer may recognize income on an annual incremental basis based on the bond's increase in redemption value or at the time the bond is redeemed.

4. Amounts Received under an Obligation to Repay -- When an amount has been received by a taxpayer and there is an obligation to repay the amount (e.g., loans, deposits), no income is considered realized.

D. Exceptions Applicable to Accrual Basis Taxpayers

1. Prepaid income generally is included in a taxpayer's income in the year of receipt, even if it has not been earned. However, deferral opportunities exist in certain situations.

2. Deferral of Advance Payments for Goods -- The seller can elect to defer the recognition of income in the case of receiving *advance payment for goods* until the goods are delivered if the taxpayer's method of accounting for the sale is the same for both book and tax purposes.

KEY TERMS
• Gross Income
• Cash, Accrual Accounting Methods
• Alimony, Child Support, Property Settlement
• Installment Method
• Below-Market Loan
• Prizes and Awards
• Social Security Benefits

3. Deferral of Advance Payments for Services -- Revenue Procedure 2004-34 permits an accrual basis taxpayer to defer recognition of income for *advance payments for services* to be performed after the end of the year of receipt. This deferral, however, *does not apply* to prepaid rent income or prepaid interest income.

III. Income Sources

A. Personal Services -- The income generated from a taxpayer's personal services must be included in the gross income of the person who performs the services. A mere assignment of income does not shift the liability for the tax.

Because of the IRS's program of computerized matching of income reported by taxpayers and their employers, taxpayers should verify that the amount of salary and other income reported to the IRS is correct. If the W-2s and Form 1099s are incorrect, a taxpayer should have them corrected as soon as possible so the IRS's records agree with the amounts shown on the individual's tax return.

B.   Income from Property
1.   Income from property, such as interest, dividends, or rents, must be included in the income of the *owner* of the property.
2.   *Interest* is considered to accrue daily. Therefore, if a gift of property is made by a cash basis donor on which interest has accrued, the donor must recognize income in the year that income is received by the donee equal to that amount which had been accrued up to the date of the gift.
3.   When there is a sale of property on which interest has accrued, a portion of the selling price is treated as interest and taxed to the seller in the year of the sale.
4.   *Dividends* do not accrue on a daily basis because their declaration is at the discretion of the corporation's board of directors. Dividends from property generally are taxed to the person who is the stockholder on the date of record. However, the Tax Court has held that a donor cannot shift the dividend income to a donee if a gift of property is made after the date of declaration and before the date of record. Generally, dividend income now is taxed at the same marginal rate that is applicable to a net capital gain (i.e., 5% or 15%).

C.   Income received by the taxpayer's agent is considered to be received by the taxpayer.

D.   Income from Partnerships, S Corporations, Trusts, and Estates
1.   Each partner in a *partnership* must report his or her distributive share of the partnership's income and deductions for the partnership's tax year ending within or with his or her tax year, even if such amounts are not actually distributed.
2.   A shareholder in an *S corporation* must report his or her proportionate share of the corporation's income and deductions for the corporation's tax year whether or not any distributions are actually made to the shareholder by the corporation.
3.   The *beneficiaries of estates and trusts* generally are taxed on income that actually is distributed or required to be distributed to them. Any income not taxed to the beneficiaries is taxed to the estate or trust.

E.   Income in Community Property States
1.   *Community property states* include Louisiana, Texas, New Mexico, Arizona, California, Washington, Idaho, Nevada, and Wisconsin. In Alaska, spouses can choose to have the community property laws apply.
2.   The basic difference between common law and community property law centers around the property rights of married persons.
3.   For example, income from personal services generally is treated as having been earned 50 percent by each spouse. The treatment of income earned from property held by married couples in community property states varies by state.

IV.   Items Specifically Included in Gross Income
A.   Alimony and Separate Maintenance Payments
1.   Alimony payments are *taxable* to the recipient and *deductible for* adjusted gross income by the payor.
2.   A transfer of property other than cash (e.g., appreciated property) to a former spouse pursuant to a divorce is not a taxable event. Instead, it is considered to be a division of property.
3.   Payments made under post-1984 agreements and decrees are

considered alimony if the following conditions are satisfied.
- a. The payments are in cash.
- b. The agreement does not specify that the cash payments are not alimony.
- c. The payor and payee are not members of the same household when the payments are made.
- d. There is no obligation to continue making the payments for any period after the death of the payee.
4. Special "front-loading" rules apply to post-1986 agreements to prevent property settlements from being disguised as alimony if payments in the first or second year exceed $15,000. Further, a special *alimony recapture* calculation must be made if changes in the amount of the payments exceed statutory limits. The recapture calculation would affect the net amounts considered alimony by the payor and payee.
5. Exceptions to the recapture rules exist in situations involving the death of the payor, if contingencies concerning property or a business exist, or if payments terminate because the payee remarries.
6. Amounts paid that represent child support are treated as nondeductible personal expenses rather than alimony.
- B. Imputed Interest on Below-Market Loans
  1. Imputed interest rules apply to several types of below-market loans.
     - a. Gift loans.
     - b. Compensation-related loans.
     - c. Corporation-shareholder loans.
     - d. Tax avoidance loans or loans that significantly affect the borrower's or lender's federal tax liability.
  2. The effects of the imputation to the borrower and lender differ depending on the type of loan involved. Exhibit 4-1 summarizes the effect of certain below-market loans on the lender and the borrower.

Exhibit 4-1
EFFECT OF CERTAIN BELOW-MARKET LOANS

Type of Loan	Lender	Borrower
Gift	Interest income Gift made	Interest Expense Gift received
Compensation-related	Interest income Compensation expense	Interest expense Compensation income
Corporation to shareholder	Interest income Dividend paid	Interest expense Dividend income

3. In certain situations, exceptions and limitations to the imputed interest rules apply.
   - a. Interest is not imputed on total outstanding *gift loans* of $10,000 or less between individuals, unless the loan proceeds are used to

purchase *income-producing property*.
- b.   The imputed interest on loans of $100,000 or less between individuals cannot exceed the *borrower's net investment income* for the year.

C.   Income From Annuities
1.   The tax accounting issue associated with receiving payments under an *annuity contract* is one of apportioning the amounts received between recovery of capital and income.
2.   Collections received before the annuity starting date equal to or less than the post-August 13, 1982 increases in the annuity's cash value are first considered gross income, and not recovery of capital. Excess amounts received are treated as recovery of capital until the taxpayer's cost has been recovered. Any additional amounts received are included in gross income.
3.   For collections received on or after the annuity starting date, an annuitant may exclude from income (as a return of capital) the proportion of each annuity payment that the investment in the contract bears to the expected return under the contract based on life expectancy tables published by the IRS.
4.   The *exclusion amount* is computed as follows.

$$\frac{Investment\ in\ contract}{Expected\ return} \quad X \quad Annuity\ payment$$

This exclusion ratio applies until the annuitant has recovered his or her investment in the contract. However, once the investment is recovered, the entire amount of subsequent payments is taxable. If the annuitant dies before the investment has been recovered, the unrecovered cost is deductible in the year the payments cease (e.g., the year of death).

D.   Prizes and Awards
1.   The fair market value of prizes and awards generally is included in income rather than being treated as tax-free "gifts."
2.   However, an award is not included in income if *all* of the following conditions are met.
- a.   It is received in recognition of religious, charitable, scientific, educational, artistic, literary, or civic achievement.
- b.   The recipient transfers the award to a qualified governmental unit or a nonprofit organization.
- c.   The recipient has been selected without any action on his or her part to enter a contest or proceeding.
- d.   There is no requirement that substantial future services be rendered as a condition to receiving the award.
3.   Another exception allows for the exclusion of certain employee achievement awards of tangible personal property (e.g., a gold watch). The awards must be made in recognition of *length of service* or *safety achievement*. The ceiling on the limitation amount generally is $400; however, a ceiling of $1,600 applies for a "qualified plan award."

E.   Group Term Life Insurance
1.   The premiums paid by an employer for group term life insurance on an employee are excluded from the employee's income for the first $50,000

of protection if the plan does not discriminate.

2. For protection received in excess of $50,000, the covered employee must include an amount in income that is calculated based on a table in the Regulations.

3. The amount calculated as includible income is generally less than the actual cost of the protection to the employer; therefore, favorable tax treatment may result for employees even when group term life insurance coverage is in excess of $50,000.

F. Unemployment Compensation -- Section 85 provides that all unemployment compensation benefits are includible in gross income.

G. Social Security Benefits

1. A portion of Social Security retirement benefits may be included in a taxpayer's gross income. The taxable amount of the benefits is determined through the application of one of two formulas that utilizes a unique measure of income -- *modified adjusted gross income (MAGI)*.

2. Generally, MAGI is the sum of a taxpayer's adjusted gross income from all sources (other than Social Security receipts), the foreign earned income exclusion, and any tax-exempt interest income received.

 Recall that the typical taxpayer pays one-half of the total contributions to the Social Security account and his or her employer pays the other half. Thus, in an ideal world, no more than one-half of Social Security benefits would be taxed upon receipt, under the recovery-of-capital doctrine.

3. In the formulas, two sets of base amounts are established. This first set is as follows.
   a. $32,000 for married taxpayers who file a joint return.
   b. $0 for married taxpayers who do not live apart for the entire year but file separate returns.
   c. $25,000 for all other taxpayers.

4. The second set of base amounts is as follows.
   a. $44,000 for married taxpayers who file a joint return.
   b. $0 for married taxpayers who do not live apart for the entire year but file separate returns.
   c. $34,000 for all other taxpayers.

5. If MAGI plus one-half of Social Security benefits exceed the first set of base amounts, but not the second set, the taxable amount of Social Security benefits is the *lesser* of the following.
   a.   .50 (Social Security benefits).
   b.   .50 [MAGI + .50 (Social Security benefits) - (first base amount)].

6. If MAGI plus one-half of Social Security benefits exceed the second set of base amounts, the taxable amount of Social Security benefits is the *lesser* of the following.
   a.   .85 (Social Security benefits).
   b.   Sum of the following.
      (1)   .85 [MAGI + .50(Social Security benefits) - (second base amount)].
      (2)   The lesser of the following.

     (a)   The amount included through application of the first formula.

     (b) $4,500 ($6,000 for married filing jointly).

"The very first Social Security check, for $22.54, was paid in 1940 to a Vermont woman who had paid $22 in Social Security taxes. By the time she died, in 1974, age 100, she had collected $20,944.42."

--Andrew Tobias

TEST FOR SELF-EVALUATION -- CHAPTER 4

True or False

Indicate which of the following statements are true or false by circling the correct answer.

T   F   1.   The recovery of capital doctrine provides that a seller can reduce gross receipts by the adjusted basis of property sold in determining gross income.

T   F   2.   Provided a taxpayer maintains adequate books and records, a fiscal year may be selected to report income.

T   F   3.   Revenue Procedure 2004-34 permits an accrual basis taxpayer to defer recognition for advance payments for goods or services to be delivered or performed after the end of the tax year of receipt.

T   F   4.   If a father "clips" interest coupons from bonds just before the interest payments are due and gives the coupons to his son, the father will still be required to pay taxes on the interest income.

T   F   5.   A security deposit received by a lessor (which will be returned if no damages are caused by the lessee) must be included in the lessor's income in the year of receipt.

T   F   6.   A salary check received on the evening of December 31, 2006 after banking hours is taxable in 2006.

T   F   7.   Payments properly classified as alimony should always be taken into income by the recipient and deducted by the payor.

T   F   8.   A taxpayer receiving an annuity applies the exclusion ratio only until his or her investment has been recovered.

T   F   9.   If a professional baseball player receives a new automobile for being the team's "outstanding fielder," he would likely be able to exclude this award from his income because it is really a gift.

T   F   10.   The actual cost to an employer for qualifying group term life insurance protection must be included in the gross income of an employee to the extent that the protection exceeds $50,000.

T   F   11.   For alimony payments under a post-1984 decree or agreement to be deductible, they must be in cash.

T   F   12.   With respect to a transfer of appreciated property to a former spouse, no gain or loss is recognized if the transfer is incident to a divorce settlement.

T   F   13.   In a transaction where a loan was extended to an employee (who is not a shareholder) by an employer at below-market rates, the employer will recognize imputed interest income and claim a compensation expense deduction, and the employee may claim an interest deduction and report compensation income.

T   F   14.   Prizes and awards are normally excluded from income because they are really gifts.

T   F   15.   Based on the doctrine of constructive receipt, an item is not brought into income until the taxpayer has actually received cash.

T   F   16.   A contestant winning $25,000 on a television game show need not report the amount as income.

T   F   17.   Tax accounting rules are not necessarily consistent with generally accepted accounting principles.

T   F   18.   A cash basis landlord collects a damage deposit from a tenant this year and ultimately returns the amount next year. The amount is taxable to the landlord this year.

T   F   19.   The courts have generally accepted the accountant's concept of income, which is based on the realization principle.

T   F   20.   The income earned by a partnership must be allocated among the partners and included in their income tax computations.

Fill-in-the-Blanks

Complete the following statements with the appropriate word(s) or amount(s).

1.   Gross income represents an increase in wealth that is recognized for tax purposes, but only after it has been _____.

2.   The _____ doctrine provides that on the sale of property, a seller can reduce the gross receipts by the adjusted basis of the property sold to determine the amount of gain or loss realized.

3.   The doctrine of _____ places certain limits on the ability of cash basis taxpayers to arbitrarily shift income from one year to another.

4.   The basic difference between _____ and _____ states centers around the property rights possessed by married persons.

5.   States within the US that have adopted community property law include _____, _____, _____, _____, _____, _____, _____, _____, _____, and _____.

6.   Gross income includes income realized in any form, whether in the form of _____, _____, or _____.

7.   The imputed interest rules generally apply to various types of _____.

8.   In general, the _____ method of accounting is required for determining purchases and sales when a taxpayer maintains an inventory.

9.   The law excludes from an employee's income the premiums paid by an employer for the first _____ of group term life insurance protection if the plan does not discriminate.

10.   As a safeguard against a divorce-related property settlement being disguised as alimony, special rules apply to post-1986 agreements if the payments in the first two years exceed _____.

11.   Based on a divorce or separation agreement, a taxpayer may receive alimony and child support payments from the former spouse. The receipt of _____ is included in gross income, but a _____ is not.

12.   The IRS may prescribe the taxpayer's method of accounting if the method chosen by the taxpayer does not _____.

13.   Under the _____ rules, a cash basis taxpayer may be required to recognize interest income before the cash is received.

14.   For a single taxpayer whose MAGI plus one-half of the Social Security benefits received does not exceed $34,000, no more than _____ percent of Social Security receipts are included in gross income. If this income threshold exceeds $34,000, up to _____ percent of the Social Security benefits are included in gross income.

15.   If a taxpayer receives $6,000 in alimony and $5,000 in child support, the amount that must be included in income is _____.

Multiple Choice

Choose the best answer for each of the following questions.

_____   1.   The following is *not* a reason why determining an annual accounting period for tax purposes is important.
            a.   Congress may change the tax rate schedule.
            b.   The entity may go out of existence.
            c.   The entity's income may rise or fall between years so that placing the income in a particular year may mean that the income is taxed at different marginal rates.
            d.   The entity may undergo a change in status and a different tax rate schedule may apply (e.g., change from a sole proprietorship to a corporation).
            e.   All of these choices are important.

_____   2.   The following doctrine places certain limits on the ability of cash basis taxpayers to arbitrarily shift income from one year to another in an effort to minimize taxes.
            a.   Claim of right doctrine.
            b.   Doctrine of the fruit and tree.

    c.   Recovery of capital doctrine.
    d.   Doctrine of constructive receipt.
    e.   None of these choices applies.

____   3.   A calendar-year cash basis taxpayer deposited $5,000 in an interest-bearing savings account at his bank. The deposit is expected to earn approximately $500 of interest income per year beginning on January 1, 20X0. He anticipates a need for cash at the end of five years (December 31, 20X4) when the account will have a balance of approximately $7,500. If the taxpayer closes the account at the end of the fifth year and assuming $500 was credited to the account at the end of each year, how much income must the taxpayer recognize in the year the account is closed?
    a. $0.
    b. $500.
    c. $2,500.
    d. $7,500.
    e.   None of these choices.

____   4.   Nel's savings account at the local credit union was credited with $600 of interest income on December 31, last year. The balance prior to the inclusion of the interest income was $2,400. On February 4, of this year, she withdraws $3,000 from her account. Nel is on the cash basis. What amount must be recognized as income last year?
    a. $0.
    b. $600.
    c. $2,400.
    d. $3,000.
    e.   None of these choices.

____   5.   Mindy and Rob are married and both are gainfully employed in Illinois. Mindy earns $38,000 as a nurse and Rob earns $44,000 as an accountant. If Mindy files a separate return, she would report how much gross income?
    a. $38,000.
    b. $41,000.
    c. $82,000.
    d.   A separate return may not be filed by Mindy.
    e.   None of these choices.

____   6.   Mindy and Rob are married and both are gainfully employed in New Mexico. Mindy earns $38,000 as a nurse and Rob earns $44,000 as an accountant. If Mindy files a separate return, she would report how much gross income?
    a. $38,000.
    b. $41,000.
    c. $82,000.
    d.   A separate return may not be filed by Mindy.
    e.   None of these choices.

____   7.   Select the *incorrect* statement.
    a.   Appreciation in the market value of an asset would be economic income but not accounting income.
    b.   For a cash basis taxpayer, the year of payment generally determines the

period in which an expense is deductible.

c.   An accrual basis taxpayer does not always recognize the same amount of net income for book and tax purposes.

d.   As long as a taxpayer follows generally accepted accounting principles, the Commissioner of the IRS cannot prescribe a change in accounting methods.

e.   None of these choices.

____ 8.   The Drayer Corporation, an accrual basis calendar-year taxpayer, sells its services under 12-month, 15-month, and 24-month contracts. The corporation services each customer every month. On October 1 of the current year, Drayer sold the following customer contracts, receiving payment as indicated.

Length of Contract	Proceeds
12 months	$9,000
24 months	8,000
36 months	4,800

The Drayer Corporation should recognize taxable income of what amount this year?

a. $3,650.
b. $12,800.
c. $18,150.
d. $21,800.
e.   None of these choices.

____ 9.   On December 1, of last year, Sandra gave her dependent son a $2,000 bond that paid 8% interest semi-annually on July 1 and January 1 (i.e., 4% twice a year). Sandra and her son are cash basis taxpayers. How much of the $80 of bond interest paid on January 1, of this year must Sandra recognize as income this year? For simplicity, assume a year has 360 days and each month has 30 days.

a. $0.
b. $40.
c. $67.
d. $80.
e.   None of these choices.

____ 10.   Eleanor purchased a ten-year annuity for $10,000 a number of years ago. She is to receive $4,000 per year for 10 years. How much gross income must Eleanor include in income in year 1?

a. $0.
b. $1,000.
c. $3,000.
d. $4,000.
e.   None of these choices.

____ 11.   Eleanor purchased a ten-year annuity for $10,000 a number of years ago. She is to receive $4,000 per year for 10 years. How much gross income must Eleanor *include* in income in year 4?

a. $0.
b. $1,000.

     c. $3,000.
     d. $4,000.
     e.   None of these choices.

12.   Leon retired five years ago on December 31 from Dart Company. Prior to his retirement, he had contributed $30,000 of after-tax earnings to an employee annuity plan. He had a life expectancy of 10 years at the time of retirement. Leon is to receive $1,000 per month for life beginning in January in the year following retirement. Leon should *include* the following amount in taxable income for the current year.
     a. $12,000.
     b. $9,000.
     c. $3,000.
     d. $0.
     e.   None of these choices.

13.   Which of the following is *not* a requirement that must be met in order for an alimony payment to be deductible for settlements reached in the current year?
     a.   Legally separated or divorced parties may not be members of the same household at the time of payment.
     b.   The payment must be made in cash.
     c.   The payment must be periodic.
     d.   The payment must not be designated as anything other than alimony (e.g., child support).
     e.   All of these choices are requirements.

14.   After being married for over 15 years Duane and Sue are divorced this year (Year 1). The following support payments have been or are scheduled to be made.

Year 1	$35,000
Year 2	20,000
Year 3	15,000

    Based on the above, what is the amount of excess payments that must be recaptured in Year 3?
     a. $0.
     b. $15,000.
     c. $20,000.
     d. $35,000.
     e.   None of these choices.

15.   Lee is covered under a non-discriminatory group term life insurance policy. Lee's employer pays the entire $700 cost of the $75,000 policy. Assuming that the uniform annual premium according to the Income Tax Treasury Regulations is $8 per $1,000 of coverage, what amount is taxable to Lee?
     a. $0.
     b. $200.
     c. $250.
     d. $600.
     e.   None of these choices.

_____ 16. Lee, a highly paid employee, is covered under a group term life insurance plan that discriminates in favor of highly paid employees. Lee's employer pays the entire $700 cost of the $75,000 policy. Assuming that the uniform annual premium according to the Income Tax Treasury Regulations is $8 per $1,000 of coverage, what amount is taxable to Lee?
a. $0.
b. $200.
c. $250.
d. $600.
e. None of these choices.

_____ 17. In Dr. Dogood's medical practice, her patients usually pay their office visit charges on the date of the visit or within one month. Additionally, she makes house calls for her patients suffering from acrophobia (because Dr. Dogood's office is on the 13th floor of the local high-rise professional office building). These outside visits are billed weekly, and are usually paid within two months after the patients collect from their insurance companies. Dr. Dogood is a cash basis taxpayer. Information relating to this year is as follows.

Cash received on the date of office visits	$ 40,000
Collections on accounts receivable	100,000
Accounts receivable, beginning of year	25,000
Accounts receivable, end of year	21,000

Calculate Dr. Dogood's gross income from her medical practice for this year.
a. $136,000.
b. $140,000.
c. $161,000.
d. $165,000.
e. None of these choices.

REFER TO THE FOLLOWING INFORMATION WHEN ANSWERING THE ITEMS BELOW.

Dorothy had the following cash receipts during 2006.

Interest on life insurance proceeds from her decedent aunt's policy left on deposit with the insurance company	$ 20
Interest on state income tax refund	22
Net rent from condominiums	18,000
Advance rent from lessees of above condominiums to be applied against rent for the last two months of the 4-year lease, ending in 2010	3,000
Dividend from a mutual insurance company on a life insurance policy	600

Dividend on Blue Corporation stock. Declared on   730
November 15, 2005, mailed on December 30, 2005,
to holders of record on December 15, 2005.
Dividend was received in the mail on January 2, 2006.

Gross amount of state lottery winnings (Dorothy   1,200
spent $450 on state lottery tickets, and $525 on
state pari-mutuel horse racing, for which she
has full documentation)

Dorothy uses the standard deduction on her 2006 return. Total dividends received to-date on the life insurance policy do not exceed the aggregated premiums paid by Dorothy.

_____ 18.   How much should Dorothy include in her 2006 taxable income for interest?
    a. $0.
    b. $20.
    c. $22.
    d. $42.
    e.   None of these choices.

_____ 19.   How much should Dorothy include in her 2006 taxable income for rent?
    a. $21,000.
    b. $18,500.
    c. $18,125.
    d. $18,000.
    e.   None of these choices.

_____ 20.   How much should she report as dividend income for 2006?
    a. $1,330.
    b. $730.
    c. $600.
    d. $0.
    e.   Some other amount.

_____ 21.   What is Dorothy's total gross income for 2006?
    a. $21,772.
    b. $21,997.
    c. $22,522.
    d. $22,972.
    e.   Some other amount.

_____ 22.   Lucy, an accrual basis taxpayer, leases office buildings to commercial tenants. During 2006, she receives $10,000 from various tenants as damage deposits, $300,000 for 2006 rents, and $50,000 for 2007 rents. How much should Lucy include in her income for 2006?
    a. $300,000.
    b. $310,000.
    c. $350,000.

        d. $360,000.

        e.   None of these choices.

_____ 23. Judy, a cash basis taxpayer, leases office buildings to commercial tenants. During 2006, she receives $10,000 from various tenants as damage deposits, $300,000 for 2006 rents, and $50,000 for 2007 rents. How much should Judy include in 2006 gross income?

        a. $300,000.

        b. $310,000.

        c. $350,000.

        d. $360,000.

        e.   None of these choices.

_____ 24. The imputed interest rules on below-market loans apply to which of the following types of loans?

        a.   Gift loans.

        b.   Compensation-related loans.

        c.   Corporation-shareholder loans.

        d.   Tax avoidance loans.

        e.   All of these choices are subject to the imputed interest rules.

_____ 25. What amount of Social Security benefits is subject to tax?

        a.   In certain situations, the amount subject to tax is limited to 85 percent of the benefits received.

        b.   In certain situations, the amount subject to tax is limited to 50 percent of the benefits received.

        c.   In certain situations, the amount subject to tax is zero.

        d.   In certain situations, the amount subject to tax can exceed 50 percent of the benefits received.

        e.   Each of these choices is true.

_____ 26. During the year, Alicia, a single taxpayer, earns consulting fees of $20,000 and receives Social Security benefits of $20,000. What amount of the Social Security benefits is subject to tax?

        a. $0.

        b. $2,500.

        c. $10,000.

        d. $20,000.

        e.   None of these choices.

_____ 27. During the year, Ramon, a single taxpayer, earns consulting fees of $50,000, interest on state of California bonds of $10,000, and receives Social Security benefits of $12,000. What amount of the Social Security benefits is subject to tax?

        a. $0.

        b. $10,200.

        c. $12,000.

        d. $31,700.

        e.   None of these choices.

Code Section Recognition

Several important sections of the Internal Revenue Code are described below. Indicate, by number, the appropriate Code section.

1. _____   The term "gross income" is defined.

2. _____   Provides a limited exclusion for premiums on the first $50,000 of group term life insurance protection.

3. _____   Provides the Commissioner power to determine if the accounting method used by a taxpayer clearly reflects income.

Short Answer

1. Sally, who is single, receives $15,000 of Social Security benefits during 2006. Her other adjusted gross income is $16,000. In addition, she receives tax-exempt interest income of $4,000. Calculate the amount of the Social Security earnings subject to taxation during the year.

2. Susan's records reflect the following transactions for the year. How are they treated for tax purposes?
    - Sale of stock for $10,000, original cost of $7,500.
    - Receipt of alimony of $8,000 from former husband.
    - Share of partnership earnings $12,000. Susan withdrew $8,000 during the year.
    - Received $45,000 of group term life insurance coverage from her employer. The plan does not discriminate in favor of highly-paid employees.
    - Received the door prize at the Chamber of Commerce annual dance valued at $1,000.

SOLUTIONS TO CHAPTER 4 QUESTIONS

True or False

1.	T	The Supreme Court has held that there is no income subject to tax until the taxpayer has recovered the capital invested. [Recovery of Capital Doctrine p. 4-6]
2.	T	However, in many situations, partnerships, S corporations, and personal service corporations may not use a fiscal year. [Taxable Year p. 4-6]
3.	F	Revenue Procedure 2004-34 only applies to services, and not to goods. [Deferral of Advance Payments for Services p. 4-13]
4.	T	The "fruit and tree" doctrine is applicable. [Income from Property p. 4-14]
5.	F	Because the lessor has an obligation to return the money, no income is recognized. [Amounts Received under an Obligation to Repay p. 4-11]
6.	T	The amount is constructively received, and therefore, taxable in 2006. [Constructive Receipt p. 4-9]
7.	T	Alimony payments are deductible by the party making the payments and are includible in the gross income of the party receiving the payments. [Alimony and Separate Maintenance Payments p. 4-20]
8.	T	This approach is required to apportion the amounts received between recovery of capital and income. [Income from Annuities p. 4-27]
9.	F	Athletes have been unsuccessful in their attempt to exclude these awards as being in recognition of "artistic" achievement. Therefore, the award is taxable. [Prizes and Awards p. 4-30]
10.	F	The amount taken into an employee's income is based on tables in the Income Tax Regulations and does not necessarily reflect the actual cost of the coverage. [Group Term Life Insurance p. 4-31]
11.	T	This is one of the requirements for a transfer of wealth to be classified as alimony. [Post-1984 Agreements and Decrees p. 4-20]
12.	T	Such a transfer is not considered a taxable event (i.e., no gain or loss is realized). [Alimony and Separate Maintenance Payments p. 4-20]
13.	T	Imputed interest rules are required to prevent taxpayers from shifting income to other taxpayers without recognizing tax consequences. [Imputed Interest on Below-Market Loans p. 4-23]
14.	F	Such receipts are not treated as gifts, but as gross income subject to taxation. [Prizes and Awards p. 4-30]
15.	F	There need not be an actual receipt of cash, only its constructive receipt. [Constructive Receipt p. 4-9]
16.	F	Such amounts are treated as gross income subject to taxation. [Prizes and Awards p. 4-30]
17.	T	Differences between tax accounting and financial accounting concepts are due largely because of the different goals and objectives of the two systems. [Comparison of the Accounting and Tax Concepts of Income p. 4-5]
18.	F	The amount is not taxable because there is an obligation to repay the damage deposit (assuming no damage occurs). [Amounts Received under an Obligation to Repay p. 4-11]
19.	T	The Supreme Court expressed an inclination toward the accounting concept of income when it adopted the realization requirement. [Economic and Accounting Concepts p. 4-3]
20.	T	Each partner reports his or her share of the partnership's income and deductions for the partnership's tax year. [Income from Partnerships, S Corporations, Trusts, and Estates p. 4-16]

Fill-in-the-Blanks

1. realized [Economic and Accounting Concepts p. 4-3]
2. recovery of capital [Recovery of Capital Doctrine p. 4-6]
3. constructive receipt [Constructive Receipt p. 4-9]
4. common law, community property [Income in Community Property States p. 4-17]
5. Louisiana, Texas, New Mexico, Arizona, California, Washington, Idaho, Nevada, and Wisconsin. In Alaska, spouses can choose to have community property laws apply. [Income in Community Property States p. 4-17]
6. money, property, services [Form of Receipt p. 4-5]
7. below-market loans [Imputed Interest on Below-Market Loans p. 4-23]
8. accrual [Accounting Methods p. 4-7]
9. $50,000 [Group Term Life Insurance p. 4-31]
10. $15,000 [Front-Loading p. 4-21]
11. alimony, child support payment [Alimony and Separate Maintenance Payments p. 4-20]
12. clearly reflect income [Accounting Methods p. 4-7]
13. original issue discount [Original Issue Discount p. 4-10]
14. 50, 85 [Social Security Benefits p. 4-33]
15. $6,000 [Alimony and Separate Maintenance Payments p. 4-20]

Multiple Choice

1. b   Assessing the particular year in which the income will be taxed is important for determining when the tax must be paid. But the year an item of income is subject to tax can also affect the total tax liability over the entity's lifetime. [Taxable Year p. 4-6]
2. d   The doctrine of constructive receipt taxes an item of income in certain situations even though it has not actually been received. [Constructive Receipt p. 4-9]
3. b   Income of approximately $500 is recognized each year over the five-year period. [Interest p. 4-14]
4. b   Income of $600 is recognized last year because it was constructively received, even though it was not withdrawn last year. [Constructive Receipt p. 4-9]
5. a   Because Illinois is a common law state, Mindy must report only her salary as income on her separate return. [Income in Community Property States p. 4-17]
6. b $41,000 = .50($38,000 + $44,000) -- Because New Mexico is a community property state, this allocation is required. [Income in Community Property States p. 4-17]
7. d   See the discussion in the text regarding the comparison of accounting and taxable income. [Comparison of the Accounting and Tax Concepts of Income p. 4-5]
8. a $3,650 = (3/12 X $9,000) + (3/24 X $8,000) + (3/36 X $4,800) [Deferral of Advance Payments for Services p. 4-13]
9. c $80 X 5/6 = $67 [Interest p. 4-14]
10. c $1,000 of the $4,000 received in year 1 is a return of her investment and $3,000 is reportable income. [Collections on and after the Annuity Starting Date p. 4-28]
11. c   Same as the previous question. [Collections on and after the Annuity Starting Date p. 4-28]
12. b $9,000 = $12,000 - [($30,000/$120,000 X $12,000)] [Collections on and after the Annuity Starting Date p. 4-28]
13. c   This criterion is not required. [Post-1984 Agreements and Decrees p. 4-20]

14. a   There is no alimony recapture because payments did not decrease by *more than* $15,000 per year. [Front-Loading p. 4-21]

15. b $200 = $8 X [($75,000 - $50,000) / $1,000] [Group Term Life Insurance p. 4-31]

16. e   The amount included in income is the greater of the actual cost ($700) or the amount calculated in accordance with the Treasury Regulations ($600 = $8 X $75,000/$1,000). Thus, Lee must include $700 in income. [Group Term Life Insurance p. 4-31]

17. b $140,000 = $40,000 + $100,000 [Cash Receipts Method p. 4-7]

18. d $42 = $20 + $22 [Interest p. 4-14]

19. a $21,000 = $18,000 + $3,000 [Income from Property p. 4-14]

20. b $730. The $600 "dividend" received from the mutual insurance company is considered a reduction in the cost of Dorothy's life insurance coverage. [Dividends p. 4-15]

21. d $22,972 = $42 (interest) + $21,000 (rent) + $730 (dividends) + $1,200 (lottery winnings) [Income Sources p. 4-13]

22. c $350,000 = $300,000 + $50,000. The $50,000 of prepaid rent received may not be deferred for tax purposes, even though Lucy is an accrual method taxpayer. The damage deposits are not income because of the potential obligation to return the amounts. [Prepaid Income p. 4-12; Amounts Received under an Obligation to Repay p. 4-11]

23. c $350,000 = $300,000 + $50,000. The $50,000 of prepaid rent received may not be deferred for tax purposes. The damage deposits are not income because of the potential obligation to return the amounts. [Prepaid Income p. 4-12; Amounts Received under an Obligation to Repay p. 4-11]

24. e   Each type of loan listed is subject to the imputed interest rules. [Imputed Interest on Below-Market Loans p. 4-23]

25. e   Each statement concerning the taxation of Social Security benefits is true. [Social Security Benefits p. 4-33]

26. b   The amount taxable is the *lesser* of the following:
         .50($20,000) = $10,000 *or*
         .50[$20,000 + .50($20,000) - $25,000] = $2,500
         [Social Security Benefits p. 4-33]

27. b   The amount taxable is the *lesser* of the following:
         .85($12,000) = $10,200 *or*
         .85($66,000 - $34,000) + $4,500 = $31,700
         [Social Security Benefits p. 4-33]

Code Section Recognition

1.   61 [Definition p. 4-2]
2.   79 [Group Term Life Insurance p. 4-31]
3.   446 [Accounting Methods p. 4-7]

Short Answer

1.   The taxable amount is $1,250, the *lesser* of the following.
      - .50($15,000) = $7,500.
      - .50[$16,000 + $4,000 + .50($15,000) - $25,000] = $1,250.
      [Social Security Benefits p. 4-33]

2.   The following amounts are included in Susan's income.

Sale of stock ($10,000 - $7,500)	$ 2,500
Alimony	8,000
Partnership earnings	12,000
Group term life insurance coverage	0
Door prize	1,000
Total income	$23,500

      [Income Sources p. 4-13]

Chapter 5
Gross Income: Exclusions

CHAPTER HIGHLIGHTS

This chapter discusses items that are specifically excluded from gross income. Even though a definition of gross income is provided in the Code, Congress has considered it necessary to indicate explicitly how certain items are to be treated, either for the sake of clarity or for the purpose of insuring some sense of equity. Congress has acted on its own initiative at times in defining gross income, but judicial and administrative influences also have played important roles in the evolution of the definition and scope of gross income.

I.   Statutory Authority -- Statutory authority for excluding certain items from gross income is provided in §§ 101 through 150 of the Internal Revenue Code. Congress has enacted these provisions for various purposes (e.g., to provide indirect welfare payments, to prevent double taxation, to provide incentives for socially desirable activities, to change the effect of judicially imposed decisions).

II.   Gifts and Inheritances
     A.   General
          1.   The recipient of a gift or an inheritance excludes the value of such property from gross income. The recipient is, however, subject to tax on any income that is earned from holding or exchanging the property subsequent to its receipt.
          2.   A *gift* has been defined by the courts as "a voluntary transfer of property by one to another without adequate consideration or compensation there from" which has been made "out of affection, respect, admiration, charity, or like impulses." Thus, in many cases the issue of whether a gift has been made rests on the donor's intent.
     B.   Gifts to Employees -- A payment is not considered a gift if it represents compensation for past, present, or future services. Transfers from an employer to an employee *cannot* be excluded as a gift.

C.   Employee Death Benefits
1.   When an employer makes payments to a deceased employee's surviving spouse, children, or other beneficiaries, a fundamental question must be resolved: Do the payments represent *compensation* for prior services rendered or are they *gifts*?
2.   Generally, the IRS considers such payments to be compensation for prior services rendered by the deceased employee. However, in certain situations, some courts have held that payments to an employee's surviving spouse or other beneficiaries are gifts.

III.   Life Insurance Proceeds
A.   General Rule -- Life insurance proceeds paid to a beneficiary by reason of the death of the insured generally are exempt from income taxation.
B.   Accelerated Death Benefits
1.   Generally, if the owner of a life insurance policy cancels the policy and receives its cash surrender value, the taxpayer must recognize gain equal to the excess of the amount received over premiums paid on the policy. In this case, the insurance policy is treated as an investment. Exceptions apply, however, for terminally ill and chronically ill individuals.
2.   For the *terminally ill*, such gain realized on the collection of the cash surrender value or the assignment of the policy proceeds to a qualified third party is excluded.
3.   For a *chronically ill* patient, no gain is recognized if the proceeds of the policy are used for the long-term care of the insured.
C.   Transfer for Valuable Consideration
1.   When a life insurance policy is *transferred for valuable consideration*, the receipt of insurance proceeds are includible in the gross income of the transferee to the extent the proceeds received exceed the amount paid for the policy by the transferee plus any subsequent premiums paid.
However, this rule does not apply when the transfer is made to any one of the following.
a.   A partner of the insured.
b.   A partnership in which the insured is a partner.
c.   A corporation in which the insured is an officer or shareholder.
d.   A transferee whose basis in the policy is determined by reference to the transferor's basis (e.g., property transferred by gift).
2.   Investment Earnings on Life Insurance Proceeds -- Earnings from the reinvestment of life insurance proceeds generally are subject to tax. The annuity rules are used to apportion the interest and principal elements of an insurance installment receipt. The principal element is excludable from income while the interest portion is includible in income.

IV.   Scholarships
A.   General Information
1.   Scholarships are payments or benefits received by a student at an educational institution that are not classified as either gifts or compensation for services. Subject to limitations, such amounts are excludable from gross income if received by degree candidates. However, if amounts received represent payment for compensation or if payments are made primarily for the benefit of the employer, then the

amounts are taxable to the recipient.

2.   The exclusion is limited to amounts required to be used for tuition, and course-required fees, books, supplies, and equipment. Amounts received for room and board are not excludable and are treated as earned income for purposes of calculating the standard deduction.

B.   Timing Issues -- If the amount eligible for exclusion is not known at the time the money is received, the transaction is held *open* until the educational expenses are paid.

C.   Disguised Compensation -- The IRS has ruled that scholarships made available by employers solely to children of key employees are taxable income to the parent-employee as disguised compensation.

D.   Qualified Tuition Reduction Plans -- An employee (including a retired or disabled former employee) of a nonprofit educational institution is allowed to exclude a tuition waiver from gross income if the waiver is pursuant to a qualified tuition reduction plan.

V.   Compensation for Injuries and Sickness

    A.   Damages

        1.   The tax consequences from the receipt of damages depend on the type of harm the taxpayer has experienced. For example, reimbursement for the loss of income is taxed the same as the income that is replaced, and a payment for damaged or destroyed property is treated as income if the proceeds received exceed the property's basis.

        2.   In terms of personal injury damages, a distinction is made between compensatory damages and punitive damages. Under specified circumstances, *compensatory damages* may be excluded from gross income. Under no circumstances may *punitive damages* be excluded from gross income.

        3.   Compensatory damages are intended to compensate the taxpayer for the damages incurred. Only those compensatory damages received on account of physical personal injury or physical sickness can be excluded from gross income.

    B.   Workers' Compensation -- Congress has specifically exempted workers' compensation benefits (i.e., fixed amounts for specific job-related injuries) from inclusion in gross income.

    C.   Accident and Health Insurance Benefits -- Such benefits received are excludable from gross income if the premiums are *paid by the taxpayer*.

VI.   Employer-Sponsored Accident and Health Plans

    A.   Employees, retired former employees, and their dependents are not required to include in income the amounts *paid by their employer* to keep accident or health insurance, disability insurance, and long-term care plans in force. Further, the

---

KEY TERMS

- Gifts and Inheritances
- Life Insurance Proceeds
- Scholarships
- Employee Fringe Benefits
- Interest, Dividend Income
- Foreign Earned Income
- Tax Benefit Rule

amount paid for such a policy is deductible by the employer.
B.   As a general rule, *benefits* received from such plans are includible in income.
C.   However, payments received for medical care of the employee, spouse, and children are specifically excluded from income, unless the amounts were deducted in a prior year as a medical expense. Payments for expenses that do *not* meet the law's definition of medical care must be included in gross income. In addition, amounts received as compensation for permanent loss or use of a *member or function of the body* or permanent disfigurement of the employee, spouse, or dependent are excluded from gross income.
D.   Medical Reimbursement Plans
   1.   Reimbursements received by an employee from his or her employer to cover medical or hospital costs may be excluded from income if the benefits are received under a plan.
   2.   However, if a self-insured reimbursement plan discriminates, the benefits received are subject to taxation.
   3.   On a limited basis, *health savings accounts (HSA)* provide an alternative means of accomplishing a medical reimbursement plan for an employee. The employee is not taxed on the contributions to the health savings account by the employer, the earnings on the funds in the account, or the withdrawals made for medical expenses.
E.   Long-Term Care Insurance Benefits
   1.   Because long-term care insurance is treated as a type of accident and health insurance benefit, the employee does not recognize income when the employer pays the premiums.
   2.   However, when benefits are received from the policy, the exclusion from gross income is limited to the *greater* of the following amounts.
      a. $250 in 2006 (indexed amount for 2005 is $240) for each day the patient receives the long-term care.
      b.   The actual cost of the care.

VII.   Meals and Lodging
A.   Furnished for the Convenience of the Employer
   1.   The *value of meals* provided to an employee and the employee's spouse and dependents is excluded from the taxpayer's income if the following three requirements are met.
      a.   The meals are *furnished* by the employer.
      b.   The meals are provided on the employer's *business premises*.
      c.   The meals are provided for the *convenience of the employer*.
   2.   The *value of lodging* is excluded from a taxpayer's income if the three requirements listed above are met and, additionally, if the employee is *required* to accept the lodging as a condition of employment.
B.   Other Housing Exclusions
   1.   In certain situations, an *employee of an educational institution* may be able to exclude the value of campus housing provided by the employer.
      a.   No income is reported by the employee if annual rents equal or exceed five percent of the appraised value of the facility.
      b.   If rents paid are less than five percent of the facility's value, the deficiency is included in the employee's gross income.
   2.   *Ministers of the gospel* can exclude from income the rental value of a home furnished, a rental allowance paid to them to the extent the amount is used to rent or provide a home, or the rental value of a home owned by

the minister.
3. *Military personnel* are allowed a housing exclusion in various situations.

VIII. Other Employee Fringe Benefits
    A. Specific Benefits -- Congress has enacted several nontaxable fringe benefits in order to encourage employers to do certain things. The following fringe benefits, among others, may be received on a tax-free basis.
        1. The value (subject to certain limitations) of *child and dependent care services* provided by an employer to enable an employee to work.
        2. The value of the use of certain *on-premises athletic facilities* by employees, their spouses, and their dependents.
        3. Qualified employer-provided educational assistance at the undergraduate and graduate level is excludable from gross income up to an annual ceiling of $5,250.
        4. The employee can exclude from gross income up to $10,960 (in 2006) of expenses incurred by an employee to adopt a child where the adoption expenses are paid or reimbursed by the employer under a qualified adoption assistance program. The exclusion in 2006 is phased out as AGI increases from $164,410 to $204,410.
    B. Cafeteria Plans -- The value of certain services or noncash benefits received that are a part of a *cafeteria plan* is excluded.
    C. Flexible Spending Plans
        1. Under these plans, the employee agrees to reduce his or her cash compensation in return for the employer agreeing to pay certain costs incurred by the employee (e.g., medical expenses) without the employee recognizing gross income.
        2. If the employee's actual expenses are less than the reduction in cash compensation, the employee cannot recover the difference. Thus, these plans are often referred to as *use or lose* plans.
    D. General Classes of Excluded Benefits -- Congress has specified seven broad classes of nontaxable employee benefits that include the following.
        1. General classes
            a. No-additional-cost services.
            b. Qualified employee discounts.
            c. Working condition fringes.
            d. *De minimis* fringes.
            e. Qualified transportation fringes.
            f. Qualified moving expense reimbursements.
            g. Qualified retirement planning services.
        2. For the exclusion of these general classes of fringe benefits to be available, certain requirements must be met. For example, *nondiscrimination provisions* apply to the no-additional-cost services, qualified employee discounts, and qualified retirement planning services, which provide that if the plan discriminates in favor of highly compensated employees, the exclusion is denied to these key employees. However, the nondiscrimination rules generally do not apply to *de minimis* and working conditions fringe benefits.
    E. Taxable Fringe Benefits -- Fringe benefits received from employers that are not excluded from income by statute or do not fit into any of the general classes of excluded benefits are taxable. The amount of income is equal to the benefits' fair market value.

IX.   Foreign Earned Income
    A.   A taxpayer who has *earned income* from personal services from a foreign source may elect *either* of the following options.
        1.   Include the receipts in the gross income computation and then claim a credit for foreign taxes paid on that income.
        2.   Exclude part or all of the foreign income from US gross income.
    B.   To qualify for the *exclusion*, the taxpayer must meet one of the two following tests.
        1.   Be a bona fide resident of the foreign country (or countries).
        2.   Be present in the foreign country for 330 days during any consecutive 12-month period.
    C.   The exclusion is *limited* to $80,000 of income earned during a tax year. However, the available exclusion must be prorated on a daily basis over the year if all of the days in the tax year are not qualifying days. For married persons, both of whom have foreign earned income, the exclusion is computed separately for each spouse.
    D.   In addition, *reasonable housing costs* incurred by the taxpayer and the taxpayer's family in a foreign country in excess of a base amount may be excluded from income.

X.   Interest on Certain State and Local Government Obligations
    A.   Interest income on state and local government obligations is exempt from federal taxation.
    B.   Other types of income are not excluded by this provision, such as interest received on a condemnation award, the overpayment of a state income tax liability, or gains on the sale of tax-exempt securities.

 While most municipal bond interest is not subject to federal income taxation, capital gain income realized on the sale of the underlying bond is. An investor should be aware of this when deciding which bonds to buy, and when to sell them.

XI.   Dividends
    A.   Amounts paid by a corporation to a shareholder with respect to his or her stock is taxable to the extent the payments are made from *current* or *accumulated earnings and profits*.
    B.   Often receipts that are referred to as dividends, such as dividends on deposits with savings and loans, patronage dividends, and dividends paid to policyholders of mutual insurance companies, are *not* dividends for income tax purposes.
    C.   A *stock dividend* generally is not taxable. However, if the taxpayer has the *option* of receiving cash in lieu of additional stock, the consideration received is taxable.

XII.   Educational Savings Bonds
    A.   Interest earned on certain Series EE US government savings bonds may be excluded if the following requirements are met.
        1.   The savings bonds are issued after 1989.

2.   The bonds are redeemed to pay *qualified higher education expenses.*
3.   The bonds are issued to an individual who was at least 24 years old at the time of issuance.
For married taxpayers, the exclusion is not available if a separate return is filed.

B.   Qualified higher education expenses consist of tuition and fees paid to an eligible educational institution for the taxpayer, spouse, or dependents.

C.   If the redemption proceeds exceed the qualified expenses, only a pro-rata amount of the expenses will qualify for the exclusion.

D.   The benefit of the exclusion is phased out as the taxpayer's *modified adjusted gross income* exceeds $63,100 ($94,700 on a joint return) for 2006.

E.   Modified adjusted gross income is adjusted gross income prior to the foreign earned income exclusion and the educational savings bond exclusion.

 With the top marginal income tax rate applicable to individuals at or exceeding 40 percent when considering both federal and state taxes, certain investors will likely be attracted to municipal bonds and educational savings bonds. Be certain that this decision makes sense after-tax, given the investor's tax rate, and the taxable and exempt rates of return.

XIII.   Qualified Tuition Programs

A.   No tax consequences fall to the parent if the amount the parent contributes is used for qualified higher education expenses of the child. However, if the parent receives a refund, the excess of the amount refunded over the amount contributed by the parent is included in the parent's gross income.

B.   The earnings of the fund, including the discount on tuition charged to participants, are not included in gross income provided that the contributions and earnings are used for qualified higher education expenses.

XIV.   Tax Benefit Rule

A.   If a taxpayer obtains a deduction for an item in one year and in a later year recovers a portion of the amount that caused the prior deduction, the recovery produces income in the year of receipt.

B.   No income must be recognized on the recovery of the deduction or portion of the deduction if a tax benefit was not received in a previous year.

XV.   Income from Discharge of Indebtedness

A.   The transfer of appreciated property in satisfaction of a debt is treated as a sale of the property followed by a payment of the debt. Foreclosure by a creditor is also treated as a sale or exchange of the property. Income is realized in such cases and is generally taxable.

B.   The discharge of indebtedness in the following situations is subject to special treatment.
1.   Creditors' gifts.
2.   Discharges under federal bankruptcy law.
3.   Discharges when the debtor is insolvent.
4.   A solvent farmer whose farm debt is discharged.
5.   Discharge of real estate debt on qualified real property used in a trade or

business.
6. A seller's cancellation of the buyer's indebtedness.
7. A shareholder's cancellation of the corporation's indebtedness.
8. Forgiveness of certain loans to students.

TEST FOR SELF-EVALUATION -- CHAPTER 5

True or False

Indicate which of the following statements are true or false by circling the correct answer.

T   F   1.   In general, if a beneficiary receives a death benefit from a decedent's former employer, the amount is excluded from income because it is treated the same as life insurance.

T   F   2.   Life insurance proceeds are always excluded from income.

T   F   3.   If a taxpayer has received various types of income during the year from foreign sources, the taxpayer may either include all of that foreign income in the regular tax computation and then take a foreign tax credit, or the taxpayer may exclude all of such income, subject to an overall limitation.

T   F   4.   A dividend received by a policyholder from a mutual insurance company is not taxable income.

T   F   5.   On the receipt of a stock dividend, the taxpayer generally does not recognize income.

T   F   6.   There are currently no interest income exclusion provisions in the law applicable to individuals.

T   F   7.   Interest received on certain state and local government obligations is excluded from federal income taxation.

T   F   8.   A voluntary transfer of property to another where adequate consideration is not exchanged is included in the recipient's gross income if the transfer is made out of affection, respect, admiration, charity, or like impulses.

T   F   9.   Payments received as compensation for services (e.g., for teaching) in certain educational degree programs may be excluded from income if all students are required to engage in the activity.

T   F   10.   The value of a parking space provided by an employer must be included in the income of an employee.

T   F   11.   In order to qualify for exclusion from income, a qualified employee discount for the receipt of services may not exceed 15% of the customer price.

T   F   12.   Alfred is an employee of his employer's car rental business. His employer also operates a regional bus company. As an employee, Alfred may exclude the value of a free bus trip and the use of a rental car received from the company's "vacation plan" fringe benefit package that is available to all employees.

T   F   13.   One of the requirements that must be met for meals and lodging to be excluded from a recipient's income is that they must be provided for the convenience of the employee.

T   F   14.   Interest earned on certain Series EE US government savings bonds may be excluded if the proceeds from a bond's redemption are used to pay qualified higher education expenses.

T   F   15.   A cash payment received by an employee from his or her employer can qualify for the gift exclusion in certain cases.

T   F   16.   Gain realized on the sale of a bond issued by a state or municipality is not recognized.

T   F   17.   No portion of a scholarship received that is used for tuition, room, and board is included in income.

T   F   18.   Receipts from illegal sources (e.g., embezzlement) are not taxable because the government would never expect the recipient to voluntarily report the amounts.

T   F   19.   Workers' compensation benefits are not taxable.

T   F   20.   Generally, a debtor whose debt is forgiven has enjoyed the receipt of income that must be recognized for tax purposes.

Fill-in-the-Blanks

Complete the following statements with the appropriate word(s) or amounts(s).

1.   The _____ rule provides that if a taxpayer obtains a benefit from a deduction for an item in one year and later recovers a portion or all of the prior deduction, the recovery produces taxable income in the year received.

2.   Up to _____ of adoption expenses incurred by an employee to adopt a child where the adoption expenses are paid or reimbursed by the employer may be excluded from income.

3.   The _____ portion, but not the _____ portion of amounts collected on a life insurance policy received in installments are excluded from gross income.

4.   In order for meals provided by the employer to be excluded from income of the employee, three tests must be met. These tests are (1) _____ (2) _____ (3) _____.

5.   For lodging provided by an employer to be excluded from income of the employee, the following additional test (over and above the three tests listed in the preceding question) must be met: _____.

6.   The interest earned from certain _____ and _____ obligations is excluded from

federal income tax.

7.   Certain amounts of scholarships may be excluded from income by _____ candidates, but similar amounts may not be excluded by _____ candidates.

8.   The maximum amount of foreign earned income that may be excluded from gross income in 2006 by a taxpayer is _____.

9.   There are _____ broad categories of nontaxable employee fringe benefits that have been specified by Congress in § 132.

10.   A _____ plan provision permits a covered employee to choose one or more benefits from among several taxable or nontaxable fringe benefits that may be offered by the employer.

11.   The benefit of the exclusion from Educational Savings Bonds is phased out as a taxpayer's _____ exceeds certain amounts.

12.   A scholarship recipient may exclude from gross income the amount used for _____ and _____.

13.   Fred gave a corporate bond, valued at $10,000, to Debbie at the beginning of the year. If $800 of interest was generated by the bond during the year, Debbie would have to report _____ of taxable income.

14.   Emily gave a municipal bond, valued at $10,000, to David at the beginning of the year. If $800 of interest was generated by the bond during the year, David would have to report _____ of taxable income.

15.   While cash dividends are taxable to the recipient, _____ dividends generally are not taxable to the recipient.

Multiple Choice

Choose the best answer for each of the following questions.

_____   1.   A widow and her two sons each received $5,000 from their husband's and father's former employer by reason of the death of their loved-one. Unless an exception to the IRS's position applies, what amount of the death benefit must be *included* in the surviving spouse's income in the year of receipt?
        a. $0.
        b. $1,667.
        c. $3,333.
        d. $5,000.
        e. $15,000.

_____   2.   Which of the following items is not normally excluded from an individual's gross income?
        a.   Punitive damages.
        b.   Life insurance proceeds received by reason of death.

      c.   *De minimis* fringe benefits.
      d.   A gift received by a child from his or her parents.
      e.   All of these choices normally are excluded from taxation.

____   3.   Emily, an undergraduate majoring in tax accounting, receives a $5,000 scholarship from the accounting department at the University of the Midwest during the year. The amount was spent in the following ways.

Tuition	$2,000
Room	1,000
Board	1,000
Books	500
Incidental living expenses	500

How much can Emily *exclude* from gross income?
      a. $5,000.
      b. $3,500.
      c. $2,500.
      d. $2,000.
      e.   Some other amount is excluded.

____   4.   Which of the following statements is true?
      a.   The receipt of a scholarship is always taxable.
      b.   A limited income exclusion is available to nondegree candidates who receive a scholarship.
      c.   A deduction is available for scholarship receipts spent for tuition by a degree candidate.
      d.   The *de minimis* fringe benefit rule could apply on the receipt of "supper money" by an employee.
      e.   None of these choices is true.

____   5.   Mr. and Mrs. Pease receive the following distributions during the current year from entities in which they hold securities.

Mr. Pease	General Motors Corporation cash dividends	$125
	City of Dallas bond interest income	200
Mrs. Pease	IBM Corporation cash dividends	30
	Mexican Foods (a Mexican corporation) bond interest	100
	Continental National Bank (stock dividends paid on common stock)	20

Mr. and Mrs. Pease file a joint return. What amount of the above income is subject to tax for the year after available exclusions?
      a. $75.
      b. $100.
      c. $200.
      d. $300.
      e.   None of these choices.

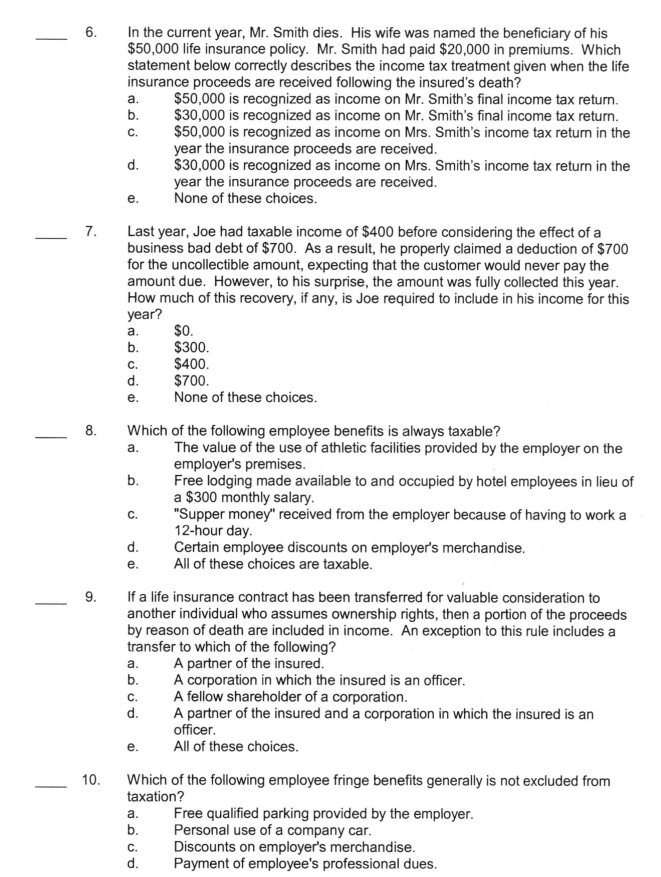

_____   6.   In the current year, Mr. Smith dies. His wife was named the beneficiary of his
            $50,000 life insurance policy. Mr. Smith had paid $20,000 in premiums. Which
            statement below correctly describes the income tax treatment given when the life
            insurance proceeds are received following the insured's death?
            a. $50,000 is recognized as income on Mr. Smith's final income tax return.
            b. $30,000 is recognized as income on Mr. Smith's final income tax return.
            c. $50,000 is recognized as income on Mrs. Smith's income tax return in the
                    year the insurance proceeds are received.
            d. $30,000 is recognized as income on Mrs. Smith's income tax return in the
                    year the insurance proceeds are received.
            e.   None of these choices.

_____   7.   Last year, Joe had taxable income of $400 before considering the effect of a
            business bad debt of $700. As a result, he properly claimed a deduction of $700
            for the uncollectible amount, expecting that the customer would never pay the
            amount due. However, to his surprise, the amount was fully collected this year.
            How much of this recovery, if any, is Joe required to include in his income for this
            year?
            a. $0.
            b. $300.
            c. $400.
            d. $700.
            e.   None of these choices.

_____   8.   Which of the following employee benefits is always taxable?
            a.   The value of the use of athletic facilities provided by the employer on the
                    employer's premises.
            b.   Free lodging made available to and occupied by hotel employees in lieu of
                    a $300 monthly salary.
            c.   "Supper money" received from the employer because of having to work a
                    12-hour day.
            d.   Certain employee discounts on employer's merchandise.
            e.   All of these choices are taxable.

_____   9.   If a life insurance contract has been transferred for valuable consideration to
            another individual who assumes ownership rights, then a portion of the proceeds
            by reason of death are included in income. An exception to this rule includes a
            transfer to which of the following?
            a.   A partner of the insured.
            b.   A corporation in which the insured is an officer.
            c.   A fellow shareholder of a corporation.
            d.   A partner of the insured and a corporation in which the insured is an
                    officer.
            e.   All of these choices.

_____   10. Which of the following employee fringe benefits generally is not excluded from
            taxation?
            a.   Free qualified parking provided by the employer.
            b.   Personal use of a company car.
            c.   Discounts on employer's merchandise.
            d.   Payment of employee's professional dues.

e.   All of these choices are excluded from taxation as a matter of policy.

_____ 11.   Sarah, a cash basis taxpayer, practices law as an employee of a firm where she earns an annual salary of $100,000. She receives the following fringe benefits from her employer this year.

Personal use of copying machine	$ 45
Free qualified parking (provided only to highly-paid employees and partners)	360
Personal letters typed	105
Membership in the U-R-Fit Athletic Club	500
Personal use of the firm's beach cottage	150

What amount related to the receipt of these fringe benefits must be *included* in Sarah's gross income?
a. $500.
b. $605.
c. $650.
d. $695.
e.   None of these choices.

_____ 12.   Which of the following categories of fringe benefits do not qualify for exclusion?
a.   No-additional-cost services.
b.   *De minimis* fringe benefits.
c.   Qualified tuition reductions.
d.   Certain working condition fringes.
e.   All of these choices qualify for exclusion.

_____ 13.   The maximum amount of foreign earned income that may be excluded in 2006 from a US taxpayer's gross income is limited to the following amount.
a. $78,000.
b. $80,000.
c. $85,000.
d.   All foreign earned income may be excluded.
e.   None of these choices.

_____ 14.   What fringe benefits (if any) will be excludable from an individual's gross income only if provided by his employer on a "nondiscriminatory" basis?
a.   No-additional-cost services.
b.   Discounts to below cost on goods sold to the public.
c.   Discounts on services exceeding 25% of the selling price.
d.   None of these choices.
e.   All of these choices.

_____ 15.   Lisa receives the following interest payments during the year.

Interest on refund of federal income tax for the prior year	$520
Interest on award for personal injuries sustained in an automobile accident last year	460
Interest on municipal bonds	900

Interest on Series H US savings bonds	650

How much should she report as gross income?
a. $0.
b. $980.
c. $1,630.
d. $2,530.
e.   None of these choices.

_____ 16. Mike sustains serious injuries in the course of his employment as a Washington, D.C. hot dog vendor. As a result of his injuries, Mike receives the following payments during the current year.

Damages for physical personal injuries	$3,250
Worker's compensation	6,400
Reimbursement from his employer's accident and health plan for medical expenses paid by Mike and not deducted by him	2,500

Compute his gross income from these items.
a. $12,150.
b. $9,650.
c. $5,750.
d. $0.
e.   None of these choices.

_____ 17. Which of the following is *not* excluded from a taxpayer's gross income for federal income tax purposes?
a.   Earned income from a foreign source in amounts up to $85,000.
b.   Gifts received from one's parents.
c.   Interest earned on bonds issued by the State of California.
d.   Accelerated death benefits received by a terminally ill or chronically ill individual.
e.   All of these choices are excluded.

_____ 18. Carmen, the owner of a $50,000 life insurance policy, decides to cancel the policy. She has paid premiums of $12,000 during the years the policy has been in force, while the current cash surrender value received on the cancellation is $20,000. Carmen must recognize income of what amount?
a. $0.
b. $8,000.
c. $12,000.
d. $20,000.
e.   None of these choices.

_____ 19. Ivan, the owner of a $50,000 life insurance policy, had planned to cancel the policy. However, he was killed in a tragic automobile accident prior to contacting his insurance agent. He had paid premiums totaling $12,000 during the years since the policy's acquisition. At the time of Ivan's death, the policy had a cash surrender value of $20,000. What amount is taxable on the receipt of the $50,000 proceeds?

a. $0.
b. $30,000.
c. $38,000.
d. $50,000.
e.   None of these choices.

_____ 20. Jane receives a $15,000 scholarship from Boatright College in August, 2006 to be used for tuition, fees, and related expenses during the 2006-2007 academic year. She actually incurs qualifying expenditures as follows.

August-December, 2006	$6,000
January-May, 2007	7,000

Compute Jane's gross income.
a. $1,500 in 2006.
b. $9,000 in 2006.
c. $500 in 2007.
d. $2,000 in 2007.
e.   None of these choices.

_____ 21. Lane receives the following compensation and benefits during the year.

Salary	$60,000
Overtime bonus	12,000
Value of medical insurance coverage	5,000
Medical insurance reimbursements	3,000
Total	$80,000

What amount is *included* in Lane's current year tax computation assuming he has always used the standard deduction?
a. $60,000.
b. $72,000.
c. $77,000.
d. $80,000.
e.   None of these choices.

_____ 22. Rick, a plumber, was fatally injured on the job and his widow, Jane, receives the following as a result of his death.

Accrued earnings	$ 5,000
Death benefit paid by the employer	3,000
Group term life insurance proceeds	9,000
Total	$17,000

Compute the inclusion of the above items in Rick and Jane's gross income for the year of his death.
a. $0.
b. $3,000.
c. $5,000.
d. $9,000.
e. $17,000.

f.   None of these choices.

23.   Ross, a full time student at Keller College, serves as a teaching assistant in exchange for tuition and board. Normally the tuition is $10,000 per year, while board is $3,000 per year. What must be *included* in income for tax purposes due to this arrangement?

     a. $0, because the value received is classified as a scholarship.
     b. $0, because teaching is a requirement of Ross's degree program.
     c. $3,000, because only $10,000 is classified as a scholarship.
     d. $13,000 must be included in Ross's gross income because it is compensation.
     e.   None of these choices.

24.   Mitchell is employed as the general manager of a local hotel. His employer gave him the choice of two compensation arrangements:

     Cash salary of $30,000 per year, *or*
     Cash salary of $24,000 per year plus free lodging at the hotel valued at $5,000

     If Mitchell chose the second option, what amount would be *included* in his gross income?

     a. $24,000.
     b. $29,000.
     c. $30,000.
     d.   None of these choices.

25.   The provision under § 119 excludes the value of lodging from an employee's gross income if the following requirements are met.

     a.   The lodging is provided for the convenience of the employer.
     b.   The lodging is furnished by the employer.
     c.   The lodging is on the employer's business premises.
     d.   The employee is required to accept the lodging as a condition of employment.
     e.   All of these conditions must be present.

26.   The following are dividends generally subject to current taxation.

     a.   Cash dividends on publicly traded stock.
     b.   Stock dividends on publicly traded stock.
     c.   Dividends paid by a mutual insurance company on an unmatured life insurance policy.
     d.   Cash dividends on publicly traded stock and stock dividends on publicly traded stock.
     e.   Cash dividends on publicly traded stock and dividends paid by a mutual insurance company on an unmatured life insurance policy.
     f.   None of these choices.

Code Section Recognition

Several important sections of the Internal Revenue Code are described below. Indicate, by number, the appropriate Code section.

1. _____   The general rules for the taxability of scholarships and fellowships are provided here.

2. _____   This section excludes the value of meals and lodging from gross income when certain conditions are met.

3. _____   Provides guidance regarding the taxation of seven categories of fringe benefits.

4. _____   Provides an exclusion associated with the funding of higher education with Educational Savings Bonds.

Short Answer

1. Margaret receives a $15,000 scholarship to attend State University during the current school year. Her records reflect the following expenditures.

Tuition	$10,000
Books and fees	500
Room	2,000
Board	2,000
	$14,500

    Comment on how the scholarship proceeds are taxed.

2. Identify the seven broad classes of nontaxable employee benefits.

SOLUTIONS TO CHAPTER 5 QUESTIONS

True or False

1. F   Generally, such benefits are treated as compensation for prior services rendered by the deceased employee. [Employee Death Benefits p. 5-6]
2. F   Normally this is the case, but exceptions do exist. For example, such proceeds may be income to an assignee to the extent that they exceed the amount paid for the policy plus subsequent premiums paid. [Life Insurance Proceeds p. 5-6]
3. F   The special treatment where foreign income may be excluded is available only for *earned* income. [Foreign Earned Income p. 5-26]
4. T   Such a receipt is not considered a "dividend" for tax purposes; rather, it is considered a reduction in the premium. [General Information p. 5-28]
5. T   While exceptions exist, the receipt of a stock dividend generally is not taxable. [Stock Dividends p. 5-29]
6. F   Interest received on certain state and local government obligations is exempt from taxation. [Interest on Certain State and Local Government Obligations p. 5-27]
7. T   Such exclusion generally leads to a lower coupon rate on the obligation. [Interest on Certain State and Local Government Obligations p. 5-27]
8. F   Gifts are not included in the recipient's gross income. [Gifts and Inheritances p. 5-4]
9. F   Such a receipt is not treated as an excludable scholarship. The amounts received are considered compensation for services rendered. [Scholarships p. 5-9]
10. F   The value is not included if it is considered qualified parking, which is a qualified transportation fringe benefit. [Qualified Transportation Fringes p. 5-23]
11. F   The discount exclusion may not exceed 20% of the selling price. [Qualified Employee Discounts p. 5-21]
12. F   Alfred may exclude the value of the rental car fringe benefit received but may not exclude the value of the free bus trip because of the "line of business" limitation. [No-Additional-Cost Services p. 5-20]
13. F   They must be provided for the convenience of the *employer* to be excluded, not the *employee*. [Furnished for the Convenience of the Employer p. 5-15]
14. T   The exclusion applies only if the savings bonds are issued after December 31, 1989 and if they are issued to an individual who is at least 24 years old at the time of issuance. [Educational Savings Bonds p. 5-29]
15. F   Such receipts are considered to be in exchange for services rendered. [Gifts and Inheritances p. 5-4]
16. F   The exclusion available pertains to interest income generated by such obligations. [Interest on Certain State and Local Government Obligations p. 5-27]
17. F   The portion of the scholarship not used for tuition and related expenses is included in income. [Scholarships p. 5-9]
18. F   The amounts are taxable because a provision exempting such receipts does not exist. [Items Specifically Excluded from Gross Income p. 5-2]
19. T   Congress has specifically exempted workers' compensation from income even though the payments are intended, in part, to compensate for a loss of income. [Workers' Compensation p. 5-12]
20. T   Generally, the income realized by the debtor from the forgiveness of a debt is taxable. [Income from Discharge of Indebtedness p. 5-31]

Fill-in-the-Blanks

1. tax benefit [Tax Benefit Rule p. 5-31]
2. $10,960 [Specific Benefits p. 5-18]
3. principal, interest [Life Insurance Proceeds p. 5-6]
4. The meals must be (1) furnished by the employer, (2) furnished on the employer's business premises, and (3) furnished for the convenience of the employer. [Meals and Lodging p. 5-15]
5. The employee is required to accept the lodging as a condition of employment. [Required as a Condition of Employment p. 5-17]
6. state, municipal [Interest on Certain State and Local Government Obligations p. 5-27]
7. degree, nondegree [General Information p. 5-9]
8. $80,000 [Foreign Earned Income p. 5-26]
9. seven [General Classes of Excluded Benefits p. 5-20]
10. cafeteria [Cafeteria Plans p. 5-19]
11. modified adjusted gross income [Educational Savings Bonds p. 5-29]
12. tuition, related expenses [Scholarships p. 5-9]
13. $800 [Interest on Certain State and Local Government Obligations p. 5-27]
14. $0 [Interest on Certain State and Local Government Obligations p. 5-27]
15. stock [Stock Dividends p. 5-29]

Multiple Choice

1. d   In general, the IRS considers such payments to be compensation for prior services rendered by the deceased employee. [Employee Death Benefits p. 5-6]
2. a   Because the amounts received as punitive damages may actually place the victim in a better economic position than before the harm was experienced, they are included in gross income. [Personal Injury p. 5-11]
3. c   The cost of tuition ($2,000) and books ($500) may be excluded as a scholarship. [General Information p. 5-9]
4. d   Supper money is specifically included as a *de minimis* fringe in a congressional report because accounting for such costs would be impractical given the small amount. [*De Minimis* Fringes p. 5-22]
5. e $255 = $125 + $30 + $100 [Interest on Certain State and Local Government Obligations p. 5-27; Dividends p. 5-28]
6. e   Life insurance proceeds paid to the beneficiary because of the death of the insured are exempt from income tax. [Life Insurance Proceeds p. 5-6]
7. c   Income is recognized in the year of recovery to the extent the deduction reduced taxable income ($400) in the earlier year. [Tax Benefit Rule p. 5-31]
8. b   Because acceptance of the lodging is not a condition of employment, its value is taxable. [Required as a Condition of Employment p. 5-17]
9. d   These exceptions facilitate the use of insurance contracts to fund buy-sell agreements. [Transfer for Valuable Consideration p. 5-8]
10. b   Only certain fringe benefits specified by law are excluded from taxation. [General Classes of Excluded Benefits p. 5-20]
11. c

Athletic club membership	$500
Use of firm's beach cottage	150
Total	$650

[General Classes of Excluded Benefits p. 5-20]

12. e   Each of the fringes listed qualifies for exclusion. [General Classes of Excluded

Benefits p. 5-20]

13.   b   This amount is set by law and is available if the taxpayer is willing to forgo the use of the tax credit for foreign taxes paid. [Foreign Earned Income p. 5-26]

14.   a   For no-additional-cost services, qualified employee discounts, and qualified retirement planning services, if the plan is discriminatory in favor of highly compensated employees, these key employees are denied exclusion treatment. [Nondiscrimination Provisions p. 5-24]

15.   c $1,630 = $520 + $460 + $650 [Interest on Certain State and Local Government Obligations p. 5-27]

16.   d   None of the amounts received is subject to taxation. [Compensation for Injuries and Sickness p. 5-11]

17.   a   The exclusion is available on foreign earned income of up to $80,000 in 2006. [Foreign Earned Income p. 5-26]

18.   b $8,000 = $20,000 - $12,000 [Transfer for Valuable Consideration p. 5-8]

19.   a   Life insurance proceeds paid to the beneficiary because of the death of the insured are exempt from income tax. [General Rule p. 5-6]

20.   d   The amount received in excess of qualifying expenses is included in gross income. [Timing Issues p. 5-10]

21.   b   Only the salary and the overtime bonus are included in the tax computation. The other items are excluded from taxation. [Employer-Sponsored Accident and Health Plans p. 5-13]

22.   f $8,000 = $5,000 (accrued earnings) + $3,000 (death benefit paid by the employer). The IRS generally considers death benefit payments to be compensation for prior services rendered by the deceased employee. [Employee Death Benefits p. 5-6]

23.   d   Payments received that represent compensation for services rendered are included in gross income. [General Information p. 5-9]

24.   b   Because the employee has the option of receiving cash or lodging, the required test is not met and the value of the lodging must be included in gross income. [Required as a Condition of Employment p. 5-17]

25.   e   Each of the conditions must be met in order to exclude the value of lodging from gross income. [Furnished for the Convenience of the Employer p. 5-15]

26.   a   Some payments frequently referred to as dividends are not considered dividends for tax purposes. Further, the receipt of stock dividends generally is not subject to taxation. [Dividends p. 5-28]

Code Section Recognition

1.   117 [Scholarships p. 5-9]
2.   119 [Meals and Lodging p. 5-15]
3.   132 [General Classes of Excluded Benefits p. 5-20]
4.   135 [Educational Savings Bonds p. 5-29]

Short Answer

1. Of the $15,000 received, the $10,500 spent on tuition, books, and fees is excluded from taxation. The remaining $4,500 ($15,000 - $10,500) is subject to taxation. [General Information p. 5-9]

2. No-additional-cost services.
    Qualified employee discounts.
    Working condition fringes.
    De minimis fringes.
    Qualified transportation fringe.
    Qualified moving expense reimbursement.
    Qualified retirement planning services.
    [General Classes of Excluded Benefits p. 5-20]

Chapter 6
Deductions and Losses: In General

CHAPTER HIGHLIGHTS

The courts have established the principle that unless an expenditure is provided by the Code as being deductible, then it is *not* deductible. Generally, however, deductions are allowable for items of expense incurred in a trade or business or in the production of income as well as for some items of a personal nature. These expenditures are deductible in determining taxable income, either as deductions in arriving at adjusted gross income or as deductions subtracted from adjusted gross income. Business and certain nonbusiness losses also are deductible, but with some limitations. Moreover, a number of disallowance possibilities exist in situations where otherwise deductible items are not deductible in part or in full. This chapter includes discussion of these concepts and issues.

I.   Classification of Deductible Expenses
     A.   Scheme of the Treatment of Deductions and Losses
          1.   Expenditures and losses are *not* deductible unless a provision in the law provides for such deduction.
          2.   Deductible expenses may be deducted either *for* adjusted gross income (AGI) (i.e., deductions subtracted from gross income in calculating adjusted gross income) or *from* AGI.
          3.   Deductions *for* AGI may be claimed whether or not the taxpayer itemizes. However, deductions *from* AGI produce a tax benefit only if they aggregate more than the taxpayer's standard deduction. Thus, deductions *for* AGI may be more valuable to the taxpayer than deductions *from* AGI.
          4.   AGI is an important amount because it is used as a factor in the limitation of certain itemized deductions (e.g., medical expenses, charitable contributions).
     B.   Deductions *for* Adjusted Gross Income -- Section 62 specifies those expenses that are deductible *for* adjusted gross income. These items include (among others) the following.

1. Trade or business deductions.
2. Certain reimbursed employee business expenses.
3. Rent and royalty expenses.
4. Alimony payments.
5. Keogh and traditional IRA deductions.
6. Losses, within limits, on the sale or exchange of property other than personal use property.
7. One-half of the self-employment tax paid by a self-employed taxpayer.
8. Moving expenses.
9. The deduction for interest paid on student loans.
10. The deduction for medical insurance premiums paid by a self employed taxpayer.

C. Itemized Deductions -- The following lists some of the more commonly encountered expenses deductible *from* adjusted gross income.
   1. Expenses allowed by § 212 that are paid or incurred:
     a. For the production or collection of income (other than rent or royalty income).
     b. For the management, conservation, or maintenance of property held for the production of income (other than rent or royalty income).
     c. In connection with the determination, collection, or refund of any tax.
   2. Deductible Personal Expenses:
     a. Medical expenses.
     b. Certain state and local taxes.
     c. Interest incurred on a personal residence.
     d. Charitable contributions.
     e. Personal casualty losses.

D. Trade or Business Expenses and Production of Income Expenses
   1. Section 162(a) permits a deduction for all *ordinary and necessary* expenses paid or incurred in carrying on a trade or business. Unfortunately, a clear and unambiguous definition of *trade or business* does not exist. Such expenses are deductible *for* AGI.
   2. Certain types of expenses, such as charitable contributions, bribes, and fines and penalties, are not classified as trade or business expenses.
   3. An expense must be both *ordinary* and *necessary* in order to be deductible under § 162. However, the words ordinary and necessary are not defined in the Code; but rather, they have been defined over time by the courts.
   4. An expense is considered to be *necessary* if a prudent businessperson would incur such an expense and if the expense is expected to be appropriate and helpful in the taxpayer's business.
   5. An expense is *ordinary* if it is normal, usual, or customary in the taxpayer's business. The amount cannot be capital in nature and it need not be a recurring expenditure.
   6. Reasonableness Requirement -- Salaries and other compensation for personal services must be of a *reasonable* amount to be deducted. Further, the courts have held that for other business expenses to be ordinary and necessary, they must also be reasonable in amount. What constitutes reasonable is a *question of fact*.

E. Business and Nonbusiness Losses

1.   Section 165 allows a deduction for the following losses.
        a.   Losses incurred in a trade or business.
        b.   Losses incurred in any transaction entered into for profit.
        c.   Personal casualty losses.
2.   Personal casualty losses are reduced by $100 *per casualty* and the *aggregate of all casualty losses* is reduced by 10 percent of the taxpayer's adjusted gross income.
3.   These losses may be deducted either *for* or *from* adjusted gross income, depending on the nature of the loss.

II.   Deductions and Losses -- Timing of Expense Recognition
    A.   Importance of Taxpayer's Method of Accounting -- The *method of accounting* used by a taxpayer controls the timing as to when an item is includible in income and deductible from income in the determination of taxable income. The method selected must clearly reflect the taxpayer's income and must be applied consistently.

> Generally, it is prudent to time income and expenditures so that they are taken into account on either side of the taxpayer's year-end—depending on which alternative produces the greatest tax benefit.

    B.   Cash Method Requirements
        1.   Expenses are deductible only when an amount is actually or constructively paid with cash or other property. However, payment does not assure a current deduction.
        2.   A deduction can be generated by paying with borrowed funds, but issuing a note or promising to pay will not give rise to a deduction.
        3.   If an expenditure creates an asset that has a life which extends substantially beyond the close of the tax year, the amount must be capitalized.
        4.   Limitations on Who Can Use the Cash Method -- Certain taxpayers are not allowed to use the cash method (see Chapter 16).
    C.   Accrual Method Requirements
        1.   To deduct an expense under the accrual method, the *all events test* and the *economic performance test* must be met. A deduction cannot be claimed until (1) all the events have occurred to create the taxpayer's liability and (2) the amount of the liability can be determined with reasonable accuracy. Once these requirements are satisfied, the deduction is permitted only if economic performance has occurred. The

KEY TERMS
• Deduction *For, From* AGI
• Trade or Business Expense (§ 162)
• Income Production Expense (§ 212)
• Hobby Loss
• Vacation Home

economic performance test is met when the service, property, or use of property giving rise to the liability is actually performed for, provided to, or used by the taxpayer.

        2.   Exceptions to the economic performance test apply in the case of certain recurring items.

        3.   Reserves for estimated expenses that may be claimed for financial accounting purposes are *not* deductible for tax purposes because the economic performance test cannot be satisfied.

III.   Disallowance Possibilities

    A.   Public Policy Limitation

        1.   A payment that is in *violation of public policy* is not considered a necessary expense and therefore is not deductible.

        2.   Several nondeductible expenses fall under this limitation.

              a.   Payments for illegal bribes and kickbacks.

              b.   Fines and penalties paid to a government for violation of a law.

              c.   Two-thirds of the treble damage payments made to claimants resulting from violation of antitrust law.

        3.   Legal expenses are deductible if they are incurred in connection with trade or business activity or relate to property held for the production of income or relate to the determination of a tax liability. However, legal fees incurred for personal reasons are not deductible.

        4.   The normal expenses of operating an illegal business, other than those expenses that are contrary to public policy, are deductible. An exception to this rule applies to ordinary and necessary business expenses incurred with regard to illegal trafficking in drugs. Such expenses are not deductible.

    B.   Political Contributions and Lobbying Activities

        1.   Generally, a business deduction is not allowed for direct or indirect payments made for political purposes.

        2.   Taxpayers may not deduct expenses associated with political campaigns or attempts to influence voters or the public. In addition, any lobbying expenses incurred in attempting to influence state or federal legislation or the actions of high ranking government officials are not deductible. The disallowance also applies to a pro rata portion of the membership dues of trade associations and other groups used for lobbying activities.

        3.   The disallowance does not apply to activities devoted solely to monitoring legislation or to lobbying expenses at the local government level.

    C.   Excessive Executive Compensation -- The compensation deduction allowable to a publicly held corporation may be limited to $1 million for each covered executive. The provision is applicable to the compensation paid to the chief executive officer and the four other most highly compensated officers. Exceptions to this limitation exist and include (among others) certain performance-based compensation.

    D.   Investigation of a Business

        1.   If a taxpayer investigating a business is already in a business similar to or the same as the business being investigated, the relevant expenses incurred are deductible.

        2.   Investigation expenses incurred are not deductible if the taxpayer who is not in the same or similar business does not acquire the new business. If such new business is acquired, the investigation costs are capitalized as

startup expenses. However, at the election of the taxpayer, up to $5,000 of the expenses can be deducted; any excess amount can be amortized over a period of 180 months or more.

E.   Hobby Losses
1.   If an individual can show that a business or investment activity (that may have personal pleasure attributes) has been conducted with the purpose of earning a profit, then any losses from the activity are deductible in full.
2.   The *hobby loss* rules under § 183 apply if the activity is considered not to be engaged in for profit.
3.   A rebuttable presumption in the Code provides that if an activity shows a profit in *at least three of any five consecutive years* (two years out of seven for activities involving horses), then the activity is considered to be profit-seeking and the hobby loss rules do *not* apply.
4.   If an activity is deemed to be a hobby, expenses are deductible only to the extent of the income from the hobby. However, some expenses may be deducted in full as allowed by other sections of the Code (e.g., property taxes). These expenses must be considered before other types of expenses in computing the overall hobby loss limitation. Hobby deductions are deductible *from* AGI as itemized deductions, but only to the extent they exceed two percent of AGI.

 If a taxpayer chooses self-employment over a second job to earn additional income, care must be given to avoid the hobby loss rules if a loss is incurred. The IRS looks at a number of tests, not just the elements of personal pleasure or recreation involved in the activity.

F.   Rental of Vacation Homes
1.   Depending on the relative amount of time a vacation residence is used for personal and rental purposes, the tax treatment will vary. Three possible classifications exist.
      a.   When the structure is devoted primarily to *personal use.*
      b.   When the home is used primarily for *rental purposes.*
      c.   When the residence is characterized as *personal/rental property.*
2.   If the residence is rented for less than 15 days in a year, the property is treated as a personal residence. Rental income would be excluded, and mortgage interest and real estate taxes incurred would be itemized deductions. No other expenses would be deductible.
3.   If the residence is not used for more than 14 days (or more than 10 percent of the total days rented) for personal use, the residence is treated as a rental property. Expenses must be allocated between personal and rental days if there are any personal days. Deductible rental losses may result.
4.   If the residence is rented for 15 or more days and is used for personal purposes for the greater of more than 14 days or more than 10 percent of the rental days, it is treated as personal/rental property. In such case, the rental expenses are allowed only to the extent of rental income.

 One of the very few instances when the law considers income to be nontaxable is where property is rented for less than 15 days. Residents of Augusta, Georgia, for example, have an annual opportunity to rent their houses for a short period during the Masters Golf Tournament and earn income that is not taxable.

G.   Expenditures Incurred for Taxpayer's Benefit or Taxpayer's Obligation -- For an expense to be deductible, it must be incurred for the taxpayer's benefit or arise from the taxpayer's obligation.

H.   Disallowance of Personal Expenditures
    1.   Unless a deduction is provided in the law, no deduction is allowed for personal, living, or family expenses.
    2.   Examples of deductible personal expenses include the following.
        a.   Medical expenses (§ 213).
        b.   Charitable contributions (§ 170).
        c.   Moving expenses (§ 217).
    3.   Legal fees incurred in connection with a divorce are deductible only if they relate solely to tax advice. For example, fees attributable to the determination of dependency exemptions or the determination of the tax consequences of a property settlement are deductible.

I.   Disallowance of Deductions for Capital Expenditures
    1.   Amounts paid for new buildings or for permanent improvements that tend to add value or prolong the life of a property or adapt the property to a new or different use, must be *capitalized* rather than currently deducted.
    2.   When an item is capitalized rather than expensed, a deduction is, at best, deferred and, at worst, lost forever. Nonetheless, in some situations, a taxpayer may prefer to capitalize an item (such as when the deduction would create an unusable net operating loss). However, in some situations, a taxpayer may elect to expense an item rather than capitalize it.

J.   Transactions between Related Parties
    1.   Restrictions are placed on the recognition of losses resulting from transactions occurring between *related parties* because of the myriad opportunities to create tax savings from transactions that have no economic substance.
    2.   Section 267 *disallows* the recognition of losses when property is sold or exchanged between related parties. However, a previously unrecognized loss may *reduce* any realized gain on the subsequent sale of the property to an unrelated person.
    3.   Section 267 *defers* a deduction by an *accrual basis taxpayer* (when the party to receive a payment is related and is on the *cash basis*) until the period when the amount is included in the income of the recipient.
    4.   Related parties include the following.
        a.   Brothers, sisters (including half-blood), spouse, ancestors, and lineal descendants of the taxpayer.
        b.   A corporation owned *more than* 50 percent by the taxpayer.
        c.   Two corporations that are members of a controlled group.

5. Constructive ownership rules are applied in order to determine whether taxpayers are related. These rules provide that for loss and expense deduction disallowance purposes, stock owned by certain relatives or related entities is *deemed* to be owned by the taxpayer.

K. Substantiation Requirements

1. Appropriate documentation and substantiation of events and transactions are usually advisable, and generally required by law.

2. The law provides that in order for travel, entertainment, or business gift expenditures to be deductible, the following information must be kept.

   a. The amount of the expense.

   b. The time and place of the travel or entertainment (or date of gift).

   c. The business purpose of such expense.

   d. The business relationship of the taxpayer to the person entertained (or receiving the gift).

Credit card issuers have been responsive to requirements imposed by the tax law, in that they often provide a form on each charge slip on which the person doing the entertaining can enter all of the Code-required information to substantiate the deduction. However, whether taxpayers are conscientious about filling in the required information may be another story.

L. Expenses and Interest Relating to Tax-Exempt Income

1. Generally, expenses incurred for purposes of producing tax-exempt income are *not* deductible.

2. It is often very difficult to show a direct relationship between borrowings and investments in tax-exempt securities. Judicial interpretation generally has tried to show "reasonableness" in the disallowance of expenses under this Code section.

TEST FOR SELF-EVALUATION -- CHAPTER 6

True or False

Indicate which of the following statements are true or false by circling the correct answer.

T   F   1.   The courts have established a doctrine that stipulates that an expenditure is not deductible unless a Code section provides for its deduction.

T   F   2.   Section 212 allows a deduction for "all ordinary and necessary expenses paid or incurred during the taxable year in carrying on any trade or business."

T   F   3.   Section 162 business expenses are deductions *for* adjusted gross income and can be taken whether or not an individual taxpayer itemizes.

T   F   4.   To obtain a deduction under § 212, it is necessary for the property to which the deduction relates to be producing income currently.

T   F   5.   For a salary expense to be deductible, it must be ordinary and necessary and also, it must be reasonable in amount.

T   F   6.   Legal fees pursuant to a criminal defense are deductible if the taxpayer is declared not guilty.

T   F   7.   Any deductible loss relating to an asset is limited to the taxpayer's cost basis of the asset involved.

T   F   8.   Section 267 operates to disallow or defer losses and deductions between related parties.

T   F   9.   The amount of deductible travel and entertainment expenses may be estimated if adequate records have not been maintained.

T   F   10.   Interest expense incurred is always deductible by an individual taxpayer.

T   F   11.   An accrual basis taxpayer may claim a deduction for an amount owed to a related cash basis taxpayer if the amount is paid within two and a half months of the accrual taxpayer's year-end.

T   F   12.   Because a rental activity is not considered to be a trade or business, rental expenses are not deductible *for* adjusted gross income.

T   F   13.   The amount of deductions taken *for* adjusted gross income can never have an impact on the amount of itemized deductions.

T   F   14.   Alimony expenditures are deductible *for* adjusted gross income.

T   F   15.   Because they are related to a taxpayer's trade or business, unreimbursed employee expenses are deductible *for* adjusted gross income.

T   F   16.   As a general rule, cash basis taxpayers cannot claim an immediate deduction for capital expenditures.

T   F   17.   Legal and accounting expenses incurred in connection with rental property are itemized deductions.

T   F   18.   If Father pays Daughter's mortgage interest obligation, Father may claim a deduction on his income tax return for the amount paid.

T   F   19.   Even if Father pays Daughter's mortgage interest obligation, Daughter may claim a deduction on her income tax return for the amount paid by Father because the payment pertains to Daughter's obligation.

T   F   20.   Unrealized losses can be deducted in certain situations.

Fill-in-the-Blanks

Complete the following statements with the appropriate word(s) or amount(s).

1.   For individual taxpayers, deductions are claimed either _____ adjusted gross income or _____ adjusted gross income.

2.   Corporations are not subject to the separate classification scheme of classifying deductions as *for* or *from* because the term _____ does not appear in the corporate tax formula.

3.   A qualifying expenditure will be deductible *from* adjusted gross income as an itemized deduction if the total amount of itemized deductions exceeds the taxpayer's _____.

4.   The _____ rules apply only if an activity that has personal and profit-seeking attributes is not engaged in for profit.

5.   Section 183 provides that hobby expenses are deductible only to the extent of _____.

6.   The Code provides a rebuttable presumption that an activity (that does not involve horses) is profit-seeking if it shows a profit in at least _____ of any _____ consecutive years ending with the taxable year in question.

7.   One of the basic concepts in the tax law is that a deduction can be taken only when a loss has actually been _____.

8.   All income received from the rental of a residence is excluded if the residence is rented for less than _____ days.

9.   The period in which an accrual basis taxpayer can deduct an expense is determined by applying the _____ test.

10.   Generally, in order for an expense to be deductible, it must be incurred for the taxpayer's

_____ or arise from the taxpayer's _____.

11. The so-called millionaires' provision, applicable to publicly held corporations, can limit the amount the employer can deduct for the compensation of a covered executive to _____ annually.

12. Trade or business expenses are deductible only if they possess the following three attributes. Such expenses must be _____, _____, and _____.

13. Whether and to what an extent an expenditure is deductible depends on a notion referred to as _____.

14. All itemized deductions *from* adjusted gross income are reported on _____ of Form 1040.

15. A vacation home used 10 days for personal purposes and 4 months for rental purposes is treated as _____ property.

Multiple Choice

Choose the best answer for each of the following questions.

_____ 1. Which of the following is not a deduction *for* adjusted gross income?
   a. Alimony payments.
   b. Ordinary and necessary business expenses.
   c. Reimbursed travel expenses incurred in the capacity of an employee.
   d. Charitable contributions made by a sole proprietor.
   e. All of these choices are deductions *for* adjusted gross income.

_____ 2. Which of the following expenditures are not deductible?
   a. Expenses incurred for the production or collection of income.
   b. Expenses incurred for the management, conservation, or maintenance of property held for the production of income.
   c. Expenses related to the management, conservation, or maintenance of a personal residence.
   d. Expenses incurred in connection with the determination, collection, or refund of any tax.
   e. All of these choices are deductible.

_____ 3. Which of the following expenses are not deductible *from* adjusted gross income?
   a. Alimony payments.
   b. Safe deposit box rentals.
   c. Investment counseling fees.
   d. Interest on home mortgage.
   e. All of these choices are deductible *from* adjusted gross income.

_____ 4. In connection with the hobby loss rules, indicate which of the following is *incorrect.*
   a. If a taxpayer can show that an activity has been conducted with the intent to earn a profit, losses from the activity are fully deductible.

b.   Section 183 provides that hobby expenses are deductible only to the extent of hobby income.

c.   The Code provides a rebuttable presumption that an activity is profit-seeking if it shows a profit in two of any five consecutive years.

d.   If an activity is deemed to be a hobby, some expenses incurred may be deductible by virtue of other sections in the Code.

e.   All of these choices are true.

_____ 5.   Irene, not a dealer in securities, sold common stock (basis of $15,000) to her son Victor for $10,000. What is Irene's deductible loss from this transaction?

a. $0.

b. $5,000.

c. $10,000.

d. $15,000.

e.   Some other amount.

_____ 6.   Irene, not a dealer in securities, sold common stock (basis of $15,000) to her son Victor for $10,000. Victor sells the stock subsequently for $12,000 to an unrelated third party. In the year of sale, what amount of gain or loss should Victor recognize for tax purposes?

a. $2,000 gain.

b. $3,000 loss.

c.   No gain or loss.

d.   None of these choices.

_____ 7.   Select the *correct* statement.

a.   Reserves for estimated expenses that are frequently employed for financial accounting purposes are also deductible for tax purposes.

b.   Legal expenses paid to affect a divorce generally are not deductible because they are personal expenditures.

c.   A mother who pays her son's home mortgage payments would be able to deduct the related interest expense on her federal income tax return.

d.   Expenses incurred in connection with municipal bond interest income are deductible within certain limitations.

e.   None of these choices is correct.

_____ 8.   On January 1, Rashad sold stock with a cost of $12,000 to his sister Cora for $10,000, its fair market value. On July 1, Cora sold the same stock to Miguel for $12,500 in an arms-length transaction. What is the result of these transactions?

a.   Neither Rashad nor Cora has a recognized gain or loss.

b.   Rashad has a $2,000 recognized loss.

c.   Cora has a $500 recognized gain.

d.   Cora has a $2,500 recognized gain.

e.   None of these choices.

REFER TO THE FOLLOWING INFORMATION WHEN ANSWERING THE ITEMS BELOW.

Davidson leases his vacation home for three months and uses it for one month during his vacation. Gross rental income from the property was $12,000. Davidson incurred the following expenses during the year.

Taxes and interest	$ 8,800
Utilities	1,000
Depreciation	2,000
Maintenance	500
Total	$12,300

_____ 9.   Compute the allowable deduction available to offset rental income (i.e., the
            amount that is not otherwise deductible) assuming that Davidson believes that
            the IRS's approach to allocating expenses between rental and personal days is
            appropriate.
            a. $0.
            b. $9,225.
            c. $12,000.
            d. $12,300.
            e.   None of these choices.

_____ 10.   If Davidson does not use the property any of the time for personal purposes, what
            is the allowable deduction that may be claimed (prior to considering possible
            implications of the passive activity rules)?
            a. $0.
            b. $9,225.
            c. $12,000.
            d. $12,300.
            e.   None of these choices.

_____ 11.   Which of the following are *not* "related parties" under § 267?
            a.   Taxpayer and a great, great grandparent.
            b.   Taxpayer and an uncle.
            c.   Taxpayer and a child.
            d.   Taxpayer and a corporation in which more than 50% of the stock of the
                  corporation is held by the taxpayer.
            e.   All of these choices are "related parties."

_____ 12.   Which of the following is deductible when paid by a cash basis taxpayer who
            itemizes deductions?
            a.   Acquisition of a building by a sole proprietor.
            b.   Fines paid by a sole proprietor.
            c.   Prepaid interest expense.
            d.   Medical expenses paid for a physical examination to be performed next
                  year.
            e.   Charitable contributions.

_____ 13.   Choose the *correct* statement.
            a.   A cash basis taxpayer always receives equal tax benefit for an amount
                  paid whether it be deductible *for* or *from* adjusted gross income.
            b.   An expense related to the maintenance of a personal residence is
                  deductible as an itemized deduction.

      c.   The courts have held that an expense is "necessary" for business purposes if a prudent businessperson would incur such an expense.

      d.   Business prepaid rent is includible in the gross income of the landlord and deductible by the tenant as a deduction *for* adjusted gross income in the year paid.

      e.   None of these choices.

_____ 14.   Mr. Amor, a self-employed massage parlor owner, incurred the following expenses during the year.

Rent expense	$ 1,000
Wages	20,000
Bribes to police	5,000
Expenses incurred to influence the public on a massage parlor bill in the state legislature	800
Interest expense on a loan used to purchase municipal bonds	900

Determine the amount of deductions *for* adjusted gross income that Mr. Amor may take currently.

      a. $21,800.
      b. $22,700.
      c. $26,000.
      d. $26,800.
      e.   None of these choices.

_____ 15.   Based on advice from his financial analyst, Tracy made the following long-term investments at par:

      $3,000 general obligation bonds of Fairfax County (wholly tax-exempt)
      $9,000 debentures of McIntire Corporation (16% effective yield)

Tracy did not have the cash readily available to finance these purchases so she obtained a $12,000 loan from Jefferson Bank. She paid the following amounts as interest expense during the year.

Home mortgage	$4,500
Jefferson Bank	1,800
	$6,300

What amount can Tracy deduct currently as interest expense?

      a. $0.
      b. $4,500.
      c. $5,850.
      d. $6,300.
      e.   Some other amount.

_____ 16.   Rich is the president of Masters Corporation and has owned 75 percent of its outstanding stock since its inception. During the year, Rich purchased from the corporation depreciable property with an adjusted tax basis of $60,000 for

$45,000, its fair market value. Masters had placed this property in service five years ago. What is the available loss that Masters Corporation can claim for the current year?
   a. $11,250 ordinary loss.
   b. $15,000 capital loss.
   c. $15,000 ordinary loss.
   d. $0 loss.
   e.   Some other amount.

_____   17.   After 25 years of marriage, Victor and Paula divorced during the year. The settlement included the following payments to Paula from Victor. The alimony would cease upon her death or remarriage.

Lump-sum property distribution	$60,000
Annual alimony payments	5,000

Victor does not itemize his deductions. How much may he deduct *for* AGI in the current year?
   a. $0.
   b. $5,000.
   c. $60,000.
   d. $65,000.
   e.   Some other amount.

_____   18.   Which of the following may be considered a trade or business expense?
   a.   Travel expenses incurred by a self-employed CPA.
   b.   Charitable contributions.
   c.   Illegal bribes and kickbacks.
   d.   Fines and penalties.
   e.   All of these choices.

_____   19.   An exception to the economic performance requirement for accrual basis taxpayers provides that certain recurring items may be deducted if which of the following conditions are met?
   a.   Such items are treated consistently.
   b.   Either they are not material in amount or such accrual results in better matching of income and expenses.
   c.   The all-events test is met.
   d.   Economic performance occurs within a reasonable period but not more than 8 and one-half months after year-end.
   e.   All of these choices are conditions that must be met.

_____   20.   Choose the *correct* statement.
   a.   Personal legal expenses may be deductible if they relate to the determination of a tax liability.
   b.   For legal expenses to be deductible *for* adjusted gross income, the taxpayer must be able to show that the origin and character of a related claim pertaining to the legal services rendered are directly related to a trade or business or an income-producing activity.
   c.   Legal expenses may be deductible either *for* or *from* adjusted gross income, depending on the circumstances.

     d.   Legal expenses that are deductible *from* adjusted gross income only produce a tax benefit to the extent they exceed 2 percent of adjusted gross income.

     e.   Each of these choices is correct.

_____ 21.   Bonnie incurs $15,000 of travel and other expenses during the investigation of a business opportunity in Bermuda. Specifically, she has heard that the hotel business in that part of the world normally proves to be a wonderful investment. Whether and how the $15,000 expenditure produces a tax benefit is *not* dependent on the following.

     a.   Bonnie's current business.

     b.   The length of time Bonnie has been in the current business.

     c.   The extent to which the investigation has proceeded.

     d.   Whether or not the acquisition actually takes place.

     e.   Each of these choices is a relevant factor.

_____ 22.   Which of the following expenditures is deductible *from* adjusted gross income (i.e., as an itemized deduction), and at the same time, the size of the deduction is dependent on the amount of the taxpayer's adjusted gross income?

     a.   Mortgage interest expense.

     b.   Moving expense.

     c.   Casualty loss.

     d.   State and local income taxes.

     e.   None of these choices.

_____ 23.   Which of the following is deductible?

     a.   Commuting expenses.

     b.   Unrealized losses.

     c.   Unreimbursed employee business expenses.

     d.   Interest expense incurred to purchase a City of Richmond bond.

     e.   None of these choices is deductible.

_____ 24.   Pat, who is single, had gross income during the year of $22,000 and incurred the following expenses.

Traditional IRA contribution	$2,000
Commuting expense	1,000
Mortgage interest expense	2,500
Loss realized on XYZ stock	2,000
Legal fees related to his divorce	500
Total	$8,000

What is Pat's adjusted gross income?

     a. $16,000.

     b. $18,000.

     c. $20,000.

     d. $22,000.

     e.   Some other amount.

_____ 25.   Bubba owns and operates a very successful automotive service station. Every weekend and during vacations from school, his son Junior (age 12) works full time, earning $50 per hour. During the years, Junior has become very knowledgeable about this type of business. However, on other occasions when Junior cannot work and heavy traffic is anticipated, Bubba hires high school students at $8 per hour. With respect to Junior's wages, what amount probably is deductible by Bubba's business?

a. $0.
b. $8 per hour.
c. $50 per hour.
d.   None of these choices.

Code Section Recognition

Several important sections of the Internal Revenue Code are described below. Indicate, by number, the appropriate Code section.

1. _____   Allows a deduction for "all ordinary and necessary" business expenses.

2. _____   Provides a deduction for losses incurred in a trade or business, losses incurred in any transaction entered into for a profit, and casualty losses.

3. _____   Deductions are allowed for expenses involved in the production or collection of income; for expenses incurred in the management, conservation, or maintenance of property held for the production of income; and for expenses in connection with the determination, collection, or refund of any tax.

4. _____   Determines which expenditures are deductible *for* AGI.

5. _____   Determines the treatment of expenses incurred in the conduct of an activity not engaged in for profit (i.e., the "hobby loss" rules).

6. _____   Disallows losses arising from transactions between related parties.

Short Answer

1. Indicate whether the following expenses are deductible *for* or *from* AGI.

Expense Item	Deductible *for* AGI	Deductible *from* AGI
Medical expenses		
Rent expenses		
Unreimbursed moving expenses		
Charitable contributions		
Trade or business expenses		

2. David and Eleanor own a mountain cabin where they live for two months in the summer. However, each fall, their cabin is rented for 2 weeks to Eleanor's mother for $2,000 (an arms-length rental). The vacation home is vacant for the rest of the year. In addition, real property taxes of $600 and utility payments of $500 are incurred during the year. How are these receipts and expenditures treated for tax purposes?

3. John makes pottery in his spare time and occasionally sells it to the public. In the current year, he and his wife have AGI of $50,000 before any income or loss from his pottery activity. John earns $4,500 from selling the pottery. He uses 10 percent of their home for the pottery activity. The mortgage interest and real estate taxes on the home total $15,000 and total depreciation is $3,500. John incurs other expenses related to the activity of $6,000. John and his wife have no other expenses. What amount of income or loss results if (1) the activity is treated as a trade or business versus (2) the activity being treated as a hobby?

SOLUTIONS TO CHAPTER 6 QUESTIONS

True or False

1. T   Courts have held that whether and to what extent deductions are allowed depends on legislative grace. [Classification of Deductible Expenses p. 6-2]

2. F   Section 162 allows deductions of this nature, not § 212. [Deductions for Adjusted Gross Income p. 6-3]

3. T   In order for these business expenses to be deductible, they must be considered ordinary and necessary in carrying on a trade or business. [Deductions for Adjusted Gross Income p. 6-3]

4. F   The property needs only to be *held* for the production of income. [Section 212 Expenses p. 6-4]

5. T   In addition, executive compensation deductions are limited in certain situations. [Reasonableness Requirement p. 6-7]

6. F   They are deductible only if the crime is associated with the taxpayer's trade or business activity. [Legal Expenses Incurred in Defense of Civil or Criminal Penalties p. 6-12]

7. T   The maximum allowable loss represents the portion of an asset's basis that is not recovered in a disposition. [Deductions for Adjusted Gross Income p. 6-3]

8. T   This prohibition of loss recognition is intended to thwart transactions between related parties that have no economic substance. [Transactions between Related Parties p. 6-25]

9. F   The law provides that a deduction must be properly substantiated. [Substantiation Requirements p. 6-26]

10. F   Section 265 disallows a deduction for an expense incurred for the production of tax-exempt income. Further, deductions for "consumer interest" are prohibited. [Expenses and Interest Relating to Tax-Exempt Income p. 6-27]

11. F   Such amounts cannot be deducted by the accrual basis taxpayer until payments are made. [Unpaid Expenses and Interest p. 6-25]

12. F   The law specifically provides that rental expenses are deductible *for* AGI. [Deductions for Adjusted Gross Income p. 6-3]

13. F   For example, as deductions reduce AGI, itemized deductions such as medical expenses and personal casualty and theft losses that are modified by a percentage of AGI, may become deductible to a greater extent. [Classification of Deductible Expenses p. 6-2]

14. T   This type of expenditure is specifically allowed as a deduction *for* AGI by § 62 [Deductions for Adjusted Gross Income p. 6-3]

15. F   These are always deductible *from* AGI. [Reporting Procedures p. 6-8]

16. T   Initially, a capital expenditure generally is capitalized and then possibly subject to depreciation or cost recovery over the asset's life. [Disallowance of Deductions for Capital Expenditures p. 6-24]

17. F   Expenses related to rental property are deductible *for* AGI. [Deductions for Adjusted Gross Income p. 6-3]

18. F   Because Father is not obligated to make the payment, he may not claim the interest deduction. [Expenditures Incurred for Taxpayer's Benefit or Taxpayer's Obligation p. 6-23]

19. F   In order for Daughter to qualify to claim a deduction, she must be the one who makes the payment. [Expenditures Incurred for Taxpayer's Benefit or Taxpayer's Obligation p. 6-23]

20.   F   Losses can never be deducted until they are realized. [Deductions for Adjusted
               Gross Income p. 6-3]

Fill-in-the-Blanks

1.   for, from [Classification of Deductible Expenses p. 6-2]
2.   adjusted gross income [Deductions for Adjusted Gross Income p. 6-3]
3.   standard deduction [Classification of Deductible Expenses p. 6-2]
4.   hobby loss [Hobby Losses p. 6-15]
5.   hobby income [General Rules p. 6-16]
6.   three, five [Presumptive Rule of §183 p. 6-16]
7.   realized [Deductions for Adjusted Gross Income p. 6-3]
8.   15 [Primarily Personal Use p. 6-18]
9.   economic performance [Accrual Method Requirements p. 6-10]
10.   benefit, obligation [Expenditures Incurred for Taxpayer's Benefit or Taxpayer's Obligation
       p. 6-23]
11. $1 million [Excessive Executive Compensation p. 6-13]
12.   ordinary, necessary, reasonable [Trade or Business Expenses and Production of Income
       Expenses p. 6-5]
13.   legislative grace [Classification of Deductible Expenses p. 6-2]
14.   Schedule A [Reporting Procedures p. 6-8]
15.   rental [Primarily Rental Use p. 6-19]

Multiple Choice

1.   d   Charitable contributions made by a sole proprietor are deductible as itemized
               deductions *from* adjusted gross income. [Deductions for Adjusted Gross Income
               p. 6-3; Deductible Personal Expenses p. 6-5]
2.   c   Deductions are disallowed unless a specific provision in the tax law permits them.
               There is no provision in the law providing for the deduction of such expenses
               relating to a personal residence. [Classification of Deductible Expenses p. 6-2]
3.   a   An alimony payment is deductible *for* AGI. [Deductions for Adjusted Gross Income
               p. 6-3]
4.   c   Except for horses, a profit must be shown in *three* out of five years. [Presumptive
               Rule of §183 p. 6-16]
5.   a   Because Irene and Victor are related, the loss realized by Irene on the sale is not
               deductible. [Transactions between Related Parties p. 6-25]
6.   c   In this situation, gain is not recognized because the realized gain of $2,000 is
               reduced by an amount up to the previously disallowed loss ($5,000).
               [Transactions between Related Parties p. 6-25]
7.   b   Personal legal fees are not deductible. [Legal Expenses Incurred In Defense of
               Civil or Criminal Penalties p. 6-12]
8.   c $500 = [($12,500 - $10,000) - $2,000 (previously disallowed loss)] [Transactions
               between Related Parties p. 6-25]
9.   b $9,225 = $12,300 X .75. The .75 factor reflects three months of rental use out of
               the four months the property was used. [Personal/Rental Use p. 6-20]
10.   d   Because the property is rental property, a loss may result. [Primarily Rental Use p.
               6-19]
11.   b   An uncle is not considered related under this tax provision. [Relationships and

Constructive Ownership p. 6-26]

12.   e   This is an example of a personal expense for which Congress has granted a deduction. [Deductible Personal Expenses p. 6-5; Cash Method Requirements p. 6-9]

13.   c   For any business expense to be deductible, it must be ordinary and necessary. [Ordinary and Necessary Requirement p. 6-5]

14.   e $21,000 (rent expense and wages) [Trade or Business Expenses and Production of Income Expenses p. 6-5]

15.   c $5,850 = $4,500 + [($9,000/$12,000) X $1,800]   The deduction is not limited by the investment interest restrictions (see Chapter 10) assuming $1,440 (i.e., 16% yield) has been received on the McIntire Corporation debentures during the year. Interest expense related to the Fairfax County bond is not deductible. [Expenses and Interest Relating to Tax-Exempt Income p. 6-27]

16.   d   No loss is deductible because Rich and Masters are related parties. [Transactions between Related Parties p. 6-25]

17.   b   Only the alimony payment is deductible *for* adjusted gross income. [Deductions for Adjusted Gross Income p. 6-3]

18.   a   Travel expenses incurred by a self-employed taxpayer are considered ordinary and necessary business expenses. [Trade or Business Expenses and Production of Income Expenses p. 6-5]

19.   e   Each of the conditions listed must be met. [Accrual Method Requirements p. 6-10]

20.   e   Each of the statements pertaining to legal expenses is correct. [Legal Expenses Incurred In Defense of Civil or Criminal Penalties p. 6-12]

21.   b   The taxpayer need not have been in the business for any particular period of time for the investigation expenses to be deductible. [Investigation of a Business p. 6-14]

22.   c   A personal casualty loss can be claimed only to the extent it exceeds an aggregate floor of 10 percent of AGI and a $100 floor per casualty. [Classification of Deductible Expenses p. 6-2; Deductible Personal Expenses p. 6-5]

23.   c   Business expenses incurred by an employee may be deductible. If the expenses are not reimbursed by the employer, the expenses are deductible *from* AGI. [Reporting Procedures p. 6-8]

24.   b

Gross income	$22,000
Less: Traditional IRA contribution	(2,000)
Loss on XYZ stock	(2,000)
Adjusted gross income	$18,000

[Deductions for Adjusted Gross Income p. 6-3]

25.   b   The reasonableness requirement would apply, which would undoubtedly prohibit Bubba from deducting Junior's salary at the $50 per hour rate. [Reasonableness Requirement p. 6-7]

Code Section Recognition

1.   162 [Trade or Business Expenses and Production of Income Expenses p. 6-5]
2.   165 [Business and Nonbusiness Losses p. 6-7]
3.   212 [Section 212 Expenses p. 6-4]
4.   62 [Deductions for Adjusted Gross Income p. 6-3]
5.   183 [Hobby Losses p. 6-15]
6.   267 [Transactions between Related Parties p. 6-25]

Short Answer

1.

Expense Item	Deductible *for* AGI	Deductible *from* AGI
Medical expenses		X
Rent expenses	X	
Unreimbursed moving expenses	X	
Charitable contributions		X
Trade or business expenses	X	

[Classification of Deductible Expenses p. 6-2]

2. Because the property is not rented for at least fifteen days, it is treated as a personal residence and, as a result, the $2,000 of rent income is excluded from taxation. The real property tax is an itemized deduction and the utility payments are nondeductible personal expenses. [Primarily Personal Use p. 6-19]

3.

	Trade or Business	Hobby
Hobby income included in gross income		$4,500
Income from trade or business	$4,500	
Less: Mortgage interest and real estate taxes (10% X $15,000)	(1,500)	(1,500)
Subtotal	$3,000	$3,000
Less: Other expenses	(6,000)	(3,000)*
Depreciation (10% X $3,500)	(350)	0**
Effect of 2%-of AGI-limitation***		1,090
Net taxable income (loss) from activity	($3,350)	$1,090

*   Limited to $3,000 of hobby income less other deductible items.
**   Limited by hobby income less other related expenses.
***   AGI = $54,500 ($50,000 + $4,500 income from activity). Therefore, 2% of AGI equals $1,090 ($54,500 X 2%).

[Determining the Amount of the Deduction p. 6-17]

Chapter 7
Deductions and Losses:
Certain Business Expenses and Losses

CHAPTER HIGHLIGHTS

T he discussion relating to certain business expenses and losses is continued in this chapter. Specifically, bad debts, worthless securities, § 1244 stock, casualty and theft losses, research and experimental expenditures, the domestic production activities deduction, and net operating losses are discussed. As the discussion suggests, while §§ 162 and 165 provide for the deductibility of business expenses and losses in general, additional guidance has been developed in defining the procedural details and limitations that apply to the expenses and losses covered in this chapter.

I.   Bad Debts
      A.   A bad debt deduction is allowed in the year an account receivable that was previously included in income becomes *worthless*. No such deduction is allowed if the taxpayer uses the *cash basis* of accounting.
      B.   Specific Charge-Off Method -- Most taxpayers are required to use the *specific charge-off* method. Under the specific charge-off method, a deduction is available when a specific *business debt* becomes either *partially* or *totally worthless*. Further, this method is available when a specific *nonbusiness debt* becomes *wholly worthless*.

 A taxpayer using the specific charge-off method is allowed to claim a deduction in the year in which a debt becomes uncollectible. To strengthen the claim of uncollectibility, it would be helpful to create a paper trail showing the steps taken in attempting to collect the debt.

C.   Business versus Nonbusiness Bad Debts
1.   A debt is considered to be *nonbusiness* if it is not related to the taxpayer's trade or business either when the debt was created or when it becomes worthless.
2.   A business bad debt is always deductible as an *ordinary loss* in the year incurred. A nonbusiness bad debt, however, is treated as a *short-term capital loss* and is subject to capital loss limitations (i.e., the maximum net short-term loss that is deductible annually by an individual is $3,000).
D.   Loans Between Related Parties
1.   A question can be raised whether a transfer of funds made between relatives is a *bona fide loan* or a *gift*.
2.   Some considerations which would indicate that a debtor-creditor relationship exists include the following.
a.   Whether a note was properly executed.
b.   Whether there is a reasonable rate of interest stated.
c.   Whether there is collateral.
d.   What collection efforts have been made.
e.   What was the intent of the parties.

II.   Worthless Securities
A.   Generally, a loss deduction is allowed for securities (e.g., shares of stock, bonds, notes, or other evidence of indebtedness of a corporation or government) that become *completely worthless* during the year. This loss is considered to have occurred as of the *last day* of the year in which the loss occurred and it is usually considered to be capital.
B.   Small Business Stock
1.   *Individuals* may receive *ordinary loss* treatment, within limitations, on the sale or exchange of stock if such stock is classified as *§ 1244 stock*. The treatment as an ordinary loss is limited to $50,000 ($100,000 for married individuals filing jointly) per year.
2.   Were it not for this provision, a shareholder would always receive capital loss treatment on such a disposition of stock. Section 1244 applies only to *losses*.
3.   Section 1244 stock can be either common or preferred stock.

III.   Losses of Individuals
A.   An individual may deduct a loss in the following circumstances.
1.   For losses incurred in a trade or business.
2.   For losses incurred in a transaction entered into for profit.
3.   For losses caused by fire, storm, shipwreck, or other casualty or by theft.
B.   A *casualty* is usually defined as destruction of property resulting from an event due to some *sudden*, *unexpected*, or *unusual* cause. Further, the loss must result from an event that is identifiable and damaging to the property. However, a deduction for a casualty loss from an automobile accident can be taken only if the damage was not caused by the taxpayer's willful act or willful negligence.
C.   Events That Are Not Casualties -- Not all "acts of God," such as erosion, are casualty losses for income tax purposes; an event must be sudden, unusual, or unexpected to qualify.
D.   Theft Losses
1.   Theft includes larceny, embezzlement, and robbery. However, the term does *not* include lost or misplaced items.

      2.   A theft loss is taken in the year of *discovery,* not in the year of theft, if the two are different.

      3.   If in the year of discovery a claim exists, such as against an insurance company, and there is a reasonable expectation of recovering the fair market value of the asset, no deduction is allowed.

      4.   A partial deduction may be available if the recovery is less than the asset's adjusted basis.

E.   When to Deduct Casualty Losses

      1.   General Rule

           a.   Usually, a casualty loss is deducted in the year during which the loss occurs.

           b.   A casualty loss is not permitted if a reimbursement claim exists with a *reasonable prospect of (full) recovery.*

           c.   If a reimbursement is received for a loss previously sustained and deducted, the taxpayer must include the amount in gross income when received to the extent that the previous deduction produced a tax benefit.

> ## KEY TERMS
>
> - Bad Debt Deduction
> - § 1244 Stock
> - Casualty, Theft Loss
> - Research and Experi-
>   mental Expenditures
> - Domestic Production
>   Activities Deduction
> - Net Operating Loss

      2.   Disaster Area Losses -- An exception to the general rule allows a taxpayer to *elect* to deduct a loss in the year *preceding* the taxable year in which a disaster occurred if the loss results from a casualty sustained in an area designated as a disaster area by the President of the United States.

F.   Measuring the Amount of Loss

      1.   Amount of Loss

           a.   The computation of the amount of a casualty loss depends on whether the property is held for personal use or for business use and whether the property was partially or completely destroyed.

           b.   The amount of the deduction for *partial losses* to both business and personal-use property and for the *complete* destruction of personal-use property is the *lesser* of the following.

                (1)   The adjusted basis of the property.

                (2)   The difference between the fair market value of the property before the casualty and the fair market value immediately after the casualty.

           c.   If *business* property is *completely* destroyed, the deduction is equal to the property's adjusted basis at the time of the destruction.

           d.   Any insurance recovery reduces the loss for business and personal-use casualties. However, in the case of losses arising from insured *personal use* property, if the taxpayer chooses not to file a timely claim against the insurance company, a deduction will *not* be allowed. If insurance proceeds exceed the amount of the loss, a taxable gain results.

 If a taxpayer plans to claim a deduction for a casualty or theft loss, it is important that as much supporting evidence as possible be gathered. Newspaper clippings about a storm, police reports, and insurance reports may all be helpful in documenting the nature of the casualty or theft and when it occurred. Remember, the taxpayer will want to be in the position to show that a casualty occurred and that the loss was a direct result of the casualty.

    2.   Reduction for $100 and 10 Percent-of-AGI -- A casualty loss on *personal-use* property must be reduced by a $100 statutory floor when computing the deduction. Further, an additional floor, which is equal to 10 percent of the taxpayer's AGI, also applies to the *aggregate* of all personal losses incurred during the year after reducing *each* loss by the $100 floor.

G.   Statutory Framework for Deducting Losses of Individuals

    1.   Losses incurred by an individual in connection with a trade or business are deductible *for* AGI. These losses are not subject to the $100 per event and 10 percent-of-AGI limitations.

    2.   Losses incurred by an individual in a transaction entered into for profit are not subject to the $100 per event and 10 percent-of-AGI limitations. If such losses relate to rents and royalties, they are deducted *for* AGI. Otherwise (such as in the case of the theft of a security), they are deducted *from* AGI as other miscellaneous itemized deductions.

    3.   Casualty and theft losses incurred which pertain to personal property are deductible *from* AGI and are subject to the $100 per event floor and the 10 percent-of-AGI limitation.

H.   Personal Casualty Gains and Losses

    1.   If *personal casualty gains* exceed *personal casualty losses*, the gains and losses are treated as dispositions of capital assets. The result can be either long-term or short-term, depending on the length of time that the taxpayer held the various assets involved in the casualty.

    2.   If the losses exceed the gains, all of the gains and losses are treated as ordinary items. In this case, the losses, to the extent of the gains, offset the gains in computing AGI while the excess losses are deductible *from* AGI to the extent they exceed 10 percent-of-AGI.

IV.   Research and Experimental Expenditures

A.   The law permits three alternatives for handling *research and experimental expenditures.*

    1.   The expenditures may be expensed in the year paid or incurred.

    2.   They may be deferred and amortized.

    3.   The costs may be capitalized.

B.   In addition, a credit to encourage research and experimentation activities may be claimed equal to 20 percent of certain *incremental* research and experimentation expenditures.

 The incremental research credits and deductions are aimed at encouraging expenditures related to manufacturing and other industries that create physical products. No such incentive exists at this time to bolster the software, publishing, or other "intellectual property" industries.

V.   Domestic Production Activities Deduction -- The production activities deduction (PAD) is available to manufacturers based on income from manufacturing activities.
    A.   Operational Rules
        1.   The production activities deduction is based on the lesser of:
            a.   Three percent times qualified production activities income (PAI), or
            b.   Three percent times taxable (or modified adjusted gross) income or alternative minimum taxable income.
        2.   The production activities deduction cannot exceed 50 percent of W-2 wages paid by the taxpayer during the year.
        3.   The three percent rate increases to six percent for 2007-2009 and to nine percent for 2010 and thereafter.
        4.   Qualified production activities income (QPAI) is the excess of domestic production gross receipts (DPGR) over the sum of:
            a.   Cost of goods sold allocated to such receipts.
            b.   Other deductions, expenses, or losses directly allocated to such receipts.
            c.   Ratable portion of deductions, expenses, and losses not directly allocable to such receipts or another class of income.
    B.   The deduction is available to individuals, partnerships, S corporations, C corporations, cooperatives, estates, and trusts.

VI.   Net Operating Losses
    A.   A net operating loss deduction is allowed which is designed to provide partial relief from potential inequitable tax treatment that may arise because of the requirement that every taxpayer is to file an income tax return annually.
    B.   Carryback and Carryover Periods
        1.   Generally, a net operating loss must be applied initially to the two taxable years preceding the loss. If the loss is not fully used up in the carryback period, it may be carried forward for up to 20 years.
        2.   A three year carryback period is available for any portion of an individual's net operating loss resulting from a casualty or theft loss. The three-year carryback rule also applies to net operating losses attributable to Presidentially declared disasters that are incurred by certain small businesses.
        3.   A taxpayer may *elect* to only carry forward a net operating loss.
    C.   Computation of the Net Operating Loss
        1.   A net operating loss is intended as a relief provision for *business* income and losses. Therefore, in its computation, an individual must make several adjustments in the net operating loss computation for personal items taken in arriving at taxable income (e.g., personal exemption, standard deduction).
        2.   The net operating loss must reflect the taxpayer's *economic* loss.

TEST FOR SELF-EVALUATION -- CHAPTER 7

True or False

Indicate which of the following statements are true or false by circling the correct answer.

T   F   1.   The reserve method for bad debts is available for all taxpayers who sell goods or services on credit and use the accrual method of accounting.

T   F   2.   Assuming a timely insurance claim is filed, a personal casualty loss is potentially deductible only to the extent that it is not covered by insurance.

T   F   3.   A nonbusiness bad debt is deductible by individuals as a short-term capital loss.

T   F   4.   The net operating loss provisions for individuals apply only to business-related or economic losses.

T   F   5.   Personal casualty losses are never deductible in the year prior to the actual occurrence of the casualty event.

T   F   6.   All taxpayers who qualify to obtain a tax benefit for bad debts incurred in a trade or business may use either the specific write-off method or the reserve method.

T   F   7.   An individual taxpayer who recognizes a loss from the disposition of stock held as an investment always would recognize a capital loss assuming the stock is a capital asset in the taxpayer's hands.

T   F   8.   A deduction may be claimed by an individual when stock held for investment becomes partially worthless.

T   F   9.   Items that are lost or misplaced may not be deducted as a personal casualty or theft loss.

T   F   10.   The measure of a personal casualty loss deduction is always the decline in the property's fair market value as a result of the casualty event.

T   F   11.   Personal casualty and theft loss deductions are subject to the $100 per event and 10 percent-of-AGI limitations.

T   F   12.   Business and nonbusiness bad debts receive the same tax treatment.

T   F   13.   The business bad debt deduction may not be claimed if the taxpayer uses the cash method of accounting.

T   F   14.   The reserve method for computing deductions for bad debts is allowed for certain financial institutions.

T   F   15.   A taxpayer may deduct a casualty loss for termite damage to her personal residence incurred over a ten-year period.

T   F   16.   A taxpayer may elect to not carry back a net operating loss, but instead only to carry it forward to future years.

T   F   17.   A deduction is allowed on the partial worthlessness of a business bad debt.

T   F   18.   Because the deduction for a theft loss must be claimed in the year in which the loss occurs, filing an amended income tax return may sometimes be necessary.

T   F   19.   Research and experimental expenditures must be expensed in the year in which they are incurred.

T   F   20.   The special treatment available for § 1244 stock applies equally to gains and losses.

Fill-in-the-Blanks

Complete the following statements with the appropriate word(s) or amount(s).

1.   A business bad debt is deductible as a(n) _____ loss in the year incurred, whereas a nonbusiness bad debt is always treated as a(n) _____ loss.

2.   A shareholder may claim an ordinary loss rather than a capital loss on the sale or exchange of stock if the stock has been classified as _____, which is also known as _____.

3.   If business property or property held for the production of income is completely destroyed, the measure of the deduction is always the _____ at the time of the destruction.

4.   A taxpayer may deduct an ordinary loss of up to _____ (_____ if filing a joint return) in the year of disposition of § 1244 stock.

5.   The amount of a personal casualty loss deduction is the lesser of its _____ or the decline in its _____.

6.   In general, a net operating loss deduction may be carried back _____ years and then any unused amounts may be carried forward for up to _____ years.

7.   Assuming no capital asset transactions, a nonbusiness bad debt may be deducted in an amount of up to _____ in any given year.

8.   The amount of a casualty loss for personal use property must be reduced by a _____ per event floor as well as the _____ percent-of-AGI aggregate floor.

9.   If personal casualty gains and losses net to a gain, all of the assets involved in the casualty events will be considered to be _____ assets.

10.   Casualty losses connected to rental or royalty property are deductible _____ AGI.

11.   Transfers of funds between related parties raise the issue of whether the transfers were bona fide loans or _____.

12.   A nonbusiness bad debt incurred by a taxpayer is always treated as a _____.

13.   If a taxpayer holds corporate securities for investment purposes that become worthless, they are generally treated as _____ losses deemed to have occurred on the _____ of the taxable year.

14.   A deduction for bad debts is not allowed if a taxpayer uses the _____ method of accounting.

15.   No deduction is allowed for the partial worthlessness of a _____ bad debt.

16.   In 2006, the domestic production activities deduction is calculated by multiplying the lesser of qualified production activities income or taxable income by _____ percent.

Multiple Choice

Choose the best answer for each of the following questions.

_____ 1.   John uses the cash receipts and disbursements method in his business and has the following income and expenses during the year.

Gross receipts	$30,000
Business expenses	32,000
Uncollectible customer accounts	4,000

Compute his bad debt deduction.
a. $0.
b. $1,000.
c. $2,000.
d. $4,000.
e.   None of these choices.

_____ 2.   John uses the accrual method of accounting in his business and has the following income and expenses during the year.

Gross receipts	$30,000
Business expenses	32,000
Uncollectible customer accounts	4,000

Compute his bad debt deduction.
a. $0.
b. $1,000.
c. $2,000.
d. $4,000.

e.   None of these choices.

REFER TO THE FOLLOWING INFORMATION WHEN ANSWERING THE ITEMS BELOW

During the year, Wayne had the following personal casualty losses that were fully covered by an insurance policy and which all resulted from the same casualty. His AGI for the year was $20,000.

Asset	Adjusted Basis	Fair Market Value Before	After
Auto	$5,000	$3,000	$ 0
Boat	1,600	2,400	1,900
Television	600	700	0

_____ 3.   What is Wayne's casualty loss deduction for the year, assuming he had not requested a reimbursement from his insurance company?
    a. $1,800.
    b. $2,000.
    c. $4,100.
    d. $6,100.
    e.   None of these choices.

_____ 4.   If Wayne did not have insurance coverage for the assets, what is Wayne's casualty loss deduction?
    a. $1,800.
    b. $2,000.
    c. $4,100.
    d. $6,100.
    e.   None of these choices.

_____ 5.   Assume Wayne did not have insurance coverage for the assets and that each of the casualties occurred in separate events. What is Wayne's casualty loss deduction?
    a. $1,800.
    b. $2,000.
    c. $4,100.
    d. $6,100.
    e.   None of these choices.

_____ 6.   Which of the following would be deductible as a personal casualty loss before considering any ceilings or limitations?
    a.   Termite damage to the foundation of your home.
    b.   Moth damage to out-of-style clothes that you had in storage.
    c.   Reduction in the value of your home because it was near a disaster area.
    d.   A car window broken due to vandalism.
    e.   All of these choices are personal casualty losses.

_____ 7. Select the correct statement.
   a. Harry, a calendar year taxpayer, bought Ivy Corporation stock on December 1, 2006 as an investment. Ivy Corporation went bankrupt on March 15, 2007. Harry may take a short-term capital loss for 2007.
   b. A deduction for theft is allowed in the year in which the taxpayer discovers the loss, and not necessarily in the year during which the loss actually occurred.
   c. The nature of a debt depends on whether the borrower was engaged in a business or used the loan for a nonbusiness reason.
   d. Misplaced or lost valuables that have value greater than $100 and the 10 percent-of-AGI limitation may be allowed as casualty loss deductions.
   e. None of these choices is correct.

_____ 8. Robert, the sole stockholder in his corporation, suffered the following uninsured casualty losses.

Asset	Adjusted Basis	Fair Market Value Before Casualty	Fair Market Value After Casualty
Company car	$1,000	$1,500	$ 300
Theft of wife's diamond ring	2,000	3,000	0
Company boat (shipwreck)	1,100	1,700	1,400

   What is the *personal* casualty loss deduction on Robert's and his wife's joint income tax return assuming AGI of $10,000?
   a. $2,300.
   b. $2,400.
   c. $3,300.
   d. $3,400.
   e. None of these choices.

_____ 9. On November 1, 2005, Holkham Corporation and Ed (a single taxpayer) each purchased $75,000 worth of stock in the newly formed Johnson Corporation. On September 1, 2006, the company suddenly went bankrupt and the stock became totally worthless. The stock was § 1244 stock. How should the loss be reported, assuming Holkham and Ed both are calendar year taxpayers?

	Holkham Corporation	Ed
a.	$25,000 LTCL $50,000 Ordinary Loss	$75,000 STCL
b.	$75,000 Ordinary Loss	$75,000 Ordinary Loss
c.	$75,000 LTCL	$50,000 Ordinary Loss $25,000 LTCL
d.	$50,000 Ordinary Loss $25,000 LTCL	$50,000 Ordinary Loss $25,000 LTCL
e.	None of these choices.	

_____ 10. Louie, who had an AGI of $20,000 during the year, suffered a theft loss of a ring worth $6,000 (adjusted basis was $7,000) and a $3,000 casualty loss due to a boat accident. What amount would be deductible (assuming no insurance coverage)?

    a. $6,800.
    b. $6,900.
    c. $8,800.
    d. $8,900.
    e. $9,000.

11.   In November of last year, Bill was seriously injured when he was riding on rugged terrain in the Blue Ridge Mountains on his all-terrain vehicle. Unfortunately, because of the seriousness of the accident, he had to be flown to the trauma center for care at the closest local hospital. The all-terrain vehicle, which cost Bill $2,000, had a FMV of approximately $1,600 immediately before the accident. After his release from the hospital on January 5 of the current year, Bill traded in the all-terrain vehicle for a new set of snow skis and was given an allowance of $600. Bill also received a settlement of $500 under his homeowners insurance policy on February 26. What amount can he deduct as a casualty loss before the 10 percent-of-AGI limitation, and in which year should the deduction be taken?
    a. $400 last year.
    b. $400 this year.
    c. $500 last year.
    d. $500 this year.
    e.   None of these choices.

12.   Womack and Co., a professional accounting corporation, extended a loan ($10,000) last year to one of its trusted employees, Charles, who promptly and permanently left the country at the beginning of this year. As a consequence, the loan will never be collected. Womack and Co. may deduct what amount?
    a. $10,000 ordinary loss this year.
    b. $3,000 short-term capital loss this year and has a $7,000 carryover.
    c. $10,000 ordinary loss on last year's tax return.
    d. $3,000 short-term capital loss last year, $3,000 short-term capital loss this year, and has a $4,000 carryover.
    e.   None of these choices.

13.   Margaret operates a pet shop that specializes in the sale of rare breeds of cats. During the year, she has sales of $300,000. However, she has determined that $8,000 will never be collected from some of her customers who have moved out of town. Assuming Margaret uses the accrual method of accounting in her business, she may claim the following bad debt deduction.
    a. $0.
    b. $8,000.
    c.   A specified percentage of her sales.
    d.   Some other amount.

14.   Margaret misjudged the integrity of one of her best customers, Kathleen, whose $8,000 account receivable had been written-off last year. Kathleen made payment on her $2,400 debt in the current year. Margaret must report the following amount of income.
    a. $0.
    b. $2,400.
    c. $8,000.
    d   The $2,400 multiplied by Margaret's gross profit percentage.

     e. Some other amount.

_____ 15. Meghan and Travis loaned $4,000 to their next door neighbor, Dan, so that he could buy some new living room furniture. Dan's business, his sole source of income, fell on "hard times" and he informed Meghan and Travis that he could not repay the loan. What are the tax consequences to Meghan and Travis in the year of the loss, assuming the only other items on their income tax return are their salaries?

     a. No deduction is available.
     b. $3,000 short-term capital loss.
     c. $4,000 short-term capital loss.
     d. $4,000 ordinary loss.
     e. $4,000 itemized deduction.
     f. Some other treatment.

_____ 16. Select the correct statement.

     a. Individuals could never be in a situation that would generate a net operating loss deduction.
     b. A net operating loss must be carried back before it is carried forward to offset income of future years.
     c. A business loss incurred by an individual may create a net operating loss.
     d. An individual's net operating loss for a year is the excess of all of the taxpayer's deductions *for* and *from* AGI over gross income.
     e. None of the statements is correct.

_____ 17. An individual may deduct the following types of losses.

     a. Losses incurred in a trade or business.
     b. Losses incurred in a transaction entered into for profit.
     c. Losses caused by fire, storm, shipwreck, or other casualty or by theft.
     d. Any of these types of losses may be deducted.
     e. None of these choices may be deducted.

_____ 18. The law allows which of the following alternatives for the handling of research and experimental expenditures:

     Option I. Expensing in the year paid or incurred.
     Option II. Deferral and amortization.
     Option III. Capitalization.

     a. Only Option III.
     b. Option II or III.
     c. Only Option II
     d. Options I, II, or III.
     e. None of these choices.

_____ 19. During 2005, Champaign Corporation incurred research and experimental expenses of $10,000. In 2006, the business incurred another $40,000 of such expenditures relating to the same project and began to enjoy benefits from the project on July 1, 2006. If the taxpayer elects the deferral and amortization method, what amount may be deducted in 2006?

     a. $4,000.

   b. $5,000.
   c. $8,000.
   d. $10,000.
   e.   None of these choices.

20.   During 2005, Champaign Corporation incurred research and experimental
      expenditures of $10,000. In 2006, the business incurred another $40,000 of such
      expenditures relating to the same project and began to enjoy benefits from the
      project on July 1, 2006. If the taxpayer uses the expense method for the
      research and experimental expenditures, what amount may be deducted?
      a. $10,000 in 2005.
      b. $40,000 in 2006.
      c. $50,000 in 2006.
      d.   Both $10,000 in 2005 and $40,000 in 2006 are correct.
      e.   None of these choices.

21.   Pedro is in the business of lending money. Two years ago Pedro lent $3,000 to
      Abby for nonbusiness purposes. Last year, Abby declared bankruptcy, but
      expected to be able to pay all of her creditors at the rate of $.60 on the dollar.
      However, this year, Abby was only able to pay in final settlement $.10 on the
      dollar. How should Pedro have treated the loss on *last year's* return?
      a.   No deduction is available.
      b. $1,200 ordinary loss.
      c. $1,200 short-term capital loss.
      d. $2,700 ordinary loss.
      e.   None of these choices.

22.   Ross is in the business of lending money. Two years ago Ross lent $3,000 to
      Carlos for nonbusiness purposes. Last year, Carlos declared bankruptcy, but
      expected to be able to pay all of his creditors at the rate of $.60 on the dollar.
      However, this year, Carlos was only able to pay in final settlement $.10 on the
      dollar. How should Ross treat the loss on *this year's* return?
      a.   No deduction is available.
      b. $1,500 ordinary loss.
      c. $1,500 short-term capital loss.
      d. $2,700 ordinary loss.
      e.   None of these choices.

23.   On October 31, 2005, Kathleen acquired Concord Corporation § 1244 stock from
      the corporation for $5,000. On September 30, 2006, the stock was considered to
      be worthless. How is the loss treated?
      a. $5,000 ordinary loss.
      b. $5,000 short-term capital loss.
      c. $5,000 long-term capital loss.
      d.   No loss is available in any year because this was a personal investment.
      e.   Some other amount.

24.   On September 30, 2005, Kathleen (a calendar year taxpayer) acquired Concord
      Corporation stock (not § 1244 stock) from the corporation for $5,000. On May 31,
      2006, the stock was considered to be worthless. How is the loss treated?
      a. $5,000 ordinary loss.

    b.　　$5,000 short-term capital loss.

    c.　　$5,000 long-term capital loss.

    d.　　No loss is available in any year because this was a personal investment.

    e.　　Some other amount.

25.　Molly suffered the following casualty events, in a year when her AGI totaled $20,000.

Personal casualty gain (asset held 4 years)	$2,000
Personal casualty loss (after $100 floor)	6,000

What is her casualty loss deduction?

    a.　　$2,000.

    b.　　$3,800.

    c.　　$4,000.

    d.　　$6,000.

    e.　　None of the amounts is correct.

Code Section Recognition

Several important sections of the Internal Revenue Code are described below. Indicate, by number, the appropriate Code section.

1.　_____　Provides for a bad debt deduction.

2.　_____　Rules relating to small business stock.

3.　_____　Provides for the deduction for worthless securities.

4.　_____　Provides for a deduction for personal and casualty theft losses.

5.　_____　Provides a deduction for qualified production activities.

Short Answer

1.　Hector, who is single, owns 100 shares of stock in Blue Corporation that he purchased four years ago for $200,000. The stock meets all of the requirements of § 1244. How will the following transactions be treated for tax purposes under the following scenarios?

    a.　　In the current year, he sold the stock for $75,000.

    b.　　In the current year, he sold the stock for $225,000.

2.   Dan incurs the following personal casualty losses in separate incidents during the year. Calculate the casualty loss for each item before application of the 10 percent-of-AGI limitation.

Asset	Adjusted Basis	FMV Before Casualty	FMV After Casualty	Insurance Recovery
A	$500	$600	$400	$200
B	$500	$600	$ 50	$150
C	$500	$600	$400	$400
D	$500	$600	$250	$300

SOLUTIONS TO CHAPTER 7 QUESTIONS

True or False

1.   F   The reserve method is not available for income tax purposes for most taxpayers. [Specific Charge-Off Method p. 7-3]

2.   T   No casualty loss may be deducted if a reasonable prospect of full recovery exists. If a partial claim exists, a deduction may be claimed for only the amount that is not reimbursed by insurance. [General Rule. p. 7-9]

3.   T   The nature of the debt dictates the nature of any loss associated with the debt. [Business versus Nonbusiness Bad Debts p. 7-4]

4.   T   The NOL provision is intended to serve as a form of relief for business income and losses. [Net Operating Losses p. 7-19]

5.   F   A taxpayer may elect to deduct the amount in the prior year if the President of the United States declares the area in which the casualty occurred a disaster area. [Disaster Area Losses p. 7-9]

6.   F   Only the specific charge-off method may be used by most taxpayers. [Specific Charge-Off Method p. 7-3]

7.   F   Dispositions of § 1244 stock at a loss will produce an ordinary loss within certain limitations. [Small Business Stock p. 7-6]

8.   F   The stock must be fully worthless in this situation. [Worthless Securities p. 7-5]

9.   T   Theft does not include items that are simply lost or misplaced. [Theft Losses p. 7-9]

10.   F   The deduction is equal to the property's adjusted basis if such amount is less than the decline in fair market value. [Amount of Loss p. 7-10]

11.   T   These two limitations tend to significantly reduce the value of a casualty and theft loss deduction. [Reduction for $100 and 10 Percent-of-AGI Floors p. 7-11]

12.   F   Business bad debts are treated as ordinary losses while nonbusiness bad debts are considered short-term capital losses. [Business versus Nonbusiness Bad Debts p. 7-4]

13.   T   The deduction is allowed only if income arising from the creation of the account receivable was previously included in income. [Bad Debts p. 7-3]

14.   T   Only certain financial institutions may use the reserve method. [Specific Charge-Off Method p. 7-3]

15.   F   Such damage would not likely meet the suddenness test. [Events That Are Not Casualties p. 7-8]

16.   T   Such an election is irrevocable. [Election to Forgo Carryback p. 7-20]

17.   T   In contrast to a business bad debt, a nonbusiness bad debt must be completely worthless in order to be deductible. [Business versus Nonbusiness Bad Debts p. 7-4]

18.   F   The theft loss deduction is claimed in the year in which the loss is discovered. [Theft Losses p. 7-9]

19.   F   Three alternatives are available: expensing, deferral and amortization, and capitalization. [Research and Experimental Expenditures p. 7-15]

20.   F   The special treatment only applies to losses. [Small Business Stock p. 7-6]

Fill-in-the-Blanks

1.   ordinary, short-term capital [Business versus Nonbusiness Bad Debts p. 7-4]

2.   small business stock, § 1244 stock [Small Business Stock p. 7-6]

3.   adjusted basis of the property [Amount of Loss p. 7-10]
4. $50,000, $100,000 [Small Business Stock p. 7-6]
5.   adjusted basis, fair market value [Amount of Loss p. 7-10]
6.   2, 20 [General Rules p. 7-20]
7. $3,000 [Business versus Nonbusiness Bad Debts p. 7-4]
8. $100, 10 [Reduction for $100 and 10 Percent-of-AGI Floors p. 7-11]
9.   capital [Personal Casualty Gains and Losses p. 7-13]
10.   for [Statutory Framework for Deducting Losses of Individuals p. 7-13]
11.   gifts [Loans between Related Parties p. 7-5]
12.   short-term capital loss [Business versus Nonbusiness Bad Debts p. 7-4]
13.   capital, last day [Worthless Securities p. 7-5]
14.   cash [Bad Debts p. 7-3]
15.   nonbusiness [Business versus Nonbusiness Bad Debts p. 7-4]
16.   three [Domestic Production Activities Deduction p. 7-17]

Multiple Choice

1.   a   A bad debt expense deduction is not available to cash basis taxpayers. [Bad Debts p. 7-3]

2.   d   A bad debt expense deduction is available to accrual basis taxpayers. [Bad Debts p. 7-3]

3.   e   No deduction for such a loss would be allowed unless a timely insurance claim is filed. [Amount of Loss p. 7-10]

4.   b
Auto ($3,000 - $0)	$3,000
Boat ($2,400 - $1,900)	500
Television	600
	$4,100
Less: Statutory floor per event	(100)
Less: 10% of AGI	(2,000)
Deduction	$2,000

[Reduction for $100 and 10 Percent-of-AGI Floors p. 7-11]

5.   a
Auto ($3,000 - $100)	$2,900
Boat ($500 - $100)	400
Television ($600 - $100)	500
	$3,800
Less: 10% of AGI	(2,000)
Deduction	$1,800

[Multiple Losses p. 7-11]

6.   d   This is a casualty loss because the event is (1) identifiable, (2) damaging to property, and (3) sudden, unexpected, and unusual in nature. [Losses of Individuals p. 7-7]

7.   b   A theft loss is deducted in the year of discovery, not the year of the theft (unless the discovery occurs in the same year as the theft). [Theft Losses p. 7-9]

8.   e $900; the loss from the theft of the diamond ring is the only *personal* casualty loss incurred [$2,000 - $100 - 10%($10,000) = $900]. Robert's corporation would report the other casualties. [Multiple Losses p. 7-11]

9.   c   Only individuals and partnerships are eligible to take advantage of the beneficial provisions of § 1244. [Small Business Stock p. 7-6]

10.   a $6,800 = [($6,000 - $100) + ($3,000 - $100)] - ($20,000 X 10%) [Multiple Losses p. 7-11]

11.   a $1,000 decline in FMV (net of allowance) - $500 insurance reimbursement - $100 floor = $400. The deduction would be taken last year (i.e., the year of the accident) because the anticipated insurance recovery would not be enough to offset the entire amount of the loss. [General Rule p. 7-9]

12.   a   Business bad debts produce ordinary loss deductions. [Business versus Nonbusiness Bad Debts p. 7-4]

13.   b   The specific write-off method is required in this situation. [Bad Debts p. 7-3]

14.   b   Income must be recognized in the year of recovery to the extent the amount produced a tax benefit in a previous year. [Specific Charge-Off Method p. 7-3]

15.   b   The nonbusiness bad debt is treated as a STCL and limited to $3,000 in the year of the loss. [Business versus Nonbusiness Bad Debts p. 7-4]

16.   c   The NOL provision is intended as a form of relief for business income and losses. [Net Operating Losses p. 7-19]

17.   d   Each of the losses identified may be deducted by individuals. [Losses of Individuals p. 7-7]

18.   d   The law offers three alternatives for handling of research and experimental expenditures. [Research and Experimental Expenditures p. 7-15]

19.   b $5,000 = ($10,000 + $40,000) / 60 months X 6 months. [Deferral and Amortization Method p. 7-16]

20.   d   A taxpayer may elect to expense all of the research and experimental expenditures incurred in the current year and all subsequent years. [Expense Method p. 7-15]

21.   b   Loan amount $3,000
          Less: Expected recovery ($3,000 X 60%)   (1,800)
          Expected loss $1,200
          [Specific Charge-Off Method p. 7-3]

22.   b   Total loss ($3,000 - $300) $2,700
          Less: Loss claimed last year   (1,200)
          Current year's loss $1,500
          [Specific Charge-Off Method p. 7-3]

23.   a   Ordinary loss treatment is available on losses related to § 1244 stock. [Small Business Stock p. 7-6]

24.   c   The loss is treated as a capital loss deemed to have occurred on the last day of the taxable year. [Worthless Securities p. 7-5]

25.   a   Casualty loss in excess of casualty gain $4,000
          Less: 10% of AGI (10% X $20,000)   (2,000)
          Allowable deduction $2,000
          [Personal Casualty Gains and Losses p. 7-13]

Code Section Recognition

1.   166 [Bad Debts p. 7-3]
2.   1244 [Small Business Stock p. 7-6]
3.   165 [Worthless Securities p. 7-5]
4.   165 [Losses of Individuals p. 7-7]
5.   199 [Domestic Production Activities Deduction p. 7-17]

Short Answer

1. a. Of the total $125,000 loss on the sale of § 1244 stock, §1244 treats $50,000 as an ordinary loss while the remaining $75,000 loss is capital.

    b. The stock is sold at a $25,000 gain. The gain is treated as a long-term capital gain because the stock is a capital asset to Hector. Section 1244 has no impact when stock is sold at a gain.

    [Small Business Stock p. 7-6]

2.

Asset	Loss	Insurance Recovery	Net Gain/Loss before $100 floor	$100 floor	Net Gain or Loss
A	($200)	$200	$ 0	$ 0	$ 0
B	($500)	$150	($350)	$100	($250)
C	($200)	$400	$200	$ 0	$200
D	($350)	$300	($ 50)	$100	$ 0

[Measuring the Amount of Loss p. 7-10]

Chapter 8
Depreciation, Cost Recovery, Amortization, and Depletion

CHAPTER HIGHLIGHTS

Many assets acquired for use in a trade or business or held for the production of income do not produce tax benefits in the year of acquisition equal to their costs because their lives extend substantially beyond the close of the tax year. This chapter discusses the procedures by which a tax benefit is received over an asset's useful life or some other specified period of time. The write-off of an asset's cost (or other adjusted basis) is referred to as depreciation, cost recovery, amortization, or depletion. Depreciation and cost recovery are terms associated with tangible property, amortization pertains to intangible property, and depletion relates to certain natural resources. These provisions have been changed numerous times over the years and, as a result, have produced something of a nightmare for taxpayers who own long-lived assets. Further, distinctions, such as whether an asset has a business or personal use, whether it is realty or personalty, or whether it is tangible or intangible, are important when determining the tax treatment of an asset.

I. Overview
  A. General
    1. The tax law provides for a deduction for the consumption of the cost of an asset through depreciation, cost recovery, amortization, or depletion. The concept of depreciation is based on the premise that the asset acquired (or improvement made) benefits more then one accounting period. The selection of the appropriate depreciation or cost recovery provision depends on when a particular asset is placed into service. A summary of the provisions that apply to depreciable assets is provided in Exhibit 8-1.
    2. Taxpayers may write off the cost of certain assets that are used in *a trade or business* or *held for the production of income*. The write-off takes the form of depreciation, depletion, or amortization. Generally, no deduction is allowed for an asset that does not have a determinable useful life.
  B. Concepts Relating to Depreciation
    1. Nature of Property -- Depreciable property includes both realty and

personalty. Realty generally includes land and buildings permanently affixed to the land. Write-offs are not available for land, however, because land does not have a determinable useful life. Personalty includes furniture, machinery, and equipment. Personalty should not be confused with *personal use* property. Personal use property includes assets *not* put to a business or income-producing use. Personal use property may not be written off.

Exhibit 8-1
DEPRECIATION AND COST RECOVERY: RELEVANT TIME PERIODS

System	Date Property is Placed in Service
Pre-1981 depreciation	*Before January 1, 1981, and certain property placed in service after December 31, 1980.*
Original accelerated cost recovery system (ACRS)	*After December 31, 1980, and before January 1, 1987.*
Modified accelerated cost recovery system (MACRS)	*After December 31, 1986.*

2. Assets used in a trade or business or for the production of income are eligible for cost recovery if they are subject to wear and tear, decay or decline from natural causes, or obsolescence.
3. Placed in Service Requirement -- The key date for the commencement of depreciation is the date an asset is placed in service.
4. The basis of cost recovery property must be reduced by the cost recovery *allowed* and by not less than the *allowable* amount.
5. The basis for cost recovery purposes generally is the adjusted basis used to determine gain if the property is sold or otherwise disposed of. However, if personal use assets are converted to business or income-producing use, the basis for cost recovery and for loss is the *lower* of the adjusted basis or the fair market value at the time the property was converted.

II. Modified Accelerated Cost Recovery System (MACRS)
   A. General
      1. MACRS provide separate tables for *realty* (real property) and *personalty* (personal property).
      2. Under MACRS, the cost of an asset is recovered over a predetermined period that generally is shorter than the useful life of the asset or the period over which the asset is used to produce income.
   B. Personalty: Recovery Periods and Methods
      1. Classification of Property -- Accelerated depreciation is allowed for six different classes of personal property: 3-year, 5-year, 8-year, 10-year, 15-

year, and 20-year. For each class, the cost recovery deduction is computed by multiplying the asset's basis by the percentages found in the appropriate table.

2.   Taxpayers may *elect* the straight-line method to compute cost recovery allowances for these classes of property. Further, certain assets do not qualify to be depreciated using the accelerated methods and must be depreciated using the alternative depreciation system (ADS) discussed below.

> **KEY TERMS**
>
> - ACRS, MACRS, ADS
> - Straight-Line Election
> - § 179 Expense Election
> - Listed Property
> - Amortization
> - Cost Depletion
> - Percentage Depletion

3.   Under MACRS, all personalty is subject to the half-year convention in the year of acquisition *and* in the year of disposition or retirement. Thus, in a practical sense, the write-off periods are 4, 6, 8, 11, 16, and 21 years.

4.   Mid-Quarter Convention -- The half-year convention may not be used if more than 40 percent of the value of property other than eligible real estate is placed in service during the last quarter of the year. In this situation, the *mid-quarter convention* applies whereby the asset acquisitions are grouped and depreciated depending on the quarter during which the assets are acquired. (See Exhibit 8-2 below.) On the property's subsequent disposition, the property is treated as though it were disposed of at the midpoint of the quarter.

Exhibit 8-2
MID-QUARTER CONVENTION

Assets Acquired in	Amount of Depreciation
1st Quarter	10.5 months
2nd Quarter	7.5 months
3rd Quarter	4.5 months
4th Quarter	1.5 months

C.   Realty: Recovery Periods and Methods

1.   Real property placed in service after December 31, 1986 is subject to MACRS rules, which vary depending on whether an asset is *residential rental property* or *nonresidential real estate*.

2.   For residential rental property (property for which 80 percent or more of the gross rental revenues are from non-transient dwelling units), costs are recovered over 27.5 years on a straight-line basis using the mid-month convention. Low-income housing is classified as residential rental property.

3.   Nonresidential real estate has a life of 39 years, during which the straight-line method is used. For nonresidential realty subject to MACRS that was placed in service before May 13, 1993, the recovery period is 31.5 years.

By carefully analyzing the tax benefits associated with cost recovery deductions, a taxpayer may find it more advantageous to make a planned acquisition in one year rather than another. In addition, the effect of various elections and methods of cost recovery on taxable income must be carefully assessed.

D.   Straight-Line Election -- Although straight-line depreciation is currently required under MACRS for all eligible real property, a taxpayer may *elect* to use the straight-line method for personalty. In this situation, the taxpayer depreciates the asset using a half-year or mid-quarter convention over the entire class life of the asset. The election is available on a class-by-class and year-by-year basis.

E.   Election to Expense Assets

     1.   Up to $108,000 (in 2006) of the cost of tangible personal property used in a trade or business may be written off under § 179 in the year the property is placed into service. This provision is elective and the amount expensed is not capitalized. The maximum amount that may be expensed varies as shown in Exhibit 8-3 below, which depends on the year in which the asset(s) is placed in service.

Exhibit 8-3
ELECTION TO EXPENSE ASSETS: CEILING AMOUNTS

Tax Year Beginning in	Amount
2004	$102,000
2005	105,000
2006	108,000

     2.   In addition to the ceiling on the deduction, two other limits apply.

         a.   The ceiling amount on the deduction is reduced dollar-for-dollar when property (other than eligible real estate) placed in service during the taxable year exceeds $430,000 in 2006 ($420,000 in 2005).

         b.   The amount expensed under this election cannot exceed the aggregate amount of taxable income derived from the conduct of any trade or business by the taxpayer.

     3.   If expensed property is converted to personal use, recapture income results.

The § 179 election is designed to enable typical small businesses to expense immediately the full extent of acquisitions made in a normal year. Consequently, with this provision many taxpayers can avoid completely the complex MACRS rules.

F.   Business and Personal Use of Automobiles and Other Listed Property
1.   MACRS deductions are limited for automobiles and other listed property used for both business and personal purposes.
2.   If the property is used *predominantly for business*, the statutory percentage method may be taken. Otherwise, costs are recovered using the straight-line method.
3.   *Listed property* includes the following.
    a.   Any passenger automobile.
    b.   Any other property used as a means of transportation.
    c.   Any property of a type generally used for entertainment, recreation, or amusement.
    d.   Any computer or peripheral equipment unless used exclusively at a regular business establishment.
    e.   Any cellular telephone or other similar telecommunications equipment.
    f.   Any other property specified by the Regulations.

> The IRS has exempted vehicles that are not likely to be used more than a minimal amount for personal purposes from the restrictive depreciation rules. In general, such "qualified nonpersonal use" vehicles include light duty trucks and vans. A florist's delivery van modified with shelving to carry flowers and finished arrangements is an example of a qualifying vehicle.

4.   Listed property is used predominantly for business if it is used *more than 50 percent* of the time in business (not including the time spent for the production of income).
5.   Special limitations apply to *passenger automobiles* used for business. For passenger automobiles, the annual MACRS deduction, which is adjusted each year for inflation, is limited as shown in Exhibit 8-4.

Exhibit 8-4
COST RECOVERY DEDUCTION LIMITS FOR PASSENGER AUTOMOBILES

First year	*$2,960*
Second year	*4,700*
Third year	*2,850*
Each succeeding year	*1,675*

6.   The dollar caps must be reduced if qualified business use is less than 100 percent. In addition, the limitation includes any amount expensed under § 179. If the regular MACRS percentages produce a lesser amount, the lesser amount is used.
7.   For certain vehicles (e.g., large SUVs) not subject to these statutory dollar limits, the § 179 deduction is limited to $25,000.

8. If listed property is *not* used predominantly for business, its costs must be recovered using the straight-line method. Under MACRS, the straight-line method used is that required under the alternative depreciation system (ADS) described below. This system requires a five-year recovery period for automobiles. Further, the cost recovery limitations listed above for passenger automobiles cannot be exceeded.

9. *Cost recovery recapture* is triggered if an asset, which has been used predominantly for business, is not continued to be used in business for more than 50 percent of the time. The amount recaptured is included in the taxpayer's income tax return as ordinary income.

10. A taxpayer who leases a passenger automobile must report an *inclusion amount* (computed from an IRS table) in gross income. This provision is intended to prevent taxpayers from circumventing the cost recovery limitations by leasing.

11. Listed property is subject to the substantiation requirements of § 274. However, the substantiation requirements do not apply to vehicles that are not likely to be used more than a *de minimis* amount for personal purposes.

The purchase of business equipment and its related maintenance are generally deductible to a business. Rather than an individual attempting to deduct the business use of a personal computer at home, a taxpayer should negotiate with the employer to supply a home computer based on its ability to increase productivity for the business.

G. Alternative Depreciation System (ADS)
1. The *ADS* rules must be used to calculate cost recovery in the following situations.
    a. For the portion of depreciation treated as an adjustment for purposes of the alternative minimum tax (see Chapter 15).
    b. For the depreciation expense for the following assets.
        (1) Used predominantly outside of the US.
        (2) Leased or otherwise used by tax-exempt entities.
        (3) Financed with proceeds from tax-exempt bonds.
        (4) Imported from certain foreign countries.
    c. For depreciation allowances calculated for corporate E&P purposes (see Chapter 19).
2. In general, ADS depreciation is computed using the straight-line method without regard to salvage value. However, the computation for alternative minimum tax purposes for personalty is computed using the 150 percent declining balance method, followed by a switch to straight-line.
3. The half-year or the mid-quarter convention applies to all property other than eligible real estate. For real property, the mid-month convention is used.
4. The ADS recovery periods follow.
    a. Personalty: ADR mid-point life if not in the 5-year (e.g., technological equipment, automobiles, and light-duty trucks) or the 12-year (e.g., personal property with no class life) class.

b.   Realty: 40 years.

5.   In lieu of depreciation under the regular MACRS method, taxpayers may elect straight-line under ADS for property that qualifies for the regular MACRS method. The election is available on a class-by-class and year-by-year basis for property other than eligible real estate. The election for eligible real estate is on a property-by-property basis.

III. Amortization

A.   Intangible property used in a trade or business or in the production of income may be *amortized* if the property has a limited life that can be determined with reasonable accuracy.

B.   Generally, intangible property is amortized using a straight-line method.

C.   Under current law, taxpayers who acquire goodwill, going-concern value, and certain other customer-based intangibles are permitted under § 197 to amortize the costs of these assets over a 15-year period.

D.   Startup expenditures

1.   Startup expenditures are partially amortizable if the taxpayer so elects. Otherwise, they are capitalized.

2.   The elective treatment allows the taxpayer to deduct the lesser of:

a.   The amount of the trade or business startup expenditures, or

b. $5,000, reduced (but not below zero) by the amount by which the startup expenditures exceed $50,000.

3.   Any startup expenditures not deducted may be amortized ratably over a 180-month period.

IV. Depletion

A.   Intangible Drilling and Development Costs (IDC) -- These costs may be treated in *either* one of two ways by the taxpayer.

1.   They may be charged off as an expense in the year they are incurred.

2.   They may be capitalized and written off through depletion.

B.   Depletion Methods

1.   The owner of an interest in a wasting asset is entitled to deduct depletion. Like depreciation, depletion is a deduction *for* adjusted gross income.

2.   There are two methods of calculating depletion: cost depletion and percentage depletion. The choice between the two methods is made by an annual election and generally the method producing the *higher* expense is taken.

3.   The *cost depletion* per unit is calculated by using the adjusted basis of the natural resource. The depletion per unit is then multiplied by the number of units *sold* to arrive at the cost depletion deduction for a given year.

4.   The *percentage depletion* amount is calculated by multiplying a specified percentage provided in the Code by the gross income received from the property during a given year. In no event should the depletion deduction computed by this method exceed 50 percent of taxable income from the property before the allowance for depletion.

5.   IDC affects the depletion deduction in two ways: the depletion deduction may be increased if the IDC are capitalized; whereas, if the IDC are expensed, the taxable income from the property would be reduced and could invoke the depletion limitation of 50 percent of taxable income as described above.

TEST FOR SELF-EVALUATION -- CHAPTER 8

True or False

Indicate which of the following statements are true or false by circling the correct answer.

T   F   1.   Taxpayers must use the statutory percentage method of depreciation under MACRS.

T   F   2.   To be depreciable, property must be used in a trade or business or held for the production of income.

T   F   3.   The amount that may be expensed under § 179, Election to Expense Certain Depreciable Assets, generally is limited to $108,000 in 2006.

T   F   4.   For all real property placed in service after 1986, the 39-year cost recovery period applies.

T   F   5.   Limitations exist relating to the aggregate amount of depreciation deductions that may be claimed for automobiles.

T   F   6.   Goodwill is amortizable for tax purposes over a period that is arbitrarily determined by the taxpayer.

T   F   7.   Under the MACRS depreciation rules, the estimated salvage value of an asset is ignored.

T   F   8.   The depletion deduction calculation can be based either on the cost depletion or percentage depletion methods.

T   F   9.   For real property placed in service in the current year, a straight-line method of depreciation *must* be used.

T   F   10.   For real property placed in service in the current year, depreciation may be claimed in the years of acquisition and disposition.

T   F   11.   A mid-quarter convention applies to the depreciation of personal tangible property placed in service during the year if more than 40 percent of the property is placed in service during the last 4 months of the year.

T   F   12.   The use of the alternative depreciation system is in all cases elective.

T   F   13.   For tangible personal property placed in service in the current year, a straight-line method of depreciation *must* be used.

T   F   14.   For intangible property placed in service in the current year, a straight-line method of amortization *must* be used.

T   F   15.   The mid-quarter convention would apply whether or not the taxpayer uses an accelerated method or the straight-line method of cost recovery.

T   F   16.   Assuming the mid-quarter convention does not apply, the half-year convention is used in the year of acquisition if tangible personalty is placed in service on January 1, 2006.

T   F   17.   Only one-half year's worth of depreciation is available in the year of acquisition if realty is placed in service on January 1, 2006.

T   F   18.   The amount expensed under § 179 cannot exceed the aggregate amount of taxable income derived from the conduct of any trade or business by the taxpayer.

T   F   19.   The amount of the § 179 deduction otherwise available is not affected by the amount of real estate placed into service during the year.

T   F   20.   A passenger automobile is classified as listed property even if it is used exclusively for business.

Fill-in-the-Blanks

Complete the following statements with the appropriate word(s) or amount(s).

1.   When a personal use asset is converted to business or income producing use, the basis for depreciation purposes is the lower of its _____ or _____ on the date of conversion.

2.   The basis of a depreciable asset is reduced by the depreciation actually _____, but never by a lesser amount than that _____.

3.   The two methods available to compute depletion are the _____ method and the _____ method.

4.   The regular cost recovery periods under MACRS for personal property are _____ years, _____ years, _____ years, _____ years, _____ years, and _____ years.

5.   For _____ property placed in service subject to MACRS, cost recovery may be deducted in the year of acquisition as well as in the year of disposition using the half-year convention.

6.   Automobiles and computers are examples of property meeting the definition of _____ property.

7.   Under the MACRS rules, the normal recovery period for residential realty is _____ years, but for nonresidential realty, the recovery period is _____ or _____ years.

8.   The half-year convention applies to _____ property, but not to _____ property under MACRS.

9.   The election to expense immediately up to $108,000 (in 2006) in the year of acquisition applies only to purchased tangible _____ property used in a trade or business.

10.   In order to claim *any* portion of the $108,000 immediate expensing deduction during 2006, the aggregate acquisitions (excluding real estate) may not exceed _____.

11.   Listed property that is not used predominantly for business must be depreciated using the _____ method.

12.   For listed property to be considered as predominantly used in business, the percentage of use for business must exceed _____ percent.

13.   _____ depletion is computed without regard to basis.

14.   All cost recovery deductions under MACRS for _____ property are calculated using the mid-month convention.

15.   The first year cost recovery deduction for a passenger automobile is limited to _____.

Multiple Choice

Choose the best answer for each of the following questions.

_____ 1.   On April 1, 2006, Robert acquired equipment for $208,000 for use in his business. The equipment has a 5-year recovery period. Robert elects straight-line depreciation. Given this was his sole acquisition for the year, Robert desires otherwise to maximize his first year write-off on the equipment. Calculate the maximum Robert may deduct due to the purchase and use of the machine during the year, assuming the mid-quarter convention is not appropriate.
    a. $128,000.
    b. $118,000.
    c. $41,600.
    d. $20,800.
    e.   None of these choices.

_____ 2.   On April 1, 2006, Robert acquired equipment for $208,000 for use in his business. The equipment has a 5-year recovery period. Robert desires to use § 179 and the MACRS provisions to recover the cost of his investment. If this was his sole acquisition for the year, determine the total depreciation expense for the year, assuming the mid-quarter convention is not appropriate.
    a. $148,000.
    b. $128,000.
    c. $118,000.
    d. $41,600.
    e.   None of these choices.

_____ 3.   On April 1, 2006, Robert acquired equipment for $550,000 for use in his business. The equipment has a 5-year recovery period. Robert desires to use § 179 and the MACRS provisions to recover the cost of his investment. If this was his sole acquisition for the year, determine the total depreciation expense for the year, assuming the mid-quarter convention is not appropriate.
    a. $55,000.

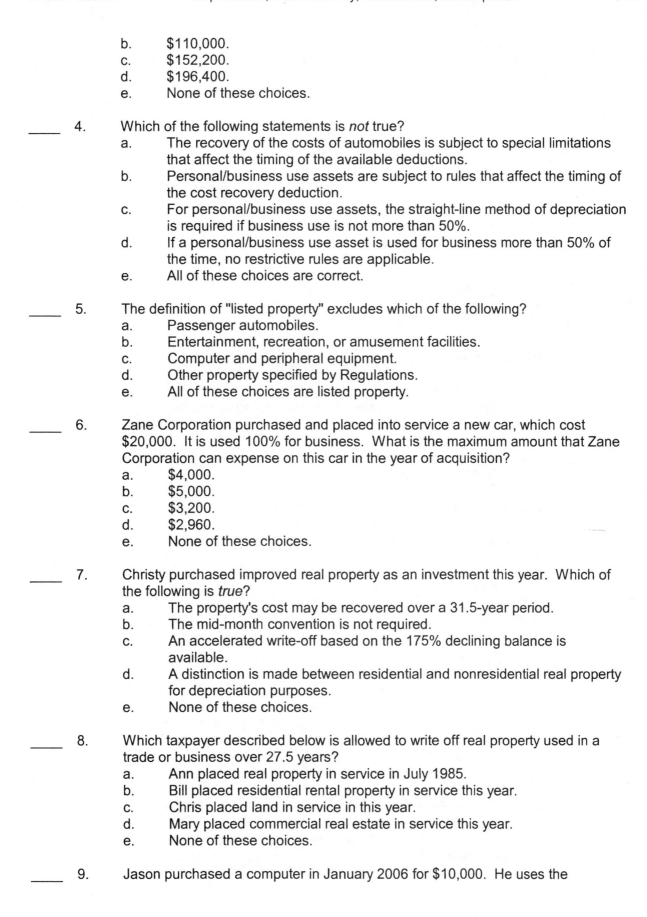

        b. $110,000.
        c. $152,200.
        d. $196,400.
        e.   None of these choices.

_____ 4. Which of the following statements is *not* true?
        a.   The recovery of the costs of automobiles is subject to special limitations that affect the timing of the available deductions.
        b.   Personal/business use assets are subject to rules that affect the timing of the cost recovery deduction.
        c.   For personal/business use assets, the straight-line method of depreciation is required if business use is not more than 50%.
        d.   If a personal/business use asset is used for business more than 50% of the time, no restrictive rules are applicable.
        e.   All of these choices are correct.

_____ 5. The definition of "listed property" excludes which of the following?
        a.   Passenger automobiles.
        b.   Entertainment, recreation, or amusement facilities.
        c.   Computer and peripheral equipment.
        d.   Other property specified by Regulations.
        e.   All of these choices are listed property.

_____ 6. Zane Corporation purchased and placed into service a new car, which cost $20,000. It is used 100% for business. What is the maximum amount that Zane Corporation can expense on this car in the year of acquisition?
        a. $4,000.
        b. $5,000.
        c. $3,200.
        d. $2,960.
        e.   None of these choices.

_____ 7. Christy purchased improved real property as an investment this year. Which of the following is *true*?
        a.   The property's cost may be recovered over a 31.5-year period.
        b.   The mid-month convention is not required.
        c.   An accelerated write-off based on the 175% declining balance is available.
        d.   A distinction is made between residential and nonresidential real property for depreciation purposes.
        e.   None of these choices.

_____ 8. Which taxpayer described below is allowed to write off real property used in a trade or business over 27.5 years?
        a.   Ann placed real property in service in July 1985.
        b.   Bill placed residential rental property in service this year.
        c.   Chris placed land in service in this year.
        d.   Mary placed commercial real estate in service this year.
        e.   None of these choices.

_____ 9. Jason purchased a computer in January 2006 for $10,000. He uses the computer for business exactly 50% of the time. What is the maximum depreciation deduction he can take currently, assuming a five-year classification and that the § 179 election is not available?

a. $10,000.
b. $5,000.
c. $2,000.
d. $1,000.
e.   None of these choices.

_____ 10. Jason purchased a computer in January 2006 for $10,000. He uses the computer for business exactly 60% of the time. What is the maximum depreciation deduction he can take currently, assuming a five-year classification and that the § 179 election is not available?

a. $2,000.
b. $1,200.
c. $1,000.
d. $600.
e.   None of these choices.

_____ 11. Which statement concerning the alternative depreciation system is *not* true?

a.   There is only one depreciation class for all types of real property.
b.   In certain situations, a taxpayer may elect to use ADS.
c.   The half-year convention is required for all assets other than realty under ADS.
d.   ADS must be used to compute the depreciation adjustment amount for alternative minimum tax purposes.
e.   All of these choices are true.

_____ 12. Emily acquired a new automobile on January 1, 2006. The automobile, which cost $20,000, is used 80 percent for business. Determine the maximum depreciation that may be taken in the year of acquisition.

a. $10,000.
b. $8,000.
c. $4,000.
d. $3,200.
e. $2,960.
f. $2,368.
g.   Some other amount.

_____ 13. Emily acquired a new automobile on January 1, 2006. The automobile, which cost $20,000, is used 20 percent for business. Determine the maximum depreciation that may be taken in the year of acquisition.

a. $4,000.
b. $2,960.
c. $800.
d. $592.
e.   Some other amount.

_____ 14. On February 26 of the current year, Ivy Corporation placed in service a *new* warehouse costing $1 million. Determine the cost recovery for the year.

a. $34,850.

       b. $31,820.
       c. $27,780.
       d. $22,470.
       e.   Some other amount.

_____   15.   On February 26 of the current year, Ivy Corporation placed in service a *used* warehouse costing $1 million. Determine the cost recovery for the year.
       a. $34,850.
       b. $31,820.
       c. $27,780.
       d. $22,470.
       e.   Some other amount.

_____   16.   On March 15 of the current year, Crozet Corporation placed in service a new apartment building costing $1 million. Calculate the cost recovery deduction for this year.
       a. $18,181.
       b. $28,790.
       c. $34,850.
       d. $36,360.
       e.   None of these choices.

_____   17.   On March 15 of the current year, Crozet Corporation placed in service a new apartment building costing $1 million. Calculate the cost recovery deduction for the second year.
       a. $18,181.
       b. $28,790.
       c. $34,850.
       d. $36,360.
       e.   None of these choices.

_____   18.   On March 15 of the current year, Crozet Corporation placed in service a new apartment building costing $1 million. Assuming the taxpayer elects ADS, calculate the cost recovery deduction for the year of acquisition.
       a. $18,181.
       b. $28,790.
       c. $34,850.
       d. $36,360.
       e.   None of these choices.

_____   19.   On March 15, 2006, Crozet Corporation placed in service a new apartment building costing $1 million. The taxpayer elects ADS. Assuming the building is sold on October 31, 2010, determine the cost recovery deduction for the year of disposition.
       a. $12,500.
       b. $19,792.
       c. $21,875.
       d. $25,000.
       e.   None of these choices.

_____   20.   Crystal Corporation acquired a used machine (8-year property) on May 15, 2006

for $100,000. Assuming neither the § 179 election nor the straight-line method is used, determine the cost recovery for the current year.
a. $7,145.
b. $14,290.
c. $24,000.
d. $33,330.
e. Some other amount.

____ 21. Crystal Corporation acquired a machine (5-year property) on December 15, 2006 for $100,000, which was its sole acquisition for the year. Assuming that neither the § 179 election nor the straight-line method is used, calculate the cost recovery deduction for the current year.
a. $5,000.
b. $10,000.
c. $14,290.
d. $20,000.
e. Some other amount.

____ 22. Canary Corporation acquired an asset (5-year property) on March 15 for $100,000. The asset is listed property (not an automobile) and it is used 35 percent for business, 50 percent for the production of income, and the remainder of the time it is used for personal use. Assuming the § 179 election is not made, calculate the maximum cost recovery for the current year.
a. $8,500.
b. $10,000.
c. $17,000.
d. $20,000.
e. Some other amount.

____ 23. Canary Corporation acquired an asset (5-year property) on March 15 for $100,000. The asset is listed property (not an automobile) and it is used 50 percent for business, 35 percent for the production of income, and the remainder of the time it is used for personal use. Assuming the § 179 election is not made, determine the maximum cost recovery for the current year.
a. $8,500.
b. $10,000.
c. $17,000.
d. $20,000.
e. Some other amount.

____ 24. Canary Corporation acquired a used asset (5-year property) on March 15 for $100,000. The asset is listed property (not an automobile) and it is used 51 percent for business, 34 percent for the production of income, and the remainder of the time it is used for personal use. Assuming the § 179 election is not made, determine the maximum cost recovery for the current year.
a. $8,500.
b. $10,000.
c. $17,000.
d. $20,000.
e. Some other amount.

_____ 25.   On February 26, Jennifer purchased the rights to a depletable asset for
             $1,000,000. At the time of its acquisition, it was estimated that the number of
             tons that could be mined would be 250,000. During the year, 50,000 tons were
             mined and 30,000 tons were sold for $750,000. Expenses other than depletion
             totaled $500,000. If the depletion rate is 22 percent, calculate the maximum
             depletion deduction.
             a. $120,000.
             b. $125,000.
             c. $165,000.
             d. $200,000.
             e.   Some other amount.

Code Section Recognition

Several important sections of the Internal Revenue Code are described below. Indicate, by
number, the appropriate Code section.

1.   _____ The MACRS rules appear in this section.

2.   _____ Describes the limitations on depreciation for luxury automobiles.

3.   _____ Provides substantiation requirements for listed property.

Short Answer

1.   Identify the MACRS cost recovery period for the following assets:
      a.   Automobile.
      b.   Copier.
      c.   Office furniture.
      d.   Land improvements.
      e.   Computer.

2. Betty acquires commercial real estate and residential real estate for $1 million each in March, 2006. Assuming that each asset is depreciable, compute the annual cost recovery deduction under MACRS and under ADS for the assets' first two years of use.

	MACRS	ADS
Commercial		
Year 1		
Year 2		
Residential		
Year 1		
Year 2		

SOLUTIONS TO CHAPTER 8 QUESTIONS

True or False

1.   F   A taxpayer may use a method other than the statutory percentage method under MACRS. If appropriate, a taxpayer may elect to use either the ADS system or the straight-line method over the MACRS recovery period. Further, no assets placed in service prior to 1987 may be depreciated using MACRS. [Straight-Line Election p. 8-10]

2.   T   Depreciation deductions are not allowed for personal use assets. [Overview p. 8-2]

3.   T   The election is an annual election and applies to the acquisition cost of tangible personal property placed in service that year. [Election to Expense Assets p. 8-10]

4.   F   For real property placed in service after December 31, 1986, the recovery period is either 27.5 years (for residential realty) or 39 years (for nonresidential realty). For nonresidential realty subject to MACRS that was placed in service before May 13, 1993, the recovery period is 31.5 years. [Realty: Recovery Periods and Methods p. 8-8]

5.   F   The limitation concerns the *timing* of the deductions and not the total or aggregate *amount* that may be claimed over the asset's recovery period. [Limits on Cost Recovery for Automobiles p. 8-12]

6.   F   Goodwill is amortizable over a 15-year period. [Amortization p. 8-19]

7.   T   An asset's salvage value does not reduce the basis used to determine the cost recovery deduction. [Overview p. 8-2]

8.   T   The choice between cost and percentage depletion is an annual election. [Depletion Methods p. 8-20]

9.   T   All realty placed in service in the current year is depreciated using a straight-line method. [Realty: Recovery Periods and Methods p. 8-8]

10. T   The mid-month convention is used in both the years of acquisition and disposition. [Realty: Recovery Periods and Methods p. 8-8]

11. F   The convention applies if more than 40 percent is placed in service during the last 3 (not 4) months of the year. [Mid-Quarter Convention p. 8-7]

12. F   The ADS rules are required in several situations, including when calculating the alternative minimum tax and corporate earnings and profits. [Alternative Depreciation System (ADS) p. 8-17]

13. F   Accelerated methods of cost recovery are available under MACRS for tangible personal property. [Personalty: Recovery Periods and Methods p. 8-5]

14. T   The cost of an asset subject to amortization is recovered over a 15-year period using a straight-line method. [Amortization p. 8-19]

15. T   Without regard to the method of depreciation used, the mid-quarter convention applies to the depreciation of personal tangible property placed in service during the year if more than 40 percent of the property is placed in service during the last 3 months of the year. [Mid-Quarter Convention p. 8-7]

16. T   MACRS views personal property as placed in service in the middle of the year of acquisition. [Personalty: Recovery Periods and Methods p. 8-5]

17. F   The mid-month convention applies. [Realty: Recovery Periods and Methods p. 8-8]

18. T   This is one of the annual limitations that may restrict the amount that may be expensed under this election. [Annual Limitations p. 8-10]

19. T   Realty acquisitions in a particular year will not have an impact on the deduction

amount allowable under § 179. [Annual Limitations p. 8-10]
20.   T   The definition of listed property includes any passenger automobile. [Business and Personal Use of Automobiles and Other Listed Property p. 8-11]

Fill-in-the-Blanks

1.   adjusted basis, fair market value [Cost Recovery Basis for Personal Use Assets Converted to Business or Income-Producing Use p. 8-4]
2.   allowed, allowable [Cost Recovery Allowed or Allowable p. 8-3]
3.   cost, percentage [Depletion Methods p. 8-20]
4.   3, 5, 7, 10, 15, 20 [Personalty: Recovery Periods and Methods p. 8-5]
5.   personal [Personalty: Recovery Periods and Methods p. 8-5]
6.   listed [Business and Personal Use of Automobiles and Other Listed Property p. 8-11]
7.   27.5, 39, 31.5 [Realty: Recovery Periods and Methods p. 8-8]
8.   personal, real [Personalty: Recovery Periods and Methods p. 8-5; Realty: Recovery Periods and Methods p. 8-8]
9.   personal [Election to Expense Assets p. 8-10]
10. $538,000 = $108,000 + $430,000 [Annual Limitations p. 8-10]
11.   straight-line [Automobiles and Other Listed Property Not Used Predominantly in Business p. 8-14]
12.   50 [Automobiles and Other Listed Property Used Predominantly in Business p. 8-12]
13.   Percentage [Percentage Depletion p. 8-22]
14.   real [Realty: Recovery Periods and Methods p. 8-8]
15. $2,960 [Limits on Cost Recovery for Automobiles p. 8-12]

Multiple Choice

1.   b $118,000 = $108,000 + [($100,000 / 5 yrs.) X ½] [Straight-Line Election p. 8-10; Election to Expense Assets p. 8-10]
2.   b $128,000 = $108,000 + ($100,000 X .20) [Election to Expense Assets p. 8-10]
3.   b   Robert may not use § 179 because the cost of his acquisition exceeds the $538,000 ceiling amount. Therefore, the total cost recovery for the year is $110,000 = $550,000 X.20. [Annual Limitations p. 8-10]
4.   d   Luxury automobiles are subject to special restrictions even when they are used predominantly (i.e., more than 50%) for business. [Limits on Cost Recovery for Automobiles p. 8-12]
5.   e   Each of the items indicated is included in the definition of listed property. [Business and Personal Use of Automobiles and Other Listed Property p. 8-11]
6.   d   The deduction is limited to $2,960 in the year of acquisition. This deduction is less than the amount that would otherwise be available ($20,000 X 20% = $4,000). Note that this limitation is indexed annually. [Limits on Cost Recovery for Automobiles p. 8-12]
7.   d   The two types of realty have cost recovery periods of different lengths. [Realty: Recovery Periods and Methods p. 8-8]
8.   b   The current cost recovery period for residential realty placed in service in the current year is 27.5 years. [Realty: Recovery Periods and Methods p. 8-8]
9.   e $500 = $10,000 X .50 X .10. The half-year convention is used in the year of acquisition; the straight-line method is required. [Automobiles and Other Listed Property Not Used Predominantly in Business p. 8-14]

10.   b $1,200 = $10,000 X .60 X .20. Because the taxpayer uses the computer predominantly for business, it may be depreciated using an accelerated method (MACRS). [Automobiles and Other Listed Property Used Predominantly in Business p. 8-12]

11.   e   Each of the statements is true. [Alternative Depreciation System (ADS) p. 8-17]

12.   f $2,368 -- Lesser of:
            $20,000 X .80 X .20 = $3,200 or $2,960 X .80 = $2,368
          The limitation is indexed annually. [Limits on Cost Recovery for Automobiles p. 8-12]

13.   e $400 -- Lesser of:
            $20,000 X .20 X .10 = $400 or $2,960 X .20 = $592
          The half-year convention is used in the year of acquisition. Note that this limitation is indexed annually. [Automobiles and Other Listed Property Not Used Predominantly in Business p. 8-14]

14.   d $22,470 = $1,000,000 X .02247. [Realty: Recovery Periods and Methods p. 8-8]

15.   d $22,470 = $1,000,000 X .02247. There is no distinction between new and used property in the cost recovery calculation. [Realty: Recovery Periods and Methods p. 8-8]

16.   b $28,790 = $1,000,000 X .02879. [Realty: Recovery Periods and Methods p. 8-8]

17.   d $36,360 = $1,000,000 X .03636. [Realty: Recovery Periods and Methods p. 8-8]

18.   e $19,790 = $1,000,000 X .01979. [Realty: Recovery Periods and Methods p. 8-8]

19.   b $19,792 = $1,000,000 X .025 X 9.5/12. [Realty: Recovery Periods and Methods p. 8-8]

20.   b $14,290 = $100,000 X .1429. [Personalty: Recovery Periods and Methods p. 8-5]

21.   a $5,000 = $100,000 X .05. The mid-quarter convention applies. [Mid-Quarter Convention p. 8-7]

22.   a $8,500 = $100,000 X .10 X .85. The property is listed property; straight-line depreciation must be used because the business usage test is not met. [Automobiles and Other Listed Property Not Used Predominantly in Business p. 8-14]

23.   a $8,500 = $100,000 X .10 X .85. The property is listed property; straight-line depreciation must be used because the business usage test is not met (i.e., *more* than 50 percent for business). [Automobiles and Other Listed Property Not Used Predominantly in Business p. 8-14]

24.   c $17,000 = $100,000 X .20 X .85. The property is listed property; however, the straight-line depreciation need not be used because the business usage test is met. [Automobiles and Other Listed Property Used Predominantly in Business p. 8-12]

25.   b $1,000,000/250,000 tons = $4/ton.
          30,000 tons X $4/ton = $120,000 cost depletion.
          22% X $750,000 = $165,000 percentage depletion.
          Percentage limit ($750,000 - $500,000) X 50% = $125,000.
          [Depletion Methods p. 8-20]

Code Section Recognition

1.   168 [Modified Accelerated Cost Recovery System (MACRS) p. 8-4]
2.   280F [Limits on Cost Recovery for Automobiles p. 8-12]
3.   274 [Substantiation Requirements p. 8-16]

Short Answer

1. a.   Automobile -- 5-year property.
    b.   Copier -- 5-year property.
    c.   Office furniture -- 8-year property.
    d.   Land improvements -- 15-year property.
    e.   Computer -- 5-year property.
    [Personalty: Recovery Periods and Methods p. 8-5]

2.

	MACRS	ADS
Commercial		
Year 1	$20,330	$19,790
Year 2	$25,640	$25,000
Residential		
Year 1	$28,790	$19,790
Year 2	$36,360	$25,000

[Realty: Recovery Periods and Methods p. 8-8; Alternative Depreciation System (ADS) p. 8-17]

Chapter 9
Deductions: Employee and
Self-Employed-Related Expenses

CHAPTER HIGHLIGHTS

Discussions concerning the deductibility and treatment of many commonly incurred employee and self-employed related expenses are included in this chapter. Specifically, the provisions that govern transportation, travel, moving expenses, education, entertainment, and certain other expenses are explained and illustrated. In addition, the substantiation requirements that must be met to support a deduction are discussed. Finally, the rules governing the classification of deductions as either *for* or *from* adjusted gross income are discussed in detail.

I.   Employee versus Self-Employed
 A.   When one person performs services for another, the person performing the service is either an employee or self-employed (i.e., an independent contractor).
 B.   Expenses incurred by an independent contractor in a trade or business are deductible *for* AGI; whereas, expenses incurred as a result of an employment relationship generally may be deductible *from* AGI.
 C.   Generally, an employer-employee relationship exists when the employer has the right to specify the end result of a task and the ways and means by which the end result is to be achieved.
 D.   *Statutory employees*, a special category of employees (e.g., full-time insurance salespersons, homeworkers, traveling salespersons), are allowed to deduct expenses *for* AGI.

II.   Employee Expenses -- In General -- Once employee status has been established, employee expenses fall into one of the following categories. These expenses are not necessarily limited to employees.
 A.   Transportation.
 B.   Travel.
 C.   Moving.
 D.   Education.
 E.   Entertainment.

      F.   Other.

III.   Transportation Expenses
    A.   Qualified Expenditures
          1.   An employee is allowed a deduction *from* AGI for transportation expenses incurred for the purpose of transporting him/herself from one place to another in the course of employment when the employee is not *away from home* in a travel status.
          2.   *Commuting expenses* are nondeductible. However, certain costs incurred by an employee who uses an automobile to transport heavy tools to work may be deductible. Further, expenses incurred for transportation from one job to another are deductible as are expenses incurred for transportation associated with *temporary* or minor assignments beyond the general area of the tax home.
    B.   Computation of Automobile Expenses
          1.   A taxpayer may compute the deduction for automobile expenses in *either* one of two ways.
              a.   The taxpayer may deduct the actual operating expenses incurred in the pursuit of business.
              b.   The taxpayer may use the automatic mileage method and deduct 44.5 cents (in 2006) per business mile driven. Parking fees and tolls are also allowed when using the automatic mileage method (also called the standard mileage method).
          2.   Actual operating expenses include depreciation (cost recovery), gas, oil, repairs, licenses, and insurance. Records must be kept to document the automobile's personal and business use. Complex depreciation rules apply if the actual expense method is used.

IV.   Travel Expenses
    A.   Definition of Travel Expenses -- Travel expenses are more broadly defined in the law than transportation expenses. In addition to transportation expenses, travel expenses include meals and lodging while away from home in pursuit of business. In contrast to transportation expenses, the taxpayer must be *away from home overnight* in order to deduct travel expenses.
    B.   Away-from-Home Requirement
          1.   To be deductible, travel expenses must be incurred by a taxpayer for a period while away from home substantially longer than an ordinary day's work, and for a period where rest, sleep or a relief-from-work period is required.
          2.   Under ordinary circumstances, there is no problem in determining the location of a taxpayer's tax home. However, in some circumstances, controversy may exist.

KEY TERMS

- Employee vs. Self-Employed Status
- Two percent-of-AGI Floor
- Travel and Entertainment
- Accountable Plan
- Moving Expenses
- Education Expenses
- Office in the Home

      C.   Restrictions on Travel Expenses
            1.   Deductions related to attending a convention, seminar, or similar meeting are disallowed unless they are associated with the taxpayer's trade or business. In addition, stringent restrictions on the deductibility of travel expenses for the taxpayer's spouse or dependent exist.
            2.   No deduction is allowed for travel that by itself is considered by the taxpayer to be educational.
      D.   Combined Business and Pleasure Travel -- If a trip combines business and personal objectives, the following points are relevant.
            1.   Transportation expenses are deductible (for domestic trips) only if the trip is *primarily for business*.
            2.   No transportation expenses may be deducted if the trip is *primarily for personal pleasure*; however, other expenses incurred that specifically relate to business are deductible.
            3.   If the trip is *outside the United States*, special rules apply.
            4.   Special restrictive rules apply to the deductibility of expenses paid or incurred to attend conventions held in locations outside the North American area.

V.   Moving Expenses
      A.   General Requirements -- Moving expenses incurred (either as an employee or as a self-employed individual) in connection with the commencement of work at a new principal place are deductible. To be deductible, the *distance and time tests* must be met.
      B.   Distance Test
            1.   For moving expenses to be deductible, the taxpayer's new job location must be *at least* 50 miles farther from the old residence than the old residence was from the former place of employment.
            2.   This test eliminates the deduction for taxpayers who purchase a new home in the same general area without acquiring new employment, if a new job in the same general area does not necessitate a move, or if the move is for personal reasons.
      C.   Time Test -- To be eligible for the moving expense deduction, an employee must be employed on a full-time basis for 39 weeks in the 12-month period following the move; or if the person is self-employed, he or she must work for 78 weeks during the next two years in the new location.
      D.   Treatment of Moving Expenses
            1.   What is Included -- Qualified moving expenses include *reasonable* expenses incurred for the following purposes.
                  a.   Moving household goods and personal effects.
                  b.   Traveling from the former residence to the new place of residence. Traveling for this purpose includes lodging, but not meals, for the taxpayer and members of the household. The taxpayer can elect to use actual auto expenses (no depreciation is allowed) or the automatic mileage method. In this case, moving expense mileage is limited to 18 cents (in 2006) per mile for each automobile. These expenses are also limited by the reasonableness standard.
            2.   What is Not Included
                  a.   The cost of meals incurred while traveling to the new location.
                  b.   Loss on the sale of a residence.
                  c.   Pre-move house-hunting expenses.

        d.   Temporary living expenses.
    3.   How treated
        a.   Qualified moving expenses that are paid (or reimbursed) by the employer are not reported as part of the gross income of the employee.
        b.   Moving expenses paid (or reimbursed) by the employer that are not qualified moving expenses are included in the employee's gross income and are not deductible.
        c.   The qualified expenses that are not reimbursed or those of self-employed taxpayers are reported as deductions *for* AGI.

VI.   Education Expenses
    A.   General Requirements
        1.   An employee may deduct education expenses if they are incurred in either of the following situations.
            a.   To maintain or improve existing skills required in the present job.
            b.   To meet the stated requirements of the employer or to meet requirements imposed by law to retain his or her employment status.
        2.   In general, education expenses are not deductible in the following situations.
            a.   If they are incurred to meet the minimum educational standards for qualification in the taxpayer's existing job.
            b.   If they qualify the taxpayer for a new trade or business.
    B.   Requirements Imposed by Law or by the Employer for Retention of Employment -- Teachers often qualify under this provision, which provides for the deduction of education expenses incurred if they are required by their employer or by law to take additional courses. However, if the required education is the minimum required for the job, no deduction is allowed.
    C.   Maintaining or Improving Existing Skills -- This requirement has been difficult for taxpayers and the courts to interpret. The successful application of the rule is often dependent on subtleties of the particular case under consideration.
    D.   Classification of Specific Items -- Educational expenses include expenses for books, tuition, typing, transportation, and travel. Unless the expenses are reimbursed by the taxpayer's employer, the amounts are deductible as miscellaneous itemized deductions, subject to the two percent-of-AGI floor. In addition, the 50 percent rule (discussed below) applies to meals.
    E.   A Limited Deduction Approach -- In certain situations, a taxpayer may deduct qualified tuition and related expenses incurred to acquire basic skills. This deduction for higher education expenses is claimed *for* AGI and phases out when the taxpayer's income reaches a prescribed threshold. To preclude a "double benefit" from occurring, the deduction must be coordinated with various other education provisions. Further, this deduction is not available to a taxpayer who qualifies as another's dependent.

VII.   Entertainment Expenses
    A.   Cutback Adjustment
        1.   Only 50 percent of meal and entertainment expenses are allowed as a deduction. The limitation applies in both the context of employment or self-employment status. However, the 50 percent cutback gradually is reduced in certain situations (e.g., truck and bus drivers, air transportation

flight crews) until reaching the point where 80 percent of the cost of meals is allowed as a deduction.

2. Although the reduction can apply to *either* the employer or the employee, it will *not* apply twice.

3. Transportation expenses are not affected by this provision.

4. The 50 percent limitation does not apply in the following situations.

    a. Where the full value of the meals or entertainment is included in the compensation of the employee (or independent contractor).

    b. Where the *de minimis* fringe benefit rule is met.

    c. Employer-paid recreational activities for employees (e.g., spring picnic).

 With only 50 percent of meals and entertainment expenses being deductible, taxpayers should consider sending gifts instead of taking their clients out to eat. Sending flowers, gift certificates, or tickets to the theater may make a bigger impact than dining out, and the cost may be deductible in full, up to $25 per person.

B. Classification of Expenses -- Entertainment expenses may be categorized as follows.

1. Those *directly related to business* -- related to an actual business meeting or discussion.

2. Those *associated with business* -- must serve a specific business purpose.

C. Restrictions Upon Deductibility

1. The cost of business meals are deductible only in certain situations.

    a. The meal is directly related to or associated with the active conduct of a trade or business.

    b. The expense is not lavish or extravagant under the circumstances.

    c. The taxpayer (or employee) is present at the meal.

2. No deduction is allowed for *club dues* for any type of club organized for business, pleasure, or any other purpose. However, this prohibition does not apply to clubs whose primary purpose is public service and community volunteerism (e.g., Kiwanis, Lions, Rotary). This limitation is true regardless of the business usage of the club. However, meal and entertainment expenses incurred at a club may be deductible.

3. Ticket Purchases for Entertainment

    a. The deduction for the cost of an entertainment event is subject to several limitations. Assuming an expenditure is otherwise deductible, its deduction is limited to 50 percent of the face value of the ticket (including any ticket tax). Thus, to the extent a premium is paid for a ticket (e.g., to a "scalper"), none of the excess over face value is deductible.

    b. A special rule for skyboxes provides that expenditures for the rental or use of a luxury skybox at a sports arena are deductible only to the extent of the face value of the regular tickets.

4. Business gifts are deductible to the extent of $25 per donee per year. Records must be maintained to substantiate business gifts.

VIII.   Other Employee Expenses
    A.   Office in the Home
        1.   No deduction is allowed unless a portion of the residence is used *exclusively* and on a *regular basis* in either of the following two ways.
            a.   As the principal place of business for any trade or business of the taxpayer.
            b.   As a place of business that is used by patients, clients, or customers.
        2.   Employees must meet an additional test: the use must be for the *convenience of the employer* as opposed to being merely *appropriate and helpful.*
        3.   An office in the home qualifies as a principal place of business if:
            a.   The office is used by the taxpayer to conduct administrative or management activities of a trade or business and
            b.   There is no other fixed location of the trade or business where the taxpayer conducts these activities.
        4.   The allowable home office expense may not exceed the gross income from the business reduced by all other business expenses attributable to the activity.
    B.   Miscellaneous Employee Expenses
        1.   Other employee expenses, which are generally deductible *from* AGI and subject to the two percent-of-AGI limitation, include the following. These expenses are deductible *for* AGI only if they are reimbursed.
            a.   Union dues.
            b.   Professional expenses (e.g., membership dues).
            c.   Special clothing.
            d.   Job hunting expenses.
        2.   Up to $250 of qualifying unreimbursed expenses incurred by elementary and secondary school teachers may be deducted *for* AGI.

IX.   Contributions to Retirement Accounts
    A.   Congress encourages planning for retirement security by providing significant tax advantages to both employees and self-employed persons.
    B.   Employee IRAs
        1.   Under one approach, contributions made to a retirement plan by an employee are excluded from current taxation. An employee's participation in a Sec. 401(k) plan is an example of where this approach is used. The contribution may be funded entirely or partially by means of a salary reduction.
        2.   The other approach to retirement planning for employees is followed by the traditional IRA. The amount contributed, limited to $4,000 for 2006, is deducted *for* AGI. Income taxation is deferred until distributions are made to the employee-participant.
        3.   With a Roth IRA, no tax benefit results from the initial contribution. Instead, later distributions are recovered tax-free.
    C.   Self-Employed Keogh (H.R. 10) Plans -- The plans for self-employed taxpayers follow the deduction approach of traditional IRAs (i.e., contributions under the plan are deducted *for* AGI and grow on a tax-deferred basis).

Congress has created numerous tax-advantaged ways for individuals to plan for their financial security during retirement. But what is the effect on the U.S. Treasury? With a traditional IRA, for example, (a) the immediate deduction moves the income tax system toward a consumption tax model, (b) encourages citizens to save for the future, and (c) creates sizable liabilities in the future, when the funds and the related investment income are withdrawn from the account.

IX.   Classification of Employee Expenses
    A.   If employee expenses are reimbursed by an employer under an accountable plan, they are not reported by the employee.
    B.   If the expenses are reimbursed under a nonaccountable plan or are not reimbursed at all, then they are classified as deductions *from* AGI and can only be claimed if the employee-taxpayer itemizes.
    C.   Moving expenses and the employment-related expenses of a qualified performing artist are deductible *for* AGI.
    D.   Accountable Plans
        1.   An *accountable plan* requires the employee to satisfy the following requirements.
            a.   The employee must adequately account for, or substantiate, the expenses incurred.
            b.   The employee must return any excess reimbursement or allowance to the employer.
        2.   Proper *substantiation* of expenses involves maintaining adequate records that contain the following information.
            a.   The amount of the expense.
            b.   The time and place of travel or entertainment, or date of gift.
            c.   The business purpose of such expense.
            d.   The business relationship of the taxpayer to the person entertained or receiving the gift.

The IRS announced that receipts are not required for business expenses under $75. Until this announcement, documentation was required to support any expenditure of $25 or more. This is the first time that the threshold for receipts has been increased since it was introduced in 1962. The current threshold will likely reduce the amount of documentation businesses and individuals will be required to accumulate in support of deductions on their returns. Not retaining receipts, however, is not the same as not having to keep records. Adequate records are still required to support all deductions.

        3.   To reduce paperwork, some employers reimburse employees for travel

away from home based on a flat dollar amount per day of business travel (a *per diem*). The amount *deemed substantiated* is equal to the *lesser* of the per diem allowance or the amount of the federal per diem rate.

a.   Use of the standard federal per diem for meals constitutes an adequate accounting. Further, an employee who receives a reimbursement of not more than the standard mileage rate allowed for tax purposes for the use of an automobile will be treated as rendering an adequate accounting.

b.   Only the *amount* of the expense is considered substantiated under the deemed substantiated method. The other substantiation requirements mentioned above must also be met.

c.   Limitations apply that prohibit the use of the per diem method as an adequate accounting for certain parties related to the employer.

The value of a deduction depends on the tax bracket of the taxpayer incurring an expense. For example, if a taxpayer who incurs an employee business expense of $100 is in the 15 percent tax bracket, the net after-tax cost of a deductible expenditure to the employee is $85. That is, the taxpayer is out-of-pocket by $85. This treatment, however, may be dependent on whether the deduction is subject to further limitations (e.g., the two percent-of-AGI limitation).

E.   Nonaccountable Plans -- A *nonaccountable plan* is one in which an adequate accounting or return of excess amounts is not required, or both. All reimbursements are fully included as income and deductible in the same manner as unreimbursed expenses.

1.   Unreimbursed employee expenses -- Meal and entertainment expenses are subject to the 50 percent limit. Total unreimbursed employee business expenses are reported as miscellaneous itemized deductions subject to the two percent-of-AGI floor.

2.   Failure of an employee to follow the rules of an accountable plan causes nonaccountable plan treatment.

F.   Reporting Procedures -- Requirements range from no reporting at all (accountable plans when all requirements are met) to the use of some or all of several forms (i.e., Form W-2, Form 2106, Form 2106-EZ, and Schedule A) for nonaccountable plans and unreimbursed expenses.

XI.   Limitations on Itemized Deductions

A.   *Miscellaneous itemized deductions* are classified as components of either one of two groups. Certain of these miscellaneous itemized deductions are aggregated and reduced by two percent-of-AGI, while certain other itemized deductions are not subject to this limitation.

B.   Other itemized deductions that are not miscellaneous itemized deductions *may* be subject to their own limitations. Such deductions include charitable contributions, interest expenses, taxes, medical expenses, and certain casualty losses (see Chapters 6 and 10).

C.   Miscellaneous itemized deductions that must be aggregated and then reduced by two percent-of-AGI include the following.

1. All § 212 expenses, except expenses of producing rent and royalty income. (Rent and royalty expenses are deductible *for* AGI.)
2. All unreimbursed employee expenses (after the 50 percent reduction for meal and entertainment expenditures, if applicable) except moving expenses.
3. Professional dues and subscriptions.
4. Union dues and work uniforms.
5. Employment-related educational expenses (except for § 222 qualified tuition and related expenses).
6. Malpractice insurance premiums.
7. Expenses of job hunting.
8. Home office expenses.
9. Legal, accounting, and tax return preparation fees.
10. Hobby expenses (up to hobby income).
11. Investment expenses.
12. Custodial fees relating to income-producing property.
13. Any fees paid to collect interest or dividends.
14. Appraisal fees incurred to establish a casualty loss or charitable contribution.

D. Other miscellaneous itemized deductions are not subject to the two percent-of-AGI floor. Included in this group are the following.
1. Impairment-related work expenses of handicapped individuals.
2. Gambling losses to the extent of gambling winnings.

Many professionals who incur business-related expenses, such as professional dues and subscriptions, cellular phones, and the business use of a personal car, can deduct these expenses on their federal income tax return as itemized deductions, but only to the extend they exceed two percent-of-AGI. For many professionals, this restriction essentially eliminates any hope of gaining a tax deduction. A preferred approach may be for the taxpayer to negotiate with his or her employer to provide reimbursement for these working condition fringe benefits. Assuming appropriate substantiation to the employer and the return of any unspent advances, the amounts would be excluded from the taxpayer's income and at the same time, the employer would be able to claim a deduction.

TEST FOR SELF-EVALUATION -- CHAPTER 9

True or False

Indicate which of the following statements are true or false by circling the correct answer.

T   F   1.   Expenses of self-employed individuals incurred in a trade or business are always deductible *for* AGI.

T   F   2.   An employee may never deduct employee related expenses *for* AGI.

T   F   3.   For tax purposes, transportation expenses and travel expenses incurred by an employee are always deductible *for* AGI.

T   F   4.   For persons who qualify, payments to traditional Individual Retirement Accounts are deductible *for* AGI.

T   F   5.   Transportation expenses and travel expenses are synonymous terms.

T   F   6.   Moving expenses are deductible without limit if they are related to an employee's trade or business.

T   F   7.   A taxpayer's daily costs of traveling from his home in Richmond, VA to his job in Washington, D.C. are deductible because he is traveling out of town.

T   F   8.   Special clothing, such as that worn by a police officer, may be deductible as a miscellaneous employee expense.

T   F   9.   All employee expenses reimbursed under a nonaccountable plan by an employer are deductible *for* AGI.

T   F   10.   A taxpayer may compute the deduction for automobile expenses in either one of two ways: the taxpayer may deduct the actual operating expenses incurred in the pursuit of business, or the taxpayer may deduct a standard allowance for every business mile driven.

T   F   11.   Like other employee expenses deductible *from* AGI as miscellaneous itemized deductions, moving expenses are subject to the two percent-of-AGI limitation.

T   F   12.   The deduction for meals and entertainment is always limited to 50 percent of the cost incurred.

T   F   13.   The tax treatment of business expenses applicable to employees and independent contractors is essentially the same.

T   F   14.   Statutory employees are allowed to deduct related expenses *for* AGI.

T   F   15.   Unreimbursed employee expenses, such as for travel, are miscellaneous itemized deductions subject to the two percent-of-AGI floor.

T   F   16.   Lavish or extravagant meal and entertainment expenses are excluded after application of the 50 percent rule.

T   F   17.   For a plan to be an accountable plan, participating employees only must render an adequate accounting of expenses.

T   F   18.   Commuting expenses are never deductible.

T   F   19.   The law does not allow a deduction for travel expenses related to attending a convention, seminar, or similar meeting unless the expenses are related to a trade or business of the taxpayer.

T   F   20.   An example of a qualifying educational expense is one that enables an employee to meet the minimum educational standards for qualification in the taxpayer's existing job.

Fill-in-the-Blanks

Complete the following statements with the appropriate word(s) or amount(s).

1.   If a taxpayer utilizes the automatic method in 2006 for computing the allowable automobile expense deduction, the deduction is based on _____ cents per mile.

2.   Unreimbursed moving expenses are deductible _____ AGI.

3.   To be eligible for the moving expense deduction, a taxpayer must meet two basic tests: _____ and _____.

4.   Moving expenses incurred by a self-employed taxpayer are deductible _____ AGI.

5.   In order to be deductible, entertainment expenses must be categorized as either _____ or _____.

6.   Business gifts generally are deductible to the extent of _____ per donee per year.

7.   In order for _____ expenses to be deductible, a taxpayer must meet the "away from home" requirement.

8.   An absence by a taxpayer of more than _____ from his or her tax home automatically causes a change in the tax home.

9.   In 2006, a single individual may contribute up to _____ per year to a traditional IRA.

10.   Certain miscellaneous itemized deductions are deductible *from* AGI to the extent that they exceed _____ percent of the taxpayer's AGI.

11.   No deduction is allowed for a home office unless the office space is used _____

and _____ for trade or business activity.

12.   The tax treatment of employee business expenses depends on whether the expenses
       are _____ or _____ and, if reimbursed, whether the expenses are reimbursed
       under an _____ plan or a _____ plan.

13.   In most situations, _____ and _____ expenses are reduced by 50 percent of
       the amount incurred.

Multiple Choice

Choose the best answer for each of the following questions.

_____ 1.   Kathleen incurred the following expenses when her employer transferred her from
            Chicago to New York City.

Continental Movers	$1,900
House-hunting trip to New York City	1,400
Loss on sale of old residence	5,000
Installation of carpeting in new home	800
Real estate commissions on residences	1,000
Lodging costs en route to new residence	400

            Assuming Kathleen is not reimbursed by her employer, she may deduct what
            amount as her moving expenses?
            a. $9,700.
            b. $8,900.
            c. $6,100.
            d. $5,700.
            e.   None of these choices.

_____ 2.   David, an employee of Able Accountants, Inc., incurs a total of $4,500 in business
            expenses, consisting of the following.

Transportation (other than commuting)	$1,200
Lodging while away from home	1,800
Professional dues	750
Dues and subscriptions	750
Total	$4,500

            David received a reimbursement of $3,000 from his employer under an
            accountable plan. His itemized deductions, based on the above and before any
            limitations, would be what amount?
            a. $1,500.
            b. $1,000.
            c. $500.
            d. $250.
            e.   None of these choices.

_____ 3.   Matt had incurred the following expenses at the Downtown Society Social Club.

Matt was not reimbursed by his employer for any of these expenses.

Annual dues	$5,500
Business meals "directly related to"	1,700
Business meals "associated with"	300
Personal meals and charges	2,000
Days directly related to business	120
Days associated with business	30
Days of personal use	70

The deduction attributable to the above before the two percent-of-AGI limitation and the 50 percent limitation is what amount?

a. $2,000.
b. $5,000.
c. $5,750.
d. $7,500.
e.   None of these choices.

_____ 4.   James, a traveling sales representative (i.e., a statutory employee), incurred the following job related expenses as an employee of Jones, Inc.

Transportation	$3,000
Travel	1,000
Entertainment and dues	2,000

His employer reimbursed him to the extent of $4,000, which was intended to cover all of James's expenses. Before the 50 percent limitation, what amount may James deduct as a deduction *for* AGI?

a. $4,000.
b. $4,667.
c. $5,333.
d. $6,000.
e.   None of these choices.

_____ 5.   Steve moved from Wyoming to Dallas after earning a Masters in Tax degree and accepting a job at a public accounting firm. During the move from Wyoming, Steve incurred the following expenses.

Truck rental	$ 250
New grips on golf clubs	50
Cost of shipping pet Bengal tiger	1,000
Lodging during trip	500
House-hunting costs after securing new job	1,000
Hotel, first 60 days in Dallas	1,100
Miles traveled in car	556

Assuming Steve's AGI is $40,000, what is the deduction *for* AGI for moving expenses?

a. $850.
b. $900.

c. $1,850.
d. $3,950.
e.   None of these choices.

6.   Nancy teaches French at Central High School. The local school board requires that she take professional development courses to maintain her professional status--and to retain her position on the faculty. The expenses incurred in meeting this requirement during the year at a college in another city are as follows.

Transportation	$ 600
Meals (while out of town)	200
Lodging	300
Trip to France to maintain general familiarity with the culture	1,500
Tuition and books	700
Total	$3,300

Unfortunately, the school board does not reimburse its employees for such expenditures. Nancy's AGI is $40,000. What is her deduction *from* AGI?
a. $900.
b. $1,000.
c. $1,700.
d. $1,800.
e. $2,500.
f.   None of these choices.

7.   In celebration of the oldest locally-owned hardware store's 100th anniversary, the owners decide to make some business gifts to its valued employees. Because the 10 employees had served for varying lengths of time, gifts of different values were presented to the employees. These gifts, which were not considered to be compensation, had the following fair market values: two at $20 each, three at $25 each, three at $50 each, and two at $500 each. What amount pertaining to these gifts is deductible as a business expense?
a. $1,265.
b. $250.
c. $240.
d. $115.
e. $0.

8.   Tami works as an employee for Lincolnshire and Company, CPAs. During the current year she incurred and paid the following expenses. Her employer's reimbursement procedure is pursuant to the terms of an accountable plan.

Airfare for business trips (reimbursed in full by employer)	$800
Use of personal auto for company business (reimbursed by employer for $400)	500
Professional dues	300
Safety deposit box rental where she keeps US Savings Bonds	50
Cost of preparing her will	100

If Tami were to itemize her personal deductions, what amount should she claim as miscellaneous deductible expenses, before considering any limitations?
a. $450.
b. $850.
c. $950.
d. $1,750.
e.   None of these choices.

_____   9.   Mary and Joseph decided that it was time to take a second honeymoon to Niagara Falls. However, Joseph decided to incorporate some business into the trip in order to be able to deduct a portion of the costs. Luckily, the headquarters office of one of his business clients is located in Niagara Falls. Round-trip airfare from their home to Niagara Falls was $260 per passenger. Of the ten days out of town, Joseph consulted with his client for two days. How much of the airfare may Mary and Joseph deduct?
a. $520.
b. $260.
c. $104.
d. $52.
e.   None of these choices.

_____   10.   Which of the following expenses is *not* classified as a miscellaneous itemized deduction subject to the two percent-of-AGI floor?
a.   Moving expense.
b.   Home office expense.
c.   Investment expense.
d.   Unreimbursed employee expense.
e.   All of these choices are miscellaneous itemized deductions subject to the two percent-of-AGI floor.

_____   11.   Select the *correct* statement.
a.   Meal and entertainment deductions are always subject to the 50 percent limitation.
b.   Unreimbursed employee expenses are deductible *from* AGI.
c.   Commuting expenses may be deducted by an employee if the distance between the taxpayer's home and employment exceeds 50 miles.
d.   The terms transportation expense and travel expense are synonymous.
e.   None of these choices is correct.

_____   12.   Sam and Susan are both employed and earn $25,000 and $25,000, respectively. They file a joint federal income tax return. What is the maximum amount that may be contributed to a traditional IRA and deducted by Sam and Susan?
a. $0 by Sam and $0 by Susan.
b. $4,000 by Sam and $4,000 by Susan.
c. $2,000 by Sam and $2,000 by Susan.
d. $4,000 allocated between Sam and Susan as they agree.
e.   None of these choices.

_____   13.   Ramon and Alicia are both employed and earn $25,000 and $25,000, respectively. They file a joint federal income tax return. What is the maximum amount that may be contributed to a Roth IRA and then deducted by Ramon and

Alicia?
- a. $0 by Ramon and $0 by Alicia.
- b. $4,000 by Ramon and $4,000 by Alicia.
- c. $2,000 by Ramon and $2,000 by Alicia.
- d. $4,000 allocated between Ramon and Alicia as they agree.
- e.   None of these choices.

____ 14.   Select the *correct* statement below.
- a.   The tax treatment of employee business expenses generally depends on whether the expenses are reimbursed or unreimbursed.
- b.   The tax treatment of reimbursed employee business expenses depends on whether the expenses were reimbursed under an accountable plan or a nonaccountable plan.
- c.   A reimbursement plan is considered an accountable plan if the employee renders an adequate accounting of the expenses and returns any excess reimbursement or allowance.
- d.   Only the *amount* of an employee business expense is considered substantiated under the deemed substantiated method.
- e.   All of these choices are correct.

____ 15.   The following does *not* qualify as a deductible employee education expense.
- a.   Expenses incurred to maintain or improve existing skills required in the present job.
- b.   Fees incurred for professional qualification exams.
- c.   Amounts incurred to meet the express requirements of the employer to retain employment status.
- d.   Amounts incurred to meet the express requirements imposed by law to retain employment status.
- e.   All of these choices qualify as deductible education expenses.

____ 16.   Which of the following is *not* a miscellaneous itemized deduction subject to the two percent-of-AGI floor?
- a.   Unreimbursed employee expenses.
- b.   Union and professional dues.
- c.   Employment-related educational expenses.
- d.   Moving expenses.
- e.   All of these choices are miscellaneous itemized deductions subject to the two percent-of-AGI floor.

____ 17.   The following is *not* an exception to the 50 percent rule for meals and entertainment.
- a.   Where the full value of meals or entertainment is included in the compensation of an employee.
- b.   Where the full value of meals or entertainment is included in the compensation of an independent contractor.
- c.   Where the expense relates to traditional employer-paid recreation expenses for employees.
- d.   Where the taxpayer can prove the validity of the expense in the conduct of the business.
- e.   All of these choices are exceptions.

____ 18. Dena incurs unreimbursed employee meal and entertainment expenses of $2,400 in her job as an accountant. If her AGI is $45,000 and she has no other miscellaneous itemized deductions, what is the amount of her deduction?
a. $300.
b. $600.
c. $900.
d. $1,200.
e. None of these choices.

____ 19. Harry, whose AGI is $90,000 this year (without considering the expenditures below), incurs the following expenses.

Unreimbursed moving expenses	$3,000
Tax return preparation fee	500
Unreimbursed employee expenses	1,000
Safe deposit box rental	100
Total	$4,600

Assuming Harry itemizes his deductions, what is the total deductible amount resulting from the above expenditures?
a. $1,600.
b. $2,800.
c. $3,000.
d. $4,600.
e. None of these choices.

____ 20. Harry, whose AGI is $90,000 this year (without considering the expenditures below), incurs the following expenses.

Deductible moving expenses	$3,000
Tax return preparation fee	500
Unreimbursed employee expenses	1,000
Safe deposit box rental	100
Total	$4,600

Assuming Harry itemizes his deductions, what is the total itemized deductions resulting from the above expenditures?
a. $0.
b. $2,800.
c. $3,000.
d. $4,600.
e. None of these choices.

____ 21. Records that are to substantiate expenses incurred need not include which of the following items?
a. The amount of the expense.
b. The time and place at which the expense was incurred.
c. The business purpose of the expense.
d. The business relationship of the taxpayer to the person for whom the expense was incurred.
e. All of these choices are necessary.

22. Which of the following is *not* a deductible employee expense?
    a. Expense incurred for daily travel from home in Baltimore, MD to office in Washington, D.C.
    b. Expense of traveling from taxpayer's office to client's office.
    c. Expense of traveling from one job (day-time job) to another job (evening job).
    d. All of these choices are deductible.
    e. None of these choices is deductible.

23. Which of the following is *not* true?
    a. Travel expenses are allowed if the taxpayer clearly demonstrates a realistic expectation as to the temporary nature of the job.
    b. If an assignment is indefinite in length rather than temporary, no deduction will be allowed for the travel expenses.
    c. For travel expenses to be deductible, the taxpayer must be away from home overnight.
    d. If a trip is primarily for pleasure, the amount of deductible transportation expense is determined based on the relative time spent on personal and business matters.
    e. All of these choices are true.

24. A self-employed accountant attends a tax seminar and incurs the following expenses.

Air transportation	$ 500
Local transportation	50
Airport parking	50
Meals	320
Lodging	275
Tips to hotel maid and bellhops	25
Total	$1,220

    The taxpayer may claim a deduction *for* AGI for the following amount.
    a. $1,035.
    b. $1,060.
    c. $1,075.
    d. $1,220.
    e. None of these choices.

25. A self-employed physician attends a tax seminar and incurs the following expenses.

Air transportation	$ 500
Local transportation	50
Airport parking	50
Meals	320
Lodging	275
Tips to hotel maid and bellhops	25
Total	$1,220

The taxpayer may claim a deduction *for* AGI for the following amount.
a. $1,035.
b. $1,060.
c. $1,075.
d. $1,220.
e.   None of these choices.

Code Section Recognition

Several important sections of the Internal Revenue Code are described below. Indicate, by number, the appropriate Code section.

1.   _____   The location of employee related expenses on the tax return and the definition of AGI are discussed here.

2.   _____   Restrictions on the deductibility of entertainment expenses.

3.   _____   Provides the rules which govern the deductibility of moving expenses.

Short Answer

1.   James, an employee of Wren Corporation, accepts a promotion that requires a move to another city. In the move, the following expenses are incurred.

Transportation costs during the move	$ 500
Cost of meals enroute to new location	200
Charge for professional movers	3,000
House-hunting expenses	1,200
Temporary housing expenses at new location (four nights)	400
Real estate commission on sale of old home	1,600

Compute the amount of the moving expense deduction James may claim on his income tax return, assuming the expenses are not reimbursed by his employer.

2.   Jane, is an employee of an accounting firm in Gainesville, Florida and is in need of CPE credit to maintain her certification to practice in Florida. Therefore, she attends the AICPA National Tax Education Program and incurs the following expenses, none of which are reimbursed by her employer.

Transportation	$ 600
Tuition and materials	1,200
Meals	300
Lodging	500

Compute the amount Jane may treat as an itemized deduction and describe how the deduction is treated (i.e., is it subject to any limitations?).

SOLUTIONS TO CHAPTER 9 QUESTIONS

True or False

1. T   Trade or business expenses incurred by a self-employed individual are deductible *for* AGI while similar expenses incurred by an employee generally are deductible *from* AGI. [Employee versus Self-Employed p. 9-2]

2. F   Unreimbursed employee expenses *generally* are deducted *from* AGI, but such expenses which are reimbursed by the employer are given treatment which is equivalent to a deduction *for* AGI, assuming the reimbursement is under an accountable plan (i.e., neither the reimbursements nor the expenses are reported). In addition, unreimbursed moving expenses are deducted *for* AGI. [Employee versus Self-Employed p. 9-2; How Treated p. 9-12]

3. F   If these expenses have not been reimbursed by the employer, they are deductible *from* AGI. [Qualified Expenditures p. 9-4; Definition of Travel Expenses p. 9-7]

4. T   To the extent a deduction is available for a contribution to a traditional IRA, it is taken *for* AGI (i.e., in the computation of AGI). [Contributions to Retirement Accounts p. 9-23]

5. F   Travel expenses are incurred when the taxpayer is away from home, whereas the away from home status is not required for transportation expenses. Further, the term travel expenses has a broader meaning than does the term transportation expenses. [Definition of Travel Expenses p. 9-7]

6. F   Only qualifying unreimbursed moving expenses of a reasonable amount are deductible. Indirect moving expenses (e.g., commissions on the sale of an old residence) and the cost of meals are not deductible. [How Treated p. 9-12]

7. F   Commuting expenses are not deductible. [Commuting Expenses p. 9-4]

8. T   To be deductible, special clothing must be both specifically required as a condition of employment and not adaptable for regular wear. [Miscellaneous Employee Expenses p. 9-22]

9. F   The expenses are classified as deductions *from* AGI and can only be claimed if the employee-taxpayer itemizes. [Nonaccountable Plans p. 9-26]

10. T   Generally, a taxpayer may elect either method for any particular year. [Computation of Automobile Expenses p. 9-5]

11. F   Unreimbursed moving expenses are deductible *for* AGI. [How Treated p. 9-12]

12. F   Several exceptions to the 50 percent rule exist. [What Is Not Covered p. 9-18]

13. F   Expenses incurred by self-employed taxpayers are deductible *for* AGI while similar expenses incurred by employees are deductible either *for* or *from* AGI, depending on the circumstances. [Employee versus Self-Employed p. 9-2]

14. T   Statutory employees, who are not common law employees, are allowed to file Schedule C to report income and deduct expenses *for* AGI. [Employee versus Self-Employed p. 9-2]

15. T   Certain miscellaneous itemized deductions, including most unreimbursed employee business expenses, are aggregated and then reduced by two percent of AGI. [Miscellaneous Itemized Deductions Subject to the 2 Percent Floor p. 9-27]

16. F   Such expenses are excluded *before* application of the 50 percent rule. [Business Meals p. 9-19]

17. F   In addition, the employee must return any excess reimbursement or allowance. [In General p. 9-24]

18. F   While commuting expenses generally are not deductible, several exceptions exist

(e.g., to transport heavy tools, to travel to a second job).   [Commuting Expenses p. 9-4]

19.   T   For travel expenses to be deductible, a convention or meeting must be directly related to the taxpayer's trade or business. [Conventions p. 9-8]

20.   F   Educational expenses incurred that enable an employee to meet minimum educational standards generally are not deductible. However, a limited exception allows a deduction for certain qualifying higher education expenses. [General Requirements p. 9-13]

Fill-in-the-Blanks

1.   44.5 [Computation of Automobile Expenses p. 9-5]
2.   *for* [How Treated p. 9-12]
3.   distance, time [Moving Expenses p. 9-11]
4.   *for* [How Treated p. 9-12]
5.   directly related to business, associated with business [Classification of Expenses p. 9-18]
6. $25 [Business Gifts p. 9-20]
7.   travel [Away-From-Home Requirement p. 9-7]
8.   one year [Temporary Assignments p. 9-7]
9. $4,000 [Contributions to Retirement Accounts p. 9-23]
10.   two [Miscellaneous Itemized Deductions Subject to the 2 Percent Floor p. 9-27]
11.   exclusively, on a regular basis [Office in the Home p. 9-20]
12.   reimbursed, unreimbursed, accountable, nonaccountable [Classification of Employee Expenses p. 9-24]
13.   meal, entertainment [What is Covered p. 9-18]

Multiple Choice

1.   e | Continental Movers | $1,900 |
           | Lodging costs en route to new residence | 400 |
           | Total deductible moving expenses | $2,300 |
           [Treatment of Moving Expenses p. 9-12]

2.   a   The unreimbursed expenses of $1,500 ($4,500 - $3,000), subject to limitation, are deductible *from* AGI as itemized deductions. [Classification of Employee Expenses p. 9-24]

3.   a $2,000 = $1,700 + $300 [Club Dues p. 9-19]

4.   d   Statutory employee expenses are deductible *for* AGI. [Employee versus Self-Employed p. 9-2]

5.   c | Truck rental | $ 250 |
           | Cost of shipping pet | 1,000 |
           | Lodging during trip | 500 |
           | Mileage (556 miles X $.18) | 100 |
           | Total moving expense deduction | $1,850 |
           [Treatment of Moving Expenses p. 9-12]

6.   a | Transportation | $ 600 |
           | Meals (50% X $200) | 100 |
           | Lodging | 300 |
           | Tuition and books | 700 |

Subtotal	$1,700
Less: $40,000 X .02	(800)
Total education expense deduction	$ 900

[Classification of Specific Items p. 9-14]

7.   c $240 = (2 X $20) + (8 X $25) [Business Gifts p. 9-20]

8.   a $450 = $100 (unreimbursed auto expense) + $300 (professional dues) + $50 (safety deposit box rental) [Reporting Procedures p. 9-26]

9.   e   Nothing may be deducted because the trip was not *primarily* for business. Of the ten days out of town, only two were devoted to business. [Domestic Travel p. 9-9]

10.   a   Moving expenses are deductible *for* AGI. [How Treated p. 9-12]

11.   b   In certain cases the 50 percent limitation does not apply. Commuting expenses generally are not deductible. Travel expenses are more broadly defined than transportation expenses. [Classification of Employee Expenses p. 9-24]

12.   b   Each may make a deductible contribution to a traditional IRA for up to $4,000. [Contributions to Retirement Accounts p. 9-23]

13.   a   Up to $4,000 each may be *contributed* by Ramon and Alicia to their Roth IRAs, but the contributions are *not deductible*. [Contributions to Retirement Accounts p. 9-23]

14.   e   Each of these statements is true. [Classification of Employee Expenses p. 9-24]

15.   b   Fees incurred for professional qualification exams (e.g., CPA exam) are not deductible because they lead to a taxpayer qualifying for a new trade or business. [General Requirements p. 9-13]

16.   d   Moving expenses are deductible *for* AGI, not *from* AGI. [Miscellaneous Itemized Deductions Subject to the 2 Percent Floor p. 9-27]

17.   d   This is not a condition under which a taxpayer may be excused from the 50 percent rule for meals and entertainment expenses. [What is Not Covered p. 9-18]

18.   a

Expenses incurred	$2,400
Less: 50%	(1,200)
Subtotal	$1,200
Less: 2%-of-AGI	(900)
Deduction	$ 300

[Reporting Procedures p. 9-26]

19.   c

Deduction *for* AGI		
Moving expense		$3,000
Deduction subject to the 2%-of-AGI floor		
($500 + $1,000 + $100)	$1,600	
Less: 2%-of-AGI [($90,000 - $3,000 moving		
expense deducted *for* AGI) X 2%]	(1,740)	(0)
Total deduction		$3,000

[Reporting Procedures p. 9-26]

20.   a   Moving expenses are deductible *for* AGI. The other expenditures ($1,600) are not deductible because they are offset by the 2 percent-of-AGI floor [($90,000 - $3,000 moving expense deducted *for* AGI) X 2% = $1,740]. [How Treated p. 9-12; Reporting Procedures p. 9-26]

21.   e   All of the information must be specified in the taxpayers records. [Substantiation p. 9-24]

22.   a   Commuting expenses generally are not deductible. [Commuting Expenses p. 9-4]

23.   d   For any of the transportation expenses to be deductible, the trip must be primarily for business. [Domestic Travel p. 9-9]

24.   b $1,060 = $500 + $50 + $50 + ($320 X .50) + $275 + $25 [Conventions p. 9-8]
25.   e   None of the travel expense incurred is deductible. The law does not allow a
               deduction for travel expenses related to attending a seminar unless the expenses
               are related to the taxpayer's trade or business. A tax seminar is not related to a
               physician's trade or business. [Conventions p. 9-8]

Code Section Recognition

1.   62 [Employee versus Self-Employed p. 9-2]
2.   274 [Restrictions upon Deductibility p. 9-19]
3.   217 [Moving Expenses p. 9-11]

Short Answer

1.   Only certain moving expenses are deductible *for* AGI.

Transportation costs during the move	$ 500
Charge for professional movers	3,000
Total deductible moving expenses	$3,500

[How Treated p. 9-12]

2.
Transportation	$ 600
Tuition and materials	1,200
Meals ($300 X 50%)	150
Lodging	500
Total	$2,450

The deduction of $2,450 is subject to the two percent-of-AGI floor limitation. Therefore, the amount actually deducted by Jane must be reduced by two percent of her AGI. [Reporting Procedures p. 9-26]

Chapter 10
Deductions and Losses: Certain Itemized Deductions

CHAPTER HIGHLIGHTS

S ection 262 of the Code specifically provides that personal expenditures are not allowed as deductions in computing taxable income. However, certain expenses that are essentially personal in nature become deductible in the tax computation because of *legislative grace*. These personal expenses, which are deductible *from* adjusted gross income as itemized deductions, include medical expenses, certain taxes, interest expenses on a home mortgage, charitable contributions, personal casualty and theft losses, and certain miscellaneous expenditures. The details relating to these deductible items and the required computational procedures and limitations are discussed in this chapter.

I.   General Classification of Expenses
    A.   As a general rule, personal expenditures are disallowed by statute as deductions in arriving at taxable income. If the Code does not specifically provide for a deduction of a personal expenditure, then it is *not* deductible.
    B.   There are some personal expenses that, because of *legislative grace*, are deductible. In general, these amounts are deductible *from* adjusted gross income (in lieu of claiming the standard deduction) and are referred to as *itemized deductions*.

II.   Medical Expenses
    A.   General Requirements -- Within limitations (to the extent eligible expenses *exceed* 7.5 percent of adjusted gross income) and to the extent not reimbursed by insurance or otherwise, medical expenses paid for the care of the taxpayer, spouse, and dependents are allowed as an itemized deduction.
    B.   Medical Expenses Defined
        1.   The term *medical care* includes expenditures incurred for the "diagnosis, cure, mitigation, treatment, or prevention of disease, or for the purpose of affecting any structure or function of the body."
        2.   Deductible expenses include those that are incurred to cure any specific ailment or disease and do not include those expenses incurred for enhancing the general health of the taxpayer. However, costs incurred as

preventive measures (e.g., annual physical exam) are deductible. The costs of prescription drugs and insulin are included as medical expenses.

3.   Amounts paid for discretionary *cosmetic surgery* are not deductible medical expenses. Such surgery would only be considered necessary when it ameliorates the following.

      a.   A deformity arising from a congenital abnormality.
      b.   A personal injury.
      c.   A disfiguring disease.

4.   The deductibility of *nursing home expenses* depends on the medical condition of the patient and the nature of the services rendered.

5.   *Tuition expense* of a dependent at a special school may be deductible as a medical expense if the individual's condition is such that the resources of the school for alleviating such infirmities are a principal reason for the individual's presence there.

C.   Capital Expenditures for Medical Purposes

1.   A capital expenditure that qualifies as a medical expense is deductible in the year incurred.

2.   A capital improvement (e.g., swimming pool, elevator) that would otherwise qualify as a medical expenditure is deductible to the extent the expenditure *exceeds* the increase in value of the related property.

3.   The full cost of certain home-related capital expenditures incurred for the benefit of a physically handicapped individual qualifies as a medical expense. Qualifying costs include the following.

      a.   Construction of entrance and exit ramps to the residence.
      b.   Widening doorways at a residence's entrances and exits.
      c.   Modifying (e.g., widening) doorways and hallways to accommodate wheelchairs.
      d.   Installation of railings, support bars, etc. in bathrooms to accommodate handicapped individuals.
      e.   Modifying kitchen cabinets and equipment to accommodate access by handicapped individuals.
      f.   Adjustment of electrical outlets and fixtures.

D.   Medical Expenses Incurred for Spouse and Dependents

1.   A taxpayer's medical expense deduction includes medical expenses paid or incurred on behalf of a spouse and dependents.

2.   In determining dependency status for medical expense purposes, neither the gross income nor the joint return tests applies (see Chapter 3).

3.   Medical expenses paid on behalf of a former spouse may be deductible as a medical expense or as alimony, depending on the circumstances.

4.   Special rules apply to a noncustodial parent in the situation of divorced persons with children.

E.   Transportation, Meal, and Lodging Expenses for Medical Treatment

1.   Expenditures incurred for *transportation* (for the patient and parent or other attendant) to and from a point of treatment are deductible. The IRS currently allows a deduction of 18 cents per mile (in 2006) instead of actual out-of-pocket expenses if an automobile is used in such transit.

2.   *Lodging* expenses of up to $50 *per* night for *each* person (i.e., for the patient, and in some situations another person) may be deducted in certain cases while receiving medical care away from home.

F.   Amounts Paid for Medical Insurance Premiums -- Medical insurance premiums paid by the taxpayer are treated like any other medical expense and are subject to the 7.5 percent-of-AGI limit. However, if a taxpayer is self-employed, insurance premiums paid for medical coverage are deductible *for* AGI as a business expense. Premiums paid on qualified long-term care insurance contracts also may be treated as a medical expense, subject to limitations.

G.   Year of Deduction
1.   Medical expenses are deductible in the year *paid*, regardless of the taxpayer's method of accounting.
2.   In most situations, lump-sum prepayments for medical services are not deductible in the year of payment if the services are to be received in future years. However, exceptions may exist if the taxpayer is under an obligation to make such prepayments.

H.   Reimbursements
1.   When an insurance reimbursement is received for medical expenses that were deducted in a previous year, the reimbursement must be included in gross income to the extent a *tax benefit* was received in the earlier year.
2.   If the taxpayer did not *itemize* deductions in the year the expenses were incurred, a subsequent reimbursement is *not* included in gross income.

KEY TERMS

- Medical Expense
- Personal Interest
- Investment Interest
- Home Mortgage Interest
- Charitable Contributions
- Miscellaneous Itemized Deductions

I.   Health Savings Accounts (HSAs)
1.   An HSA, when coupled with a high-deductible medical insurance policy, provides an opportunity for taxpayers to decrease the overall cost of medical coverage. Expenses not covered by the insurance policy can be paid with funds withdrawn from the HSA.
2.   Contributions made to an HSA by individuals are deductible *for* AGI within limits. Therefore, the taxpayer need not itemize deductions in order to take a deduction.

HSAs are designed to help qualifying individuals gain access to an alternative form of health insurance. Additionally, HSAs provide incentives for individuals to better manage their health care expenditures. HSAs are most appropriate for individuals who are in good health and who are not operating under a tight budget.

3.   The taxation of earnings on HSAs depends on the way the HSA funds are used.
a.   Distributions are excluded from gross income if they are used to pay for medical expenses not covered by the high-deductible policy.

        b.   Distributions not used to pay for medical expenses are included in gross income and also may be subject to an additional ten percent penalty.

III.   Taxes -- The deduction of certain state, local, and foreign taxes paid or accrued by a taxpayer is allowed in order to relieve the burden of multiple taxation upon the same source of revenue.

    A.   Deductibility as a Tax

        1.   A distinction is made between a *tax* and a *fee*. Certain taxes (i.e., enforced contributions) are deductible, whereas fees are not deductible *unless* they are incurred as ordinary and necessary business expenses or for the production of income.

        2.   The following taxes are listed in the Code as being deductible.

            a.   State, local, and foreign real property taxes.

            b.   State and local personal property taxes.

            c.   State, local, and foreign income taxes.

            d.   The environmental tax.

        3.   Taxes that may *not* be deducted include the following.

            a.   Federal income taxes, including any social security and railroad retirement taxes paid by the employee.

            b.   Estate, inheritance, and gift taxes.

            c.   Federal, state, and local excise taxes.

            d.   Foreign income taxes, if the foreign tax credit is claimed.

            e.   Taxes on real property to the extent that such taxes are apportioned and treated as imposed on another taxpayer.

    B.   Property Taxes

        1.   Real and personal property taxes are generally deductible by the person against whom the tax is imposed.

        2.   Personal property taxes must be *ad valorem* (i.e., assessed in relation to the value of the property) to be deductible.

        3.   As a general rule, real property taxes do not include amounts assessed for local benefits (e.g., sidewalks, curbing in front of a taxpayer's home). Such assessments are added to the adjusted basis of the taxpayer's property.

        4.   Assessments are deductible as taxes if the taxpayer can show that the amounts are incurred for the purpose of maintenance or repair, or for the purpose of meeting interest charges with respect to such benefits.

        5.   Real estate taxes for the entire year must be apportioned between a buyer and seller of real property, regardless of who actually pays the tax and without regard to a proration in the purchase agreement, based on the number of days the property was held by each party during the real property tax year.

        6.   In making such an apportionment, the real estate tax year serves as the basis for apportionment, and the assessment and lien dates are disregarded.

    C.   State and Local Income Taxes and Sales Taxes

        1.   State, local, or foreign income taxes imposed on individuals are deductible as itemized deductions, even if the taxpayer's sole source of income is from business, rents, or royalties.

        2.   The amounts are deductible in the year withheld by a taxpayer's employer or paid by an individual, even if the amounts paid relate to a prior or

subsequent year.

3.   A refund received in a later year due to excessive withholdings and/or estimated tax payments must be included in gross income to the extent that a deduction provided a *tax benefit* in the prior year.

4.   Individuals can *elect* to deduct either their state and local income taxes or their sales and use taxes beginning in 2004. The deduction is based either on actual sales and use taxes paid or an amount from an IRS table.

> A taxpayer should be careful not to include too much of a state tax refund in income. State tax refunds may not be taxable if the taxpayer did not receive a tax benefit from the previous year's deduction. For example, if a taxpayer used the standard deduction in the year the taxes were paid, the refunded amount is not included in income.

IV.   Interest

     A.   Disallowed and Allowed Items

         1.   Generally, only certain types of interest paid or accrued on indebtedness within the taxable year are deductible. However, even in situations when interest is allowable as a deduction, restrictions may be present in the law that limit the amount of its deductibility.

         2.   *Interest* has been defined as compensation for the use or forbearance of money.

         3.   The general rule is that *personal (consumer) interest* is *not* deductible. Personal interest generally is any interest other than the following.

             a.   Interest on qualified education loans.

             b.   Trade or business interest.

             c.   Investment interest.

             d.   Interest on passive activities.

             e.   Home mortgage interest to a limited extent if it is qualified residence interest.

         4.   Taxpayers who pay interest on a *qualified education loan* may deduct the interest as a deduction *for* AGI. The maximum deduction for 2006 is $2,500 and is phased out for taxpayers with modified AGI in excess of certain amounts. The deduction is not allowed for taxpayers who are claimed as dependents or for married taxpayers filing separately.

         5.   The amount of *investment interest* expense (i.e., interest incurred on funds borrowed to acquire investment assets) that may be deducted for the year is limited to net investment income.

             a.   *Net investment income* is the excess of investment income over investment expenses.

             b.   When investment expenses fall into the category of miscellaneous itemized deductions that are subject to the two percent-of-AGI floor, some may not enter into the calculation of net investment income because of the floor.

         6.   *Qualified residence interest* is interest paid or accrued on indebtedness (subject to limitations) secured by a *qualified residence* of the taxpayer. Qualified residence interest falls into two categories: interest on *acquisition indebtedness* and interest on *home equity* loans. A qualified

residence includes the *principal residence* and *one other residence* of the taxpayer or spouse.

7. In most cases, qualified interest is fully deductible; however, limitations apply.

    a. The interest deduction may be taken on indebtedness secured by a qualified residence of $1,000,000 or less ($500,000 married, filing separate returns). Acquisition indebtedness is debt incurred in acquiring, constructing, or substantially improving a qualified residence of the taxpayer. Debt in excess of these limits generates interest expense that is not deductible under these rules.

    b. In addition, interest on aggregate home equity indebtedness of up to $100,000 ($50,000 for married persons filing separate returns) is deductible. However, the deductible interest is limited to home equity loans that do not exceed the fair market value of the residence reduced by the acquisition indebtedness. The use to which the proceeds from home equity indebtedness are put is irrelevant insofar as the deductibility of the related interest expense, even if the proceeds are used for personal purposes.

8. The deductibility of interest paid on mortgages secured by a third or more residences or on indebtedness that exceeds the allowable limitations depends on the use of the proceeds. If the proceeds are used for personal purposes, the interest is nondeductible. However, if the proceeds are used for business, the interest may be fully deductible. Alternatively, if the proceeds are used for investment purposes or in passive activities, the restrictions pertaining to these types of activities apply.

9. Interest Paid for Services

    a. To qualify as deductible interest, *points* paid by a borrower (i.e., buyer) must be considered compensation to a lender solely for the use or forbearance of money as opposed to being a form of service charge or compensation for specific services. A buyer also may deduct seller-paid points in the year they are paid in certain situations.

    b. In contrast to points paid in connection with the purchase or improvement of the residence, points incurred when refinancing a residential mortgage are not deductible in a lump sum. Such expenditures should be capitalized, and then amortized and deducted over the life of the loan.

Depending on the mortgage deal the taxpayer negotiates, either the buyer or the seller may pay the points. The IRS treats these two situations slightly differently.

10. Prepayment penalties that may be incurred if loans are paid off early are considered to be interest (e.g., personal, qualified residence, investment) in the year paid.

11. If related parties are involved where the debtor is an accrual basis

taxpayer and the creditor is a cash basis taxpayer, the interest expense must be actually paid by the accrual basis taxpayer in order for a deduction to be taken.

12. An interest deduction is not allowed when the related indebtedness is incurred to *purchase or carry* tax-exempt securities.

B. Restrictions on Deductibility and Timing Considerations

1. For interest expense to be deductible, the underlying debt must be a bona fide obligation of the taxpayer. Additionally, there must be intent to repay the loan.

2. Unless the taxpayer uses the accrual method, payment must be made to secure the deduction. Under the accrual method, interest is deductible ratably over the life of the loan.

3. Prepaid interest payments must be capitalized and allocated to the subsequent periods to which the interest payments relate, even if the taxpayer otherwise uses the cash basis.

C. Classification of Interest Expense

1. If indebtedness is incurred in connection with a business or for the production of rent or royalty income, the related interest expense is deductible *for* adjusted gross income.

2. Otherwise, the related interest expense is deductible *from* adjusted gross income.

V. Charitable Contributions

A. Overview -- Charitable contributions made to qualified domestic organizations may be deducted *from* adjusted gross income. The government, by allowing this deduction, believes that it encourages charitable giving by individuals and corporations.

B. Criteria for a Gift

1. A *charitable contribution* is defined as a gift made to a qualified organization.

2. The following major elements are needed to qualify a contribution as a gift.

   a. Donative intent.
   b. Absence of consideration received by the donor.
   c. Acceptance of the contribution by the donee.

3. Generally, to the extent a tangible benefit is derived from a contribution, the value of such benefit cannot be deducted.

4. However, if a taxpayer contributes an amount and receives in return the *right* to purchase athletic tickets from a college or university, then 80 percent of the amount paid to or for the benefit of the institution qualifies as a charitable contribution deduction.

5. A deduction is not allowed for a contribution of one's services to a qualified charitable organization. However, unreimbursed expenses related to the services rendered are deductible.

6. The following do *not* qualify as charitable contributions.

   a. Country club dues, fees, and bills.
   b. Raffle, bingo, and lottery tickets.
   c. Gifts to individuals.
   d. The rental value of property used by a qualified charity.

C. Qualified Organizations

1. To qualify as a deductible charitable contribution, a payment must be

made to one of the following organizations.

    a.   A state or possession of the United States, or any subdivision thereof.

    b.   Certain organizations situated in the United States organized and operated exclusively for religious, charitable, scientific, literary or educational purposes or for the prevention of cruelty to children or animals.

    c.   A veteran's organization.

    d.   A fraternal organization operating under the lodge system.

    e.   A cemetery company.

2.   Gifts made to a donee in an individual capacity rather than as a representative of a qualifying organization are *not* deductible.

D.   Time of Deduction

1.   A charitable contribution generally is deductible, by either cash or accrual basis individual taxpayers, in the year payment is made. A contribution made by check is considered paid on the date of mailing.

2.   An *accrual basis corporate taxpayer* may claim a charitable contribution deduction in the year prior to payment if the actual payment or contribution is made within two and one-half months of the close of the taxable year *and* the board of directors has authorized such payment prior to the end of the year.

E.   Recordkeeping and Valuation Requirements

1.   No deduction is allowed for a contribution of $250 or more unless the taxpayer obtains *written substantiation* from the charitable organization.

2.   Additional information is required if the value of the donated property is over $500 but not over $5,000. If the noncash contribution exceeds $5,000 in claimed value ($10,000 in the case of nonpublicly traded stock), an appraisal of the property's fair market value must be obtained by the taxpayer.

3.   Donated property is generally valued at its *fair market value* at the time of the gift.

4.   The only guidance provided in the Code and Regulations with respect to the meaning of the term fair market value is as follows: "The fair market value is the price at which the property would change hands between a willing buyer and a willing seller, neither being under any compulsion to buy or sell and both having reasonable knowledge of relevant facts."

F.   Limitations on Charitable Deductions

1.   Individual taxpayers are subject to overall ceiling limitations on the aggregate amount that may be deducted for the tax year.

    a.   If the qualifying contributions for the year total 20 percent or less of adjusted gross income, they are fully deductible.

    b.   If the contributions are more than 20 percent of adjusted gross income, the deductible amount may be limited to either 20 percent, 30 percent, or 50 percent of adjusted gross income, depending on the type of property given and the type of organization to which the donation is made.

    c.   In any case, the maximum charitable contribution deduction may not exceed 50 percent of adjusted gross income for the tax year.

2.   Corporations also are subject to an overall limitation (see Chapter 17). Moreover, in some situations, the deduction allowed is less than the fair market value of the property contributed.

deductible only to the extent that they exceed two percent of the taxpayer's adjusted gross income.

T   F   15.   Cosmetic surgery could never qualify as a deductible medical expense.

T   F   16.   Property taxes are deducted in the year paid whether or not the taxpayer uses the cash or accrual method of accounting.

T   F   17.   All taxes must be *ad valorem* in order to be deductible.

T   F   18.   The investment interest expense deduction can never include amounts paid to enable a taxpayer to purchase a tax-exempt bond.

T   F   19.   Interest paid on a home equity line may be deducted only if the loan proceeds are used on home improvement projects.

T   F   20.   No deduction is allowed for a contribution of one's services to a qualified charitable organization.

Fill-in-the-Blanks

Complete the following statements with the appropriate word(s) or amount(s).

1.   The deduction for property donated to a charity is generally measured by its _____ at the time the gift is made.

2.   A distinction must be made between a fee and a tax because a _____ is not deductible unless it is incurred as a business expense or incurred in the production of income.

3.   When apportioning real estate taxes between a buyer and a seller of property, the _____ date and the _____ date are disregarded.

4.   Many miscellaneous itemized deductions may not be deducted unless they exceed _____ percent of adjusted gross income.

5.   All of the itemized deductions of individual taxpayers are reported on Schedule _____ of Form _____.

6.   _____ expense has been defined by the Supreme Court as compensation for the use or forbearance of money.

7.   The deductibility of investment interest expense is limited to the amount of the taxpayer's _____.

8.   The major elements needed to qualify a contribution as a gift are _____, _____, and _____.

9.   An individual may claim a charitable contribution deduction only _____, regardless of whether the cash or accrual method of accounting is used.

TEST FOR SELF-EVALUATION -- CHAPTER 10

True or False

Indicate which of the following statements are true or false by circling the correct answer.

T   F   1.   In general, personal expenditures are disallowed by the Code as deductions in arriving at taxable income.

T   F   2.   Tuition expenses of a dependent at a special school are never deductible as a medical expense.

T   F   3.   A capital improvement, such as a swimming pool at one's personal residence that would otherwise qualify as a medical expenditure, is fully deductible.

T   F   4.   The term "medicine and drugs" includes only prescribed drugs and insulin.

T   F   5.   Fees paid or incurred for automobile inspections, automobile titles and registration, and bridge and highway tolls are never deductible because they are not taxes.

T   F   6.   Both the state income tax and the federal income tax are deductible under the Code.

T   F   7.   The real estate taxes incurred in a year of sale are apportioned between the buyer and the seller of a property on the basis of the number of days the property was held by each party.

T   F   8.   State income taxes imposed on an individual are deductible only as an itemized deduction except if the taxpayer's sole source of income is from business, rents, or royalties.

T   F   9.   A service charge is not deductible as an interest expense.

T   F   10.   The amount of interest on investment indebtedness that may be deducted is unlimited.

T   F   11.   Charitable contributions made in any one year that are in excess of the appropriate limitation may be carried over for up to four years.

T   F   12.   The limitation percentage applicable to charitable contributions made to private nonoperating foundations varies depending on the type of property contributed.

T   F   13.   The unrealized appreciation related to real property contributed to a charitable organization may produce a charitable contribution deduction in certain situations.

T   F   14.   Qualifying medical expenditures incurred by an individual are normally

           3.   Tax return preparation fees.
           4.   Job-hunting expenses.
           5.   Safe deposit box rental.
           6.   Hobby losses to the extent of hobby income.
           7.   Subscription costs to professional journals.
           8.   Uniforms.
    B.   These expenses are deductible only to the extent that they exceed two percent of the taxpayer's adjusted gross income.

VII.   Other Miscellaneous Deductions -- If a taxpayer itemizes deductions and incurs the following costs, then they may be deducted without being subject to the two percent-of-AGI limitation.
    A.   Gambling losses to the extent of gambling earnings.
    B.   Impairment-related work expenses of a handicapped person.
    C.   Federal estate tax on income in respect of a decedent.
    D.   Deduction for repayment of amounts under a claim of right if more than $3,000.
    E.   Unrecovered investment in an annuity contract when the annuity ceases by reason of death.

VIII.   Overall Limitation on Certain Itemized Deductions
    A.   High-income taxpayers are subject to a limitation on itemized deductions when their AGI exceeds certain levels. The *threshold amount* (the figure where the limitation begins to take effect) for 2006 is $150,500 ($75,250 for married persons filing a separate return). For 2005, the threshold amounts were $145,950 and $72,975, respectively. In 2006 and 2007, the overall limitation is itself reduced-- the limitation is 2/3 of the otherwise applicable limitation amount.
    B.   The limitation applies to all itemized deductions *except* the following.
           1.   Medical expenses.
           2.   Investment interest.
           3.   Nonbusiness casualty and theft losses.
           4.   Gambling losses.
    C.   The limitation requires itemized deductions to be reduced by three percent of AGI to the extent of its excess over the threshold amount. However, in no case may the reduction be more than 80 percent of the covered itemized deductions.
    D.   This adjustment is applied *after* taking into account other Code provisions that reduce allowable deductions (e.g., the two percent-of-AGI limitation that applies to miscellaneous itemized deductions).

3.   If *ordinary income property* is contributed, the deduction is equal to the fair market value of the property reduced by the amount of ordinary income that would have been recognized if the property had been sold. Ordinary income property is any property that, if sold, would result in the recognition of ordinary income (e.g., inventory).

4.   As a general rule, the deduction for a contribution of *capital gain property* (i.e., property that would have produced a long-term capital gain or § 1231 gain if it had been sold) is equal to the fair market value of the property.

5.   Generally, if capital gain property is contributed to a private *nonoperating* foundation, then the contribution is reduced by the long-term capital gain that would have been recognized had the property been sold. Such reduction is generally not required for contributions of intangible or real tangible capital gain property to public charities.

6.   With respect to capital gain *tangible personalty* given to a public charity, the deduction must be reduced by the long-term capital gain element if the property is put to an *unrelated use* by the charity.

 Especially with respect to large national charities, it may be difficult for the benefactor to determine exactly what the charity plans to do with the donated property, let alone determine whether the asset is put to a related or unrelated use. Often, boards of the donee charities have specific policies about what to do with gifts of in-kind assets, such as immediate liquidation into cash, or review by an investment committee. None of these contingencies makes it easy to determine the amount of the donor's deduction by the due date of the tax return.

7.   Contributions made to public charities, all private operating foundations, or certain other private nonoperating foundations may not exceed 50 percent of an individual's adjusted gross income for the year. Excess contributions may be carried over for five years.

8.   If appreciated *capital gain property* is contributed to an organization to which the 50 percent limitation applies or if a contribution of cash or ordinary income property is made to a private nonoperating foundation, then the deduction is limited to 30 percent of the taxpayer's adjusted gross income. Any unused or excess contribution may be carried forward for up to five years.

9.   Contributions of appreciated long-term capital gain property made to private nonoperating foundations are limited to 20 percent of adjusted gross income. Any unused excess contribution may be carried forward for up to five years.

VI.   Miscellaneous Itemized Deductions
A.   A number of miscellaneous itemized deductions related to employment are reported on Schedule A. Examples of such miscellaneous deductions include the following.
1.   Unreimbursed business expenses.
2.   Professional dues.

made to one of the following organizations.

    a.   A state or possession of the United States, or any subdivision thereof.

    b.   Certain organizations situated in the United States organized and operated exclusively for religious, charitable, scientific, literary or educational purposes or for the prevention of cruelty to children or animals.

    c.   A veteran's organization.

    d.   A fraternal organization operating under the lodge system.

    e.   A cemetery company.

2.   Gifts made to a donee in an individual capacity rather than as a representative of a qualifying organization are *not* deductible.

D.   Time of Deduction

1.   A charitable contribution generally is deductible, by either cash or accrual basis individual taxpayers, in the year payment is made. A contribution made by check is considered paid on the date of mailing.

2.   An *accrual basis corporate taxpayer* may claim a charitable contribution deduction in the year prior to payment if the actual payment or contribution is made within two and one-half months of the close of the taxable year *and* the board of directors has authorized such payment prior to the end of the year.

E.   Recordkeeping and Valuation Requirements

1.   No deduction is allowed for a contribution of $250 or more unless the taxpayer obtains *written substantiation* from the charitable organization.

2.   Additional information is required if the value of the donated property is over $500 but not over $5,000. If the noncash contribution exceeds $5,000 in claimed value ($10,000 in the case of nonpublicly traded stock), an appraisal of the property's fair market value must be obtained by the taxpayer.

3.   Donated property is generally valued at its *fair market value* at the time of the gift.

4.   The only guidance provided in the Code and Regulations with respect to the meaning of the term fair market value is as follows: "The fair market value is the price at which the property would change hands between a willing buyer and a willing seller, neither being under any compulsion to buy or sell and both having reasonable knowledge of relevant facts."

F.   Limitations on Charitable Deductions

1.   Individual taxpayers are subject to overall ceiling limitations on the aggregate amount that may be deducted for the tax year.

    a.   If the qualifying contributions for the year total 20 percent or less of adjusted gross income, they are fully deductible.

    b.   If the contributions are more than 20 percent of adjusted gross income, the deductible amount may be limited to either 20 percent, 30 percent, or 50 percent of adjusted gross income, depending on the type of property given and the type of organization to which the donation is made.

    c.   In any case, the maximum charitable contribution deduction may not exceed 50 percent of adjusted gross income for the tax year.

2.   Corporations also are subject to an overall limitation (see Chapter 17). Moreover, in some situations, the deduction allowed is less than the fair market value of the property contributed.

taxpayer and the creditor is a cash basis taxpayer, the interest expense must be actually paid by the accrual basis taxpayer in order for a deduction to be taken.

12.   An interest deduction is not allowed when the related indebtedness is incurred to *purchase or carry* tax-exempt securities.

B.   Restrictions on Deductibility and Timing Considerations

    1.   For interest expense to be deductible, the underlying debt must be a bona fide obligation of the taxpayer. Additionally, there must be intent to repay the loan.

    2.   Unless the taxpayer uses the accrual method, payment must be made to secure the deduction. Under the accrual method, interest is deductible ratably over the life of the loan.

    3.   Prepaid interest payments must be capitalized and allocated to the subsequent periods to which the interest payments relate, even if the taxpayer otherwise uses the cash basis.

C.   Classification of Interest Expense

    1.   If indebtedness is incurred in connection with a business or for the production of rent or royalty income, the related interest expense is deductible *for* adjusted gross income.

    2.   Otherwise, the related interest expense is deductible *from* adjusted gross income.

V.   Charitable Contributions

A.   Overview -- Charitable contributions made to qualified domestic organizations may be deducted *from* adjusted gross income. The government, by allowing this deduction, believes that it encourages charitable giving by individuals and corporations.

B.   Criteria for a Gift

    1.   A *charitable contribution* is defined as a gift made to a qualified organization.

    2.   The following major elements are needed to qualify a contribution as a gift.

        a.   Donative intent.

        b.   Absence of consideration received by the donor.

        c.   Acceptance of the contribution by the donee.

    3.   Generally, to the extent a tangible benefit is derived from a contribution, the value of such benefit cannot be deducted.

    4.   However, if a taxpayer contributes an amount and receives in return the *right* to purchase athletic tickets from a college or university, then 80 percent of the amount paid to or for the benefit of the institution qualifies as a charitable contribution deduction.

    5.   A deduction is not allowed for a contribution of one's services to a qualified charitable organization. However, unreimbursed expenses related to the services rendered are deductible.

    6.   The following do *not* qualify as charitable contributions.

        a.   Country club dues, fees, and bills.

        b.   Raffle, bingo, and lottery tickets.

        c.   Gifts to individuals.

        d.   The rental value of property used by a qualified charity.

C.   Qualified Organizations

    1.   To qualify as a deductible charitable contribution, a payment must be

10.   For charitable contribution purposes, _____ property is any property that, if sold, will result in the recognition of ordinary income.

11.   Generally, when making a charitable contribution of property (other than publicly traded securities) that has a claimed value exceeding _____, an independent appraisal must be conducted.

12.   Interest expense on a home equity loan of up to _____ may be fully deducted regardless of the use to which the loan proceeds are put.

13.   Currently, transportation costs for medical purposes are deductible at _____ per mile while transportation costs for charitable contribution purposes are deductible at _____ per mile.

14.   The threshold amount for 2006 for the overall limitation of certain itemized deductions is _____ (_____ for married persons filing separate returns).

15.   While the overall limitation of certain itemized deductions adjustment is _____ percent of the excess of AGI over the threshold amount, in no case may the reduction be for more than _____ percent of the covered itemized deductions.

Multiple Choice

Choose the best answer for each of the following questions.

_____   1.   Which of the following taxes are not deductible?
        a.   State or local income taxes.
        b.   Personal and real property taxes.
        c.   Foreign income taxes.
        d.   Estate, inheritance, and gift taxes.
        e.   All of these choices are deductible.

_____   2.   Steve sold his home to Penny on May 1 of this year and it was agreed that Penny would pay the property taxes of $800 when due. The tax year for Albemarle County, which is where the real property is located, is January 1 to December 31. The assessment date is April 1 and the lien date is October 1. How much of the tax payment is attributed to Penny assuming that this year is not a leap year?
        a. $197.
        b. $263.
        c. $537.
        d. $603.
        e. $800.

_____   3.   Which of the items listed is not deductible as interest?
        a.   Points paid by a purchaser of a personal residence.
        b.   Mortgage interest on primary residence.
        c.   Mortgage interest on a taxpayer's second home.
        d.   Finance charges on a homeowner's utility bill.
        e.   All of these choices are deductible.

____ 4.   Which of the items listed is deductible as interest?
           a.   Mortgage prepayment penalty.
           b.   Interest on a loan used to purchase a new family automobile.
           c.   Interest expense incurred to buy or carry tax-exempt securities.
           d.   Service charges.
           e.   None of these choices is deductible.

____ 5.   During the current year, Gene contributed land to a qualifying private
           nonoperating foundation, which he had purchased as an investment four years
           ago for $1,000. The fair market value of the land on the date of contribution was
           $1,600. What is Gene's current charitable contribution deduction based on the
           above information assuming that his adjusted gross income is $7,500?
           a. $1,000.
           b. $1,240.
           c. $1,500.
           d. $1,600.
           e.   None of these choices.

____ 6.   During the current year, Gene contributed land to the University of the Southeast,
           which he had purchased as an investment four years ago for $1,000. The fair
           market value of the land on the date of contribution was $1,600. What is Gene's
           current charitable contribution deduction based on the above information
           assuming that his adjusted gross income is $7,500?
           a. $1,000.
           b. $1,240.
           c. $1,500.
           d. $1,600.
           e.   None of these choices.

____ 7.   Mary Ann paid $1,545 to various parties during the year as follows.

State cigarette tax	$ 50
State gasoline tax	90
Real estate tax on vacation home	400
State income tax	900
City personal property tax (*ad valorem*)	60
State driver's license and car license	45

           Mary Ann's federal income tax return should include a deduction for taxes paid in
           the following amount.
           a. $850.
           b. $900.
           c. $1,360.
           d. $1,450.
           e.   None of these choices.

____ 8.   Bill made the following charitable contributions during the current year.

           •   Allowed the United Way to use a building he owned, without requiring the
                 normal $3,000 rent payment

- Gift of $10,000 cash to his alma mater, Southeast University
- Gift of his services as a CPA to his church audit committee (valued at $2,000)

Assuming Bill's AGI this year is $30,000, calculate his charitable contribution deduction.
a. $10,000.
b. $12,000.
c. $13,000.
d. $15,000.
e.   None of these choices.

_____ 9.   During the year, Elizabeth and George incurred the following expenses.

Prescription drugs	$ 300
Medical insurance premiums	600
Illegal drugs	200
Hospital bills	1,000
Doctors bills	800
Foreign real property tax	1,000
Mortgage interest expense	8,200
Reimbursed employee travel expenses	500

If Elizabeth and George's AGI is $20,000 and neither is self-employed, calculate their itemized deductions for the year.
a. $0.
b. $10,400.
c. $10,700.
d. $10,900.
e. $11,200.

_____ 10.   Select the *incorrect* statement.
a.   State, local, and foreign real property taxes are deductible by an accrual basis taxpayer whether paid or accrued during the taxable year.
b.   Real estate taxes are apportioned between the buyer and seller of property on the basis of the number of days each person owned the property during the year sold.
c.   State sales tax on major purchases, such as a new car, is routinely deductible.
d.   No deduction is allowed for interest paid on debt incurred to purchase or carry tax-exempt securities.
e.   The only medicines and drugs deductible as a medical expense are prescription drugs and insulin.

_____ 11.   Jacob, whose AGI is $40,000 this year, desires to give $12,000 in value (not cash) to a charity. He is considering several alternatives and comes to you for some tax planning advice. Which of the following alternatives, from a tax planning perspective, is the optimal course of action for Jacob?
a.   Jacob can donate the use of a building to the American Red Cross, a public charity, for use in the collection of blood during the year. The building has a fair market rental of $1,000 per month.

b. Jacob can donate a painting that has a cost basis of $3,000 and a fair market value of $12,000 to Goodwill, a public charity. Goodwill plans to sell the painting at a special auction to raise funds for new collection dumpsters.

c. Jacob can donate land that he purchased as an investment for $3,000 several years ago and that has a fair market value of $12,000 to the Jones Foundation, a 20% private nonoperating charity. Jacob then expects to take his deduction over this tax year and next.

d. Jacob can donate municipal bonds purchased as an investment three years ago for $3,000 and maturing next year to St. Jude's Hospital, a 50% charity. The bonds have a fair market value of $12,000.

e. Jacob can donate stock purchased as an investment for $20,000 five years ago. The stock now has a fair market value of $12,000. The donee is a 50% charity.

12. In 2006, Maria traveled 500 miles in her personal automobile while doing volunteer work for the United Way. She contributed 10 hours of services as an accountant, valued at $600. By how much would her charitable contributions deduction be increased because of this work?

a. $0.
b. $60.
c. $70.
d. $670.
e. None of these choices.

13. Mr. and Mrs. Burke made the following payments during the year.

Interest on loan to purchase auto	$1,000
Interest on home mortgage	2,700
Prepayment penalty on home mortgage	800
Finance charges on bank credit card	1,000

What amount can the Burkes deduct as interest expense in calculating their itemized deductions?

a. $2,700.
b. $3,100.
c. $3,700.
d. $3,900.
e. $5,500.
f. None of these choices.

14. Betsy's adjusted gross income was $80,000 for the year and she made the following contributions to qualified public charitable organizations.

• $6,000 cash
• 1,500 shares of common stock of the Crenshaw Corporation with a fair market value of $14,000. The stock was purchased for $10,000 in 1973.

What is the maximum amount that Betsy can deduct for charitable contributions this year?

a. $6,000.

        b. $16,000.
        c. $20,000.
        d. $30,000.
        e.   None of these choices.

____   15.   Jim and Mary Smith are married and file a joint return. Their adjusted gross
              income for the year is $40,000, and they paid the following medical expenses.

Physician bills for themselves	$1,200
Physician bills for Mary's mother	3,420
Physician bill for their son	175

              Their son qualifies as a dependent, while Mary's mother would qualify as their
              dependent except for the fact that she earned too much gross income during the
              year. What amount can the Smiths deduct as qualifying medical expenses on
              their joint return?
        a. $1,200.
        b. $1,375.
        c. $1,795.
        d. $4,795.
        e.   Some other amount.

____   16.   James is single and made the following cash expenditures during the year.

Interest on loan to purchase taxable securities	
(net investment income = $1,500)	$300
Finance charges on bank credit card	250
Interest on home mortgage	900

              How much interest expense can James include on his schedule of itemized
              deductions?
        a. $0.
        b. $900.
        c. $1,200.
        d. $1,450.
        e.   None of these choices.

____   17.   Mimi made the following personal cash outlays during the current tax year.

State and local gasoline excise taxes paid	$400
State and local real property taxes paid	900
State income taxes paid for last year	450
Federal gift taxes paid	325

              How much can Mimi deduct as taxes on her schedule of itemized deductions for
              the year?
        a. $0.
        b. $1,350.
        c. $1,750.
        d. $2,075.
        e.   None of these choices.

_____ 18.   During 2006, Megan's records reflect the following information.

Salary	$100,000
Interest income	75,500
Qualified residence interest expense	10,000
Charitable contributions	12,000
State income taxes	13,000

Assuming Megan is single, compute the amount of itemized deductions that she may claim on her federal income tax return.
a. $32,750.
b. $34,250.
c. $34,500.
d. $35,000.
e.   None of these choices.

_____ 19.   During 2006, Hal's records reflect the following information.

Salary	$225,000
Interest income	75,500
Medical expenses (after the 7.5%-of-AGI floor)	15,000
Qualified residence interest expense	5,000
Investment interest expense	15,000

Assuming Hal is single, compute the amount of itemized deductions that he may claim on his federal income tax return.
a. $30,500.
b. $31,000.
c. $32,333.
d. $35,000.
e.   None of these choices.

_____ 20.   During the year, Warner incurred medical expenses of $6,000. But in addition, his physician recommended that he install a home dust elimination system to help mitigate his breathing problems. The cost of the new system was $3,500, but it increased the home's fair market value by $2,000. Assuming Warner's AGI is $20,000, what is the amount of his medical expense deduction?
a. $4,500.
b. $6,000.
c. $7,500.
d. $8,000.
e.   None of these choices.

_____ 21.   Which of the following taxes are deductible by individual taxpayers?
a.   Federal income taxes.
b.   FICA taxes imposed on employees.
c.   Foreign real property taxes.
d.   Federal and state gift taxes.
e.   None of these choices.

_____ 22.   Tami is single and employed as controller of a major industrial company. Her financial records for the year reflect the following.

Net investment income	$23,000
Investment interest expense	25,000
Mortgage interest expense	5,000
Home equity line interest expense (proceeds used to fund a vacation to Florida)	2,000
Bank credit card interest expense	1,000

How much interest expense can Tami deduct currently?
a. $30,000.
b. $31,000.
c. $32,000.
d. $33,000.
e.   None of these choices.

_____ 23.   Ray made a $1,000 contribution to Central State University's athletic booster club. This payment provided Ray the right to purchase tickets in a preferred section of the football and basketball facilities; and in addition, Ray would be invited to the coaches' luncheons every Monday. The value of these benefits was immeasurable in Ray's view. In addition, Ray forwarded $500 to the school for season football and basketball tickets. What amount may Ray deduct on his tax return for these expenditures?
a. $0.
b. $800.
c. $1,000.
d. $1,500.
e.   None of these choices.

_____ 24.   Which of the following is deductible as a charitable contribution?
a.   Country club fees.
b.   Raffle or bingo tickets.
c.   Donation of blood.
d.   Gifts to homeless individuals.
e.   None of these choices.

_____ 25.   Which of the following miscellaneous itemized deductions is subject to the two percent-of-AGI floor?
a.   Job-hunting costs.
b.   Moving expenses.
c.   Casualty and theft losses.
d.   Medical expenses.
e.   None of these choices.

Code Section Recognition

Several important sections of the Internal Revenue Code are described below. Indicate, by number, the appropriate Code section.

1. _____ Personal expenditures are specifically disallowed as deductions in arriving at adjusted gross income.

2. _____ Determines the medical expense deduction.

3. _____ Lists a number of taxes that are deductible if they are paid or accrued during a taxable year.

4. _____ Provides that an interest deduction is not allowed for interest on debt incurred to purchase or carry tax-exempt securities.

5. _____ Determines the deduction for charitable contributions.

Short Answer

1. Sandra made the following contributions to bona fide public charitable organizations during the year.

> Cash--$1,000.
> Green Corporation stock--Cost, $1,200; FMV, $1,000; held for 3 years.
> Blue Corporation stock--Cost, $1,200; FMV, $1,500; held for 2 years.
> Old clothing to the Salvation Army--Cost, $500; FMV, $200.
> Value of services rendered serving on her church's finance committee--$500.

Determine the amount that may be deducted on her return before any AGI limitations.

2. Indicate whether each of the following is subject to the 2%-of-AGI limitation.
   a. Moving expense.
   b. Professional dues.
   c. Tax return preparation fees.
   d. Medical expenses.
   e. Safe deposit box used to store investment-related records.
   f. Hobby loss expenses up to the amount of hobby income.

SOLUTIONS TO CHAPTER 10 QUESTIONS

True or False

1.   T   However, in certain situations, specific Code sections exist that override this general disallowance of personal expenditures. [General Classification of Expenses p. 10-2]

2.   F   In certain situations, such expenditures are deductible. [Medical Expenses Defined p. 10-3]

3.   F   With the acquisition of an item such as a swimming pool, the cost is deductible to the extent that the expenditure exceeds the increase in value of the related property. [Capital Expenditures for Medical Purposes p. 10-4]

4.   T   The meaning of this term essentially excludes nonprescription drugs. [Medical Expenses Defined p. 10-3]

5.   F   They would be deductible if they were incurred as a business expense under § 162 or for the production of income under § 212. [Deductibility as a Tax p. 10-10]

6.   F   The federal income tax is not deductible. However, the state income tax is deductible. [Deductibility as a Tax p. 10-10]

7.   T   This apportionment, based on the number of days each party held the property during the tax year, is required. [Apportionment of Real Property Taxes between Seller and Purchaser p. 10-12]

8.   F   State income taxes imposed on individuals are always deductible as itemized deductions. [State and Local Income Taxes and Sales Taxes p. 10-13]

9.   T   To be deductible as interest, payments for services must be considered compensation for the use or forbearance of money. [Interest Paid for Services p. 10-17]

10.   F   The amount deductible generally is limited to net investment income. [Investment Interest p. 10-14]

11.   F   A five-year carryover provision is available. [Contribution Carryovers p. 10-27]

12.   T   The 30 percent limitation applies to contributions of cash and ordinary income property while the 50 percent limitation can apply to certain contributions of capital gain property. [Limitations on Charitable Contribution Deduction p. 10-23]

13.   T   A charitable contribution deduction for the unrealized appreciation is available in certain situations involving capital gain property. [Capital Gain Property p. 10-24]

14.   F   A 7.5 percent-of-adjusted gross income threshold applies. [General Requirements p. 10-2]

15.   F   Cosmetic surgery may be deductible if it is considered *necessary* (i.e., when it ameliorates a deformity arising from a congenital abnormality, a personal injury, or a disfiguring disease). [Medical Expenses Defined p. 10-3]

16.   F   An accrual basis taxpayer may deduct property taxes in the year that fixes the right to deductibility. [Taxes p. 10-10]

17.   F   The restriction only applies to personal property taxes. [Property Taxes p. 10-11]

18.   T   Investment expenses are those *deductible* expenses that are directly connected with the production of investment income. [Investment Interest p. 10-14]

19.   F   The use of the proceeds is irrelevant. [Qualified Residence Interest p. 10-16]

20.   T   No deduction is allowed for a contribution of one's services to a qualified charitable organization. [Contribution of Services p. 10-21]

Fill-in-the-Blanks

1.   fair market value [Valuation Requirements p. 10-22]
2.   fee [Deductibility as a Tax p. 10-10]
3.   assessment, lien [Apportionment of Real Property Taxes between Seller and Purchaser p. 10-12]
4.   two [Miscellaneous Itemized Deductions p. 10-27]
5.   A, 1040 [Comprehensive Example of Schedule A p. 10-28]
6.   Interest [Allowed and Disallowed Items p. 10-14]
7.   net investment income [Investment Interest p. 10-14]
8.   donative intent, the absence of consideration, acceptance by donee [Criteria for a Gift p. 10-20]
9.   in the year of payment [Time of Deduction p. 10-22]
10.   ordinary income [Ordinary Income Property p. 10-23]
11. $5,000 [Record-Keeping Requirements p. 10-22]
12. $100,000 [Qualified Residence Interest p. 10-16]
13.   18 cents, 14 cents [Transportation, Meal, and Lodging Expenses for Medical Treatment p. 10-6; Contribution of Services p. 10-21]
14. $150,500, $75,250 [Overall Limitation on Certain Itemized Deductions p. 10-29]
15.   three, 80 [Overall Limitation on Certain Itemized Deductions p. 10-29]

Multiple Choice

1.   d   [Taxes p. 10-10]
2.   c $537 = $800 - (120/365 X $800) Steve used the property for 120 days while Penny used the property for 245 days. [Apportionment of Real Property Taxes between Seller and Purchaser p. 10-12]
3.   d   Personal (consumer) interest is not deductible [Interest p. 10-13]
4.   a   Neither personal (consumer) interest, interest to purchase or carry tax-exempt securities, nor service charges constitutes deductible interest. [Interest p. 10-13]
5.   a $1,000--Limited to the land's basis because the contribution is made to a private nonoperating foundation. The AGI limit is moot in this case. [Capital Gain Property p. 10-24]
6.   d   Limited to 30% X $7,500 (AGI), or $2,250. Therefore, the entire $1,600 contribution is deducted. [Thirty Percent Ceiling p. 10-25]
7.   c $1,360 = $400 + $900 + $60. [Taxes p. 10-10]
8.   a   The contribution of $10,000 of cash is deductible. [Contribution of Services p. 10-21; Nondeductible Items p. 10-21]
9.   b   Medical expense deduction (net of 7.5%-of-AGI floor)

[$2,700 - (7.5% X $20,000)]	$ 1,200
Foreign real property tax	1,000
Mortgage interest expense	8,200
Total	$10,400

The $500 of reimbursed employee expenses are deductible *for* AGI. [Medical Expenses p. 10-3; Taxes p. 10-10]
10.   c   State sales taxes are deductible only if the taxpayer elects to do so and does not claim a deduction for state income taxes. [Itemized Deduction for Sales Taxes Paid p. 10-13]
11.   d   Notice that in each case $12,000 of value is contributed but differing tax

consequences result. [Charitable Contributions p. 10-20]

12. c $70 = 500 miles X $0.14; the value of services rendered are not deductible.
         [Contributions of Services p. 10-21]
13. f $3,500 = $2,700 + $800 [Interest p. 10-13]
14. c $20,000 = $6,000 + $14,000 [Thirty Percent Ceiling p. 10-25]
15. c $1,795 = [$1,200 + $3,420 + $175 - ($40,000 X 7.5%)] [Medical Expenses
         Incurred for Spouse and Dependents p. 10-5]
16. c $1,200 = $900 + $300 [Interest p. 10-13]
17. b $1,350 = $900 + $450 [Taxes p. 10-10]
18. c $34,500 = $35,000 - {2/3 X .03[$175,500 (AGI) - $150,500 (threshold amount)]}
         In 2006 and 2007, the overall limitation is itself reduced--the limitation is 2/3 of the
         otherwise applicable limitation amount. [Overall Limitation on Certain Itemized
         Deductions p. 10-29]
19. c   Deductions *not* subject to the 3 percent limitation

Medical expenses	$15,000
Investment interest expense	15,000

Deductions subject to the 3 percent limitation

Qualified residence interest expense		5,000
Less: The smaller of--		
[2/3 X .03($300,500 - $150,500)] [3% rule]	$3,000	
[2/3 X .80($5,000) [80% rule]	2,667	(2,667)
Allowable itemized deductions		$32,333

         In 2006 and 2007, the overall limitation is itself reduced--the limitation is 2/3 of the
         otherwise applicable limitation amount. [Overall Limitation on Certain Itemized
         Deductions p. 10-29]
20. b

Medical expenses	$6,000
Cost of dust elimination system, net of the increase in the home's value ($3,500 - $2,000)	1,500
Total medical expenses	$7,500
Less: 7.5% of AGI ($20,000 X .075)	(1,500)
Medical expense deduction	$6,000

         [Medical Expenses p. 10-2]
21. c   Foreign real property tax is the only tax listed that is deductible. [Taxes p. 10-11]
22. a $30,000 = $23,000 + $5,000 + $2,000 [Interest p. 10-13]
23. b $800 = $1,000 X 80%   [Benefit Received Rule p. 10-20]
24. e   None of these qualifies under the tax law as a charitable contribution.
         [Nondeductible Items p. 10-21]
25. a   Only the job-hunting costs are subject to the two-percent-of-AGI limit.
         [Miscellaneous Itemized Deductions p. 10-27]

Code Section Recognition

1.   262 [General Classification of Expenses p. 10-2]
2.   213 [Medical Expenses p. 10-2]
3.   164 [Taxes p. 10-10]
4.   265 [Tax-Exempt Securities p. 10-18]
5.   170 [Charitable Contributions p. 10-20]

Short Answer

1.
Cash	$1,000
Green Corporation stock	1,000
Blue Corporation stock	1,500
Old clothing to the Salvation Army	200
Value of services rendered	0
Total	$3,700

[Charitable Contributions p. 10-20]

2. a.   Moving expense--No, this expense is deductible *for* AGI and not as an itemized deduction.
    b.   Professional dues--Yes.
    c.   Tax return preparation fees--Yes.
    d.   Medical expenses--No.
    e.   Safe deposit box used to store investment-related records--Yes.
    f.   Hobby loss expenses up to the amount of hobby income--Yes.
    [Miscellaneous Itemized Deductions p. 10-27]

Chapter 11
Passive Activity Losses

CHAPTER HIGHLIGHTS

T he tax law includes two sets of complex rules that limit the numerous opportunities which were available to taxpayers under prior law to avoid or reduce their income tax liability through tax shelter investments. These rules, the at-risk limitations and the passive loss limitations, are the topics discussed in this chapter. In essence, the at-risk rules limit a taxpayer's deductions from an investment to the amount the taxpayer would stand to lose if the investment became worthless. The passive loss rules stipulate that deductions attributable to passive activities, as a general rule, may be used only to offset passive income. Thus, in most situations passive losses may not be used to offset active or portfolio income.

I. The Tax Shelter Problem
    A. Under prior law, *tax shelter* investments were successfully used for tax avoidance purposes (i.e., to either avoid or reduce the income tax liability).
    B. The *at-risk limitations* and the *passive activity rules* are now intended to help curb such abuse.

II. At-Risk Limits
    A. Rules apply to individuals and closely held corporations that limit the amount of deductible losses to the amount that the taxpayer has at risk (i.e., the amount the taxpayer could actually lose) in the activity. These rules apply to losses from business and income-producing activities.
    B. The initial amount considered at risk includes the following.
        1. Cash and the adjusted basis of property contributed to the activity.
        2. Amounts borrowed for use in the activity for which the taxpayer has personal liability or has pledged as security property not used in the activity.
        However, the amount at risk varies as the entity recognizes income and losses, obtains and pays down qualifying debt, and distributes assets (e.g., cash withdrawals) to the owners.

C. Any losses disallowed for any given year by the at-risk rules may be deducted in the first succeeding year in which the rule does not prevent the deduction. However, such losses will be subject to the passive loss limitations if they are generated by a passive activity.

D. Recapture of previously allowed losses is required to the extent the at-risk amount is reduced below zero.

 Losses from previous years may have sufficiently reduced a taxpayer's basis in an investment to the point that a current loss may not be claimed. Therefore, it is important to check a taxpayer's at risk basis before the end of each year to determine whether an additional investment is required in order to benefit currently from losses.

III. Passive Loss Limits
A. Classification and Impact of Passive Income and Losses
1. Classification -- The passive loss rules require the classification of income and losses into one of three categories: active, passive, and portfolio.
a. *Active income* includes the following.
(1) Amounts for services rendered (e.g., salary, commissions).
(2) Profit from a trade or business in which the taxpayer is a material participant.
(3) Gain on the disposition of an asset used in a trade or business.
(4) Income from intangible property if the taxpayer's personal efforts significantly contributed to the creation of the property.
b. *Portfolio income* includes the following.
(1) Interest, dividends, annuities, and royalties not derived in the ordinary course of a trade or business.
(2) Gain or loss from the disposition of property that produces portfolio income or that is held for investment purposes.
c. *Passive income or loss* includes the following.
(1) Income or loss from any trade or business or production of income activity in which the taxpayer does not materially participate.
(2) Any rental activity regardless of whether the taxpayer materially participates, with the exception of certain real estate activities discussed later in the chapter.
2. General Impact
a. Losses or expenses generated by passive activities can be deducted only to the extent of income from all of the taxpayer's passive activities. Unused passive losses are suspended and carried forward to future years to offset passive income in those years.
b. A loss is suspended under the passive loss rules only after the application of the at-risk rules as well as other provisions relating to the measurement of taxable income.
3. Impact of Suspended Losses -- On the disposition of an entire interest in a

passive activity in a fully taxable disposition, any realized but suspended loss may be recognized and used to offset nonpassive income.

 An appropriate strategy to consider in the event that large passive loss carryovers pile up is to sell passive assets. The sale of an entire interest in a passive activity may free up the losses for use in the current year.

4.   Carryovers of Suspended Losses
   a.   The suspended loss for an activity is determined by allocating the passive activity losses among all activities in which the taxpayer has a loss during the year.
   b.   Suspended losses are carried over indefinitely and may be deductible from the activities to which they relate in the immediately succeeding taxable year.
5.   Passive Credits -- Passive credits are limited much like passive losses and can be utilized only against the regular tax attributable to passive income.
6.   Carryovers of Passive Credits -- While unused passive credits can generally be carried forward indefinitely, they can be lost forever when the activity is disposed of in a taxable transaction.
7.   Passive activity changes to active -- If a formerly passive activity becomes an active one, suspended losses are allowed to the extent of income from the now active business.

 When considering potential new investments from a tax perspective, it would probably be unwise to invest in passive activities that are expected to produce passive losses or credits, unless sufficient passive income is available to absorb those passive losses and credits. However, if a taxpayer currently owns passive investments that are generating passive losses, passive activities that generate passive income should be sought.

B.   Taxpayers Subject to the Passive Loss Rules
   1.   The passive loss rules apply to the following taxpayers.
      a.   Individuals.
      b.   Estates.
      c.   Trusts.
      d.   Personal service corporations.
      e.   Closely held C corporations.
   2.   For investments in partnerships or S corporations that are passive activities, the passive activity rules are applied at the owner level.
   3.   Application of the passive loss limitation to personal service corporations is intended to prevent taxpayers from sheltering personal service income

by creating personal service corporations and acquiring passive activities at the corporate level.

4.   Application of the passive loss rules to closely held (non-personal service) C corporations also is intended to prevent individuals from incorporating to avoid the passive loss limitations.

 If a taxpayer owns a corporation (other than an S corporation or a personal service corporation), consideration should be given to transferring investments generating passive losses to the corporation. A tax benefit could result given that regular corporations can deduct passive losses against its active business income.

C.   Passive Activities Defined -- Passive activities are defined to include the following.

    1.   Any *trade or business* or *production of income* activity in which the taxpayer does not *materially participate*.

    2.   Subject to certain exceptions, all *rental activities*.

D.   Identification of an Activity

    1.   Identifying what constitutes an *activity* is of critical importance in applying the passive loss limitations.

    2.   Regulations provide rules for grouping a taxpayer's trade or business activities and rental activities for purposes of applying the passive loss limitations. The rules provide a *facts and circumstances test* to determine whether a taxpayer's activities constitute an *appropriate economic unit*. Taxpayers may use *any reasonable method* in applying the facts and circumstances test.

    3.   In general, one or more trade or business or rental activity will be treated as a single activity if they constitute an appropriate economic unit. Taxpayers may use any reasonable method in applying the facts and circumstances.

    4.   Regrouping of activities

        a.   Once activities have been grouped, they cannot be regrouped unless the original grouping was clearly inappropriate or there has been a material change in the facts and circumstances.

        b.   In certain situations, the IRS is allowed to regroup activities.

    5.   Special rules deal specifically with the grouping of rental activities. These provisions are designed to prevent taxpayers from grouping rental activities, which are generally passive, with other businesses in a way that would result in a tax advantage.

E.   Material Participation -- To be a material participant, the taxpayer must participate on a *regular*, *continuous*, and *substantial* basis. If a taxpayer does not materially participate in a nonrental trade or business activity, any loss will be treated as a passive loss. Temporary Regulations provide seven tests for determining whether a taxpayer is a material participant.

    1.   *Tests Based on Current Participation* -- Four quantitative tests of a taxpayer's participation require measurement in terms of hours of activity during the year.

    2.   *Tests Based on Prior Participation* -- Two tests require a taxpayer in

certain situations to be classified as a material participant, even though a high level of activity is no longer maintained, if the taxpayer was formerly a material participant.

3. *Test Based on Facts and Circumstances* -- The criteria of regular, continuous, and substantial participation are used in applying this test. However, the definition of these terms has not yet been fully developed.

4. Participation Defined -- Participation generally includes any work done by an individual in an activity that he or she owns. However, work done in an individual's capacity as an investor is not counted in applying the material participation tests.

5. Limited Partners -- While exceptions exist, a *limited partner* generally is not deemed to materially participate.

F. Rental Activities Defined

1. Rental activities generally are treated as passive activities.

2. A *rental activity* is defined as any activity where payments are received principally for the use of tangible property.

3. However, Temporary Regulations provide six exceptions involving rentals of real and personal property that are *not* to be *treated* as rental activities. However, such activities will be subject to the material participation tests for final determination as to their passive status. The exceptions involve the following circumstances.

   a. The average period of customer use for such property is seven days or less.

   b. The average period of customer use for such property is 30 days or less, and significant personal services are provided by the owner of the property.

   c. Extraordinary personal services are provided by the owner of the property.

   d. The rental of such property is treated as incidental to a nonrental activity of the taxpayer.

   e. The taxpayer customarily makes the property available during defined business hours for nonexclusive use by various customers.

   f. The property is provided for use in an activity conducted by a partnership, S corporation, or joint venture in which the taxpayer owns an interest.

KEY TERMS

- At-Risk Limitation
- Passive Activity Rules
- Material Participation
- Active Participation
- Suspended Loss on Taxable Disposition

G. Interaction of the At-Risk and Passive Activity Limits -- The determination of whether a loss is suspended under the passive loss rules is made after application of the at-risk rules, as well as other provisions relating to the measurement of taxable income. In other words, a loss that is not allowed for the year because the taxpayer is not at risk is suspended under the at-risk provisions and not under the passive loss rules.

 Tax planning that could minimize the impact of the passive loss rules include (a) finding assets that generate passive income in an amount that roughly offsets suspended passive losses, (b) using the Regulations' definitions of passive activity to one's advantage (e.g., in counting hours spent in generating passive income and loss), and (c) turning over passive investments more frequently, so as to access any suspended losses and preserve the value of resulting deductions.

H.   Special Passive Activity Rules for Real Estate Activities -- Two exceptions allow all or part of rental real estate losses to be used to offset active or portfolio income even though the activity may otherwise be a passive activity.
   1.   Material Participation in a Real Property Trade or Business -- Losses from rental real estate activities are not treated as passive losses for certain real estate professionals. In order to qualify for nonpassive treatment, a taxpayer must satisfy the following requirements.
      a.   More than half of the personal services that the taxpayer performs in trades or businesses are performed in real property trades or businesses in which the taxpayer materially participates.
      b.   The taxpayer performs more than 750 hours of services in these real property trades or businesses as a material participant.
   2.   The second exception allows individuals to deduct up to $25,000 of losses on rental real estate activities against active and portfolio income.
      a.   The annual $25,000 deduction is reduced to zero by 50 percent of the taxpayer's adjusted gross income in excess of $100,000. In the case of a married taxpayer not filing a joint return and living apart for the entire year, the allowable $12,500 deduction is reduced by 50 percent of the adjusted gross income in excess of $50,000. Married individuals who live together at any time during the taxable year and file separate returns receive no benefit from the $25,000 allowance. For this purpose, adjusted gross income is computed without regard to IRA deductions, the taxable Social Security benefits amount, interest deductions on education loans, and the net losses from passive activities. The loss allowance is phased out completely once AGI exceeds $150,000 ($75,000 for married couples filing separately).
      b.   In order for the relief provision to be available, a taxpayer must meet the following criteria.
         (1)   Actively participate in the rental real estate activity.
         (2)   Own at least 10 percent of the value of all interests in the activity during the entire tax year or the period during which the taxpayer held an interest.
         Note that the *active participation* requirement is different (and less rigorous) than the *material participation* requirement.
      c.   The $25,000 allowance is an aggregate of both deductions and credits in deduction equivalents (i.e., the amount of deductions that would reduce the tax liability for the taxable year by an amount

equal to the credit).

 Since the interest costs incurred when borrowing to finance a passive investment generally are treated as part of any passive loss, a taxpayer should try to realign his or her personal finances to avoid any unnecessary borrowing costs.

I.   Dispositions of Passive Interests -- Special rules apply to dispositions of passive activities other than those that are fully taxable transactions.
      1.   Disposition of a passive activity at death.
      2.   Disposition of a passive activity by gift.
      3.   Installment sale of a passive activity.
      4.   Nontaxable exchange of a passive activity.

TEST FOR SELF-EVALUATION -- CHAPTER 11

True or False

Indicate which of the following statements are true or false by circling the correct answer.

T   F   1.   Net losses from passive activities never produce a deduction.

T   F   2.   The passive activity rules apply to the limitation of net losses and tax credits.

T   F   3.   Net passive income is recognized only to the extent of passive losses incurred.

T   F   4.   The passive loss rules generally disallow all of the net losses from passive activities held by an individual taxpayer.

T   F   5.   The at-risk rules limit a taxpayer's tax deductions from an activity for any taxable year to the amount the taxpayer has at risk at the end of the year.

T   F   6.   An interest in a limited partnership is automatically characterized as an interest in a passive activity.

T   F   7.   An individual is considered to be a material participant if he/she participates in an activity for at least 400 hours during the year.

T   F   8.   Rental activities include both real estate rentals and rentals of tangible personal property.

T   F   9.   Generally, up to $25,000 of losses on rental real estate or tangible personal property rental activities of an individual may be deducted against active or portfolio income.

T   F   10.   Suspended losses related to a passive activity may be used to offset gains realized on a fully taxable disposition of a portion of the taxpayer's interest.

T   F   11.   In order for a taxpayer to qualify for the rental real estate exception which provides for deductions of up to $25,000, the taxpayer must be a material participant in the activity.

T   F   12.   The passive activity limitations apply only to individuals, estates, trusts, closely held C corporations, and personal service corporations.

T   F   13.   The at-risk provisions, which limit the ability to claim deductions for losses from business and income-producing activities, apply only to individuals.

T   F   14.   The amount that a taxpayer has at risk is always limited to the amount the taxpayer has invested in the business or income producing venture.

T   F   15.   The at-risk rules impose an important limitation because if a taxpayer is denied losses for a particular year by the at-risk rules, they can never be deducted in future years.

T   F   16.   Recapture of previously allowed losses is required to the extent the at-risk amount is reduced below zero.

T   F   17.   Closely held C corporations (other than personal service corporations) may offset passive losses against active income, but not against portfolio income.

T   F   18.   If a taxpayer actively participates in a nonrental activity, any loss from that activity can be offset against active income.

T   F   19.   The tax law stipulates that material participation must entail regular, continuous, and substantial involvement in the operations of an activity.

T   F   20.   By virtue of the definition of a limited partner, such a taxpayer could never be a material participant in an activity.

Fill-in-the-Blanks

Complete the following statements with the appropriate word(s) or amount(s).

1.   In certain situations involving rental real estate activities, an individual taxpayer may deduct up to _____ of losses against nonpassive income. However, for a single individual or for a taxpayer who files a joint return, the allowance is completely phased out once the taxpayer's AGI exceeds _____.

2.   _____ are recognized on the taxable disposition of an entire interest in a passive activity.

3.   In terms of the interaction of the at-risk and passive activity limits, the determination of whether a loss is suspended under the _____ rules is made after application of the _____ rules.

4.   The passive activity rules require classification of income into one of three categories: _____ income, _____ income, or _____ income.

5.   To be a material participant, the taxpayer must participate on a _____, _____, and _____ basis.

6.   The passive activity rules apply to any trade or business activity if the taxpayer does not _____.

7.   If a taxpayer materially participates in an activity, income or loss from the activity is considered active, not _____.

8.   _____ arising from passive activities are limited much like passive losses.

9.   In terms of levels of participation in an activity by a taxpayer, _____ participation

requires more involvement than does _____ participation.

10.   A closely held C corporation (other than a personal service corporation) may offset passive losses against _____ income, but not against _____ income.

11.   Identifying what constitutes an _____ is a necessary first step in applying the passive loss limitations.

12.   As required by the passive loss rules, interest, dividends, and annuities are classified as _____ income.

13.   As a general rule, taxpayers who are subject to the passive loss limitations cannot offset passive losses against _____ income or _____ income.

14.   The _____ rules apply to individuals and closely held corporations, while the _____ rules apply to individuals, estates, trusts, closely held C corporations, and personal service corporations.

15.   The _____ rules are designed to prevent a taxpayer from deducting losses in excess of the actual economic investment in an activity.

Multiple Choice

Choose the best answer for each of the following questions.

____ 1.   The rules restricting losses and credits from passive activities apply to the following taxpayers.
   a.   Individuals.
   b.   Trusts and estates.
   c.   Personal service corporations.
   d.   Closely held C corporations.
   e.   All of these choices.

____ 2.   A passive activity is defined as any of the following.
   a.   Any trade or business in which the taxpayer does not materially participate.
   b.   Any rental activity, subject to certain exceptions.
   c.   Both of the following are passive activities: any trade or business in which the taxpayer does not materially participate and any rental activity, subject to certain exceptions.
   d.   None of these choices.

____ 3.   If a taxpayer materially participates in an activity, income or loss from the activity is considered active, and not passive. Material participation is achieved by meeting any one of seven tests. Which of the following is not one of those tests?
   a.   The individual participates in the activity for more than 500 hours during the year.
   b.   The individual's participation in the activity for the taxable year constitutes substantially all of the participation in the activity of all individuals for the year.

      c.   The individual participates in the activity for more than 100 hours during the year, and the individual's participation in the activity for the year is not less than the participation of any other individual for the year.

      d.   Based on all of the facts and circumstances, the individual participates in the activity on a regular, continuous, and substantial basis during such year.

      e.   Each of these choices is a qualifying test.

____ 4.   Margaret has investments in three passive activities with the following income and losses for the year.

Activity X	($40,000)
Activity Y	(30,000)
Activity Z	20,000
Net passive loss	($50,000)

Which of the following statements is true?

      a.   Current deductible losses total $70,000.

      b.   The deductible losses are allocated equally among Activities X, Y, and Z.

      c.   The deductible losses are allocated equally between Activities X and Y.

      d.   The total suspended loss is $50,000.

      e.   None of these choices is true.

____ 5.   Sue disposes of her entire interest in a passive activity at a $20,000 gain while she continues to hold investments in several other passive activities. Associated with the activity disposed of were suspended losses of $50,000. Which of the following describes the tax result of the disposition?

      a.   None of the suspended loss is deductible because she continues to hold investments in other passive activities.

      b.   All $50,000 of suspended losses may be used this year.

      c.   Only $20,000 of the $50,000 in the suspended losses may be used this year.

      d.   The amount of the $50,000 loss that may be used this year depends on the returns from the other passive activities during the current year.

      e.   None of these choices.

____ 6.   Sue disposes of her entire interest in a passive activity at a $20,000 gain while she continues to hold investments in several other passive activities. Associated with the activity disposed of were suspended losses of $50,000. In addition, a $10,000 suspended credit also exists at the time of disposition. The suspended tax credit is treated as follows.

      a.   All of the credit may be used in the year of disposition.

      b.   None of the credit may be used in the year of disposition or in future years.

      c.   A portion of the credit may be used in the year of disposition.

      d.   None of the credit may be used in the year of disposition, but it may be carried forward and used in future years.

      e.   None of these choices is true.

REFER TO THE FOLLOWING INFORMATION WHEN ANSWERING THE ITEMS BELOW.

_____ 7.   Woody, who files a joint return with his wife, actively participates in a rental activity (a beach cottage) from which a $60,000 loss results from current operations. Assuming he owns a 50 percent interest in this property and that their other AGI (solely from salary) totals $75,000, the current deduction from this property is what amount?
a. $0.
b. $25,000.
c. $30,000.
d. $60,000.
e.   None of these choices.

_____ 8.   Assume the same facts as in the preceding problem, except their AGI (solely from salary) this year, exclusive of the rental loss, is $125,000. What amount of the loss is currently deductible?
a. $0.
b. $25,000.
c. $30,000.
d. $60,000.
e.   None of these choices.

_____ 9.   Assume the same facts as in the preceding problem, except that Woody and his wife file separately instead of jointly, even though they continue to be married and live together for the entire year. What amount may Woody deduct on his return this year?
a. $0.
b. $25,000.
c. $30,000.
d. $60,000.
e.   None of these choices.

_____ 10.   A taxpayer in the 28 percent tax bracket with $10,000 of tax credits from a passive activity would have a deduction equivalent of what amount?
a. $0.
b. $2,800.
c. $10,000.
d. $35,714, but limited to $25,000.
e. $35,714.

_____ 11.   During the year, a taxpayer in the 28 percent tax bracket realizes a $10,000 tax credit from a passive activity. In addition, the following is noted.

•   The taxpayer's share of passive income or loss during the current year from the activity (or any others) is zero.
•   The tax credit arises from an investment in a rental real estate venture in which the taxpayer actively participates.

Based on the above, what is the maximum deduction equivalent that may be used currently by the taxpayer?

- a. $0.
- b. $2,800.
- c. $10,000.
- d. $25,000.
- e. $35,714.

____ 12. The at-risk limitations apply to which of the following types of taxpayers?

- a. Partnerships.
- b. Individuals.
- c. Closely held corporations.
- d. Publicly held corporations.
- e. Individuals and closely held corporations.
- f. Partnerships, individuals, and closely held corporations.
- g. All of these choices.

____ 13. Samantha made an investment in three passive activities during the current year. The following income and losses result from operations during the year.

Activity X	($60,000)
Activity Y	(40,000)
Activity Z	50,000
Net passive loss	($50,000)

What is the amount of suspended loss allocated to Activity Y?

- a. $0.
- b. $20,000.
- c. $25,000.
- d. $40,000.
- e. $50,000.
- f. Some other amount.

____ 14. Tom sells an apartment house during the year that has an adjusted basis of $80,000. The sales price of the property is $120,000. Suspended losses associated with the rental property total $60,000. Assuming Tom has no other passive activities, which of the following is true?

- a. Suspended losses of $40,000 reduce the gain recognized to zero and $20,000 of the suspended losses are lost.
- b. Suspended losses of $40,000 reduce the gain recognized to zero and $20,000 of the suspended losses remain suspended until passive income of at least $20,000 is generated.
- c. The total gain of $40,000 is offset by the suspended losses and the remaining $20,000 of suspended losses are used to offset Tom's active and portfolio income.
- d. The total gain recognized on the transaction is $40,000 because the suspended losses are not relevant.
- e. None of these choices is true.

____ 15. Molly, who earns a salary of $90,000, invests $25,000 for a 50 percent interest in a partnership venture. The entity acquires assets worth $3 million through the use of $2,400,000 in nonrecourse financing. Molly's share of the partnership's loss for the current year is $80,000. Assuming she is a material participant, how much may Molly deduct this year?

a. $0.
b. $25,000.
c. $40,000.
d. $80,000.
e.   None of these choices.

_____ 16.   Molly, who earns a salary of $90,000, invests $25,000 for a 50 percent interest in a partnership venture. The entity acquires assets worth $3 million through the use of $2,400,000 in recourse financing (i.e., Molly is personally liable for one-half of the debt). Molly's share of the partnership's loss for the current year is $80,000. Assuming she is a material participant, how much may Molly deduct this year?

a. $0.
b. $25,000.
c. $40,000.
d. $80,000.
e.   None of these choices.

_____ 17.   Darlene, who earns salary of $20,000 and portfolio income of $60,000, invests $25,000 for a 50 percent interest in a partnership venture. The entity acquires assets worth $3 million through the use of $2,400,000 in recourse financing (i.e., Darlene is personally liable for one-half of the debt). Darlene's share of the partnership's loss for the current year is $80,000. Assuming she is not a material participant, how much may Darlene deduct this year?

a. $20,000.
b. $25,000.
c. $40,000.
d. $80,000.
e.   None of these choices.

_____ 18.   Because of the at-risk limitations, Iris has been unable to deduct a $30,000 loss from previous years' operations of an oil partnership investment. However, this year, Iris invests an additional $5,000 in cash and the partnership generates net income, of which her share is $10,000. What amount of the loss carryover from previous years remains, after accounting for this year's activities, assuming Iris materially participates in the venture?

a. $0.
b. $15,000.
c. $20,000.
d. $30,000.
e.   None of these choices.

_____ 19.   Orange Corporation, a closely held C corporation (not a personal service corporation), has $45,000 of passive losses from a rental activity, $30,000 of active income, and $15,000 of portfolio income. What amount of the passive losses may be deducted this year by Orange?

a. $0.

b. $15,000.
c. $30,000.
d. $45,000.
e. None of these choices.

_____ 20. Blue Corporation, a personal service corporation, has $45,000 of passive losses from a rental activity, $30,000 of income generated from personal services, and $15,000 of portfolio income. What amount of the passive losses may be deducted this year by Blue?
a. $0.
b. $15,000.
c. $30,000.
d. $45,000.
e. None of these choices.

_____ 21. Sarah owns the following businesses and participates as indicated in each of the activities.

Activity	Hours of Participation
1	100
2	130
3	300
4	250

In which activities is Sarah considered to be a material participant?
a. None of them.
b. Only activities 3 and 4.
c. Activities 2, 3, and 4.
d. All of them.
e. Some other answer.

_____ 22. Sarah owns the following businesses and participates as indicated in each of the activities.

Activity	Hours of Participation
1	101
2	130
3	300
4	250

In which activities is Sarah considered to be a material participant?
a. None of them.
b. Only activities 3 and 4.
c. Activities 2, 3, and 4.
d. All of them.
e. Some other answer.

_____ 23. Sarah owns the following businesses and participates as indicated in each of the activities.

Activity	Hours of Participation

1	101
2	130
3	250

In which activities is Sarah considered to be a material participant?
a.   None of them.
b.   Only activities 2 and 3.
c.   All of them.
d.   Some other answer.

_____ 24.   Suzanne's adjusted basis in a passive activity is $20,000 at the beginning of the year. Her loss from the activity during the year is $15,000. She has investments in no other passive activities. Which of the following is true?
a. $5,000 year-end basis; $0 deductible loss.
b. $20,000 year-end basis; $0 deductible loss.
c. $5,000 year-end basis; $15,000 deductible loss.
d. $20,000 year-end basis; $15,000 deductible loss.
e.   None of these choices is true.

Code Section Recognition

Several important sections of the Internal Revenue Code are described below. Indicate, by number, the appropriate Code section.

1. _____   Prescribes limitations on the deduction of losses to the extent that a taxpayer is at risk.

2. _____   Provides that net losses and credits from passive activities are limited.

Short Answer

1.   Identify those taxpayers who are subject to the passive loss rules.

2.   What activities or endeavors are considered to be passive?

SOLUTIONS TO CHAPTER 11 QUESTIONS

True or False

1.　F　A carryover of net passive losses is available to offset passive income in future years; further, special rules allow deductions for real estate rental losses incurred by certain real estate professionals and up to a $25,000 loss deduction from rental real estate activities. [General Impact p. 11-6; Special Passive Activity Rules for Real Estate Activities p. 11-19]

2.　T　The passive activity loss rules limit both net losses and tax credits that have been generated by a passive activity. [General Impact p. 11-6; Passive Credits p. 11-8]

3.　F　There is no limitation on the recognition of passive income. [General Impact p. 11-6]

4.　T　In general, passive losses generated by individuals, estates, trusts, personal service corporations and closely held C corporations are deductible only to the extent of passive income. [General Impact p. 11-6; Taxpayers Subject to the Passive Loss Rules p. 11-9]

5.　T　The at-risk basis, computed as of the end of the year, serves as the ceiling on the amount of losses that may be deducted by a taxpayer subject to the at risk rules. [At-Risk Limits p. 11-3]

6.　F　Generally, a limited partner is not deemed to materially participate unless certain exceptions apply. However, if the exceptions are met, losses from such an interest would not be subject to the passive activity rules. [Limited Partners p. 11-16]

7.　F　The standard provided in the Regulations requires more than 500 hours of participation during the year. [Tests Based on Current Participation p. 11-13]

8.　T　Rental activities are defined to include rentals of both tangible realty and personalty. [Rental Activities Defined p. 11-16]

9.　F　The exception applies only to real estate rental activities. [Real Estate Rental Activities p. 11-20]

10.　F　In order to utilize suspended losses, the taxable disposition must be of the taxpayer's *entire* interest. [Impact of Suspended Losses p. 11-6]

11.　F　The taxpayer must be an *active* participant. [Real Estate Rental Activities p. 11-20]

12.　T　Each of these types of taxpayers is subject to the passive loss rules. Investments in partnerships and S corporations are subject to the passive loss rules at the owner level. [Taxpayers Subject to the Passive Loss Rules p. 11-9]

13.　F　The provisions apply to individuals and closely held corporations. [At-Risk Limits p. 11-3]

14.　F　The amount at risk is adjusted periodically to reflect the taxpayer's share of income, losses, and withdrawals from the activity. [At-Risk Limits p. 11-3]

15.　F　Losses disallowed under the at-risk rules generally can be carried over and used in future years to the extent an at-risk basis becomes available. [At-Risk Limits p. 11-3]

16.　T　Previous losses that were allowed must be offset by the recognition of enough income to bring the at-risk amount up to zero. [At-Risk Limits p. 11-3]

17.　T　In contrast to active income, portfolio income may not be offset by passive losses incurred by a closely held C corporation that is not a personal service corporation. [Closely Held C Corporation p. 11-9]

18. F   The taxpayer must be a *material* participant to deduct such losses against active income. [Material Participation p. 11-12]
19. T   The level of participation that constitutes material participation is specified by a series of tests found in the Regulations. [Material Participation p. 11-12]
20. F   Such a taxpayer could be a material participant if Test 1, 5, or 6 as described in the text is met. [Material Participation p. 11-12]

Fill-in-the-Blanks

1. $25,000, $150,000 [Real Estate Rental Activities p. 11-20]
2.   Suspended losses [Impact of Suspended Losses p. 11-6]
3.   passive loss, at-risk [Interaction of the At-Risk and Passive Activity Limits p. 11-18]
4.   active, portfolio, passive [Classification and Impact of Passive Income and Losses p. 11-5]
5.   regular, continuous, substantial [Material Participation p. 11-12]
6.   materially participate [Passive Activities Defined p. 11-10]
7.   passive [Classification and Impact of Passive Income and Losses p. 11-5]
8.   Tax credits [Passive Credits p. 11-8]
9.   material, active [Real Estate Rental Activities p. 11-20]
10. active, portfolio [Closely Held C Corporations p. 11-9]
11. activity [Identification of an Activity p. 11-10]
12. portfolio [Classification and Impact of Passive Income and Losses p. 11-5]
13. active, portfolio [General Impact p. 11-6]
14. at-risk, passive activity [At-Risk Limits p. 11-3; Taxpayers Subject to the Passive Loss Rules p. 11-9]
15. at-risk [At-Risk Limits p. 11-3]

Multiple Choice

1.   e   Each of these types of taxpayers is subject to the passive activity rules. For investments held in partnerships and S corporations, the passive loss rules are applied at the owner level. [Taxpayers Subject to the Passive Loss Rules p. 11-9]
2.   c   Activities subject to the passive loss rules are ones in which either the owner does not materially participate or, subject to certain exceptions, is rental property. [Passive Activities Defined p. 11-10]
3.   e   The level of participation that constitutes material participation is specified by a series of tests found in the Regulations. Each of the scenarios illustrates participation that is considered material. [Material Participation p. 11-12]
4.   d   Of the $70,000 loss generated, $20,000 is deductible in the current year. Therefore, $50,000 of the loss is suspended. [Carryovers of Suspended Losses p. 11-7]
5.   b   Since the taxpayer disposes of her *entire* interest in the passive activity, all of the suspended losses may be utilized in the year of disposition. [Impact of Suspended Losses p. 11-6]
6.   b   A suspended credit that cannot be used in the year of the related activity's disposition is lost forever. [Carryovers of Passive Credits p. 11-8]
7.   b   This loss qualifies under the real estate rental activity exception, but only $25,000 of his share of the current loss (i.e., $30,000) is deductible this year. [Real Estate Rental Activities p. 11-20]

8.   e $12,500 = $25,000 - [50% ($125,000 - $100,000)]. [Real Estate Rental Activities p. 11-20]
9.   a   If married individuals file separately, the $25,000 deduction is reduced to zero unless they lived apart for the entire year. [Real Estate Rental Activities p. 11-20]
10.   e $35,714 = $10,000 / 28%. [Real Estate Rental Activities p. 11-20]
11.   d $10,000 / 28% = $35,714, but limited in the current year to $25,000. [Real Estate Rental Activities p. 11-20]
12.   e   Individuals and closely held corporations are subject to the at risk rules. [At-Risk Limits p. 11-3]
13.   b $20,000 = $50,000 X ($40,000 / $100,000). [Carryovers of Suspended Losses p. 11-7]
14.   c   In the year of disposition of a passive activity, all current and suspended passive losses associated with the activity may be used. [Impact of Suspended Losses p. 11-6]
15.   b   The loss deduction is limited to the amount at risk, the $25,000 investment. [At-Risk Limits p. 11-3]
16.   d   The amount at risk includes Molly's share of the recourse debt. Therefore, all of the loss is deductible. [At-Risk Limits p. 11-3]
17.   e   Because the taxpayer is not a material participant in the venture, the passive activity rules limit the amount of the deduction to the amount of passive income she generates during the year, which is zero. [General Impact p. 11-6; Material Participation p. 11-12]
18.   b   The additional contribution and the partnership net income increases the at risk amount, allowing for the deduction of $15,000 of previously suspended losses. [At-Risk Limits p. 11-3]
19.   c   Passive losses may be used to offset active income, but not portfolio income. [Closely Held C Corporations p. 11-9]
20.   a   Passive losses incurred by a personal service corporation may be used to offset passive income, but not portfolio or active income. [Personal Service Corporations p. 11-9]
21.   c   Material participation is achieved based on Test 4. [Material Participation p. 11-12]
22.   d   The material participation standard has been met for all of the activities based on Test 4. [Material Participation p. 11-12]
23.   a   None of the tests of material participation as specified in the Regulations has been met. [Material Participation p. 11-12]
24.   a   Even though the taxpayer has sufficient basis in her activity, none of the passive loss is deductible because of the lack of passive income. [Interaction of the At-Risk and Passive Activity Limits p. 11-18]

Code Section Recognition

1.   465 [At-Risk Limits p. 11-3]
2.   469 [Passive Loss Limits p. 11-5]

Short Answer

1.   The passive loss rules apply to individuals, estates, trusts, closely held C corporations, and personal service corporations. [Taxpayers Subject to the Passive Loss Rules p. 11-9]

2.   The following types of activities are treated as passive.
        •   Any trade or business or income-producing activity in which the taxpayer does not materially participate.
        •   Subject to certain exceptions, all rental activities.
        [Classification and Impact of Passive Income and Losses p. 11-5]

Chapter 12
Tax Credits

CHAPTER HIGHLIGHTS

Tax credits are used often by Congress to implement its tax policy objectives. Tax credits have a substantially different impact on the determination of a tax liability than do tax deductions: tax credits offset a tax liability dollar for dollar, whereas tax deductions merely reduce the tax base on which a tax liability is calculated. Some observers contend that tax credits provide benefits to taxpayers on a more equitable basis than those benefits received as a result of tax deductions. Numerous tax credits are available to individuals and businesses. The attributes of the various credits differ: the calculations for some of the credits are complex and some are not; some credits are refundable and some are nonrefundable. Many of these tax credits and their attributes are discussed in this chapter.

I.   Tax Policy Considerations
    A.   A tax credit should not be confused with an income tax deduction. A tax credit is generally worth substantially more to a taxpayer than a deduction of a similar amount since a credit directly offsets the tax liability. On the other hand, a deduction merely reduces taxable income.
    B.   Tax credits, as opposed to deductions, generally provide benefits to taxpayers on a more equitable basis.
    C.   Generally, tax credits are used by Congress to achieve social or economic objectives or to promote equity among different groups or types of taxpayers.
    D.   Congress has used the tax credit provisions liberally in implementing tax policy. However, budget constraints and economic considerations often dictate whether a credit survives or is to be repealed. Some credits have been retained, or even enhanced, based on economic, equity, or social considerations (e.g., low-income housing credit, earned income credit, credit for child and dependent care expenses).

II.   Overview and Priority of Credits
    A.   Refundable versus Nonrefundable Credits
        1.   Two basic types of credits exist: refundable and nonrefundable. *Refundable credits* (e.g., taxes withheld on wages, earned income credit)

are available to the taxpayer even if they exceed the taxpayer's tax liability; whereas, *nonrefundable credits* (e.g., foreign tax credit, tax credit for the elderly or disabled) are not available if the credits exceed the tax liability.

2. Some of the nonrefundable credits are subject to carryover provisions if they cannot be used in a given year (e.g., foreign tax credit), while some of the nonrefundable credits are lost forever if they cannot be used in the year in which they arise (e.g., tax credit for the elderly or disabled).

3. A prioritized ranking by which tax credits are utilized to reduce a tax liability is specified by law. The major refundable and nonrefundable credits are shown in the text in Exhibit 12-1.

B. General Business Credit -- This credit is comprised of a number of other credits, each of which is computed separately under its own set of rules. This credit combines these credits into one amount to limit the amount of business credits that can be used to offset a taxpayer's income tax liability. Special rules apply to the general business credit.

1. Any unused credit must first be carried back 1 year, then forward 20 years.

2. The general business tax credit is limited for any tax year: the maximum allowable credit is limited to the taxpayer's *net income tax* reduced by the greater of the following.

   a. The *tentative minimum tax*.

   b. 25 percent of *net regular tax liability* that exceeds $25,000.

C. Treatment of Unused General Business Credits -- Unused credits are initially carried back one year. Any remaining unused credits are then carried forward for 20 years. The FIFO method is applied to the carrybacks, carryovers, and utilization of credits earned during a specific year.

III. Specific Business-Related Tax Credit Provisions

A. Tax Credit for Rehabilitation Expenditures

1. A tax credit is available for rehabilitation expenditures incurred on industrial and commercial buildings and on certified historic structures.

2. The operating features are summarized below in Exhibit 12-1.

Exhibit 12-1
REHABILITATION TAX CREDIT RATES

Rate of Credit for Rehabilitation Expenses	*Nature of Property*
10%	Nonresidential buildings and residential rental property, other than certified historic structures, originally placed in service before 1936
20%	Nonresidential and residential certified historic structures

3.   The basis of a rehabilitated building must be reduced by the amount of the credit taken, and the taxpayer is required to depreciate the rehabilitated structure using the straight-line method.

4.   To qualify for the credit, the building must be substantially rehabilitated. The building is considered to have been substantially rehabilitated if the rehabilitation expenditures exceed the greater of the following.
a.   The adjusted basis of the property.
b. $5,000.

5.   If the rehabilitated building is disposed of prematurely (before five years) or if it ceases to be qualifying property, part or all of the credit must be recaptured.

B.   Work Opportunity Tax Credit

1.   The credit was enacted to encourage employers to hire individuals from one or more targeted and economically disadvantaged groups. Examples of such targeted persons include qualified ex-felons, high-risk youth, food stamp recipients, veterans, and persons receiving certain welfare benefits.

2.   The credit generally is equal to 40 percent of the first $6,000 of wages (per eligible employee) for the first 12 months of employment. In cases where the employee has not worked at least 400 hours for the employer, the rate is reduced to 25 percent provided the employee meets a minimum employment level of at least 120 hours of service.

KEY TERMS

- Refundable Credit
- Nonrefundable Credit
- Foreign Tax Credit
- Rehabilitation Credit
- Child Tax Credit
- Earned Income Credit
- Research Credit

---

3.   The credit is not available for any wages paid to an employee after his or her first year of employment. However, if the employee's first year overlaps two of the employer's tax years, the employer may take the credit over two tax years.

4.   If the credit is elected, the employer's tax deduction for wages is reduced by the amount of the credit.

5.   For an employer to qualify, the employees must be certified by a designated local agency as being a member of one of the targeted groups.

C.   Welfare-to-Work Credit

1.   The welfare-to-work credit is available to employers hiring individuals who have been long-term recipients of family assistance welfare benefits. This credit is available for qualified wages paid for the first two years of employment. The employer's tax deduction for wages is reduced by the amount of the credit.

2.   The credit is equal to 35 percent of the first $10,000 of wages paid to an employee in the first year of employment, plus 50 percent of the first $10,000 of qualified wages in the second year of employment. Thus, the maximum credit per qualified employee is $8,500.

3.   The employer may not claim both the work opportunity credit and the welfare-to-work credit for wages paid to a qualified employee in a given

tax year.

D.   Research Activities Credit

1.   A credit is allowed for the purpose of encouraging research and experimentation. It is available for qualifying expenditures paid or incurred paid by a taxpayer. The credit is the *sum* of two components: an incremental research activities credit and a basic research credit.

2.   Incremental Research Activities Credit

a.   The credit applies at a 20 percent rate to the *excess* of *qualified research expenses* for the current taxable year over the *base amount.*

b.   A statutory rule defines the nature of expenditures qualifying for the credit.

c.   The credit may be claimed on these expenditures and, in addition, the taxpayer may choose among several alternatives insofar as their deduction is concerned. One of the following options may be used.

(1)   Use the full credit and reduce the expense deduction for research expenses by 100 percent of the credit.

(2)   Retain the full expense deduction and reduce the credit by the product of 100 percent times the maximum corporate tax rate.

(3)   Use the full credit, and capitalize the research expenses and amortize them over 60 months or more.

3.   Basic Research Credit

a.   A credit is allowed for *basic research expenditures* incurred in *excess* of a base amount, at the rate of 20 percent. *Basic research* payments are amounts paid in cash to a qualified basic research organization, such as a college or university.

b.   Basic research is any original investigation for the advancement of scientific knowledge not having a specific commercial objective.

E.   Low-Income Housing Credit

1.   Owners of qualified low-income housing may claim a credit that is intended to encourage the provision of affordable housing to low-income individuals. The credit may be claimed annually in equal amounts for ten years if the property continues to meet the required conditions.

2.   Several important characteristics of the credit follow.

a.   The appropriate rate for computing the credit is set monthly by the IRS.

b.   The amount of the credit is based on the qualified basis of the property, which depends on the number of units rented to low-income tenants.

c.   Once declared eligible, the property must meet the required conditions continuously throughout an extended period. Recapture rules apply in the case of noncompliance.

F.   Disabled Access Credit

1.   The disabled access credit is designed to encourage small business taxpayers to make their businesses more accessible to disabled individuals.

2.   The credit is available for *eligible access expenditures* paid or incurred by an *eligible small business* (i.e., certain sole proprietorships, partnerships, and regular or S corporations).

3. The credit is calculated at the rate of 50 percent of the eligible expenditures that exceed $250 but do not exceed $10,250.
4. To the extent the credit is available, no deduction or credit is allowed under any other provision of the tax law (e.g., for depreciation).

G. Credit for Small Employer Pension Plan Startup Costs
1. Small businesses are entitled to a nonrefundable credit for administrative costs associated with establishing and maintaining certain qualified plans.
2. The credit is available for eligible employers at the rate of 50 percent of qualified startup costs.
   a. An eligible employer is one with fewer than 100 employees who have earned compensation of at least $5,000.
   b. Qualified startup costs include ordinary and necessary expenses incurred in connection with establishing or maintaining an employer plan and retirement-related education costs, such as payroll system changes and consulting fees.
3. The maximum credit is $500, which is based on a maximum of $1,000 of qualifying expenses times 50 percent. The deduction for the startup costs incurred is reduced by the amount of the credit.

H. Credit for Employer-Provided Child Care
1. Employers are allowed to claim a credit for qualifying expenditures incurred while providing child care facilities to their employees during normal working hours.
2. The credit for employer-provided child care, limited annually to $150,000, is comprised of the aggregate of two components: 25 percent of qualified child care expenses and 10 percent of qualified child care resource and referral services.
   a. Qualified child care expenses include costs of acquiring, constructing, and operating a child care facility.
   b. Child care resource and referral services include amounts paid or incurred under a contract to provide child care and resource and referral services to an employee.
3. To prevent the possibility of a double benefit arising from claiming a credit and the associated deductions on the same expenditures, any qualifying expenses deductible by the taxpayer must be reduced by the amount of the credit. In addition, the taxpayer's basis for any property acquired or constructed and used for qualifying purposes is reduced by the amount of the credit.
4. If within 10 years of a child care facility being placed in service, it ceases to be used for a qualified use, the taxpayer will be required to recapture a portion of the credit previously claimed.

IV. Other Tax Credits
A. Earned Income Credit
1. The earned income credit has been part of the tax law for many years. It is intended to provide equity to the working poor.
2. The *earned income credit* is determined by multiplying a maximum amount of earned income by the appropriate credit percentage. However, the maximum earned income credit is phased out, beginning when the taxpayer's earned income or adjusted gross income exceeds a certain amount. The phase-out rates and thresholds vary depending on the number of the taxpayer's qualifying children and whether the taxpayer files

a joint return. See Exhibit 12-2 below for the current factors used in the calculation of the earned income credit.

Exhibit 12-2
EARNED INCOME CREDIT AND PHASE-OUT PERCENTAGES

Tax Year	Number of Qualifying Children	Maximum Earned Income	Credit Percentage	Phase-out Begins	Phase-out Percentage	Phase-out Ends
2006	Married, Filing Joint:					
	One child	$ 8,080	34.00	$16,810	15.98	$34,001
	Two or more children	11,340	40.00	16,810	21.06	38,348
	No qualifying child	5,380	7.65	8,740	7.65	14,120
	Other Taxpayers:					
	One child	$ 8,080	34.00	$14,810	15.98	$32,001
	Two or more children	11,340	40.00	14,810	21.06	36,348
	No qualifying child	5,380	7.65	6,740	7.65	12,120
2005	Married, Filing Joint:					
	One child	$ 7,830	34.00	$16,370	15.98	$33,030
	Two or more children	11,000	40.00	16,370	21.06	37,263
	No qualifying child	5,220	7.65	8,530	7.65	13,750
	Other Taxpayers:					
	One child	$ 7,830	34.00	$14,370	15.98	$31,030
	Two or more children	11,000	40.00	14,370	21.06	35,263
	No qualifying child	5,220	7.65	6,530	7.65	11,750

3.   The IRS issues a table that may be used to determine the proper amount of the credit.

4.   In general, to be *eligible* for the credit, not only must certain income thresholds not be exceeded, but the taxpayer must also have a *qualifying child*.

5.   The earned income credit also is available for low-income workers who do not have any qualifying children, as long as the worker (or his or her spouse) is over age 25 (and less than 65) and is not claimed as a dependent on another return. See Exhibit 12-2 for the current factors used in the calculation of the earned income credit.

 The earned income credit is unusual in several ways: (a) the taxpayer need not spend money to obtain it, (b) he or she can collect the credit throughout the year through a withholding adjustment, and (c) the credit is generally thought of as a "negative income tax" (i.e., if the credit exceeds the tax due for the year, the Treasury still pays the difference).

6.   The earned income credit is not available if the taxpayer's unearned income (e.g., interest, dividends) exceeds $2,800 in 2006 ($2,700 in 2005).

7.   The earned income credit is refundable to the extent that it exceeds the taxpayer's tax liability.

B.   Tax Credit for the Elderly or Disabled Taxpayers

1.   The retirement income credit is a relief provision for certain elderly (age 65 and over) taxpayers and/or certain taxpayers who are permanently and totally disabled.

2.   Individuals under age 65 also are eligible for this credit, but only if they retire with a permanent and total disability and have disability income from a public or private employer on account of that disability.

3.   The *maximum* allowable credit is $1,125 (15% X $7,500 of qualifying income).

4.   The credit is based on an initial ceiling amount of $5,000 (designated as the base amount) for a single taxpayer. The base amount is also $5,000 for married taxpayers filing a joint return when only one spouse is 65 or older. However, this amount increases to $7,500 for married taxpayers filing jointly when both spouses are 65 or older. If married taxpayers file separately, the base amount is $3,750.

5.   This initial ceiling amount is *reduced* by (1) social security, railroad retirement, and certain excluded pension benefits and (2) one-half of the taxpayer's adjusted gross income in excess of $7,500. To compute the credit, the remainder is multiplied by 15 percent.

6.   The adjusted gross income factor of $7,500 for single taxpayers described above is increased to $10,000 for married taxpayers filing jointly. For married taxpayers filing separately, the amount is $5,000. The amount is also $7,500 for a head of household or a surviving spouse.

C.   Foreign Tax Credit

1.   A tax credit (as an alternative to a deduction) may be claimed by individual or corporate taxpayers on income earned and subject to a tax in a foreign country or U.S. possession.

2.   The credit, which is generally more favorable than a deduction, is designed to mitigate the problem of double taxation.

3.   The credit is limited by the following formula.

$$\frac{\text{Foreign-source taxable income}}{\text{Worldwide taxable income}} \times \frac{\text{US tax before}}{\text{the FTC}} = \text{Overall limitation}$$

The foreign tax credit is the *lesser* of the foreign taxes actually imposed or the overall limitation amount. Only foreign income taxes, war profits taxes, and excess profits taxes qualify for the credit.

  4. Unused foreign tax credits may be carried back one year and then forward ten years.

D. Adoption Expenses Credit

  1. Qualifying adoption expenses paid or incurred by a taxpayer may give rise to the adoption expenses credit. The provision is intended to assist taxpayers who incur nonrecurring costs directly associated with the adoption process, such as legal costs, social service review costs, and transportation costs.

  2. In 2006, up to $10,960 ($10,630 in 2005) of costs incurred to adopt an eligible child qualify for the credit. An eligible child is one who meets one of the following conditions.

   a. Under 18 years of age at the time of the adoption.

   b. A person who is physically or mentally incapable of taking care of himself or herself.

  3. The credit is claimed in the year qualifying expenses are paid or incurred if they are paid or incurred during or after the year in which the adoption is finalized. For expenses paid or incurred in a tax year prior to the year when the adoption is finalized, the credit must be claimed in the tax year following the tax year in which the expenses are paid or incurred.

  4. The amount of the credit that is otherwise available is phased out beginning when a taxpayer's AGI (modified for this purpose) exceeds $164,410 (in 2006). The credit is totally eliminated when the AGI reaches $204,410. The resulting credit is calculated by reducing the allowable credit (determined without this reduction) by the amount that equals the ratio of the excess of the taxpayer's AGI over $164,410 to $40,000 multiplied by the amount of the credit. This threshold amount is indexed annually for inflation.

  5. The credit is nonrefundable and available to taxpayers only in a year in which this credit and the other nonrefundable credits do not exceed the taxpayer's tax liability. However, an unused adoption expenses credit may be carried over for up to five years and utilized on a first-in, first-out basis.

D. Child Tax Credit

  1. Individual taxpayers may take a tax credit based solely on the number of their qualifying children under age 17.

  2. The maximum credit is $1,000 per qualifying child. The credit, however, is phased out for higher income taxpayers beginning when AGI reaches $110,000 for joint filers and $75,000 for single taxpayers.

F. Credit for Child and Dependent Care Expenses

  1. This credit was enacted to benefit taxpayers who incur employment-related expenses for child or dependent care. The credit is equal to a specified percentage of expenses incurred to enable the taxpayer to work or seek employment.

  2. To be eligible, an individual taxpayer must have either of the following qualifying individual(s).

   a. A dependent under age 13.

   b. A dependent or spouse who is physically or mentally incapacitated and who lives with the taxpayer for more than one-half of the year.

3.   Eligible expenses include amounts paid for household services and care of a qualifying individual(s) that are incurred to enable a taxpayer to be employed. The amount of employment-related expenses that may be considered in the computation of the credit is limited to an individual's earned income. For married taxpayers, this limitation applies to the spouse with the *lesser* amount of earned income.

4.   The credit is equal to a percentage (ranging from 20 to 35 percent) of employment-related expenses up to $3,000 for one qualifying individual and $6,000 for two or more individuals. The rate used to compute the credit is dependent on the taxpayer's adjusted gross income.

5.   A taxpayer is not allowed to exclude an amount from gross income under a qualifying dependent care assistance program and compute the child and dependent care credit on the same amount. Therefore, the allowable child and dependent care expenses are reduced by any amount received pursuant to a dependent care assistance program.

G.   Education Tax Credits

1.   The HOPE scholarship credit and lifetime learning credit are available to help defray the cost of higher education. They are available for qualifying tuition and related expenses incurred by students pursuing undergraduate or graduate degrees, or vocational training.

2.   Maximum Credit

a.   The HOPE scholarship credit permits a maximum credit in 2006 of $1,650 per year for the first two years of post-secondary education.

b.   The lifetime learning credit permits a maximum credit of 20 percent of tuition expenses of up to $10,000 per year. This credit may not be claimed in the same year as the HOPE scholarship credit. The lifetime learning credit is intended for individuals who are beyond the first two years of post-secondary education.

3.   Eligible Individuals -- The education credits are available for qualifying expenses incurred by a taxpayer, taxpayer's spouse, or taxpayer's dependent. The HOPE scholarship credit is available per eligible student, while the lifetime learning credit is calculated per taxpayer.

4.   Income Limitations -- Both education credits are subject to income limitations and are combined for purposes of the limitation calculation.

5.   Taxpayers are prohibited from receiving a double tax benefit associated with qualifying education expenses (e.g., scholarship and employer-paid educational assistance).

H.   Credit for Certain Retirement Plan Contributions

1   Taxpayers may claim a nonrefundable credit for contributions of up to $2,000 to certain eligible retirement plans established after 2001.

2.   Contributions to certain qualified retirement plans, such as traditional and Roth IRAs and § 401(k) plans, qualify for the credit.

3.   The credit rate applied to the eligible expenses depends on the taxpayer's AGI and filing status; however, the maximum credit allowed to an individual is $1,000 ($2,000 X 50%). As one's AGI increases, the rate applied to the contributions in calculating the credit is reduced and once the taxpayer's AGI exceeds the upper end of the applicable range, no credit is available.

4.   To qualify for the credit, the taxpayer must be at least 18 years of age and cannot be a dependent of another taxpayer or a full-time student.

TEST FOR SELF-EVALUATION -- CHAPTER 12

True or False

Indicate which of the following statements are true or false by circling the correct answer.

T   F   1.   A tax credit is always worth more than a tax deduction of an equal dollar amount.

T   F   2.   One rationale for the use of tax credits as a means of implementing tax policy is that tax credits provide benefits on a more equitable basis than do tax deductions.

T   F   3.   For a building to qualify as being substantially rehabilitated for purposes of the rehabilitation tax credit, the rehabilitation expenditures must exceed the greater of the adjusted basis of the property or $10,000.

T   F   4.   To qualify for the tax credit for the elderly or disabled taxpayers, an individual under 65 years of age need only be retired with a permanent and total disability.

T   F   5.   Rehabilitation tax credit recapture may be triggered on disposing of property on which the rehabilitation tax credit had been claimed.

T   F   6.   Unused foreign tax credits may be carried back one year and forward ten years.

T   F   7.   The maximum amount of employment-related expenses that qualify for purposes of computing the credit for child and dependent care expenses for a taxpayer is $3,000.

T   F   8.   The earned income tax credit is a form of negative income tax.

T   F   9.   Eligible employment-related expenses allowable in computing the credit for child and dependent care expenses include amounts paid for household services.

T   F   10.   The amount of the earned income credit may be dependent on the number of the taxpayer's qualifying children.

T   F   11.   Unused general business tax credits must first be carried back for one year and then carried forward for 20 years.

T   F   12.   In order to be eligible for the earned income credit, the taxpayer must have at least one qualifying child.

T   F   13.   Refundable credits are paid to the taxpayer even if the amount of the credit (or credits) exceeds the taxpayer's tax liability.

T   F   14.   The low-income housing credit is an example of a refundable credit.

T   F   15.   A LIFO method is applied to the carryovers, carrybacks, and the utilization of unused general business credits used in a particular year.

T   F   16.   The rehabilitation tax credit must be recaptured if the property is disposed of or ceases to be qualifying property within ten years of incurring the rehabilitation expenditures.

T   F   17.   The research activities credit is the sum of two components: an incremental research activities credit and a basic research credit.

T   F   18.   Qualified research and experimentation expenditures not only are eligible for the 20 percent credit but also can be expensed in the year incurred.

T   F   19.   A food stamp recipient is one of the types of individuals targeted by the work opportunity tax credit.

T   F   20.   The adoption expenses credit in 2006 is available for qualifying expenses of up to $5,000.

T   F   21.   The two education credits available are the HOPE scholarship credit and the lifetime learning credit. They are available only for students seeking undergraduate degrees.

T   F   22.   An employer is prohibited from taking both the work opportunity credit and the welfare-to-work credit for wages paid to a qualified employee in a given tax year.

Fill-in-the-Blanks

Complete the following statements with the appropriate word(s) or amount(s).

1.   While a tax deduction merely reduces _____, a tax credit reduces the _____.

2.   A tax credit is available for rehabilitation expenditures incurred on certain commercial and industrial buildings as well as _____.

3.   The _____ method is applied to the carryovers, carrybacks, and the utilization of general business credits earned during a particular year.

4.   A _____ percent tax credit for rehabilitation expenditures is allowed on certified historic structures.

5.   The disabled access credit is available at the rate of _____ percent of the eligible expenditures that exceed _____ but do not exceed _____.

6.   A taxpayer may either claim a _____ or a _____ with respect to taxes paid on income earned from foreign sources.

7.   The maximum credit for child and dependent care expenses allowable to a taxpayer who

maintains a household for one dependent is _____.

8.   In computing the tax credit for the elderly or disabled taxpayers, after the initial ceiling amount is reduced for certain items, the remainder is multiplied by _____ percent.

9.   The credit for child and dependent care expenses is a percentage of the employment-related expenses, ranging from _____ to _____ percent.

10.   The research activities credit is the sum of two components: an _____ and a _____.

11.   All tax credits are of one or two types: they are either _____ or _____.

12.   The _____ credit was introduced as a part of tax law to discourage the relocation of businesses from older, economically distressed areas to newer locations and to preserve historic structures.

13.   For the incremental research activities credit, if research is conducted by persons outside the taxpayer's business (i.e., under contract), generally only _____ percent of the amount paid qualifies for the credit.

14.   The work opportunity tax credit is equal to _____ percent of the first _____ of wages paid per eligible employee for the first year of employment.

15.   If a taxpayer claims the work opportunity tax credit, the _____ for wages is reduced by the amount of the credit.

16.   The welfare-to-work credit is available to an employer for wages paid over a _____ period that can result in a maximum credit per qualified employee of _____.

17.   Individual taxpayers are permitted to take a tax credit based solely on the number of their qualifying children under age 17. The maximum child tax credit is _____ per qualifying child.

Multiple Choice

Choose the best answer for each of the following questions.

_____   1.   Which of the following is a refundable tax credit?
         a.   Earned income credit.
         b.   Foreign tax credit.
         c.   Credit for certain retirement plan contributions.
         d.   Disabled access credit.
         e.   None of these choices is a refundable tax credit.

_____   2.   Several years ago, David purchased a non-historic structure for $170,000 that was originally placed in service in 1933. In the current year, he incurred qualifying rehabilitation expenditures of $180,000. The amount of the tax credit for rehabilitation expenditures, and the amount by which the building's basis for

cost recovery would increase as a result of the rehabilitation expenditures are the following amounts:
- a. $18,000 credit, $162,000 basis.
- b. $18,000 credit, $200,000 basis.
- c. $18,000 credit, $350,000 basis.
- d. $36,000 credit, $144,000 basis.
- e.   None of the above.

_____   3.   Two and one-half years ago, Westphal placed in service a non-historic building on which expenditures were incurred that qualified for the rehabilitation tax credit. Qualifying rehabilitation expenditures incurred were $800,000. If Westphal sold the building at a loss this year, what amount of rehabilitation tax credit recapture is due?
- a. $32,000.
- b. $48,000.
- c. $80,000.
- d.   None because the building was disposed of at a loss.
- e.   None of these choices.

_____   4.   Select the *correct* statement.
- a.   The only taxpayer eligible to claim the earned income credit would be one who either is married and has a qualifying child, or is a surviving spouse.
- b.   Because of the ceiling limitation imposed, the foreign tax credit may not eliminate completely the effect of multiple taxation.
- c.   The LIFO method is applied to the carryovers, carrybacks, and the utilization of general business tax credits earned during a particular year.
- d.   An intangible asset used in a trade or business with a useful life of three years or more is eligible for the rehabilitation tax credit.
- e.   None of these choices is correct.

_____   5.   Select the *incorrect* statement below pertaining to the research activities credit.
- a.   The research credit is the sum of two components: an incremental credit and a basic research credit.
- b.   The incremental research activities credit is 20 percent of the amount of qualified research expenses that exceeds the base amount.
- c.   Qualifying expenditures not only are eligible for the research credit, but also can be expensed in the year incurred.
- d.   Corporations, but not S corporations or personal service corporations, are eligible for the basic research credit.
- e.   Each of these choices is correct.

_____   6.   Sam and Tanya, married filing a joint return, have two children. In 2006, their earned income is $18,000. Calculate their earned income credit for 2006.
- a. $0.
- b. $251.
- c. $4,285.
- d. $4,536.
- e.   Some other amount.

_____   7.   John and Susie are married, file jointly, and have one dependent daughter, Sarah. During the year, qualifying child care expenditures of $3,200 were incurred in order that both parents could work outside the home. John earned $7,500 and

Susie earned $17,000; however, their adjusted gross income was $25,000. What is the allowable credit for child and dependent care expenses?
a. $870.
b. $900.
c. $928.
d. $960.
e. Some other amount.

8. John and Susie are married, file jointly, and have two dependent daughters, Sarah and Emily. During the year, qualifying child care expenditures of $3,200 were incurred in order that both parents could work outside the home. John earned $7,500 and Susie earned $17,000; however, their adjusted gross income was $25,000. What is the allowable credit for child and dependent care expenses?
a. $870.
b. $900.
c. $928.
d. $960.
e. Some other amount.

9. Jane and Bobby have three dependent children aged 3, 5, and 14. Jane has been physically disabled since March 1, 2006 and unable to work or care for the children. Since March 1, 2006, Jane and Bobby have incurred $7,200 of child care expenses. Bobby's salary (and adjusted gross income) was $30,000. Jane had no earnings in January or February, 2006. Bobby and Jane may claim a credit for child and dependent care expenses of what amount?
a. $1,944.
b. $1,640.
c. $1,350.
d. $0.
e. None of these choices.

10. Burke Corporation had $250,000 in income from Scotland, which imposes a 50% income tax on income earned within its borders. Burke also had income of $500,000 from within the United States. The tentative U.S. tax on the $750,000 total income is $255,000. What is Burke's foreign tax credit for the year?
a. $0.
b. $42,500.
c. $85,000.
d. $125,000.
e. None of these choices.

11. Which of the following taxes qualify for purposes of calculating the foreign tax credit?
a. VAT (value added taxes).
b. War profits taxes.
c. Property taxes.
d. Sales taxes.
e. None of these choices qualify.

12. Which of the following statements concerning the earned income credit is *true*?

a.   The credit can only be offset against any net tax liability after considering withholdings and estimated tax payments.

b.   The credit can result in a refund only when the taxpayer has had taxes withheld.

c.   The credit can result in a refund even if the taxpayer has had no taxes withheld and has no tax liability.

d.   None of these choices is true.

_____ 13.   The general business credit is *not* comprised of which of the following?

a.   Tax credit for rehabilitation expenditures.

b.   Credit for small employer pension plan startup costs.

c.   Low-income housing credit.

d.   Foreign tax credit.

e.   All of these choices are components of the general business credit.

_____ 14.   Herold Corporation's general business credit for the year is $85,000. The business's net income tax is $125,000, while the tentative alternative minimum tax is $50,000. Assuming Herold Corporation has no other credits for the year, the general business credit allowed for the year is what amount?

a. $50,000.

b. $75,000.

c. $85,000.

d. $100,000.

e.   Some other amount.

_____ 15.   Herold Corporation's general business credit for the year is $85,000. The business's net income tax is $125,000, while the tentative alternative minimum tax is $15,000. Assuming Herold Corporation has no other credits for the year, the general business credit allowed for the year is what amount?

a. $15,000.

b. $85,000.

c. $100,000.

d. $110,000.

e.   Some other amount.

_____ 16.   Traylor Corporation spent $75,000 to rehabilitate a non-historic building that had originally been placed in service in 1921 in the inner city. Traylor had acquired the building early this year for $100,000. The amount of the rehabilitation expenditures credit available to the taxpayer is the following.

a. $7,500.

b. $15,000.

c. $17,500.

d. $35,000.

e.   None of these choices.

_____ 17.   Traylor Corporation spent $75,000 to rehabilitate a certified historic structure located in the inner city. Traylor had acquired the building early this year for $50,000. The amount of the rehabilitation expenditures credit available to the taxpayer is the following.

a. $7,500.

b. $12,500.

    c. $15,000.
    d. $25,000.
    e.   None of these choices.

_____ 18.   Skyline Corporation, desiring to make their business more accessible to disabled individuals, incurred $8,000 in eligible access expenditures. The amount of disabled access credit arising from these expenditures is what amount?
    a. $0.
    b. $3,875.
    c. $4,000.
    d. $5,000.
    e.   Some other amount.

_____ 19.   Skyline Corporation, desiring to make their business more accessible to disabled individuals, incurred $18,000 in eligible access expenditures. The amount of disabled access credit arising from these expenditures is what amount?
    a. $3,875.
    b. $5,000.
    c. $8,875.
    d. $9,000.
    e.   Some other amount.

_____ 20.   Viola, a single taxpayer who is 26 years old, is not claimed as a dependent on another tax return and she has no children. During 2006, her earned income was $8,000. She qualifies for the following amount of earned income credit.
    a. $0.
    b. $96.
    c. $316.
    d. $412.
    e.   None of these choices.

_____ 21.   During the current year, Green Hills Corporation had $250,000 in income from Ireland, which imposes a 10% income tax on income earned within its borders. Green Hills also had income of $500,000 from within the United States. The tentative U.S. tax on the $750,000 total income is $255,000. How much is Green Hill's foreign tax credit for the year?
    a. $0.
    b. $8,333.
    c. $25,000.
    d. $85,000.
    e.   None of these choices.

_____ 22.   To qualify for the credit for child and dependent care expenses, the taxpayer must have the following:
    a.   A dependent under age 13.
    b.   A dependent of any age.
    c.   A dependent or spouse who is physically or mentally incapacitated and who lives with the taxpayer for more than one-half of the year.
    d.   A dependent of any age or a dependent or spouse who is physically or mentally incapacitated and who lives with the taxpayer for more than one-half of the year.

e.   A dependent under age 13 or a dependent or spouse who is physically or mentally incapacitated and who lives with the taxpayer for more than one-half of the year.
f.   All of these choices qualify.

_____ 23.   Good Hands Company hires four individuals who qualify for the work opportunity tax credit. Each individual worked 1,000 hours for wages of $8,000 during the first year of employment. What is the amount of the work opportunity tax credit and the wages deduction related to the employment of these four individuals by Good Hands?
a. $9,600; $22,400.
b. $9,600; $32,000.
c. $12,800; $19,200.
d. $12,800; $32,000.
e.   None of these choices.

_____ 24.   Which of the following statements regarding the adoption expenses credit is *not* true?
a.   The provision is intended to assist taxpayers who incur certain costs in the process of adopting an eligible child.
b.   Costs that qualify for the credit are limited to $10,960 in 2006.
c.   The credit always is claimed in the year in which the qualifying costs are incurred.
d.   The amount of the credit that is otherwise available is reduced if a taxpayer's modified AGI exceeds $164,410 in 2006.
e.   None of these choices is false.

_____ 25.   Regarding the work opportunity credit and the welfare-to-work credit, which of the following attributes relevant in their computations are *similar*?
a.   The type of employee targeted by the credit.
b.   The amount of qualified expenses incurred.
c.   The number of years that the payment of qualified expenses give rise to the credit for a particular employee.
d.   The credit's impact on the employer's calculation of the wages deduction.
e.   None of these attributes is the same for both credits.

_____ 26.   John and Fay are married and file a joint return showing AGI of $105,000. Their children are ages 12, 13, 17, and 20. The 20-year-old is a full-time student at State University. What amount may John and Fay as a child credit in 2006?
a. $1,000.
b. $2,000.
c. $3,000.
d. $4,000.
e.   Some other amount.

_____ 27.   Nancy and Steve file a joint income tax return where their AGI is calculated at $75,000. Their daughter, Kathleen, is attending State Polytechnic Institute where the tuition costs over the four undergraduate years are expected to be $10,000 per year. If Nancy and Steve's income stays about the same over the four-year period and the HOPE scholarship credit rules remain as they currently exist, what is the maximum amount of HOPE scholarship credit available to them over the

four-year period?
a. $0.
b. $1,650.
c. $3,300.
d. $6,600.
e.   Some other amount.

Code Section Recognition

Several important sections of the Internal Revenue Code are described below. Indicate, by number, the appropriate Code section.

1.   _____   Requires recapture of the rehabilitation tax credit in certain situations.

2.   _____   Provides a tax credit to multinational taxpayers to relieve double taxation.

3.   _____   Taxpayers who incur qualifying child care expenditures may claim a credit.

Short Answer

1.   During 2006, Bob and Tami incur child care expenses of $4,000 on behalf of their two preschool-age sons, Mitchell and Lane. Bob's earnings for the year are $3,800 and Tami's earnings total $22,000. Assuming they had no other income, determine their credit for child and dependent care expenses.

SOLUTIONS TO CHAPTER 12 QUESTIONS

True or False

1. T A tax credit reduces the tax liability dollar for dollar whereas a tax deduction only reduces the tax base. [Tax Policy Considerations p. 12-3]

2. T While the tax benefit received from a tax deduction depends on the tax rate, a tax credit is not affected by the tax rate of the taxpayer. [Tax Policy Considerations p. 12-3]

3. F The expenditures must exceed the greater of the adjusted basis or $5,000. [Tax Credit for Rehabilitation Expenditures p. 12-7]

4. F The taxpayer must also have disability income from a public or private employer on account of that disability. [Tax Credit for Elderly or Disabled Taxpayers p. 12-16]

5. T The recapture occurs if the rehabilitated property is disposed of prematurely or if it ceases to be qualifying property. [Recapture of Tax Credit for Rehabilitation Expenditures p. 12-8]

6. T Unused foreign tax credits may be carried back and then carried forward. [Computation p. 12-18]

7. F The maximum amount is $6,000 if expenditures are incurred on behalf of two or more dependents. [Calculation of the Credit p. 12-21]

8. T It is viewed as a form of negative income tax because it is refundable for those taxpayers who do not have a tax liability. [Advance Payment p. 12-16]

9. T Such expenses, along with those incurred for the care of a qualifying individual, are intended to enable the taxpayer to be employed. [Eligible Employment-Related Expenses p. 12-21]

10. T In situations where the taxpayer has one or more qualifying children, the rate varies depending on whether one child or two or more children are involved. [Earned Income Credit p. 12-14]

11. T The general business credit must be carried back and used to the extent allowable before it is carried forward. [General Business Credit p. 12-5]

12. F While this generally is true, a reduced earned income credit is available for a low-income taxpayer if he/she (or his or her spouse) is over 25 and under age 65 and is not claimed as a dependent on another return. [Eligibility Requirements p. 12-16]

13. T Receiving a benefit from a refundable credit, unlike a nonrefundable credit, is not dependent on the existence of a taxpayer liability. [Refundable versus Nonrefundable Credits p. 12-4]

14. F The low-income housing credit is not a refundable credit. [Low-Income Housing Credit p. 12-12]

15. F A FIFO method is used. [Treatment of Unused General Business Credits p. 12-6]

16. F The amount recaptured is based on a holding period requirement of five years. [Recapture of Tax Credit for Rehabilitation Expenditures p. 12-8]

17. T The nature and the computation of the two components of the credit differ but a taxpayer is allowed to claim tax benefits for undertaking certain research in both categories. [Research Activities Credit p. 12-10]

18. T In regard to expensing qualified research and experimentation expenditures, taxpayers have several options. [Incremental Research Activities Credit p. 12-10]

19. T Other types of individuals targeted include ex-felons, high-risk youths, veterans, summer youth employees, and persons receiving certain welfare benefits. [Work Opportunity Tax Credit p. 12-8]

20.   F   Qualifying expenses of up to $10,960 in 2006 give rise to the adoption expenses credit. [Adoption Expenses Credit p. 12-19]
21.   F   The lifetime learning credit is available for individuals pursuing undergraduate or graduate degrees, or vocational training. [Education Tax Credits p. 12-23]
22.   T   A taxpayer must choose between these two credits. [Welfare-to-Work Credit p. 12-9]

Fill-in-the-Blanks

1.   taxable income, tax liability [Tax Policy Considerations p. 12-3]
2.   certified historic structures [Tax Credit for Rehabilitation Expenditures p. 12-7]
3.   FIFO [Treatment of Unused General Business Credits p. 12-6]
4.   20 [Tax Credit for Rehabilitation Expenditures p. 12-7]
5.   50, $250, $10,250 [Disabled Access Credit p. 12-13]
6.   deduction, credit [Foreign Tax Credit p. 12-17]
7. $1,050 (i.e., $3,000 X 35%) [Calculation of the Credit p. 12-21]
8.   15 [Tax Credit for the Elderly or Disabled Taxpayers p. 12-16]
9.   20, 35 [Calculation of the Credit p. 12-21]
10.   incremental research activities credit, basic research credit [Research Activities Credit p. 12-10]
11.   refundable, nonrefundable [Refundable versus Nonrefundable Credits p. 12-4]
12.   rehabilitation expenditures [Tax Credit for Rehabilitation Expenditures p. 12-7]
13.   65 [Incremental Research Activities Credit p. 12-10]
14.   40, $6,000 [Computation of the Work Opportunity Tax Credit: General p. 12-8]
15.   tax deduction [Computation of the Work Opportunity Tax Credit: General p. 12-8]
16.   two-year, $8,500 [Maximum Credit p. 12-10]
17. $1,000 [Maximum Credit and Phaseouts p. 12-20]

Multiple Choice

1.   a   The earned income credit is the only refundable tax credit listed. [Refundable versus Nonrefundable Credits p. 12-4]
2.   a   Credit: $18,000 = $180,000 X 10%; basis increase: $162,000 = $180,000 (rehabilitation expenditures) - $18,000 (credit). [Tax Credit for Rehabilitation Expenditures p. 12-7]
3.   b   Original credit ($800,000 X .10) $80,000
           Less: Amount of credit earned ($80,000 X .40)   (32,000)
           Recapture tax $48,000
           [Recapture of Tax Credit for Rehabilitation Expenditures p. 12-8]
4.   b   The overall limitation may result in some of the foreign income being subjected to double taxation. [Computation p. 12-18]
5.   e   Each of the statements correctly relates an aspect of the research activities credit. [Research Activities Credit p. 12-10]
6.   c   Maximum credit ($11,340 X 40%) $4,536
           Less: 21.06% ($18,000 - $16,810)   (251)
           Allowable earned income credit $4,285
           [Earned Income Credit p. 12-14]
7.   b $900 = $3,000 X 30% [Calculation of the Credit p. 12-21]
8.   d $960 = $3,200 X 30% [Calculation of the Credit p. 12-21]

9.	c	$1,350 = $6,000 X 10/12 X .27 [Calculation of the Credit p. 12-21]
10.	c	$85,000 = $250,000/$750,000 X $255,000 [Computation p. 12-18]
11.	b	In general, qualifying taxes must be based on income (e.g., war profits). [Computation p. 12-18]
12.	c	The earned income credit is a refundable credit. [Advance Payment p. 12-16]
13.	d	The general business credit includes only certain credits and does not include the foreign tax credit. [Refundable versus Nonrefundable Credits p. 12-4]

14. b

Net income tax	$125,000
Less: The greater of	
• $50,000 (tentative minimum tax)	
• $25,000 [25% X ($125,000 - $25,000)]	(50,000)
Allowable business credit	$ 75,000

[General Business Credit p. 12-5]

15. b

Net income tax	$125,000
Less: The greater of	
• $15,000 (tentative minimum tax)	
• $25,000 [25% X ($125,000 - $25,000)]	(25,000)
Maximum business credit allowed	$100,000
Allowable business credit limited to amount of credit available	$ 85,000

[General Business Credit p. 12-5]

16.	e	The rehabilitation expenditures credit is not available because the building has not been substantially rehabilitated (i.e., the amount of the expenditures incurred did not exceed the greater of $5,000 or the adjusted basis of the building prior to the rehabilitation). [Tax Credit for Rehabilitation Expenditures p. 12-7]
17.	c	$15,000 = $75,000 X 20% [Tax Credit for Rehabilitation Expenditures p. 12-7]
18.	b	$3,875 = ($8,000 - $250) X 50% [Disabled Access Credit p. 12-13]
19.	b	$5,000 = ($10,250 - $250) X 50% [Disabled Access Credit p. 12-13]

20. c

Initial credit ($5,380 X 7.65%)	$412
Less: 7.65% ($8,000 - $6,740)	(96)
Allowable earned income credit	$316

[Eligibility Requirements p. 12-16]

21.	c	$85,000 = $250,000/$750,000 X $255,000. But, the maximum credit is limited to the amount of foreign tax actually paid (i.e., $25,000). [Computation p. 12-18]
22.	e	To qualify, a taxpayer must have either a dependent under age 13 or a dependent or spouse who is physically or mentally incapacitated and who lives with the taxpayer for more than one-half of the year. [Eligibility p. 12-21]
23.	a	$9,600 credit = 4 X $6,000 X 40% $22,400 wages deduction = $32,000 - $9,600 [Computation of the Work Opportunity Tax Credit: General p. 12-8]
24.	c	A taxpayer may claim the credit in the year qualifying expenses were paid or incurred if they were paid or incurred during or after the tax year in which the adoption was finalized. For qualifying expenses paid or incurred in a tax year prior to the year when the adoption was finalized, the credit must be claimed in the tax year following the tax year during which the expenses are paid or incurred. [Adoption Expenses Credit p. 12-19]
25	d	In each case, the wages deduction is reduced by the amount of the credit. [Work Opportunity Tax Credit p. 12-8; Welfare-to-Work Credit p. 12-9]
26.	b	Their credit is $2,000, or $1,000 each for the children ages 12 and 13. A credit may not be claimed with respect to either of the older children. [Child Tax Credit p. 12-20]

27.   c   The maximum HOPE credit under current rules is $3,300 over the period, or
                 $1,650 per year for the first two years of post-secondary education. The HOPE
                 scholarship credit is not available during the final two years Kathleen is in college.
                 However, the taxpayers should consider the availability of the lifetime learning
                 credit for Kathleen's last two years of college. [Education Tax Credits p. 12-23]

Code Section Recognition

1.   50 [Recapture of Tax Credit for Rehabilitation Expenditures p. 12-7]
2.   901 [Foreign Tax Credit p. 12-17]
3.   21 [Credit for Child and Dependent Care Expenses p. 12-20]

Short Answer

1.   Qualifying expenses--$4,000, but limited to Bob's earnings $3,800
        Rate (based on AGI of $25,800)   X 29%
        Credit amount $1,102
        [Credit for Child and Dependent Care Expenses p. 12-20]

Chapter 13
Property Transactions: Determination of Gain or Loss, Basis Considerations, and Nontaxable Exchanges

CHAPTER HIGHLIGHTS

Tax consequences generally result when a sale or other disposition of property occurs. In such cases, any gain or loss realized is recognized for tax purposes. Thus, income tax would be payable on a gain recognized or a loss deduction would be available on a loss recognized in the year of sale or disposition. However, in some situations gains or losses realized are not recognized for tax purposes in the year of disposition. Examples of transactions where gains or losses realized may not be recognized currently for tax purposes include like-kind exchanges and involuntary conversions. Thus, these nonrecognition provisions, which may or may not be mandatory, can provide for temporary deferral of gain or loss recognition. Further, one provision provides for a permanent forgiveness of gain recognition of up to $250,000 (or $500,000 for certain married couples) on the sale of a principal residence.

I.   Determination of Gain or Loss
    A.   Realized Gain or Loss
        1.   A *realized gain* or *loss* is measured by the difference between the amount realized from the sale or other disposition of property and its adjusted basis on the date of disposition.
        2.   A realized gain results if the amount realized exceeds the property's adjusted basis. A loss is realized if the adjusted basis exceeds the amount realized.
        3.   The term *sale or other disposition* includes virtually any disposition of property, such as trade-ins, casualties, sales and exchanges, or condemnations.
        4.   The *amount realized* from the disposition of property is the sum of money received, plus the fair market value of property received, plus the release of any liability on the property disposed of, less selling expenses relating to the sale.

          5.   The *adjusted basis* of property disposed of is the original basis (usually cost), plus capital additions or improvements, less capital recoveries. The result reflects the unrecovered cost or other basis of the property on the date of disposition.

          6.   Capital additions, which may be distinguished from ordinary repair and maintenance expenditures, include the cost of capital improvements and betterments made to property by a taxpayer.

          7.   The following are examples of capital recoveries (i.e., reductions in an asset's basis).

               a.   Depreciation and cost recovery allowances.

               b.   Casualties and thefts.

               c.   Certain corporate distributions.

               d.   Amortizable bond premium.

               e.   Easements.

    B.   Recognized Gain or Loss

          1.   *Recognized gain* is an amount of realized gain that is included in a taxpayer's gross income.

          2.   A *recognized loss* is an amount of realized loss that is deductible for tax purposes.

          3.   As a general rule, all realized gains and losses are recognized.

    C.   Nonrecognition of Gain or Loss -- Several situations where realized gains and/or losses are not recognized include the following.

          1.   Nontaxable exchanges.

          2.   Losses realized on personal use assets, except in the case of thefts or casualties.

          3.   Gains realized on the sale of a personal residence.

          4.   Realized losses on certain transactions between related parties.

    D.   Recovery of Capital Doctrine

          1.   A taxpayer is entitled to recover the cost or other original basis of property acquired and, therefore, is not taxed on that amount.

          2.   The cost or other original basis is recovered through annual depreciation or cost recovery deductions.

          3.   On a sale or other disposition, the unrecovered cost is compared to the amount realized to determine realized gain or loss.

II.   Basis Considerations

    A.   Determination of Cost Basis

          1.   The basis of property is generally its cost -- the amount paid for the property in cash or other property. However, the basis of property received in a *bargain purchase* is its fair market value.

          2.   Cost identification problems are frequently encountered in securities transactions. Unless a taxpayer can adequately identify the particular stock that has been sold, a security sold is presumed to come from the first lot or lots purchased (i.e., a FIFO presumption).

          3.   It is often necessary to allocate the lump-sum purchase price of multiple assets acquired for the purpose of determining the basis of each individual asset involved. The lump-sum cost is allocated on the basis of the relative fair market value of the individual assets acquired. If a business is purchased and *goodwill* is involved, a special allocation rule applies. Further, a special allocation may be required in the case of when *nontaxable stock dividends* are received.

 When selling shares of stock or interests in a mutual fund, be certain that the asset's basis is properly stated. Income and capital gains generated by the fund can increase the investment's basis. The effect of these adjustments is to reduce the amount of gain or increase the amount of loss to be reported from the sale.

B.   Gift Basis
1.   Because there is no cost to the recipient on the receipt of a gift, a basis must be assigned to the property. However, the basis for gain and the basis for loss may not be the same amount. In general, the donee's basis depends on the following.
   a.   The date of the gift.
   b.   The basis of the property to the donor.
   c.   The amount of the gift tax paid.
   d.   The fair market value of the property.
2.   The basis rules for gifts made in 1921 or after require the following.
   a.   If the donee subsequently disposes of the property and a gain is realized, the basis to the donee is the same as the donor's adjusted basis.
   b.   If the donee subsequently disposes of the property in a transaction which results in a loss, the basis to the donee is the lower of the donor's adjusted basis or the fair market value on the date of the gift.
3.   If, on a sale by the donee, the amount of sales proceeds is between the basis for gain and the basis for loss, then no gain or loss is recognized.
4.   Gift taxes paid by the donor are often added, in part or in full, to the basis of property given to the donee.
   a.   For gifts made after 1976, the amount of the gift tax added is that amount attributed to the *net unrealized appreciation* up to the date of the gift.
   b.   For gifts made prior to 1977, the full amount of the gift tax paid is added to the donor's basis, up to the fair market value of the property.
5.   If the donor's adjusted basis of property received by gift is the basis to the donee, then the *holding period* begins on the date the property was acquired by the donor. The holding period begins on the date of the gift if the fair market value is the basis to the donee.
6.   The basis for depreciation on depreciable gift property is the donor's adjusted basis (i.e., the donee's basis for gain).
C.   Property Acquired from a Decedent
1.   The basis of property acquired from a decedent is generally its fair market value at the date of the decedent's death. In some situations, an estate's executor or administrator may *elect* the *alternate valuation amount*, which generally, is the property's fair market value six months after the decedent's death.
2.   Survivor's Share of Property
   a.   With *community property*, both the decedent's share and the

survivor's share assume a basis equal to fair market value on the date of the decedent's death.

      b.   With property in a *common law* state, only one-half of jointly held property of spouses is included in the decedent's estate. No adjustment of the basis is permitted for the excluded property interest.

    3.   The holding period of property acquired from a decedent is *deemed* to be *long-term* (i.e., held for the required long-term holding period).

D.   Disallowed Losses

    1.   Related Taxpayers

      a.   Direct and indirect losses realized from sales or exchanges of property between certain related parties are *not* recognized.

      b.   The basis of business or income producing property to the transferee in a related party transaction is its cost.

      c.   The original transferee may reduce any realized gain on a subsequent disposition of the property to the extent of the previously disallowed loss.

      d.   The holding period includes only the period of time the property was held.

    2.   Wash Sales -- A realized loss will not be recognized if the taxpayer sells or exchanges stock or securities and, within 30 days before or after such sale or exchange, acquires *substantially identical* stock or securities. Any realized loss not recognized is added to the basis of the substantially identical stock or securities acquired. The holding period of the new stock or securities includes the holding period of the old stock or securities. These rules relate to transactions known as *wash sales*.

E.   Conversion of Property From Personal Use to Business or Income-Producing Use

    1.   The *original basis for loss* on personal use assets converted to business or income-producing use is the *lower* of the property's adjusted basis or fair market value on the date of conversion.

    2.   The *gain basis* for converted property is equal to its adjusted basis on the date of conversion.

    3.   The basis for loss serves as the basis for depreciating the converted property.

III.   Nontaxable Exchanges

A.   In a *nontaxable exchange*, realized gains or losses are not recognized until the property received in the nontaxable exchange is subsequently disposed of in a taxable sale or exchange. That is, the recognition of such gains and losses is *postponed* or *deferred*.

B.   Gain or loss is not recognized in a nontaxable exchange based on the theory that a taxpayer merely has changed the *form*, but not the *substance*, of his or her relative economic position. That is, the property received is viewed as being a

---

KEY TERMS

- Amount Realized
- Adjusted Basis
- Realized and Recognized Gain or Loss
- Related Party Gain or Loss
- Involuntary Conversion
- Like-Kind Exchange
- Sale of a Residence

continuation of the old investment.

IV.   Like-Kind Exchanges -- § 1031
    A.   Section 1031 provides that "no gain or loss shall be recognized if property held for productive use in a trade or business or for investment is exchanged solely for property of a *like-kind* to be held either for productive use in a trade or business or for investment."
    B.   Property held for personal use, inventory, partnership interests, or securities do *not* qualify for deferral of gain or loss under the like-kind provisions. Further, US real property and foreign real property are not like-kind under these provisions. Moreover, personal property used predominantly within the US and personal property used predominantly outside the US are not like-kind property.
    C.   The like-kind provisions are not elective -- they are *mandatory* if the following requirements are satisfied.
        1.   The form of the transaction is an exchange.
        2.   Both the property transferred and the property received are held either for productive use in a trade or business or for investment.
        3.   The property is like-kind property.
    D.   However, in most situations, a like-kind exchange between related parties loses its nonrecognition status if, within two years of the exchange, one of the parties disposes of the property it acquired in the exchange.
    E.   Like-Kind Property
        1.   The words *like-kind* have reference to the nature or character of the property and not to its grade or quality.
        2.   Under this definition, real estate may be exchanged only for other real estate, and personalty may be exchanged only for other personalty. It is irrelevant whether the real estate is improved or unimproved.
    F.   Exchange Requirement
        1.   To qualify as a like-kind exchange, a transaction generally must involve a direct exchange.
        2.   The sale of old property and the purchase of new property, even though like-kind, is generally not an exchange. However, the IRS may treat the two transactions as a like-kind exchange if the transactions are mutually dependent.

> Like-kind exchanges are not limited to direct exchanges between two parties. Instead, if an agreement cannot be reached with someone owning property the taxpayer desires, a multi-party exchange could be arranged. This could result in a solution that would satisfy both parties, while at the same time still achieve tax deferral.

    G.   Boot
        1.   *Boot* is cash or property other than like-kind property.
        2.   Realized gain is recognized to the extent of any boot *received*; however, boot received has no effect on the recognition of realized losses.
        3.   Cash *given* in a like-kind exchange has no effect on the recognition of realized gains or losses. However, if appreciated or depreciated non like-kind property (i.e., boot) is given, realized gain or loss will be recognized.

H.   Basis of Property Received
1.   The basis of the property received in a like-kind exchange must be adjusted to reflect any postponed gain or loss.
2.   The basis may be computed using either of the two methods shown in Exhibit 13-1.

Exhibit 13-1
LIKE-KIND EXCHANGE BASIS CALCULATIONS

Method 1   The basis of the property received in the exchange is its *fair market value less postponed gain* or *plus postponed loss*

Method 2   Adjusted basis of property surrendered
   Plus: Adjusted basis of boot given
   Plus: Gain recognized
   Less: Fair market value of boot received
   Less: Loss recognized
   Equals: Basis of like-kind property received

---

3.   The *holding period* of the like-kind property given up carries over and "tacks on" to the holding period of the like-kind property received. For any boot received, the holding period will begin from the date of the exchange.

V.   Involuntary Conversions -- § 1033
A.   General Scheme
1.   This relief provision specifies that if a taxpayer suffers an involuntary conversion of property, he or she may postpone recognition of *gain* (but not loss) realized from the conversion.
2.   The basic rules of the provision follow.
a.   If the amount realized (e.g., from insurance proceeds) exceeds the amount reinvested in replacement property, realized gain is recognized to the extent of the *excess*.
b.   If the amount reinvested in replacement property equals or exceeds the amount realized, realized gain is *not* recognized.
B.   Involuntary Conversion Defined -- An *involuntary conversion* is the result of the complete or partial destruction, theft, seizure, requisition or condemnation, or the sale or exchange under threat or imminence of requisition or condemnation of the taxpayer's property.
C.   Computing the Amount Realized -- The amount realized from a condemnation of property generally includes only the amount received as compensation for the property. Amounts designated as *severance damages* are not generally included as part of the amount realized. Such severance damage awards reduce the basis of the property.
D.   Replacement Property
1.   A basic requirement is that the replacement property be *similar or related in service or use* to the involuntarily converted property. This rule is more restrictive than the § 1031 like-kind rules.

        2.   *Owner-investors* are subject to the *taxpayer use test* in selecting qualified replacement property. That is, the replacement property must be used by the taxpayer in a similar endeavor.

        3.   Replacement property is subject to the *functional use test* if acquired by *owner-users*. This test requires that the taxpayer's use of the replacement property and the involuntarily converted property be the same.

        4.   Business or investment realty need only be replaced by like-kind property if it has been condemned.

  E.   Time Limitation on Replacement -- The taxpayer has a two-year period (three years for condemnation of realty used in a trade or business or held for investment) to replace the property after the close of the taxable year in which any gain is realized from the involuntary conversion.

  F.   Nonrecognition of Gain

        1.   If the conversion is made *directly* into replacement property rather than into money, then the nonrecognition of realized gain is *mandatory* and the basis of the replacement property is the same as the adjusted basis of the converted property.

        2.   If the conversion is first into money and then into property, which is the usual situation, then the provision is *elective*. In such case, the basis of the replacement property is its cost *less* postponed gain.

        3.   The provision applies *only* to the nonrecognition of gains. Losses are recognized if the property is held for business or income-producing purposes or the conversion is the result of a personal casualty.

  G.   Involuntary Conversion of a Personal Residence

        1.   The tax consequences of an involuntary conversion of a personal residence depend on whether a gain or loss results and whether the conversion is due to a condemnation or a casualty.

        2.   Special tax relief is allowed for taxpayers whose principal residence (and/or its contents) is involuntarily converted in a Presidentially declared Federal disaster area.

        3.   Loss Situations

            a.   If a loss is due to a *condemnation*, the realized loss is not recognized.

            b.   If a loss is due to a *casualty*, the loss is recognized but is subject to the personal casualty loss limitations.

        4.   Gain Situations -- If a gain results from a *casualty, theft, or condemnation*, the taxpayer may defer the gain under § 1033 or exclude the gain under § 121. In certain situations, the taxpayer may use both the § 121 exclusion of gain and the § 1033 postponement of gain provisions.

  H.   Reporting Considerations -- Even though a taxpayer may have elected to postpone a gain, the facts of the transaction should be disclosed in the taxpayer's return.

VI.   Sale of a Residence -- § 121

  A.   Because a taxpayer's *personal residence* is a personal use asset, a loss realized from its sale is not recognized. However, subject to the exclusion under § 121, any gain realized is subject to taxation. The amount of the exclusion is $250,000, and $500,000 in certain situations involving married couples.

  B.   Requirements for Exclusion Treatment

        1.   At the date of sale, the property must have been *owned* and *used* by the taxpayer as the principal residence for at least two years during the 5-year

period ending on the date of sale.   Thus, this exclusion is available even if the property is not the taxpayer's personal residence at the time of the sale.

2. The Code, however, generally precludes the application of § 121 to any sales occurring within two years of the provision's last use.

3. However, to mitigate potential hardship in situations that are beyond the control of the taxpayer, the two year ownership and use requirements may be waived in the following events.

    a. Change of employment.

    b. Health.

    c. Other unforeseen circumstances, to the extent provided in the Regulations.

However, under this relief provision, the full § 121 exclusion is not available.

The § 121 personal residence provision works to protect the gains accumulated over time by taxpayers who live according to the "American Dream" (i.e., they keep moving into bigger and bigger houses during their working years, and then they retire to an apartment or care facility at the end of their careers). Under this scenario, no gain (or loss) on home sales will ever be recognized by the typical homeowner over his or her lifetime.

C. Calculation of the Amount of the Exclusion

  1. General Provisions

    a. The amount of the exclusion available on the sale of a personal residence is $250,000.

    b. Realized gain is calculated in the normal manner. Therefore, *amount realized* includes items such as the following, but does not include repair and maintenance expenses incurred as an aid in selling the property.

      (1) Advertising costs.

      (2) Real estate broker commissions.

      (3) Legal fees in connection with the sale.

      (4) Loan placement fees.

  2. Effect on Married Couples -- If a married couple files a joint return, the $250,000 amount is increased to $500,000 when the following requirements are satisfied.

    a. Either spouse meets the at least two years *ownership* requirement.

    b. Both spouses meet the at least two years *use* requirement.

    c. Neither spouse is ineligible for the exclusion on the sale of the current residence because of the sale of a prior personal residence within the prior two years.

  3. Relief Provision – If the relief provisions discussed above apply, the § 121 exclusion amount ($250,000 or $500,000) is multiplied by a fraction, the numerator of which is the number of qualifying months and the denominator of which is 24 months. The resulting amount is the excluded gain.

           4.   Basis of New Residence – As § 121 is an exclusion provision rather than a gain deferral provision, the basis of a new residence is its cost.

    D.   Principal Residence

           1.   For this provision to apply, the residence must be the taxpayer's *principal residence*. The residence must have been owned and used by the taxpayer as the principal residence during at least two years during the 5-year window prior to the sale.

           2.   Whether a residence is the taxpayer's principal residence "… depends upon all of the facts and circumstances in each case."

           3.   A residence does not have to be a house in the traditional sense. It can be a houseboat, a house trailer, or a motor home.

    E.   Involuntary Conversion and Using § 121 and § 1033 – A taxpayer can use both the § 121 exclusion of gain provision and the § 1033 postponement of gain provision. The taxpayer initially can elect to exclude realized gain under § 121 to the extent of the statutory amount; then, a qualified replacement of the residence under § 1033 can be used to postpone the remainder of realized gain.

If a taxpayer attempting to sell his or her personal residence is in the midst of a slow real estate market, the residence can be rented temporarily (while still trying to sell the home) without jeopardizing the gain exclusion. In addition, a tax loss resulting from the rental activity may be available.

VII.   Other Nonrecognition Provisions

    A.   Exchange of Stock for Property -- § 1032 -- No gain or loss is recognized by a corporation when it deals in its own stock.

    B.   Certain Exchanges of Insurance Policies -- § 1035 -- No gain or loss is recognized as a result of the following exchanges.

           1.   The exchange of life insurance contracts.

           2.   The exchange of life insurance contracts for endowment or annuity contracts.

           3.   The exchange of certain endowment contracts.

           4.   The exchange of endowment contracts for annuity contracts.

           5.   The exchange of annuity contracts.

    C.   Exchange of Stock for Stock of the Same Corporation -- § 1036 -- No gain or loss is recognized from the exchange of common stock solely for common stock or from the exchange of preferred stock solely for preferred stock.

    D.   Certain Reacquisitions of Real Property -- § 1038 -- Although gain may be recognized to a limited extent, no loss is recognized from the repossession of real property which is sold on an installment basis.

    E.   Transfer of Property Between Spouses Incident to Divorce -- § 1041 -- Property transfers made between *spouses* or *former spouses incident to a divorce* are nontaxable transactions. The recipient has a carryover basis in the property received.

    F.   Rollovers into Specialized Small Business Investment Companies -- § 1044 -- If the amount realized on the sale of publicly traded securities is reinvested in the common stock or partnership interest of a specialized small business investment company, the realized gain, subject to limitations, is not recognized. Any amount not reinvested will trigger the recognition of the realized gain on the sale.

G. Rollover of Gain from Qualified Small Business Stock into Another Qualified Business Stock -- § 1045

   a. Realized gain from the sale of qualified small business stock held for more than six months many be postponed if the taxpayer acquires other qualified small business stock within 60 days.

   b. Any amount not reinvested will trigger the recognition of the realized gain on the sale to the extent of the deficiency.

   c. In calculating the basis of the acquired qualified small business stock, the amount of the purchase price is reduced by the amount of the postponed gain.

TEST FOR SELF-EVALUATION -- CHAPTER 13

True or False

Indicate which of the following statements are true or false by circling the correct answer.

T   F   1. Realized gain or loss is measured by the difference between the amount realized from the sale or other disposition of property and the property's adjusted basis on the date of disposition.

T   F   2. Depreciation is an example of a capital recovery.

T   F   3. Realized gains and losses are always recognized for tax purposes.

T   F   4. The basis of property received by a gift is assigned depending on the date of the gift, gift tax paid (if any), the basis of the property to the donor, and the fair market value of the property on the date of the gift.

T   F   5. The basis of property received by gift is dependent on whether the property is later sold at a gain or a loss.

T   F   6. The basis of property acquired from a decedent is always its fair market value at the date of the decedent's death.

T   F   7. The holding period of property acquired from a decedent is always deemed to be long-term.

T   F   8. The like-kind exchange provisions under § 1031 are mandatory.

T   F   9. The nonrecognition provisions for involuntary conversions apply only to gains.

T   F   10. A realized loss on the sale of a personal residence is never recognized.

T   F   11. Like-kind treatment under § 1031 is not available for exchanges of partnership interests.

T   F   12. A personal casualty loss deduction pertaining to one's personal residence does not reduce the property's basis.

T   F   13. The wash sale rules disallow the recognition of realized gains and losses in certain sales or exchanges of stock or securities.

T   F   14. An exchange of idle farmland for an apartment building could qualify as a nontaxable like-kind exchange.

T   F   15. A bakery destroyed in a fire could be replaced by its owner-user with idle farmland in a qualifying nontaxable involuntary conversion.

T   F   16. The use of the involuntary conversion provision allowing for the deferral of gain recognition is always elective.

T   F   17.   The tax consequences of the involuntary conversion of a personal residence depend on whether a realized loss or gain results.

T   F   18.   The opportunity to exclude the recognition of gain under § 121 is only available if both the old and new residences qualify as the taxpayer's principal residence.

T   F   19.   The opportunity available to taxpayers to exclude gain on the sale or exchange of their personal residence is limited to $250,000.

T   F   20.   In computing the amount realized on the sale of a personal residence, expenses such as broker commissions and repairs incurred to aid the sale are taken into account.

Fill-in-the-Blanks

Complete the following statements with the appropriate word(s) or amount(s).

1.   If a taxpayer sells his or her principal residence, the taxpayer may exclude up to _____ (_____ in the case of certain married couples) of the gain realized.

2.   On dispositions due to involuntary conversions, _____, but not _____ may be deferred.

3.   The basis of property received by a beneficiary from a decedent's estate generally is equal to the _____ of the property on the date of the decedent's death.

4.   For property received by gift, if the donee ultimately disposes of the property in a transaction that results in a gain, the basis of the property to the donee is the same as the _____.

5.   A(n) _____ is the result of the complete or partial destruction, theft, seizure, requisition or condemnation, or the sale or exchange under threat or imminence of requisition or condemnation of the taxpayer's property.

6.   The basis of like-kind property received in an exchange is its fair market value _____ postponed gain or _____ postponed loss.

7.   In like-kind exchanges, realized gain is recognized if _____ is received.

8.   The _____ rules specify that if a taxpayer sells or exchanges stock or securities and within _____ days before or after the date of such sale or exchange acquires substantially identical stock or securities, any loss realized from the sale or exchange is not recognized.

9.   The holding period of property acquired by gift begins on the date the property was acquired by the donor if the donor's _____ is the basis to the donee. The holding period begins on the date of the gift if the property's _____ serves as the basis to the

donee.

10.   Section 1031 requires the recognition of gain in some situations, but only if _____ is
       received by the taxpayer and only if _____ is realized on the transaction.

11.   A like-kind exchange between related parties may lose its nonrecognition status if, within
       _____ years of the exchange, one of the parties disposes of the property it acquired.

12.   For personal property converted to business or income-producing use, the loss basis is
       the lower of the property's _____ or _____ on the date of conversion, while the
       gain basis is the property's _____ on the date of conversion.

13.   If the amount realized from a sale or other disposition of property received by gift is
       _____ the basis for loss and the basis for gain, no gain or loss is realized.

14.   Under the involuntary conversion rules, the _____ test applies to owner-users and
       the _____ test applies to owner-investors.

15.   In general, the _____ doctrine provides that a taxpayer is entitled to recover the cost
       or other original basis of property acquired and is not taxed on that amount.

Multiple Choice

Choose the best answer for each of the following questions.

_____   1.   Edward exchanged an apartment house held for investment for unimproved land
               to be held for investment. The old property had an adjusted basis of $80,000 and
               a fair market value of $140,000 and the new property has a fair market value of
               $100,000. As a part of the exchange, Edward received $10,000 cash and the
               other party to the exchange assumed a $30,000 mortgage on the old property.
               Calculate Edward's recognized gain.
               a. $0.
               b. $30,000.
               c. $40,000.
               d. $60,000.
               e.   None of these choices.

_____   2.   Edward exchanged an apartment house held for investment for unimproved land
               to be held for investment. The old property had an adjusted basis of $80,000 and
               a fair market value of $140,000 and the new property has a fair market value of
               $100,000. As a part of the exchange, Edward received $10,000 cash and the
               other party to the exchange assumed a $30,000 mortgage on the old property.
               What would be Edward's basis in the new property?
               a. $80,000.
               b. $90,000.
               c. $100,000.
               d. $110,000.
               e.   None of these choices.

_____   3.   Catherine was given a parcel of land this year. The donor had originally purchased the land for $15,000; however, on the date of the land's transfer, the value of the land was $32,000 and amount of the taxable gift was $20,000. Assume the gift tax paid by the donor on the transaction was $2,000. The basis of the property to Catherine, if the property were to later be sold at a gain, would be what amount?

a. $15,000.
b. $16,700.
c. $17,000.
d. $20,000.
e.   Some other amount.

_____   4.   Mitchell inherited some prime horse grazing land this year from his long-lost uncle. The uncle had purchased the land in 1978 for $25,000, and over the years, the uncle had added over $16,000 of improvements to the land. The fair market value of the property at the date of the uncle's death was $75,000. The basis of the property in Mitchell's hands would be what amount?

a. $25,000.
b. $41,000.
c. $75,000.
d.   Some other amount.

_____   5.   Mitchell inherited some prime horse grazing land this year from his long-lost uncle. The uncle had purchased the land in 1978 for $25,000, and over the years, the uncle had added over $16,000 of improvements to the land. The fair market value of the property at the date of the uncle's death was $40,000. Mitchell sold the land five months later for $45,000. Assuming the estate made no special elections, Mitchell's basis of the property would be what amount?

a. $25,000.
b. $40,000.
c. $41,000.
d. $45,000.
e.   Some other amount.

_____   6.   Mitchell inherited some prime horse grazing land this year from his long-lost uncle. The uncle had purchased the land in 1978 for $25,000, and over the years, the uncle had added over $16,000 of improvements to the land. The fair market value of the property at the date of the uncle's death was $40,000. Mitchell sold the land five months later for $45,000. Assuming the estate made no special elections, Mitchell will recognize the following on the sale of the land (assumed to be held for investment).

a.   Short-term capital gain of $4,000.
b.   Short-term capital gain of $5,000.
c.   Long-term capital gain of $4,000.
d.   Long-term capital gain of $5,000.
e.   Some other answer.

_____   7.   The following statement regarding the § 121 exclusion on the sale of a principal residence is *true*.

a.   Unlimited in terms of the amount of gain that can be excluded.
b.   No stated limit on the number of times the provision may be used during a taxpayer's lifetime.

c.   Applies to both gains and losses.
d.   Available on the sale of principal residential property only if the property had formerly been used and owned by the taxpayer as his principal residence for three years during the five year period ending on the date of the sale.
e.   None of these choices is true.

_____ 8.   The permanent exclusion available to single taxpayers on the sale of a principal residence is limited to what amount?
a. $100,000.
b. $125,000.
c. $250,000.
d.   The amount of recognized gain.
e.   None of these choices.

_____ 9.   Douglas sold an apartment building this year that had an adjusted basis of $150,000. The buyer agreed to pay $60,000 in cash, agreed to take the title to the building subject to the $140,000 mortgage on the building, and agreed to pay $50,000 plus interest at the current market rate one year from the date of the sale. What is Douglas's gain or loss realized on the sale?
a. $34,000 loss realized.
b. $40,000 loss realized.
c. $100,000 gain realized.
d. $106,000 gain realized.
e.   None of these choices.

_____ 10.   Select the *incorrect* statement.
a.   The cost on the date of acquisition plus capital additions less capital recoveries equals the adjusted basis of property on date of disposition.
b.   The amount realized from the sale of property includes related liabilities assumed by the buyer.
c.   When a taxpayer acquires multiple assets in a lump-sum purchase, the taxpayer must allocate the cost among the individual assets because some may be depreciable and others not.
d.   Gift taxes paid by the donor that are attributable to the net unrealized appreciation up to the date of the gift are subtracted from the basis of the property given to the donee.

_____ 11.   This year, David made gifts to his two daughters, Sarah and Emily. To Sarah he gave 100 shares of ABC stock that had a basis to him of $5,000 and a fair market value of $4,000 at the date of the gift. To Emily he gave XYZ stock that had a basis of $3,000 and a fair market value of $4,000 at the date of the gift. Late in the same year, both Sarah and Emily sold their gifts to unrelated third parties for $3,500 and $4,500, respectively. What gains or losses must Sarah and Emily recognize in the year of disposition?

	Sarah	Emily
a.	$1,500 loss	$1,500 gain.
b.	$500 loss	$500 gain.
c.	$0 gain or loss	$1,500 gain.
d.	$500 loss	$1,500 gain.

e. $1,500 loss $500 gain.

___ 12.   This year, Ralph gave his son common stock with a fair market value of $50,000.
          He had purchased the stock four years earlier for $20,000. The son
          subsequently sells the stock to an unrelated third party late in the current year for
          $40,000. The son should recognize a gain or loss this year of the following.
          a.   No gain or loss.
          b. $20,000 gain.
          c. $10,000 loss.
          d.   None of these choices.

___ 13.   Which of the following statements is *incorrect*?
          a.   Real business property which has been condemned may be replaced by
                 "like-kind" property within three years and qualify for treatment under
                 involuntary conversion rules.
          b.   In involuntary conversions and "like-kind" exchanges, the recognized gain
                 may never exceed the realized gain.
          c.   A taxpayer who sells property because of threat of condemnation may
                 defer gain on a sale under the involuntary conversion rules.
          d.   A taxpayer who exchanges a tract of land held for investment for an
                 apartment building may elect to either recognize gain on the exchange or
                 defer gain under the like-kind rules.
          e.   None of these choices is incorrect.

REFER TO THE FOLLOWING INFORMATION WHEN ANSWERING THE ITEMS BELOW.

___ 14.   Robert sells his home (where he had lived for the past 10 years) for $100,000 on
          July 1. The real estate agent's commission is 5 percent of the sales price. On
          July 15 he pays $2,000 for painting and ordinary repairs. He pays $1,000 more
          on September 30 for additional fix-up repairs. The adjusted basis of his old home
          is $50,000. On July 30 he buys a new home for $80,000. The realized gain on
          the sale of his home is the following.
          a. $50,000.
          b. $45,000.
          c. $43,000.
          d. $42,000.
          e.   None of these choices.

___ 15.   The adjusted basis of Robert's new home is what amount?
          a. $30,500.
          b. $44,500.
          c. $49,500.
          d. $80,000.
          e.   None of these choices.

___ 16.   Robert may exclude gain of the following amount.
          a. $42,000.
          b. $45,000.
          c. $50,000.
          d. $250,000.

e.   None of these choices.

___ 17.   Patrick Co. and Mitchell Co. exchanged machinery used in their separate businesses. Patrick Co. transferred to Mitchell Co. a machine with an adjusted basis of $150,000 (FMV $300,000) which was subject to a mortgage of $60,000 (assumed by Mitchell Co.). In return Patrick Co. received a machine with a FMV of $190,000 (adjusted basis $100,000) and cash of $50,000. What is Patrick Co.'s recognized gain?
   a. $50,000.
   b. $60,000.
   c. $110,000.
   d. $150,000.
   e.   None of these choices.

___ 18.   Joseph purchased stock in Ace Corporation for $45,000 in 1972. In January of 1982, when the stock was worth $15,000, he gave it to his son, Marvin. In January of 2006, Marvin sold the stock for $18,500. How much gain or loss should Marvin recognize in 2006?
   a. $0 gain or loss.
   b. $3,500 gain.
   c. $26,500 loss.
   d. None of these choices.

___ 19.   An apartment building held for rental purposes owned by Britton was condemned by the state on September 12, 2003. However, the condemnation award was not received until February 26, 2004. In order to defer any gain realized on the involuntary conversion, what is the latest date on which Britton can purchase qualified replacement property?
   a.   September 12, 2005.
   b.   September 12, 2006.
   c.   December 31, 2006.
   d.   February 26, 2007.
   e.   December 31, 2007.
   f.   None of these choices.

___ 20.   On January 7, 2006, Susan sold a vacant lot for $65,000. She had received the lot from the estate of her father who died on September 9, 2005, when the land had a fair market value of $63,000. Susan's father had purchased the land in 1985 for $47,500. What is Susan's basis in the lot?
   a. $63,000.
   b. $47,500.
   c. $0.
   d.   None of these choices.

___ 21.   On January 7, 2006, Susan sold a vacant lot for $65,000. She had received the lot from the estate of her father who died on September 9, 2005, when the land had a fair market value of $63,000. Susan's father had purchased the land in 1985 for $47,500. What is Susan's holding period for the lot?
   a.   Long-term.
   b.   Mid-term.

    c.   Short-term.

    d.   The classification is always irrelevant in the situation when receiving property from a decedent.

    e.   None of these choices.

____ 22.   The following information applies to the acquisition of new machinery received by Al in a like-kind exchange. Al is a self-employed bricklayer, and the machine is used 100 percent in his business.

Original cost of machinery traded in	$17,000
Adjusted basis of machinery traded in	7,000
FMV of new machinery	21,000
Cash payment made by Al	12,000

What amount of gain must Al recognize on the exchange?
    a. $0.
    b. $2,000.
    c. $4,000.
    d. $9,000.
    e.   None of these choices.

____ 23.   In October 1976, John bought 50 shares of common stock in BC Coal Co. for $11,000. In December 1984, when the fair market value of the shares was $8,000, he gave them to his son, Bob. This year in January, Bob sold the stock for $14,000. How much gain should Bob report this year?
    a. $0.
    b. $3,000.
    c. $6,000.
    d.   None of these choices.

____ 24.   Willie died this year leaving his entire estate to his sister, Beth. The executor of Willie's estate properly made the alternate valuation date election. Willie's estate included 1,000 shares of ABC Co. stock for which Willie's basis was $200,000. The stock was distributed to Beth seven months after Willie's death. Fair market values for the stock were as indicated.

On the date of Willie's death	$356,000
Six months after Willie's death	270,000
Seven months after Willie's death	272,000

What is Beth's basis in the stock?
    a. $200,000.
    b. $270,000.
    c. $272,000.
    d. $356,000.
    e.   None of these choices.

____ 25.   Joe converted his personal residence to rental property. At the time of the conversion, the property had an adjusted basis of $75,000 (land $5,000, building $70,000) and a fair market value of $50,000 (land $5,000, building $45,000). What is Joe's gain basis, loss basis, and basis for depreciation?

a.   Gain basis $50,000; loss basis $50,000; depreciation basis $50,000.
b.   Gain basis $50,000; loss basis $75,000; depreciation basis $45,000.
c.   Gain basis $75,000; loss basis $50,000; depreciation basis $45,000.
d.   Gain basis $75,000; loss basis $75,000; depreciation basis $70,000.
e.   None of these choices.

Code Section Recognition

Several important sections of the Internal Revenue Code are described below. Indicate, by number, the appropriate Code section.

1.   _____ Gains and losses are not recognized on a like-kind exchange.

2.   _____ Gains are not recognized on involuntary conversions.

3.   _____ The permanent exclusion of gain on the disposition of a principal residence is provided.

Short Answer

1.   Calculate the gain or loss recognized on the disposition of the properties in the following transactions.

a.   Judy disposes of stock for $5,000 that had been received as a gift 5 years ago when its value was $3,000. The donor purchased the stock for $2,000 and paid no gift tax on the transfer.

b.   Judy disposes of stock for $5,000 that had been received as a gift 5 years ago when its value was $3,000. The donor purchased the stock for $4,000 and paid no gift tax on the transfer.

c.   Judy disposes of stock for $2,000 that had been received as a gift 5 years ago when its value was $3,000. The donor purchased the stock for $4,000 and paid no gift tax on the transfer.

2.   Fran, who is 42 years of age, sells her personal residence for $150,000 during the current year. She had received the house eight years ago as a bequest from her mother when it was worth $115,000. Her mother had purchased the home 20 years prior to her death for $45,000. Fran incurred selling expenses (commissions) of $7,500 and fix-up expenses of $2,000. Following the sale of her old residence, Fran purchases a new personal residence for $145,000. Calculate the gain or loss recognized on the sale and Fran's basis in her new home.

SOLUTIONS TO CHAPTER 13 QUESTIONS

True or False

1.   T   This is the fundamental model used in property transactions to determine the amount of gain or loss realized. [Realized Gain or Loss p. 13-3]

2.   T   Capital recoveries, such as depreciation, reduce a taxpayer's basis in property. [Capital Recoveries p. 13-5]

3.   F   Certain situations exist (e.g., like-kind exchanges) when realized gains and losses are not recognized on realization. [General Concept of a Nontaxable Exchange p. 13-22]

4.   T   Each of these factors plays a role in determining the basis of property received by gift. [Gift Basis p. 13-12]

5.   T   If the donee subsequently disposes of gift property in a transaction that results in a loss, the basis to the donee is the lower of the donor's adjusted basis or the fair market value on the date of the gift. However, if the donee subsequently disposes of gift property in a transaction that results in a gain, the basis to the donee is the same as the donor's adjusted basis. [Gift Basis p. 13-12]

6.   F   An election may be made in certain situations to value the estate using the alternate valuation date. In such cases, the basis of property to the recipient generally is its fair market value six months following the decedent's death. [Property Acquired from a Decedent p. 13-14]

7.   T   The holding period is deemed to be long term regardless of whether the property is disposed of at a gain or a loss. [Holding Period of Property Acquired from a Decedent p. 13-17]

8.   T   The like-kind exchange provisions are mandatory rather than elective. If a taxpayer desires to recognize gain or loss, the transaction must be structured to avoid the statutory requirements of a like-kind exchange. [Like-Kind Exchanges-- § 1031 p. 13-25]

9.   T   The provision is intended to provide relief to the taxpayer who has suffered hardship and does not have the wherewithal to pay the tax on any gain realized from the conversion. [Involuntary Conversions--§ 1033 p. 13-32]

10.   T   Because a personal residence is a personal use asset, a loss realized on its sale is not recognized. [Sale of a Residence--§ 121 p. 13-37]

11.   T   This is a statutory exception to the like-kind provisions. [Like-Kind Exchanges--§ 1031 p. 13-25]

12.   F   A casualty or theft may result in the reduction of the adjusted basis of property. [Capital Recoveries p. 13-5]

13.   F   The wash sale rules apply only to transactions on which *losses* occur. [Wash Sales p. 13-18]

14.   T   It is immaterial whether real estate is improved (apartment building) or unimproved (farmland). [Like-Kind Property p. 13-25]

15.   F   The functional use test would require owner-users to replace the bakery with another facility of similar functional use. [Functional Use Test p. 13-34]

16.   F   If the conversion is made directly into replacement property rather than into money, nonrecognition of realized gain is mandatory. [Direct Conversion p. 13-35]

17.   T   In addition, the tax consequences depend on whether the conversion is a casualty or condemnation. [Involuntary Conversion of a Personal Residence p.

13-36]
18.   F   Only the property *sold* must qualify as the principal residence. In fact, there is no requirement that a new principal residence be purchased. [Requirements for Exclusion Treatment p. 13-37]
19.   F   The exclusion amount increases to $500,000 for certain married couples filing a joint return. [Effect on Married Couples p. 13-40]
20.   F   The broker commissions reduce the amount realized but repair expenses incurred as an aid in selling the property are not included. [Calculation of the Amount of the Exclusion p. 13-40]

Fill-in-the-Blanks

1. $250,000, $500,000 [Calculation of the Amount of the Exclusion p. 13-40]
2.   gains, losses [Involuntary Conversions--§ 1033 p. 13-32]
3.   fair market value [Property Acquired from a Decedent p. 13-14]
4.   donor's adjusted basis [Gift Basis Rules if No Gift Tax Is Paid p. 13-12]
5.   involuntary conversion [Involuntary Conversion Defined p. 13-32]
6.   less, plus [Basis and Holding Period of Property Received p. 13-29]
7.   boot [Boot p. 13-28]
8.   wash sale, 30 [Wash Sales p. 13-18]
9.   adjusted basis, fair market value [Holding Period p. 13-14]
10.   boot, gain [Boot p. 13-28]
11.   two [Like-Kind Property p. 13-25]
12.   adjusted basis, fair market value, adjusted basis [Conversion of Property From Personal Use to Business or Income-Producing Use p. 13-19]
13.   between [Gift Basis Rules if No Gift Tax Is Paid p. 13-12]
14.   functional use, taxpayer use [Replacement Property p. 13-33]
15.   recovery of capital [Recovery of Capital Doctrine p. 13-8]

Multiple Choice

1.   c $40,000 ($10,000 cash + $30,000 release of liability); realized gain ($60,000) is recognized only to the extent boot was received. [Boot p. 13-28]
2.   a $100,000 (fair market value) - $20,000 (gain not recognized) = $80,000 [Basis and Holding Period of Property Received p. 13-29]
3.   b $15,000 + [$17,000 X $2,000] = $16,700
                    $20,000
      [Adjustment for Gift Tax p. 13-13]
4.   c   Fair market value at the date of the uncle's death. [Property Acquired from a Decedent p. 13-14]
5.   b   Fair market value at the date of the uncle's death. [Property Acquired from a Decedent p. 13-14]
6.   d $5,000 = $45,000 - $40,000   The holding period is deemed to be long-term. [Property Acquired from a Decedent p. 13-14]
7.   b   The only limitation placed on the frequency with which the provision can be used is that the residence must have been owned and used by the taxpayer as the principal residence for at least two years during the five-year period ending on the date of the sale. [Requirements for Exclusion Treatment p. 13-37]
8.   c   The ceiling on the amount of gain excludible for taxpayers who are not married is

$250,000. [Calculation of the Amount of the Exclusion p. 13-40]

9. c   Amount Realized: Cash $ 60,000
                            Mortgage   140,000
                            Note   50,000
        Total amount realized $250,000
        Less: Adjusted Basis   (150,000)
        Gain Realized $100,000
        [Realized Gain or Loss p. 13-3]

10. d   A portion of the gift taxes paid is *added* to the property's basis. [Adjustment for Gift Tax p. 13-13]

11. d   Sarah: ($500) = $3,500 - $4,000; Emily: $1,500 = $4,500 - $3,000 [Gift Basis Rules if No Gift Tax Is Paid p. 13-12]

12. b   Because the stock is sold at a gain, the donee's basis is equal to the donor's basis. [Gift Basis Rules if No Gift Tax Is Paid p. 13-12]

13. d   Because this qualifies as a like-kind exchange, the deferral of gain realized is mandatory, not elective. [Like-Kind Exchanges--§ 1031 p. 13-25]

14. b   Selling Price $100,000
        Less: Selling Expenses (Agent's Commissions)   (5,000)
        Amount Realized $ 95,000
        Less: Adjusted Basis   (50,000)
        Gain Realized $ 45,000
        [Calculation of the Amount of the Exclusion p. 13-40]

15. d   Robert's basis in his new home is its cost, or $80,000. [Basis of New Residence p. 13-42]

16. b   The gain excluded is limited to the gain realized, or $45,000. [Calculation of the Amount of the Exclusion p. 13-40]

17. c   Amount Realized: Machine $190,000
                            Liability   60,000
                            Cash   50,000
        Total amount realized $300,000
        Less: Adjusted Basis   (150,000)
        Gain Realized $150,000
        Gain Recognized $110,000
        [Boot p. 13-28]

18. a   No gain or loss is recognized because the amount realized on the sale is between the basis used to compute a gain (i.e., $45,000) and the basis used to compute a loss (i.e., $15,000). [Gift Basis Rules if No Gift Tax Is Paid p. 13-12]

19. e   Three years from the end of the year in which gain is realized (2004). [Time Limitation on Replacement p. 13-34]

20. a   FMV at date of decedent's death. [Property Acquired from a Decedent p. 13-14]

21. a   Property received from a decedent's estate is always considered long-term. [Holding Period of Property Acquired from a Decedent p. 13-17]

22. a $0; $21,000 - ($7,000 + $12,000) = $2,000 gain realized. However, because Al received no boot, the gain realized is not recognized in the like-kind exchange. [Boot p. 13-28]

23. b $3,000 = $14,000 - $11,000 [Gift Basis Rules if No Gift Tax Is Paid p. 13-12]

24. b   Value as of six months after decedent's death ($270,000), unless distributed earlier. [Property Acquired from a Decedent p. 13-14]

25. c   Note that land is not depreciable. [Conversion of Property from Personal Use to Business or Income-Producing Use p. 13-19]

Code Section Recognition

1.   1031 [Like-Kind Exchanges--§ 1031 p. 13-25]
2.   1033 [Involuntary Conversions--§ 1033 p. 13-32]
3.   121 [Sale of a Residence--§ 121 p. 13-37]

Short Answer

1.   a.   Sales price $5,000
             Less: Basis to Judy   (2,000)
             Gain on the disposition $3,000

       b.   Sales price $5,000
             Less: Basis to Judy   (4,000)
             Gain on the disposition $1,000

       c.   Sales price $2,000
             Less: Basis to Judy   (3,000)
             Loss on the disposition   ($1,000)
       [Gift Basis Rules if No Gift Tax Is Paid p. 13-12]

2.   Amount Realized ($150,000 - $7,500) $142,500
       Less: Adjusted Basis   (115,000)
       Realized Gain $ 27,500

       Recognized gain (all gain excluded under § 121) $ 0

       Basis of new residence $145,000
       [Sale of a Residence--§ 121 p. 13-37]

Chapter 14
Property Transactions: Capital Gains and Losses, Section 1231, and Recapture Provisions

CHAPTER HIGHLIGHTS

Capital gain provisions were enacted originally with the intention of helping promote the formation of capital investment and risk-taking by investors. These provisions allow for beneficial treatment of gains for noncorporate taxpayers on certain sales or exchanges of capital assets. In addition, on dispositions of certain non-capital assets (e.g., depreciable and real property used in a trade or business), the beneficial treatment associated with a net capital gain also may result. Recapture provisions, however, provide that certain gains, which might have otherwise qualified for the beneficial capital gain treatment, receive ordinary income treatment. Thus, the character of gain or loss as capital or ordinary and its impact in the tax calculation are significant factors under the law.

I.   General Considerations
    A.   Rationale for Separate Reporting of Capital Gains and Losses
        1.   Capital gains may effectively be taxed at a lower rate than ordinary gains. Therefore, separating capital asset transactions from other types of transactions is important, and required by law.
        2.   Capital losses initially offset capital gains. Only *net capital gains* receive preferential treatment.
        3.   However, if a *net capital loss* results, it is deductible by noncorporate taxpayers, but only to the extent of $3,000 per tax year. Excess losses are carried forward to future tax years.
        4.   Because of the unique treatment that applies to capital gains and losses, individual income tax forms include extensive reporting requirements for these transactions.
    B.   General Scheme of Taxation
        1.   Proper classification of gains and losses depends on the following.
            a.   The tax status of the property.
            b.   The manner of the property's disposition.
            c.   The holding period of the property.

2.   There are three possible *tax statuses* of property.
        a.   Capital assets.
        b.   Section 1231 assets.
        c.   Ordinary assets.

3.   Capital gain or loss characterization results from the sale or exchange of a capital asset. In addition, capital gain treatment can result from the sale or exchange of § 1231 assets in some cases. Otherwise, ordinary income or loss results.

4.   There are two holding periods for capital assets: short-term (one year or less) and long-term (more than one year).

II.   Capital Assets
    A.   Definition of a Capital Asset

1.   A capital asset is property held by a taxpayer that is *not* one of the following types.
        a.   Inventory or property held primarily for sale to customers in the ordinary course of a business.
        b.   Accounts and notes receivable acquired from the sale of inventory or acquired for services rendered in the ordinary course of business.
        c.   Depreciable property or real estate used in a business.
        d.   Certain copyrights; literary, musical, or artistic compositions; or letters or memoranda or similar property.
        e.   Certain US government publications.
        f.   Supplies of a type regularly used or consumed in the ordinary course of a business.

2.   The principal capital assets held by *individual* taxpayers include personal-use assets, such as a personal residence or an automobile, or assets held for investment purposes, such as investments in mutual funds, land, and corporate stock. Often, the only *business* asset that is a capital asset is goodwill.

    B.   Effect of Judicial Action

1.   Because of the way the Code defines the term *capital asset* and because of the *sale or exchange* requirement, whether capital asset treatment is appropriate has at times been uncertain. The courts have often resolved this uncertainty.

2.   The court decisions often revolve around whether an asset is held for investment purposes (capital asset) or business purposes (ordinary asset). Further, in order to make the distinction between capital and ordinary, the taxpayer's motive, or the *use* to which property has been put, may be relevant.

    C.   Statutory Expansions

1.   To help reduce uncertainty, Congress has statutorily *expanded* the scope of the general definition of what is a capital asset in several cases.

2.   If a *securities dealer* clearly identifies certain securities as being held for investment purposes by the close of business on *the date of their acquisition*, gain from their sale normally will be capital. Losses are capital if the dealer has *at any time* identified the securities as being held for investment.

3.   *Noncorporate investors* in real estate who engage in limited development activities may receive capital gain treatment to a limited extent.

III.   Sale or Exchange
   A.   For a gain or loss to receive capital treatment, a *sale or exchange* of a capital asset must occur. Although the term sale or exchange is not defined by the Code, a sale generally involves the receipt of money and/or the assumption of liabilities for property, and an exchange involves the transfer of property for other property.
   B.   Worthless Securities and § 1244 Stock
      1.   If a security that is a capital asset in the hands of the taxpayer becomes worthless during a taxable year, it is treated as a sale or exchange of a capital asset that has occurred on the *last day* of that same taxable year.
      2.   Section 1244 allows an *ordinary* loss, rather than a capital loss, on the disposition of qualifying small business corporation stock. However, the ordinary loss treatment is limited to $50,000 ($100,000 on a joint return) per year.

KEY TERMS

- Capital Gains and Losses
- Long-Term, Short-Term
- Net Capital Gains
- Worthless Security
- § 1231 Gains and Losses
- § 1231 Look-Back Rule
- Depreciation Recapture

   C.   Special Rule -- Retirement of Corporate Obligations
      1.   The collection of the redemption value of a debt obligation, such as a bond or note payable, may result in a gain or loss if the instrument was purchased at a discount or premium.
      2.   Under the general rule, the collection of a debt obligation (issued after June 8, 1997) is *treated* as a sale or exchange. Therefore, any gain or loss can be a capital gain or capital loss because a sale or exchange has taken place.
   D.   Options
      1.   The sale or exchange of an *option* to buy or sell property generally results in capital gain or loss if the property subject to the option is or would be a capital asset in the hands of the option holder.
      2.   If an option holder fails to exercise the option, the *lapse* is considered to be a sale or exchange on the option expiration date and a loss is recognized.
      3.   If an option is *exercised*, the amount paid for the option by the grantee is added to the cost basis of the property subject to the option. With respect to the grantor, the amount paid for the option is added to the selling price of the property subject to the option.
   E.   Patents
      1.   If all *substantial rights* relating to a patent are transferred by a qualifying holder, the disposition will be treated as a sale or exchange of a capital asset.
      2.   If the requirements are met, any gain or loss is *automatically* a long-term capital gain or loss regardless of whether the patent is a capital asset, whether the transfer is a sale or exchange, and how long the patent was held by the transferor.
      3.   The *holder* of a patent is usually (but not always) the creator of the invention. The creator's employer and certain parties related to the

creator do not qualify as "holders."
F. Franchises, Trademarks, and Trade Names
 1. A *franchise* is an agreement that gives the franchisee the right to distribute, sell, or provide goods, services, or facilities within a specified area.
 2. The transfer of a franchise, trademark, or trade name shall be considered a disposition of a capital asset if the transferor does not retain any *significant power, right, or continuing interest.*
 3. When the transferor retains a significant power, right, or continuing interest, the transferee's *noncontingent* payments to the transferor will be ordinary income to the transferor. The franchisee capitalizes the payments and amortizes them over 15 years.
 4. *Contingent* franchise payments produce ordinary income for the franchisor and ordinary deductions for the franchisee.
 5. The standard franchise rules also apply to sports franchises.
G. Lease Cancellation Payments
 1. Payments received by a *lessee* in consideration of a lease cancellation produce capital gains if the lease is a capital asset. In certain situations, a lessee's lease can be an ordinary asset or a § 1231 asset.
 2. Payments received by a *lessor* are always ordinary income because they are considered to be made in lieu of rental payments.

IV. Holding Period
A. The holding period of property must be determined in order to properly characterize any gain or loss resulting from its disposition as either long-term or short-term. For example, if an asset is not held for the required long-term holding period, short-term treatment is appropriate.
B. Review of Special Holding Period Rules
 1. The holding period of property received in a nontaxable exchange includes the holding period of the former asset if the property that has been exchanged is a capital or a § 1231 asset.
 2. If a transaction is nontaxable and the basis of the property to the former owner carries over to the new owner, the holding period of a former owner of property *tacks on* to the present owner's holding period.
 3. In situations involving disallowed losses, a new holding period begins when the property is transferred.
 4. The holding period for property that has been inherited is treated as long-term no matter how long the property is actually held by the heir.
C. Special Rules for Short Sales
 1. A *short sale* occurs when a taxpayer sells borrowed property and repays the lender with *substantially identical property* (e.g., other shares of the same stock) either held on the date of the sale or purchased after the sale.
 2. The general rule is that the holding period of the property sold short is determined by the how long the property used to close the short sale was held. However, exceptions to the general rule exist.
 3. The purpose of the special rule is to prevent taxpayers from engaging in short sales in order to convert short-term capital gains to long-term capital gains or to convert long-term capital losses to short-term capital losses.

Appreciating assets and long-term growth investments may be more attractive than assets that generate ordinary income thanks to the substantial difference between the capital gains and the top ordinary tax rates. The tax savings from the alternative tax calculation range from a low of 5 percentage points (10% - 5%) to a high of 20 percentage points (35% - 15%).

V.   Tax Treatment of Capital Gains and Losses of Noncorporate Taxpayers -- Taxpayers must net all gains and losses within each holding period category to determine the appropriate tax treatment.

    A.   Capital Gain and Loss Netting Process

        1.   Holding Periods for Capital Gain and Loss Netting

            a.   There are two holding periods for purposes of the capital gain and loss netting process.

                (1)   *Short-term* -- Assets held one year or less: Net short-term capital gains are not eligible for special tax treatment.

                (2)   *Long-term* -- Assets held more than one year: NLTCGs are eligible for one or more of four alternative tax rates of 5%, 15%, 25%, and 28%. The 25% gain is technically called the *unrecaptured § 1250 gain* and is related to gain from the disposition of § 1231 assets (discussed later in the chapter). The 28% rate applies to collectibles and § 1202 gain (see Chapter 5).

            b.   When the net long-term capital gain exceeds net short-term capital loss, a net capital gain (NCG) exists. A NCG qualifies for beneficial alternative tax treatment.

            c.   Because of the different holding periods and the various rates that may apply, an ordering procedure is required to net the capital gains and losses against each other. Consequently, many unique final results of the ordering procedure can occur.

        2.   Use of Capital Loss Carryovers

            a.   A short-term capital loss carryover to the current year retains its character as short-term and is combined with the short-term items of the current year.

            b.   A long-term net capital loss carries over as a long-term capital loss and is combined with the current long-term items.

        3.   Collectibles do not qualify for the 5%/15% alternative tax and include items such as works of art, rugs or antiques, metals and gems, stamps, alcoholic beverages, and most coins.

    B.   Qualified Dividend Income -- Dividends paid from current or accumulated earnings and profits of domestic and certain foreign corporations are eligible to be taxed at the 5%/15% long-term capital gain rates if they constitute qualified dividend income. See Chapter 4.

    C.   Alternative Tax on Net Capital Gain

        1.   The alternative tax is the special calculation that provides preferential treatment for net capital gains. This applies only if taxable income includes net capital gain.

2. The net capital gain is made up of various *rate layers*. The layers are taxed in the following order: 25% gain, 28% gain, the 5% portion of the 5%/15% gain, and then the 15% portion of the 5%/15% gain.

3. The alternative tax computation allows the taxpayer to pay the lower of the regular tax or the alternative tax on each layer of net capital gain or portion of each layer of net capital gain.

D. Treatment of Capital Losses

1. The determination of *net capital losses* involves the same netting process as described above.

2. Net capital losses are deductible by noncorporate taxpayers, generally up to a maximum of $3,000 per year.

3. Individual taxpayers may carry over any unused capital losses for an *indefinite* period. Unused short-term capital losses carried over retain their original nature as short-term. Likewise, long-term capital losses retain their character.

4. If a taxpayer has both a capital loss deduction and negative taxable income, a special computation of the capital loss carryover is required.

VI. Tax Treatment of Capital Gains and Losses of Corporate Taxpayers -- The treatment of a corporation's capital gains and losses is different from that of a noncorporate taxpayer.

A. The capital gains are taxed at the ordinary corporate tax rates. Long-term gains are subject to a maximum rate of 35 percent.

B. No deduction against ordinary income is allowed for net capital losses. Capital losses offset only capital gains.

C. There is a three-year carryback and a five-year carryforward allowed for net capital losses. The carrybacks and carryforwards are always treated as short-term, regardless of their original nature.

VII. Section 1231 Assets

A. Relationship to Capital Assets

1. Under current law, it is necessary to identify § 1231 assets and to make the special § 1231 computations in relevant sales and exchanges.

2. Section 1231 provides that on the sale or exchange or involuntary conversion of depreciable personal property or real property used in business, *capital gain treatment* may be allowed if the transaction results in a *net gain* and the assets have been held for a period of time that meets the long-term holding period requirement. Therefore, capital gain *treatment* may result even though the applicable assets are not capital assets.

3. *Net losses* on such property, however, are recognized as *ordinary losses* rather than as capital losses. These losses are deductible *for* adjusted gross income.

B. Justification for Favorable Tax Treatment -- The scheme of § 1231 and the dichotomy of capital gain/ordinary loss treatment evolved due to economic considerations existing in 1938 and in 1942.

C. Property Included -- Property covered by § 1231 generally *includes* the following if it is held for more than one year.

1. Depreciable or real property used in business or for the production of income.

2. Timber, coal, or domestic iron ore.

3. Livestock held for draft, breeding, dairy, or sporting purposes.

            4.   Unharvested crops on land used in business.

            5.   Certain *purchased* intangible assets (such as patents and goodwill) that are eligible for amortization.

            6.   Until these assets have been held for more than one year they are ordinary assets. Only then do they become § 1231 assets.

  D.   Property Excluded -- Section 1231 property generally does *not* include the following.

            1.   Property *not* held for the normal long-term holding period (except unharvested crops and certain livestock).

            2.   Nonpersonal use properties that produce casualty losses in excess of casualty gains.

            3.   Inventory and property held primarily for sale to customers.

            4.   Other property such as copyrights, literary compositions, and certain US Government publications.

            5.   Accounts receivable and notes receivable arising in the ordinary course of a trade or business.

  E.   Section 1231 Assets Disposed of by Casualty or Theft

            1.   First, the casualty gains and losses from § 1231 assets and the casualty gains and losses from long-term nonpersonal use capital assets are determined. The gains and losses from these transactions are then netted.

            2.   If the result is a *net loss*, the gains are treated as ordinary gains, the § 1231 casualty and theft losses are deductible *for* AGI, and the nonpersonal use capital asset losses are deductible *from* AGI subject to the two percent-of-AGI limitation.

            3.   If the result is a *net gain*, the net gain is treated as a § 1231 gain.

            4.   Involuntary conversion gains may be deferred if conversion proceeds are reinvested. Involuntary conversion losses are recognized currently regardless of whether the conversion proceeds are reinvested.

            5.   Gains *recognized* from an *involuntary conversion* due to condemnation of assets held for the long-term holding period and used in business or for the production of income are given § 1231 treatment.

  F.   General Procedure for § 1231 Computation

            1.   Net all recognized long-term gains and losses from casualties of § 1231 assets and nonpersonal use capital assets. Personal use property casualty gains and losses are not subject to the § 1231 rules.

                a.   If gains exceed losses, add the excess to the other § 1231 gains for the year.

                b.   If losses exceed gains, exclude from any further § 1231 computation. Section 1231 casualty losses are deductible *for* adjusted gross income.

            2.   After adding any net casualty gains from above, net all of the § 1231 gains and losses.

                a.   If gains exceed losses, the excess is treated as a long-term capital gain.

                b.   If losses exceed gains, all gains produce ordinary income and all losses are deductible either *for* or *from* adjusted income, as appropriate.

            3.   In addition, net § 1231 gains must be offset by the *nonrecaptured* net § 1231 losses for the five preceding years (i.e., the *§ 1231 lookback*). Capital gain treatment results only after the *non-recaptured § 1231 losses*

from the preceding years have been offset.

VIII.   Section 1245 Recapture
    A.   Section 1245 was enacted to prevent taxpayers from receiving the dual benefits of depreciation deductions that offset ordinary income plus long-term capital gain treatment provided under § 1231.
    B.   Section 1245 recapture provides in general that the portion of recognized gain from the sale or other disposition of § 1245 property is treated as *ordinary income* to the extent of depreciation taken. Any gain in excess of the amount not recaptured as ordinary income may be § 1231 gain.
    C.   Section 1245 Potential
        1.   Recapture is limited to the amount of recognized gain that represents depreciation claimed on the disposed property.
        2.   Depreciation recapture rules do not apply to *losses*. Generally, the loss will be a § 1231 loss unless the form of the disposition is a casualty.

> Very few depreciable assets subject to § 1245 generate § 1231 gain upon their disposal. Section 1231 gain results only when the market value of the asset increases during its period of use. In most cases, application of an asset in a business setting consumes the asset's utility, thereby reducing its market value. Consequently, any gain realized is recognized fully as ordinary income depreciation recapture. Recapture potential typically is a very large number, approaching the full purchase price. Only unusual assets, such as those that become antiques or prototypes, show an increase in value between the acquisition and disposal dates.

    D.   Section 1245 Property -- Section 1245 property includes the following.
        1.   All depreciable personalty.
        2.   Livestock on which depreciation has been claimed.
        3.   Amortizable personalty such as goodwill, patents, copyrights, leaseholds, and professional football and baseball player contracts.
        4.   Amortization of reforestation expenditures.
        5.   Expensing of costs to remove architectural and transportation barriers that restrict the handicapped and/or elderly.
        6.   Immediate expensing of costs under § 179.
        7.   Elevators and escalators acquired before January 1, 1987.
        8.   Certain depreciable tangible real property employed as an integral part of the manufacturing and production process.
        9.   Pollution control facilities, railroad grading and tunnel bores, on-the-job training, and child care facilities on which amortization is taken.
        10. Single purpose agricultural and horticultural structures and petroleum storage facilities.
        11. Certain real property placed in service after 1980 and before 1987, including 15-year, 18-year, or 19-year nonresidential real property if the statutory percentage ACRS method is used, which is not subject to § 1250 (see below).

E.   Observations on Section 1245
1.   Section 1231 gain will not result unless the § 1245 property is disposed of for *more* than its original cost.
2.   Recapture applies to the total amount of depreciation allowed or allowable.
3.   Recapture applies regardless of the holding period of the property.
4.   Losses normally receive § 1231 treatment.
5.   Gains from the disposition of § 1245 assets may also be treated as passive gains.

IX.   Section 1250 Recapture
A.   Section 1250 recapture was enacted for *depreciable real property* for reasons similar to those supporting the enactment of § 1245. Section 1250 provides for the recapture of *additional depreciation* deducted by the taxpayer. Additional depreciation is the *excess* of accelerated depreciation actually taken over the depreciation that would have been allowed had the straight-line method been used. Section 1250 does not apply to dispositions of real property that was depreciated using the straight-line method. Thus, *since real property placed in service after 1986 can only be depreciated using the straight-line method, there will be no § 1250 depreciation recapture on such property.* Further, the recapture provisions do not apply in situations where a loss is recognized; rather, § 1231 or casualty loss treatment generally would be appropriate. Generally, § 1250 property is depreciable real property that is not subject to § 1245.
B.   Computing Recapture on Nonresidential Real Property
1.   The amount treated as ordinary income is limited to the *lesser* of the gain recognized or the additional depreciation (i.e., depreciation taken in excess of straight-line).
2.   If the property is held for one year or less, *all* depreciation taken, even under the straight-line method, is additional depreciation.
3.   Any gain not recaptured as ordinary income is treated under § 1231.
C.   Computing Recapture on Residential Rental Housing
1.   The computation of depreciation recapture on the disposition of residential realty acquired before 1987 differs from the depreciation recapture rules for nonresidential realty.
2.   Essentially, the rules for residential rental housing are the same as for other § 1250 property, except that only the post-1975 additional depreciation may be recaptured.
3.   If straight-line depreciation is used, there is no § 1250 recapture potential unless the property is disposed of in the first year of use. Thus, for real property placed in service after 1986, § 1250 will have no application unless the property is disposed of in the year of its acquisition.
D.   Section 1250 Recapture Situations
1.   Residential rental real estate acquired before 1987.
2.   Nonresidential real estate acquired before 1981.
3.   Real property used predominantly outside the United States.
4.   Certain government-financed or low-income housing described in § 1250(a)(1)(B).
E.   Unrecaptured § 1250 Gain (Real Estate 25% Gain)
1.   This gain is an element in the alternative tax computation for net capital gains discussed earlier. Unrecaptured § 1250 gain is some or all of the § 1231 gain that is treated as long-term gain and relates to a sale of

depreciable real estate. Such gain is subject to a 25% tax rate.
2. The maximum amount of this 25% gain is the depreciation taken on the real property sold at a gain. However, the gain subject to this treatment can be reduced in certain situations.

X. Considerations Common to Sections 1245 and 1250 -- Exceptions -- Recapture under §§ 1245 and 1250 does not apply to the following transactions.
   A. Gifts -- However, the recapture potential carries over to the donee.
   B. Death -- Recapture potential does *not* carry over from a decedent to an estate or heir.
   C. Charitable Transfers -- The recapture potential reduces the amount of the charitable contribution deduction.
   D. Certain Nontaxable Transactions -- In certain tax-free transactions, the recapture potential carries over to the transferee.
   E. Like-kind Exchanges and Involuntary Conversions -- To the extent gain is recognized, the nature of such gain may be governed by §§ 1245 or 1250. Realized losses are not recognized in like-kind exchanges, but are recognized in involuntary conversions.

XI. Special Recapture Provisions
   A. Special Recapture for Corporations
      1. Corporations may have ordinary income in addition to that required by § 1250 when selling depreciable real estate.
      2. The provision calls for an *ordinary income adjustment* equal to 20 percent of the excess of the § 1245 potential recapture over the § 1250 recapture amount.
   B. Gain from Sale of Depreciable Property between Certain Related Parties
      1. In general, in the case of a sale or exchange, directly or indirectly, of depreciable property between an individual and his or her controlled corporation or partnership, any gain recognized is ordinary if the property is depreciable in the hands of the *transferee*.
      2. Control for purposes of this section means ownership of *more* than 50 percent in the value of the corporation's outstanding stock or *more* than 50 percent of the capital interest or profits interest of a partnership. Constructive ownership rules apply in such circumstances.
   C. Intangible Drilling Costs
      1. *Intangible drilling and development costs* (IDC) are subject to recapture when the property is disposed of.
      2. Recapture does not apply if the property is disposed of at a loss.

XII. Reporting Procedures -- Noncapital gains and losses are reported on Form 4797, Sales of Business Property. Form 4684, Casualty and Thefts, will also be required if such transactions have occurred.

TEST FOR SELF-EVALUATION -- CHAPTER 14

True or False

Indicate which of the following statements are true or false by circling the correct answer.

T   F   1.   Net short-term capital losses are preferable to net long-term capital losses on an individual's income tax return.

T   F   2.   The principal capital assets held by individuals include personal residences, personal use automobiles, and corporate stock held for investment.

T   F   3.   If a security that is a capital asset becomes worthless during the taxable year, the resulting loss shall be treated as a loss from the sale or exchange of a capital asset on the last day of the taxable year.

T   F   4.   As a general rule, the sale or exchange of an option to buy or sell property results in capital gain or loss if the property subject to the option is a capital asset in the hands of the grantor of the option.

T   F   5.   Patents have not been given capital asset treatment because Congress believes that by doing so would inhibit technological progress.

T   F   6.   A capital asset acquired on the last day of any month must not be disposed of until on or after the first day of the thirteenth succeeding month to be considered held for more than twelve months.

T   F   7.   Special preference is provided to individual taxpayers in the taxation of net capital gains.

T   F   8.   In some situations, § 1231 treatment is available for capital assets.

T   F   9.   Gain on § 1245 property, to the extent that it exceeds all recapture potential, will be § 1231 gain.

T   F   10.   Casualty and theft gains and losses of personal use property are not subject to the provisions of § 1231.

T   F   11.   A capital asset is characterized as long-term if held for more than 12 months.

T   F   12.   The depreciation recapture rules have an impact on the *nature* of gain recognized rather than on the *timing* of the recognition of gain.

T   F   13.   For depreciable real property placed in service by a noncorporate taxpayer after 1986, the depreciation recapture rules of § 1245 apply.

T   F   14.   As a general rule, securities held by a dealer are considered to be inventory and are not, therefore, subject to capital gain or loss treatment.

T   F   15.   Dealers in securities can never hold securities as investments and have them receive capital gain or loss treatment.

T   F   16.   The treatment provided to capital gains and losses is identical for both corporate and noncorporate taxpayers.

T   F   17.   For individual taxpayers, personal use assets are never capital assets.

T   F   18.   A franchise is an agreement that gives the franchisee the right to distribute, sell, or provide goods, services, or facilities within a specified area.

T   F   19.   Short-term capital losses receive the same treatment as ordinary losses.

T   F   20.   Real property used in a trade or business is § 1231 property.

Fill-in-the-Blanks

Complete the following statements with the appropriate word(s) or amount(s).

1. _____ is some or all of the § 1231 gain that is treated as long-term capital gain and relates to a sale of depreciable real estate. The tax rate that applies to this element is 25 percent.

2. Depreciation recapture is not triggered in certain situations such as _____, _____, and _____.

3. To obtain capital asset treatment, two things are required: the transaction must be a _____ and the item disposed of must be a _____.

4. _____ acquired after 1986 and sold at a gain is not subject to the depreciation recapture rules because such property is required to be depreciated using the straight-line method.

5. The transfer of a franchise will be deemed a sale or exchange of a capital asset except when the _____ retains any significant power, right, or continuing interest.

6. The required holding period for long-term capital gains or losses is _____.

7. The holding period of property received in a nontaxable exchange includes the holding period of the former asset if the property that has been exchanged is a _____ asset or a _____ asset.

8. The excess of _____ over _____ is defined as a net capital gain.

9. The net capital loss deduction in any one year for individuals is limited to _____.

10. The statutory provision that enables the net capital gain to be taxed at special rates is referred to as the _____ on net capital gain.

11.   Net capital losses that cannot be used in the current year by a corporate taxpayer may be carried back initially for _____ years and then forward for _____ years.

12.   On the sale of stock investments by individual taxpayers, the alternative tax on net capital gains subjects such gains to a maximum tax rate of _____ percent.

13.   A business § 1231 loss incurred by an individual taxpayer is deductible _____ adjusted gross income.

14.   If the transfer of a patent meets the requirements of § 1235, any gain or loss is automatically treated as a _____ gain or loss (i.e., considered to have been held for more than _____ months).

15.   To the extent that any § 1231 gain remains after the required netting and consideration of the depreciation recapture provisions and the lookback rules, this gain is treated as

      _____.

16.   Unrecaptured § 1250 gain is some or all of the _____ gain that is treated as long-term capital gain and relates to a sale of _____.

17.   The maximum amount of 25% gain is equal to the _____ taken on the real property sold at a gain.

Multiple Choice

Choose the best answer for each of the following questions.

_____   1.   In the current year, Nancy had the following capital transactions.

Long-term gain	$ 4,000
Long-term loss	6,000
Short-term gain	8,000
Short-term loss	11,000

Before consideration of the above capital transactions, Nancy had taxable income of $32,500. Calculate (1) Nancy's current taxable income or loss after considering the capital transactions and (2) the capital loss carryforward.
   a. $27,500, $0 carryforward.
   b. $29,500, $2,000 long-term carryforward.
   c. $29,500, $0 carryforward.
   d. $32,500, $2,000 long-term carryforward and $3,000 short-term carryforward.
   e.   None of these choices.

_____   2.   Select the *correct* statement.
   a.   Noncorporate dealers in real estate routinely treat gains and losses from their business as capital transactions.
   b.   The holding period of property received in a nontaxable exchange includes the holding period of the former asset if the exchanged property is a capital or § 1231 asset.

c. With a short sale of stock, if substantially identical property is acquired after the date of the short sale and on or before the closing date, the gain or loss may be long-term.
d. In general, the sale or exchange of an option to buy or sell property could result in a capital gain or loss if the property subject to the option is not a capital asset to the holder of the option.
e. None of these choices.

_____ 3. Elizabeth had the following recognized gains and losses during the year.

- Theft loss of a painting from her home, owned for six months, net of the $100 floor, $700.
- Gain from an insurance recovery on a business machine, owned for two years and assuming no depreciation recapture potential, $3,000.
- Sale of a business machine for $40,000. The machine was purchased six years ago for $45,000. Depreciation of $8,000 was taken on the machinery prior to sale.

Calculate Elizabeth's net § 1231 gain or loss. Assume the § 1231 lookback procedure does not apply.
a. $6,000.
b. $5,300.
c. $2,300.
d. $3,000.
e. None of these choices.

_____ 4. Mitchell had the following capital gains and losses.

LTCG $15,000   STCG $20,000
LTCL 5,000   STCL 5,000

Calculate Mitchell's net long-term and net short-term capital gains.
a. NLTCG $15,000; NSTCG $20,000.
b. NLTCG $20,000; NSTCG $25,000.
c. NLTCG $35,000; NSTCG $0.
d. NLTCG $10,000; NSTCG $15,000.
e. NLTCG $10,000; NSTCG $25,000.

_____ 5. Ida and Woody are married, and both are under 65 years of age. They have no dependents. The current year's income tax facts are as follows.

Ida's salary	$ 9,000
Woody's salary	26,000
Interest income	2,000
Short-term capital gain	5,000
Long-term capital loss carryover from the previous year	4,000

What is their adjusted gross income for the year?
a. $37,400.
b. $38,000.
c. $40,000.

      d. $42,000.

      e.   Some other amount.

____   6.   Carpenter Corporation sold an automobile on March 27 for $15,000 when its adjusted basis was $12,000. The automobile had originally been purchased on the previous December 31 for $14,000. How should Carpenter Corporation report the transaction?

      a. $2,000 § 1231 gain and $1,000 ordinary income.

      b. $1,000 § 1231 gain and $2,000 ordinary income.

      c. $3,000 § 1231 gain.

      d. $3,000 ordinary income.

      e.   None of these choices.

____   7.   Carpenter Corporation sold an automobile on March 27 for $14,500 when its adjusted basis was $12,000. The automobile was purchased about 16 months ago for $14,000. How should Carpenter Corporation report the transaction?

      a. $2,500 ordinary income.

      b. $2,500 capital gain.

      c. $2,500 § 1231 gain.

      d. $500 § 1231 gain and $2,000 ordinary income.

      e.   Some other answer.

____   8.   Robert acquired nonresidential real property in 2002 to be used in his business. The building cost $70,000. *Assume* that during the time he held the building, the cost recovery deductions were $17,000. If the statutory percentage method had been available, the cost recovery deductions would have been $23,000.. If the building is sold during the year for $80,000, before considering the § 1231 lookback rules, how should Robert report the transaction?

      a. $27,000 ordinary income.

      b. $27,000 capital gain.

      c. $17,000 25%/§ 1231 gain and $10,000 § 1231 gain.

      d. $6,000 ordinary income and $21,000 § 1231 gain.

      e.   None of these choices.

____   9.   Otto gives his mother § 1245 property that was used in his business. He bought the property for $50,000 and took $25,000 in accelerated depreciation before giving it to her this year. Which of the following statements is *correct*?

      a.   Otto will recapture $25,000 as ordinary income on the gift to his mother.

      b.   When the mother later sells the property, Otto will recapture $25,000 as ordinary income.

      c.   The mother will recapture the excess of accelerated depreciation over straight-line depreciation as ordinary income on the sale of the property.

      d.   The first $25,000 of the recognized gain will be ordinary income to the mother when she sells the property.

      e.   The first $25,000 of proceeds received on the sale of the property will be ordinary income to the mother.

____   10.   Which of the following is *false* regarding § 1245 recapture?

      a.   It can reduce the amount of charitable contribution deduction if § 1245 property is donated.

      b.   It can apply to like-kind exchanges.

      c.   It does not apply to any real property placed in service after 1986.

      d.   It can apply to involuntary conversions.

      e.   None of these choices is false.

11.   Caroline had the following transactions during 2006.

January 15	Theft of bicycle she purchased for $250 on November 15, 2004. It was not insured.
February 21	Sale of personal auto for $1,000; it was purchased on January 1, 1994 for $6,000.
March 1	Sold IBM stock for $3,000; the stock was purchased on September 1, 2005 for $1,500.
March 15	Theft of a diamond necklace she received from her friend Oscar on February 15, 2005; it had a fair market value of $75,000, and an adjusted basis of $60,000; $70,000 was received as reimbursement from the insurance company.

What should Caroline report on her 2006 return under the assumption that the § 1231 lookback rule does not apply?

      a.   Section 1231 gain $11,500; itemized deduction $150.

      b.   Section 1231 gain $ 6,500; itemized deduction $150.

      c.   Section 1231 gain $10,000; STCG $1,500; itemized deduction $150.

      d.   Section 1231 gain $ 5,000; LTCG $1,500; itemized deduction $150.

      e.   None of these choices.

12.   Which is not or could not be § 1245 property?

      a.   Elevators and escalators.

      b.   Professional baseball and football contracts.

      c.   Section 179 immediate expensing of depreciable tangible personal property costs.

      d.   A copyright on § 1245 property.

      e.   All are or could be § 1245 property.

13.   On November 15, 2005, Alfred acquired 3,000 shares of stock in Heights Corporation (not a "small business corporation") for $50 per share. On March 29, 2006, the Heights Corporation stock was considered worthless. What type and amount of deduction should Alfred take for 2006 assuming no other capital transactions?

      a. $3,000 loss deduction and $147,000 STCL carryforward.

      b. $50,000 ordinary loss deduction and $100,000 LTCL carryforward.

      c. $3,000 loss deduction and $147,000 LTCL carryforward.

      d. $3,000 loss deduction and $144,000 LTCL carryforward.

      e.   None of these choices.

14.   On January 6 of this year, Jason sold some § 1245 business equipment that had an adjusted basis of $5,000. He purchased the equipment for $10,000 five years ago. If he sold it for $8,000, how should Jason treat the transaction?

      a.   Section 1231 gain of $3,000.

      b.   Section 1245 gain of $3,000.

      c.   Section 1231 loss of $2,000.

      d.   Capital gain of $3,000.

    e.   None of these choices.

15.   On January 1, Rose Marie sold machinery for $68,000. The machinery was
       purchased on January 1, four years earlier, for $60,000 and using accelerated
       depreciation had an adjusted basis of $30,000 as of the date of the sale. Using
       the straight-line method, the adjusted basis would have been $40,000. In the
       year of sale, Rose Marie should report the following.
       a.   Section 1231 gain of $28,000.
       b.   Section 1231 gain of $38,000.
       c.   Ordinary income of $38,000.
       d.   Section 1231 gain of $8,000; ordinary income of $20,000.
       e.   Section 1231 gain of $8,000; ordinary income of $30,000.

16.   Last year, Emily sustained a § 1231 loss of $4,000 and was able to deduct the
       loss in full as an ordinary loss. This year, Emily realized a $5,000 gain on the
       disposition of a § 1231 asset. Assuming there were no other property
       transactions, how should this year's transaction be treated?
       a. $5,000 capital gain.
       b. $5,000 ordinary income.
       c. $4,000 capital gain and $1,000 ordinary income.
       d. $4,000 ordinary income and $1,000 capital gain.
       e.   Some other answer.

17.   The following assets were among those owned by the Gray Corporation at year
       end.

           Delivery truck $11,000
           Inventory   15,000
           Trade accounts receivable   6,000

       The capital assets total the following.
       a. $0.
       b. $11,000.
       c. $17,000.
       d. $32,000.
       e.   Some other answer.

18.   If a § 1231 gain is incurred in the current year, to how many years must a
       taxpayer "look back" in order to determine whether any nonrecaptured net § 1231
       losses exist?
       a.   0. The lookback rule has been repealed.
       b.   3.
       c.   4.
       d.   5.
       e.   None of these choices.

19.   Black Corporation had § 1231 gains of $5,000 in the current year before
       considering the "lookback" provision. The taxpayer also had "nonrecaptured net
       § 1231 losses" from the previous five years of $3,500. What is the character of
       the gain recognized this year?
       a. $3,500 § 1231 gain and $1,500 ordinary income.

  b. $5,000 ordinary income.
  c. $1,500 § 1231 gain and $3,500 ordinary income.
  d. $5,000 § 1231 gain.
  e.   None of these choices.

20.   Gary and Gail are married and file a joint return. After offsetting their capital
      gains, what is the maximum net capital loss they can deduct this year?
      a. $0.
      b. $1,000.
      c. $1,500.
      d. $3,000.
      e.   None of these choices.

21.   On January 1 of the current year, Freddie owned the following assets.

      Personal residence $165,000
      ABC Corporation stock   6,000
      Antique automobile   12,000

      What is the total amount of his capital assets?
      a. $183,000.
      b. $177,000.
      c. $171,000.
      d. $18,000.
      e.   None of these choices.

22.   In 2002, Charlie purchased a crane for $225,000 that had been depreciated on
      an accelerated basis. Straight-line depreciation would have produced cost
      recovery deductions of $50,000 less than what was actually claimed. In the
      current year, when Charlie's basis in the crane was $150,000, he exchanged it for
      a new crane worth $275,000. What is Charlie's reportable gain on this
      transaction?
      a. $75,000 § 1245 gain.
      b. $50,000 § 1245 gain.
      c. $125,000 § 1231 gain.
      d. $0 gain.
      e.   None of these choices.

23.   Which of the following is a capital asset?
      a.   Inventory.
      b.   Machinery and equipment.
      c.   Land used as a parking lot.
      d.   Personal use automobile.
      e.   None of these choices.

24.   Craft Timber Company purchased an option to buy 100 acres of nearby farmland.
      Craft Timber Company purchased the option for $2,000 which gave it the right to
      buy the property at $200,000 at anytime during the next 3 months. If the option is
      exercised, the following treatment results.
      a.   Craft Timber Company increases its basis in the land purchased by
            $2,000 to $202,000.

        b.   Craft Timber Company deducts the $2,000 as an ordinary business expense.

        c.   The grantor of the option treats the $2,000 as the receipt of ordinary income because the land had been used to produce inventory (i.e., crops for sale).

        d.   Craft Timber Company holds an asset that can never be recovered for tax purposes until the business is liquidated.

        e.   None of these choices.

_____   25.   Brown Company purchased an option to buy 10,000 shares of stock that it planned to hold as an investment. Brown Company purchased the option for $2,000 that gave it the right to buy the stock at $200,000 at anytime during the next 3 months. If the option lapses, the following treatment results.

        a.   Brown Company has an ordinary loss of $2,000.

        b.   Brown Company has a long-term capital loss of $2,000.

        c.   Brown Company has a § 1231 loss of $2,000.

        d.   Brown Company has a short-term capital loss of $2,000.

        e.   None of these choices.

_____   26.   Net capital gain may consist of the following.

        a.   5%/15% gain.

        b.   25% gain.

        c.   28% gain.

        d.   All of these choices.

        e.   None of these choices.

Code Section Recognition

Several important sections of the Internal Revenue Code are described below. Indicate, by number, the appropriate Code section.

1.   _____   Defines a capital asset.

2.   _____   Provides detailed rules for determining the holding period of an asset.

3.   _____   Provides that in certain cases, long-term capital gain treatment applies to sales and exchanges of certain business assets.

4.   _____   Provides for depreciation recapture on the disposition of all depreciable personal property.

5.   _____   Provides for depreciation recapture on the disposition of depreciable residential realty acquired before 1987.

Short Answer

1.   Because of the two holding periods for capital assets held by individuals and the various tax rates that may apply, an ordering procedure is necessary to net the gains and losses. Describe the ordering procedure required to net them against each other.

2.   Calf Mountain Company sells depreciable property during the year that is subject to §
        1245 recapture. The property had been used for three years. The relevant data follow:

Original cost	$10,000
Depreciation taken	4,000

Determine the amount and nature of the gain or loss in the following situations.
a.   The property is sold for $8,000.
b.   The property is sold for $12,000.
c.   The property is sold for $4,000.

SOLUTIONS TO CHAPTER 14 QUESTIONS

True or False

1. F   Either of the two types of net capital losses may be used by individuals to offset up to $3,000 of other income. [Treatment of Capital Losses p. 14-25]

2. T   Personal use assets and investment assets are the most common capital assets owned by individual taxpayers. [Definition of a Capital Asset p. 14-3]

3. T   This last-day rule may have the effect of converting what otherwise would have been a short-term capital loss into a long-term capital loss. [Worthless Securities and § 1244 Stock p. 14-8]

4. F   This is true with respect to the option holder, not the option's grantor. [Sale of an Option p. 14-10]

5. F   Gains from the disposition of patents *do* receive capital asset treatment. [Patents p. 14-11]

6. T   To compute the holding period, a taxpayer starts counting on the day after the property was acquired and includes the day of disposition. [Holding Period p. 14-15]

7. T   The calculation providing this special preference is referred to as the alternative tax on net capital gains. [Alternative Tax on Net Capital Gain p. 14-24]

8. T   If § 1231 asset casualty gains and losses and the nonpersonal use capital asset casualty gains and losses are netted together and a net loss results, the § 1231 casualty gains and the nonpersonal use capital asset casualty gains are treated as ordinary gains, the § 1231 casualty losses are deductible *for* AGI, and the nonpersonal use capital asset casualty losses are deductible *from* AGI subject to the 2 percent-of-AGI limitation. [Section 1231 Assets Disposed of by Casualty or Theft p. 14-31]

9. T   However, one must remember to consider the § 1231 lookback procedure. [General Procedure for §1231 Computation p. 14-32; Section 1245 Recapture p. 14-36]

10. T   Such gains and losses of personal use property are netted separately rather than being netted with § 1231 gains and losses. [General Procedure for §1231 Computation p. 14-32]

11. T   For capital assets sold that have not been held for more than one year, short-term capital gain or loss results. If held for more than one year, long-term treatment results. [Holding Periods for Capital Gain and Loss Netting Purposes p. 14-20]

12. T   The recapture provisions only affect the nature, and not the amount or timing of gain recognized. [Section 1245 Recapture p. 14-36; Section 1250 Recapture p. 14-39]

13. F   This type of property is subject to the recapture provisions of § 1250. [Section 1250 Recapture p. 14-39]

14. T   However, capital gain or loss treatment is available for such taxpayers to the extent that they clearly identify the securities that are being held for investment (and not as inventory). [Dealers in Securities p. 14-6]

15. F   If a dealer clearly identifies certain securities as held for investment purposes, capital treatment can result. [Dealers in Securities p. 14-6]

16. F   Differences exist with respect to the treatment of both net capital gains and net capital losses. [Tax Treatment of Capital Gains and Losses of Noncorporate Taxpayers p. 14-19; Tax Treatment of Capital Gains and Losses of Corporate Taxpayers p. 14-28]

17. F   For individuals, both personal use assets and investment assets are capital
            assets. [Definition of a Capital Asset p. 14-3]
18. T   Tax consequences with respect to franchises may result with the granting of a
            franchise, a transfer by one franchisee to another person, or the renewal of a
            franchise. [Franchises, Trademarks, and Trade Names p. 14-12]
19. F   Short-term capital losses are initially netted against capital gains. Further, if a net
            capital loss results, its current deductibility may be limited. [Tax Treatment of
            Capital Gains and Losses of Noncorporate Taxpayers p. 14-19; Tax Treatment of
            Capital Gains and Losses of Corporate Taxpayers p. 14-28]
20. T   Depreciable or real property used in a business or for the production of income
            that is held for the long-term holding period is a § 1231 asset. [Property Included
            p. 14-30; Property Excluded p. 14-31]

Fill-in-the-Blanks

1.   Unrecaptured § 1250 gain (25% gain) [Unrecaptured § 1250 Gain (Real Estate 25%
     Gain) p. 14-42]
2.   gifts, charitable transfers, certain nontaxable transactions. Also, death, like-kind
     exchanges, and involuntary conversions. [Exceptions p. 14-44]
3.   sale or exchange, capital asset [Sale or Exchange p. 14-8]
4.   Real property [Section 1250 Recapture p. 14-39]
5.   transferor [Franchises, Trademarks, and Trade Names p. 14-12]
6.   more than 12 months [Holding Period p. 14-15]
7.   capital, § 1231 [Nontaxable Exchanges p. 14-15]
8.   net long-term capital gain, net short-term capital loss [Holding Periods for Capital Gain
     and Loss Netting Purposes p. 14-20]
9. $3,000 [Treatment of Net Capital Loss p. 14-26]
10. alternative tax [Alternative Tax on Net Capital Gain p. 14-24]
11. three, five [Tax Treatment of Capital Gains and Losses of Corporate Taxpayers p. 14-
     28]
12. 15 [Alternative Tax on Net Capital Gain p. 14-24]
13. for [Relationship to Capital Assets p. 14-29]
14. long-term capital, 12 [Patents p. 14-11]
15. long-term capital gain [Relationship to Capital Assets p. 14-29]
16. § 1231, depreciable real estate [Unrecaptured § 1250 Gain (Real Estate 25% Gain) p.
     14-42]
17. depreciation [Unrecaptured § 1250 Gain (Real Estate 25% Gain) p. 14-42]

Multiple Choice

1.   b   Up to $3,000 of net capital losses may be deducted per year by an individual
            taxpayer. Any unused net capital losses are carried forward to future years. The
            short-term capital losses are counted first toward the $3,000 annual limitation.
            [Treatment of Net Capital Loss p. 14-26]
2.   b   In certain nontaxable transactions involving a substituted basis, the holding
            period of the former property is tacked on to the holding period of the newly
            acquired property. [Nontaxable Exchanges p. 14-15]
3.   d   The theft of personal use property and gain from the sale of depreciable property
            (which is subject to depreciation recapture) are not included. [General Procedure

for § 1231 Computation p. 14-32]

4.   d   Since there are both short- and long-term capital gains and losses and because the long-term capital gains may be taxed at various rates, a netting procedure is required. [Holding Periods for Capital Gain and Loss Netting Process p. 14-20]

5.   b

Salary and interest		$37,000
STCG	$5,000	
Less: LTCL carryover	(4,000)	1,000
AGI		$38,000

[Carryovers p. 14-26]

6.   d   All of the gain is ordinary income because the automobile was not held for more than the long-term holding period. [Property Excluded p. 14-31]

7.   d   The gain to the extent of the depreciation claimed ($2,000) is ordinary income because of the § 1245 depreciation recapture rules. The remaining $500 gain is given § 1231 treatment.. [Section 1245 Recapture p. 14-36]

8.   c   The $27,000 gain recognized ($80,000 sales price - $53,000 adjusted basis) is treated as 25%/§ 1231 gain to the extent of depreciation taken ($17,000) and the remaining amount ($10,000) is given § 1231 treatment. The statutory percentage method of cost recovery may not be used for real property placed in service after 1986. [Unrecaptured § 1250 Gain (Real Estate 25% Gain p. 14-42]

9.   d   In the case of a gift, the recapture potential carries over to the donee. [Gifts p. 14-44]

10. e   Each statement is true. [Section 1245 Property p. 14-38]

11. e   STCG $1,500 on the sale of stock; net personal casualty gain $9,850 ($10,000 gain from the necklace - $150 loss from the bicycle, net of $100 floor). The loss on the sale of the personal auto is not deductible. [General Procedure for § 1231 Computation p. 14-32]

12. e   Each of the items could meet the definition of § 1245 property. [Section 1245 Property p. 14-38]

13. c   The loss on the stock is deemed to have occurred as the result of a sale or exchange on the last day of the tax year. Therefore, of the $150,000 LTCL, $3,000 is deducted in the current year and $147,000 is carried forward to future years. [Worthless Securities and § 1244 Stock p. 14-8]

14. b   Because the amount of gain recognized is less than the depreciation recapture potential, all of the gain is ordinary. [Section 1245 Recapture p. 14-36]

15. e   The amount of gain treated as ordinary is limited to the amount of depreciation recapture potential under § 1245. [Section 1245 Recapture p. 14-36]

16. d   The lookback rules apply. [Step 3: § 1231 Lookback Provision p. 14-32]

17. a   These types of assets are specifically excluded from the definition of a capital asset. [Definition of a Capital Asset p. 14-3]

18. d   The lookback period is five years. [Step 3: § 1231 Lookback Provision p. 14-32]

19. c   To the extent of the nonrecaptured net § 1231 loss, the current-year net § 1231 gain is ordinary income. [Step 3: § 1231 Lookback Provision p. 14-32]

20. d   Noncorporate taxpayers may deduct up to $3,000 of a net capital loss per year. [Treatment of Net Capital Loss p. 14-26]

21. a   Personal use assets and investment assets held by an individual meet the definition of capital assets. [Definition of a Capital Asset p. 14-3]

22. d   The transaction qualifies for like-kind treatment under § 1031. Further, any depreciation recapture potential does not trigger the recognition of any realized gain. [Like-Kind Exchanges (§ 1031) and Involuntary Conversions (§ 1033) p. 14-45]

23. d   Personal use assets qualify under the definition of capital assets. [Definition of a

Capital Asset p. 14-3]

24.   a   If an option is exercised, the amount paid for the option is added to the optioned property's basis. [Exercise of Options by Grantee p. 14-10]

25.   d   If an option holder fails to exercise the option, the lapse of the option is considered a sale or exchange on the option expiration date. Thus, the loss is a capital loss if the property subject to the option is or would be a capital asset in the hands of the grantee. [Failure to Exercise Options p. 14-10]

26.   d   Net capital gains can be subject to any of these rates, depending on the circumstances. [Alternative Tax on Net Capital Gain p. 14-24]

Code Section Recognition

1.   1221 [Definition of a Capital Asset p. 14-3]
2.   1223 [Review of Special Holding Period Rules p. 14-15]
3.   1231 [Section 1231 Assets p. 14-29]
4.   1245 [Section 1245 Recapture p. 14-36]
5.   1250 [Section 1250 Recapture Situations p. 14-42]

Short Answer

1.   The ordering procedure involves the following steps:

   Step 1: Group all gains and losses into short-term and 28%, 25%, and 5%/15% long-term.
   Step 2: Net the gains and losses within each group.
   Step 3: Offset the net 28% and net 25% amounts if they are of opposite sign.
   Step 4: Offset the result after step 3 against the 5%/15% amount if they are of opposite sign. If the 5%/15% amount is a loss, offset it against the highest taxed gain first. After this step, there is a net long-term capital gain or loss.
   Step 5: Offset the short-term amount against the results of step 4 if they are of opposite sign. The netting rules offset net short-term capital loss against the highest taxed gain first.

   If the result of step 5 is only a short-term capital gain, the taxpayer is not eligible for a reduced tax rate. If the result of step 5 is a loss, the taxpayer may be eligible for a capital loss deduction. If there was not offsetting in step 5 because the short-term and step 4 results were both gains *or* if the result of the offsetting is a long-term gain, a net capital gain exists, and the taxpayer may be eligible for a reduced tax rate.
   [Holding Periods for Capital Gain and Loss Netting Purposes p. 14-20]

2. a.   The property is sold for $8,000:
         Amount realized $8,000
         Less: Adjusted basis   (6,000)
         Amount of gain recognized $2,000

         Nature of gain recognized
              § 1245 $2,000
              § 1231 $ 0

    b.   The property is sold for $12,000:
         Amount realized $12,000
         Less: Adjusted basis   (6,000)
         Amount of gain recognized $ 6,000

         Nature of gain recognized
              § 1245 $4,000
              § 1231 $2,000

    c.   The property is sold for $4,000:
         Amount realized $4,000
         Less: Adjusted basis   (6,000)
         Amount of loss recognized   ($2,000)

         Nature of loss recognized
              § 1245 $ 0
              § 1231 $2,000

    [Section 1245 Recapture p. 14-36]

Chapter 15
Alternative Minimum Tax

CHAPTER HIGHLIGHTS

For most taxpayers, no special tax considerations are required beyond computing their regular income tax liabilities. For those taxpayers, the regular income tax formula applies. However, some taxpayers may be subject to the alternative minimum tax, which was designed to insure that every taxpayer with specified levels of income pays at least a minimum amount of tax. The alternative minimum tax applies to individuals, corporations, trusts, and estates, and in essence, represents a parallel tax system, separate and distinct from the regular income tax system. In order to determine which tax system applies, the income tax liability, based on the regular income tax system, is calculated along with the tentative alternative minimum tax liability, and the taxpayer's liability to the government is the higher of the two amounts.

I.   Introduction: Alternative Minimum Tax
       A.   The tax law contains incentives to encourage economically and socially beneficial behavior, and to provide relief for taxpayers in various situations. Examples of these incentives include: accelerated depreciation, immediate expensing of research and experimentation expenses, and exclusion of interest income received on debt obligations of state and local governmental units.
       B.   Because some taxpayers with large economic incomes had been so successful in reducing (or eliminating) their tax liabilities due to their use of these and other incentives, Congress felt compelled to institute a system that would alleviate the resulting sense of inequity.
       C.   The *alternative minimum tax* (AMT) was enacted as a backup to the regular income tax to insure that taxpayers who benefit from such preferential treatment under the income tax law pay at least a minimum amount of tax.

II.   Individual Alternative Minimum Tax
       A.   AMT Formula for Alternative Minimum Taxable Income (AMTI)
              1.   The AMT is separate from, but parallel to, the regular income tax system. Consequently, alternative minimum taxable income (AMTI) will differ from regular taxable income.

2.   In some cases, certain items are included in both the regular income tax and AMT computations, but the amounts are different (e.g., income from some long-term contracts).

3.   Most income and expense items are treated the same way for both regular income tax and AMT purposes (e.g., salary and alimony).

4.   Alternatively, some income and expense items are treated differently for regular income tax and AMT purposes (e.g., personal and dependency exemptions).

5.   The approach taken by the tax forms to calculate AMTI uses regular taxable income (calculated *before* the deduction for personal and dependency exemptions) as the starting point and essentially reconciles taxable income to AMTI by accounting for the differences between the regular income tax provisions and AMT provisions. These reconciling items are referred to as AMT *adjustments* and *tax preferences*. The AMTI computation is shown in Exhibit 15-1 below.

Exhibit 15-1
FORMULA FOR ALTERNATIVE MINIMUM TAXABLE INCOME (AMTI)

Taxable income

<u>*Plus*</u>: *Positive AMT adjustments*

<u>*Minus*</u>: *Negative AMT adjustments*

<u>*Equals*</u>: *Taxable income after AMT adjustments*

<u>*Plus*</u>: *Tax preferences*

<u>*Equals*</u>: *Alternative minimum taxable income*

---

6.   Adjustments may *increase or decrease* taxable income in the AMTI formula.

     a.   Many of the adjustments arise as a result of *timing differences* related to deferral of income or acceleration of deductions. Examples include differences related to depreciation calculations and immediate expensing options.

     b.   When these timing differences reverse, *negative adjustments* are made.

     c.   A few adjustments do not relate to timing differences and result in a permanent difference between regular taxable income and AMTI.

7.   Tax preferences are additional tax benefits that have been singled out in the AMTI formula. The presence of tax preferences in a given year always *increases* the AMTI base. Examples include excess depreciation on certain assets, interest on certain private activity bonds, and seven percent of the exclusion from gross income associated with gains on the sale of certain small business stock.

B.   AMT Formula: Other Components
    1.   Other formula components must be considered when moving from AMTI to AMT as shown in Exhibit 15-2.
    2.   If the regular tax liability exceeds the tentative AMT, then the AMT is zero. If the tentative AMT exceeds the regular tax liability, the amount of the excess is the AMT.

Exhibit 15-2
ALTERNATIVE MINIMUM TAX FOR NONCORPORATE TAXPAYERS

Regular taxable income

Plus or minus: *Adjustments*

Equals: *Taxable income after AMT adjustments*

Plus: *Tax preferences*

Equals: *Alternative minimum taxable income*

Minus: *Exemption*

Equals: *Alternative minimum tax base*

Times: *26% x first $175,000 plus 28% x amounts greater than $175,000*

Equals: *Tentative minimum tax before foreign tax credit*

Minus: *Alternative minimum tax foreign tax credit*

Equals: *Tentative minimum tax*

Minus: *Regular tax liability*

Equals: *Alternative minimum tax (if amount is positive)*

---

    3.   Exemption amount
        a.   An exemption of one of the following amounts is allowed in the computation of the AMT.
            (1)   Married taxpayers filing a joint return -- $58,000.
            (2)   Single taxpayers -- $40,250.
            (3)   Married taxpayers filing separate returns -- $29,000.
            (4)   These exemption amounts are scheduled to be reduced after 2005. However, Congress will likely extend them for 2006.
        b.   However, the exemption amount is phased out at a rate of 25 cents on the dollar, beginning when the AMTI exceeds a specified amount.
            (1)   Married taxpayers filing a joint return -- $150,000.

(2)   Single taxpayers -- $112,500.
(3)   Married taxpayers filing separate returns -- $75,000.

The number of individual taxpayers subject to the AMT is increasing, due in part to the fact that personal and dependency exemptions and tax brackets for regular income tax purposes are indexed for inflation, while the AMT exemption amounts and tax bracket break points are not.

4.   AMT rate schedule -- The AMT rates for noncorporate taxpayers are 26 percent for the first $175,000 of the tax base and 28 percent for the tax base in excess of $175,000. Any net capital gain and qualified dividend income included in the AMT base are taxed at the favorable tax rates for capital gains (i.e., 15% or 5%) rather than the AMT statutory rates.

5.   Regular Tax Liability -- The AMT is equal to the tentative minimum tax minus the *regular tax liability*. The regular tax liability for AMT purposes is equal to the gross income tax liability reduced by the allowable foreign tax credit. In an AMT year, the taxpayer's total tax liability is equal to the tentative minimum tax.

Currently, the AMT rates on net capital gains conform to the alternative tax rates for net capital gains for noncorporate taxpayers. Without this conformity, taxpayers enjoying a capital gain could find themselves receiving little or no benefit from the lower capital gains rate. This is because the highest statutory AMT rate is higher than the alternative tax rates for capital gains (15% or 5%).

C.   AMT Adjustments
1.   Direction of Adjustments -- With each of the adjustments, it is necessary to determine not only the *amount* of the adjustment, but also whether the adjustment is *positive* or *negative*.
2.   Circulation expenditures may be expensed in the year incurred for regular income tax purposes; however, such expenses must be capitalized and amortized ratably over a three-year period for AMT purposes. The difference between the regular income tax deduction and the amortization allowed for AMT purposes is the required adjustment for circulation expenditures.
3.   Depreciation of Post-1986 Real Property
        a.   The AMT depreciation adjustment for real property applies only to real property placed in service before January 1, 1999. Therefore, for real property placed in service after December 31,

KEY TERMS
• AMT Income
• AMT Adjustments
• AMT Preferences
• AMT Credit
• AMT Exemption
• AMT Asset Basis

1998, conformity exists between the AMT and the regular income tax depreciation calculations.

    b.   Otherwise, the difference between AMT depreciation and regular income tax depreciation is treated as an adjustment for real property placed in service after 1986 and before January 1, 1999. The AMT depreciation is computed using a life (i.e., 40 years) that is longer than that used for the regular income tax depreciation computation (i.e., 27.5, 31.5, or 39 years). Therefore, after an asset has been fully depreciated for regular income tax purposes it continues to be depreciated for AMT purposes, resulting in a negative adjustment.

4.   Depreciation of Post-1986 Personal Property – The adjustment for post-1986 personal property placed in service before January 1, 1999 is equal to the difference between the MACRS deduction and the amount of depreciation computed using the *alternative depreciation system* (ADS), which assumes longer lives and a lower rate. The taxpayer may elect to use ADS for regular income tax purposes. If the election is made, no adjustment is required because the depreciation deduction for both purposes is the same. For personalty placed in service *after* 1998, this adjustment is either reduced or eliminated because of the availability of less onerous depreciation rules for AMT purposes.

5.   The adjustment for certified pollution control facilities placed in service after 1986 and before January 1, 1999 is equal to the difference between the regular income tax deduction (i.e., the cost may be amortized over a 60-month period) and the deduction allowed for the calculation of AMT (i.e., depreciated using ADS over the appropriate class life). This adjustment is reduced for pollution control facilities placed in service *after* 1998.

6.   Mining exploration and development costs may be deducted for regular tax purposes in the year paid or incurred for exploration. However, for AMT purposes, these costs must be capitalized and amortized ratably over a 10-year period. The difference between what was deducted under the regular tax system and what would have been amortized over 10 years is the AMT adjustment. The taxpayer may *elect* the same treatment for regular tax purposes as is required for AMT purposes.

7.   With respect to research and experimental expenditures that are expensed for regular income tax purposes in the year paid or incurred, the AMT adjustment is equal to the difference between the regular tax deduction and the amount that would have been allowed if the expenditures had been capitalized and amortized ratably over a 10-year period. This adjustment may be avoided if the taxpayer *elects* to write the expenditures off over the 10-year period for regular income tax purposes.

8.   Because the completed contract method is not allowed for AMT purposes, an adjustment is required if that method is used for regular income tax purposes. The adjustment is equal to the difference between the income that would have been reported under the percentage of completion method and the amount reported using the completed contract method.

9.   For taxpayers with incentive stock options, the excess of the fair market value of stock over the exercise price is treated as an adjustment in the first taxable year in which the rights in the stock are freely transferable or are not subject to a substantial risk of forfeiture.

10.   Adjusted gain or loss -- Because the basis of property may be different for

regular income tax purposes than for AMT purposes, the gain or loss for regular income tax purposes will be different than gain or loss for AMT purposes. Consequently, a positive or negative adjustment will be required in the year of a sale or other disposition.

11. Net losses incurred on passive activities are not deductible in computing *either* the regular income tax or the AMT. However, this does not eliminate the possibility of adjustments attributable to passive activities.

12. The regular income tax NOL is modified for AMT adjustments and tax preferences with the result being the ATNOLD. Preferences and adjustment items that have benefited the taxpayer in computing the regular income tax NOL are added back, thereby reducing or eliminating the ATNOLD.

13. Itemized Deductions

   a. Itemized deductions allowed for AMT purposes are limited to casualty losses, gambling losses, charitable contributions, medical expenses in excess of 10 percent of AGI, estate tax on income in respect of a decedent, and qualified interest. Therefore, the effect of any other itemized deductions claimed for regular income tax purposes must be removed from the AMT calculation.

   b. The 3 percent cutback adjustment that disallows a portion of high-income taxpayer's itemized deductions for regular income tax purposes does not apply for AMT purposes.

   c. For AMT purposes, medical expenses are deductible only to the extent they exceed 10 percent of AGI while for regular income tax purposes, they are deductible to the extent that they exceed 7.5 percent of AGI.

   d. The AMT itemized deduction for interest expense includes only *qualified housing interest, investment interest to the extent of net investment income that is included in the determination of AMTI,* and *qualified interest on student loans.* The AMT term *qualified housing interest* has a different meaning than the regular income tax term *qualified residence interest.*

14. Other adjustments may be necessary in the computation of AMTI. Taxpayers who do not itemize deductions must include the standard deduction as an adjustment in computing AMTI. In addition, a positive adjustment is required for personal and dependency exemptions.

 Taxpayers living in high-tax-rate states, such as Minnesota, Massachusetts, and Wisconsin might be especially vulnerable to the AMT, as they depend upon the itemized deduction for state and local taxes paid to reduce their regular tax liability. This shows how a broader AMT tax base can affect taxpayers with similar income situations in different ways.

D. AMT Preferences -- Tax preferences *increase* the AMT base.

1. The percentage depletion preference is equal to the excess of the regular income tax deduction for depletion over the adjusted basis of the property at the end of the taxable year.

2. Excess intangible drilling costs (IDC) for the year are treated as a

preference item.

3.   Tax-exempt interest on private activity bonds is a tax preference item.

4.   Depreciation preference -- For real property and leased personal property placed in service before 1987, the preference is equal to the excess of accelerated depreciation over straight-line depreciation, computed on an item-by-item basis.

5.   Fifty percent of the gain on the sale of certain small business stock is excludible from gross income for regular income tax purposes. Seven percent of the excluded amount is a tax preference for AMT purposes.

E.   AMT Credit

     1.   A credit is allowed to provide equity for taxpayers when timing differences that have given rise to AMT adjustments (and an AMT liability) reverse. The *regular income tax liability* may be reduced by the AMT credit for prior years' AMT liability attributable to timing differences. The AMT credit may be carried over indefinitely.

     2.   The AMT credit is not available in connection with the following.

         a.   The standard deduction.

         b.   Personal exemptions.

         c.   Medical expenses, to the extent deductible for regular income tax purposes but not deductible in computing AMT.

         d.   Other itemized deductions not allowable for AMT purposes.

         e.   Excess percentage depletion.

         f.   Tax-exempt interest on specified private activity bonds.

If a high-bracket taxpayer is subject to the AMT in one year and expects to be subject to the regular tax the next year, income should be accelerated into the AMT year (when the marginal income tax rate is relatively lower) and deductions should be deferred into the regular income tax year (when the marginal income tax rate is relatively higher). This is the opposite of the classic income tax planning strategy of deferring income and accelerating deductions.

III.   Corporate Alternative Minimum Tax -- The corporate AMT is very similar to the individual AMT with many (but not all) of the adjustments and preferences being the same. While the corporate AMT rates and exemptions are different than those for the individual AMT, the objectives of the taxes are identical. The formula for computing the corporate AMT follows in Exhibit 15-3.

A.   Repeal of AMT for Small Corporations -- Beginning after 1997, small corporations are not subject to the AMT. Generally, a small corporation is one whose average annual gross receipts for the three-year period after 1993 is not more than $5 million. In addition, a corporation will automatically be classified as a small corporation in the first tax year of existence.

B.   AMT Adjustments

     1.   Adjustments applicable to individuals *and* corporations include the following.

         a.   Excess depreciation on property placed in service after 1986.

         b.   Excess cost recovery for pollution control facilities placed in service after 1986.

        c.   Excess mining and exploration expenditures.

        d.   Income on long-term contracts -- the percentage of completion method is required for AMT purposes instead of the completed contract method.

        e.   Dispositions of assets (if gain or loss for AMT purposes differs from gain or loss for income tax purposes).

        f.   Allowable ATNOLD (which cannot exceed 90 percent of AMTI before deduction for ATNOLD).

2.   Adjustment applicable *only* to corporations -- An adjustment applicable only to corporations is the *adjusted current earnings* (ACE) adjustment.

        a.   Corporations are subject to an AMT adjustment equal to 75 percent of the difference between ACE and AMTI before the ACE adjustment.

        b.   The adjustment can be either a positive or negative amount. Any negative adjustment is limited to the aggregate of the positive adjustments under ACE for prior years reduced by the previously claimed negative adjustments.

        c.   While ACE is similar to current earnings and profits (see Chapter 19), differences exist.

        d.   The starting point for computing ACE is AMTI, which is defined as regular taxable income after AMT adjustments (other than the ATNOLD and ACE adjustments) and tax preferences. However, other types of adjustments also are required.

C.   Tax Preferences -- Tax preference items that apply to individuals also apply to corporations.

D.   Exemption Amount

    1.   The tentative AMT, calculated at 20 percent times the AMT base, results only if the tax base exceeds the corporate exemption amount.

    2.   The exemption amount for a corporation is $40,000 reduced by 25 percent of the amount by which AMTI exceeds $150,000. The exemption amount phases out entirely when AMTI reaches $310,000.

E.   Other Aspects of the AMT -- All of a corporation's AMT is available for carryover as a minimum tax credit.

Exhibit 15-3
AMT FORMULA FOR CORPORATIONS

Taxable income

Plus: *Income tax NOL deduction*

Plus or minus: AMT adjustments

Plus: *Tax preferences*

Equals: *Alternative minimum taxable income before ATNOLD*

Minus: *ATNOLD (limited to 90% of AMTI before ATNOLD)*

Equals: *AMTI*

Minus: *Exemption*

Equals: *Alternative minimum tax base*

Times: *20% rate*

Equals: *Tentative minimum tax before AMT foreign tax credit*

Minus: *AMT foreign tax credit*

Equals: *Tentative alternative minimum tax*

Minus: *Regular tax liability before credits minus regular foreign tax credit*

Equals: *AMT if positive*

TEST FOR SELF-EVALUATION -- CHAPTER 15

True or False

Indicate which of the following statements are true or false by circling the correct answer.

T   F   1.   The maximum tax rate for individual taxpayers subject to the alternative minimum tax is 28 percent.

T   F   2.   The alternative minimum tax exemption amount for all married taxpayers filing a joint return is set at $58,000.

T   F   3.   "Adjustments" to taxable income in arriving at the alternative minimum taxable income may be either positive or negative.

T   F   4.   The adjustments that apply to individuals for AMT purposes also apply to corporations and the adjustments that apply to corporations also apply to individuals.

T   F   5.   Itemized deductions for state and local taxes and miscellaneous itemized deductions subject to the 2 percent-of-AGI floor are examples of adjustments required in the calculation of an individual's alternative minimum taxable income.

T   F   6.   A tax preference item would arise in the AMT computation if personalty acquired this year is depreciated using the MACRS method.

T   F   7.   For individual taxpayers, the personal exemption is allowed in the computation of AMTI.

T   F   8.   Both adjustments and preference items can either increase or decrease taxable income in arriving at AMTI.

T   F   9.   Interest expense incurred by individuals is fully deductible for AMT purposes.

T   F   10.   Any tax-exempt interest earned by a taxpayer is a tax preference item.

T   F   11.   The corporate AMT is calculated using the same tax rate as that which applies to the individual AMT calculation.

T   F   12.   The tax preferences that apply to individuals also apply to corporations.

T   F   13.   The AMT applies only if it produces a higher tax liability than the regular income tax computation.

T   F   14.   The AMT is based on a modification of the regular taxable income by preferences and adjustments.

T   F   15.   A negative AMT adjustment is required in the amount of the difference between qualified residence interest allowed as an itemized deduction for regular tax purposes and qualified housing interest allowed in the determination of AMTI.

T   F   16.   Alternative minimum taxable income minus the exemption equals the alternative minimum tax base.

T   F   17.   To provide equity for the taxpayer when timing differences reverse, the regular tax liability may be reduced by the AMT credit for prior years' AMT liability attributable to timing differences.

T   F   18.   The AMT exemption for corporations is $30,000 reduced by 25 percent of the amount by which AMTI exceeds $150,000.

T   F   19.   The adjusted current earnings adjustment is applicable only to C corporations.

T   F   20.   The ATNOLD is limited to 90 percent of AMTI before the ATNOLD.

Fill-in-the-Blanks

Complete the following statements with the appropriate word(s) or amount(s).

1.   A two-tier tax rate schedule applies to a noncorporate taxpayer's alternative minimum tax base: _____ percent of the tax base up to the first $175,000 and _____ percent of the tax base in excess of $175,000.

2.   The alternative minimum tax exemption amount is _____ for married taxpayers filing joint returns, _____ for single taxpayers, and _____ for married taxpayers filing separate returns.

3.   In the context of the alternative minimum tax computation, the excess tax depreciation on post-1986 realty is known as a(n) _____.

4.   The corporate alternative minimum tax rate is _____ percent.

5.   The exemption amount for a single taxpayer is phased out entirely by the time AMTI reaches _____.

6.   _____ is the sum of the regular taxable income, plus or minus adjustments, plus tax preferences.

7.   The tentative AMT is calculated only if the tax base exceeds the _____ amount.

8.   The _____ is allowed as an offset against the regular tax liability to provide equity to taxpayers when timing differences that have given rise to AMT adjustments reverse.

9.   The adjustment for certain depreciable property acquired after 1986 is equal to the difference between _____ depreciation deducted for income tax purposes and _____ depreciation deductible for AMT purposes.

10.   _____ could be either an adjustment or a tax preference item, depending on when

the related property was placed in service.

11.   The _____ applicable to noncorporate taxpayers are also applicable to corporate
        taxpayers, but some _____ differ.

12.   Corporations are subject to an AMT adjustment equal to _____ percent of the
        difference between ACE and AMTI before the ACE adjustment.

13.   A bond that produces interest income that is exempt for regular income tax purposes but
        which produces a preference for AMT purposes is known as a _____.

14.   The AMT exemption for individuals and corporations is phased out at a rate of
        _____ cents on the dollar for alternative minimum taxable income in excess of
        specified amounts.

15.   Interest on certain private activity bonds has the effect of _____ alternative
        minimum taxable income.

Multiple Choice

Choose the best answer for each of the following questions.

_____   1.   Which of the following is *not* a preference item or an adjustment for purposes of
                computing the alternative minimum tax?
        a.   Unrealized appreciation element on charitable contributions to public
                charities made during the year.
        b.   Modifications to passive activity losses deducted in computing taxable
                income.
        c.   Depreciation expense claimed for income tax purposes versus
                depreciation expense calculated over a longer life using a slower rate for
                AMT purposes.
        d.   The difference between the income reported under the percentage of
                completion method and the amount reported using the completed contract
                method.
        e.   Each of these choices is either a preference or an adjustment.

_____   2.   A married taxpayer filing a joint return has alternative minimum taxable income of
                $216,000. For purposes of the alternative minimum tax computation, what is the
                amount of the exemption?
        a. $58,000.
        b. $41,500.
        c. $40,250.
        d. $29,000.
        e.   None of these choices.

_____   3.   A single individual taxpayer has alternative minimum taxable income of $216,000.
                For purposes of the alternative minimum tax computation, what is the amount of
                the exemption?
        a. $40,250.
        b. $35,750.
        c. $25,875.

    d. $14,375.
    e.   None of these choices.

_____ 4.   Which of the following is *not* true with respect to the alternative minimum tax?
    a.   The individual AMT rate is 20 percent.
    b.   The amount of interest (other than qualified housing interest) that may be deducted in arriving at alternative minimum taxable income is limited to the taxpayer's investment income and qualified interest on student loans.
    c.   The corporate AMT rate is 20 percent.
    d.   All of these choices are true.

_____ 5.   Before any limitation, the AMT exemption amounts for taxpayers filing as single, married filing jointly, and married filing separately, respectively, are as follow.
    a. $40,250; $58,000; $0.
    b. $112,500; $150,000; $75,000.
    c. $40,250; $60,000; $40,250.
    d. $40,250; $58,000; $29,000.
    e.   None of these choices.

_____ 6.   Timothy's alternative minimum tax base for the current year is $292,500. As a result, determine the tentative minimum tax liability.
    a. $58,500.
    b. $76,050.
    c. $78,400.
    d. $81,900.
    e.   Some other amount.

_____ 7.   For the current year, Bobby and Tami's regular income tax liability on their joint return is $15,000 before considering the AMT. Their AMTI is $150,000. Determine the total amount of their tax liability for the year.
    a. $8,920.
    b. $15,000.
    c. $23,920.
    d. $39,000.
    e.   None of these choices.

_____ 8.   From your review of Fran's income tax data, you note the following.

AGI	$40,000
Medical expenses incurred	5,000
Taxable income	23,000

    Assuming that Fran is subject to the AMT this year, what is the adjustment given the information presented above?
    a. $0.
    b. $1,000.
    c. $2,000.
    d. $4,000.
    e.   None of these choices.

_____ 9.   Bill, a calendar year single taxpayer, had the following transactions.

Taxable income	$200,000
Net capital gain (included in taxable income)	50,000
Receipt of incentive stock option -- excess of current FMV over exercise price (exercisable next year)	10,000
Excess depreciation on fixed assets	50,000
Excess depletion	40,000

Based on the above, what is Bill's AMTI?
a. $240,000.
b. $290,000.
c. $300,000.
d. $350,000.
e. Some other amount.

_____ 10. Which of the following is not allowed as an itemized deduction for the individual AMT calculation?
a. Charitable contributions.
b. State income taxes.
c. Medical expenses in excess of 10 percent of AGI.
d. Qualified interest.
e. All of these choices are allowable.

_____ 11. Which of the following is an adjustment that applies only to corporations?
a. The adjustment for excess circulation expenditures.
b. The adjustment for excess depreciation on post-1986 real property.
c. The adjustment pertaining to long-term contracts.
d. The adjusted current earnings adjustment.
e. Some other answer.

_____ 12. Which of the following is an AMT adjustment?
a. Itemized deductions allowed for income tax purposes but not for AMT.
b. Net appreciation on contribution of long-term capital gain property to public charities.
c. Excess of accelerated over straight-line depreciation on real property placed in service before 1987.
d. Excess of accelerated over straight-line depreciation on leased personal property placed in service before 1987.
e. None of these choices.

_____ 13. Which of the following is an AMT preference?
a. Standard deduction if the taxpayer did not itemize.
b. Percentage depletion in excess of the property's adjusted basis.
c. Excess of MACRS depreciation over alternative depreciation on certain personal property placed in service after 1986.
d. Excess of MACRS depreciation over alternative depreciation on certain real property placed in service after 1986.
e. All of these choices are true.

_____ 14. If Green Corporation placed an office building into service in 2006 which cost $500,000 and claimed MACRS depreciation for regular income tax purposes, which of the following is true?
a. No adjustment is required this year.

          b.   A tax preference item arises from this transaction.

          c.   A negative adjustment arises this year.

          d.   If the property is held for 39 years, the adjusted basis for regular tax purposes and AMT purposes will be the same.

          e.   None of these choices.

15.   AMT adjustments for which of the following items can be avoided if the taxpayer elects to write off the expenditures for regular income tax purposes using the same method as that required for AMT purposes?

          a.   Circulation expenditures.

          b.   Depreciation of post-1986 personal property.

          c.   Mining exploration and development costs.

          d.   Accounting for long-term contracts.

          e.   All of these choices.

16.   In 2006, Kelly, a magazine publisher, incurs $33,000 of deductible circulation expenditures. This amount may be deducted in full in 2006 for income tax purposes. Which of the following is correct?

          a.   No amount is deductible for AMT purposes.

          b.   A negative adjustment of $11,000 is required in 2006.

          c.   A positive adjustment of $11,000 is required in 2007.

          d.   A negative adjustment of $11,000 is required in 2008.

          e.   None of these choices.

17.   In 2004, Richard exercised an incentive stock option (ISO) that had been granted by his employer. He had acquired 500 shares of his employer's stock for $5,000 at a time when the stock's fair market value was $15,000. The restrictions that the employer had placed on Richard's ownership of the stock lapsed in 2006. Which of the following correctly describes the treatment to Richard?

          a.   Taxable income of $10,000 is recognized in 2004.

          b.   Taxable income of $10,000 is recognized in 2006.

          c.   An AMT adjustment of $10,000 occurs in 2004.

          d.   An AMT adjustment of $10,000 occurs in 2006.

          e.   None of these choices.

18.   In 2004, Richard exercised an incentive stock option (ISO) that had been granted by his employer. He had acquired 500 shares of his employer's stock for $5,000 at a time when the stock's fair market value was $15,000. The restrictions that the employer had placed on Richard's ownership of the stock lapsed in 2006. In 2007, the stock is sold for $20,000. Which of the following correctly describes the treatment to Richard from the sale?

          a.   There is an income tax gain of $5,000.

          b.   There is an AMT gain of $5,000.

          c.   There is an AMT gain of $15,000.

          d.   There is no gain recognized for either regular income tax or AMT purposes because of the beneficial attributes of an ISO.

          e.   None of these choices.

19.   In the current year, Joyce had a net operating loss for regular income tax purposes of $50,000. This amount included the deduction for accelerated depreciation of $60,000 on real property acquired prior to 1987. Straight-line depreciation acceptable for AMT purposes would have been $45,000. Calculate

Joyce's ATNOLD carryover to the future.
a. $0.
b. $35,000.
c. $50,000.
d. $60,000.
e.   None of these choices.

_____ 20.   Blue Corporation, an oil and gas company, incurred IDC of $75,000 during the year. The amount was expensed for regular income tax purposes. During the year, Blue Corporation's net oil and gas income was $100,000. What is Blue Corporation's tax preference for IDC?
a. $0.
b. $2,500.
c. $10,000.
d. $67,500.
e.   Some other amount.

Code Section Recognition

Several important sections of the Internal Revenue Code are described below. Indicate, by number, the appropriate Code section.

1.   _____ Requires a taxpayer in certain situations to pay the alternative minimum tax.

2.   _____ All of the alternative minimum tax preference items are prescribed here.

Short Answer

1.   Indicate whether the following items are adjustments or preference items used in the calculation of AMTI.
a.   Certain itemized deductions.
b.   Tax-exempt interest on private activity bonds.
c.   Excess depreciation over straight-line depreciation on real property placed in service before 1987.
d.   Excess MACRS depreciation over ADS depreciation on property placed in service after 1986 and before 1999.
e.   Standard deduction (if taxpayer does not itemize).

2.   Shaletha, who is single, calculates her AMTI to be $238,000. Calculate her tentative minimum tax.

SOLUTIONS TO CHAPTER 15 QUESTIONS

True or False

1. T   The AMT graduated tax rates for noncorporate taxpayers are 26% and 28%. [AMT Rate Schedule p. 15-7]

2. F   The exemption amount of $58,000 is phased out at a rate of 25 cents on the dollar when the alternative minimum taxable income exceeds $150,000. No exemption is available after the taxpayer's AMTI exceeds $382,000. [Exemption Amount p. 15-7]

3. T   Most adjustments relate to timing differences that arise because of different regular income tax and AMT treatments. Adjustments that are caused by timing differences will eventually reverse; that is, positive adjustments will be offset by negative adjustments in the future, and vice versa. [Adjustments p. 15-4]

4. F   Differences (e.g., ACE adjustment) do exist between the two. [AMT Adjustments p. 15-27]

5. T   Taxes and miscellaneous itemized deductions that are subject to the 2 percent-of-AGI floor are not allowed in computing AMT. [Itemized Deductions p. 15-16]

6. F   In such situations, an *adjustment* could arise, not a *preference* item. [Depreciation of Post-1986 Personal Property p. 15-10]

7. F   The preference for personal exemptions allowed for regular income tax purposes is not allowed and, thus, increases AMTI. [Other Adjustments p. 15-19]

8. F   Tax preferences always are added to taxable income in arriving at AMTI while adjustments may be either positive or negative. [AMT Formula for Alternative Minimum Taxable Income (AMTI) p. 15-2]

9. F   Only qualified housing interest, investment interest, and qualified interest on student loans are deductible for AMT purposes. [Itemized Deductions p. 15-16]

10. F   Only tax-exempt interest earned on specified private activity bonds is a tax preference item. [Interest on Private Activity Bonds p. 15-21]

11. F   In general, the individual rates are 26 percent on the first $175,000 of the tax base and 28 percent of the tax base in excess of $175,000, while the corporate AMT rate is 20 percent. [Corporate Alternative Minimum Tax p. 15-26]

12. T   While adjustments may differ for corporate and noncorporate taxpayers, tax preferences applicable to noncorporate taxpayers also are applicable to corporate taxpayers. [Corporate Alternative Minimum Tax p. 15-26]

13. T   The taxpayer will pay whichever tax liability is greater—that calculated using the regular income tax rules or that calculated using the AMT rules. If the regular tax liability exceeds tentative AMT, then the AMT is zero. [AMT Formula: Other Components p. 15-6]

14. T   Preferences and adjustments account for the different treatment of various items for purposes of the regular taxable income and the AMT. [AMT Formula for Alternative Minimum Taxable Income (AMTI) p. 15-2]

15. F   The adjustment would be positive, not negative. [Itemized Deductions p. 15-16]

16. T   The exemption amount can be thought of as a materiality provision. As such, it enables a taxpayer with a small amount of positive adjustments and tax preferences to avoid being subject to the burden of the AMT because it is subtracted from the AMTI in arriving at the tax base. [AMT Formula: Other Components p. 15-6]

17. T   The AMT credit is applicable only for the AMT that results from timing differences. It may be carried over indefinitely. [AMT Credit p. 15-23]

18. F   The corporate exemption amount is $40,000 reduced by 25 percent of the amount by which AMTI exceeds $150,000. [Exemption p. 15-30]

19.   T   The ACE adjustment applies to C corporations (but not S corporations) and has a significant impact on both tax and financial accounting. [Adjustments Applicable Only to Corporations p. 15-28]

20.   T   A ceiling exists on the amount of the ATNOLD that can be deducted in the carryback or carryforward year. The deduction is limited to 90 percent of AMTI (before the ATNOLD) for the carryback or carryforward year. [Alternative Tax Net Operating Loss Deduction p. 15-15]

Fill-in-the-Blanks

1.   26, 28 [AMT Rate Schedule p. 15-7]
2. $58,000, $40,250, $29,000 Most commentators expect that Congress will extend these amounts for 2006, which were scheduled to decrease after 2005. [Exemption Amount p. 15-7]
3.   adjustment [Depreciation of Post-1986 Real Property p. 15-9]
4.   20 [Corporate Alternative Minimum Tax p. 15-26]
5. $273,500 [Exemption Amount p. 15-7]
6.   Alternative minimum taxable income [AMT Formula for Alternative Minimum Taxable Income (AMTI) p. 15-2]
7.   exemption [Exemption Amount p. 15-7]
8.   AMT credit [AMT Credit p. 15-23]
9.   MACRS, ADS [Depreciation of Post-1986 Real Property p. 15-9; Depreciation of Post-1986 Personal Property p. 15-10]
10.   Excess depreciation [AMT Adjustments p. 15-8; AMT Preferences p. 15-19]
11.   preferences, adjustments [Corporate Alternative Minimum Tax p. 15-26]
12.   75 [Adjustments Applicable Only to Corporations p. 15-28]
13.   private activity bond [Interest on Private Activity Bonds p. 15-21]
14.   25 [Exemption Amount p. 15-7; Exemption p. 15-30]
15.   increasing [Interest on Private Activity Bonds p. 15-21]

Multiple Choice

1.   a   Charitable contributions are allowed for AMT purposes. [Itemized Deductions p. 15-16]
2.   b $41,500 = $58,000 - [($216,000 - $150,000) X .25] [Exemption Amount p. 15-7]
3.   d $14,375 = $40,250 - [($216,000 - $112,500) X .25] [Exemption Amount p. 15-7]
4.   a   A graduated, two-tier rate schedule applies to noncorporate taxpayers (i.e., 26 percent and 28 percent). [AMT Rate Schedule p. 15-7]
5.   d   The initial exemption amounts are set by statute and subject to a phase out as AMTI exceeds certain levels. Most commentators expect that Congress will extend these amounts for 2006, which were scheduled to decrease after 2005. [Exemption Amount p. 15-7]

6.   c

AMT base	$292,500
Tentative minimum tax liability:	
$175,000 X 26%	$ 45,500
($292,500 - $175,000) X 28%	32,900
Tentative minimum tax	$ 78,400

[AMT Rate Schedule p. 15-7]

7.   c

AMTI	$150,000
Less: Exemption	(58,000)

AMT base	$ 92,000
Rate	X 26%
Tentative AMT	$ 23,920

Because the tentative AMT is higher than the regular income tax liability, the tentative AMT amount is payable. [AMT Formula: Other Components p. 15-6]

8.   b $1,000 = [$5,000 - ($40,000 X 7.5%)] - [$5,000 - ($40,000 X 10%)] [Itemized Deductions p. 15-16]

9.   b $290,000 = $200,000 (taxable income) + $50,000 (excess depreciation on fixed assets) + $40,000 (excess depletion) [Illustration of the AMT Computation p. 15-22]

10.   b   All of the items listed other than state income taxes are deductible for purposes of the AMT. [Itemized Deductions p. 15-16]

11.   d   Only the adjustment for adjusted current earnings is applicable just to corporations. All of the other items listed are adjustments that apply to all taxpayers subject to the AMT. [Adjustments Applicable Only to Corporations p. 15-28]

12.   a   Of the items listed, this is the only adjustment. [Itemized Deductions p. 15-16]

13.   b   Of the items listed, this is the only preference item. [AMT Preferences p. 15-19]

14.   a   An AMT recovery period conformity provision applies to property placed in service after December 31, 1998. Therefore, no AMT depreciation adjustment is required for the year of acquisition or subsequent years. [Depreciation of Post-1986 Real Property p. 15-9]

15.   e   The AMT adjustment can be avoided in each case. [AMT Adjustments p. 15-8]

16.   d   This difference occurs because circulation expenditures can be deducted in the year incurred for income tax purposes while for AMT purposes, circulation expenditures must be deducted over a three-year period. [AMT Formula for Alternative Minimum Taxable Income (AMTI) p. 15-2]

17.   d   For AMT purposes, the excess of the fair market value of the stock over the exercise price is treated as an adjustment in the first taxable year in which the rights in the stock are freely transferable or are not subject to a substantial risk of forfeiture. [Incentive Stock Options p. 15-12]

18.   b   The gain or loss upon disposition of the stock option is different for regular income tax purposes and AMT purposes because of the different bases under the two systems. [Incentive Stock Options p. 15-12]

19.   b $35,000 = $50,000 regular tax NOL - $15,000 tax preference item. [Alternative Tax Net Operating Loss Deduction p. 15-15]

20.   b

Intangible drilling costs expensed in the year incurred	$75,000
Minus: Deduction if IDC were amortized over ten years	(7,500)
Equals: Excess of IDC expense over amortization	$67,500
Minus: 65% of net oil and gas income	(65,000)
Equals: Tax preference item	$ 2,500

[Intangible Drilling Costs p. 15-20]

Code Section Recognition

1.   55 [AMT Formula for Alternative Minimum Taxable Income (AMTI) p. 15-2]
2.   57 [Tax Preferences p. 15-5]

Short Answer

1.   a.   Adjustment.
      b.   Preference.
      c.   Preference.
      d.   Adjustment.
      e.   Adjustment.
      [AMT Adjustments p. 15-8; AMT Preferences p. 15-19]

2.   AMTI $238,000
      Less: Exemption $40,250 - [($238,000 - $112,500) X 25%]   (8,875)
      Alternative minimum tax base $229,125
      Times: 26% X $175,000 $ 45,500
                  28% X ($229,125 - $175,000)   15,155
      Tentative minimum tax $ 60,655

      [Illustration of the AMT Computation p. 15-22]

Chapter 16

Accounting Periods and Methods

CHAPTER HIGHLIGHTS

T he computation of the income tax liability may be affected by various accounting periods and methods that are available or required to be used by taxpayers. In particular, requirements exist for the adoption and change of a tax year, various methods of accounting are available, procedures exist for changing accounting methods, and numerous requirements impact the use of the installment method and the methods of reporting long-term contracts. These issues relate to *when* income and deductions are reported by a taxpayer. These issues and the relevant restrictions that apply are discussed in this chapter.

I. Accounting Periods [p 16-2]
    A. In General -- The federal income tax determination and collection system is based on the concept of an *annual reporting* by the taxable entity. Most individuals use a *calendar year* to report income; however, a noncalendar fiscal year may be selected if the taxpayer's books are maintained on the basis of that same *fiscal year*.
    B. Specific Provisions For Partnerships, S Corporations, and Personal Service Corporations

16-1

1.   Partnerships and S corporations are subject to restrictions designed to prevent owners from shifting income from one period to another.

    a.   A partnership tax year must be the same as the tax year of the *majority interest partners*. If the majority owners do not have the same tax year, the entity must have the same tax year as its *principal partners*. Otherwise, the partnership must use a year which results in the *least aggregate deferral* of income.

    b.   Generally, S Corporations must adopt a calendar year.

    c.   However, partnerships and S Corporations can *elect* an otherwise *impermissible* year in either of the following situations.

        (1)   A business purpose for the year can be demonstrated.

        (2)   The desired year results in a deferral of not more than three months' income and the entity agrees to make required tax payments.

2.   The IRS position is that the only business purpose that would justify a fiscal year relates to the need to conform reporting to the natural business year of a business. Generally, only seasonal businesses have a natural business year.

3.   Required tax payments of a partnership or an S corporation, which are due April 15 of each year, are computed by applying the highest individual tax rate plus one percent to an estimate of the deferral period income. The deferral period runs from the end of the fiscal year to the end of the calendar year. The amount due is reduced by the amount of required tax payments for the previous year.

4.   If certain requirements are met, a personal service corporation (i.e., a corporation whose shareholder-employees provide personal services, such as medical, dental, legal, accounting, engineering, actuarial, consulting, or performing arts) may *elect* a fiscal year instead of the normally required calendar year.

C.   Making the Election -- A taxpayer makes an election for a particular tax year by the timely filing of its initial return. For all subsequent years, the same period must be used unless prior approval for change is obtained from the IRS.

D.   Changes in the Accounting Period

1.   Consent must be obtained from the IRS before a taxpayer may change his or her tax year. An application for permission to change tax years must be filed on or before the fifteenth day of the second calendar month following the close of the short period that results from the change in accounting period.

2.   The taxpayer must be able to show a substantial business purpose (e.g., a change to a tax year that coincides with the *natural business year*) before permission for the change is granted by the IRS.

3.   To establish the existence of a natural business year, the IRS applies an objective *gross receipts* test which requires that 25 percent of the entity's gross receipts for the 12-month period be realized in the final *two months* of the 12-month period for *three consecutive years*.

4.   The IRS usually establishes certain conditions that the taxpayer must accept if the approval for change is to be granted.

E.   Taxable Periods of Less Than One Year

1.   A *short year* (or short period) is a period of less than 12 calendar months. A taxpayer may have a short year in the following situations.

    a.   The first income tax return.

          b.   The final income tax return.

          c.   A change in the tax year.

To report on a fiscal year basis, a taxpayer must keep his or her books and records based on that fiscal year. Since most individual taxpayers keep their personal financial records on a calendar year basis, it is easier to use a calendar year period. It would be virtually impossible for an individual to change to a fiscal year without justification. Such justification may exist, however, when the primary or sole source of income comes from self-employment or partnership income from a cyclical business.

      2.   If a short period results from a change in the taxpayer's annual accounting period, the taxpayer is required to annualize.

      3.   Once the taxable income is annualized, the tax is computed on an annualized basis and then converted to a short period tax.

      4.   Rather than annualize the short period *income*, the taxpayer can elect to calculate the tax for a 12-month period beginning on the first day of the short period and then *allocate* the portion of the *tax* attributable to the short period.

      5.   Special adjustments must be made by individuals when annualizing.

          a.   Deductions must be itemized for the short period. The standard deduction is not allowed.

          b.   Personal and dependency exemptions must be prorated.

F.   Mitigation of the Annual Accounting Period Concept -- Relief is provided by the tax law to mitigate harsh treatment resulting from the effects of an arbitrary accounting period and a progressive rate structure. Examples include the following.

      1.   Net operating loss carryback and carryover rules.

      2.   Restoration of amounts received under a claim of right -- If the *claim of right doctrine* requires income to be recognized on receipt of an amount, a later repayment will generally give rise to a deduction. In situations where the deduction for the amount previously included in income exceeds $3,000, the taxpayer may claim the deduction in the year that would produce the greater tax benefit (i.e., either the year of original receipt or the year of repayment).

II.   Accounting Methods [p 16-10]

    A.   Permissible Methods

      1.   Taxable income must be computed using the method of accounting regularly used by the taxpayer, provided that the method *clearly reflects income*.

      2.   Three permissible overall methods are allowed by the Code.

          a.   The cash receipts and disbursements method.

          b.   The accrual method.

          c.   A hybrid method (a combination of cash and accrual).

      3.   Special methods of accounting are also permitted or required in certain situations. The taxpayer *must* use the accrual method to report sales and cost of goods sold if inventories are an income-producing factor in business. Special methods are permitted for installment sales, for long-term construction contracts, and for farmers.

4. A taxpayer who has more than one trade or business may use a different method of accounting for *each* trade or business activity.

5. The IRS may require a taxpayer to change his method of accounting if that method does not clearly reflect income.

> **KEY TERMS**
>
> - Annual tax period
> - Fiscal year, Natural business year
> - Cash, accrual, hybrid tax accounting
> - Installment Method

B. Cash Receipts and Disbursements Method -- Cash Basis

1. The popularity of this method can be largely attributed to its simplicity and flexibility. Income is recognized when the taxpayer actually or constructively receives cash or its equivalent. Deductions are generally permitted in the year of payment.

2. An item of income must be included in income if it has been *constructively* received. An item has been constructively received if it has been made available to a taxpayer so that he or she could draw on it.

3. While a deduction generally is allowed in the year of payment, there are exceptions to this rule.

    a. A taxpayer must capitalize and amortize an asset over its useful life if the asset has a useful life that extends substantially beyond the tax year.

    b. Many items that have been prepaid (e.g., rent, interest) are required to be capitalized and subsequently deducted in the years to which the payment relates.

4. To prevent opportunities to distort the measurement of income, in addition to the restrictions mentioned above, other limitations apply in the use of the cash method.

    a. The accrual method must be used by a corporation (other than an S corporation), a partnership with a corporate partner, and a tax shelter.

    b. Exceptions to this accrual requirement apply in certain situations.
        (1) A farming business.
        (2) A qualified personal service corporation.
        (3) An entity that is not a tax shelter whose average annual gross receipts for the most recent three-year period is $10 million or less.

5. Although farming operations may generally use the cash method even though inventories normally are material to farming operations, exceptions to this treatment exist. Certain farming corporations and limited partnerships may not use the cash method. In addition, capitalization of costs is generally required when the preproduction period of certain assets (e.g., an apple farmer) is greater than two years. A farmer may elect out of this capitalization requirement, but only if the alternative depreciation system is used for all farming property. Further, while the cost of purchasing an animal must be capitalized, a cash basis farmer may expense the cost of raising an animal.

C. Accrual Method

1. All Events Test for Income -- Under the accrual method, an item of income

is included in income for the year in which it is earned, regardless of when the income is collected. An item is earned when all events have occurred which fix the right to receive such income and when the amount to be received can be determined with reasonable accuracy.

2. The amount of income to be recognized is determined by looking at the amount such taxpayer has a right to receive, not the value of the obligation.

3. An expense is deductible in the year in which all events have occurred which determine the fact of the liability and the amount can be determined with reasonable accuracy. Furthermore, in most circumstances economic performance must have occurred.

4. The economic performance test is waived and year-end accruals may be deducted if certain conditions are met.

5. Generally, the *all events* and *economic performance tests* will prevent the use of reserves that are frequently used in financial reporting. However, small banks are allowed to use a bad debt reserve. Furthermore, an accrual basis taxpayer in a service business is permitted to defer recognizing revenue that appears uncollectible based on experience.

D. Hybrid Method -- A hybrid method of accounting involves the use of more than one method. However, the hybrid method may be used only if the taxpayer's income is clearly reflected.

E. Change of Method

1. If a taxpayer desires to change a method of accounting, permission must generally be obtained from the IRS. A change in the *accounting method* encompasses a change of an *overall method* of accounting as well as the treatment of any material item of income or deduction.

2. A change in accounting method is distinguishable from the *correction of an error*. Errors are corrected by a taxpayer filing an amended return.

3. To change from the use of an *erroneous method* (an incorrect rule used consistently year-after-year) to a correct method, permission must be obtained from the IRS.

4. Certain adjustments may be required to items of income and expense to prevent a distortion of taxable income resulting from the change of an accounting method.

III. Special Accounting Methods [p 16-18]

A. Installment Method -- The installment sale provisions, which provide an exception to the general rule of income recognition, allow the taxpayer to spread gain from an installment sale over the collection period. This method of accounting is an important tax planning tool because of tax deferral possibilities.

B. Eligibility and Calculations

1. The installment method applies only to *gains*, and not to losses, from the sale of property where the seller receives at least one payment *after* the year of sale. However, the method may not be used in the following cases.

     a. On gains from property held for the sale in the ordinary course of business.

     b. To the extent that depreciation recapture under §§1245 or 1250 applies.

     c. On gains from stocks or securities traded on established markets.

2. Nonelective aspect -- Regardless of the taxpayer's method of accounting, as a general rule, sales *must* be reported by the installment method. A

special election is required to report the gain by any other method.

 The taxpayer has nearly unlimited freedom to *choose* an accounting method on an initial tax return, but it often is quite difficult to get the IRS to approve a *change* from an existing method to another alternative. The tax advisor must be sure to provide full information as to the best long-term tax accounting methods available early in the taxpayer's life-cycle, so as to provide the most effective management of the resulting tax liabilities.

3. The gain reported on each sale is computed by the following formula.

$$\frac{\textit{Total Gain}}{\textit{Contract Price}} \quad x \quad \textit{Payments Received}$$

   a. The *total gain* is the selling price reduced by selling expenses and the adjusted basis of the property.
   b. The *contract price* is the amount (excluding interest) the seller will ultimately collect from the buyer. This excludes the seller's liabilities that are assumed by the buyer.
   c. *Payments received* are the collections on the contract price received in the tax year.

4. If the sum of the seller's basis and selling expenses is less than the liabilities assumed by the buyer, the difference must be added to the contract price and to the payments (treated as *deemed payments*) received in the year of sale.

5. Gain attributable to *depreciation recapture* is recognized in the year of the sale, and the remaining gain may be recognized using the installment method.

6. If a deferred payment contract for the sale of property with a selling price that is greater than $3,000 does not contain a reasonable interest rate (at least the federal rate), then an interest rate (the federal rate) is imputed. As a general rule, the buyer and seller must account for interest on the accrual basis. Several exceptions exist regarding the rate at which interest is imputed and the method of accounting for interest income and expense.

7. Restrictions and limitations apply to the use of the installment method in the case of related party sales of nondepreciable and depreciable property.

C. Disposition of Installment Obligations -- On the disposition of an installment obligation, the taxpayer generally must pay the tax on the portion of gross profit which was previously deferred.

D. Interest on Deferred Taxes -- In some situations, taxpayers are required to pay interest on taxes deferred through the use of the installment method.

 It is possible to structure a property sale so that the sale proceeds are deposited in an escrow account and then disbursed in a later year. The advantage to the seller of this arrangement is not only the security of knowing that the sale has been consummated, but the gain can be deferred for tax purposes using the installment method until the proceeds are made available to the former owner.

E.   Electing Out of the Installment Method
    1.   A taxpayer can *elect not to use* the installment method by reporting on a timely filed return the gain computed by the taxpayer's usual method of accounting (cash or accrual).
    2.   Permission of the IRS is required to revoke an election not to use the installment method.

F.   Long-Term Contracts [p 16-25]
    1.   A *long-term contract* is a building, installation, construction, or manufacturing contract that is entered into but not completed within the same tax year. Further, it is long-term *only* if the contract is to manufacture a *unique* item not normally carried in finished goods inventory.
    2.   The direct and indirect costs incurred on long-term contracts must be accumulated and allocated to individual contracts. In addition, mixed service costs must be allocated to production.
    3.   The accumulated costs are deducted when the revenue from a contract is recognized. Revenue generally is recognized using one of two methods.
        a.   The completed contract method.
        b.   The percentage of completion method.
    4.   The completed contract method may be used for home construction contracts and certain other real estate construction contracts.
    5.   Under the *completed contract method*, no revenue from the contract is recognized until the contract is completed and accepted by the customer. A taxpayer may not delay completion of a contract for the principal purpose of deferring tax.
    6.   Under the *percentage of completion method*, a portion of the gross contract price is included in income during each period as the contract is completed.
    7.   A *lookback* provision, applied in the year a contract is completed, provides that interest is paid *to* the taxpayer if there was an overpayment of taxes. Interest is payable *by* the taxpayer if there was an underpayment attributable to the percentage of completion method.
    8.   The advantage of the completed contract method over the percentage of completion method is that income is deferred.

TEST FOR SELF-EVALUATION -- CHAPTER 16

True or False

Indicate which of the following statements are true or false by circling the correct answer.

T   F   1.   The tax year for a new corporation begins on the day the corporation begins business.

T   F   2.   The request to change accounting periods is granted automatically by the IRS.

T   F   3.   Taxpayers are not required to annualize taxable income in every situation where a short year occurs.

T   F   4.   A taxpayer who has more than one trade or business may use a different method of accounting for each trade or business.

T   F   5.   For an accrual basis taxpayer, the amount of income recognized is determined by looking at the income such taxpayer has a right to receive and not the value of the assets given up.

T   F   6.   Regardless of the taxpayer's method of accounting, as a general rule, eligible sales must be reported by the installment method.

T   F   7.   An accrual basis taxpayer may not deduct an expense until economic performance has occurred even though all events have occurred which determine the fact of a liability.

T   F   8.   The contract price is the selling price less the seller's liabilities that are assumed by the buyer.

T   F   9.   The installment method may be used to report a gain on the sale of depreciable property to a controlled entity.

T   F   10.   Because of the opportunity to defer the recognition of income, the preferred method of reporting long-term contracts is the percentage of completion method.

T   F   11.   A taxpayer may never use a taxable year that exceeds twelve calendar months.

T   F   12.   Generally, S corporations must adopt a calendar year; however, they may elect an otherwise impermissible year under certain conditions.

T   F   13.   The cash method of accounting can be used to measure sales and costs of goods sold even if inventories are material to a taxpayer's business.

T   F   14.   The installment method cannot be used to report gains on property held for sale in the ordinary course of business.

T   F   15.   A personal service corporation generally must use a calendar year; however, a fiscal year can be elected under certain conditions.

Fill-in-the-Blanks

Complete the following statements with the appropriate word(s) or amount(s).

1.   A taxpayer may be able to utilize one of the following methods to report revenues earned on long-term contracts: _____ or _____.

2.   In an installment sale, the _____ is generally the amount (excluding interest) that will ultimately be collected from the buyer by the seller.

3.   If the sum of the seller's basis and selling expenses in an installment sale is less than the liabilities assumed by the buyer, the difference must be _____ to the _____ and to the payment received in the year of the sale.

4.   Generally, if a deferred payment contract does not provide a simple interest rate of at least _____, a rate equal to the federal rate is imputed.

5.   Subject to exceptions, corporations, partnerships, trusts, and tax shelters may not use the _____ method of accounting.

6.   Although exceptions exist, _____, _____, and _____ generally must adopt tax years that conform with that of their owners.

7.   Generally, a taxable year cannot exceed _____ months.

8.   A _____ provision requires the recalculation of annual profits reported on a contract accounted for by the percentage of completion method in the year a contract is completed.

9.   On the disposition of depreciable property, ordinary income gain attributable to the _____ provisions under §§1245 and 1250 is ineligible for installment reporting.

10.   The gift of an installment note _____ [will/will not] be treated as a taxable disposition by the donor.

11.   In determining the tax year for a partnership, if the principal partners do not all have the same tax year and no majority of partners have the same tax year, the partnership must use a year that results in the _____ of income.

12.   A _____ is a corporation whose shareholder-employees provide personal services such as medical, dental, legal, or accounting services.

13.   The Code recognizes the following as generally permissible methods of accounting: the _____ method, the _____ method, or a _____ method.

14.   The term _____ includes not only the overall method of accounting of the taxpayer but also the accounting treatment of any item.

15.   Under the cash method, income is not recognized until the taxpayer actually receives, or
        _____ receives, cash or its _____.

Multiple Choice

Choose the best answer for each of the following questions.

_____ 1.   In general, which of the following is not required to use the calendar year for tax
             purposes?
             a.   A partnership.
             b.   An S corporation.
             c.   A personal service corporation with annual gross receipts of $7,500,000.
             d.   An oil and gas tax shelter.
             e.   All of the above must use the calendar year of reporting for tax purposes,
                    subject to exceptions.

_____ 2.   A contractor has agreed to construct a building for you. The total contract
             amounts to $200,000. In the first year of construction, $125,000 of costs are
             incurred. At the time the contract is signed, the contractor estimates that the job
             will cost a total of $160,000. In the second year, the building is completed for an
             additional $15,000. If the contractor uses the percentage of completion method,
             how much income is recognized in year 1?
             a. $0.
             b. $25,000.
             c. $31,250.
             d. $56,250.
             e.   None of the above.

_____ 3.   A contractor has agreed to construct a building for you. The total contract
             amounts to $200,000. In the first year of construction, $125,000 of costs are
             incurred. At the time the contract is signed, the contractor estimates that the job
             will cost a total of $160,000. In the second year, the building is completed for an
             additional $15,000. If the contractor qualified to utilize the completed contract
             method of accounting for costs, the income to be recognized in year 1 is:
             a. $0.
             b. $25,000.
             c. $32,000.
             d. $60,000.
             e. $75,000.

_____ 4.   James sold farmland on March 1 of the current year which he had been holding
             as an investment. He had originally acquired the property in 1986. James's basis
             on the date of sale is $10,000. The buyer agreed to assume the $15,000
             mortgage on the property, and to make a $15,000 cash down payment, and to
             make annual payments beginning one year after the date of the sale on a 10-year
             $50,000 installment note which stipulates an appropriate rate of interest. What is
             the contract price for the sale?
             a. $50,000.
             b. $65,000.
             c. $70,000.

       d. $80,000.

       e.   None of the above.

____ 5.   James sold farmland on March 1 of the current year which he had been holding as an investment. He had originally acquired the property in 1986. James's basis on the date of sale is $10,000. The buyer agreed to assume the $15,000 mortgage on the property, and to make a $15,000 cash down payment, and to make annual payments beginning one year after the date of the sale on a 10-year $50,000 installment note which stipulates an appropriate rate of interest. How much gain is recognized in the year of the sale?

       a. $12,187.50.

       b. $15,000.00.

       c. $16,250.00.

       d. $20,000.00.

       e.   None of the above.

____ 6.   James sold farmland on March 1 of the current year which he had been holding as an investment. He had originally acquired the property in 1986. James's basis on the date of sale is $10,000. The buyer agreed to assume the $15,000 mortgage on the property, and to make a $15,000 cash down payment, and to make annual payments beginning one year after the date of the sale on a 10-year $50,000 installment note which stipulates an appropriate rate of interest. How much gain is recognized in the year of the first installment payment (i.e., one year after the sale)?

       a. $4,062.50.

       b. $5,000.00.

       c. $10,000.00.

       d. $50,000.00.

       e.   Some other amount.

____ 7.   Certain restrictions apply to the tax accounting devices used by personal service corporations. For federal income tax purposes, which of the following statements concerning such entities is *not* true?

       a.   The corporation provides services through shareholder-employees.

       b.   Substantially all of the activities of the corporation must be the performance of personal services in certain fields.

       c.   A professional accounting or law corporation could be classified as personal service corporation.

       d.   In all cases, a personal service corporation must adopt a calendar year for tax reporting purposes.

____ 8.   In general, which of the following are permissible tax accounting methods?

       a.   The cash method.

       b.   The accrual method.

       c.   The hybrid method.

       d.   All of the above are permissible methods.

       e.   None of the above methods can be used.

____ 9.   Bob sold land held for investment to Ted on March 1, 2007. Bob had acquired the land in 1986 for a cost of $10,000. Ted agreed to assume Bob's $2,000 mortgage on the land, to make a $2,000 down payment, and to make 10 annual payments of $1,000, beginning on March 1, 2008. Assuming no selling expenses

were incurred, how much gain must Bob recognize in 2007?
a. $571.
b. $667.
c. $2,000.
d.   None of the above.

_____ 10.   Bob sold land held for investment to Ted on March 1, 2007. Bob had acquired
              the land in 1986 for a cost of $1,000. Ted agreed to assume Bob's $2,000
              mortgage on the land, to make a $2,000 down payment, and to make 10 annual
              payments of $1,000, beginning on March 1, 2008. Assuming no selling expenses
              were incurred, how much gain must Bob recognize in 2007?
              a. $2,000.
              b. $2,167.
              c. $3,000.
              d. $4,000.
              e.   None of the above.

_____ 11.   White Corporation entered into a $400,000 construction contract that was to take
              two years to complete. Total costs were estimated to be $350,000. Costs
              incurred in the first year totaled $210,000. If White Corporation uses the
              percentage of completion method, how much income must it recognize in year 1
              of the project?
              a. $0.
              b. $25,000.
              c. $30,000.
              d. $50,000.
              e.   None of the above.

_____ 12.   ABC Partnership is owned equally by Albert, Beth, and Chris. Albert and Beth
              each close their tax years on January 31 while Chris uses the calendar year to
              report income. ABC's tax year must end on what date?
              a.   January 31.
              b.   December 31.
              c.   Determined based on the least aggregate deferral of income.
              d.   None of the above.

_____ 13.   Partnerships, LLCs, and S corporations may elect an otherwise impermissible
              year under which of the following conditions?
              a.   A business purpose for the year can be demonstrated.
              b.   The entity's year results in a deferral of not more than three months'
                     income, and the entity agrees to make required tax payments.
              c.   Either of the above.
              d.   None of the above.

_____ 14.   A taxpayer with inventories can avoid using the accrual method if an exception
              applies. Which of the following is *not* such an exception?
              a.   A farming business.
              b.   A defense contractor.
              c.   A qualified personal service corporation.
              d.   An entity that is not a tax shelter whose average annual gross receipts for
                     the most recent three-year period are $10 million or less.
              e.   More than one of the above is an exception.

Code Section Recognition

Several important sections of the Internal Revenue Code are described below. Indicate, by number, the appropriate Code section.

1.   _____ The cash method of tax accounting is prohibited for certain types of taxpayers.

2.   _____ This section stipulates that an entity which elects an otherwise impermissible year under certain conditions must make required tax payments.

3.   _____ Grants the IRS broad powers to determine whether the taxpayer's accounting method clearly reflects income.

Short Answer

1. Tanya, who is not a dealer in real estate, sells land for $10,000 (cash of $2,500 and $7,500 of notes payable to Tanya over the next three years). The buyer pays an adequate rate of interest. The property's adjusted basis is $8,000 on the date of disposition. Assuming Tanya does not elect out of the installment method, calculate the gain she recognizes in each year of the four-year period.

2. Jack, who is not a dealer in real estate, sells land for $10,000 (cash of $2,500 and $7,500 of notes payable to Jack over the next three years). The buyer pays an adequate rate of interest. The property's adjusted basis is $8,000 on the date of disposition and §1245 depreciation recapture potential is $500. Assuming Jack does not elect out of the installment method, calculate the gain he recognizes over the four-year period.

SOLUTIONS TO CHAPTER 16 QUESTIONS

True or False

1.   F   The tax year begins on the day the corporation comes into existence. [In General p. 16-2]
2.   F   The taxpayer must be able to establish a substantial business purpose for the change. [Changes in the Accounting Period p. 16-6]
3.   T   No annualization is required for the first or last tax year of the taxpayer. [Taxable Periods of Less Than One Year p. 16-7]
4.   T   The business' method must follow that used for its books. [Permissible Methods p. 16-10]
5.   T   Accrual basis income is recognized when it is earned. [Accrual Method p. 16-13]
6.   T   One must elect out of the installment method. Otherwise, it applies. [The Nonelective Aspect p. 16-19]
7.   T   Both tests must be met. [All Events and Economic Performance Tests for Deductions p. 16-13]
8.   T   This is the amount that the seller will receive, other than interest, from the buyer. [Computing the Gain for the Period p. 16-19]
9.   F   Installment reporting is not available for sales of property to controlled entities. [Related-Party Sales of Depreciable Property p. 16-24]
10.   F   Deferral of income recognition is an advantage of the completed contract method. [Completed Contract Method p. 16-28]
11.   F   If certain requirements are met, a taxpayer may elect to use an annual period that varies from 52 to 53 weeks. [In General p. 16-2]
12.   T   Often a tax payment accompanies this election. [Partnerships and S Corporations p. 16-4]
13.   F   The accrual method must be used in such situations. [Permissible Methods p. 16-10]
14.   T   Such gross income cannot be deferred. [Eligibility and Calculations p. 16-19]
15.   T   Often a tax payment accompanies this election. [Personal Service Corporations p. 16-4]

Fill-in-the-Blanks

1. completed contract method, percentage of completion method [Long-Tem Contracts p. 16-25]
2. contract price [Computing the Gain for the Period p. 16-19]
3. added, contract price [Computing the Gain for the Period p. 16-19]
4. the federal rate [Imputed Interest p. 16-21]
5. cash [Restrictions on Use of the Cash Method p. 16-11]
6. partnerships, S corporations, and personal service corporations [Specific Provisions for Partnerships, S Corporations, and Personal Service Corporations p. 16-4]
7. 12 [In General p. 16-2]
8. lookback [Long-Term Contracts p. 16-25]
9. depreciation recapture [Eligibility and Calculations p. 16-19]
10. will [Disposition of Installment Obligations p. 16-24]
11. least aggregate deferral [Partnerships and S Corporations p. 16-4]
12. personal service corporation [Personal Service Corporations p. 16-4]
13. cash, accrual, hybrid [Permissible Methods p. 16-10]

14.   method of accounting [Permissible Methods p. 16-10]
15.   constructively, equivalent [Cash Receipts and Disbursements Method – Cash Basis p. 16-11]

Multiple Choice

1.   e   The basic tax year for these entities is the calendar year. [Specific Provisions for Partnerships, S Corporations, and Personal Service Corporations p. 16-4]

2.   c   Revenue [$200,000 X ($125,000/$160,000)] $156,250
          Less: Costs incurred on the contract   (125,000)
                                                           $ 31,250
          [Percentage of Completion Method p. 16-28]

3.   a   No contract has been completed yet. [Completed Contract Method p. 16-27]

4.   c   Selling price $80,000
          Less: Mortgage assumption   (15,000)
          Plus: Excess of mortgage over basis   5,000
          Contract price $70,000
          [Computing the Gain for the Period p. 16-19]

5.   d $70,000 X $20,000 = $20,000
          $70,000
          [Computing the Gain for the Period p. 16-19]

6.   b $70,000 X $5,000 = $5,000
          $70,000
          [Computing the Gain for the Period p. 16-19]

7.   d   A personal service corporation may adopt a fiscal year if it can persuade the IRS that a good business reason exists for having a non-calendar year. [Personal Service Corporations p. 16-6]

8.   d   All of these methods are available to taxpayers. [Permissible Methods p. 16-10]

9.   b $667 = $4,000 (total gain) / $12,000 (contract price) X $2,000 (payments received in the current year). [Computing the Gain for the Period p. 16-19]

10. c $3,000 = $13,000 (total gain) / $13,000 (contract price) X $3,000 (payments received in the current year). [Computing the Gain for the Period p. 16-19]

11. c $30,000 = $210,000 (costs incurred this year) / $350,000 (total expected costs) X $50,000 (total expected income from the project). [Percentage of Completion Method p. 16-28]

12. a   The entity year follows that of its majority partners. [Partnerships and S Corporations p. 16-4]

13. c   Non-calendar tax years are available. [Partnerships and S Corporations p. 16-4]

14. b   No exception exists for defense contractors. [Accrual Method p. 16-13]

Code Section Recognition

1.   448   [Restrictions on Use of the Cash Method p. 16-11]
2.   444   [Required Tax Payments p. 16-5]
3.   446   [Permissible Methods p. 16-10]

Short Answer

1. Amount realized: Cash $ 2,500
                           Notes   7,500
    Total amount realized $10,000
    Less: Adjusted basis   (8,000)
    Total gain to be recognized $ 2,000

    Year 1 $2,000 (gain)
              $10,000 (contract price) X $2,500 (cash) = $625
    Year 2 $2,000 (gain)
              $10,000 (contract price) X $2,500 (cash) = $625

    Year 3 $2,000 (gain)
              $10,000 (contract price) X $2,500 (cash) = $625

    Year 4 $2,000 (gain)
              $10,000 (contract price) X $2,500 (cash) = $625

    [Computing the Gain for the Period p. 16-19]

2. Amount realized: Cash $ 2,500
                           Notes   7,500
    Total amount realized $10,000
    Less: Adjusted basis   (8,000)
    Total gain to be recognized $ 2,000

    Year 1 Recapture amount recognized in year of sale $500

              $2,000 (gain) - $500 (recapture)
              $10,000 (contract price)   X $2,500 (cash) =   375

              Total gain in year 1 $875

    Year 2 $2,000 (gain) - $500 (recapture)
              $10,000 (contract price)   X $2,500 (cash) = $375

    Year 3 $2,000 (gain) - $500 (recapture)
              $10,000 (contract price)   X $2,500 (cash) = $375

    Year 4 $2,000 (gain) - $500 (recapture)
              $10,000 (contract price)   X $2,500 (cash) = $375

    [Computing the Gain for the Period p. 16-19]

Chapter 17
Corporations: Introduction and Operating Rules

CHAPTER HIGHLIGHTS

U nlike partnerships and sole proprietorships, a corporation is a taxable entity, separate and distinct from its owners. Although the determination of gross income and many of the deductions are similar to those allowed to individuals, there are many important differences in the tax treatment of corporations. The most important of these is that a corporation is allowed only business-related deductions. Therefore, there is no concept of adjusted gross income for the corporation. Furthermore, most of the deductions from adjusted gross income are eliminated, since many of them are personal, rather than business, expenditures.

I.   Taxation of Corporations   [An Introduction to the Income Taxation of Corporations p. 17-9]
   A.   The corporate income tax is levied upon a corporate entity, usually as defined by state law. Nonetheless, some non-corporate entities also are subject to the corporate income tax, if they are classified as "associations."
   B.   A partnership or limited liability entity can be taxed as a corporation if it makes a "check the box" election. Without this election, such an entity is a tax-reporting, but not a tax-paying, entity. [Entity Classification, p. 17-9]
   C.   A trust is taxed as a corporation if it is owned by a group of associates who operate the entity as a business or for a profit motive.
   D.   All of the states and Washington DC have adopted statutes allowing limited liability companies (LLCs) as a form of doing business. These entities allow limited liability for their owners.
   E.   Like other business entities, the corporation qualifies for the deduction for manufacturing activities.

II.   The following are similarities between individual and corporate taxable income.   [An Overview of Corporate versus Individual Income Tax Treatment p. 17-9]

    A.   The concepts of gross income, deductions, and exclusions are the same. However, corporations have fewer exclusions from gross income than do individuals.

    B.   Both corporations and individuals exclude municipal bond interest from gross income.

    C.   Deductions include wages, rents, interest, taxes, and cost of goods sold.

    D.   Gross income includes rents, interest, dividends, sales proceeds, service income, and any recognized gain or loss on property transactions.

    E.   Both corporations and individuals defer recognized gain or loss on a like-kind exchange.

    F.   Cost recovery deductions are allowed, and the corresponding recapture provisions apply to both individuals and corporations. Corporations, however, have more recapture potential than do individuals.

    G.   Both corporations and individuals are disallowed losses on wash sales of securities and related party transactions.

    H.   Both individuals and certain corporations have a choice of taxable periods. However, personal service corporations and S corporations are subject to severe restrictions in the use of fiscal years.

    I.   Capital gains and losses are defined and netted in the same manner for corporations as they are for individuals.

    J.   Both corporations and individuals are subject to an alternative minimum tax (AMT). Small corporations are exempted from the AMT.

III.   The following are important differences between the taxation of individuals and corporations.   [An Overview of Corporate versus Individual Income Tax Treatment p. 17-9]

    A.   There is no concept of adjusted gross income for corporations. This means that there is no distinction between deductions for and from adjusted gross income for the corporation.

    B.   There are no standard deduction amounts or personal exemptions for corporations.

    C.   Corporations cannot use the credit for the elderly, the child care credit, or the earned income credit.

    D.   There is no exclusion of gain on the sale of a principal residence for corporations.

    E.   A corporation is not subject to any limitations on casualty loss deductions.

    F.   Organization expenses of a corporation are deductible if a timely election is made.

        1.   The first $5,000 is deducted immediately by small corporations, and the rest is amortized over 180 months or more, starting when the corporation begins to operate as a trade or business.

        2.   The deductible organization expenses must be incurred by the end of the corporation's first taxable year.

        3.   Deductible organization expenses include state registration fees, legal and accounting fees, and director and promotional fees.

        4.   Expenses associated with obtaining debt, equity, or assets are not deductible as organization expenses.

        5.   If the election is not made on a timely basis, organizational expenses cannot be deducted until the corporation ceases to do business or

liquidates.

G. Capital gains and losses of a corporation are treated differently than are the capital gains and losses of an individual.

1. A corporation cannot deduct any portion of net capital losses. Rather, the corporation's net capital losses must be offset against its net capital gains.

2. Net capital losses can be carried back three years and forward five years. All carryovers are treated as short-term capital losses for a corporation. Carryovers do not lose their identity for non-corporate taxpayers.

3. The highest tax rate on long-term capital gains of individuals usually is limited to 15%, as opposed to the 35% maximum rate applicable to ordinary income. For corporate taxpayers, capital gains are subject to the normal income tax rates.

H. The deduction for charitable contributions has different limits for a corporation.

1. The deduction for charitable contributions is limited to ten percent of taxable income before the dividends-received deduction, charitable contributions, and carrybacks of NOLs and capital losses.

2. Excess charitable contributions are carried forward for five years. The current year's contributions must be deducted first, with excess contributions from previous years deducted in chronological order.

3. An accrual-basis corporation may deduct a charitable contribution in the current year, if the contribution is authorized by year-end and paid within 2 ½ months after the tax year.

> ### KEY TERMS
>
> - Organization expenses
> - Dividends-Received deduction
> - AMT rate = 20%
> - ACE adjustment
> - Controlled corporation

I. A corporation receives a dividends-received deduction (DRD) for payments received from other US corporations.

1. This deduction is 100% of the total amount of the dividend received from a corporation that is a member of its controlled group.

2. For dividends received or accrued from a domestic corporation that is not a member of an affiliated group, the DRD percentage depends upon the ownership percentage that the recipient corporation holds in the corporation making the distribution.

a. If the percentage of ownership is less than 20%, the DRD percentage is 70%.

b. If the percentage of ownership is 20% or more, the DRD percentage is 80%.

3. There is a limitation on the deduction for dividends received from a corporation that is not a member of a controlled group.

a. The dividends-received deduction is limited to the DRD percentage of taxable income after charitable contributions, but without regard to any dividends-received deductions claimed; net operating carryovers or carrybacks; and, any capital loss carrybacks to the current year.

b. The limit on the deduction to the DRD percentage of taxable income does not apply if [Taxable Income - DRD percentage of

Dividends Received] creates or enlarges an NOL.

J.   Net operating losses are treated differently for corporations than for individuals.
    1.   A corporation does not have any non-business deductions, so there are no adjustments to taxable income when the NOL is computed.
    2.   The NOL carryover includes the dividends-received deduction.
    3.   Corporations carry their NOLs back two years, then forward twenty years.
    4.   Corporations can elect to carry the loss forward only, forgoing the carryback altogether.

K.   The passive loss rules apply to individuals, closely held C corporations and personal service corporations.
    1.   A corporation is closely held if, at any time during the taxable year, more than 50% of the value of the corporation's outstanding stock is directly or indirectly owned by five or fewer individuals.
    2.   For purposes of the passive loss provisions, a corporation is classified as a personal service corporation if:
        a.   the corporation's principal activity is the performance of personal services;
        b.   such services are substantially performed by owner-employees; and
        c.   more than ten percent of the stock (in value) is held by owner-employees.
    3.   For individuals and personal service corporations, the passive activity losses cannot be offset against either active income or portfolio income.
    4.   Closely held corporations may offset passive losses against active income, but not against portfolio income.

L.   The production activities deduction is allowed to corporations, as it is to all business taxpayers who otherwise qualify [§199].

IV.   Corporate Income Tax   [Determining the Corporate Income Tax Liability p. 17-20]
A.   A corporation must file an income tax return, regardless of whether it has any taxable income.
B.   The top corporate tax rate is 35%.
C.   Qualified personal service corporations are subject to a flat 35% income tax rate on all taxable income.

V.   Corporate Alternative Minimum Tax (AMT)   [Alternative Minimum Tax p. 17-20]
A.   Corporations also are subject to a 20% *alternative minimum tax (AMT)*. Details of the AMT are discussed in text chapter 15.
B.   The starting point in the computation of *alternative minimum taxable income (AMTI)* is the taxable income of the corporation before any net operating loss deduction. To this amount certain adjustments are added and subtracted and tax preferences are added.

The alternative minimum tax could be seen as a trial balloon that Congress is testing, mainly on equipment-intensive corporations, for adoption someday as the main tax system. The AMT has a broad base, with few deductions, other than for business expenditures, and very few credits to offset against it. As applied to individuals, it resembles a consumption tax.

C.　The alternative minimum tax is 20% of a corporation's AMTI that exceeds the exemption amount. The exemption amount of $40,000 is reduced by 25 percent of the amount by which AMTI exceeds $150,000. As a result of the required reduction, no part of the exemption is available to a corporation that has AMTI of $310,000 or more.

D.　A minimum tax credit is available to mitigate the double tax that otherwise would result. The amount that may be carried forward as a credit is equal to the entire amount of the AMT liability.

VI.　Controlled Groups　[Tax Liability of Related Corporations　p. 17-21]

A.　The Code includes the *controlled group* provisions, to discourage taxpayers from dividing Taxable Income amounts among a series of entities, thereby gaining additional tax rate discounts, exemptions, and other limitations.

B.　Members of a controlled group share a number of tax attributes. In each case, one *n*th of the attribute is available to the group member, where *n* is the number of corporations in the group. The group may use any other allocation method, however, if all of the members consent to the method. Such consent methods may be changed every year without securing IRS permission.

1.　The 15%, 25%, and 34% marginal income tax brackets.

2.　The $40,000 alternative minimum tax exemption.

C.　A controlled group exists in two distinct forms.

1.　The *brother-sister* controlled group exists where five or fewer individuals, trusts, or estates own at least fifty percent of the voting power or stock value of two or more corporations.

2.　The *parent-subsidiary* controlled group exists when one corporation owns at least eighty percent of the voting power or stock value of another corporation.

VII.　Consolidated Returns　[Consolidated Returns　p. 17-24]

A.　An *affiliated group* of corporations can elect to file its federal income tax returns on a consolidated basis. This allows one corporation's positive taxable income to be offset by another group member's operating loss. The recognition of income or loss on certain intercompany transactions also is deferred.

B.　Consolidation eliminates any intercompany pricing problems that may exist among the group members. See §§ 381 and 482.

C.　The election to consolidate brings about significant additional compliance requirements, and the election is binding on all future years, unless the make-up of the affiliated group changes.

D.　An affiliated group exists when, on every day of the tax year, one corporation owns at least eighty percent of the voting power and value of another corporation. Multiple tiers are allowed as long as there is an identifiable parent corporation for the group.

E.　Most of the rules governing consolidated returns are found in the regulations. This authority is delegated by Congress in §1502.

VIII.　Procedural Matters　[Procedural Matters　p. 17-27]

A.　A corporation reports its tax liability on Form 1120, which is due 2 ½ months after the end of the tax year, before extensions. For calendar year corporations, this date is March 15. A corporation must file a return regardless of whether it has either taxable income or tax liability.

B. Form 1120-A may be used by active, US-based corporations with limited gross receipts (< $500,000), Total Income (< $500,000), and total assets (< $500,000).

C. Quarterly estimated tax payments are required of the corporation, usually so that at least 100% percent of the year's tax liability is paid prior to the filing of the return.

D. The corporation reconciles financial accounting income with Taxable Income on Schedule M-1 or M-3 to the Form 1120. Schedule M-2 reconciles beginning and ending financial Retained Earnings.

TEST FOR SELF-EVALUATION - CHAPTER 17

True or False

Indicate which of the following statements are true or false by circling the correct answer.

T   F   1.   A limited liability company can be subject to the corporate income tax.

T   F   2.   A corporation can deduct up to $3,000 in net capital losses in a year.

T   F   3.   A corporation can elect to deduct organization expenses over a period of four years or more.

T   F   4.   Corporations are permitted to deduct eighty percent of the dividends that are received from nonaffiliated domestic corporations.

T   F   5.   Excess corporate charitable contributions may be carried back three years and then carried forward five years.

T   F   6.   An accrual-basis corporation only can deduct charitable contributions in the year paid.

T   F   7.   A corporation files its annual tax return using Form 1140.

T   F   8.   Active US-based corporations with modest income and asset amounts can file the corporate income tax return using a "short form."

T   F   9.   Schedule M-1 of the corporate return is used to reconcile financial accounting net income with taxable income.

T   F   10.   Closely held corporations may offset passive losses against active income, but not against portfolio income.

T   F   11.   An optimal tax strategy would be to split the corporation into separately incorporated divisions, each generating no more than $75,000 of Taxable Income each year.

T   F   12.   A personal service corporation with $100,000 of taxable income is subject to a $22,250 tax liability.

T   F   13.   The election to file a consolidated return is made by the parent every tax year.

T   F   14.   Most of the rules governing consolidated returns are found in the regulations.

T   F   15.   A corporation can claim the deduction for manufacturing activities.

Fill-in-the-Blanks

Complete the following sentences with the appropriate word(s) or amount(s).

1. The maximum amount of the charitable contribution deduction for a corporation is
    _____% of taxable income computed without regard to the _____, _____,
    _____, and _____.

2. The passive loss rules apply to _____ _____ C corporations and _____
    _____ corporations.

3. The top corporate tax rate is _____.

4. Net operating losses of a corporation can be carried back _____ years and then
    forward _____ years.

5. A corporation is allowed a dividends-received deduction of _____% for dividends from
    a member of the recipient's controlled group, and either a _____% or _____%
    dividends-received deduction for dividends from any other domestic corporation.

6. The limitation on the dividends-received deduction is the applicable DRD percentage of
    taxable income, unless the corporation has a _____ for the year.

7. A corporation can amortize its organization expenses over a period of _____ or more.

8. There are two types of corporate controlled groups: the _____ controlled group and
    the _____ controlled group.

9. Usually, the corporation must pay _____% of its tax liability for the year by making
    _____ estimated payments.

10. On the Form 1120, a corporation reconciles accounting and taxable income amounts on
    Schedule _____, and beginning and ending retained earnings balances on Schedule
    _____.

11. The corporation _____ (does/does not) apply the concept of Adjusted Gross Income
    in computing its tax liability.

12. A business can be conducted in the form of a _____ _____, _____
    corporation, _____ corporation, _____ _____ company, or _____.

13. Excess _____ _____ of a corporation are carried back three years and forward
    five years.

14. A corporation's excess charitable contributions are carried forward _____ years.

15. A consolidated return can be filed by a(n) _____ group of corporations.

16. When corporations file on a consolidated basis, intercompany dividends are _____ in computing group taxable income.

17. A corporation files a tax return by the _____ day of the _____ month following the close of the tax year.

18. A corporation must make payments of _____ tax unless its liability is expected to be less than _____.

Multiple Choice

Choose the best answer(s) for each of the following questions.

_____ 1. In computing taxable income, corporations and individuals are treated similarly with respect to the following item(s). More than one answer may be correct.
   a. limitation on charitable contributions.
   b. deduction of capital losses.
   c. deferral of recognized gain or loss on like-kind exchanges.
   d. deduction of net operating losses.

_____ 2. Tul Corporation has taxable income of $300,000. Tul's federal income tax liability is:
   a. $90,250.
   b. $100,250.
   c. $101,500.
   d. $102,000.

_____ 3. An accrual-basis corporation can deduct charitable contributions:
   a. in the year paid only.
   b. in the current year, if authorized by year-end and paid within 2 ½ months after the year-end.
   c. in the year authorized, if paid at any time within the next taxable year.
   d. only in the year in which they are both authorized and paid.

_____ 4. A corporation received $10,000 of dividends from an unrelated domestic corporation in which it owned 30% of the stock. Other corporate taxable income was $5,000, and operating expenses were $9,000. The dividends-received deduction is:
   a. $4,200.
   b. $4,800.
   c. $7,000.
   d. $8,000.
   e. $10,000.

_____ 5. A corporation received $10,000 of dividends from an unrelated domestic corporation in which it owned 30% of the stock. Other corporate taxable income

was $5,000, and operating expenses were $6,000. The dividends-received deduction is:
   a. $6,300.
   b. $7,000.
   c. $7,200.
   d. $8,000.
   e. $10,000.

_____ 6.   A corporation received $10,000 of dividends from an unrelated domestic corporation in which it owned 15% of the stock. Other corporate taxable income was $5,000, and operating expenses were $8,000. The dividends-received deduction is:
   a. $4,900.
   b. $5,600.
   c. $7,000.
   d. $8,000.
   e. $10,000.

_____ 7.   The cash method of accounting is available to which of the following entities? More than one answer may be correct.
   a.   C corporations.
   b.   S corporations.
   c.   Corporations with average annual gross receipts of more than $5 million.
   d.   Corporations engaged in the trade or business of manufacturing.

_____ 8.   Rip Corporation had operating income of $200,000, after deducting $12,000 for charitable contributions, but not including dividends of $20,000 received from nonaffiliated domestic corporations in which Rip held more than 20% ownership interest. How much is the base amount to which the percentage limitation should be applied in computing the maximum allowable deduction for contributions?
   a. $212,000.
   b. $215,000.
   c. $220,000.
   d. $232,000.

_____ 9.   Zoff Corporation had operating income of $9,500. In addition, Zoff had the following capital gains and losses.

Net short-term capital gain	$1,000
Net long-term capital loss	9,000

How much of the excess of net long-term capital loss over net short-term capital gain can Z offset against ordinary income?
   a. $0.
   b. $3,000.
   c. $3,500.
   d. $8,000.

_____ 10.   Arc Corporation files a consolidated return with its wholly-owned subsidiary, Bit Corporation. Bit paid a cash dividend of $10,000 to Arc. How much of this dividend is taxable on the consolidated return?
   a. $0.

        b. $ 2,000.
        c. $ 3,000.
        d. $10,000.

11.   Gopp, a closely held C corporation has $400,000 of passive losses from a rental activity, $100,000 of active business income, and $200,000 of portfolio income. How much of the passive loss may Gopp offset against its other income?
        a. $0.
        b. $100,000.
        c. $200,000.
        d. $300,000.
        e. $400,000.

12.   Gopp, a personal service corporation has $400,000 of passive losses from a rental activity, $100,000 of active business income, and $200,000 of portfolio income. How much of the passive loss may Gopp offset against its other income?
        a. $0.
        b. $100,000.
        c. $200,000.
        d. $300,000.
        e. $400,000.

13.   Bun Corporation, a calendar year taxpayer, incurred the following items . Compute B's charitable contribution deduction for the year.

Operating income	$300,000
Operating expenses	250,000
Dividend received (15% ownership)	70,000
Gift to charity, 9/14	20,000

        a. $5,100.
        b. $7,100.
        c. $12,000.
        d. $20,000.

14.   Col Corporation, a calendar year taxpayer, incurred the following items. Compute Col's net operating loss.

Operating income	$300,000
Operating expenses	350,000
Dividend received (30% ownership)	100,000

        a. $30,000.
        b. $50,000.
        c. $20,000.
        d.   None of the above. Specify_____.

Short Answer

1.   Quark Corporation is created in Year 1. It contributes $10,000 in Year 1, and $12,000 in

Year 2, to a qualifying charitable organization.

(a)   Compute the charitable contribution deduction, if other taxable income before the contribution = $(20,000) in Year 1.

(b)   Compute the charitable contribution deduction, if other taxable income before the contribution = $55,000 in Year 1 (computed after claiming a $5,000 dividends-received deduction and a $10,000 net operating loss deduction) and $130,000 in Year 2.

Year 1 deduction =

Carryforward to Year 2 =

Year 2 deduction =

Carryforward to Year 3 =

2.   Quink Corporation receives $7,000 Dividend Income. Compute its taxable income if:

(a)   The dividend is from a subsidiary corporation. Other taxable income = $60,000.

(b)   The dividend is from an unrelated domestic corporation in which the recipient corporation owns 50% of the paying corporation's stock. Other taxable income = $60,000.

(c)   The dividend is from an unrelated domestic corporation in which the recipient corporation owns 15% of the paying corporation's stock. Other taxable income = $60,000.

(d)   The dividend is from an unrelated domestic corporation in which the recipient corporation owns 50% of the paying corporation's stock. Other taxable income = $(500).

(e)   The dividend is from an unrelated domestic corporation in which the recipient corporation owns 15% of the paying corporation's stock. Other taxable income = $(500).

(f)   The dividend is from an unrelated domestic corporation in which the recipient corporation owns 20% of the paying corporation's stock. Other taxable income = $(3,000).

3.   Quelk Corporation's Taxable Income = $200,000. Compute the federal corporate income tax, if A is NOT a member of any controlled group.

4.   Quell Corporation, a calendar year accrual basis entity, was formed and began sales on July 1. The following items were incurred during its tax Year 1. If Quell makes a timely election to amortize qualifying organizational expenses, what is its Year 1 deduction?

Expenses of temporary directors	$22,500
Expenses of printing and selling stock certificates	11,000
Incorporation fee paid to state	500
Legal fees for drafting corporate charter and by-laws (paid in Year 2 on 1/17)	23,000

SOLUTIONS TO CHAPTER 17 QUESTIONS

True or False

1. T   An LLC is taxed as a corporation if its tax return "checks the box" to do so. [Entity Classification p. 17-8]
2. F   A corporation's net capital losses must be offset against its net capital gains. [Capital Losses p. 17-11]
3. F   Organization expenses may be deducted over a period of 60 months or more. [Deduction of Organizational Expenses p. 17-17]
4. F   The DRD percentage varies depending upon ownership percentage. [Dividends Received Deduction p. 17-17]
5. F   Contributions may be carried forward five years, but may not be carried back. [Charitable Contributions p. 17-13]
6. F   Such corporations may deduct contributions that are authorized by year end and paid within 2 ½ months of the next year. [Charitable Contributions p. 17-13]
7. F   Form 1120 is used by the corporation. [Filing Requirements for Corporations p. 17-27]
8. T   This is Form 1120-A. [Filing Requirements for Corporations p. 17-27]
9. T   This is a valuable self-check of the return's computations. [Reconciliation of Taxable Income and Financial Net Income p. 17-28]
10. T   This is usually to the taxpayer's advantage. [Passive Losses p. 17-12]
11. F   The controlled group rules would counter this strategy. [Tax Liability of Related Corporations p. 17-21]
12. F   The tax liability is $35,000 [35% x $100,000]. Personal service corporations are subject to a flat 35% tax rate. [Corporate Income Tax Rates p. 17-20]
13. F   The election is binding until the group membership changes. [Advantages and Disadvantages of Filing Consolidated Returns, p. 17-25]
14. T   This delegation is found in §1502. [Eligibility and the Election, p. 17-25]
15. T   The deduction is allowed, as it is for all qualifying business taxpayers.p. 17-15

Fill-in-the-Blanks

1. 10, charitable contribution deduction, net operating loss carryback, capital loss carryback, dividends-received deduction [Charitable Contributions p. 17-13]
2. closely held, personal service [Passive Losses p. 17-12]
3. 35% [Corporate Income Tax Rates p. 17-20]
4. two, twenty [Net Operating Losses p. 17-16]
5. 100, 70, 80 [Dividends Received Deduction p. 17-18]
6. net operating loss [Dividends Received Deduction p. 17-18]
7. sixty months [Deduction of Organizational Expenses p. 17-19]
8. brother/sister, parent/subsidiary [Controlled Groups p. 17-22]
9. 100, quarterly [Estimated Tax Payments p. 17-28]
10. M-1, M-2 [Reconciliation of Taxable Income and Financial Net Income p. 17-28]
11. does not [Dissimilarities p. 17-9]
12. sole proprietorship, C, S, limited liability, partnership [Tax Treatment of Various Business Forms p. 17-2]
13. capital losses [Capital Losses p. 17-12]
14. five [Charitable Contributions p. 17-13]
15. Affiliated [Consolidated Returns, p. 17-24]
16. eliminated [Advantages and Disadvantages of Filing Consolidated Returns, p. 17-25]

17.   fifteenth, third   [Filing Requirements for Corporations p. 17-27]
18.   estimated, $500   [Estimated Tax Payments   p. 17-28]

Multiple Choice

1.   c   All of the other choices are treated differently. [Similarities p. 17-10]
2.   b   [(15% x $50,000) + (25% x $25,000) + (34% x $225,000) + 5%($300,000 - $100,000)] [Corporate Income Tax Rates p. 17-20]
3.   b   Only corporations can use this grace period. [Charitable Contributions p. 17-13]
4.   d   Since a DRD of $8,000 ($10,000 x 80%) creates a NOL, the DRD is not restricted by the taxable income limitation. [Dividends Received Deduction p. 17-18]
5.   c   DRD is subject to the taxable income limitation: 80%($10,000 + $5,000 - $6,000) [Dividends Received Deduction p. 17-18]
6.   a   DRD is subject to the taxable income limitation: 70%($10,000 + $5,000 - $8,000) [Dividends Received Deduction p. 17-18]
7.   b   Manufacturing entities tend to carry receivables and inventory. [Accounting Periods and Methods p. 17-10]
8.   d   ($200,000 + $12,000 + $20,000) [Charitable Contributions p. 17-13]
9.   a   Capital losses can only be used to offset capital gains. [Capital Losses p. 17-12]
10.   a   The pertinent dividends received deduction is 100%.   [Dividends Received Deduction p. 17-18]
11.   b   X may offset the passive loss against the $100,000 active business income, but may not offset the remainder against its portfolio income. [Passive Losses p. 17-12]
12.   a   For a personal service corporation, passive losses cannot be offset against either active income or portfolio income. [Passive Losses p. 17-12]
13.   c   The ten percent limitation applies to $120,000 [$300,000 - 250,000 + 70,000]. [Charitable Contributions, p. 17-13]
14.   a $300,000 - 350,000 + 100,000 - (80% x $100,000). [Net Operating Losses p. 17-16]

Short Answer

1.   (a)   Year 1 Taxable Income = $(20,000).
             No deduction is allowed.
             Year 1 carryforward = $10,000.

      (b)   For purposes of the 10% limitation only, Year 1 Taxable Income = $70,000 ($55,000 taxable income + $5,000 DRD + $10,000 NOL deduction) before the contribution.
             Year 1 deduction = 10% x $70,000 = $7,000.
             Year 1 carryforward = $3,000.

             Year 2 deduction limit = 10% x $130,000 = $13,000.
             Use first: Year 2 contribution = $12,000.
             Use second: Year 1 carryforward = $1,000.
             Year 1 loss carryforward to Year 3 = $2,000.

      [Charitable Contributions p. 17-13]

2.   (a)   Taxable Income: $60,000   Other Income

	+ 7,000	Dividend Income
	- 7,000	100% Deduction
	$60,000	

(b)   Taxable Income:

	$60,000	Other Income
	+ 7,000	Dividend Income
	- 5,600	80% Deduction = [80% x $7,000]
	$61,400	

(c)   Taxable Income:

	$60,000	Other Income
	+ 7,000	Dividend Income
	- 4,900	70% Deduction = [70% x $7,000]
	$62,100	

(d)   Taxable Income:

	$ (500)	Other Income
	+ 7,000	Dividend Income
	- 5,200	Limitation on Deduction = [80%
	$ 1,300	Taxable Income before DRD ($6,500)]

(e)   Taxable Income:

	$ (500)	Other Income
	+ 7,000	Dividend Income
	- 4,550	Limitation on Deduction = [70%
	$ 1,950	Taxable Income before DRD ($6,500)]

(f)   The usual 80% deduction creates an NOL ($7,000 Dividend Income - $5,600 Dividends-Received Deduction - $3,000 Other Income = $1,600 NOL). So, there is no limitation on the deduction to 80% of Taxable Income.

Taxable Income:

	$ (3,000)	Other Income
	+ 7,000	Dividend Income
	- 5,600	80% Deduction = [80% x $7,000]
	$ (1,600)	

[Dividends Received Deduction p. 17-18]

3.

15% x $50,000	$7,500	
25% x $25,000	6,250	
34% x $125,000	42,500	
5% x $100,000	5,000	Extra tax on taxable income > $100,000
	$61,250	

[Corporate Income Tax Rates p. 17-20]

4.   All expenses qualify except those related to printing and selling stock. The $23,000 paid in Year 2 is allowed -- the tax year in which the item is incurred dictates the tax treatment, not the corporation's actual accounting method. [Organizational Expenses p. 17-18]

Year 1 deduction	=	$5,000 first-year immediate deduction allowed
	+	Remaining $41,000 expense x 6 months in operation / 180 months amortization period = $1,367
	=	$6,367

Chapter 18
Corporations: Organization and Capital Structure

CHAPTER HIGHLIGHTS

T he Code allows transfers of property to a corporation to be accomplished tax-free, when the person(s) transferring the property are in control of the corporation immediately after the transfer. This opportunity recognizes that (1) the taxpayer may have non-tax motivations for incorporating, and the tax system should remain neutral in this regard; and, (2) the transferor shareholder may not have any wherewithal to pay the resulting tax on the realized gain. In fact, when the new shareholder *receives* cash or other resources with which to pay the tax, a corresponding amount of the realized gain becomes recognized. The §351 provisions afford a powerful means by which to defer the tax liability on appreciated business assets, but they also force a deferral of any realized loss on the assets in the hands of the transferor.

I. Transfers to Controlled Corporations   [Organization of and Transfers to Controlled Corporations p. 18-2]
   A. Gain or loss is not recognized upon the transfer by one or more persons of property to a corporation, solely in exchange for stock in the corporation, if, immediately after the exchange, such persons are *in control* of the corporation. §351(a)
      1. The contribution of services does not qualify as property.
      2. Persons *in control* must own at least eighty percent of the total combined voting power of all classes of stock entitled to vote, *and* eighty percent of the total number of shares of all other classes of stock of the corporation.
      3. §351 is available only to the extent that stock is received by the shareholder; the receipt of money or property (often called *boot*) other than stock causes a portion of any realized gain to be recognized.
      4. Stock includes either common or preferred shares, but not stock rights or warrants.

B. Loss never is recognized in a §351 transaction. Gain, however, is recognized when cash or *boot*, (i.e., property other than stock) is received by the transferor-shareholder. The gain is limited to the lesser of the amount of cash and the fair market value of property (other than stock) received, or the realized gain. Securities received in a §351 transaction are treated as *boot*.

C. The basis of stock received by a shareholder is the same as the basis of the property transferred, increased by any gain recognized, and decreased by boot received and liabilities assumed by the corporation. Often, this is referred to as a *substituted basis*.

D. The basis of the property received by the corporation in the transfer is the same as the basis of the property in the hands of the transferor, increased by any gain recognized by the transferor. Often, this is referred to as a *carryover basis*. A basis step-down may occur in certain circumstances, so that total asset basis does not exceed the fair market value of the transferred assets.

E. A shareholder who contributes both property and services can be used in meeting the 80% control test only if the value of the contributed assets is at least ten percent of the value of the contributed services.

F. Liabilities assumed by the corporation in a §351(a) transfer usually do not create recognized gain (§357), although they decrease the shareholder's basis in the stock received. However, there are two exceptions to this non-recognition rule.

> **KEY TERMS**
>
> - §351 contribution
> - Liabilities in excess of basis
> - Gain/Loss realized, recognized
> - §1244 loss

   1. If the sum of the liabilities assumed by the corporation exceeds the total of the transferor's adjusted basis in the property transferred, the excess is taxable to the transferor-shareholder.
   2. If the primary purpose of the assumption of the liabilities is the avoidance of tax, or if there is no bona fide business purpose behind the exchange, the total liabilities assumed are treated as boot.

G. The shareholder's holding period for the stock received in a §351 transfer includes that of the capital and §1231 property transferred to the corporation. For other transferred property, the stock's holding period starts the day after the exchange. The corporation always takes a holding period which includes that of the transferor shareholder.

H. There is no recapture of ACRS/MACRS deductions in a §351 transfer, when there is no boot received. Instead, the recapture potential carries over to the corporation.

I. §351 is mandatory. The deferral procedures apply to both realized gains and losses.
   1. If the taxpayer desires a deduction for a realized loss upon incorporation, one of the §351 requirements should be violated, or the transfer of the loss assets should be delayed, so as to avoid the postponement of the deduction.
   2. Similarly, if the contributing taxpayer desires a basis in the stock, or the recipient corporation desires a higher basis in the transferred assets, than is afforded under §351, some means must be found to avoid the provision altogether.

J.   §351 also applies to subsequent asset transfers to a corporation. Thus, unless other shareholders are inclined to make a similar contribution, the subsequent contribution of assets to the entity will trigger recognized gain or loss for the less-than-eighty-percent shareholder.

K.   See Exhibit 18-1 for a summary of the basis computations in the context of a §351 exchange.

II.   Capital Structure of a Corporation   [Capital Structure of a Corporation p. 18-14]

A.   The receipt of money or property in exchange for stock produces neither gain nor loss to the recipient corporation.

B.   Using debt in the capital structure may be advantageous.
1.   Interest is deductible by the corporation.
2.   Shareholders are not taxed on the repayment of debt. An investment in stock cannot be withdrawn tax-free when the corporation has Accumulated Earnings and Profits. See Chapter 19 in the text.

C.   Using debt in the capital structure also may be disadvantageous.
1.   Securities received in a §351 transaction are treated as boot. Accordingly, the recipient-shareholder is required to recognize gain to the extent of the lesser of boot received or gain realized.
2.   In certain situations, the IRS will contend that debt is really an equity interest and will deny the corporation a deduction for interest paid with respect to the debt.   Rather, the payments that are structured as interest will be reclassified as dividends, fully taxable to the recipient to the extent of the payor's Earnings and Profits, and non-deductible to the payor corporation.
a.   This assertion often is made when the ratio of debt to outstanding equity is high, i.e., the corporation is *thinly capitalized*.
b.   The Treasury has been unsuccessful in drafting Regulations that define thin capitalization and the situations under which interest payments are to be reclassified as dividends.

D.   The Tax Court has held that legal and banking costs incurred by a company in transacting a §351 exchange are capital expenditures, rather than deductible expenses.

E.   The treatment of contributions to a corporation's capital by non-shareholders reflects the wherewithal to pay concept, as well.
1.   When an asset other than cash is contributed to a corporation, the entity recognizes no gross income. However, the transferred asset is assigned a zero basis, so that cost recovery and other deductions cannot be claimed with respect to the asset.
2.   If cash is received by a corporation as a contribution to capital from a non-shareholder, no gross income is recognized.
a.   However, the basis of any property acquired with the money during a twelve-month period, beginning on the day the contribution was received, is reduced by the amount of the contribution. Thus, only additional investments of after-tax dollars by the corporation create basis in the asset.
b.   The amount of any cash remaining after the expiration of the twelve-month period is used to reduce the basis of other corporate cost-recovery assets, relative to their relative bases.
i.   The bases of depreciable assets are reduced first.
ii.   The bases of amortizable and depletable assets then are reduced, respectively.

       iii. The bases of all other non-cash assets are reduced last.

III. Investor Losses [Investor Losses p. 18-18]
  A. Gain or loss on the worthlessness of stock or bonds depends upon whether the securities are capital assets.
    1. If the stock or bonds were capital assets, a capital loss results on the last day of the tax year in which the assets became totally worthless.
    2. If the stock or bonds were not capital assets, an ordinary loss is recognized on the day on which the assets became worthless.
  B. Bad debts must be classified as either business or nonbusiness in nature.
    1. Business bad debts constitute ordinary losses, while nonbusiness bad debts are short-term capital losses.
    2. Nonbusiness bad debts are deducted only upon total worthlessness.
    3. All bad debts of a corporation are classified as business bad debts.
  C. Stock issued as §1244 stock, upon worthlessness or a disposal at a loss, qualifies for ordinary loss treatment.
    1. No more than $1,000,000 of stock can be issued under §1244 by the corporation.
    2. The ordinary loss is limited to $50,000 ($100,000 on a joint return) per tax year. Any excess amount is a capital loss.
    3. Only the original holder of the shares can deduct an ordinary loss under §1244.

Knowing that almost nine of every ten new corporations fails within two years, the tax advisor should always counsel the new corporate client to issue stock under §1244. This is a "no-lose" technique, generally adding only one short paragraph to the corporate charter.

  D. One-half of the realized gain on the sale or other disposition of certain small business stock is excluded from gross income by the investor.
    1. The sold stock must have been held by an original holder of the shares for more than five years.
    2. At the time when the corporation was formed and the stock was issued, the corporation must not have held gross assets worth more than $50 million in the aggregate. At least 80 percent of the corporate assets must have been used in an active trade or business.
    3. The 50 percent exclusion applies to the greater of:
     a. $10 million, or
     b. Ten times the shareholder's basis in the sold stock.
    4. Recognized gain then is taxed at a 28 percent rate.

Exhibit 18-1
BASIS COMPUTATIONS WHEN §351 APPLIES

Adjusted Basis of Transferred Property

\+   Gain Recognized on Exchange

\-   Boot Received

\-   <u>Liabilities Transferred to Corporation</u>

<u>BASIS OF STOCK RECEIVED BY SHAREHOLDER</u>

Adjusted Basis of Transferred Assets

\+   <u>Gain Recognized on Exchange by Shareholder</u>

<u>BASIS OF ASSET TO CORPORATION</u>

* When built-in loss assets are contributed, the corporation's asset basis may be stepped-down to fair market value, and the shareholder may elect to reduce the basis of the shares.

TEST FOR SELF-EVALUATION - CHAPTER 18

True or False

Indicate which of the following statements are true or false by circling the correct answer.

T   F   1.   The transfer of assets to a corporation by a controlling shareholder usually is a taxable event.

T   F   2.   A corporation generally takes a carryover basis in assets that it receives from a controlling shareholder.

T   F   3.   The provisions of §351 apply when the shareholder receives stock in the entity, or when he or she receives the corporation's debt with a maturity date at least twenty years in the future.

T   F   4.   §351 applies only to contributions that "start up" a new corporation.

T   F   5.   When the provisions of §351 apply, the shareholder's realized gain is recognized to the extent of any boot that he or she receives as part of the exchange.

T   F   6.   "Boot" refers to any cash, securities, or property other than stock that is received from the controlled corporation.

T   F   7.   Liabilities always are considered boot for purposes of determining recognized gain in a §351 transfer.

T   F   8.   Gain or loss never is recognized in a §351 transfer.

T   F   9.   Depreciation recapture is recognized upon the incorporation of an entity, with respect to assets contributed in-kind by the new shareholders, even when §351 is in effect.

T   F   10.   When a corporation receives property from a non-shareholder, it recognizes gross income to the extent of the fair market value of the assets (net of any associated liabilities) on the contribution date.

T   F   11.   Under the thin capitalization doctrine, the IRS can reclassify proper interest payments as dividends.

T   F   12.   Gain from the sale of shares of qualified small business stock is fully excluded from gross income in the year of the transaction.

T   F   13.   When stock becomes worthless, a loss materializes on the day of worthlessness.

T   F   14.   Nonbusiness bad debts may be deducted only upon total worthlessness.

T   F   15.   Nonbusiness bad debts constitute long-term capital losses.

T   F   16.   Any holder of §1244 stock can qualify for ordinary loss treatment.

Fill-in-the-Blanks

Complete the following sentences with the appropriate word(s) or amount(s).

1.   When §351 applies, the shareholder recognizes gross income to the extent of any boot
       _____.

2.   The contribution of a liability to a controlled corporation triggers gain recognition if the
       debt was not incurred for a _____ _____ _____ purpose.

3.   §351 gain is triggered upon the receipt by the new shareholder of _____ corporate
       debt of the entity.

4.   The new shareholder's basis in the stock of a controlled corporation is _____ by any
       gain that he or she recognizes, and it is _____ by the face amount of any debt that he
       or she transferred to the entity.

5.   When a corporation receives non-cash property from a non-shareholder, it assigns a
       _____ basis to the asset, and it recognizes _____ gross income due to the
       contribution.

6.   When a corporation reduces the basis of its existing assets, due to the expiration of the
       _____ -month period after receiving cash from a non-shareholder, the bases are
       reduced according to their relative _____ on the date of the contribution.

7.   A new shareholder recognizes gross income to the extent of the value of any _____
       that he or she performed as a condition to receiving the stock.

8.   Gain or loss is not recognized on the transfer of property to a corporation solely in
       exchange for _____ if the person(s) transferring the property are _____
       _____ of the corporation immediately after the transfer.

9.   When other property or money is received by the transferor in an otherwise tax-free
       transfer of property to a corporation, gain is recognized to the extent of the lesser of
       _____ _____ or _____ _____.

10.   The basis of stock received in a tax-free transfer of property to a controlled corporation is
       the basis of the property transferred, increased by _____ and decreased by
       _____ and _____.

11.   The basis of property received by a corporation in a §351 transfer is the basis of the
       property prior to transfer _____ by gain recognized by the _____.

12.   In a tax-free transfer of property to a controlled corporation, any _____ recapture
       potential carries over to the corporation.

Multiple Choice

Choose the best answer(s) for each of the following questions.

USE THE FOLLOWING INFORMATION FOR PROBLEMS 1-3.

Ann, a cash basis taxpayer, incorporates her sole proprietorship. She transfers the following items to New Corporation in exchange for 100% of the corporation's stock.

	Adjusted Basis	*Fair Market Value*
Cash	$5,000	$5,000
Land	50,000	80,000
Mortgage payable	70,000	70,000
(secured by the land)		

_____ 1. The gain recognized by Ann is:
   a. $0.
   b. $30,000.
   c. $10,000.
   d. $15,000.
   e. $20,000.

_____ 2. The basis of the land to New is:
   a. $50,000.
   b. $80,000.
   c. $65,000.
   d. $85,000.

_____ 3. The basis of the stock to Ann is:
   a. $0.
   b. $55,000.
   c. $70,000.
   d. $85,000.

USE THE FOLLOWING INFORMATION FOR PROBLEMS 4-6.

Babs, a cash basis taxpayer, incorporates her sole proprietorship. She transfers the following items to New Corp. in exchange for 100% of the corporation's stock.

	Adjusted Basis	*Fair Market Value*
Cash	$5,000	$5,000
Land	90,000	80,000

_____ 4. The loss recognized by Babs is:
   a. $0.
   b. $5,000.
   c. $10,000.
   d. $15,000.
   e. $20,000.

_____ 5. The basis of the land to New Corp. is:

    a. $95,000.
    b. $90,000.
    c. $85,000.
    d. $80,000.

_____ 6.   The basis of the stock to Babs is:
    a. $0.
    b. $5,000.
    c. $80,000.
    d. $85,000.
    e. $90,000.
    f. $95,000.

USE THE FOLLOWING INFORMATION FOR PROBLEMS 7-9.

Char, a cash basis taxpayer, incorporates her sole proprietorship. She transfers the following items to New Corp. in exchange for 100% of the corporation's stock (value $185,000), and $40,000 in cash.

	Adjusted Basis	Fair Market Value
Cash	$5,000	$5,000
Land	90,000	190,000
Accounting Services Performed		30,000

_____ 7.   Gross income recognized by Char is:
    a. $0.
    b. $30,000.
    c. $40,000.
    d. $70,000.
    e. $130,000.

_____ 8.   The basis of the land to New Corp. is:
    a. $0.
    b. $90,000.
    c. $130,000.
    d. $160,000.
    e. $190,000.

_____ 9.   The basis of the stock to Char is:
    a. $0.
    b. $95,000.
    c. $125,000.
    d. $165,000.
    e. $180,000.
    f. $225,000.

USE THE FOLLOWING INFORMATION FOR PROBLEMS 10-12.

Dot, a cash basis taxpayer, incorporates her sole proprietorship. She transfers the following items to New Corp. in exchange for 100% of the corporation's stock (value $185,000), and $40,000 in cash.

	Adjusted Basis	*Fair Market Value*
Cash	$5,000	$5,000
Land	200,000	220,000

____ 10. The gain recognized by Dot is:
   a. $0.
   b. $20,000.
   c. $25,000.
   d. $40,000.

____ 11. The basis of the land to New Corp. is:
   a. $0.
   b. $200,000.
   c. $205,000.
   d. $220,000.
   e. $225,000.

____ 12. The basis of the stock to Dot is:
   a. $0.
   b. $145,000.
   c. $180,000.
   d. $185,000.
   e. $200,000.
   f. $225,000.

USE THE FOLLOWING INFORMATION FOR PROBLEMS 13-14.

On January 2, Year 1, Old Corporation received some land and improvements, worth $1,000,000, from a suburb, as an incentive to locate a new plant in that locality.

____ 13. How much gross income does Old recognize as a result of the receipt of the improved land?
   a. $0.
   b. $0 in Year 1, $1 million in Year 2 when the twelve-month period expires.
   c. $1 million in Year 1.
   d. $500,000 in Year 1, under the Economic Development Act (EDA).

____ 14. What basis does Old take in the improved land?
   a. $0.
   b. $0, until 1/2/Y2, when basis becomes $1 million.
   c. $1 million.
   d. $500,000, under the terms of the EDA.

____ 15. Under which doctrine can the IRS reclassify an interest payment as a dividend?
   a. Thin capitalization.
   b. Form over substance.
   c. Debt before equity.
   d. Federal deficit recovery.
   e. Owner reconciliation.

_____   16.   When §351 is in effect, how is depreciation recapture treated?
　　　　　　　　a.   All recapture potential is forgiven upon incorporation.
　　　　　　　　b.   All recapture potential is transferred to the new corporation.
　　　　　　　　c.   All recapture potential is assigned to the remaining business assets of the new shareholder.
　　　　　　　　d.   Any recognized gain is made up of depreciation recapture; unrecognized recapture potential transfers to the new corporation.
　　　　　　　　e.   Any depreciation recapture is taxed upon the incorporation, even though §351 is in effect.

Code Section Recognition

Several important sections of the Internal Revenue Code are described below. Indicate, by number, the appropriate Code section.

1.   _____   Allows for the tax-free transfer of property to a controlled corporation.

2.   _____   Determines the corporation's basis in property transferred in a §351 transaction.

3.   _____   Determines the consequences of contributing liabilities to a controlled corporation, in a tax-free transfer.

4.   _____   Determines the basis of stock or securities received in a tax-free transfer to a controlled corporation.

Short Answer

Zenn Corporation is formed, via the following simultaneous activities.

Taxpayer	% and Value of Only Class of Common Stock	RECEIVED		CONTRIBUTED		Corporation Assumed Taxpayer Liabilities
		Cash	One-Year Note, Fair Market Value	Asset to Corporation (Taxpayer's Basis)	Promoter Services (Fair Market Value)	
A	15% $15,000			$ 8,000		
B	15% $15,000			20,000		
C	10% $10,000	$20,000		5,000		
D	10% $10,000		$ 5,000	3,000		
E	10% $10,000	$ 6,000		15,000		
F	10% $10,000			6,000		$4,000
G	10% $10,000			7,000		8,000
H	20% $20,000			-0-	$20,000	

Complete the schedule below.

Taxpayer	Gain/Loss Realized	Gain/Loss Recognized	Basis of Assets to Zenn	Basis of Stock to Taxpayer
A				
B				
C				
D				
E				
F				
G				
H				

SOLUTIONS TO CHAPTER 18 QUESTIONS

True or False

1.   F   With exceptions, the transfer is usually tax-free. [In General p. 18-2]
2.   T   This is true when §351 applies. [Basis Determination and Related Issues p. 18-12]
3.   F   Stock not debt brings §351 into play. [Stock Transferred p. 18-5]
4.   F   Subsequent contributions to the entity also can fall under §351. [In General p. 18-2]
5.   T   Boot is usually cash or the new corporation's debt. [In General p. 18-2]
6.   T   Boot is usually cash or the new corporation's debt. [In General p. 18-2]
7.   F   Liabilities usually do not result in gain recognition, although there are some exceptions to this rule. [Assumption of Liabilities -- §357 p. 18-9]
8.   F   Gain may be recognized when boot is received by the transferor-shareholder. [In General p. 18-2]
9.   F   Recapture potential transfers to the new corporation. [Recapture Considerations p. 18-14]
10.   F   No gross income is recognized, but the transferred property takes a zero basis. [Capital Contributions p. 18-14]
11.   T   This costs the corporation a deduction, as dividends paid are nondeductible. [Reclassification of Debt as Equity (Thin Capitalization Problem) p. 18-16]
12.   F   *Fifty* percent of the gain is excluded from gross income. [Gain from Qualified Small Business Stock p. 18-21]
13.   F   The loss materializes on the last day of the tax year in which the worthlessness occurred. [Stock and Security Losses p. 18-18]
14.   T   Business bad debts are not held to this standard. [Business versus Nonbusiness Bad Debts p. 18-19]
15.   F   They are short-term capital losses. [Business versus Nonbusiness Bad Debts p. 18-19]
16.   F   Only the original holder of the shares can claim an ordinary loss. [Section 1244 Stock p. 18-20]

Fill-in-the-Blanks

1. received [In General p. 18-2]
2. bona fide business [Exception (1): Tax Avoidance or No Bona Fide Business Purpose p. 18-9]
3. any [In General p. 18-2]
4. increased, decreased [Basis of Stock to Shareholder p. 18-12]
5. zero, zero [Capital Contributions p. 18-14]
6. twelve, bases [Capital Contributions p. 18-14]
7. services [Property Defined p. 18-4]
8. stock, in control [In General p. 18-2]
9. boot received, realized gain [In General p. 18-2]
10. gain recognized, boot received, liabilities assumed [Basis of Stock to Shareholder p. 18-12]
11. increased, transferor [Basis of Stock to Shareholder p. 18-12]
12. depreciation [Recapture Considerations p. 18-14]

Multiple Choice

1. d ($70,000 Aggregate liabilities - $55,000 Aggregate basis) [Exception (2): Liabilities in Excess of Basis p. 18-10]
2. c ($50,000 basis of transferor + $15,000 gain recognized by transferor) See text Figure 18-2. [Basis of Property to Corporation p. 18-12]
3. a ($55,000 basis of contributed property + $15,000 gain recognized - $70,000 liabilities assumed) See text Figure 18-1. [Basis of Stock to Shareholder p. 18-12]
4. a §351 is mandatory and defers gain and loss realized. [In General p. 18-2]
5. b Basis carries over in a §351 transaction. [Basis of Property to Corporation p. 18-12]
6. f Basis of property given to the entity is substituted for the stock basis. [Basis of Stock to Shareholder p. 18-12]
7. d ($30,000 services + $40,000 boot received) Services meets the 10% test, so §351 applies. [Transfers for Services and Nominal Property p. 18-8]
8. c ($90,000 basis in land + $40,000 gain recognized from boot received) [Basis of Property to Corporation p. 18-12]
9. c ($95,000 basis in contributed property + $70,000 gross income recognized - $40,000 boot received) [Basis of Stock to Shareholder p. 18-12]
10. b Lesser of boot received ($40,000) or realized gain ($20,000) [In General p. 18-2]
11. d ($200,000 basis in land + $20,000 gain recognized) [Basis of Property to Corporation p. 18-12]
12. d ($205,000 basis in contributed property + $20,000 gain recognized - $40,000 boot received) [Basis of Stock to Shareholder p. 18-12]
13. a No gross income is recognized, but the transferred property takes a zero basis. [Capital Contributions p. 18-14]
14. a No gross income is recognized, but the transferred property takes a zero basis. [Capital Contributions p. 18-14]
15. a This power counters the taxpayer's advantages in issuing debt as well as stock in a start-up. [Reclassification of Debt as Equity (Thin Capitalization Problem) p. 18-16]
16. d Depreciation and credit recapture potential transfers to the new corporation. [Recapture Considerations p. 18-14]

Code Section Recognition

1. 351 [In General p. 18-2]
2. 362 [Basis of Property to Corporation p. 18-12]
3. 357 [Assumption of Liabilities -- §357 p. 18-9]
4. 358 [Basis of Stock to Shareholder p. 18-12]

Short Answer

Taxpayer	Gain/Loss Realized	Gain/Loss Recognized	Basis of Assets to Zenn	Basis of Stock to Taxpayer
A	$ 7,000	$ 0	$ 8,000	$ 8,000
B	(5,000)	0	20,000	20,000
C	25,000	20,000	25,000	5,000
D	12,000	5,000	8,000	3,000
E	1,000	1,000 υ	16,000	10,000
F	8,000	0	6,000	2,000
G	11,000	1,000 ν	8,000	0
H	20,000	20,000 λ	NONE 4	20,000 σ

υ   Limited to Gain Realized

ν   Liabilities in Excess of Basis

λ   Ordinary Service Income

4   Corporation generally is allowed a compensation deduction.

σ   Value of stock received, not services rendered

[Basis Determination and Related Issues p. 18-12]

Chapter 19

Corporations: Distributions
Not in Complete Liquidation

CHAPTER HIGHLIGHTS

Generally, corporate distributions are considered dividend income, unless the shareholder can prove otherwise. A distribution is dividend income to the extent of the corporation's Current and Accumulated Earnings and Profits. Certain stock redemptions are treated as an exchange of stock for property and, therefore, result in capital gain. When a corporation distributes appreciated property in redemption of its stock or as a property dividend, the corporation must recognize gain to the extent of the unrealized appreciation.

I. Taxable Dividends in General   [Corporate Distributions – In General p. 19-3]
    A. Shareholders do not recognize taxable income when their corporation generates earnings. (Of course, the corporation pays a corporate income tax.)
    B. The two most common sources of taxable income to shareholders are:
        1. Capital gain, when shares of stock in the corporation are sold; and,
        2. Dividend income, when a distribution is made from the corporation's Earnings and Profits. Such distributions constitute ordinary income.
    C. The amount of the dividend income for both corporate and noncorporate shareholders is equal to the amount of money distributed plus the fair market value of any other property distributed, minus any corporate liabilities assumed by the shareholder. The shareholder's basis in the property is its FMV.

II.   Sources of Corporate Distributions - see Exhibit 19-1   [Earnings and Profits p. 19-3]
        A.   First, distributions are from Current E&P.
                1.   This is ordinary income.
                2.   If there is more than one distribution during the year and total distributions
                        are greater than Current E&P, Current E&P is allocated pro rata among
                        the distributions, but Accumulated E&P is applied chronologically until it is
                        exhausted.
        B.   Second, distributions are from Accumulated E&P.
                1.   This is ordinary income.
                2.   If Current E&P for the entire year is less than zero, combine it with
                        Accumulated E&P at the date of the distribution to determine whether the
                        distribution is a dividend. Losses are allocated ratably during the year
                        unless the parties can show otherwise.
                3.   If Current E&P is positive but there was a deficit balance in Accumulated
                        E&P at the beginning of the year, distributions are dividends to the full
                        extent of Current E&P; the two accounts are *not* netted.
        C.   Third, distributions are a return of the shareholder's capital. This produces no
                taxable income, but it reduces the basis of the shareholder's investment, but not
                below zero.
        D.   Fourth, distributions will result in capital gain (or ordinary income if the stock is not
                a capital asset), to the extent of the remaining distribution.
        E.   All distributions are presumed to be from current E&P, unless the parties can
                show otherwise.

III.   Computation of Corporate E&P   [Computation of E&P p. 19-3]
        A.   Earnings and profits is the key to dividend treatment of corporate distributions. A
                distribution is taxed as a dividend only to the extent that the corporation making
                the distribution has E&P.
        B.   Earnings and profits is not defined directly in the Code. However, it is a concept
                similar to "Net Receipts Available for Dividend Payments."
        C.   Increases to E&P include:
                1.   Annual taxable income.
                2.   Non-taxable corporate receipts (e.g., tax-exempt interest income,
                        proceeds of key-employee life insurance, amount of the production
                        activities deduction).
                3.   Deduction of excess charitable contributions in succeeding taxable years
                        (note that E&P was reduced in prior year - See D.4. below).
                4.   Any dividends-received deduction.
        D.   Decreases to E&P include:
                1.   Annual corporate deficit;
                2.   Annual federal tax liability;
                3.   Dividend distributions, which include: cash paid plus the corporation's
                        basis in distributed property, increased by gain recognized on the
                        distribution, net of liabilities assumed.
                4.   Non-deductible corporate payments (e.g., premiums on key-employee life
                        insurance, charitable contributions in excess of the ten percent limitation).
                5.   Loss on sale between related parties.
                6.   A dividend never may reduce E&P below zero; E&P may be reduced
                        below zero only when the corporation generates a loss.
        E.   Other items that affect E&P:
                1.   The corporation may not reduce E&P for accelerated depreciation or
                        accelerated cost recovery deductions, including the §179 allowance. The

        corporation must use a straight-line recovery method for E&P purposes, with useful lives longer than those that apply in the ACRS/MACRS tables.

    2.   The corporation increases E&P by the increase in cash surrender value of key-employee life insurance.

    3.   A corporation's E&P is increased by the full amount of any deferred installment gain in the year of the sale.

    4.   For E&P purposes, a corporation must use the percentage-of-completion method to account for long-term contracts.

    5.   Intangible drilling costs and mineral exploration and development costs must be capitalized and amortized over a 60 month and 120 month period, respectively, for E&P purposes.

    6.   Only cost depletion can reduce E&P.

F.   Gains and losses from property transactions generally affect E&P only to the extent that they are recognized as gross income. Thus, a realized gain on an involuntary conversion that is not recognized under §1033 does not increase E&P.

G.   The AMT adjusted current earnings (ACE) adjustment is a means of capturing a measure of economic income within the corporate AMT base. ACE incorporates certain E&P adjustments, but should not be confused with current E&P.

KEY TERMS

▶   Dividend
▶   Earnings and Profits
▶   Property, Constructive, Stock Dividend
▶   Stock Redemption
▶   Attribution Rules

IV.   Consequences of a Property Dividend   [Property Dividends p. 19-12]

    A.   A corporation recognizes any realized gain (but not loss) when it distributes appreciated property as a dividend to its shareholders.

    B.   The corporation's E&P is reduced, but not below zero, by the greater of the fair market value of the distributed property or its adjusted basis, less the amount of any liability assumed by the shareholders.

    C.   E&P is increased by any gain recognized on distributed appreciated property.

    D.   The shareholder generally recognizes gross income from the dividend equal to the fair market value of the distributed assets, to the extent of the payor's E&P. Distributions in excess of E&P reduce stock basis. When stock basis reaches zero, capital gain results.

    E.   The shareholder's basis in the distributed property is the fair market value of the assets on the distribution date.

V.   Constructive Dividends   [Constructive Dividends p. 19-13]

    A.   Shareholders may receive dividend income even when no apparent distribution is made.

    B.   The IRS scrutinizes closely-held corporations (and others) for:

        1.   Unreasonable compensation paid to shareholder-employees;

        2.   Bargain sales of corporate assets to a shareholder;

        3.   Use of corporate assets at little or no cost to the shareholder (e.g., autos and recreation equipment);

        4.   Payment of shareholder debts by the corporation (e.g., loans, insurance premiums); and,

        5.   Sham loan or rental agreements between the corporation and the

shareholder.

C. Constructive distributions possess the same tax attributes as actual distributions. Accordingly, constructive distributions result in a taxable dividend only to the extent of the distributing corporation's E&P.

VI. Stock Dividends [Stock Dividends and Stock Rights p. 19-18]

A. When a corporation distributes additional shares of stock to its current shareholders, generally no taxable income results to the shareholders. In addition, there is no reduction in the corporation's E&P. This result occurs if the shareholders' proportionate interests in the corporation do not change.

B. When a stock dividend is not taxable, a portion of the basis of the stock on which the dividend is distributed must be allocated to the stock dividend. In addition, the holding period of the stock received as a dividend includes the holding period of the formerly held stock.

C. Stock dividends may be taxable if the percent of the shareholder's ownership changes. When the stock dividend is taxable, the corporation treats the distribution the same as other taxable property dividends. The amount of the dividend equals the fair market value of the property received. A taxable stock dividend may arise:

1. Where the distribution is receivable in stock or other property;

2. Where some of the shareholders receive preferred stock and others receive common stock;

3. On distributions on preferred stock;

4. When some of the shareholders receive other property, and some receive additional stock; and,

5. When common stock shareholders receive convertible preferred stock.

D. The rules for determining taxability of stock rights are identical to those for determining taxability of stock dividends.

1. If stock rights are not taxable and the value of the rights is less than fifteen percent of the value of the formerly held stock, the basis of the rights is zero unless the shareholder elects to allocate to the rights some of the basis in the formerly-held stock.

2. If the fair market value of the rights is fifteen percent of the value of the old stock and the rights are exercised or sold, the shareholder *must* allocate some of the basis in the formerly held stock to the rights.

VII. Stock Redemptions - Exchange Treatment [Stock Redemptions p. 19-20]

A. §317 defines a stock redemption as an "*exchange*" of a corporation's stock for property.

B. Thus, stock redemptions may result in recognition of long-term capital gain or loss to the shareholders. The maximum tax rate on capital gains of individual taxpayers is usually 15%, compared to the maximum rate of 35% on ordinary income. More importantly, a shareholder's recognized gain or loss is measured by the difference between the consideration received and the basis of the stock redeemed (i.e., the shareholder receives a tax-free recovery of his or her basis in the stock), rather than on the full amount of the consideration received.

C. The following types of stock redemptions result in capital gain or loss treatment:

1. Distributions "*not essentially equivalent to a dividend*" [§302(b)(1)];

2. Distributions that are "*substantially disproportionate*" in terms of shareholder effect [§302(b)(2)];

3. Distributions in *complete termination* of a shareholder's interest [§302(b)(3)]; and,

           4.   Distributions to pay a *shareholder's death taxes* [§303].

D.   A corporation recognizes gain, to the extent of the appreciation, upon the distribution of appreciated property to its shareholders in redemption of their stock. Losses never are recognized.

E.   In addition, gain is recognized on the redemption of stock with appreciated property to the extent of recapture under §§291(a), 1245, 1250, 1251, and 1252; corporate liabilities assumed by the distributor in excess of the corporation's basis for the asset; and, the excess of the fair market value over the corporation's basis in installment notes receivable that are distributed.

F.   Generally, a distribution is considered to be not essentially equivalent to a dividend [under §302(b)(1)] when there has been a meaningful reduction of the shareholder's proportionate interest in the redeeming corporation. However, few objective tests exist to determine when a redemption qualifies as not essentially equivalent to a dividend.

G.   A stock redemption is treated as *substantially disproportionate* under §302(b)(2) if two tests are met:
           1.   The shareholder owns **less than 50%** of the total combined voting power of all classes of the corporation's stock after the redemption; and,
           2.   The shareholder's interest, after the redemption, is **less than 80%** of the ownership interest that he or she held before the redemption.
           3.   For both of these tests, the stock attribution rules of §318 apply. See J. below.

H.   For purposes of the "complete termination" test of §302(b)(3), the *family* stock attribution rules of §318 are waived if the former shareholder does not have an interest in the corporation, other than as a creditor, for a ten-year period immediately after the redemption. Thus, with minor exceptions, he or she cannot be a shareholder, officer, employee, or director of the corporation over that period. In addition, the former shareholder must agree to notify the IRS of any acquisition of such stock within the ten-year period.

The effect of the stock redemption rules is that the shareholder must give up something of value, namely, control of the corporation, to obtain capital asset treatment on the exchange. This is a costly move by the shareholder in most cases, one in which the tax consequences are secondary to the effect on the dynamics and politics of the organization.

I.   Under §303, the decedent's executor may redeem, at capital gains rates (i.e., receive *exchange treatment*), an amount of corporate stock equal to the sum of the shareholder decedent's state and federal death tax liabilities and funeral and administration expenses. The value of the stock in the decedent's gross estate must exceed 35% of the decedent's adjusted gross estate to qualify for this exception to the general rule. See Chapter 27.

J.   The stock attribution rules of §318 treat the shareholder as if he or she also owned the shares that are owned by his or her:
           1.   Spouse, children, parents, and grandchildren;
           2.   Corporation, in which he or she owns at least 50% of the shares; and,
           3.   Partnership, estate, and trust, in any applicable percentage of control.

K.   The distributing corporation's Earnings and Profits are reduced as a result of a stock redemption, in an amount equal to the lesser of:

1. The redemption price; or,
2. The redeemed stock's ratable share of accumulated earnings and profits, i

$$E\&P \ x \ \frac{number \ of \ shares \ redeemed}{number \ of \ shares \ outstanding}$$

but not to exceed the sale price of the stock.

L. If §§302 and 303 do not apply, then the redemption generates dividend income to the shareholder (to the extent of the corporation's current and accumulated Earnings and Profits) in an amount equal to the cash and fair market value of the property received.

1. The shareholder's basis in the stock of the distributing corporation purportedly redeemed is applied, without increase or decrease, to the smaller number of shares retained.

2. If no shares are retained, and redemption treatment is denied as a result of the attribution rules, the basis in the stock of the distributing corporation purportedly redeemed flows to the shareholders from which there was attribution (i.e., stock that is *constructively* owned).

Exhibit 19-1
SOURCES OF CORPORATE DISTRIBUTIONS

Current Earnings and Profits* **TAXABLE**
Dividend income

Accumulated Earnings and Profits**: **TAXABLE**.
Dividend income

Return of Capital: **NONTAXABLE**; the
shareholder reduces the basis in the stock,
but not below zero

Capital Gain: **TAXABLE**, to the extent of
the amount of the distribution that remains

*If there is more than one distribution during the year AND total distributions
exceed Current E&P, allocate Current E&P pro rata among the distributions, **BUT**
apply Accumulated E&P chronologically, until it is depleted.

**If Current E&P is less than zero for the entire year, combine it with E&P at the
date of the distribution.

TEST FOR SELF-EVALUATION - CHAPTER 19

True or False

Indicate which of the following statements are true or false by circling the correct answer.

T   F   1.   When there is a deficit in accumulated E&P and a positive balance in current E&P, the two are netted on the date of a distribution in determining the taxability of the distribution to the shareholder.

T   F   2.   The distribution of appreciated property to a shareholder as a dividend results in an increase in E&P that is equal to the difference between the fair market value (FMV) and adjusted basis of the property and a decrease in E&P equal to the lesser of the Corporation's E&P or the FMV of the property.

T   F   3.   A distribution of appreciated property to a shareholder always results in the recognition of gain by the distributing corporation.

T   F   4.   When the IRS determines that a purported loan is actually a constructive dividend, the total amount of the loan will be taxable as dividend income, whether or not there is sufficient E&P to cover the distribution.

T   F   5.   A dividend may reduce E&P below zero.

T   F   6.   To qualify for exchange treatment under §302(b)(3) (complete termination), the taxpayer must agree to notify the IRS of any acquisition of such stock within a ten-year period.

T   F   7.   A distribution of depreciated property to a shareholder generally results in the recognition of loss by the distributing corporation.

T   F   8.   Under §303, the decedent's executor may redeem an unlimited amount of stock at capital gains rates.

T   F   9.   A shareholder can never recognize loss on the redemption of his or her stock.

T   F   10.   When there is more than one distribution during the year and total distributions exceed current E&P, current E&P is applied in chronological order beginning with the earliest distribution.

T   F   11.   A stock redemption reduces the corporation's E&P account in an amount not in excess of the ratable share of the corporation's E&P that is attributable to the stock redeemed.

T   F   12.   The alternative to a successful stock redemption is dividend treatment of the distribution under §301.

Fill-in-the-Blanks

Complete the following statements with the appropriate word(s) or amount(s).

1.   Stock redemptions that qualify for exchange treatment include distributions that are: not essentially equivalent to a dividend; _____ _____; in _____ _____ of a shareholder's interest; and, distributions to pay a shareholder's _____ _____.

2.   Interest income on municipal bonds _____ E&P and federal income taxes paid _____ E&P.

3.   The two sources of taxable income to a shareholder are _____ _____ when stock is sold, and _____ _____ when a corporation distributes Current or Accumulated E&P.

4.   For a shareholder, the amount of a property dividend is the _____ _____ _____ of the asset distributed.

5.   The amount of dividend income that a shareholder must recognize is limited to the corporation's _____ _____ _____.

6.   When current E&P for the entire year is less than the total of all distributions for the year, it is _____ _____ to all distributions occurring during the year.

7.   Accumulated E&P will be applied _____ to the distributions during the year, when no current E&P remains.

8.   E&P represents the corporation's _____ ability to pay a dividend without impairing its _____.

9.   Stock dividends are not taxable if they are _____ _____ distributions of stock.

10.   When a shareholder-employee receives unreasonable compensation, the distributor corporation may be forced to treat a portion of the payment as a _____ _____.

11.   A stock redemption is treated as "substantially disproportionate" if, after the redemption, the shareholder owns less than _____ of the total combined voting power of the corporation's stock and owns less than _____ of the ownership that he or she held before the redemption.

12.   When there is a deficit in accumulated E&P and a positive amount in current E&P, distributions will be regarded as dividends to the extent of _____ E&P.

13.   If stock rights received as a distribution are not taxable and the value of the rights is less than _____ of the value of the old stock, the basis of the rights is _____, unless the shareholder elects otherwise.

14.   A corporation recognizes _____, but not _____, on the distribution of property to its shareholders.

Multiple Choice

Choose the best answer for each of the following questions.

USE THE FOLLOWING INFORMATION FOR QUESTIONS 1-2.

Dill Corporation distributes a property dividend to its two equal shareholders: Bill, an individual, and Trill, a corporation. Each receives property with a basis to the corporation of $3,000 and a fair market value of $10,000. The corporation's E&P before the distribution is $8,000.

_____ 1.   How much of the distribution is treated as a dividend for Bill and Trill, respectively?
    a. $3,000, $3,000.
    b. $4,000, $4,000.
    c. $7,000, $7,000.
    d. $10,000, $10,000.

_____ 2.   What is the balance of E&P after the distribution?
    a.   ($12,000).
    b. $0.
    c. $2,000.
    d. $8,000.

USE THE FOLLOWING INFORMATION FOR QUESTIONS 3-5.

Fill Corporation made three distributions during the year, of $10,000 each, on April 1, May 30, and October 1. Current E&P for the year is $18,000. Accumulated E&P at the beginning of the year was $3,000.

_____ 3.   How much of the October 1 distribution was from Current E&P?
    a. $0.
    b. $2,000.
    c. $6,000.
    d. $10,000.

_____ 4.   How much of each of the April 1 and May 30 distributions were from Accumulated E&P?
    a. $1,000, $1,000.
    b. $2,000, $0.
    c. $2,000, $2,000.
    d. $3,000, $0.

_____ 5.   How much of the April 1, May 30, and October 1 distributions constituted return of capital, if the shareholders' bases in the stock totaled $6,000 before the distributions?

	April 1	*May 30*	*October 1*
a.	$ 0	$ 2,000	$ 2,000
b.	$ 0	$ 0	$ 3,000
c.	$ 1,000	$ 4,000	$ 1,000

d. $ 1,000 $ 4,000 $ 4,000

_____ 6.   Will Corporation, a calendar-year taxpayer, had Accumulated E&P of $15,000 on
               January 1. The following transactions took place during the year.

Taxable Income prior to taxable gains from property distributions	$5,000
Tax Liability	2,500
Excess of cost recovery over straight-line	1,000
Premium on Key-Employee life insurance	1,200
Increase in cash surrender value of Key-Employee life insurance	700
Tax-exempt interest	200
Proportionate stock dividend	3,000

What was the balance of Will's current and accumulated E&P on December 31?
- a. $15,200.
- b. $17,500.
- c. $18,000.
- d. $18,200.

USE THE FOLLOWING INFORMATION FOR QUESTIONS 7-8.

Z Corporation had 100 shares of stock outstanding. Art, Bev, and Cyd owned 90, 7, and 3
shares, respectively.

_____ 7.   On December 31, Zapp redeemed 75 of Art's shares for $25,000. These shares
               had a basis of $20,000. Zapp's Accumulated E&P on the distribution date was
               $200,000. The amount and nature of income recognized by Art is:
- a. $0 gain or loss.
- b. $5,000, capital gain.
- c. $25,000, dividend income.
- d. $25,000, capital gain.

_____ 8.   Assume instead that Zapp redeemed six shares of Bev's stock for $7,000. These
               shares had a basis of $9,000 to Bev. What is the amount and nature of income
               or loss to Bev?
- a. $0 gain or loss.
- b. $2,000 capital gain.
- c. $7,000 dividend income.
- d. $2,000 capital loss.

USE THE FOLLOWING INFORMATION FOR QUESTIONS 9-13.

Papp Corporation, which had earnings and profits of $100,000, distributed land to Ron as a
dividend in-kind. Papp's adjusted basis in this land was $3,000. The land had a fair market
value of $12,000 and was subject to a mortgage liability of $5,000, which Ron assumed.

_____ 9.   How much was Papp's recognized gain on the distribution?
- a. $0.
- b. $2,000.
- c. $4,000.

    d. $9,000.

_____ 10.   How much of the distribution was taxable to Ron as a dividend?
    a. $3,000.
    b. $4,000.
    c. $7,000.
    d. $9,000.
    e. $12,000.

_____ 11.   Ron's basis in the land is:
    a. $3,000.
    b. $4,000.
    c. $7,000.
    d. $9,000.
    e. $12,000.

_____ 12.   If Papp's E&P prior to the distribution had been $0, how much of the distribution would be taxable to Ron as a dividend?
    a. $0.
    b. $3,000.
    c. $7,000.
    d. $9,000.
    e. $12,000.

_____ 13.   If Papp's E&P prior to the distribution had been $100,000, what is the balance of E&P after the distribution?
    a. $88,000.
    b. $93,000.
    c. $97,000.
    d. $102,000.
    e.   None of the above.

USE THE FOLLOWING INFORMATION FOR QUESTIONS 14-16.

Awl Corporation, which has earnings and profits of $9,000, distributed land to Cal, an individual shareholder. Awl's basis in the land was $10,000 and, the land had a fair market value of $2,000.

_____ 14.   What is the balance of E&P after the distribution?
    a.   ($3,000).
    b.   ($1,000).
    c. $0.
    d. $7,000.

_____ 15.   As a result of the distribution, Awl Corporation recognizes:
    a. $0 gain or loss
    b. $1,000 loss.
    c. $7,000 loss.
    d. $8,000 loss.

_____ 16.   How much of the distribution was taxable to Cal as a dividend?

        a. $0.
        b. $2,000.
        c. $8,000.
        d. $9,000.
        e. $10,000.

_____ 17.   Bawl Corporation has 200 shares of stock outstanding. Of these shares, 116 shares are owned by Ann and the remaining 84 shares are owned by other unrelated individuals. If Bawl redeems 20 shares of Ann's shares, the redemption will qualify for exchange treatment because it qualifies as:

        a.   not essentially equivalent to a dividend.
        b.   substantially disproportionate.
        c.   complete termination.
        d.   redemption to pay death taxes.
        e.   the redemption does not qualify for exchange treatment.

Code Section Recognition

Several important sections of the Internal Revenue Code are listed below. Give a brief description of the provisions contained in each section.

1.   301 _____

2.   303 _____

3.   302(b)(2) _____

4.   302(b)(3) _____

5.   318 _____

Short Answer

1.   Indicate the effects on Yinn Corporation's E&P and taxable income for each of the items below.

Question	Item	Effect on Corporation's E&P	Gain/Loss Recognized by Corporation
a	Current-year Taxable Income = $65,000 **NOTE: This amount includes any gain/loss recognized by Yinn as a result of property distributions**		
b	Cash dividends paid = $6,000		
c	Federal income tax liability = $11,250		
d	Key-Employee Life Insurance: Premiums Paid = $3,000 Increase in cash surrender value = $1,400 Proceeds received, net of cash surrender value = $75,000		
e	Accelerated depreciation claimed = $8,000 [Straight-line amount = $5,000]		
f	Sale of Depreciable asset for $1,400: Original basis = $15,000 Accumulated MACRS deductions = $12,000 [Accumulated straight-line depreciation would be $8,500]		

g	Distribution of inventory:
	    Fair market value $3,800
	    LIFO basis $1,000
	    FIFO basis would be $1,800		

h	Distribution of land:
	    Fair market value $3,800
	    Basis $1,800		

i	Distribution of land:
	    Fair market value $3,800
	    Basis $1,800
	    Subject to liability $1,300		

j	Distribution of land:
	    Fair market value $2,000
	    Basis $1,800
	    Subject to liability $2,300		

k	Distribution of land:
	    Fair market value $1,800
	    Basis $3,800		

l	Distribution of §1245 asset:
	
	    Fair market value $6,600
	
	    Original basis $7,200
	
	    Accumulated straight-line
	    depreciation $2,800		

2.   Mawl Corporation has 400 shares of common stock outstanding. Ann and Bill, individuals, each own 200 shares. Each has a basis in the stock of $25,000. Mawl's E&P = $700,000.

Indicate the tax treatment to Ann if:

A)   Ann and Bill are unrelated. Mawl redeems 100 of Ann's shares for $20,000.

B)   Ann and Bill are siblings. Mawl redeems 100 of Ann's shares for $20,000.

C)   Ann and Bill are spouses. Mawl redeems 100 of Ann's shares for $20,000.

D)   Ann and Bill are spouses. Mawl redeems 200 of Ann's shares for $40,000. Ann agrees not to have any financial or operating interest in Mawl for the ten years immediately after the redemption.

E)   Ann and Bill are unrelated. Mawl redeems 60 of Ann's shares for $12,000.

3.   Complete the chart below, indicating the proper tax treatment for each of the following independent fact situations. In each case, the shareholder is an individual taxpayer.

Question	Distributed Property	E&P Before Distribution	Amount of Dividend	Effect on E&P
a	Cash, $10,000	$25,000		
b	Cash, $10,000	$8,000		
c	Land, Basis $10,000 Fair market value $13,000	$30,000		
d	Land, Basis $10,000 Fair market value $3,000	$30,000		
e	Land, Basis $3,000 Fair market value $15,000	$0		

SOLUTIONS TO CHAPTER 19 QUESTIONS

True or False

1. F   Only when there is a deficit in current E&P and a positive balance in accumulated E&P are the two netted on the date of distribution. [Allocating E&P to Distributions p. 19-7]
2. T   The entity distributes assets and recognizes gain. [Property Dividends, p. 19-12]
3. T   The entity distributes assets and recognizes gain. [Property Dividends, p. 19-12]
4. F   In all situations, a distribution is dividend income only to the extent of the corporation's E&P. [Constructive Dividends p. 19-15]
5. F   A dividend cannot reduce E&P below zero. [Earnings and Profits, p. 19-3]
6. F   The agreement waives the family attribution rules under §318. Consequently, if no family members of the redeeming shareholder own stock in the corporation, the agreement need not be made to qualify for exchange treatment under §302(b)(3). [Complete Termination Redemptions, p. 19-26]
7. F   Loss is never recognized. [Property Dividends, p. 19-12]
8. F   Only the amount of corporate stock equal to the sum of the shareholder decedent's state and federal death tax liabilities and funeral and administration expenses may be redeemed at capital gains rates. [Redemptions to Pay Death Taxes p. 19-27]
9. F   A redemption is treated as sale, therefore both gains and losses may be recognized by the shareholder. [Overview p. 19-20]
10. F   Current E&P is allocated pro rata among the distributions. [Allocating E&P to Distributions p. 19-7]
11. T   [Effect on Earnings and Profits p. 19-29]
12. T   This may be acceptable if E&P is zero or minimal in amount. [Overview p. 19-20]

Fill-in-the-Blanks

1. substantially disproportionate, complete termination, death taxes   [Overview p. 19-20]
2. increases, decreases   [Computation of E&P p. 19-3]
3. capital gain, dividend income   [Allocating E&P to Distributions p. 19-7]
4. fair market value   [Property Dividends, p. 19-11]
5. earnings and profits   [Taxable Dividends – In General p. 19-3]
6. allocated pro rata   [Allocating E&P to Distributions p. 19-7]
7. chronologically   [Allocating E&P to Distributions p. 19-7]
8. economic, capital   [Earnings and Profits, p. 19-3]
9. pro rata   [Stock Dividends and Stock Rights, p. 19-17]
10. constructive dividend   [Constructive Dividends p. 19-15]
11. 50%, 80%   [Disproportionate Redemptions p. 19-25]
12. current   [Allocating E&P to Distributions p. 19-7]
13. fifteen, zero   [Stock Dividends and Stock Rights, p. 19-18]
14. gain, loss   [Property Dividends, p. 19-10]

Multiple Choice

1. d   The dividend is equal to the fair market value of the property received. Note that the corporation has sufficient E&P, after E&P is increased by the gain from the distribution ($8,000 + $7,000 + $7,000). [Property Dividends, p. 19-10]
2. c   ($8,000 + $7,000 + $7,000 - $20,000) [Earnings and Profits, p. 19-3]
3. c   ($18,000 x $10,000/$30,000) [Allocating E&P to Distributions p. 19-7]
4. d   Accumulated E&P is applied chronologically. [Allocating E&P to Distributions p. 19-7]
5. c   Only $1,000 of the October distribution represents a return of capital ($6,000 basis - $1,000 April 1 return of capital - $4,000 May 30 return of capital = $1,000) [Allocating E&P to Distributions p. 19-7]
6. d   ($15,000 + $5,000 - $2,500 + $1,000 - $1,200 + $700 + $200) A proportionate stock dividend is not taxable and, accordingly, E&P is not reduced for such distributions. See Concept Summary 19-1 in the text. [Summary of E&P Adjustments p. 19-7]
7. c   Art owns more than 50% of Zapp Corporation after the redemption. [Disproportionate Redemptions p. 19-25]
8. d   Exchange treatment means gains or losses must be recognized. The redemption qualifies as substantially disproportionate. [Disproportionate Redemptions p. 19-25]
9. d   FMV - basis. [Property Dividends, p. 19-12]
10. c   ($12,000 - $5,000) [Property Dividends, p. 19-12]
11. e   Basis is equal to fair market value. [Property Dividends, p. 19-12]
12. c   E&P is increased by the gain recognized on the distribution. Thus, the dividend = $12,000 - $5,000 = $7,000.   [Property Dividends, p. 19-12]
13. d   [$100,000 + $9,000 gain on distribution - $7,000 ($12,000 new property basis - $5,000 assumed mortgage)] [Property Dividends, p. 19-12]
14. c   Distributions cannot reduce E&P below zero. [Earnings and Profits, p. 19-3]
15. a   Loss is not recognized on a property distribution. [Property Dividends, p. 19-12]
16. b   The dividend is equal to the FMV of the distributed property. [Property Dividends, p. 19-12]
17. e   Answer a is incorrect because Ann continues to have voting control. Answer b is incorrect because neither the 50% nor the 80% tests are met. Answer c is incorrect because Ann continues to own stock after the redemption. Answer d is incorrect because Ann did not die.   [Overview p. 19-20]

Code Section Recognition

1. Determines the tax treatment of dividends.   [Corporate Distributions – In General p. 19-3]
2. Exchange treatment for stock redemptions in a closely-held corporation, to pay death taxes. [Not Essentially Equivalent Redemptions p. 19-24]
3. Exchange treatment for substantially disproportionate redemptions of corporate stock. [Disproportionate Redemptions p. 19-25]
4. Exchange treatment for redemptions of stock that are complete terminations of the shareholder's corporate interest. [Complete Termination Redemptions p. 19-26]
5. Attribution rules for constructive stock ownership. [Stock Attribution Rules p. 19-23]

Short Answer

1.

Question	Item	Effect on Yinn Corporation's E&P	Gain/Loss Recognized by Yinn Corporation
a	Current-year Taxable Income = $65,000 *NOTE: This amount includes any gain/loss recognized by Yinn as a result of property distributions*	+$65,000	
b	Cash dividends paid = $6,000	-$6,000	
c	Federal income tax liability = $11,250	-$11,250	

d	Key-Employee Life Insurance:
	
	    Premiums Paid = $3,000
	
	    Increase in cash surrender value = $1,400
	
	    Proceeds received, net of cash surrender value = $75,000
		-$3,000
		
		+$1,400
		
		+$75,000	

e	Accelerated depreciation claimed = $8,000 [Straight-line amount = $5,000]	+$3,000	

f	Sale of Depreciable asset for $1,400: Original basis = $15,000 Accumulated MACRS deductions = $12,000 [Accumulated straight-line depreciation would be $8,500]	Taxable Income includes Recognized Loss $1,600 ($1,400 Amount Realized - 3,000 Basis) E&P should show Recognized Loss $5,100 ($1,400 - 6,500 E&P Basis Thus, the necessary adjustment is: -$3,500	

g	Distribution of inventory:
	  Fair market value $3,800
	  LIFO basis $1,000
	  FIFO basis would be $1,800
		-$3,800	$2,800 gain recognized

h	Distribution of land:
	  Fair market value $3,800
	  Basis $1,800
		-$3,800	$2,000 gain recognized

i	Distribution of land:
	  Fair market value $3,800
	  Basis $1,800
	  Subject to liability $1,300
		-$2,500	$2,000 gain recognized

j	Distribution of land:
	  Fair market value $2,000
	  Basis $1,800
	  Subject to liability $2,300
		-$0	$500 gain recognized

k	Distribution of land:
	  Fair market value $1,800
	  Basis $3,800
		-$3,800	$0 loss recognized

	Distribution of §1245 asset: Fair market value $6,600 Original basis $7,200 Accumulated straight-line depreciation $2,800	-$6,600	$2,200 gain recognized
I			

[Computation of E&P p. 19-3]

2.   A)   <u>50% test</u>:   After the redemption, Ann owns 100/300 of the shares = 33%.

        TEST PASSED

        <u>80% test</u>:   After the redemption, Ann owns 33% of the shares.
Before the redemption, Ann owned 200/400 of the shares = 50%;

        50% x 80% = <u>40%</u> > 33%

        TEST PASSED

        Thus, Ann has capital gain = $20,000 - $12,500 (basis) = <u>$7,500.</u>

Disproportionate Redemptions p. 19-25]

B)   Same as A). Stock attribution rules do NOT apply to siblings. Thus, Ann has capital gain = <u>$7,500</u>.

See Examples 33 and 34 in the text. [Disproportionate Redemptions p. 19-25]

C)   Stock attribution rules DO apply to spouses. Ann is treated as owning 100% of the stock in Mawl before and after the redemption. ***50% and 80% TESTS FAILED.***

        Thus, Ann has dividend income = $20,000.
Ann's basis of $25,000 now applies to the remaining 100 shares.

[Stock Attribution Rules p. 19-23]

D)   Under the stock attribution rules, Ann is treated as owning 100% of the stock in Mawl before and after the redemption.

        But §302(b)(3) applies -- Complete termination of Ann's interest in Mawl. Assuming that the ten-year "cooling off" period is met, the family attribution rules are waived.

Ann is treated as owning 0% of the Mawl stock after the redemption. **50% and 80% TESTS PASSED.**

Thus, Ann has capital gain = $40,000 - $25,000 = $15,000.

[Complete Termination Redemptions p. 19-26]

E) 50% test: After the redemption, Ann owns 140/340 of the shares = 41%.

TEST PASSED

80% test: After the redemption, Ann owns 41% of the shares.
Before the redemption, Ann owned 200/400 of the shares = 50%;

50% x 80% = 40% < 41%

TEST FAILED

Thus, Ann has dividend income = $12,000.
Ann's basis of $25,000 now applies to the remaining 140 shares.

[Disproportionate Redemptions p. 19-25]

3.

Question	Distributed Property	E&P Before Distribution	Amount of Dividend	Effect on E&P
a	Cash, $10,000	$25,000	$10,000	-$10,000
b	Cash, $10,000	$8,000	$8,000	-$8,000
c	Land, Basis $10,000 Fair market value $13,000	$30,000	$13,000	+$3,000 gain recognized on distribution -$13,000 FMV of distributed property

d	Land, Basis $10,000 Fair market value $3,000	$30,000	$3,000	-$10,000 [$0 loss recognized on distribution]
e	Land, Basis $3,000 Fair market value $15,000	$0	$12,000	+$12,000 gain recognized on distribution -$12,000 [a dividend cannot reduce E&P below zero]

[Property Dividends, p. 19-12]

Chapter 20

Corporate Distributions in Complete Liquidation and an Overview of Corporate Reorganizations

CHAPTER HIGHLIGHTS

 complete liquidation of a corporation generally is afforded exchange treatment in the same manner as a stock redemption. In this regard, a shareholder recognizes gain or loss equal to the difference between the basis of his or her stock and the liquidation proceeds received. Generally, the gain or loss recognized by the shareholder is a capital gain or loss. The corporation itself also recognizes gain or loss upon the distribution of its non-cash assets in a complete liquidation. However, a parent corporation that meets certain requirements can postpone recognition of gain realized upon the liquidation of a subsidiary.

The Code provides seven different types of tax-free reorganizations. Ordinarily, no gain or loss is recognized by either the acquiring or the acquired corporations who are parties to the reorganization. In addition, no gain or loss typically is recognized to the security holders of the various corporations involved in a tax-free reorganization in the exchange of their stock and securities except when they receive cash or other consideration in addition to stock and securities.

I.   Effect on the Corporation - Complete Liquidation   [Liquidations – In General p. 20-2]
    A.   Generally, corporations recognize gain or loss when distributing assets *in-kind*, or when selling assets and distributing the proceeds in complete liquidation. In determining the gain or loss on an in-kind distribution, the property is treated as

though it is sold to the distributee at fair market value. If the distributed property is subject to a liability, the deemed fair market value is an amount not less than the amount of the liability.

B. A corporation can deduct the general expenses of a liquidation. Specific liquidation expenses are offset against the selling price of the assets and thereby decrease any recognized gain or increase any recognized loss on the sale.

C. For the corporation undergoing liquidation, E&P has no tax effect on the gain or loss to be recognized by the shareholders.

II. Limitation on the Recognition of Losses [Liquidations – Effect on the Distributing Corporation p. 20-4]

 A. As a general rule, losses on the distribution of property in a complete liquidation are recognized. Exceptions to this rule, however, are provided for distributions to related parties and certain distributions of built-in loss property to unrelated parties.

  1. No loss can be recognized by a liquidating corporation on any property distributed to a shareholder who, directly or indirectly, owns more than fifty percent of the corporation's stock, unless the loss property is distributed to all shareholders on a pro rata basis **and** the property was not acquired by the liquidating corporation in a §351 transaction or as a capital contribution within five years before the distribution date.

  2. No loss can be recognized by a liquidating corporation on distributed property that it acquired shortly before the adoption of the liquidation plan.

   a. Only the amount of any built-in loss is disallowed. Subsequent declines in the value of the property can produce deductible losses where the property then is distributed to an unrelated party.

   b. The disallowance applies only to assets acquired by the corporation as a contribution to capital (eg §351).

   c. Any built-in loss property contributed within two years of the adoption of the liquidation plan is presumed to have a tax avoidance motive and is disallowed, subject to a taxpayer rebuttal.

 B. §267 does not apply to any loss of a distributee or of a distributing corporation in the case of a distribution in complete liquidation; however, such losses may be denied under other provisions.

KEY TERMS
▶ Liquidation
▶ Subsidiary liquidation
▶ Reorganization
▶ Merger
▶ Split-up, Spin-off, Split-off

III. Effect on the Shareholder - Complete Liquidation [Liquidations -- Effect on the Shareholder, p. 20-8]

 A. The general rule under Code §331 requires exchange treatment for the shareholder in a liquidation. In essence, the shareholders are treated as having sold their stock to the corporation being liquidated.

  1. Gain or loss recognized is equal to the fair market value of the assets received, net of any corporate liabilities assumed [Amount Realized] less the basis of the shareholder's stock in the corporation. Usually, the gain or loss is capital in nature.

  2. The shareholder's gain on the receipt of installment notes acquired by a liquidating corporation on the sale of its assets may be deferred until the

notes are collected. Special rules apply if the installment obligations arise from sales between certain related parties.

3.   Basis to the shareholder for assets received in the liquidation is equal to the assets' fair market value on the distribution date.

 Because a liquidation can generate taxable income at both the corporation and shareholder level, it can be an extremely expensive transaction. This consequence alone may drive investors to the S corporation, partnership, or limited liability company form of conducting the business.

B.   §332 provides for the nonrecognition of gain or loss to a parent corporation on a complete liquidation of a subsidiary. If the conditions of §332 are met, the application of its provisions are mandatory.

1.   Except for specific grandfathered acquisition provisions, the parent must directly own at least eighty percent of the voting stock and eighty percent of the total value of the subsidiary's stock.

2.   The subsidiary must distribute all of its property in complete redemption of all of its stock, within the taxable year or within three years from the close of the year in which a plan was adopted and the first distribution made.

3.   The subsidiary must be solvent and the parent must receive at least partial payment for its stock in the subsidiary.

4.   If a series of distributions occurs in the liquidation of a subsidiary, §332 applies only if the parent owns at least eighty percent of the subsidiary stock on the date the plan is adopted and at all times thereafter.

5.   Under §334(b)(1), property received by a parent corporation has the same basis as it had in the hands of the subsidiary. The parent's basis in the stock of the liquidated subsidiary disappears. In any case in which gain or loss is recognized by the liquidating corporation with respect to such property, the basis of the property in the hands of the parent is the property's FMV.

6.   Because the parent corporation takes the subsidiary's basis in its assets, the carryover limitations of §381 apply.

7.   Asset holding periods of the subsidiary carry over to the parent.

8.   A distribution to a minority shareholder in a §332 liquidation is treated in the same manner as one made pursuant to a nonliquidating redemption. Accordingly, the subsidiary must recognize gain, but not loss, on distributions to minority shareholders. The minority shareholder is subject to the §381 carryover limits.

9.   §337 provides that gain or loss generally is not recognized by the subsidiary upon the transfer of appreciated property to its parent in satisfaction of a debt. However, the parent must recognize a gain or loss.

10.   Special rules apply when a foreign subsidiary is liquidated back into its US parent.

C.   §338 allows an acquiring corporation to make an irrevocable election to treat the acquisition of a subsidiary's stock as a purchase of the assets of the acquired corporation. Therefore, the parent corporation can assign a basis to the assets of its subsidiary equal to its cost of the acquired stock. However, several conditions must be satisfied before a corporation can make a §338 election.

        1.   An irrevocable election must be made by the parent corporation by the fifteenth day of the ninth month following the acquisition month. In certain cases, the IRS may impose the election on the taxpayer.

        2.   The parent corporation must acquire eighty percent control of the corporation within twelve months.

        3.   The stock acquired in the requisite time period (i.e., twelve months) must be acquired in a taxable transaction (i.e., §351 and other non-recognition sections will not qualify).

   D.   When a §338 election is made, the following results transpire.

        1.   Generally, the target corporation recognizes gain and loss on the deemed sale. The target corporation (i.e., the purchased subsidiary) is treated as if it had sold its assets to the parent, at a deemed sale price of the parent's grossed-up basis in the target's stock. The grossed-up basis equals the value of the subsidiary's stock on the acquisition date.

        2.   The subsidiary's assets receive a new stepped-up basis. The stepped-up basis of the subsidiary's assets when a §338 election is in effect is allocated among the assets by use of the residual method.

        3.   The target corporation is treated as a new corporation. Accounting periods and methods may be elected anew.

        4.   The tax attributes of the acquired subsidiary are extinguished (i.e., no carryover of NOLs, capital losses, or E&P).

IV.   Corporate Reorganizations   [Corporate Reorganizations p. 20-14]

   A.   The Code provides the following seven types of corporate reorganizations that qualify as nontaxable exchanges.

        1.   Type A - a statutory merger or consolidation.

        2.   Type B - the acquisition by a corporation, in exchange solely for all or part of its or its parent's voting stock, of another corporation if, immediately after the acquisition, the acquiring corporation has control of the other corporation.

        3.   Type C - the acquisition by a corporation, in exchange solely for all or part of its or its parent's voting stock, of substantially all of the assets of another corporation. The acquired corporation must distribute to its shareholders the stock, securities and other property it receives in the reorganization and any of its own property.

        4.   Type D - a transfer by a corporation of all or part of its assets to another corporation if, immediately after the transfer, the transferor or one or more of the shareholders, or any combination thereof, is in control of the corporation to which the assets are transferred.

        5.   Type E - a recapitalization.

        6.   Type F - a mere change in identity, form, or place of organization.

        7.   Type G - a transfer by a corporation of all or part of its assets to another corporation in a bankruptcy or receivership proceeding.

   B.   To qualify as a tax-free reorganization, the transaction also must generally satisfy the sound business purpose, continuity of interest, and continuity of business enterprise doctrines.

VI.   Effect on the Corporation – Reorganizations   [Summary of the Tax Consequences in a Tax-Free Reorganization p. 20-17]

   A.   Generally, neither the acquiring nor the acquired corporation recognizes gain or loss in a corporate reorganization. However, the acquired corporation recognizes gain to the extent that it receives cash and other property and does not distribute such property.

B.   Property that the acquiring corporation receives from the acquired corporation retains the basis it had in the hands of the acquired corporation, increased by the gain, if any, recognized by the acquired corporation on the transfer.

VII.   Effect on the Shareholder – Reorganizations   [Summary of the Tax Consequences in a Tax-Free Reorganization p. 20-17]

A.   Certain corporate reorganizations, governed by §§361 and 368, receive tax-free status. These sections override the general result, in which a shareholder recognizes capital gain or loss on the exchange of one security for another.

B.   Although the "like-kind exchange" provisions specifically do not apply to exchanges of securities, the corporate reorganization provisions generate tax results that are very similar thereto.

C.   In general, gain or loss realized in a corporate reorganization is not recognized.

   1.   Realized gain is recognized to the extent of cash or other property received by the shareholder. To the extent of the shareholder's ratable earnings and profits, this gain is recognized as dividend income.

   2.   Loss never is recognized by the shareholder.

   3.   With respect to long-term debt, gain is not recognized if securities are surrendered in at least the same principal amount as those received.

D.   The basis of the securities in the **new** corporation received by the shareholder equals his or her basis in the **old** securities *PLUS* recognized gain and dividend income *MINUS* the amount of cash, and fair market value of other property, received. This procedure defers the unrecognized shareholder gain or loss, but it does not forgive it.

E.   The basis of other property received is the fair market value of such other property.

TEST FOR SELF-EVALUATION - CHAPTER 20

True or False

Indicate which of the following statements are true or false by circling the correct answer.

T   F   1.   By using a corporate liquidation, the entity can eliminate the dividend exposure of its shareholders.

T   F   2.   A corporation is required to recognize all gains and losses realized with respect to in-kind liquidating distributions.

T   F   3.   B reorganizations involve the exchange of stock for assets.

T   F   4.   For liquidation loss purposes, the basis of disqualified property that is later sold or distributed to an unrelated party is reduced by the excess of the property's basis on the contribution date over the property's fair market value on such date.

T   F   5.   In a §332 liquidation, the distributing corporation must recognize gain on a property distribution to minority shareholders.

T   F   6.   To meet the requirements of §332, the parent corporation generally must directly own 80% of the voting stock or 80% of the value of the outstanding stock.

T   F   7.   A corporation always recognizes gain or loss on the distribution of its assets during the liquidation period.

T   F   8.   For a corporation undergoing a liquidation, E&P has no tax impact on the gain or loss to be recognized by the shareholders.

T   F   9.   A shareholder may recognize gain or loss on the exchange of his or her stock in a tax-free reorganization.

Fill-in-the-Blanks

Complete the following statements with the appropriate word(s) or amount(s).

1.   Liquidating distributions are subject to tax both at the _____ level and at the _____ level.

2.   Except for distributions to _____ _____, the corporation recognizes losses realized relative to property distributed in a complete liquidation.

3.   C reorganizations involve the acquisition by one corporation, in exchange solely for its _____ _____, of substantially all of the _____ of another corporation.

4.   Under the general rule provided in §334(a), the basis of property received by an individual shareholder in a complete liquidation is the _____ _____ _____ of the assets.

5. If depreciated property is acquired by a liquidating corporation in a _____ _____ transaction or as a _____ _____ _____ within _____ years of the adoption of the plan of liquidation, the transaction will be deemed to have occurred for the principal purpose of providing a loss to the corporation.

6. A subsidiary does not recognize gain or loss on a liquidating distribution to a parent corporation that directly owns _____ _____ _____ of the stock of the subsidiary.

7. The nonrecognition of gain or loss on liquidating distributions under §332, does not apply to distributions to _____ shareholders.

8. To qualify for a §338 election, the stock of the target corporation must have been acquired within _____ months.

9. In a tax-free reorganization, a _____ is never recognized by a shareholder.

10. With respect to a tax-free reorganization, gain is recognized to the extent of the lesser of _____ _____ or _____ and _____ _____ received.

11. In a tax-free reorganization, the basis of stock and securities received by a shareholder is the same as the bases of _____ _____, decreased by the amount of _____ _____, and increased by the amount of _____ and _____ _____ recognized on the transaction.

Multiple Choice

Choose the best answer for each of the following questions.

USE THE FOLLOWING INFORMATION FOR QUESTIONS 1-2.

Tillie is the sole shareholder of Xan Corporation. The basis of the total assets owned by Xan is $100,000. The fair market value of these assets is $175,000. Tillie has a basis in her stock of $125,000. Xan has Accumulated E&P of $50,000. Tillie exchanges all of her shares for all of Xan's assets, in a complete liquidation of Xan.

_____ 1. What is the amount and nature of gain recognized by Tillie?
      a. $50,000 dividend income, $125,000 return of capital.
      b. $25,000 capital loss.
      c. $50,000 capital gain.
      d. $50,000 dividend income.

_____ 2. What is the basis of the assets received by Tillie?
      a. $50,000.
      b. $100,000.
      c. $125,000.
      d. $175,000.

_____ 3. In a qualified reorganization under §368, the shareholder's realized gain on the exchange is:

a.   Not recognized.
b.   Recognized to the extent of the lesser of the gain realized or the cash and FMV of other property received.
c.   Recognized in full.
d.   Recognized to the extent of E&P.

____ 4.   In a qualified reorganization under §368, the shareholder's realized loss on the exchange is:
a.   Recognized in full.
b.   Never recognized.
c.   Partially recognized, to the extent of depreciation recapture.
d.   Partially recognized, to the extent of liabilities in excess of basis.

____ 5.   The basis of securities in the "new" corporation received by a shareholder in a corporate reorganization will be equal to his or her "old" basis, adjusted by which of the following items? More than one answer may be correct.
a.   Recognized gain and dividend income.
b.   Cash received.
c.   Fair market value of other property received.
d.   Loss recognized.

USE THE FOLLOWING INFORMATION FOR QUESTIONS 6-8.

Alff Corporation distributes the following assets "in kind," in a complete liquidation of the business.

	Basis to Alff	Fair Market Value
Land	$20,000	$30,000
Inventory	4,000	14,000
Machinery (original cost $17,000)	10,000	20,000

____ 6.   The gain recognized by Alff on the distribution is:
a. $ 6,000.
b. $10,000.
c. $16,000.
d. $23,000.
e. $30,000.

____ 7.   The shareholder who receives the machinery will have a basis in these assets of:
a. $0.
b. $10,000.
c. $17,000.
d. $20,000.
e.   None of the above.

____ 8.   Kurt, the sole shareholder of Alff has a basis of $30,000 in his Alff stock. With respect to the liquidating distribution, Kurt recognizes a gain of:
a. $0.
b. $30,000.
c. $31,000.

    d. $34,000.

USE THE FOLLOWING INFORMATION FOR QUESTIONS 9-11.

Pursuant to a tax-free reorganization, Peg exchanges stock she owns in Mass Corporation for stock in Lass Corporation plus $5,000 cash. The Mass and Lass shares have a fair market value of $20,000 and $15,000, respectively.

_____ 9.   If Peg's basis in the Mass stock is $16,000, the gain Peg recognizes is:
     a. $0.
     b. $1,000.
     c. $4,000.
     d. $5,000.
     e. $15,000.

_____ 10.   If Peg's basis in the Mass stock is $22,000, the gain or loss Peg recognizes is:
     a. $0.
     b. $2,000 gain.
     c. $5,000 gain.
     d. $2,000 loss.
     e. $5,000 loss.

_____ 11.   Peg's basis in the Mass stock is $22,000. Peg's basis in the Lass stock is:
     a. $0.
     b. $15,000.
     c. $17,000.
     d. $20,000.
     e. $22,000.

USE THE FOLLOWING INFORMATION FOR QUESTIONS 12-15.

Lett Corporation owns 100 percent of the stock of Rott Corporation. Lett's basis in the Rott stock is $200,000. Rott liquidates and distributes the following assets to Lett.

	Basis	Fair Market Value
Cash	$100,000	$100,000
Installment Note	25,000	30,000
Inventory	3,000	7,000
Land	50,000	75,000
Totals	$178,000	$212,000

_____ 12.   Rott's recognized gain on the liquidation is:
     a. $0.
     b. $ 5,000.
     c. $ 8,000.
     d. $34,000.

_____ 13.   The basis of Rott's assets to Lett is:
     a. $178,000.

      b. $181,000.
      c. $183,000.
      d. $212,000.

____ 14. Assume that the requirements of §338 were met and a §338 election was made. What is the gain recognized by Rott on the liquidation?
      a. $0.
      b. $5,000.
      c. $8,000.
      d. $34,000.

____ 15. Assume the same facts as in problem 14. What is the basis of the assets to Lett?
      a. $178,000.
      b. $181,000.
      c. $183,000.
      d. $200,000.
      e. $212,000.

USE THE FOLLOWING INFORMATION FOR QUESTIONS 16-17.

Amy is the sole shareholder of Tipp Corporation, and she has a basis in the Tipp stock of $20,000. Tipp distributes the following assets "in-kind," in a complete liquidation under §331.

	Basis to Tipp	Fair Market Value
Cash	$4,000	$4,000
Inventory	6,000	6,000
Land (subject to a $15,000 mortgage)	10,000	12,000

____ 16. The gain recognized by Tipp on the distribution is:
      a. $0.
      b. $2,000.
      c. $3,000.
      d. $5,000.

____ 17. The gain or loss recognized by Amy on the distribution is:
      a. $0.
      b. $2,000 gain.
      c. $15,000 loss.
      d. $13,000 loss.

USE THE FOLLOWING INFORMATION FOR QUESTIONS 18-19.

Marty, an individual and sole shareholder of ABC Corporation, has a basis in his ABC stock of $5,000. After adopting a plan of complete liquidation early this year, ABC sold all of its assets (adjusted basis of $30,000) to an unrelated party, in exchange for $10,000 cash and installment notes of $40,000. The installment notes are payable over a five-year period, beginning in the following year. Immediately after the sale, ABC distributed the cash and installment notes to Marty.

____ 18. The gain recognized by Marty this tax year is:

a. $9,000.
b. $10,000.
c. $15,400.
d. $20,000.
e. $45,000.

____   19.   The gain recognized by Marty on the collection of each note over the next five years is:
a. $0 (entire gain was recognized in the year of liquidation).
b. $6,400.
c. $7,200.
d. $8,000.
e.   It cannot be determined from the information given.

____   20.   Pursuant to a complete liquidation, XYZ Corporation distributed to its shareholders property with a basis of $350,000 and fair market value of $500,000. The property was subject to a liability in the amount of $600,000. On the distribution, XYZ recognizes a gain of:
a. $0.
b. $100,000.
c. $150,000.
d. $250,000.

____   21.   In connection with a plan of corporate reorganization adopted in Year 4, Ruth exchanged 100 shares of B Corporation common stock for 300 shares of L Corporation common stock. Ruth had purchased the B stock in Year 1 for $5 per share. Fair market value of the L stock was $9 per share on the date of the exchange. As a result of this exchange, Ruth's long-term capital gain in Year 4 was:
a. $0.
b. $1,000.
c. $1,800.
d. $2,200.

____   22.   X Corporation acquires all of the stock of Z Corporation for $800,000 and elects to liquidate Z pursuant to an election under §338. If the fair market value of Z's physical assets is $700,000 and Z's basis in the assets is $500, how much of the purchase price must be allocated to goodwill or going concern value?
a. $0.
b. $100,000.
c. $200,000.
d. $800,000.

Code Section Recognition

Several important sections of the Internal Revenue Code are described below. Indicate, by number, the appropriate code section.

1.   ____   General rule for the treatment of complete liquidation to shareholder.

2. _____ Allows a parent corporation to treat the acquisition of a subsidiary's stock as a purchase of the subsidiary's assets.

3. _____ Allows a subsidiary to liquidate into its parent without the recognition of gain or loss.

4. _____ Allows a parent corporation to liquidate a subsidiary without the recognition of gain or loss.

5. _____ Provides the general rule for treatment of the corporation in a complete liquidation.

6. _____ Governs certain tax-free corporate reorganizations.

7. _____ Governs the determination of the basis of property received as a liquidating distribution.

Short Answer

1. XYZ Ltd. distributed the following property in light of its complete liquidation.

Asset	Basis	Fair Market Value
Inventory (FIFO basis)	$70,000	$100,000
Equipment ($40,000 of depreciation has been taken)	20,000	40,000
Securities held as an investment for four months	40,000	60,000
Supplies	0	5,000
Land purchased as an investment in 1960	5,000	90,000

Compute the nature and amount of gain or loss recognized to XYZ.

2.   Terri is the sole shareholder of Kiln Corporation. She holds shares with a basis of $25,000 and long-term debt from Kiln of $18,000.

Erg Corporation acquires Kiln in a reorganization, taking all of Kiln's assets (basis $100,000, fair market value $170,000). Erg gives Terri shares in Kiln (fair market value $60,000), long-term debt in Erg of $20,000, and $7,000 cash. Erg assumes all Kiln debt.

What is Terri's Realized Gain?

What is Terri's Recognized Gain?

What is Terri's basis in the Erg stock?

What is Erg's basis in its new assets?

3.   Albert exchanges stock he owns in Lapp Corporation for stock in Tapp Corporation worth $2,000 and $1,000 in cash. The exchange is pursuant to a tax-free reorganization. Although Albert paid $5,000 for his stock six years ago, it currently has a fair market value of $3,000.

What is Albert's realized gain or loss?

What is Albert's recognized gain or loss?

What is Albert's basis in the Tapp stock?

SOLUTIONS TO CHAPTER 20 QUESTIONS

True or False

1. T   After a liquidation, E&P disappears. [Liquidations and Other Distributions Compared p. 20-3]
2. F   The recognition of losses is subject to various limitations. [Limitation on Losses p. 20-4]
3. F   A Type B reorganization involves the exchange of stock for stock. [Summary of the Different Types of Reorganizations p. 20-16]
4. T   "Anti-stuffing" rules can lead to this result. [Built-In Loss Situations p. 20-5]
5. T   This is similar to stock redemption treatment. [Tax Treatment when a Minority Interest Exists p. 20-10]
6. F   The parent must directly own 80% of the voting stock **and** 80% of the value of the outstanding stock. [Liquidations – Parent-Subsidiary Situations p. 20-9]
7. F   Gain or loss generally is not recognized in the liquidation of a subsidiary corporation. [Liquidations – Parent-Subsidiary Situations p. 20-9]
8. T   This is more favorable than most redemption arrangements. [The General Rule p. 20-8]
9. F   Loss never is recognized. [Gain or Loss p. 20-18]

Fill-in-the-Blank

1. corporate, shareholder [Liquidations and Other Distributions Compared p. 20-3]
2. related parties [Related-Party Situations p. 20-5]
3. voting stock, assets [Summary of the Different Types of Reorganizations p. 20-16]
4. fair market value [The General Rule p. 20-8]
5. §351, contributions to capital, two [Limitations on Losses p. 20-4]
6. 80% or more [Liquidations – Parent-Subsidiary Situations p. 20-9]
7. minority [Tax Treatment when a Minority Interest Exists p. 20-10]
8. twelve [Requirements for Application p. 20-12]
9. loss [Gain or Loss p. 20-18]
10. gain realized, cash, other property [Gain or Loss p. 20-18]
11. stock surrendered, boot received, gain, dividend income [Basis p. 20-19]

Multiple Choice

1. c   ($175,000 - $125,000) [Liquidations and Other Distributions Compared p. 20-3]
2. d   Basis is equal to the fair market value of the assets received. [The General Rule p. 20-4]
3. b   This mirrors like-kind exchange treatment. [Gain or Loss p. 20-18]
4. b   This mirrors like-kind exchange treatment. [Gain or Loss p. 20-18]
5. a,b,c Loss is never recognized in a qualified reorganization. [Basis p. 20-19]
6. e   [($30,000 + $14,000 + $20,000) - ($20,000 + $4,000 + $10,000)]. [The General Rule p. 20-4]
7. d   Basis is equal to the fair market value of the machinery. [The General Rule p. 20-4]
8. d   [$64,000 (FMV of assets received) less $30,000 (basis in stock)] [The General Rule p. 20-8]

9. c   Gain recognized is limited to the lesser of gain realized ($4,000 = $20,000 - $16,000) or boot received ($5,000). [Gain or Loss p. 20-18]

10. a   Loss is not recognized in a tax-free reorganization. [Gain or Loss p. 20-18]

11. c $22,000 (basis in stock surrendered) - $5,000 (boot received). [Basis p. 20-19]

12. a   Gain is not recognized in a complete liquidation of a subsidiary. [Liquidations – Parent-Subsidiary Situations p. 20-9]

13. a   The subsidiary's basis in the assets carries over to the parent. [Basis of Property Received by the Parent Corporation – The General Rule p. 20-11]

14. d   ($212,000 - $178,000). [Tax Consequences p. 20-12]

15. d   The basis of Rott's assets is equal to Lett's basis in the stock. [Tax Consequences p. 20-12]

16. d   FMV of land cannot be computed as less than the mortgage. [The General Rule p. 20-4]

17. c   Assuming the property is not disqualified property, the loss recognized is $13,000 [$22,000 (FMV of property received) - $15,000 (mortgage) - $20,000 (basis in stock)]. [The General Rule p. 20-8]

18. a   ($10,000 cash received less the stock basis allocated to the cash $1,000 [($10,000 / $50,000) X $5,000]) [Special Rule for Certain Installment Obligations p. 20-8]

19. c   ($40,000 installment note received less $4,000 stock basis allocated to the installment note = $36,000 gross profit; $36,000 / $40,000 = 90%; 90% X $8,000 annual note collected = $7,200) [Special Rule for Certain Installment Obligations p. 20-8]

20. d   The FMV of the distributed property cannot be less than the amount of the liability. [The General Rule p. 20-4]

21. a   Gain is not recognized in an exchange of stock in a tax-free reorganization. [Gain or Loss p. 20-18]

22. b   ($800,000 - $700,000) [Allocation of Adjusted Grossed-Up Basis p. 20-13]

Code Section Recognition

1. 331   [The General Rule p. 20-8]
2. 338   [Requirements for Application p. 20-12]
3. 337   [Liquidations – Parent-Subsidiary Situations p. 20-9]
4. 332   [Liquidations – Parent-Subsidiary Situations p. 20-9]
5. 336   [The General Rule p. 20-4]
6. 368   [Summary of the Different Types of Reorganizations p. 20-17]
7. 334   [The General Rule p. 20-8]

Short Answer

1. XYZ recognizes gain on the distribution of the following property:

Asset	Gain Recognized	Nature of Gain
Inventory	$30,000	Ordinary income
Equipment	20,000	§1245 depreciation recapture
Securities	20,000	Short-term capital gain
Supplies	5,000	Ordinary income (tax benefit rule)
Land	85,000	Long-term capital gain

$160,000

[The General Rule p. 20-4]

2.

Amount Realized ($60,000 + $20,000 + $7,000)	$87,000
Adjusted Basis ($25,000 + $18,000)	-43,000
Gain Realized	$44,000
Boot Received	$7,000
Additional Long-term Debt that Terri acquired	2,000
Gain Recognized	$9,000
Basis in Kiln Stock	$25,000
Gain Recognized	+9,000
Boot Received, Excess Long-term Debt	-9,000
Basis in Erg Stock	$25,000
Basis of Assets to Kiln = **Basis of Assets to Erg**	$100,000

[Summary of the Tax Consequences in a Tax-Free Reorganization p. 20-17]

3.

Fair market value of Tapp stock	$2,000
Cash	1,000
Total amount realized	$3,000
Less: Basis in Lapp stock	5,000
Realized loss	$(2,000)
Recognized loss	$ 0

Albert cannot recognize the $2,000 realized loss, because no loss may be recognized in a tax-free reorganization. §356(c). Gain is not recognized on a boot distribution unless gain is realized on the overall transaction.

Albert's **basis in the Tapp stock** is $4,000, the same basis as the property exchanged less the cash boot received.

[Summary of the Tax Consequences in a Tax-Free Reorganization p. 20-17]

Chapter 21
Partnerships

CHAPTER HIGHLIGHTS

 partnership is not a taxable entity. Instead, the income of the partnership flows through to the partners. Income is allocated to the partners according to the partnership agreement. Many items of income and expense retain their character as they flow through to the partners. Generally, if an item of income or expense would affect a partner's income differently if it retained its character, then the character of the item flows through to the partners.

All other items are netted before they flow through to the partners. A partner's basis in his or her partnership interest is a substituted basis of the property contributed, plus any gain recognized on the transfer, plus his or her share of partnership liabilities contributed by other partners, and minus his or her liabilities that are assumed by other partners. Subject to a few exceptions, there generally is no gain or loss recognized on contributions to the partnership. A partner's basis later is adjusted for liabilities, contributions, withdrawals, profits, and losses.

A partnership takes a carryover basis in the property received. The basis of property received by the partnership is not automatically increased by the gain recognized to the partner as a result of the transfer, unless the partnership would be treated as an investment company if it was incorporated.

I. Nature of Partnerships   [Overview of Partnership Taxation p. 21-2]
    A.   Partnerships are not separate taxable entities. Rather, the partners carry on

business as "co-owners," allocating assets and liabilities, profits and losses, according to a formal or informal agreement (i.e., the aggregate concept).

B. A partnership, however, is treated as a separate taxable entity for purposes of making various tax elections, and for selecting its taxable year, depreciation method, and accounting methods (i.e., the entity concept).

C. A partnership must actively conduct a trade or business.

D. Certain unincorporated organizations may elect not to be treated as partnerships. This election generally only applies to joint ventures for the production, extraction, or use of property which will not be resold and "investment clubs" that are not engaged in a trade or business.

E. A partnership must file an information return (Form 1065) within 3 1/2 months after the end of its taxable year (i.e., April 15th for a calendar-year partnership). Each of the partnership's items is reported on Schedule K.

F. As part of its tax return, the partnership must include a Schedule K-1 for each of its partners. This schedule reports the amount and nature of income that has been allocated to the partner, according to the partnership agreement.

G. *Publicly traded partnerships* (PTPs) are partnerships whose interests are traded on an established securities market or are readily tradeable on a secondary market or the substantial equivalent of a secondary market. Generally, PTPs are treated as corporations.

H. A limited partnership is comprised of one or more general partners and one or more limited partners.

    1. Unless special rules apply, only the general partners are liable to creditors. A limited partner's risk of loss is restricted to his or her equity investment in the partnership.

    2. When a limited partnership uses nonrecourse debt to finance the purchase of property and pledges the property as collateral, usually no partner is personally liable (i.e., the debt is nonrecourse debt).

I. Limited liability companies may receive the benefits of partnership tax treatment and the limited liability afforded corporations under state law.

J. A partnership may elect large partnership status. This allows the entity to combine and pass through no more than eleven different categories of items to its partners. This simplified reporting method is available if the entity had at least one hundred partners.

II. Partner's Share of Income and Expenses   [Measuring and Reporting Income p. 21-20]

A. The following items retain their character as they pass through to the partners.

    1. Ordinary income from operations, after deducting allowable expenses.

    2. Long- and short-term capital gains/losses, and §1231 gains/losses.

    3. Charitable contributions.

    4. Tax-exempt interest.

    5. Tax preferences for the alternative minimum tax.

    6. Jobs credit and foreign tax credit.

    7. Expenses that would be itemized deductions or non-business deductions to the partner.

    8. Portfolio income (dividends, interest and royalties) and related expenses.

> **KEY TERMS**
> - Aggregate, Entity concepts
> - Special allocation
> - Guaranteed payment
> - Choice of tax year
> - Inside, outside basis
> - Basis of partnership interest

               9.   Amounts used to compute the production activities deduction.

               10.   Passive activity items (i.e., income or loss from rental real estate).

               11.   Immediately expensed tangible personal property (i.e., §179 deduction).

               12.   Meals and entertainment expenses, subject to the 50% disallowance.

               13.   Self-Employment income.

               14.   Other items specifically allocated by the partnership agreement.

     B.   All other income or expense items are netted with ordinary income. A partnership is not entitled to a dividends-received deduction or a NOL deduction. A partnership also cannot deduct payments that it makes for a partner's fringe benefits, since a partner is not considered to be an employee of the partnership.

     C.   By election, organization costs may be amortized ratably over a period of 180 months or more, starting with the month in which the partnership began business. As much as $5,000 of these expenses can be deducted in the first year of operations. In contrast, costs of promoting the sale of a partnership interest (*syndication costs*) are not deductible.

     D.   Partners may allocate specific income, deductions, or credits in any ratio identified in the partnership agreement, if such allocation has economic substance. However, when in-kind property is transferred to a partnership, any realized gain or loss as of the contribution date remains assigned to the contributing partner upon ultimate disposal by the entity in a taxable transaction.

     E.   Gain or loss is ordinary when the partnership disposes of either of the following.

               1.   Contributed receivables that were unrealized in the contributing partner's hands at the contribution date.

               2.   Contributed property that was inventory in the partner's hands on the contribution date, if the entity disposes of the property within five years of the contribution.

     F.   The tax year of a partnership generally must be the same as the taxable year of the partners owning more than 50% of profits and capital (i.e., a majority interest).

               1.   If the partners owning a majority interest do not have the same taxable year, the partnership tax year must be the same as all of its principal partners (i.e., those owning a 5% or greater interest).

               2.   If the principal partners do not have the same tax year, the partnership generally must adopt the taxable year that results in the least aggregate deferral of income.

               3.   The partnership generally can adopt any other fiscal year only if permission is received from the IRS.

               4.   Under certain circumstances, a partnership may elect to use a tax year other than a required year, provided that the income deferral is three months or less and certain tax deposits are made by the partnership with the Federal government.

     G.   The partnership tax year ends on the:

               1.   Termination of the business;

               2.   Death of a partner or termination of his or her entire interest, BUT ONLY for that partner; or,

               3.   Sale of a total of 50% or more of the partnership interests within a 12-month period. For purposes of this test, subsequent sales of the same partnership interest within a single twelve-month period are ignored.

III.   Forming a Partnership   [Formation of a Partnership: Tax Effects   p. 21-10]

     A.   Generally, no gain or loss is recognized by partners or the partnership on contributions that are made to the partnership when the partnership is formed, or contributions made subsequent to the creation of the entity. The following are

exceptions to this rule.
1. If the partnership interest is received solely for services rendered, the FMV of the interest is taxable to the partner as ordinary income;
2. Liabilities assumed by the partnership that are in excess of the partner's basis in the contributed property create taxable income to the contributor, in an amount equal to such excess;
3. If the partnership is used to effect a tax-free exchange of assets; and,
4. The contributing partner is required to recognize gain realized on the transfer of property to a partnership that would be treated as an investment company if the partnership were incorporated.

B. The holding period of a partner's interest acquired by a noncash property contribution includes the holding period of the contributed property. However, the holding period starts on the day the interest is acquired if the contributed property is neither a capital asset nor a §1231 asset in the hands of the contributing partner.

IV. Partner's Basis in the Partnership Interest
A. Each partner has an *inside basis* and an *outside basis* in partnership assets. **Inside basis** refers to the partner's share of the adjusted basis of the aggregate partnership assets, as determined from the partnership's tax accounts. A partner's **outside basis** represents the actual investment of after-tax dollars that the partner has made in the partnership.
B. The partner's original interest basis equals:
1. Money contributed,
2. *Plus* the adjusted basis (to the partner) of other property contributed,
3. *Plus* the fair market value of services the partner performed to receive the partnership interest.
4. *Plus* gain recognized by the partner under the investment company rule (See III, A.4).
5. *Plus* the partner's share of partnership liabilities, assumed from other partners on the date of entry.
6. *Minus* the share of the partner's liabilities assumed by the other partners at the date of entry.
C. The following adjustments are made to the partner's original basis.
1. *Add* additional contributions of assets to the partnership.
2. *Subtract* withdrawals and distributions of partnership assets.
   a. These payments reduce the partner's basis, but not below zero.
   b. Cash received in excess of the partner's basis will result in income recognition.
3. *Add* the partner's share of the net income of the partnership.
4. *Subtract* the partner's share of net partnership losses.
   a. Losses reduce the partner's basis, but basis cannot be reduced below zero. There is an indefinite carryover of such excess losses.
5. *Add* the partner's share of any tax-exempt income of the partnership.
6. *Subtract* the partner's share of non-deductible partnership expenses.
7. *Add* the partner's share of any increases in the partnership liabilities.
8. *Subtract* the partner's share of any reduction in the partnership liabilities.
D. Different results occur when there is a built-in gain on the contributed property, where nonrecourse debt is assumed by the entity.

V. Loss Limitations [Loss Limitations p. 21-32]
    A. Losses that flow through to a partner are eligible for deduction on his/her income tax return only to the extent that the following requirements are met, in the indicated order.
        1. There must be adequate **basis** in the partnership interest. For this purpose, basis is determined at the end of the entity's tax year, as adjusted for distributions and partnership gains, income, and losses.
        2. There must then be adequate amounts **at-risk** for the partner. Liabilities increase the at-risk amount only with respect to recourse and qualified non-recourse obligations.
        3. **Passive activity** limitations may further restrict the amount deductible for the tax year.

VI. Basis and Holding Period of Assets to Partnership   [Tax Issues Relative to Contributed Property p. 21-12]
    A. The basis of the assets to the partnership is a carryover basis from the contributing partner. The basis of property received by the partnership is not automatically increased by the gain recognized to the partner as a result of the transfer, unless the partnership would be treated as an investment company if it was incorporated.

Compare these rules with those of §351. It is much easier for a partner to make a capital contribution subsequent to the formation of a partnership than it is for a shareholder to make such a deferred contribution. In the latter case, the eighty percent group of owners must act in concert, not an easy feat in the midst of later business dealings.

    B. The holding period for an asset contributed to the partnership carries over from the partner to the partnership, i.e., it includes the time held by the partner prior to the transfer.

VII. Liquidating Distributions   [Proportionate Liquidating Distributions p. 21-44]
    A. A liquidating distribution occurs when the partner's entire interest in the entity is terminated, e.g., by sale, redemption, or death.
    B. Gain recognition and basis effects parallel those for non-liquidating distributions. See section VIII below. However, the partner's entire basis in the partnership is allocated to the assets received.
    C. A loss can be recognized on the distribution. This may occur when only cash, unrealized receivables, or inventory is received.
    D. The partnership does not recognize any gain or loss on the distribution.

VIII. Non-Liquidating Distributions   [Proportionate Nonliquidating Distributions p. 21-40]
    A. Generally, there is no gain or loss recognized by the partnership upon a non-liquidating distribution of cash or property to a partner.
        1. Gain is recognized only when money received in a distribution exceeds the basis of the partner's interest immediately preceding the distribution.
        2. Gain recognized relative to a nonliquidating distribution usually is capital in nature. However, ordinary income may be created if the partnership holds

               any §751 ("hot") assets.

B.   The partner reduces the basis of his or her interest in the partnership, but not below zero, by the adjusted basis of the property to the partnership, or by the amount of cash received. The partnership's basis in the asset carries over to the partner. However, the basis of the property received is limited to the partner's basis in the partnership. Therefore, if the basis of the partnership interest is zero, then the basis of the property distributed is zero.

IX.   Transactions Between a Partner and the Partnership   [Transactions between Partners and Partnerships p. 21-36]

A.   Transactions between a partner and a partnership are subject to close scrutiny by the Internal Revenue Service. However, subject to specific conditions, a partner may be treated as a non-partner for certain transactions.

B.   Losses on a sale between a partner and his or her more than 50% partnership (a "related party") will be disallowed. However, there is a potential offset on a gain that is recognized on a later sale to a third party.

C.   Gain on a sale between a partner and his or her more than 50% partnership will be ordinary, unless the asset is a capital asset to the purchaser.

D.   Payments made to partners for services rendered, or for use of the partner's capital determined without regard to partnership income, are called *guaranteed payments*.

        1.   Guaranteed payments are deductible by the partnership, and they are ordinary income to the partner on the last day of the partnership's taxable year, regardless of when they are actually paid.

        2.   Guaranteed payments may produce a loss for the partnership.

        3.   Guaranteed payments are a means by which income may be shifted to certain individuals.

E.   The nonrecognition treatment accorded to like-kind exchanges does not apply to exchanges between a partnership and a partner directly or indirectly owning more than 50% of the interest in the partnership, or between two partnerships in which the same persons directly or indirectly own more than 50% of the interests.

TEST FOR SELF-EVALUATION - CHAPTER 21

True or False

Indicate which of the following statements are true or false by circling the correct answer.

T   F   1.   Partnerships are subject to a flat fifteen percent federal income tax rate.

T   F   2.   Each partner can choose a different method of accounting and depreciation computation for purposes of determining his or her taxable income.

T   F   3.   If a special election is made, a partnership may choose a tax year that is different than that of all of its principal partners.

T   F   4.   *Inside basis* refers to the partner's share of the adjusted basis of the aggregate partnership assets, as determined from the partnership's tax accounts.

T   F   5.   The period of time that a partner held the asset prior to the transfer to the partnership is included in the holding period of the asset for the partnership.

T   F   6.   A partner may carry over indefinitely any operating losses in excess of his or her basis in the partnership.

T   F   7.   Nonliquidating property distributions in excess of a partner's basis result in taxable gain to the partner.

T   F   8.   Property distributed to a partner in a non-liquidating distribution always is assigned a carryover basis.

T   F   9.   §1245 gains retain their character as they pass through to the partners.

T   F   10.   Losses on sales between a partner and a partnership always are disallowed.

T   F   11.   Imposition of the income tax on individual partners and the disallowance of certain deductions and tax credits reflect the influence of the aggregate concept.

Fill-in-the-Blanks

Complete the following statements with the appropriate word(s) or amount(s).

1.   A partnership must file an information return, Form _____, within _____ months after its year-end.

2.   On a non-liquidating distribution, a partner reduces his or her basis in the partnership by

the _____ received and the partnership's _____ _____ in the property received.

3.   Taxable gain is recognized on a non-liquidating distribution when _____ is received in excess of the partner's basis in the partnership.

4.   Losses are disallowed on sales between a partnership and a partner whose direct or _____ interest in the capital or profits of the partnership is more than _____ percent.

5.   Ordinary income is recognized on a sale between a partner and a partnership, if more than _____ percent of the capital or profits interest is owned directly or indirectly by the same person or persons, unless the property is a capital asset in the hands of the _____.

6.   A partner's _____ basis accounts for the actual investment of after-tax dollars that the partner has made in the partnership.

7.   In a _____ partnership, creditors are protected by the partner's and the partnership's assets.

8.   The tax year of a partnership generally must be the same as the taxable year of the partners owning a _____ _____.

9.   A limited partnership must have at least _____ general partner(s).

10.   Partners may allocate specific income, deductions, or credits in any ratio identified in the partnership agreement provided the allocation has _____ _____.

11.   The _____ concept treats partners and partnerships as separate units.

Multiple Choice

Choose the best answer for each of the following questions.

USE THE FOLLOWING INFORMATION FOR QUESTIONS 1-4.

Rip and Dot created the RD Partnership. Rip contributed cash of $10,000 and property with a basis of $5,000 and a fair market value of $50,000, for a 60% interest. Dot contributed $20,000 cash and rendered legal and financial services worth $20,000, for a 40% interest.

_____   1.   What is the gain recognized to the partnership as a result of these contributions?
              a. $ 0.
              b. $ 20,000.
              c. $ 45,000.
              d. $100,000.

_____   2.   What is the amount of gain or ordinary income recognized by Rip and Dot, respectively?
              a. $0; $0.
              b. $60,000; $40,000.

        c. $45,000; $20,000.
        d. $0; $20,000.

3.   What is the basis of the property (excluding cash) to the partnership?
        a. $5,000.
        b. $45,000.
        c. $50,000.
        d. $0.

4.   What is the basis of Rip and Dot's partnership interests, respectively?
        a. $0, $0.
        b. $60,000, $40,000.
        c. $60,000, $20,000.
        d. $15,000, $40,000.

5.   Which of the following items do **not** retain their character as they flow through to the partners? More than one answer may be correct.
        a.   Long-term capital gains.
        b.   Short-term capital gains.
        c.   §1245 gains.
        d.   Dividend income.

6.   Sal and Nan owned 90% and 10% of the SN Partnership, respectively. SN operated a foundry. Sal sold stock in ExxonMobil with a basis of $4,000 to the partnership for $6,000. The amount and character of gain recognized to Sal is:
        a. $0.
        b. $2,000 ordinary.
        c. $2,000 capital gain.
        d. $6,000 ordinary.

7.   Sal and Nan owned 90% and 10% of the SN Partnership, respectively. SN operated a foundry. Sal sold a machine, capital asset to him but to be used in the SN business operations, with a basis of $4,000 to the partnership for $6,000. The amount and character of gain recognized to Sal is:
        a. $0.
        b. $2,000 ordinary.
        c. $2,000 capital gain.
        d. $6,000 ordinary.

8.   Bob and Lyn were equal unrelated partners in the BL Partnership. Bob sold an old truck to the partnership for $3,000. The truck had been used in Bob's sole proprietorship prior to the sale. It had a basis of $5,000 to Bob. What amount and character of loss should Bob recognize?
        a. $0.
        b. $2,000 §1231 loss.
        c. $2,000 ordinary.
        d. $5,000 ordinary.

9.   Bob and Lyn were unrelated partners in the BL Partnership, Bob owning a 70 percent interest and Lyn all of the rest. Bob sold an old truck to the partnership for $3,000. The truck had been used in Bob's sole proprietorship prior to the

sale. It had a basis of $5,000 to Bob. What amount and character of loss should Bob recognize?

a. $0.
b. $2,000 §1231 loss.
c. $2,000 ordinary.
d. $5,000 capital.

____ 10.   Bob and Lyn were unrelated partners in the BL Partnership, Bob owning a 70 percent interest and Lyn all of the rest. Bob sold an old truck to the partnership for $3,000. The truck had been used in Bob's sole proprietorship prior to the sale. It had a basis of $5,000 to Bob. The partnership sold the truck to an unrelated third-party for $3,525 ten days after purchasing it from Bob. What is the amount and character of the gain or loss to the partnership from its sale of the truck?

a. $0.
b. $525 §1231 gain.
c. $525 ordinary gain.
d. $1,475 ordinary loss.

____ 11.   Mal and Nell owned 30% and 70% of the MN Partnership, respectively. The partnership incurred the following items of income and loss.

Sales	$7,000
Cost of sales	2,000
Dividend income	3,000
§1231 loss	2,000
§1245 gain	1,000

How much must Nell report as her share of net partnership ordinary income?

a. $1,800.
b. $3,500.
c. $4,200.
d. $4,900.

____ 12.   Zoe is a calendar year taxpayer who owns a 25% interest in the XYZ Partnership. The partnership's fiscal year ends on June 30. Zoe received guaranteed payments of $1,000 on October 15, Year 1 and $500 on April 15, Year 2. For the fiscal year ending June 30, Year 2, the partnership income before deducting the guaranteed payments is $80,000. Using only these facts, what is Zoe's reportable income from the partnership for calendar Year 2?

a. $21,500.
b. $20,375.
c. $21,125.
d. $20,500.
e.   None of the above.

____ 13.   The adjusted basis of Pop's partnership interest was $70,000. In a non-liquidating distribution, he received $40,000 in cash, as well as land with a fair market value of $38,000 and an adjusted basis to the partnership of $28,000. What is the amount and nature of the gain to Pop resulting from the receipt of the distribution?

a. $8,000 capital gain.

        b. $8,000 ordinary income.

        c. $0.

        d.   None of the above.

____   14.   The adjusted basis of Pop's partnership interest was $70,000. In a non-liquidating distribution, he received $40,000 in cash, as well as land with a fair market value of $38,000 and an adjusted basis to the partnership of $28,000. What is Pop's basis in the partnership and the land respectively, after the distribution?

        a. $0, $38,000.

        b. $2,000, $38,000.

        c. $0, $28,000.

        d. $2,000, $28,000.

        e. $0, $30,000.

____   15.   The adjusted basis of Pop's partnership interest was $70,000. In a non-liquidating distribution, he received $74,000 in cash, as well as land with a fair market value of $38,000 and an adjusted basis to the partnership of $28,000. What is the amount and nature of Pop's gain and his basis in the distributed property, respectively?

        a. $4,000 capital gain, $0.

        b. $0, $28,000.

        c. $4,000 capital gain, $28,000.

        d. $4,000 ordinary income, $0.

____   16.   The MC partnership sustained an ordinary loss of $84,000. The partnership and its two partners are on a calendar year basis. The partners share profits and losses equally and materially participate in the partnership's business. Callie had an adjusted basis of $36,000 for her partnership interest, before considering the loss. On her individual income tax return, Callie should deduct a(n):

        a.   Ordinary loss of $36,000.

        b.   Ordinary loss of $42,000.

        c.   Ordinary loss of $36,000 and capital loss of $6,000.

        d.   Capital loss of $42,000.

____   17.   On July 1, Ann received a 10% interest in the AT partnership, for past services rendered. Partnership net assets at July 1 had a basis of $140,000 and a fair market value of $200,000. What income should Ann include in her current tax return for the partnership interest transferred to her by the other partners?

        a. $0.

        b. $14,000 ordinary income.

        c. $20,000 ordinary income.

        d. $20,000 long-term capital gain.

USE THE FOLLOWING INFORMATION FOR QUESTIONS 18 AND 19

On May 1, Year 1, Ally was admitted to the AB partnership. Ally's contribution to capital consisted of 500 shares of stock in Dark Corporation, purchased in Year 0 for $20,000, and which had a fair market value of $100,000 on May 1, Year 1. Ally's interest in the partnership's capital and profits is 25%. On May 1, Year 1, the fair market value of the partnership's net assets (after Ally was admitted) was $400,000.

____ 18.   What was Ally's gain on the exchange of the Dark stock for Ally's partnership
            interest?
            a. $0.
            b. $80,000 ordinary income.
            c. $80,000 long-term capital gain.
            d. $80,000 §1231 gain.

____ 19.   On June 1, Year 3, the partnership distributed the 500 shares of Dark stock to
            partner Kate. The fair market value of the stock on the date of distribution was
            $90,000. What is Ally's recognized gain on the distribution?
            a. $0.
            b. $17,500.
            c. $70,000.
            d. $80,000.

____ 20.   Ash, Blue, Cream, and Donnie formed the ABCD partnership. Each partner owns
            a 25% interest in the entity. Ash and Blue use taxable years ending June 30.
            Cream and Donnie have taxable years ending September 30. Accordingly,
            ABCD's taxable year ends on:
            a.   June 30.
            b.   September 30.
            c.   Either June 30 or September 30, at each partner's discretion.
            d.   December 31.

Short Answer

1.　ABC Services is owned by individuals Ann, Bev, and Cal. They share profits and losses 40-30-30. Ann and Bev have tax years ending June 30th; Cal uses the calendar year.

　　ABC data for the tax year ending 6-30-Year 2:

Sales	$300,000	§1231 Gain, 10-15-Y1	$30,000
Cost of Sales	120,000	Municipal Bond Interest	10,000
Jobs Credit	3,000	Charitable Contribution	2,000

　　ABC purchased business equipment, a seven-year MACRS asset, for $80,000 on 11-1-Y1. MACRS deductions in excess of the §179 first-year amount are included in Cost of Sales.

A)　Cal received guaranteed payment of $5,000/month through the year ending 6-30-Y2. These were increased to $7,000/month for the year ending 6-30-Y3.

　　Allocate ABC's income and other items to the three partners for their tax years ending in Year 2.

B)　Cal received guaranteed payments of $9,000/month through the year ending 6-30-Y2. These were increased to $10,000/month for the year ending 6-30-Y3.

　　Bev received guaranteed payments of $7,000/month for the year ending 6-30-Y2, and $7,500/month for the year ending 6-30-Y3.

　　Ann received draws from her capital account: $2,500/month.

　　Allocate ABC's income and other items to the three partners for their tax years ending in Year 2.

2.   Three individuals form the PST Partnership. The partner's contributions to the
      partnership are:

      Pat   Cash, $30,000.
      Sal   Organizational Services, fmv $30,000.
      Tim   Store Building, fmv $30,000; book and tax basis to T, $27,500.

      Each partner receives an equal profits interest in the new business. The profit-sharing
      ratio is used to allocate minimum gain and debt, under the partnership agreement.

      A)   Compute each partner's original basis in the partnership interest.

      B)   What is the basis of the store to PST?

3.   Frankie owns a 75% interest in the FG Repairs partnership. Both the partners and the
      partnership use the calendar year for tax purposes. Frankie's basis in the partnership
      interest at the beginning of the year is $30,000. FG financial data for Year 1 includes the
      following.

FG ordinary income	$ 20,000
Frankie's Draws	30,000
12/31 Cash Distribution to the partners	15,000
12/31 Distribution of Land to Frankie:	
Fair market value	$ 6,000
Basis to FG	5,000
FG Payables, 1/1	$27,000
FG Payables, 12/31	20,000
FG Municipal Bond Interest Income	$ 4,000

A)   What is Frankie's basis in the FG partnership before the 12/31 distributions?
      (Assume that the distributions were NOT in liquidation.)

B)   What is her basis in the land distributed?

C)   What is Frankie's basis in the FG partnership after the distribution?

D)   What if the cash distributions were $20,000, instead of $15,000?

E)   What if the cash distributions were $5,000, instead of $15,000?

SOLUTIONS TO CHAPTER 21 QUESTIONS

True or False

1.   F   A partnership is not a tax-paying entity. [Partnership Taxation p. 21-5]
2.   F   Depreciation methods are selected at the partnership, rather than the partner, level. [Tax Accounting Elections p. 21-14]
3.   T   See §444. [Alternative Tax Years p. 21-19]
4.   T   Cost recovery deductions turn on inside basis amounts. [Inside and Outside Bases p. 21-14]
5.   T   The holding period of contributed property carries over to the partnership. [Tax Issues Relative to Contributed Property p. 21-12]
6.   T   Assuming that the taxpayer remains a partner in the on-going entity. [Overall Limitation p. 21-32]
7.   F   Distributions of assets from a partnership generally are not taxable to the recipient partner. [Distributions from the Partnership p. 21-39]
8.   F   It could have a lower basis if the partner does not have sufficient basis in his or her partnership interest to allocate to the distribution. [Property Distributions p. 21-42]
9.   F   §1245 gains are netted with other income, loss, and deduction items to determine ordinary income from operations. [Income Measurement p. 21-20]
10. F   Losses are disallowed only with respect to partners whose direct or indirect interest in the capital or profits of the partnership is more than 50 percent. [Sales of Property p. 21-8]
11. T   Under the aggregate concept, the entity is treated as a collection of investors. [Conceptual Basis for Partnership Taxation p. 21-8]

Fill-in-the-Blanks

1.   1065, 3 ½ [Partnership Reporting p. 21-6]
2.   cash, adjusted basis   [Proportionate Nonliquidating Distributions p. 21-40]
3.   cash   [Proportionate Nonliquidating Distributions p. 21-40]
4.   indirect, 50   [Sales of Property p. 21-8]
5.   50, purchaser   [Sales of Property p. 21-8]
6.   outside   [Inside and Outside Bases p. 21-14]
7.   general   [What is a Partnership? p. 21-4]
8.   majority interest   [Required Taxable Years p. 21-18]
9.   one   [What is a Partnership? p. 21-4]
10. economic substance   [Partnership Allocations p. 21-23]
11. entity   [Conceptual Basis for Partnership Taxation p. 21-8]

Multiple Choice

1.   a   The partnership does not recognize gain upon the contribution of property. [Gain or Loss on Contributions to the Partnership p. 21-9]
2.   c   Dot recognizes $20,000 ordinary income for the interest received in exchange for providing legal services. [Services p. 21-11]
3.   a   Property basis carries over from the partner to the partnership, increased by any investment-company gain recognized by the partner. No such gain was

recognized here. [Tax Issues Relative to Contributed Property p. 21-12]

4.   d   Rip: $10,000 basis + 5,000 basis.   Dot: $20,000 basis + 20,000 gain. [Tax Issues Relative to Contributed Property p. 21-12]

5.   c   §1245 gains are part of ordinary partnership income. [Income Measurement p. 21-20]

6.   c   The Exxon stock is a capital asset to the partnership. [Sales of Property p. 21-38]

7.   b   The machine is not a capital asset to the partnership. To get capital gain for the partner, the asset must be capital to both partner and partnership. [Sales of Property p. 21-38]

8.   b   Bob does not have a more than 50% interest in the partnership. [Sales of Property p. 21-38]

9.   a   Since Bob owns more than a 50% interest in the partnership, the loss is not recognized. [Sales of Property p. 21-38, Concept Summary 21-3]

10.   a   No gain is recognized, because it does not exceed the loss previously disallowed. [Sales of Property p. 21-38]

11.   c   [70% x ($7,000 - $2,000 + $1,000)] [Income Measurement p. 21-20]

12.   c   [$1,000 + $500 + (25% x $78,500)] [Guaranteed Payments p. 21-36]

13.   c   The cash distribution is less than the basis in the partnership. [Ordering Rules p. 21-42]

14.   d   Basis = $2,000 ($70,000 - $40,000 - $28,000); basis in land = $28,000 (basis carries over from partnership). [Ordering Rules p. 21-42]

15.   a $74,000 - $70,000 basis in partnership. Pop's basis in the partnership after the cash distribution is zero; thus, there is no remaining basis to allocate to the land. [Ordering Rules p. 21-42]

16.   a   The deduction for losses is limited to the partner's basis. [Overall Limitation p. 21-32]

17.   c $200,000 x 10%. [Services p. 21-11]

18.   a   Generally, no gain is recognized on contributions made to the partnership. [Gain or Loss on Contributions to the Partnership p. 21-9]

19.   c   A's recognized gain is the lesser of $80,000 (the built-in gain at the time of contribution of the stock) or $70,000 (the gain that would be recognized by the partnership if the stock was sold for its FMV at the time of distribution). [Precontribution Gain or Loss p. 21-24]

20.   a   Since partners owning a majority interest and the principal partners do not have the same taxable year, the partnership's tax year ends June 30; this year-end results in the least aggregate deferral of income. [Required Taxable Years p. 21-18]

Short Answer

1.   A)   Ordinary Income: Sales $300,000
                                Cost of Sales   -120,000
                                Guaranteed Payments (12 x $5,000)   - 60,000
                                        Total $120,000

Allocation of tax items for the partners' tax years ending in Year 2

	Ann	Bev	Cal
Ordinary income	$48,000	$36,000	$36,000
Guaranteed Payments	-	-	60,000
§1231 Gain	12,000	9,000	9,000
Jobs Credit	1,200	900	900
Charitable Contribution	800	600	600
Municipal Bond Interest (for state tax)	4,000	3,000	3,000
§179 Cost Recovery	7,000	5,250	5,250

There is no special treatment for the regular MACRS deductions. The partnership's elections are effective for all of the partners. All income and deduction items flow through on the last day of the partnership's tax year.

      B)   Ordinary Income: Sales $300,000
                                Cost of Sales   -120,000
                                Guaranteed Payments (12 x ($7,000 + 9,000)   -192,000
                                        Total $(12,000)

Allocation of tax items for the partners' tax years ending in Year 2

	Ann	Bev	Cal
Ordinary Income	$(4,800)	$(3,600)	$(3,600)
Guaranteed Payments	-	84,000	108,000
§1231 Gain	12,000	9,000	9,000
Jobs Credit	1,200	900	900
Charitable Contribution	800	600	600
Municipal Bond Interest (for state tax)	4,000	3,000	3,000
§179 Cost Recovery	7,000	5,250	5,250

Ann's draws do not affect partnership income. Guaranteed payments can produce a loss for the partnership.

[Measuring and Reporting Income, p. 21-20]

2. A)

	Pat	Sal	Tim
Cash Contributions	$30,000		
Basis of Other Property			$27,500
Gain Recognized on Contribution	-	$30,000*	
Original Interest Basis	$30,000	$30,000	$27,500

*Ordinary Income: Compensation for services

B)   Basis of Store $27,500

[Gain or Loss on Contributions to the Partnership p. 21-9]

3. A)

Basis, 1/1	$30,000
Distributive Share of Ordinary Income (75%)	+15,000
Draws	-30,000
Share of Exempt Income (75%)	+ 3,000
Share of Decrease in Liabilities (75%)	- 5,250
Basis before 12/31 Distribution	$12,750

B)

Apply Cash Distribution First (75%)	-11,250
Balance: Frankie's Basis in the Land Received	$1,500

C)   Basis of Partnership to Frankie, 1/1 $ 0

D)   Frankie incurs a capital gain of $2,250, because her share of the cash distributions ($15,000) exceeds her predistribution basis in the partnership interest ($12,750). F's basis in the land and her partnership interest now are zero.

E)   Frankie does not incur a capital gain as a result of the distribution, because her share of the cash distributions ($3,750) does not exceed her pre-distribution basis in the partnership interest ($12,750). Frankie's basis in the land now is $5,000 (i.e., carryover basis), and her basis in the partnership interest now is $4,000.

[Tax Issues Relative to Contributed Property p. 21-12]

Chapter 22
S Corporations

CHAPTER HIGHLIGHTS

Subchapter S is an elective provision of the Code that allows some "small business corporations" to become non-taxable entities. Income and losses of the corporation pass through directly to its shareholders, who recognize their pro-rata share of the income or loss on their individual returns, in the year with or within which the corporate year ends. Both income and losses pass through to the shareholders on the basis of pro-rata daily ownership. This pass-through of income directly to the shareholders helps to mitigate the effect of double taxation. In addition, shareholders who materially participate in the operations of the business can use the corporate losses to offset any other income that they have.

I.   Subchapter S Provisions [Introduction p. 22-2]

    A.   The Subchapter S provisions of the Code allow certain "small business corporations" to become non-taxable entities.

    B.   S corporations are regular corporations in the legal sense.

    C.   Subchapter S is an elective provision. Failure to make the election, or comply with the requirements once such an election has been made, results in the corporation being taxed as a regular (C) corporation.

    D.   Certain states do not recognize some or all of the Subchapter S provisions. Therefore, in such states, S corporations are subject to state corporate income taxes.

    E.   An S corporation is not subject to the alternative minimum tax . An S corporation, however, may be subject to a corporate-level tax on: built-in gains; excessive passive income; and, state income tax. In addition, upon the conversion from a C corporation to an S corporation, the S corporation must include in income a LIFO recapture amount.

F.   An S corporation cannot deduct its expenditures in providing fringe benefits to a shareholder-employee owning 2% or more of the corporation's stock.

G.   An S corporation cannot join in the filing of a consolidated return.

II.   Definition of A Small Business Corporation [Qualifying for S Corporation Status p. 22-5]

A.   A "small" business corporation must be a domestic corporation.

B.   The number of shareholders is limited to 100. For this purpose, family members are counted as a single shareholder, regardless of the manner in which they own the stock.

C.   Shareholders may be individuals, estates, or certain trusts. However, a non-resident alien may not be a shareholder. In addition, another corporation or a partnership may not be a shareholder.

D.   A qualifying "small" business corporation may have only one class of stock. However, differences in voting rights among shares of common stock are permitted.

E.   A small business corporation may not be an ineligible corporation, e.g., it may not be a bank or insurance company. This rule does not apply if the affiliated corporations are inactive.

F.   An S corporation can be part of an affiliated group. The S corporation may own up to one hundred percent of a C corporation, and it may have a wholly owned S corporation subsidiary.

III.   Making the Election [Making the Election p. 22-8]

A.   All shareholders must elect S corporation status, by consenting and filing Form 2553. A husband and wife who both own stock must both consent.

B.   In community property jurisdictions, both the husband and the wife must sign the consent even though the stock is owned by only one of the spouses.

C.   An election must be made before the fifteenth day of the third month of the election year, or at any time in the preceding year, to obtain S status for the current tax year.

IV.   Loss of an S Election [Loss of the Election p. 22-10]

A.   When a corporation ceases to meet the definition of a small business corporation, the election is terminated. The termination is effective as of the date on which the disqualifying event occurs. The IRS can validate an S election that is inadvertently defective due to a failure to meet a qualification requirement, or due to a missing shareholder consent.

B.   An S election is terminated at the beginning of the fourth year when the S corporation has Subchapter C accumulated earnings and profits, and passive income exceeds 25% of gross receipts for three consecutive years. Moreover, a penalty tax equal to the highest corporate rate of tax will be imposed on the lesser of the excess net passive income or the corporation's taxable income as computed under §1374. This penalty tax applies only if the S corporation has Subchapter C accumulated earnings and profits. The passive income, however, will not trigger an involuntary termination unless it exceeds 25% of gross receipts for three consecutive years.

$$\textbf{Excess net}\ \textbf{passive income} = \frac{\text{Passive investment income in excess of 25\% of gross receipts for the year}}{\text{Passive investment}} \times \begin{array}{l}\text{Net passive}\\ \text{investment income}\\ \text{for the year}\end{array}$$

income for the year

C. In addition, a majority of the shareholders may revoke the election voluntarily. The revocation must be filed by the fifteenth day of the third month of the tax year for which the revocation will be effective, or at any time in the preceding year.

D. A new shareholder of an S corporation (after the initial election) does not have the power to terminate the election, unless he or she owns more than one-half of the corporation's stock.

KEY TERMS
- **Qualifying S Corporation**
- **Pass-Through Items, Basis of shares**
- **Accumulated Adjustments Account**
- **Built-In Gains Tax**
- **Fiscal Year, Fringe Benefits**

E. After termination or revocation, a new S election typically cannot be made for a period of five years. The IRS may permit an early reelection in either of the following situations.
   1. There is a more than 50% change in ownership after the first year for which the termination is applicable, or
   2. The event causing the termination was not reasonably within the control of the S corporation or its majority shareholders.

V. Taxable Income of an S Corporation [Computation of Taxable Income p. 22-12]
   A. Generally, the taxable income or loss of an S corporation is determined according to the tax rules that are applicable to partnerships.
   B. Some deductions that usually are allowable only to individuals are allowed to S corporations. However, an S corporation cannot claim deductions for the standard deduction amount, personal exemptions, foreign taxes, net operating losses, medical and dental expenses, alimony paid, personal moving expenses, and expenses for the care of certain dependents.
   C. Income, losses, deductions, and credits that could uniquely affect the tax liability for any of the shareholders are separated from the S corporation's ordinary income or loss. Items that flow through separately include: short- and long-term capital gains and losses; §1231 gains and losses; the production activities deduction; passive gains, losses and credits under §469; charitable contributions; tax-exempt interest; certain portfolio income; investment interest income and expenses; foreign tax credits; business credits; and tax preference items.
   D. The dividends-received deduction is not available to S corporations.
   E. Nonseparate income and deduction items are lumped together into an undifferentiated amount that constitutes Subchapter S ordinary income or loss.
   F. The separate income, deduction, and credit items are passed through to the shareholders, on a pro rata per-share daily ownership basis. However, if a shareholder dies or stock is transferred during the taxable year, income, deduction and credits may be allocated under the pro rata approach or the shareholders may make a per-books election.
   G. An S corporation is required to make estimated tax payments for its tax liability that is attributable to the built-in gains tax and passive investment income tax.
   H. Generally, all S corporations must adopt a calendar year unless there is a bona fide business purpose for a different tax year or a special election under §444 is made to retain a fiscal year.
      1. If a special election is made to retain a fiscal year, the S corporation must make a special tax deposit with the IRS.

2.   This deposit is approximately equal to the revenue that the government loses as a result of the S corporation's retention of a fiscal year.

VI.   The Order and Sources of Distributions by an S Corporation *without* Accumulated Earnings and Profits   [Tax Treatment of Distributions to Shareholders p. 22-15]

    A.   Distributions to an S corporation shareholder are measured by the fair market value of the cash and other distributed property.

    B.   First, distributions are tax-free up to the amount of the shareholder's stock basis.

    C.   Any residual is treated as a gain from the sale or exchange of property.

VII.   The Order and Sources of Distributions by an S Corporation *with* Accumulated Earnings and Profits [Tax Treatment of Distributions to Shareholders p. 22-15]

    A.   First, distributions are tax-free up to the amount in the accumulated adjustments account (AAA), limited to the stock basis at the time of the distribution.

        1.   The AAA is a corporate account that represents the cumulative total of undistributed net income items for S corporation taxable years beginning after 1982.

        2.   The AAA is adjusted in a similar manner to the shareholder's stock basis except there is no adjustment for tax-exempt income and related expenses or for Federal taxes attributable to a C corporation tax year. In addition, when the AAA balance is negative, any decreases in stock basis have no impact on the AAA.

        3.   The AAA can have a negative balance. All losses decrease the AAA balance, even those in excess of the shareholder's stock basis. However, distributions may neither increase a negative AAA balance nor take the balance below zero.

    B.   Second, distributions are tax-free up to the amount of the corporation's previously taxed income (PTI), under prior Subchapter S rules.

    C.   Third, a distribution in excess of the sum of the AAA and any PTI is treated as a taxable dividend to the extent of Subchapter C accumulated earnings and profits.

    D.   Fourth, any residual amount is a return of capital to the extent of the shareholder's remaining basis in the S corporation's stock.

    E.   Fifth, distributions in excess of the shareholder's basis in his or her stock are taxable as capital gains.

    F.   With the consent of all shareholders, an S corporation may elect to have a distribution treated as made from accumulated earnings and profits, rather than from the AAA.

    G.   See Exhibit 22-1 to compare this scheme to that for a C corporation.

    H.   An S corporation recognizes gain when it distributes appreciated property to its shareholders. The character of the gain will depend upon the type of asset distributed. Loss is not recognized on the distribution of depreciated property. However, an S corporation recognizes both gain or loss on liquidating distributions.

VIII.   Built-in Gains Tax [Tax on Pre-Election Built-In Gains p. 22-26]

    A.   An S corporation is taxed on **built-in gains** to the extent of the lesser of:

        1.   The recognized built-in gains for the tax year; or,

        2.   The amount of taxable income the corporation would have recognized if it were not an S corporation. For purposes of this computation, NOLs and special corporate deductions are not taken into account.

    The lesser amount then is reduced by the unexpired C corporation NOL, capital loss or business credit carryforwards. In addition, alternative minimum tax credits carried over from prior C corporation years can be used against the built-in gains tax resulting in post-conversion years.

B.   The tax does **not** apply to:

    1.   a corporation that had an S election in effect for the ten previous taxable years;

    2.   a new corporation (in existence for fewer than eleven years), if the S election was made in the first year of the corporation's operation; or,

    3.   a corporation that made its S election prior to 1987.

C.   Net recognized built-in gain that is not subject to the built-in gains tax due to the net income limitation is carried forward and is subject to the built-in gains tax to the extent that the corporation subsequently has other taxable income (that is not already subject to the built-in gains tax) for any tax year within the ten-year recognition period.

D.   Net unrealized built-in gain is the excess of the aggregate FMV of the corporation's assets as of the beginning of its first S corporation taxable year, over the aggregate adjusted basis of its assets at that time.

E.   Recognized built-in gain is any gain recognized during the ten-year period beginning with the first day of the taxable year that the corporation becomes an S corporation. All gains recognized during this period are deemed to be built-in gains, unless the S corporation can prove:

    1.   The asset was not held by the corporation as of the beginning of the first taxable year as an S corporation, or

    2.   The gain recognized is in excess of the FMV of the asset at the beginning of the corporation's first taxable year as an S corporation, over its adjusted basis at that time.

F.   The tax rate is equal to the highest corporate tax rate, now 35%.

G.   Built-in gains, less the built-in gains tax, flow through to the shareholders. The character of the gain is retained as it flows through.

IX.   LIFO Recapture Tax   [LIFO Recapture Tax p. 22-30]

A.   When a corporation uses the FIFO method for its inventory in the last tax year before making an S election, any built-in gain is recognized and taxed as the inventory is sold, as described above.

B.   A corporation using the LIFO method for its last year before making an S election must include in gross income for its last C year the excess of the inventory's value under FIFO over its LIFO basis. No negative adjustment is allowed where the LIFO basis exceeds the FIFO value at the time of the election.

X.   Net Operating Losses   [Treatment of Losses p. 22-23]

A.   NOLs pass through to an S corporation's shareholders.

B.   A loss is deductible by the shareholders for the year with or within which the corporation's tax year ends.

C.   NOLs are allocated to the shareholders on a daily basis, in proportion to the percent of stock owned. When a shareholder has acquired stock at different times and for different amounts, a separate-share approach is required.

D.   NOLs reduce the shareholder's basis in the stock.

E.   A shareholder's deduction for the NOL pass-through is limited to the shareholder's adjusted basis in the stock plus the basis of any loans that he or she has made to the corporation. To the extent that the NOL exceeds this amount, the NOL deduction can be carried over indefinitely to another tax year.

Probably the chief attraction of the S election over time is the shareholder's ability to deduct pass-through losses against salary and other income. Any restriction on this ability should be avoided or planned for, to preserve the valuable resulting deductions.

Any loss so carried forward may be deducted only by the same shareholder. Loss carryovers remaining at the end of a one-year S corporation post-termination period are lost forever.

F.   S corporation shareholders are subject to the §469 passive loss rules. Therefore, shareholders who do not materially participate in operating the business can apply the corporate losses and credits only against income from other passive activities.

XI.   Shareholder's Tax Basis in S Corporation Stock   [Shareholder's Basis p. 22-20]
A.   Initial basis is computed in the same manner as would be the case for the basis in the stock of a regular corporation, e.g., purchase price of the shares.
B.   The basis of stock in an S corporation is increased further by taxable income, by tax-exempt income, by additional shareholder capital contributions, and by the excess of the deductions for depletion over the basis of the property that is subject to depletion.
C.   The basis of S corporation stock is reduced by the amount of money and the fair market value of property distributed, by the sum of current and prior years' distributive share of deductible losses, and by the shareholder's share of nondeductible expenditures.
D.   If a loss and a distribution occur in the same tax year, the distribution reduces stock basis first.
E.   The shareholder's basis in the stock cannot fall below zero. Excess basis reductions decrease the shareholder's basis in his or her loans to the corporation. When basis is restored (e.g., via additional corporate income or shareholder capital contributions), the basis of the loan is restored before the basis of the stock is increased.
F.   If a loan is repaid in an amount that exceeds its basis (e.g., because of an NOL pass-through), the excess constitutes a capital gain to the shareholder, provided that the debt is evidenced by an instrument such as a note, bond, or debenture that is a capital asset in the shareholder's hands. If the debt is not evidenced by an instrument, then the character of the gain recognized will be ordinary.

XII.   Advantages of S Corporation Status   [Tax Planning Considerations p. 22-31]
A.   Income of an S corporation is not subject to double taxation, i.e., at both the corporate and the shareholder levels.
B.   Use of the corporate entity allows the owners limited liability.
C.   The corporation can choose desirable tax accounting methods. Thus, the shareholders can control (to a certain degree) the nature and amount of much of their income from an S corporation. However, a corporation that makes an S election is required to use either a calendar year, some other fiscal year for which a business purpose can be established, or make special deposits to retain its current fiscal year.

D.   Unlike a regular corporation, an S corporation may use the cash method of accounting.
E.   Net operating losses, net long-term and short-term capital gains and losses, and other types of income and deductions, and tax credits, flow through to the shareholders.
F.   Income can be shifted to lower-bracket family members, by transferring to them some of the shares in the corporation. However, any family member who renders services or furnishes capital to an S corporation must be paid reasonable compensation, or the IRS may make adjustments to reflect the value of such services or capital.
G.   S corporations are not subject to the alternative minimum tax.

XIII. Disadvantages of S Corporation Status   [Tax Planning Considerations p. 22-31]
A.   Corporate income tax rates may be lower than those applicable to high-bracket individuals. Thus, an S corporation may generate unnecessary income tax liability.
B.   It is difficult to elect a fiscal year for an S corporation.
C.   The S corporation may be subject to a corporate-level tax on built-in gains, or excess passive investment income. In addition, the S election is not recognized by the District of Columbia and by a few states; therefore, in those jurisdictions, some or all of the corporation's income may be subject to a state corporate income tax.
D.   C corporations that use the LIFO inventory method are subject to a LIFO recapture tax when they convert to S status.
E.   Tax-free fringe benefits are not available to more-than-2% owner-employees.
F.   Under the passive loss rules, the deductibility of pass-through losses for inactive owners is limited.
G.   Carryovers from subchapter C years are not available to an S corporation for regular tax purposes, but may be available for built-in gains tax purposes.

Exhibit 22-1
SOURCES OF CORPORATE DISTRIBUTIONS

S CORPORATION	C CORPORATION
Accumulated Adjustments Account: Tax-free.	Current E&P: Taxable. Cash or other property. Dividend income.
Previously Taxed Income remaining from pre-1983 years: Non-Taxable. Cash only. Nontransferable. S election required for year of distribution.	
Accumulated E&P from prior (and Non-Subchapter S) years: Taxable. Cash or other property. Dividend income. *	Accumulated E&P from prior years: Taxable. Cash or other property. Dividend income.
Return of Capital: Non-Taxable (Reduce Basis).	Return of Capital: Non-Taxable (Reduce Basis).
Capital Gain: Taxable.	Capital Gain: Taxable.

*   With the consent of all shareholders, an S corporation may elect to have a distribution treated as made from accumulated earnings and profits rather than from the AAA.

Refer to text Chapter 19 for additional explanations concerning distributions from regular corporations.

TEST FOR SELF-EVALUATION - CHAPTER 22

True or False

Indicate which of the following statements are true or false by circling the correct answer.

T   F   1.   A corporation with over $50 million in sales cannot elect S status.

T   F   2.   A new shareholder of an S corporation does not have the power to terminate the election by affirmatively refusing to consent to the election, unless he or she owns 50% or more of the voting stock.

T   F   3.   A husband and wife are considered to be a single shareholder, for purposes of making an S election on Form 2553.

T   F   4.   The limited liability company may be more attractive to many businesses than the S corporation.

T   F   5.   S status is lost if different shares have different voting rights.

T   F   6.   Any net gains from the recapture of depreciation constitute separately stated income.

T   F   7.   When an S corporation's election is involuntarily terminated, the entity is taxed as a regular corporation starting on the day after the date on which the disqualifying event occurred.

T   F   8.   After an S election is voluntarily terminated, there usually is a ten-year waiting period before a new election can be made.

T   F   9.   When one S corporation shareholder transfers stock to another shareholder, any AAA on the purchase date is fully available to the purchaser.

T   F   10.   The built-in gains tax applies to all corporations that made an S election after 1986.

T   F   11.   An S corporation cannot own 80% or more of the stock of another corporation.

T   F   12.   An annual ordinary loss reduces shareholders' basis in S stock.

Fill-in-the-Blanks

Complete the following statements with the appropriate word(s) or amount(s).

1.   The pass-through of ordinary income _____ (increases/decreases) shareholders' basis in S stock.

2.   The S corporation rules _____ (do/do not) place a ceiling on the asset value of the entity.

3.   An S corporation election can be made at any time during the preceding taxable year, or by the _____ day of the _____ month of the election year.

4.   Unexpired C corporation _____s, and _____ _____ can be used against the built-in gains tax.

5.   An S corporation with accumulated earnings and profits from Subchapter C years is subject to the regular corporate income tax to the extent that its _____ income exceeds _____ percent of its gross receipts.

6.   The order of S corporation distributions is: (1) _____ _____ _____, (2) _____ _____ _____, (3) _____ _____ _____ _____, (4) _____ _____ _____, and (5) capital gain.

7.   An S election can be terminated in any of the following ways: voluntary _____; cessation of small business _____ _____; or the corporation fails the _____ _____ limitation.

8.   No more than _____ investors can hold shares in an S corporation.

9.   S corporation shareholders receive a ratable share of the corporation's income and losses, based upon their _____ _____ _____.

10.   The deduction for an NOL may not exceed a shareholder's basis in the _____, plus the basis of any _____ that he or she has made to the corporation.

11.   A shareholder's share of an S corporation's NOL can be _____ _____ to future taxable years, to the extent that it exceeds the basis of the shareholder's stock and the loans made to the corporation.

12.   If a calendar-year S corporation wishes voluntarily to terminate its election retroactive to the beginning of the year, shareholders owning _____ than _____ percent of the voting stock must notify the IRS to this effect.

13.   A _____ cannot own stock in an S corporation.

14.   Any net gains from depreciation recapture constitute _____ computed S corporation income.

15.   After an S shareholder's basis in her stock and loans to the corporation have been depleted by the flow-through of corporate NOLs, corporate income will flow through and first restore the basis of her _____.

Multiple Choice

Choose the best answer for each of the following questions.

_____ 1.   A qualifying small business corporation:
            a.   May have both common and preferred stock.
            b.   Must be a domestic corporation.
            c.   May have another corporation as a shareholder.
            d.   May not have a trust as a shareholder.
            e.   b and c.

_____ 2.   A business that made an S election upon incorporation may be subject to the
            following corporate-level taxes. More than one answer may be correct.
            a.   State corporate income tax.
            b.   Passive investment income tax.
            c.   Federal income tax on built-in gains.
            d.   Capital gains tax.
            e.   a and b.

_____ 3.   An S election may be terminated when:
            a.   Gross receipts exceed five million dollars for the year.
            b.   Any one of the shareholders chooses to revoke the election.
            c.   A new shareholder forgets to make the election on his own.
            d.   A new 75 percent shareholder revokes the election.
            e.   c and d.

_____ 4.   The following items retain their tax character as they flow through to the
            shareholder from an S corporation. More than one answer may be correct.
            a.   Long-term capital gain.
            b.   Short-term capital gain.
            c.   Tax-exempt income.
            d.   §162 expenses.
            e.   §1245 recapture.

_____ 5.   On January 1, Don Baker owned 10% of the stock of Electing Corp., which is a
            calendar-year S corporation. On June 14, Baker acquired another 10% of
            Electing Corp's stock. For the calendar tax year, Electing Corp's nonseparately
            computed income is $36,500. What is Baker's share of Electing Corp's income?
            a. $3,650.
            b. $5,475.
            c. $5,660.
            d. $7,300.

_____ 6.   The following entity will not qualify as a small business corporation: (More than
            one answer may be correct.)
            a.   A corporation that has 116 shareholders, consisting of 31 married couples
                  and 54 unrelated individuals.
            b.   An active corporation that is a wholly-owned subsidiary.
            c.   A corporation with six individual shareholders and income of over $250
                  million.
            d.   A corporation that has an estate as a shareholder.
            e.   A corporation that issues both common and preferred stock.

_____ 7.   Income of an S corporation is allocated among the shareholders on a pro rata
            basis, according to the:
            a.   Profit and loss ratio.

      b.   Allocation method described in the corporate charter.

      c.   Number of shares owned on the last day of the taxable year.

      d.   Pro-rata number of shares owned, on a daily basis.

____ 8.   Pinn, a calendar year S corporation, distributes $500 to its only shareholder, Ann, on December 31, Year 2. A's basis in his stock is $200 on December 31, Year 1. For Year 2, Pinn had $800 of nonseparately stated income, $300 of capital losses and $100 of tax-exempt income. What is Ann's basis in her stock as of December 31, Year 2?

      a. $0.

      b. $100.

      c. $200.

      d. $300.

      e. $800.

____ 9.   A shareholder's basis in S corporation stock is:

      a.   Unaffected by property distributions.

      b.   Decreased by a distribution from accumulated E&P.

      c.   Originally computed in a manner similar to that used for regular corporations.

      d.   Unaffected by cash distributions.

____ 10.   Deductions for NOLs are limited to: (More than one answer may be correct)

      a.   A shareholder's basis in the stock.

      b. $100,000 per shareholder per year.

      c.   The basis of stock plus any liabilities owed to the corporation.

      d.   The basis of the stock plus the basis of any debt owed by the corporation to the shareholder.

      e.   The amount determined under the passive loss rules.

____ 11.   A valid calendar-year S corporation issues a second class of stock on April 1, Year 1. What is the tax effect of this action?

      a.   The election is lost, effective 1-1, Year 1.

      b.   The election is lost, effective 4-1, Year 1.

      c.   The election is lost, effective 4-2, Year 1.

      d.   The election is lost, effective 1-1, Year 2.

      e.   There is no effect. The election is not lost.

USE THE FOLLOWING INFORMATION FOR QUESTIONS 12 THROUGH 14.

In Year 1, Cheryl Brown, the sole shareholder of a calendar-year S Corporation, received a loss pass-through that exceeds her basis in the corporate stock by $10,000. During Year 2, the corporation incurred a $30,000 loss. During year 3, the corporation generated taxable income of $12,000.

On December 31, Year 2, Brown contributed $25,000 to the capital of the corporation.

On December 31, Year 1, Brown did not have any loans outstanding to the corporation. On January 1, Year 2, Brown loaned $10,000 to the corporation.

____ 12.   What is the amount of loss that Cheryl may deduct in Year 2?

        a. $0.
        b. $10,000.
        c. $30,000.
        d. $35,000.
        e. $40,000.

____ 13. What is the amount of Cheryl's loss carryforward to Year 3?
        a. $0.
        b. $5,000.
        c. $10,000.
        d. $30,000.

____ 14. What is Cheryl's basis in the S corporation's stock and the loan to the corporation, respectively, at December 31, Year 3?
        a. $0, $0.
        b. $0, $7,000.
        c. $2,000, $10,000.
        d. $3,500, $3,500.
        e. $7,000, $0.

____ 15. The basis of shareholder X's stock in her valid calendar-year S corporation is $10,000. Ms. X owns 100 percent of the stock in the corporation, and she has no loans outstanding to the corporation. The corporation's NOL is $12,000. Which statement is true?
        a.   Ms. X claims a $12,000 deduction.
        b.   Ms. X claims a $10,000 deduction. She can carry back the $2,000 excess for three years.
        c.   Ms. X claims a $10,000 deduction. There is no carryback allowed, but she can carryforward the $2,000 excess indefinitely.
        d.   Ms. X claims a $10,000 deduction. There is no carryover of the disallowed loss.

____ 16. Which of the following will prevent a corporation from making a valid election to be taxed as an S corporation?
        a.   Having 140 individual shareholders, each of which is married to one other shareholder.
        b.   Owning 50% of the stock of a domestic corporation.
        c.   Having a partnership as a shareholder.
        d.   Deriving 40% of its gross receipts from passive income services.
        e.   Owning 100 percent of an inactive corporation.

____ 17. Which of the following items will not pass through as a separately stated item to an S corporation shareholder?
        a.   Production activities deduction.
        b.   Tax-exempt bond interest income.
        c.   §1245 gains.
        d.   §1231 gains and losses.
        e.   Tax preference items.

____ 18. An NOL that exceeds the S corporation shareholder's adjusted basis in his or her stock and loans made to the S corporation may be:
        a.   Carried forward for twenty years.

b. Carried back two years and forward twenty years.

c. Carried forward indefinitely and deducted when and if the basis is restored by any shareholder who owns or purchases the stock.

d. Carried forward indefinitely and deducted only by the same shareholder when and if the basis is restored.

_____ 19. A C corporation that made an S election this year may be subject to which of the following taxes. More than one answer may be correct.

a. State corporate income tax.

b. Built-in gains tax.

c. Passive investment income tax.

d. National sales tax.

_____ 20. On January 31, year 1, Zed Corporation sold all of its stock in its wholly owned subsidiary, Xenon Corporation, to individuals Ann and Babs. Xenon is a calendar-year corporation and, Ann and Babs filed an S election on March 14, year 1. The earliest date that Xenon's S election can be effective is:

a. January 1, Y1.

b. February 1, Y1.

c. March 14, Y1.

d. March 15, Y1.

e. January 1, Y2.

_____ 21. Which of the following is NOT a requirement for a corporation to elect S corporation status? More than one answer may be correct.

a. Must not have any accumulated earnings and profits.

b. Must confine stockholders to individuals, estates, and certain qualifying trusts.

c. Must be a domestic corporation.

d. Must have only one class of stock.

e. Must not have a nonresident alien shareholder.

_____ 22. Which of the following rules pertain to S corporations? More than one answer may be correct.

a. Municipal bond interest income of the corporation passes through to the shareholders, retaining its tax-exempt status.

b. The hobby loss provisions of §183 are applicable.

c. An S corporation is not subject to the alternative minimum tax, but preferences and adjustments flow through to the shareholders.

d. Any family member who renders services to an electing corporation must be paid a reasonable salary.

e. All of the above.

Short Answer

1.   Cann Corporation has a valid S election in effect. Cann has no accumulated E&P from Subchapter C years. On 1-1-Y1, Art owns all of the 100 outstanding shares in Cann. On 10-1-Y1, he sells twenty shares to Babs for $30,000. All taxpayers use the calendar year.

                Y1 Salaries: Art $75,000;   Babs $15,000
                Y1 Cash Distributions: $10,000 on 5-1-Y1 and $10,000 on 11-1-Y1

    A)   Cann's Y1 Non-Separately-Stated Income = $200,000
              LTCG = $30,000, on a sale that was completed 2-1-Y1
              Charitable Contribution = $55,000, made 12-15-Y1
              Compute Art's and Babs' Y1 gross income from Cann.

    B)   Same as A, but Non-Separately-Stated Income = ($90,000).

    C)   Same as A, but Cann's fiscal year ends on 1-31-Y2.

2.   Ruth is the sole shareholder of Hitt, a calendar-year S corporation. Ruth purchased her shares on 1-1-Y1, for $100,000. Ruth loans Hitt $17,000 on 2-1-Y1. Hitt loans Ruth $7,000 on 11-1-Y1. Year 1 activities of Hitt include:

Non-Separately-Stated Income	$15,000
Net Long-Term Capital Gain	3,000
Exempt Interest Income	4,000
Dental Expenses of Ruth's mother, paid by Hitt	750
Cash Distribution, 12-31-Y1	111,000

A)   What is Ruth's basis in her Hitt shares on 1-1-Y2?

B)   Same as A, but Non-Separately-Stated Income is ($120,000).

3.   Keepp Corporation has made a valid S election. It has Accumulated Earnings and Profits, from Subchapter C years, of $30,000. This year, Keepp recognizes:

Sales Receipts	$60,000
Interest Income--AT&T bonds	40,000
Brokerage Fees	5,000

A)   Compute Keepp's passive income penalty tax.

B)   Same as A, but Keepp had operating expenses of $85,000 in addition to the brokerage fees.

SOLUTIONS TO CHAPTER 22 QUESTIONS

True or False

1.   F   S status turns on various technical qualifications, one of which is not sales volume. [Definition of a Small Business Corporation p. 22-5]
2.   F   The shareholder must own more than 50% of the S corporation's stock. [Loss of the Election p. 22-10]
3.   F   Although a husband and wife are considered to be one shareholder for purposes of the number of shareholders requirement, each spouse must consent to the election. [Number of Shareholders p. 22-6]
4.   T   Recent developments have made the LLC more desirable than the S corporation for many businesses. [An Overview of S Corporations p. 22-3]
5.   F   Differential voting rights do not violate the one-class-of-stock requirement. [One Class of Stock p. 22-5]
6.   F   Depreciation recapture amounts are included in the corporation's ordinary income (i.e., nonseparately stated income). [Computation of Taxable Income p. 22-12]
7.   F   The entity is taxed as a regular corporation starting on the date on which the disqualifying event occurred. But the IRS could validate the election if it was due to an "inadvertent" termination. [Loss of the Election p. 22-10]
8.   F   There usually is a five-year waiting period. [Reelection after Termination p. 22-12]
9.   T   AAA is a corporate account. [AEP from C Corporation Years p. 22-16]
10. F   This tax only applies to C corporations that made an S election after 1986. [Tax on Pre-Election Built-In Gain p. 22-26]
11. F   An S corporation may own up to one hundred percent of a C corporation, and it may have a wholly owned S corporation subsidiary. [Definition of a Small Business Corporation p. 22-5]
12. T   These items are reported on the Schedule K-1. [Shareholder's Basis p. 22-20]

Fill-in-the-Blanks

1.   decreases [Shareholder's Basis p. 22-20]
2.   do not [Definition of a Small Business Corporation p. 22-5]
3.   fifteenth, third [Making the Election p. 22-8]
4.   NOL, capital loss [Treatment of Losses p. 22-23]
5.   passive, 25 [Passive Investment Income Penalty Tax p. 22-29]
6.   accumulated adjustment account, previously taxed income, accumulated earnings and profits, return of capital [Tax Treatment of Distributions to Shareholders p. 22-15]
7.   revocation, corporation status, passive investment [Loss of the Election p. 22-10]
8.   100 Special counting rules apply to family members [Number of Shareholders p. 22-6]
9.   daily stock ownership [Allocation of Income and Loss p. 22-14]
10.   stock, loans [Net Operating Loss p. 22-24]
11.   carried over [Net Operating Loss p. 22-24]
12.   more, fifty [Voluntary Revocation p. 22-10]
13.   nonresident alien [Definition of a Small Business Corporation p. 22-5]
14.   nonseparately [Computation of Taxable Income p. 22-12]
15.   loans [Net Operating Loss p. 22-24]

Multiple Choice

1. b   An S corporation has strict stock ownership requirements. [Definition of a Small Business Corporation p. 22-5]
2. a   A corporation that has always been an S corporation is not subject to the passive investment income tax, or to the built-in gains tax. [Tax on Pre-Election Built-In Gain p. 22-26]
3. d   Only a majority shareholder can bring this about. [Voluntary Revocation p. 22-10]
4. a, b Separately stated items can be treated differently by different shareholders. [Computation of Taxable Income p. 22-12]
5. c   [$3,650 + 10% ($36,500 x 201/365)]. [Allocation of Income and Loss p. 22-14]
6. e   An S corporation cannot issue more than one class of stock. [Definition of a Small Business Corporation p. 22-5]
7. d   See Example 16 in the text. [Allocation of Income and Loss p. 22-14]
8. d   [$200 + $800 - $300 + $100 - $500 (distribution)]. [Shareholder's Basis p. 22-22]
9. c   The original basis is cost, gross estate value, donor's basis, etc. [Shareholder's Basis p. 22-20]
10. d, e Passive loss restrictions apply to flow-through S losses. [Net Operating Loss p. 22-24]
11. b   The C tax year starts on the day that the requirement is violated. [Loss of the Election p. 22-10]
12. d   ($10,000 loan to corporation + $25,000 capital contribution) [Net Operating Loss p. 22-24]
13. b   [$40,000 ($10,000 Y2 loss + $30,000 Y3 loss) - $35,000 loss allowed in Y3] [Net Operating Loss p. 22-24]
14. b $12,000 taxable income less $5,000 loss carryforward from Y3. The basis in the loan to the corporation is restored before the stock basis.
15. c   [Net Operating Loss p. 22-24]
16. c   An S corporation has strict stock ownership requirements. [Definition of a Small Business Corporation p. 22-5]
17. c   Separately stated items can be treated differently by different shareholders. [Computation of Taxable Income p. 22-12]
18. d   Provided also that the deduction finally occurs in a year in which the S election is still effective, or by the end of the one-year post-termination transition period. [Net Operating Loss p. 22-24]
19. a, b, c Other taxes may make the S corporation a tax-paying entity. [When the Election is Advisable p. 22-31]
20. e   The election is not effective until January 1, Y2 because the corporation was owned by a regular corporation for part of Y1, and accordingly, is not eligible to receive S status for Y1. [Definition of a Small Business Corporation p. 22-5]
21. a   An S corporation with accumulated E&P may be subject to additional taxes, though. [Definition of a Small Business Corporation p. 22-5]
22. e   All of these rules apply. [Other Operational Rules p. 22-30]

Short Answer

1. Ownership Weights:

    Art [100% X 273/365] + [80% X 92/365]   = .95

Babs [20% X 92/365]   = .05

A)

	Art	*Babs*
Salary	$75,000	$15,000
Dividends	0	0
Non-Separately-Stated Income	190,000	10,000
Long-Term Capital Gain	28,500	1,500
Charitable Contribution	52,250	2,750

B)

	Art	*Babs*
Salary	$75,000	$15,000
Dividends	0	0
Non-Separately-Stated Income	(85,500)	(4,500)
Long-Term Capital Gain	28,500	1,500
Charitable Contribution	52,250	2,750

C)

	Art	*Babs*
Salary	$75,000	$15,000
Dividends	0	0
Non-Separately-Stated Income	0*	0*
Long-Term Capital Gain	0*	0*
Charitable Contribution	0*	0*

*   Pass-Through will appear on Art's and Babs' year 2 returns. (Note, though, that ownership weights then will change.)

[Allocation of Income and Loss p. 22-14]

2.   A)

Original Basis of Stock	$100,000
Income ($15,000 + $3,000)	+ 18,000
Exempt Income	+ 4,000
Non-Deductible Expenditures	- 750
Subtotal	$121,250
Distribution	- 111,000
Basis of stock, 1-1-Y2	$ 10,250

The distribution is received tax-free, reducing Ruth's stock basis to $10,250.

B)

Original Basis of Stock	$100,000
Capital Gain	+ 3,000
Exempt Income	+ 4,000
Non-Deductible Expenditures	- 750
Subtotal	$106,250
Distribution	$111,000
Basis of stock, 1-1-Y2 ($106,250 - $111,000)	$ 0

The distribution reduces Ruth's stock basis to $0, and she recognizes a $4,750 capital gain (Distribution $111,000 – Stock basis $106,250). Distributions to shareholders do not reduce loan basis.

Under the Losses Last rule, now account for the pass-through of the NOL. Stock basis is zero, so Ruth deducts $17,000, reducing loan basis to $0. Do not net the two loans together.   She carries forward the remaining $103,000 loss to Year 2.

[Shareholder's Basis p. 22-20]

3.   A) 35% Tax Rate   X $35,000 Net Passive Income ($40,000 - $5,000)

$$X \frac{\$40,000 \text{ Passive Income} - \$25,000 \text{ (1/4 of Gross Receipts)}}{\$40,000 \text{ Passive Income}}$$

= $4,593.75 Passive Income Penalty Tax

B) 35% Tax Rate x lesser of:
$$\frac{\$40,000 - \$25,000}{\$40,000}$$
(1) $35,000 x   = $13,125; or,

(2) $10,000 (Taxable Income; $100,000 - $90,000) = $3,400 Passive Income Penalty Tax. Note: The tax base is limited to taxable income.

[Passive Investment Income Penalty Tax p. 22-29]

Chapter 23
Exempt Entities

CHAPTER HIGHLIGHTS

A lthough the primary objective of the Federal tax law is the raising of revenue, economic, social, equity and political considerations play a significant role in the development of tax laws. Social consideration objectives resulted in the enactment of Subchapter F of the Code. Based on the theory that the government is compensated for the loss of revenue by its relief from the financial burden which would otherwise be satisfied by appropriations from public funds and by the benefits resulting from the promotion of the general welfare, certain organizations are provided exemption from Federal income taxation. Depending on the nature and scope of the entity, an organization may be partially or completely exempt from Federal income taxation. In addition, an organization may engage in activities, or fail to act in certain circumstances, that are subject to special taxation.

I. Requirements for Tax-Exempt Status [Requirements for Exempt Status p. 23-4]
   A. IRC §501 provides tax-exempt status for over twenty types of organizations. An organization qualifies for exempt status only if it fits into one of these categories. The most prevalent types of tax-exempt organizations include:
      1. Entities organized and operated exclusively for the following purposes: religious, charitable, scientific, literary, educational, testing for public safety, fostering national or international amateur sports, or prevention of cruelty to children or animals [§501(c)(3)].
      2. Civic leagues operated exclusively for the promotion of social welfare, and local associations of employees whose association net earnings are

used exclusively for charitable, educational, or recreational purposes [§501(c)(4)].

3. Business leagues, chambers of commerce, real estate boards, boards of trade, and professional football leagues [§501(c)(6)].

4. Fraternal beneficiary societies operating under the lodge system and having a system for the payment of insurance benefits to members and their dependents [§501(c)(8)].

5. Voluntary employees' beneficiary associations having a system for the payment of insurance benefits to members, their dependents, or their designated beneficiaries [§501(c)(9)].

6. Credit unions without stock organized for mutual purposes [§501(c)(14)].

B. Frequently, exempt status requires more than the mere classification in one of the categories of exempt organizations. The definitional requirements of many of the organizations that qualify for tax-exempt status generally include, within the statutory language or by implication, the following factors.

1. The organization serves some type of common good.

2. The organization is not a for-profit entity.

3. The net earnings of the organization do not inure to the benefit of any private shareholder or individual.

4. The organization does not exert political influence.

II. Tax Consequences of Exempt Status   [Tax Consequences of Exempt Status: General p. 23-7]

A. Although an exempt organization generally is exempt from Federal income taxation, engaging in specific transactions or activities will subject the organization to taxation.

1. If an exempt organization engages in a prohibited transaction, it will be subject to tax.

2. A *feeder* organization is subject to tax.

3. A private foundation may be partially subject to tax.

4. An exempt organization is subject to tax on its unrelated business taxable income.

B. If an exempt organization engages in a prohibited transaction, part or all of its income may be subject to Federal income taxation, or the organization may forfeit its exempt status.

1. An organization or its executives may be subject to intermediate sanctions, generally a series of fines, if they engage in prohibited transactions, or convey excessive benefits to the management of the entity.

2. Organizations exempt under §501(c)(3), i.e., religious, charitable, educational, or similar organizations, generally will forfeit their exempt status if the organization attempts to influence legislation (lobbying activities) or participates in political campaigns.

3. Qualifying §501(c)(3) organizations may make an affirmative election that will permit such organizations to participate in lobbying activities on a limited basis without losing their exempt status. When the election is made, a ceiling is placed on lobbying expenditures. Exceeding the ceiling amount can lead to forfeiture of exempt status. Even though the ceiling is not exceeded, a tax may be imposed on some of the lobbying expenditures.

a. *Lobbying expenditures* are expenditures made for the purpose of influencing legislation through attempting to affect the opinions of the general public or communicating with any legislator or staff member, or with any government official or staff member who may participate in the formulation of legislation. The statutory ceiling on lobbying expenditures is computed as follows.

150% x Lobbying nontaxable amount = Ceiling amount

The lobbying nontaxable amount is the lesser of $1,000,000 or the amount from a rate schedule in IRC §4911.

    b.   *Grass roots expenditures* are expenditures made for the purpose of influencing legislation through attempting to affect the opinions of the general public. The statutory ceiling on grass roots expenditures is computed as follows.

150% x Grass roots nontaxable amount = Ceiling amount

The grass roots nontaxable amount is 25 percent of the lobbying nontaxable amount.

    4.   A §501(c)(3) organization that elects to make lobbying expenditures on a limited basis is subject to tax on the its *excess lobbying expenditures*.

        a.   The tax rate is 25 percent.

        b.   Excess lobbying expenditures are the greater of:

            (1) the excess of the lobbying expenditures for the taxable year over the lobbying nontaxable amount; or,

            (2) the excess of the grass roots expenditures for the taxable year over the grass roots nontaxable amount.

    5.   Under §503, certain exempt organizations lose their exempt status if they engage in a prohibited transaction.

    6.   A feeder organization carries on a trade or business for the benefit of an exempt organization and is not exempt from Federal income taxation. The following activities, however, are not subject to the feeder organization rules.

        a.   An activity that generates rental income that would be excluded from the definition of "rent" for purposes of the unrelated business income tax.

        b.   Activities that normally would constitute a trade or business, but for which substantially all of the work is performed by volunteers.

        c.   Activities that normally would constitute the trade or business of selling merchandise, but for which substantially all the merchandise has been received as contributions or gifts.

III.   Tax Consequences of Private Foundation Status   [Private Foundations p. 23-11]

    A.   Classification as a private foundation is less beneficial than that as a public charity.

        1.   The deduction consequences to the donor may be less favorable than would be the case if the organization were a public charity.

        2.   A private foundation may be partially subject to tax.

    B.   The Code defines a private foundation by enumerating the §501(c)(3) exempt organizations that are **not** private foundations. The following §501(c)(3) organizations are included among those that are defined as being outside of the definition of a private foundation.

1. Churches; educational institutions; hospitals and medical research organizations; charitable organizations receiving a major portion of their support from the general public or governments; and, governmental units.

2. Organizations that are broadly supported by the general public (excluding disqualified persons), by governmental units, or by organizations described in 1. above. To satisfy the broadly supported provision, the one-third-support test and the not-more-than-one-third-support test must be met.

> **KEY TERMS**
>
> ➤ Tax exemption
> ➤ Private foundation
> ➤ Lobbying, Grass roots amounts
> ➤ Unrelated business income
> ➤ Debt-financed income

   a. Under the **one-third-support test**, the organization *normally* must receive more than one-third of its support each taxable year from: gifts; grants; contributions; membership fees; and gross receipts from admissions, sales of merchandise, performance of services, or the furnishing of facilities, in an activity that is not an unrelated trade or business. However, such gross receipts from any person or governmental agency in excess of the greater of $5,000 or one percent of the organization's support for the taxable year are not counted.

   b. Under the **not-more-than-one-third-support test**, the amount of support *normally* received from gross investment income and unrelated business income net of the related tax is limited to one-third of the organization's support for the taxable year.

   c. The term *normally* refers to the tests being satisfied for the four taxable years preceding the current taxable year. Satisfying the test for the current taxable year will result in the subsequent taxable year being treated as satisfying the test.

3. Organizations organized and operated exclusively for the benefit of organizations described in 1. and 2.

4. Organizations organized and operated exclusively for testing for public safety.

C. A private foundation may be subject to numerous taxes including: tax based on investment income; tax on self-dealing; tax on failure to distribute income; tax on excess business holdings; tax on investments that jeopardize charitable purposes; and, tax on taxable expenditures. These taxes serve to restrict the permitted activities of private foundations.

IV. Unrelated Business Income Tax [Unrelated Business Income Tax p. 23-16]

A. To be characterized as an activity that generates unrelated business income (UBI), the following three factors generally must be present in the exempt organization.

1. The organization must conduct a trade or business.

2. The trade or business must be regularly carried on.

3. The trade or business must not be substantially related to the

              performance of the organization's exempt function.

B. Even in cases where the three factors are present, the following activities are *not* classified as an unrelated trade or business.

1. Substantially all the work of the trade or business is performed by volunteers.

2. The trade or business consists of merchandise sales, and substantially all of the merchandise has been received as gifts or contributions.

3. With respect to §501(c)(3) organizations and state colleges or universities, the trade or business is conducted primarily for the convenience of the organization's members, students, patients, officers, or employees.

4. With respect to most employee unions, the trade or business consists of selling to members, at their usual place of employment, work-related clothing and equipment and items normally sold through vending machines, snack bars, or food dispensing facilities.

5. Payments received for corporate sponsorships, eg for bowl games. The payor must receive no benefit from the use of its name, logo, or product line, if the amounts are to excluded from UBI.

C. In determining whether an activity is an unrelated trade or business, special rules apply to the following activities.

1. Bingo games.

2. The distribution of low-cost articles.

3. Rental or exchange of membership lists.

4. Qualified public entertainment activities.

5. Qualified convention and trade show activities.

6. Certain services provided at cost or less by a hospital to small hospitals.

7. Certain pole rentals by telephone companies.

D. UBI is the income derived from the unrelated trade or business.

E. In computing unrelated business taxable income, a deduction of $1,000 is permitted.

F. The formula for the unrelated business income tax is illustrated in Exhibit 23-1.

In avoiding the UBIT, the "exempt function" rule, the "volunteers" test, the "convenience of" test, and the $1,000 deduction are the most important. In addition, if the business activity is not regularly carried on, eg because it occurs only once or twice a year, the tax can be avoided.

V. Unrelated Debt-Financed Income [p 23-22]

A. Unrelated debt-financed income increases unrelated business taxable income, and unrelated debt-financed deductions decrease unrelated business taxable income.

B. *Debt-financed income* is the gross income generated from debt-financed property.

C. *Debt-financed property* is all of the property of the organization held to produce income and on which there is acquisition indebtedness except for the following.

1. Property for which at least 85 percent of the use of the property is for the achievement of the exempt purpose of the organization.

2. Property whose gross income is otherwise treated as UBI.

3. Property whose gross income is derived from certain research and is not

otherwise treated as unrelated business income.

4. Property used in a trade or business that is treated as not being an unrelated trade or business under one of the statutory exceptions.

5. Certain land that is acquired for exempt use within ten years (property acquired for prospective exempt use).

D. *Acquisition indebtedness* consists of the following debts with respect to debt-financed property.

1. Debt incurred in acquiring or improving the property.

2. Debt incurred prior to the acquisition or improvement of the property but which absent such acquisition or improvement, would not have been incurred.

3. Debt incurred subsequent to the acquisition or improvement of the property but which would have not been incurred and whose incidence was reasonably foreseeable at the time of acquisition or improvement.

E. The portion of the debt-financed income and deductions that is unrelated debt-financed income and deductions is determined by the following formula.

$$\frac{\textbf{\textit{Average acquisition indebtedness for the property}}}{\textbf{\textit{Average adjusted basis of the property}}} = \begin{array}{c} \textbf{\textit{Debt/basis}} \\ \textbf{\textit{percentage}} \end{array}$$

1. The *average acquisition indebtedness* for a debt-financed property is the average amount of the outstanding debt (ignoring interest) for the taxable year.

2. The *average adjusted basis* of the debt-financed property is the average of the property's adjusted basis at the beginning and at the end of the taxable year.

3. If debt-financed property is disposed of during the taxable year at a gain, average acquisition indebtedness in the formula is replaced with highest acquisition indebtedness. *Highest acquisition indebtedness* is the largest amount of the property's acquisition indebtedness for the twelve-month period preceding the date of disposition.

Exhibit 23-1
UNRELATED BUSINESS INCOME TAX FORMULA

	Gross Unrelated business income
-	**Directly connected income**
	Net unrelated business income
+	**Charitable contributions in excess of 10% of unrelated business taxable income**
+	**Net unrelated debt-financed income**
+	**Certain interest, annuity, royalty, and rental income not included in net unrelated business income, received from an organization controlled by the entity (This provision overrides the negative adjustment modification of these items)**
-	**Income, net of directly related deductions, from dividends, interest, and annuities**
-	**Net royalty income**
-	**Net rental income from real property**
-	**Net rental income from certain personal property**
-	**Gains and losses from the sale, exchange, or other disposition of property, other than inventory**
-	**Certain net research income**
-	**Certain charitable contributions (Note: the total deduction for charitable contributions cannot exceed 10% of unrelated business taxable income)**
-	**$1,000 statutory deduction**
	Unrelated business taxable income
x	**Corporate tax rates**
	Unrelated Business Income Tax

TEST FOR SELF-EVALUATION - CHAPTER 23

True or False

Indicate which of the following statements are true or false by circling the correct answer.

T   F   1.   In recognition of the equity considerations objective, the Code contains provisions that permit certain organizations to be either partially or completely exempt from Federal income taxation.

T   F   2.   The statutory authority for certain organizations to be exempt from Federal income taxation is provided in Subchapter F of the Code.

T   F   3.   An organization that is classified as a feeder organization is exempt from Federal income taxation.

T   F   4.   Qualifying §501(c)(3) organizations that make an affirmative election are subject to a 35% tax on excess lobbying expenditures.

T   F   5.   Organizations exempt under §501(c)(3), i.e., religious, charitable, educational, or similar organizations, will forfeit their exempt status if the organization participates in any lobbying activities.

T   F   6.   Lobbying expenditures are expenditures made for the purpose of influencing legislation through attempting to affect the opinions of the general public or any segment thereof.

T   F   7.   The general objective of the tax on unrelated business income is to tax such income as if the entity were subject to the individual income tax.

T   F   8.   Bingo games generally constitute unrelated trades or businesses.

T   F   9.   In determining unrelated business taxable income, gains and losses from the sale, exchange, or other dispositions of property (other than inventory) are subtracted from net unrelated business income.

T   F   10.   Acquisition indebtedness includes debt incurred in acquiring or improving debt-financed property.

T   F   11.   An organization will be exempt from taxation only if it fits into one of the categories enumerated in the Code.

T   F   12.   Exempt organizations that qualify as private foundations receive more beneficial tax treatment than do those that qualify as public charities.

T   F   13.   If an exempt organization conducts an unrelated trade or business, it may lose its exempt status.

T   F   14.   In computing unrelated business taxable income, a $5,000 statutory deduction generally is available to all exempt organizations.

T   F   15.   A trade or business is not an unrelated trade or business if the persons who perform substantially all the work are volunteers.

T   F   16.   An exempt organization is subject to tax on its unrelated debt-financed income.

T   F   17.   Charitable contributions of an exempt entity are limited to ten percent of UBTI.

T   F   18.   Intermediate sanctions penalize an exempt entity without jeopardizing its exempt status.

Fill-in-the Blanks

Complete the following statements with the appropriate word(s) or amount(s).

1.   In recognition of the _____ considerations objective, Subchapter _____ of the Code provides that certain organizations are exempt from Federal income taxation.

2.   IRC §501(c)(3) provides exemption from income taxation for entities organized and operated exclusively for the following purposes: _____, _____ scientific, literary, educational, testing for public safety, fostering national or international amateur sports and prevention of cruelty to children or animals.

3.   The underlying rationale for all exempt organizations is that they serve some type of _____ _____.

4.   For failure to distribute all of its income, a tax may be imposed on a nonoperating _____ _____ in the form of an initial tax and an additional tax.

5.   _____ _____ expenditures are those made for the purpose of influencing legislation through attempting to affect the opinions of the general public or any segment thereof.

6.   A _____ organization carries on a trade or business for the benefit of an exempt organization.

7.   In general, _____ _____ _____ is income from activities not related to the exempt purpose of the exempt organization.

8.   A _____ or _____ includes any activity conducted for the production of income through the sale of merchandise or the performance of services.

9.   With respect to debt-financed property, _____ _____ is debt sustained by an exempt organization in association with the acquisition of property.

10.   For an exempt organization to be subject to the tax on unrelated business income, the organization must conduct a _____ or _____ that is not substantially related to the _____ _____ of the organization and is regularly _____ on by the

organization.

11.   The election by a §501(c)(3) organization to be eligible to make lobbying expenditures on a limited basis subjects the exempt organization to tax on _____ _____ _____.

12.   Classification as a private foundation may have an adverse impact on the _____ received by the donee exempt organization and may result in _____ at the organization level.

13.   Unrelated business income is taxed at the same rates as those applicable to _____ taxpayers.

14.   If an exempt entity passes an excessive benefit to one of its executives, fines may apply under the _____ _____ rules.

Multiple Choice

Choose the best answer for each of the following questions.

_____   1.   Which of the following statements generally is *not* included in the definitional requirements of many of the organizations that qualify for exemption?
         a.   The organization serves some type of common good.
         b.   The organization is not a for-profit entity.
         c.   The organization does not engage in any unrelated trades or businesses.
         d.   The organization does not exert political influence.
         e.   The net earnings of the organization do not benefit the members of the organization.

_____   2.   A private foundation may be subject to which of the following taxes: (More than one answer may be correct.)
         a.   Tax on failure to distribute income.
         b.   Tax on built-in gains.
         c.   The environmental tax.
         d.   Tax on taxable expenditures.
         e.   Tax on excess distributions.

_____   3.   For an exempt organization to be subject to the tax on unrelated business income, the following factors must be present: (More than one answer may be correct)
         a.   The organization conducts a trade or business that is regularly carried on.
         b.   The trade or business is conducted primarily for the convenience of the organization's members.
         c.   The trade or business is substantially related to the exempt purpose of the organization.
         d.   The organization does not use the funds generated by the trade or business to provide income to help defray the costs of conducting the exempt purpose.
         e.   The trade or business is not substantially related to the exempt purpose of the organization.

_____ 4.   Factors to be considered in determining whether a trade or business is regularly
            carried on include: (More than one answer may be correct.)
            a.   The frequency of the activity.
            b.   The continuity of the activity.
            c.   Whether the activity generates income.
            d.   The manner in which the activity is pursued.
            e.   The number of persons employed in the activity.

_____ 5.   In computing unrelated business taxable income, which of the following is not a
            subtraction modification?
            a.   Dividend income.
            b.   Royalty income.
            c.   Gains and losses from the sale, exchange, or other dispositions of
                    property except inventory.
            d.   Unrelated debt-financed income.
            e.   The $1,000 statutory deduction.

_____ 6.   Xircon, a qualifying §501(c)(3) organization, made an election to be eligible to
            make lobbying expenditures on a limited basis. During the year, Xircon incurs
            lobbying expenditures of $800,000 and determined its lobbying nontaxable
            amount to be $600,000. The election results in:
            a.   The loss of Xircon's exempt status.
            b.   Imposition of tax on $800,000 of excess lobbying expenditures.
            c.   A tax liability of $68,000.
            d.   Imposition of tax on $200,000 of excess lobbying expenditures.
            e.   The election neither results in the imposition of tax nor the loss of exempt
                    status.

_____ 7.   In determining whether a §501(c)(3) organization is broadly supported by the
            general public, governmental units or certain exempt organizations, and thus, is
            not a private foundation, which of the following tests must be satisfied? (More
            than one answer may be correct.)
            a.   The one-third-support test.
            b.   The gross income test.
            c.   The normal source of income test.
            d.   The not-more-than-one-third-support test.
            e.   The $5,000 gross receipts test.

_____ 8.   During the taxable year, a §501(c)(3) organization received the following support.

                    General public for services rendered $10,000
                    US governmental unit for services rendered   8,000
                    State A, for services rendered   15,000
                    Contributions from disqualified persons   10,000
                    Gross investment income   12,000

            Which of the following statements are accurate? (More than one answer may be
            correct.)
            a.   The one-third-support test has been met.
            b.   The $5,000 gross receipts test has been satisfied.
            c.   The organization is a private foundation.
            d.   The not-more-than-one-third-support test is satisfied.

e.   The organization is subject to the unrelated business income tax.

____ 9.   Which of the following activities would constitute an unrelated trade or business for a state university?
a.   A laundry operated by the university for laundering dormitory linens and students' clothing.
b.   Operation by the university of parking facilities for faculty and students.
c.   Operation by the university of banquet facilities that are available to the general public.
d.   Operation by the university of a bookstore that only sells textbooks.
e.   None of the above.

____ 10.   An exempt organization may incur an unrelated business income tax on which of the following items of income generated from an unrelated trade or business?
a.   Dividends.
b.   Interest.
c.   Gain from the sale of inventory.
d.   Royalties.
e.   None of the above.

____ 11.   Entities organized and operated exclusively for religious, charitable and educational purposes are exempt from Federal income taxation under the following Code section?
a.   501(c)(2).
b.   501(c)(3).
c.   501(2)(c).
d.   501(3)(c).
e.   None of the above.

____ 12.   Z, a qualifying religious organization, made an election to be eligible to make lobbying expenditures on a limited basis. Z's excess lobbying expenditures for the current tax year are $100,000. Z's resulting tax liability is:
a. $0.
b. $10,000.
c. $22,250.
d. $25,000.
e. $34,000.

____ 13.   §501(c)(3) organizations that are not classified as private foundations are called:
a.   Feeder organizations.
b.   Nonprivate foundations.
c.   Private charities.
d.   Public charities.
e.   None of the above.

____ 14.   Assuming that each of the following is held by an exempt organization to produce income and there is acquisition indebtedness on each, which of the following is debt-financed property? (More than one answer may be correct.)
a.   Property used in a trade or business that is treated as not being an unrelated trade or business under one of the statutory exemptions.
b.   Property whose gross income is otherwise treated as unrelated business income.

    c.   Property for which at least 75% of the use of the property is for the achievement of the organization's exempt purpose.

    d.   Property whose gross income is derived from research for a hospital and is not otherwise treated as unrelated business income.

    e.   None of the above.

_____ 15.   Egg-On, an exempt organization, owns an office building that it leases to Zip-Off Corporation for $200,000 per year. The acquisition indebtedness at the beginning and end of the tax was $400,000 and $500,000, respectively. The adjusted basis of the building at the beginning and end of the year was $1,000,000 and $800,000, respectively. Egg-On's unrelated debt-financed income is:

    a. $0.

    b. $80,000.

    c. $100,000.

    d. $135,000.

    e. $200,000.

SOLUTIONS TO CHAPTER 23 QUESTIONS

True or False

1.   F   The tax laws providing exemption from income taxation for certain organizations is based on the social consideration objective. [General Considerations p. 23-2]
2.   T   The Code authorizes only exemption from the federal income tax. [General Considerations p. 23-2]
3.   F   Feeder organizations are not exempt from federal income taxation. [Feeder Organizations p. 23-10]
4.   F   Excess lobbying expenditures are subject to a 25% tax. [Election Not to Forfeit Exempt Status for Lobbying p. 23-7]
5.   F   Qualifying §501(c)(3) organizations may make an affirmative election that will permit such organizations to participate in lobbying activities on a limited basis without losing their exempt status. [Election Not to Forfeit Exempt Status for Lobbying p. 23-7]
6.   T   Lobbying expenditures are expenditures made for the purpose of influencing legislation through: (1) attempting to affect the opinions of the general public or any segment thereof; or (2) communicating with any legislator or staff member or with any government official or staff member who may participate in the formulation of legislation. [Election Not to Forfeit Exempt Status for Lobbying p. 23-7]
7.   F   The general objective is to tax such income as if the entity were subject to the corporate income tax.   [Unrelated Business Income Tax p. 23-16]
8.   F   Qualified bingo games are not unrelated trades or businesses. [Special Rule for Bingo Games p. 23-18]
9.   T   Inventory gain/loss is not such an adjustment.   [General Tax Model p. 23-21]
10. T   The amount includes outstanding debt principal.   [Definition of Acquisition Indebtedness p. 23-23]
11. T   Exempt status is not open-ended under the Code.   [Types of Exempt Organizations p. 23-4]
12. F   For private foundations, deduction tax consequences to the donor may be less favorable than that available for public charities; the classification as a private foundation may result in taxation at the organization level.   [Tax Consequences of Private Foundation Status p. 23-11]
13. T   The usual penalty for conducting an unrelated trade or business is liability for the UBIT. [Unrelated Business Income Tax p. 23-16]
14. F   The statutory deduction is $1,000.   [General Tax Model p. 23-19]
15. T   *Substantially all* of the work must be done by volunteers.   [Unrelated Trade or Business p. 23-16]
16. T   This is a positive adjustment in computing the UBIT.   [General Tax Model p. 23-19]
17. T   This is a positive adjustment in computing the UBIT.   [General Tax Model p. 23-19]
18. T   Exempt status will be revoked only in extreme circumstances.   [Intermediate Sanctions p. 23-8]

Fill-in-the-Blanks

1.   social, F   [General Considerations p. 23-2]
2.   religious, charitable [General Considerations p. 23-2]

3.   common good   [Serving the Common Good p. 23-4]
4.   private foundation   [Private Foundations p. 23-11]
5.   grass roots   [Election Not to Forfeit Exempt Status for Lobbying p. 23-7]
6.   feeder   [Feeder Organizations p. 23-10]
7.   unrelated business income   [Unrelated Business Income Tax p. 23-16]
8.   trade or business   [Definition of Trade or Business p. 23-17]
9.   acquisition indebtedness   [Definition of Acquisition Indebtedness p. 23-23]
10.   trade, business, exempt purpose, carried   [Unrelated Business Income Tax p. 23-16]
11.   excess lobbying expenditures   [Election Not to Forfeit Exempt Status for Lobbying p. 23-7]
12.   contributions, taxation   [Private Foundations p. 23-11]
13.   corporate   [Unrelated Business Income Tax p. 23-16]
14.   Intermediate sanctions   [Intermediate Sanctions p. 23-8]

Multiple Choice

1.   c   Although the income from an unrelated trade or business is subject to Federal income taxation, exempt organizations are not prohibited from engaging in such activities, as long as such activities are not the primary purpose of the organization. [Requirements for Exempt Status p. 23-4]

2.   a, d   The taxes restrict the activities of the private foundation. [Taxes Imposed on Private Foundations p. 23-13]

3.   a, e   The tax increases the costs of a commercial activity conducted by an exempt entity. [Unrelated Business Income Tax p. 23-16]

4.   a, b, d   The business need not be profitable. [Definition of Trade or Business p. 23-17]

5.   d   In computing unrelated business taxable income, unrelated debt-financed income constitutes an addition modification. [General Tax Model p. 23-19]

6.   d   ($800,000 lobbying expenditures - $600,000 lobbying nontaxable amount) [Election Not to Forfeit Exempt Status for Lobbying p. 23-7]

7.   a, d   [Definition of a Private Foundation p. 23-11]

8.   a, d   The one-third support test is met: [$20,000 ($10,000 from general public + $5,000 from U.S. governmental unit + $5,000 from state A) / $55,000 (Total support)] is more than 33.33%. The not-more-than-one-third support test also is met: [$12,000 (investment income) / $55,000 (total support)] is less than 33.33%. [Definition of a Private Foundation p. 23-11]

9.   c   The "convenience" test is failed. [Unrelated Trade or Business p. 23-16]

10.   c   Inventory gain/loss is not such an adjustment. [General Tax Model p. 23-19]

11.   b   Over two dozen specific exemptions exist. See text Exhibit 23-1. [Types of Exempt Organizations p. 23-4]

12.   d   ($100,000 x 25%). [Election Not to Forfeit Exempt Status for Lobbying p. 23-7]

13.   d   Public charity status is preferable to being a private foundation. [Tax Consequences of Private Foundation Status p. 23-11]

14.   c   To be excluded from the definition of debt-financed property, at least 85% of the property's use must be for the achievement of the organization's exempt purpose. [Definition of Debt-Financed Income p. 23-23]

15.   c   {[($400,000 + $500,000) / 2] / [($1,000,000 + $800,000) / 2] x $200,000] [Average Adjusted Basis p. 23-23]

Chapter 24
Multistate Corporate Taxation

CHAPTER HIGHLIGHTS

For most businesses, forty percent or so of the total tax burden is paid to state and local governments. Location decisions as to new and expanded facilities are partly determined such that this state and local tax burden can be optimized. The sheer number of state and local jurisdictions, coupled with the propensity of each to develop tax bases and computations that differ from their neighbors', mean that the state and local tax burden is in a constant state of flux. Current open issues include the taxation of catalog and internet sales, the collection of use taxes in small amounts, and the reduction of the compliance complexity that faces the business taxpayer.

I.   Income Taxes [Overview of Corporate State Income Taxation, p. 24-3]
    A.   Forty-six states and the District of Columbia impose some sort of taxed that is based on the taxable income of a corporation. Each state uses its own tax base, but most states use a formula that:
        1.   Applies modifications to federal taxable income, to reflect a desire for a different tax base, or to reflect limitations attributable to the local constitution or statutes as to what can be taxed and how.
        2.   **Allocate** nonbusiness income to the location where it is earned, and **apportion** business income on a formulary basis.
        3.   Allow tax credits and other incentives to reduce the resulting tax liability.

A few states levy an alternative minimum tax similar to that of federal law. Most states coordinate audit efforts with those of the IRS.

B.   Commonly encountered state modifications include the following. [State Modifications, p. 24-6]

1.   Addition modifications -- they are added to federal taxable income.
        a.   Interest income on state and local bonds, net of expenses.
        b.   State and local income taxes deducted in determining federal taxable income.
        c.   Differences in cost recovery computations.
        d.   Differences in asset basis when an sale takes place.
        e.   Federal NOL deductions.

2.   Subtraction modifications -- they are subtracted from federal taxable income.
        a.   Interest on federal bonds, bills, and notes, net of expenses.
        b.   Refunds of state and local income taxes that were included in federal taxable income.
        c.   Dividends received from out-of-state corporations, to the extent included in federal taxable income.
        d.   State/local NOL deductions.

C.   Jurisdiction to tax. [Jurisdiction to Impose Tax: Nexus and Public Law 86-272, p. 24-9]

1.   A jurisdiction can apply its income tax to the taxpayer only if the taxpayer has a sufficient degree of contact with the jurisdiction. If such **nexus** is established, as defined under local law, allocation and apportionment of the taxpayer's income can occur.

2.   The federal Public Law 86-272 further restricts the right of a state to tax the business on its sales of tangible personal property. Only if the taxpayer's activities exceed a mere solicitation of sales can the income tax be applied.
        a.   Advertising campaigns, inventory review, and the use of a company car by a travelling sales representative generally do not exceed the solicitation standard of PL 86-272, and sales resulting therefrom are immune from state income tax.
        b.   If the sales representative approves or accepts and order, determines the creditworthiness of the customer, provides training or supervisory services for the customer, or coordinates shipping and delivery of the goods, the sale exceeds the allowed solicitation and is subject to state income tax.

D.   Allocation and Apportionment. [Allocation and Apportionment of Income, p. 24-9]

1.   A business apportions its taxable business income (after modifications) among the states in which it does business. Nonbusiness income is allocated, although some states require an apportionment of *all* of the taxpayer's taxable income by failing to distinguish between business and nonbusiness income.

2.   Nonbusiness income generally includes investment gains and losses, rental and royalty operations, and dealings in intangible assets. Business income is that arising from or integrally related to the taxpayer's regular trade or business.

3.   Most states use an apportionment procedure that assigns to the state a portion of state taxable income equal to the average of the:
        a.   **Payroll factor** = In-State Payroll / Total Payroll
        b.   **Property factor** = Instate Property / Total Property

    c.   **Sales Factor** = In-State Sales / Total Sales

4.   Some states place a higher weight on the sales factor in determining the apportionment percentage for its taxpayers. This has the effect of shifting a disproportionate share of the state tax burden to out-of-state businesses.

5.   The sales factor is based on the "ultimate destination" rule, such that a sale "belongs" to the state where the goods or services finally are consumed. If the state has adopted a **throwback rule**, the sales factor includes sales made into states that do not have an income tax, and into states with which the taxpayer does not have nexus.

KEY TERMS

✓ Nexus
✓ Allocation and Apportionment
✓ Sales, property, payroll factors
✓ Unitary theory
✓ Sales/Use Taxation

---

6.   The payroll factor sometimes excludes executive compensation, or contributions to retirement plans. An employee's salary "belongs" solely to the state in which he/she has a permanent situs. Payments to independent contractors are not included in the payroll factor.

7.   The property factor includes the rental value of leased property, at eight times the annual rental. Construction in progress is included in the property factor. Property in-transit is sourced to its destination state. Mobile property "belongs" proportionately to the states in which it resided during the year.

8.   Only property used in the regular business of the taxpayer is included in the apportionment formulas. Nonbusiness receipts, payroll, and property are excluded from the factors.

E.   Unitary Businesses. [The Unitary Theory, p. 24-21]

    1.   When the taxpayer is part of an integrated or "unitary" business, apportionment factors are computed using the sales, property, and payroll of all of the group members.

    2.   If the other members of the unitary group are less profitable than the taxpayer, or if they operate in lower-tax jurisdictions than does the taxpayer.

    3.   Most of the states determine whether a unitary business exists based on a number of subjective factors, looking for shared management and services, common procedures, and overlapping ownership. About half of the states apply or allow unitary computations in deriving taxable income.

F.   State Taxation of S Corporations [Taxation of S Corporations, p. 24-25]

    1.   Most of the states allow the flow-though treatment of income, deduction, and credit to the shareholders of a federal S corporation. A few states require a state-specific S election form, and a few allow a federal S corporation to *elect out* of S status for state purposes. Most of them require the corporation to withhold state income tax on out-of-state shareholders.

    2.   In non-S states, the entity computes state income tax as would any C corporation, using apportionment and allocation to derive the tax base.

G.   Taxation of Partnerships and LLCs [Taxation of Partnerships and LLCs, p. 24-26]

    1.   Most states apply a pass-through model to partnerships, limited liability entities, and their owners.

2.   Difficult issues include whether the owner creates nexus for the entity or vice versa, and the computation of credits for taxes paid to other states.

II.   Other Taxes [Other State and Local Taxes. p. 24-27]

    A.   Sales and use taxes are applied by most of the states and by many local jurisdictions.

        1.   The tax is due when a local taxpayer is the ultimate consumer of a sales-taxable good or service. Generally, the vendor providing the good or service collects the tax on behalf of the state.

        2.   The vendor must collect the tax only if it has sales-tax nexus with the state.

        3.   Most states allow exemptions from the tax for medical goods, professional services, groceries, and educational materials. An item that is purchased for resale is not subject to the tax

        4.   A use tax is due when the in-sate consumer acquired the good out of state and brings it across the border for its ultimate consumption.

    B.   Property taxes are collected by nearly all local jurisdictions. This is an *ad valorem* tax that is based on the current "assessed" value of the taxed property.

        1.   Property taxes on realty often apply to residences and commercial property.

        2.   Property taxes on personalty usually apply to business property, luxury goods, and automobiles.

    C.   Many jurisdictions apply other taxes and fees, including franchise and capital stock taxes on businesses, incorporation and stock transfer taxes on investments, and realty transfer and mortgage recording taxes and licenses on individuals.

III.   Multistate tax planning [Tax Planning Considerations, p. 24-29]

Taxpayers who wish to manage their multistate tax liabilities often employ a combination of the following strategies.

    A.   Create nexus in low-tax states, and avoid it with high-tax states.

    B.   Apply the unitary theory where the taxpayer's affiliates are less profitable or operate in lower-tax jurisdictions.

    C.   Put less profitable operations in low-tax states, and profitable activities in higher-tax jurisdictions.

    D.   Place profitable operations in states that levy no income tax, with which the taxpayer has no nexus, or where it is protected by PL 86-272.

    E.   Use the apportionment factors to the taxpayer's benefit.

        1.   Re-arrange delivery methods so that the destination state is a no- or low-tax state.

        2.   Keep idle and investment assets out of the property factor. Expand operations into states with relatively lower property factor weightings.

        3.   Use independent contractors to reduce the payroll factor.

    F.   Remember that some states assess sales tax when assets flow in and out of new corporations, e.g., as a result of a merger or liquidation. This can add great expense to an otherwise tax-favorable deal.

TEST FOR SELF-EVALUATION - CHAPTER 24

True or False

Indicate which of the following statements are true or false by circling the correct answer.

T   F   1.   In many cases, state and local taxes account for two-thirds of the total tax burden of a business.

T   F   2.   Nontax considerations drive most decisions of the business as to location and expansion, not the tax consequences.

T   F   3.   About a dozen states "piggyback" their state income tax with the federal tax, such that the federal government collects the state tax and then remits the money to the state at a later date.

T   F   4.   Most states use federal taxable income, with several state modifications, as their tax base.

T   F   5.   Most states require the taxpayer to use the same tax year for state purposes as it does on federal tax returns.

T   F   6.   The audit divisions of most states communicate fully with federal tax auditors, so that completion of a federal audit often is followed by an inquiry from the state.

T   F   7.   Typical modifications to the state tax base include an addition for federal-bond interest income, and a subtraction for local-bond interest.

T   F   8.   Some states allow a subtraction modification for federal income taxes paid.

T   F   9.   The taxpayer has nexus with a state if its activities in the state are substantial in nature and amount.

T   F   10.   PL 86-272 allows immunity from state income tax for a taxpayer that merely solicits sales from customers in the state.

T   F   11.   Business income is apportioned and nonbusiness income is allocated.

T   F   12.   All of the states apportion taxable income using an equal weighting of the payroll, property, and sales factors.

T   F   13.   The sum of all states' taxable incomes may be more or less than federal taxable income.

T   F   14.   A rental building owned by a manufacturer is included in the property factor.

T   F   15.   When the taxpayer is part of a unitary business, data for all of the affiliates might be used in computing the apportionment percentage.

T   F   16.   About half of the states require or allow unitary computations in deriving state taxable income.

T   F   17.   A few states tax federal S corporations as C corporations.

T   F   18.   A use tax complements a state's sales tax provisions.

Fill-in-the Blanks

Complete the following statements with the appropriate word(s) or amount(s).

1.   In computing state taxable income, interest income from a US Treasury bond usually is a(n) _____ modification.

2.   In computing state taxable income, the federal NOL deduction often is a(n) _____ modification.

3.   In computing state taxable income, state income tax refunds usually are a(n) _____ modification.

4.   In computing state taxable income, the state NOL deduction usually is a(n) _____ modification.

5.   In computing state taxable income, a federal taxes paid deduction might be a(n) _____ modification.

6.   In applying the PL 86-272 rule for mere order solicitation, picking up damaged property from the customer (does/does not) _____ exceed the standard for immunity.

7.   In applying the PL 86-272 rule for mere order solicitation, approving orders from the customer (does/does not) _____ exceed the standard for immunity.

8.   In applying the PL 86-272 rule for mere order solicitation, carrying sample goods for the customer to review (does/does not) _____ exceed the standard for immunity.

9.   In applying the PL 86-272 rule for mere order solicitation, maintaining a home office in-state for the sales representative (does/does not) _____ exceed the standard for immunity.

10.   In applying the PL 86-272 rule for mere order solicitation, operating a purchasing office in-state (does/does not) _____ exceed the standard for immunity.

11.   The throwback rule is an exception to the _____ _____ concept of the sales factor.

12.   Some states exclude executive compensation from the _____ factor.

13.   In computing the property factor, leased assets are included at _____ times the

annual rental charge.

14.   A(n) _____ business might exist where the taxpayer shares marketing and accounting functions with related corporations.

15.   Affiliates of a unitary business might be required to file a _____ return.

Multiple Choice

Choose the best answer for each of the following questions.

_____   1.   Sporting's federal taxable income is $1 million. It earned $20,000 from City of Boise bonds, and $30,000 from US Treasury bonds. Sporting's state taxable income is:
           a. $1,050,000.
           b. $1,030,000.
           c. $1,010,000.
           d. $990,000.
           e.   Some other amount. Specify _____

_____   2.   Sprinting's federal taxable income is $1 million. Its federal cost recovery deduction was $50,000. The correct amount for state purposes is $35,000. Sprinting's state taxable income is:
           a. $1,050,000.
           b. $1,015,000.
           c. $1,000,000.
           d. $965,000.
           e.   Some other amount. Specify _____

_____   3.   Jogging's federal taxable income is $1 million. Its federal NOL deduction is $40,000. This year's state NOL deduction is $100,000. Jogging's state taxable income is:
           a. $860,000.
           b. $900,000.
           c. $1,000,000.
           d. $1,060,000.
           e.   Some other amount. Specify_____

_____   4.   Lilting's federal taxable income is $1 million. Its deduction for state income taxes paid is $50,000. Federal income taxes incurred in the period were $70,000. Lilting's state taxable income is:
           a. $880,000.
           b. $980,000.
           c. $1,000,000.
           d. $1,020,000.
           e.   Some other amount. Specify _____

_____   5.   Tripping's federal taxable income is $1 million. Its deduction for advertising expenses is $40,000. Deductible business supplies totaled $55,000. Tripping's state taxable income is:

    a. $905,000.
    b. $960,000.
    c. $1,000,000.
    d. $1,040,000.
    e.   Some other amount. Specify _____

____   6.   Hiking is based in State A. It also makes sales into states B and C. Hiking has nexus with all three states. All of the states have adopted a throwback rule. Compute Hiking's sales factor for state A, assuming the following data.

Sales to A customers	$1 million
Sales to B customers	$2 million
Sales to C customers	$2 million

    a.   0%.
    b.   20%.
    c.   33%.
    d.   100%.
    e.   Some other amount. Specify _____

____   7.   Hiking is based in State A. It also makes sales into states B and C. Hiking has nexus with A and B, but not C. All of the states have adopted a throwback rule. Compute Hiking's sales factor for state A, assuming the following data.

Sales to A customers	$1 million
Sales to B customers	$2 million
Sales to C customers	$2 million

    a.   0%.
    b.   20%.
    c.   60%.
    d.   100%.
    e.   Some other amount. Specify _____

____   8.   Hiking is based in State A. It also makes sales into states B and C. Hiking has nexus with all three states. All of the states have adopted a throwback rule. B double-weights the sales factor. Compute Hiking's sales factor for state A, assuming the following data.

Sales to A customers	$1 million
Sales to B customers	$2 million
Sales to C customers	$2 million

    a.   0%.
    b.   14%.
    c.   20%.
    d.   100%.
    e.   Some other amount. Specify _____

____   9.   Hiking is based in State A. It also makes sales into states B and C. Hiking has nexus with all three states. All of the states have adopted a throwback rule. A double weights the sales factor. Compute Hiking's sales factor for state A, assuming the following data.

Sales to A customers	$1 million
Sales to B customers	$2 million
Sales to C customers	$2 million

 a. 0%.
 b. 20%.
 c. 33%.
 d. 100%.
 e. Some other amount. Specify _____

_____ 10. Hiking is based in State A. It also makes sales into states B and C. Hiking has nexus with all three states. All of the states have adopted a throwback rule. A uses sales-factor-only apportionment. Compute Hiking's sales factor for state A, assuming the following data.

Sales to A customers	$1 million
Sales to B customers	$2 million
Sales to C customers	$2 million

 a. 0%.
 b. 20%.
 c. 33%.
 d. 100%.
 e. Some other amount. Specify _____

_____ 11. Hiking is based in State A. It also makes sales into states B and C. Hiking has nexus with A and B, but not C. None of the states have adopted a throwback rule. Compute Hiking's sales factor for state A, assuming the following data.

Sales to A customers	$1 million
Sales to B customers	$2 million
Sales to C customers	$2 million

 a. 0%.
 b. 20%.
 c. 33%.
 d. 100%.
 e. Some other amount. Specify _____

_____ 12. Hiking is based in State A. It also makes sales into states B and C. Hiking has nexus with A and B, but not C. None of the states have adopted a throwback rule. Compute Hiking's sales factor for state C, assuming the following data.

Sales to A customers	$1 million
Sales to B customers	$2 million
Sales to C customers	$2 million

 a. 0%.

        b.   20%.

        c.   33%.

        d.   100%.

        e.   Some other amount. Specify _____

____ 13.   Walking is based in state A, and it makes sales into states B and C. It has nexus with all three states. Applying the states' apportionment formulas, Walking's apportionment percentage for each state is as follows.

        A   40%

        B   35%

        C   35%

        a.   Due to differences in statutes and apportionment weightings, this result can occur.

        b.   This result cannot occur. Apportionment percentages always sum to 100%

        c.   This result cannot occur. Apportionment percentages can sum to less than, but never more than, 100%, according to the Supreme Court.

        d.   This result can occur, and it is evidence of good tax planning by the taxpayer.

____ 14.   Over-weighting the sales factor, such that its weight is greater than one-third:

        a.   Is found in only a few states today.

        b.   Is found in a majority of states today.

        c.   Shifts a greater share of the state's tax burden to those basing their operations in the state.

        d.   Is unconstitutional after 1992.

____ 15.   In working to manage its state income tax liabilities, a non-unitary taxpayer typically should:

        a.   Place a nonprofitable research affiliate in a high-tax state with other profitable operations.

        b.   Avoid nexus with a high-tax state.

        c.   Merge a nonprofitable marketing affiliate into a profitable sales affiliate.

        d.   Give a sales representative order-approval authority in a low-tax state.

        e.   All of the above are productive tax planning techniques.

SOLUTIONS TO CHAPTER 24 QUESTIONS

True or False

1. F   The correct proportion is forty to fifty percent. [Introduction, p. 24-2]
2. T   Tax consequences are an important, but seldom the key, decision factor. [Introduction, p. 24-2]
3. F   Federal law allows this, but no states currently have adopted such piggybacking. [Overview of Corporate State Income Taxation, p. 24-3]
4. T   Only a few states compute state taxable income "from scratch." [Overview of Corporate State Income Taxation, p. 24-3]
5. T   Accounting methods usually must follow federal elections as well. [Overview of Corporate State Income Taxation, p. 24-3]
6. T   Such communication is returned by the state auditors too. [Overview of Corporate State Income Taxation, p. 24-3]
7. F   The opposite is true. [Overview of Corporate State Income Taxation, p. 24-3]
8. T   This is an unusual modification, though. [Overview of Corporate State Income Taxation, p. 24-3]
9. T   Nexus grants the state authority to tax the business. [Overview of Corporate State Income Taxation, p. 24-3]
10. T   The standard of solicitation is strict. See text Exhibit 24-2. [Overview of Corporate State Income Taxation, p. 24-3]
11. T   Some states fail to distinguish between business and nonbusiness income, but most states use both allocation and apportionment in computing state taxable income. [Allocation and Apportionment of Income, p. 24-9]
12. F   Most states weight the sales factor greater than the other factors. [Allocation and Apportionment of Income, p. 24-9]
13. T   Because of the different definitions of taxable income, factor weightings, and item modifications, aggregate state taxable income almost never equals federal taxable income. [Allocation and Apportionment of Income, p. 24-9]
14. F   Only business assets are included in the property factor. [Allocation and Apportionment of Income, p. 24-9]
15. T   Depending on the profitability of the affiliates, the tax liability of the unitary taxpayer may increase or decrease. Not all states require or allow the unitary concept. [The Unitary Theory, p. 24-21]
16. T   This represents fewer states than was the case several decades ago. [The Unitary Theory, p. 24-21]
17. T   These states include Connecticut, Michigan, and Tennessee. [Taxation of S Corporations, p. 24-25]
18. T   Use tax applies when the good was acquired out of state. [Other State and Local Taxes, p. 24-27]

Fill-in-the-Blanks

1. subtraction   [Overview of Corporate State Income Taxation, p. 24-3]
2. addition   [Overview of Corporate State Income Taxation, p. 24-3]
3. subtraction   [Overview of Corporate State Income Taxation, p. 24-3]
4. subtraction   [Overview of Corporate State Income Taxation, p. 24-3]
5. subtraction   [Overview of Corporate State Income Taxation, p. 24-3]
6. does [Overview of Corporate State Income Taxation, p. 24-3]
7. does [Overview of Corporate State Income Taxation, p. 24-3]

8.   does not [Overview of Corporate State Income Taxation, p. 24-3]
9.   does [Overview of Corporate State Income Taxation, p. 24-3]
10.   does [Overview of Corporate State Income Taxation, p. 24-3]
11.   ultimate destination [Allocation and Apportionment of Income, p. 24-9]
12.   payroll [Allocation and Apportionment of Income, p. 24-9]
13.   eight [Allocation and Apportionment of Income, p. 24-9]
14.   unitary [The Unitary Theory, p. 24-21]
15.   combined [The Unitary Theory, p. 24-21]

Multiple Choice

1.   d   Municipal bond interest is an addition modification, and US Treasury interest is a subtraction modification. [Overview of Corporate State Income Taxation, p. 24-3]
2.   b   Federal depreciation is an addition modification, and state depreciation is a subtraction modification. [Overview of Corporate State Income Taxation, p. 24-3]
3.   e $940,000. The federal NOL is an addition modification, and the state NOL is a subtraction modification. [Overview of Corporate State Income Taxation, p. 24-3]
4.   b   State taxes paid is an addition modification, and federal taxes paid is a subtraction modification. [Overview of Corporate State Income Taxation, p. 24-3]
5.   c   §162 expenses are neither an addition modification nor a subtraction modification. [Overview of Corporate State Income Taxation, p. 24-3]
6.   b $1 A sales / $5 million total sales [Allocation and Apportionment of Income, p. 24-9]
7.   c $3 A sales after throwback / $5 million total sales [Allocation and Apportionment of Income, p. 24-9]
8.   c $1 A sales / $5 million total sales. B's weighting does not affect the A computation. [Allocation and Apportionment of Income, p. 24-9]
9.   c $2 A sales / $6 million total sales, both after double weighting [Allocation and Apportionment of Income, p. 24-9]
10. b $1 A sales / $5 million total sales. The sales factor doesn't change, but its weighting (100%) does. [Allocation and Apportionment of Income, p. 24-9]
11. c $1 A sales / $3 million total sales into nexus states [Allocation and Apportionment of Income, p. 24-9]
12. a   A sales factor exists only for nexus states [Allocation and Apportionment of Income, p. 24-9]
13. a   Apportionment percentages typically sum to some total other than 100%. [Allocation and Apportionment of Income, p. 24-9]
14. b   Over-weighting the sales factor has become very popular among the states in the last two decades. [Allocation and Apportionment of Income, p. 24-9]
15. e   All of the above reduce state tax liabilities for the typical taxpayer [Tax Planning Considerations, p. 24-29]

Chapter 25
Taxation of International Transactions

CHAPTER HIGHLIGHTS

Assignment of income, identification of deductions and exclusions, and computation of the foreign tax credit are issues of importance to the US taxpayer doing business abroad, and to the foreign investor looking for tax-advantaged means by which to enter the US market. Generally, governmental bodies wish to ensure that income earned within their jurisdictions does not escape taxation. Conversely, the taxpayer desires to eliminate the possibilities of multiple taxation, and to identify jurisdictions in which the overall tax liability can be optimized. In this chapter, an introduction to the elements of the taxation of international transactions is presented. In addition, problems relative to foreign currency translation and the individual's residency requirements are introduced.

I. Definitions   [Overview of International Taxation p. 25-2]
   A. The structure of the federal income tax with respect to international transactions is familiar to us, i.e., computations of taxable income and identification of taxable entities are carried out in a manner that resembles that for fully-US transactions. Several special definitions are employed in this context, however.

B.   *Incidence of Taxation* -- The federal income tax applies to nonresident aliens and to foreign corporations, to the extent of both US-source income and income that is effectively connected with an active US business.

C.   *Nonresident Alien* -- An individual who has not secured a "green card," i.e., official immigration status, and who is not a resident of the US.

D.   *Residency* -- For an individual, residency is determined according to official immigration status, or by satisfying the "substantial presence" test with presence in the US for at least 183 days in the current calendar year or within a three-year period. For estate and gift tax purposes, however, other actions or intentions of the taxpayer may be considered in making the classification.

E.   *US Business* -- A foreign entity operates an active US business if sufficient production, management, distribution, and other business functions are conducted in the US. Securities trading usually is not an active US business, regardless of where the trading is conducted.

F.   *Effectively Connected* -- A taxpayer's activities are effectively connected with a US business if it generates income from assets used by the business, or if the business provided the capital from which the income was generated.

G.   *Foreign Corporation* -- An entity that was not incorporated in the US. The definition may include trusts or partnerships that exhibit sufficient corporate characteristics.

H.   *FIRPTA* -- The Foreign Investment in Real Property Tax Act, enacted in 1980 to assure that foreign taxpayers would not be exempted from paying appropriate income taxes on the sale or exchange of US realty. The Act classifies as effectively connected income any sale of US realty by a nonresident alien or a foreign corporation.

I.   *Controlled Foreign Corporation (CFC)* -- A foreign entity in which more than fifty percent of the value or voting power of the corporation is owned by US shareholders on any day during the entity's taxable year. For this purpose, indirect and constructive ownership is counted, but shareholders owning (directly or otherwise) less than ten percent of the voting power are ignored.

II.   Tax Treaties [Tax Treaties p. 25-3]

The US has entered into tax treaties with over fifty countries relative to the income tax, and with about thirty countries with respect to the estate and gift tax. The provisions of a treaty commonly override those of the general income tax law. Under such a treaty, definitions and primary taxing rights are established, generally assigning the tax to the resident country of the taxpayer or the country in which permanent assets are constructed, to minimize the opportunity for double taxation.

III.   Identifying US-source and Foreign-source Income   [Sourcing of Income and Deductions p. 25-5]

A.   One must classify income and expense items as either US- or foreign-source in computing the FTC. In addition, US citizens and resident individuals are allowed an exclusion for foreign earned income. Foreign corporations and individual aliens are subject to tax only on their US-source income.

B.   Interest income is US-source if it is received on debt issued by the US government, a US corporation, or a noncorporate US resident. The interest is foreign-source, however, if the US corporation or resident alien conducts eighty percent of its business out of the US, or if the interest is received on amounts deposited with a foreign branch of a US bank.

C.   Dividend income is classified according to the country in which the payor was incorporated: payments from a US corporation are US-source, and distributions from a foreign corporation are foreign-source.

D.   Income from personal services is classified according to the situs at which the services were performed. Personal service income can be derived wherever capital is not a material income-producing factor, even by a corporation. US service income is treated as foreign-source if the performer is a nonresident alien who earned no more than $3,000, stayed in the US for no more than ninety days during the tax year, and performed the services on behalf of a foreign entity that is not engaged in a US trade or business or a business maintained in a foreign country by a US entity.

E.   Rent and royalty income for tangible property is classified according to the location of the underlying property. Income from intangible assets is assigned to the country in which the patent, copyright, or similar property is used.

F.   Gain or loss from the sale of real estate is assigned to the country in which the realty is located, i.e., the sale of US real estate produces US-source income. Gain or loss on the sale of personal property is treated as follows.

> **KEY TERMS**
>
> ▶ Source of income
> ▶ Foreign tax credit
> ▶ Baskets of income
> ▶ Domicile, residency
> ▶ Outbound, inboundTax treaty FIRPTA
> ▶ Controlled foreign corporation
> ▶ Subpart F income
> ▶ Earnings stripping
> ▶ Effectively connected US trade or business

     1.   Generally, income is assigned to the resident country of the seller, and loss is assigned to the country in which the related (sales or other operating) income had been generated prior to the sale.

     2.   Inventory sales are assigned to the country in which the sale took place.

     3.   Sales of manufactured goods are classified pro rata between the countries of production and sale, based upon independent transfer prices. Lacking such a pricing structure, the income is partitioned on the basis of the underlying sales activities and asset holdings of the seller.

     4.   Gain on the sale of depreciable property is assigned to the country in which the depreciation deductions had been claimed.

     5.   Gain attributable to an office or plant is US-source if the US location is operated by a nonresident alien, and foreign-source if the foreign location is operated by a US resident or corporation.

G.   Income from transportation and communication is US-source if both sender and receiver are located in the US. Such income is fifty percent US-source if only one node of the activity is located in the US.

H.   Deductions and losses are directly *allocated* to specific US- or foreign-sources if they relate to identifiable assets or income. Other deductions and losses, including interest charges, then are *apportioned* to US- and foreign-sources, according to some reasonable computational basis, such as relative asset holdings or income generated.

I.   The IRS is empowered to reassign income, loss, and credit items among related persons, by making IRC §482 adjustments, to more clearly reflect the taxable income of the members of the group.

J.   The 20% accuracy-related penalty applies to valuation misstatements where:

1.   A net §482 transfer price adjustment exceeds $10 million of taxable income or AMT income;
2.   The amount paid for goods or services exceeds 200% of the adjusted §482 price; or,
3.   The amount received is less than 50% of the §482 price.

One way around the dangers of a challenge by the IRS to a transfer pricing system is to reach an Advanced Pricing Agreement with the Service before the related tax return is filed. About 1,000 taxpayers currently have executed or are working on such agreements with the IRS, although others are scared off by the nature and extent of the (often proprietary) information that must be given to the Service to justify the pricing figures.

III.   Dealing with Non-US Currency [Foreign Currency Transactions p. 25-11]

A taxpayer must include in gross income gain or loss from foreign currency transactions. Such gain or loss arises from changes in exchange rates between the purchase and payment dates of a closed transaction that is denominated in a foreign currency. In determining gain or loss, such transactions are denominated in the functional currency of the taxpayer, and the currency gain or loss is treated separately from the gain or loss on the underlying sale. An implied currency gain or loss is computed when a foreign corporation makes a distribution from earnings and profits: the taxpayers must use the weighted average exchange rate for the post-1986 years in which the distributed earnings were generated.

IV.   Tax Effects of "Outbound" Transactions [US Persons with Foreign Income p. 25-14]
   A.   A credit is allowed against the US tax relative to certain foreign taxes paid, to mitigate the possibility that the taxpayer will be subject to similar taxes in various countries on the same income.
   B.   The overall limitation on the foreign tax credit (FTC) relates to the proportion of the taxpayer's overall income that is derived from foreign sources.

$$\text{US Tax before FTC} \quad X \quad \frac{\textbf{Foreign-Source Taxable Income}}{\textbf{Worldwide Taxable Income}}$$

   C.   The following two other limitations are placed upon the FTC calculation, so that the credit does not exceed actual or implied foreign tax payments. A *direct* credit is allowed dollar-for-dollar for foreign tax payments. An *indirect* credit is allowed for US corporate taxpayers who receive dividends from foreign corporations; the credit relates to foreign taxes that were paid with respect to the dividend distribution, proportionately to the payor's post-1986 undistributed earnings.

$$\textit{Indirect FTC} \quad = \quad \textbf{Dividend Paid} \quad X \quad \frac{\textbf{Foreign Taxes Paid on Post-1986 Earnings}}{\textbf{Undistributed Post-1986 Earnings}}$$

The dividend income received from the foreign corporation must be *grossed up* by the amount of the deemed-paid taxes (i.e., the amount of the indirect FTC is treated as additional dividend income). The indirect credit is allowed only to a domestic corporation that owns at least ten percent of the payor foreign corporation. The credit can be claimed relative to no more than five tiers of the foreign corporation's subsidiaries.

D. The foreign tax credit is allowed only with respect to foreign taxes that resemble an income tax, i.e., it is not allowed relative to transfer, excise, or extraction taxes.

E. The foreign tax credit must be computed with respect to distinct *baskets* of income, and the limitations are applied to each basket separately, so that credits from taxes in high-rate countries cannot be used to augment those for low-rate countries or activities. A look-through rule is applied to identify the constitution of the income underlying a dividend distribution, with respect to controlled foreign corporations.

F. Any foreign taxes that are used in computing the FTC that are disallowed under the *basket* computations are carried back one year and then forward ten years. FTC carryback and carryforward provisions apply only *within* the separate income baskets.

G. The FTC can be used to reduce the taxpayer's alternative minimum tax liability, taking into account the elements of alternative minimum taxable income.

H. In lieu of claiming a foreign tax credit, foreign tax payments can be *deducted* by the taxpayer, but one cannot claim both a credit and a deduction for the same tax in the same year. A taxpayer, however, can take a deduction in the same year as a FTC for foreign taxes that are not creditable, e.g., for *soak up* taxes.

I. Under Subpart F of this portion of the Code, US shareholders in a controlled foreign corporation (CFC) must include in US gross income a pro rata portion of Subpart F income and increase in earnings that the CFC has invested in US property for the tax year, regardless of whether such earnings have been distributed to them. *Subpart F income* qualifying for this pass-through includes the following.

    1. Foreign sales, service, shipping, personal holding company, and oil-related income.

    2. Insurance income.

    3. Illegal bribes.

If the first two of these categories does not exceed the lesser of $1 million or five percent of the entity's worldwide gross income, the corporation is treated as having no such income for the year.

J. The tax year of a CFC generally must conform to the tax year of its majority US shareholder, i.e., a US shareholder owning more than 50% of the total outstanding stock.

V. Tax Effects of "Inbound" Transactions [US Taxation of Nonresident Aliens and Foreign Corporations p. 25-30]

A. US tax provisions relative to non-US entities conducting business in this country ("inbound" transactions) include numerous reporting requirements.

B. The usual federal income taxes apply to the US-source income of nonresident aliens (NRAs) and foreign corporations, and to the foreign-source income of such entities that is *effectively connected* with an active US business. Non-US corporations usually qualify for the same exemptions from US taxation regarding interest and dividend income as do NRA individuals.

C. Income is effectively connected with a US trade or business if it is derived from assets used in the trade or business (*asset-use test*), or if the activities of the trade or business were a material factor in the production of the income (*business-activities test*).

D. A flat thirty percent tax (or in certain cases, a lower treaty rate) is applied to US-source gross income that is not effectively connected with a US business, including portfolio and other fixed, determinable, annual, or periodic (FDAP) income.

E. NRAs can claim the itemized deductions for casualties and charitable contributions, and they can claim one personal exemption.

F. The US gross estate of an NRA includes assets located in the US, including any stock or bonds issued by a US corporation or government. However, the US gross estate includes neither the NRA's life insurance proceeds, nor amounts held on deposit by foreign branches of US banks.

 1. Higher tax rates and a lower unified transfer tax credit apply to an NRA.

 2. No marital deduction is allowed for assets that pass to a nonresident surviving spouse unless the property passes through a *qualified domestic trust (QDT)*. However, a $100,000 annual gift tax exclusion is allowed on transfers to a noncitizen spouse.

G. A thirty percent branch profits tax is applied to the "dividend equivalent amount" of a foreign corporation. The tax base, limited to effectively connected and previously untaxed post-1986 E&P, includes the effectively connected income of the entity, *minus* any additional investments made in US assets during the year, or *plus* any decrease in such investments.

H. Under FIRPTA, all gains and losses from sales of US realty are treated as effectively connected to a US business.

I. An exclusion against US gross income is allowed with respect to the foreign earned income of a US citizen or resident, to allow for the payment of market or incentive wages in the context of a foreign relocation. The exclusion is allowed if the US individual is physically present in a foreign country for at least 330 full days during twelve consecutive months. The exclusion cannot exceed the excess of foreign earned income over a standard housing cost allowance. A self-employed individual cannot claim the housing cost exclusion, but he or she may be able to deduct foreign housing expenses.

J. A corporation's deduction may be deferred for interest expense paid or accrued to a related party that is not fully subject to US income tax on the interest income. This rule is referred to as the *earnings stripping* provision. For this purpose, a related party generally must be affiliated through more than 50% stock ownership.

 1. If the payor corporation's debt-to-equity ratio exceeds 1.5 to 1, related party interest will be deferred and subject to limitation in the succeeding year to the extent that total interest expense, reduced by taxable interest income, exceeds 50% of the corporation's adjusted taxable income plus the amount by which the 50% income limit has exceeded net interest expense in the prior three years.

 2. Adjusted taxable income for this purpose is the corporation's taxable income prior to deductions for interest, NOLs, depreciation, amortization, and depletion.

TEST FOR SELF-EVALUATION - CHAPTER 25

True or False

Indicate which of the following statements are true or false by circling the correct answer.

T   F   1.   For taxpayers using the cash method of accounting for tax purposes, an election is available to take the foreign tax credit in the year in which the foreign tax accrues.

T   F   2.   The *indirect* foreign tax credit is available only to non-corporate US taxpayers, with respect to actual or deemed dividends received.

T   F   3.   An indirect foreign tax credit can be claimed for payments received from up to four tiers of subsidiaries by the parent.

T   F   4.   The foreign tax credit is the *lesser* of the taxes paid or the general limitation amount.

T   F   5.   Taxes paid that qualify for the foreign tax credit include foreign income, value-added, and oil extraction fees.

T   F   6.   In a single tax year, a taxpayer's return may reflect both a credit and a deduction for foreign tax payments.

T   F   7.   Interest on US Treasury bills always is classified as US-source income.

T   F   8.   Income from personal services is assigned to the country of residence of the performer of the services.

T   F   9.   Income from rental agreements relative to tangible assets is assigned to the country in which the income-producing property is located.

T   F   10.   Gain on the sale of inventory is assigned to the resident country of the seller.

T   F   11.   Interest expenses are assigned to the country that issued the debt.

T   F   12.   An individual without official US immigration status still can qualify as a US resident for income tax purposes.

T   F   13.   A nonresident alien individual making portfolio investments is subject to a flat forty percent US income tax on his/her US-source dividend income.

T   F   14.   Tax treaties usually involve three to five countries and the taxation of the citizens of each.

T   F   15.   Almost every international tax issue requires consideration of currency exchange implications.

T   F   16.   Subpart F income is passed through to US shareholders, whether or not distributed, with respect to controlled foreign corporations.

T   F   17.   Despite §351, realized gain is recognized when assets are transferred to a new, non-US corporation.

T   F   18.   From the standpoint of a US investor, the Cayman Islands represent an attractive tax haven.

T   F   19.   A controlled foreign corporation is a foreign entity in which 80% or more of the value or voting power of the corporation is owned by US shareholders.

T   F   20.   For foreign tax credit purposes, taxes paid in a foreign currency are translated to US dollars at the average exchange rate in effect during the year in which the taxes are paid or accrued.

Fill-in-the-Blanks

Complete the following statements with the appropriate word(s) or amount(s).

1.   The _____ _____ _____ allows a dollar-for-dollar reduction of the US income tax for similar taxes paid to other countries.

2.   To claim the indirect foreign tax credit, the recipient must hold a minimum ownership level of _____ percent in each subsidiary.

3.   To prevent the use of the foreign tax credit derived from specific types of income against the tax liabilities of functionally different types of income, the credit must be applied for each of several "_____s" of income. Excess taxes that are unused under this provision can be carried back _____ and then forward _____ years.

4.   Terms of a tax _____ can override the provisions of the Internal Revenue Code.

5.   Tax treaties often include provisions to _____ the rate of withholding tax on specified income items.

6.   Under the provisions of _____, income from the sale of _____ property is assigned to the country in which the assets were located. When personal property is sold, the resulting gain is assigned to the resident country of the _____.

7.   An immigrant can establish US residency for income tax purposes either by obtaining a "_____ _____" or by meeting the _____ _____ test.

8.   A nonresident alien is subject to a flat thirty percent withholding rate of US income tax on his or her portfolio dividend income, unless a lower _____ rate applies.

9.   So-called _____ income is taxed as a flow-through to the CFC's US shareholders.

10.   US source income of a US citizen who leaves the country to reduce US taxes still is subject to US taxation for the _____ years following expatriation.

11.   A _____ _____ _____ is one in which more than _____ percent of the outstanding stock is held by US shareholders on any day in the entity's taxable year. In meeting this test, indirect and attributed ownership is counted, but those holding less than _____ percent of the shares are ignored.

12.   In computing a taxpayer's gain or loss from foreign currency transactions, all exchanges are to be denominated in the taxpayer's _____ currency.

13.   A taxpayer can not take a _____ and a _____ for the same foreign income taxes.

14.   Under §482, the IRS has the power to _____ income among organizations owned or controlled by the same interests.

Multiple Choice

Choose the best answer for each of the following questions.

____   1.   Frank, a US citizen, paid $35,000 in income taxes to Hibernia, the country in which he was assigned to work this year. Hibernia and the US have not enacted any tax treaty to date. Absent any consideration of the foreign taxes paid, assume Frank would owe $38,000 in US income taxes on the Hibernia-source income. Compute Frank's direct foreign tax credit.
     a. $0.
     b. $3,500 (10% limitation).
     c. $35,000.
     d. $210,000.
     e.   None of the above.

USE THE FOLLOWING INFORMATION FOR PROBLEMS 2 THROUGH 4

FSub, a foreign corporation, pays a $200,000 dividend to its sole shareholder/parent, DCorp, a domestic corporation, this year. Since 1986, FSub has paid $800,000 in foreign taxes on its $4,000,000 earnings for the period.

____   2.   Compute DCorp's indirect foreign tax credit relative to the FSub dividend.
     a. $0.
     b. $20,000 (10% TRA86 limitation).
     c. $40,000.
     d. $200,000.
     e.   None of the above.

____   3.   Derive DCorp's taxable income from the dividend.
     a. $0.
     b. $40,000 (after dividends-received deduction).
     c. $200,000.
     d. $240,000.
     e.   None of the above.

____   4.   DCorp's own taxable income for the year totals $10,000,000, and its US tax on this amount, before credits, is $3,400,000. The FSub dividend, and all of DCorp's other foreign transactions which aggregate taxable income of $6,000,000, are included in both of these figures. Derive DCorp's overall limit on the foreign tax credit.

a. $0 (DCorp has more than one foreign subsidiary).
b. $340,000 (10% FIRPTA limitation).
c. $2,040,000.
d. $3,400,000.
e.   None of the above.

_____ 5.   For tax year 2007, which of the following is an income basket to be used in computing the foreign tax credit limitation?

a.   Passive income.
b.   Financial services income.
c.   Shipping income.
d.   All of the above are treated as income baskets.

_____ 6.   Compute DCorp's foreign tax credit with respect to dividends received this year from its two foreign subsidiaries. DCorp's worldwide taxable income amounts to $10,000,000, and its US tax liability on that amount, before the foreign tax credit, is $3,100,000.

Payor	Type of Income	Dividend	Related Foreign Tax
Attina	Passive	$400,000	$55,000
Bulovah	General	400,000	162,500
Totals		$800,000	$217,500

a. $55,000.
b. $124,000.
c. $162,500.
d. $217,500.
e.   None of the above.

_____ 7.   Compute DCorp's US-source income relative to dividends received from its three subsidiaries. All of the subsidiaries operate outside the US.

		Incorporated in
Arriva	$1,000	Aldonza
Balbona	$1,000	West Aldonza
Cheetah	$1,000	United States

a. $0.
b. $1,000.
c. $2,000.
d. $3,000.
e.   Some other amount. Specify _____.

_____ 8.   Milway Airlines operates a flight from Raleigh to Paris. On Flight 101 to Raleigh, Milway carries forty US passengers and sixty French passengers, and it earns $110,000. Compute Milway's US-source income from the flight.

a. $0.

  b. $44,000.
  c. $55,000 (50-50 presumption).
  d. $66,000.
  e. $110,000.

_____ 9. Compute the US-source taxable income derived by the Boucher Realty Corporation for the year. General overhead expenses amounted to $75,000.

Activity	Income/Net Gain	Direct Expenses
German rentals	$200,000	$ 40,000
Sales of German buildings	$200,000	$ 15,000
US rentals	$200,000	$ 65,000
Totals	$600,000	$120,000

  a. $60,000.
  b. $110,000.
  c. $135,000.
  d. $200,000.
  e. None of the above.

_____ 10. This year, FCorp began to sell its equipment in the US through DSub, a 100%-owned subsidiary. DSub's net investment in US assets increased $200,000 during the year, and its current US taxable income would have been $750,000. Compute the tax base for the branch profits tax on FCorp for the year.
  a. $0 (three-year exemption).
  b. $550,000.
  c. $750,000.
  d. $950,000.
  e. None of the above.

_____ 11. This year, FCorp began to sell its equipment in the US through DSub, a 100%-owned subsidiary. DSub's net investment in US assets increased $200,000 during the year, and its current US taxable income would have been $750,000. What is the applicable rate for FCorp's branch profits tax?
  a. 10%
  b. 34%
  c. 35%
  d. 50%
  e. None of the above.

_____ 12. Which of the following does *not* constitute Subpart F income?
  a. Illegal bribes.
  b. Foreign base company interest income.
  c. Foreign base company sales and service income.
  d. Insurance income.
  e. All of the above are included in Subpart F income.

_____ 13. Most observers would identify which of the following as a "tax haven?"
  a. The Bahamas.
  b. The Isle of Man.
  c. The US Virgin Islands.

d.   Monaco.
e.   All of the above can be seen as tax havens.

_____ 14.   FSub, a foreign corporation, sells a computer on 12-1-X1 to DCorp, a US corporation. DCorp paid the full purchase price on 12-15-X1. FSub's functional currency is the Kronos (K). The sale is made for 100,000K. Both entities use the calendar year. Determine the amount of DCorp's X1 currency gain on the purchase.

Date	Exchange Rate
1-1-X1	1K : $1
12-1-X1	1.1K : $1
12-15-X1	1.3K : $1
12-31-X1	1.4K : $1
1-15-X2	1.5K : $1

a. $0.
b. $13,986.
c. $19,480.
d. $20,000.
e. $23,077.

_____ 15.   FSub, a foreign corporation, sells a computer on 12-1-X1 to DCorp, a US corporation. DCorp is to remit the full purchase price on 1-15-X2. FSub's functional currency is the Kronos (K). The sale is made for 100,000K. Both entities use the calendar year. Determine the amount of DCorp's X1 currency gain on the purchase.

Date	Exchange Rate
1-1-X1	1K : $1
12-1-X1	1.1K : $1
12-15-X1	1.3K : $1
12-31-X1	1.4K : $1
1-15-X2	1.5K : $1

a. $0.
b. $13,986 .
c. $19,480.
d. $24,242.
e.   None of the above.

SOLUTIONS TO CHAPTER 25 QUESTIONS

True or False

1. T   This election is made every year. [The Foreign Tax Credit p. 25-24]
2. F   It is available only to corporate taxpayers who have received such dividends during the year. [The Indirect Credit p. 25-26]
3. F   The credit is available only for up to a six-tier arrangement (parent and five levels of subsidiaries), if certain requirements are met. [The Indirect Credit p. 25-26]
4. T   Carryovers are available if the general limitation amount is less. [FTC Limitations p. 25-27]
5. F   If the levy conveys a specific benefit to the taxpayer, like a natural resource extraction fee, it does not qualify for the credit. [Other Considerations p. 25-30]
6. T   This is allowed if, for instance, the taxpayer is subject to tax in more than one foreign country, or to more than one type of tax in the same country, but not with respect to the same tax in the same country. [The Foreign Tax Credit p. 25-24]
7. F   Counter-examples include such income earned on amounts deposited in a foreign branch of a US bank. [Interest p. 25-5]
8. F   It is assigned to the country in which the services are performed. [Personal Services Income p. 25-6]
9. T   The situs rule prevails. [Rents and Royalties p. 25-7]
10. F   It is assigned to the country in which the sale took place. [Sale or Exchange of Property p. 25-7]
11. F   It is assigned to the countries on the basis of the taxpayer's asset bases. [Allocation and Apportionment of Deductions p. 25-9]
12. T   The taxpayer could base his or her US residency on the substantial presence test. [Residency p. 25-32]
13. F   The rate is a flat thirty percent.   [Nonresident Aliens Not Engaged in a US Trade or Business p. 25-33]
14. F   US tax treaties are bilateral agreements only. [Tax Treaties p. 25-3]
15. T   Changes in relative currency values affect debt and asset valuations, and gain and loss amounts [Foreign Currency Transactions p. 25-11]
16. T   This anti-abuse provision makes it more difficult for a US taxpayer to relocate taxable income in lower-tax jurisdictions.   [Foreign Corporations Controlled by US Persons p. 25-19]
17. F   §367 anti-deferral rules may apply. [Cross-Border Asset Transfers, p. 25-15]
18. T   More such countries are listed in text Exhibit 25-2. [Tax Havens p. 25-18]
19. F   A CFC is a foreign entity in which more than 50% of the value or voting power of the corporation is owned by US shareholders, on any day during the entity's tax year. [Foreign Corporations Controlled by US Persons p. 25-19]
20. T   There are some narrow exceptions to this rule. [Foreign Taxes p. 25-13]

Fill-in-the-Blanks

1.   foreign tax credit [The Foreign Tax Credit p. 25-24]
2.   ten [The Indirect Credit p. 25-26]
3.   basket, one, ten [FTC Limitations p. 25-27]
4.   treaty [Tax Treaties p. 25-3]
5.   reduce [Tax Treaties p. 25-3]

6.   FIRPTA, real, seller   [The Foreign Investment in Real Property Act p. 25-35]
7.   green card, substantial presence   [Residency p. 25-32]
8.   treaty   [Withholding Provisions p. 25-34]
9.   Subpart F   [Foreign Corporations Controlled by US Persons p. 25-19]
10.   ten   [Expatriation to Avoid US Taxation p. 25-37]
11.   controlled foreign corporation, fifty, ten   [Foreign Corporations Controlled by US Persons
       p. 25-19]
12.   functional   [Functional Currency p. 25-12]
13.   credit, deduction   [Foreign Tax Credit p. 25-24]
14.   reallocate   [Section 482 Considerations p. 25-10]

Multiple Choice

1.   c   The lesser of $35,000 or $38,000. [The Foreign Tax Credit p. 25-24]
2.   c $200,000 X ($800,000 / $4,000,000) [The Indirect Credit p. 25-26]
3.   d   Gross up taxable income by the amount of the credit. [The Indirect Credit p. 25-26]
4.   c $3,400,000 X ($6,000,000 / $10,000,000) [FTC Limitations p. 25-27]
5.   a   [FTC Limitations p. 25-27]
6.   e   Limit under the basket concept = $179,000, rather than $217,500
           Passive limit = Lesser of $55,000 or [$400,000 X ($3,100,000 / $10,000,000)] =
           $124,000
           General limit = Lesser of $162,500 or [$400,000 X ($3,100,000 / $10,000,000)] =
           $124,000. [FTC Limitations p. 25-27]
7.   b   Sourced to the location of the payor.   [Dividends p. 25-5]
8.   c   Transportation income is assigned fifty-fifty to the originating and destination
           countries.   [Transportation and Communication Income p. 25-8]
9.   b $200,000 - $65,000 - [$75,000 X ($200,000 / $600,000)]   [Allocation and
           Apportionment of Deductions p. 25-9]
10.   b   Decrease the tax base for increases in US investments. [Branch Profits Tax p.
           25-34]
11.   e   The tax is applied at a 30% rate. [Branch Profits Tax p. 25-34]
12.   b   Such income is not subject to Subpart F flowthrough. [Subpart F Income p. 25-
           22]
13.   e   More such countries are listed in text Exhibit 25-2. [Tax Havens, p. 25-18]
14.   b   Gain is computed only with respect to the period between the purchase and
           payment dates. [Foreign Currency Transactions p. 25-11]

100,000*K* / 1.1*K*	$90,909
100,000*K* / 1.3*K*	- 76,923
Currency Gain	$13,986

15.   a   The transaction is not closed in X1. [Foreign Currency Transactions p. 25-11]

Chapter 26

Tax Administration and Practice

CHAPTER HIGHLIGHTS

Although the tax system in the United States is based upon the concept of self-assessment, many returns are audited each year, to ensure taxpayer compliance. Audits may take the form of a mere letter from the IRS, or they may be full-scale undertakings conducted at the taxpayer's place of business. After an audit, an agent will attempt to reach an agreement with the taxpayer concerning the amount of the additional assessment, if any. Where an agreement cannot be reached, the taxpayer is given an opportunity to argue before the appeals division of the IRS. When an agreement cannot be reached at the appeals level, the taxpayer's only choice is to take the case to court. In addition to knowing the procedures for negotiating a settlement in cases of dispute, tax practitioners must become aware of the requirements imposed upon them, and of penalties for failure to comply with the requirements. In recent years, Congress has been encouraging the IRS to more strictly enforce the Code's penalty provisions.

I.   IRS Procedure - Individual Rulings   [IRS Procedure – Letter Rulings p. 26-4]
    A.   Individual Rulings are issued by the National Office of the IRS.
    B.   They represent the current position of the IRS on the tax consequences of a particular transaction with a given set of facts.
    C.   Individual Rulings frequently are declared obsolete or superseded.
        1.   Revocation usually is not retroactive.

2.   The IRS may revoke any Ruling if, upon subsequent audit, the agent finds a material misstatement of fact.

D.   The IRS issues rulings on uncompleted, actual transactions or on transactions that have been completed prior to the filing of the tax return.

E.   The IRS will not rule on all issues.
  1.   It will not rule on a question of fact only.
  2.   It will not rule on a hypothetical issue.

F.   Although a ruling may be relied upon only by the taxpayer who requested and received it, the ruling may provide substantial authority for a position that is taken in a tax return, and thus, eliminate the imposition of a penalty for the substantial understatement of a taxpayer's income tax.

G.   The IRS ruling policy is an attempt to promote a uniform application of the tax laws.

H.   Generally, the taxpayer must pay a user fee when requesting a ruling from the IRS.

II.   IRS Procedures - Other Issuances   [IRS Procedures – Other Issuances p. 26-4]

A.   Revenue Procedures are published statements of current internal practices and policies of the IRS.

B.   Determination letters are issued for completed transactions, when the issues are covered by judicial or statutory authority, Regulations, or Rulings.

C.   Technical Advice Memoranda are issued by the National Office of the IRS upon a request from IRS personnel.

III.   The Audit Process   [The Audit Process p. 26-7]

A.   Selection of returns for audit is done in the following ways.
  1.   The IRS uses computerized formulas to select the returns that are most likely to have errors and render positive tax liabilities after review.
  2.   Certain groups of taxpayers are more likely to be audited, e.g., individuals with gross incomes greater than $100,000, self-employed individuals, and cash-oriented businesses.
  3.   A return may be audited if a corresponding information return does not match the information on the tax return, if an individual's itemized deductions or other deductions are excessive, or if a past audit led to the assessment of a substantial deficiency.

B.   A *correspondence audit* occurs when an obvious error is made on a return, e.g., where the taxpayer has made a math error, or where he or she has failed to use a statutory limitation.
  1.   A letter of explanation and a bill for the additional taxes will be sent to a taxpayer.
  2.   Taxpayers usually are able to handle such errors through direct correspondence, without a visit to an IRS office.

C.   An *office audit* is used for individuals with few or no items of business income.
  1.   The audit is conducted by local IRS personnel.
  2.   The individual usually is asked to substantiate a deduction, credit, or item of income.

D.   A *field audit* most often is used for business returns.
  1.   Such an audit is conducted by an IRS agent at the office or home of the taxpayer.
  2.   A field audit usually is more extensive, covering many more items than would an office audit.
  3.   Upon the showing of reasonable cause, a taxpayer can have an office

audit changed to a field audit.

E.   Taxpayers' Rights.
1.   Prior to, or at the initial interview, the IRS must provide the taxpayer with an explanation of the audit process that is the subject of the interview and describe the taxpayer's rights under that process.
2.   Upon advance request, a taxpayer may make an audio recording of any in-person interview with an IRS officer or employee concerning the determination and collection of any tax.

F.   A taxpayer may attempt to settle with an agent after the audit.
1.   The agent must adhere strictly to IRS policy. He or she cannot attempt to settle an unresolved issue based upon a perceived probability of winning in court.
2.   Questions of fact usually can be solved at the agent level.
3.   Following an audit, the IRS may either accept the return as filed or recommend certain adjustments. The agent's findings are summarized in a *Revenue Agent's Report* (RAR).
4.   If an agreement is reached, Form 870 is signed by the taxpayer.
     a.   The signing of this form stops the running of interest on the additional assessment thirty days after the form is filed.
     b.   The taxpayer is barred from appealing to a higher level of the IRS or taking the issue to Tax Court after filing Form 870.
     c.   However, a taxpayer may pay the tax and file a claim for refund in the Claims Court or a Federal District Court.

IV.   The Taxpayer Appeal Process   [The Taxpayer Appeal Process p. 26-10]
A.   When an agreement cannot be reached at the agent level, the taxpayer receives a copy of the RAR and a letter stating that he or she has 30 days to request an administrative appeal.
1.   If an appeal is not made, a statutory notice of deficiency, i.e., 90-day letter, will be issued to the taxpayer.
2.   A request for appeal must be accompanied by a written protest. However, if the proposed deficiency does not exceed $10,000 or if the deficiency resulted from a correspondence or office audit, a formal letter of protest is not required.

B.   The Appeals Division of the IRS may settle disputes based on a perceived probability of winning in court (i.e. hazards of litigation).

C.   The Appeals Division usually will not raise new issues on appeal. However, if the disputed tax is substantial, and the issue has a significant administrative impact, the Appeals Division will raise a new issue.

D.   Both the Appeals Division and the taxpayer have the right to request technical advice from the National Office of the IRS.

E.   If the taxpayer cannot reach an agreement with the Appeals Division, the Service then will issue a statutory letter of deficiency. After receiving the deficiency letter, the taxpayer has 90 days to file a suit in the Tax Court.

F.   If an agreement is reached at the appeals level, the taxpayer must file Form 870AD, which is a binding agreement for both the IRS and the taxpayer absent fraud, malfeasance, concealment, or misrepresentation of material fact.

G.   The Code provides specific authority for the IRS to negotiate a compromise where there is doubt as to the taxpayer's ability to pay the tax. Form 656 (Offer in Compromise) must be filed.
1.   When there is doubt as to the amount of tax liability involved, a closing agreement may be appropriate.

2.   The IRS has statutory authority to enter into a written agreement allowing payment of taxes on an installment basis if such agreement will facilitate collection.

V.   Interest [Interest p. 26-12]

A.   During negotiations, interest accrues with respect to overpayments, deficiencies, and unpaid taxes.

B.   The taxpayer may stop the running of interest by signing Form 870 and paying the tax.

C.   Interest begins to accrue from the unextended due date for filing the tax return and continues to accrue until 30 days after the filing of the Form 870.

D.   Interest on overpayments is not allowed on refunds returned within 45 days from the date the return was filed or due, whichever is later.

E.   Interest rates are adjusted on a quarterly basis as of January 1, April 1, July 1, and October 1 of each year.

F.   Interest that accrues is compounded daily.

G.   The interest rate charged on underpayments is one percentage point higher than the interest rate charged on overpayments, for C corporation taxpayers. For all others, the rates are the same.

H.   For C corporations that have an underpayment of tax that exceeds $100,000 for any single taxable period, the interest rate charged on the underpayment is increased by two percentage points.

I.   Interest paid by an individual taxpayer to the IRS is characterized as personal interest. No portion of personal interest is deductible.

VI.   Penalties [Taxpayer Penalties p. 26-13]

A.   Penalties are imposed to ensure that the self-assessment features of the tax system function efficiently. They are an addition to the tax liability and are not deductible by the taxpayer.

B.   A penalty of 5 percent per month of the tax due is imposed on a taxpayer who *fails to timely file* a tax return. The total penalty is limited to 25 percent of the tax due. If the failure to file is fraudulent, the penalty is increased to 15 percent per month, up to a maximum of 75 percent of the tax due.

C.   A penalty of 1/2 percent per month of the tax due is assessed, when the taxpayer *fails to pay the tax* due on the return in a timely manner. The penalty is increased to one percent of the underpaid tax per month after the IRS notifies the taxpayer of the underpayment. The maximum penalty that may be imposed is 25 percent of the outstanding tax.

D.   For purposes of both the failure to file and failure to pay penalties, the term "tax due" refers to the net balance due, rather than the total tax shown on the return.

E.   When both the failure to file and the failure to pay penalties are incurred, the failure to file penalty is reduced by the failure to pay penalty, provided that a return was filed. However, if a return never was filed, both penalties will apply without reduction.

F.   A valid extension of time to file a tax return will eliminate the failure to file penalty, but it will not eliminate the failure to pay penalty.

G.   The negligence, substantial understatement and valuation penalties have been consolidated into a single *accuracy-related* penalty. The accuracy-related penalty is imposed at the rate of 20 percent on the portion of any underpayment attributable to

1.   negligence;

2.   substantial understatement of income tax;

         3.   substantial valuation overstatement;

         4.   substantial estate or gift tax valuation understatement; or

         5.   substantial overstatement of pension liabilities.

The accuracy-related penalty, however, will not be imposed where reasonable cause is shown for the underpayment and the taxpayer acted in good faith.

Many tax practitioners today believe that the elaborate penalty and disclosure system has made them operate as agents of the IRS, rather than as taxpayer advocates. The voluntary compliance aspect of the tax system sometimes is difficult to see when discussing matters of collection and enforcement of the revenue laws.

     H.   A 75 percent penalty on the amount of underpayment is imposed on any underpayment resulting from fraud. The fraud penalty only applies to the part of an underpayment that actually is attributable to fraud, i.e., not the entire underpayment. In addition to the civil fraud penalties, the Code contains various criminal sanctions, carrying various monetary fines and/or imprisonment.

     I.   A penalty is imposed for the failure to make adequate and timely estimated tax payments. The penalty is based on the amount and duration of the underpayment and the interest rate that currently is established by the Code.

     J.   Failure to make deposits of taxes, and overstatement of deposits, result in the following penalties.

         1.   Up to 15 percent of the underdeposited amount, depending on when the underpayment is corrected and whether the taxpayer received a delinquency notice;

         2.   25 percent of the overstated deposits;

         3.   Various criminal penalties; and,

         4.   100 percent of the overstatement or underdeposit, if the employer's actions are willful.

     K.   There is a $500 penalty on individuals who file incomplete returns or returns that are obviously incorrect. The tax law also imposes a civil penalty of $500 when a taxpayer claims withholding allowances based on false information.

     L.   The IRS has the authority to waive the underpayment penalty if the underpayment is due to casualty, disaster, or other unusual circumstance.

VII.   Administrative Powers of the IRS   [Administrative Powers of the IRS   p. 26-6]

     A.   The IRS can issue summons to responsible parties to appear before the IRS and to produce the books and records that are necessary for determining the correct amount of tax due.

     B.   The IRS may assess a deficiency, and demand payment of the tax, when the taxpayer has failed to file a return.

     C.   No assessment or effort to collect the tax may be made until 90 days after the issuance of a statutory notice of deficiency (i.e., a 90-day letter).

     D.   Following the assessment of tax, a taxpayer usually is given thirty days to pay the tax before collection efforts are begun. If the taxpayer neglects or refuses to pay the tax after receiving the demand for payment, a lien in favor of the IRS is placed on all property of the taxpayer.

     E.   The IRS may negotiate a compromise in the deficiency when there is doubt as to the amount of the liability or the taxpayer's ability to pay.

     F.   A Closing Agreement is binding on the government and the taxpayer, except upon a subsequent showing of fraud, malfeasance or misrepresentation of a material fact.

VIII.   The Statute of Limitations   [Statutes of Limitations p. 26-21]

A.   The statute of limitations defines the period of time during which one party may pursue an action against the other.

KEY TERMS

➢ Tax preparer
➢ Audit selection
➢ Letter ruling
➢ Correspondence, office, field audit
➢ Thirty-, ninety-day letters
➢ Statutory notice of deficiency
➢ Statute of limitations
➢ Ethics of tax practice

B.   Any tax imposed must be assessed within three years of the filing of the tax return, or the due date of the tax return, whichever is later.

    1.   If no return is filed or a fraudulent return is filed, the assessment can be made at any time, i.e., the statute of limitations never begins to run.

    2.   Where the taxpayer understates gross receipts by 25% or more, the statute of limitations is extended to six years. There is no comparable rule for an overstatement of deductions.

    3.   The statute of limitations also can be extended by mutual consent of the parties.

C.   A claim for refund must be filed within three years of the date the return was filed, or within two years from the payment of the tax if this was later. However, a seven-year period of limitations applies to refund claims relating to bad debts and worthless securities.

IX.   The Tax Practitioner   [The Tax Practitioner p. 26-22]

A.   Practice before the IRS generally is limited to CPAs, attorneys, and other persons enrolled to practice before the IRS.

B.   Exceptions to the above include the following.

    1.   A taxpayer always can represent himself or herself;

    2.   Regular full-time employees may represent their employer;

    3.   Corporations may be represented by a bona fide officer;

    4.   Partnerships may be represented by any partner;

    5.   A taxpayer may be represented at the agent level by whomever prepared the tax return; and,

    6.   A person may represent a member of his or her immediate family if no compensation is received for such services.

C.   The following requirements are imposed upon those governed to practice before the IRS.

    1.   An obligation to make the client aware of any error or omission made on the return;

    2.   A duty to submit records or information lawfully requested by the Service or the taxpayer;

    3.   An obligation to exercise due diligence in preparing the return, and to apply the best practices of the tax profession in doing so;

    4.   A restriction against causing unreasonable delay in the disposal of a disputed issue;

    5.   A restriction against charging "an unconscionable fee;" and,

    6.   A restriction against representing clients with conflicting interests.

D.   Anyone, regardless of his or her educational background, can prepare a return, subject to the following requirements.

1. A person holding himself out as a "tax expert" will be liable for penalties upon filing negligent returns.
2. All paid preparers must sign the client's return as preparer.
3. Penalties for the filing of a fraudulent return are applied to every preparer who was aware of the misstated facts.
4. There are penalties for disclosing tax information to unauthorized parties.
5. Non-attorneys must be careful to avoid the unauthorized practice of law.
6. A tax preparer may be subject to numerous other penalties.

X. Ethical Considerations: Statements On Standards for Tax Services -- Issued by the AICPA [AICPA Statements on Standards for Tax Services p. 26-26]

A. A CPA must sign every return prepared by him or her, whether or not it was prepared for a fee.
B. A CPA need not sign a return that he or she merely has reviewed for errors.
C. A CPA should sign a return only if he or she has made an appropriate effort to find an answer for all questionable items.
D. A CPA may prepare returns using estimates that are derived in a generally acceptable manner.
E. A CPA may sign a return containing a departure from the treatment of an item determined in a prior administrative proceeding.
F. A CPA should advise a client promptly upon the discovery of an error.
G. When a CPA is representing a client in an administrative proceeding with respect to a return in which there is a material error known to the CPA, the CPA should request the taxpayer's permission to disclose the error to the IRS. If the client refuses, the CPA should consider withdrawing from the engagement.
H. A CPA may rely on the information furnished to him or her by the client, i.e., without a detailed audit of the summarized data. However, a CPA should make reasonable inquires if the information appears to be incorrect, incomplete, or inconsistent.
I. A CPA may take a position contrary to the Treasury Department or IRS interpretation. However, in order to do so the CPA must have a good faith belief that the position has a realistic possibility of being sustained administratively or judicially on its merits if challenged.
J. In providing tax advice to a client, the CPA must use judgement to ensure that the advice reflects professional competence and appropriately serves the client's needs.

TEST FOR SELF-EVALUATION - CHAPTER 26

True or False

Indicate which of the following statements are true or false by circling the correct answer.

T   F   1.   The IRS will issue an individual ruling on any issue requested by the taxpayer.

T   F   2.   A letter ruling may be relied upon only by the taxpayer who requested and received it.

T   F   3.   Determination Letters are issued for completed transactions only.

T   F   4.   With respect to noncorporate taxpayers, the rate of interest that the IRS charges on an underpayment is one percentage point less than the rate of interest that it pays on an overpayment.

T   F   5.   Persons other than CPAs, attorneys, and enrolled agents are not allowed to practice before the IRS.

T   F   6.   When a taxpayer overstates deductions by more than 25% of the gross income stated on the return, the statute of limitations is increased to six years.

T   F   7.   If the IRS believes the assessment or collection of a deficiency is in jeopardy, it may assess the deficiency and demand immediate payment.

T   F   8.   The statute of limitations for an assessment of taxes never can extend beyond three years from the filing of a return.

T   F   9.   The statute of limitations for a claim for refund resulting from a bad debt deduction is six years.

T   F   10.   Both the Appeals Division and the taxpayer have the right to request technical advice from the National Office of the IRS.

T   F   11.   According to the AICPA, a CPA may prepare a tax return using estimates received from a taxpayer.

T   F   12.   The IRS requires all persons who prepare tax returns for a fee to sign as preparer of the return.

Fill-in-the-Blanks

Complete the following statements with the appropriate word(s) or amount(s).

1.   CPAs must conduct their tax practices following the AICPA's _____ _____
_____ _____ _____ _____.

2.   A _____ audit usually is handled through the mail, without requiring an office visit by the taxpayer.

3.   A _____ audit generally is used for corporate returns, or for returns of individuals engaged in business or professional activities.

4.   In most cases involving proposed deficiencies of $10,000 or more, a request for an appeal from an agent's decision must be accomplished by a written _____.

5.   After signing a Form 870 and paying the tax, the taxpayer may file a suit for refund in the _____ Court or the _____ Court, but not in the _____ Court.

6.   A tax preparer who is not a _____, _____ or _____ _____ may represent a taxpayer at the agent level.

7.   The Code provides specific authority for the IRS to negotiate a compromise if there is doubt either in determining the _____ of the actual liability or in the taxpayer's _____ _____ _____.

8.   A claim for refund must be filed within _____ years of the date the return was filed, or _____ years from the payment of the tax, whichever is later.

9.   Willful failure to make deposits of withholding tax can result in a penalty equal to _____% of the amount not deposited.

10.   Interest on overpayment of taxes will not accrue when a refund is made within _____ days from the date the return was filed or due, whichever is later.

11.   _____ _____, which was issued by the Treasury Department, prescribes the rules governing practice before the IRS.

12.   A _____ _____ _____ defines the period of time during which one party may pursue against another party a cause of action or other suit allowed under the governing law.

Multiple Choice

Choose the best answer for each of the following questions.

_____   1.   When is a request for technical advice appropriate? (More than one answer may be correct.)
          a.   The issue in dispute is not treated by law or precedent and/or published rulings or regulations.
          b.   There is reason to believe that the tax law is not being administered consistently by the IRS.

c.   The taxpayer does not know how the tax law affects his or her transaction.

d.   The question involves a hypothetical situation for which the IRS has declined to issue a private ruling.

_____ 2.   Individual Rulings will be issued on which of the following? More than one answer may be correct.

a.   Hypothetical transactions.

b.   Questions of fact.

c.   Proposed transactions.

d.   Completed transactions for which a return has not been filed.

_____ 3.   Which of the following is issued as an opinion on the classification of a completed transaction, during an on-going audit?

a.   Individual Ruling.

b.   Determination Letter.

c.   Technical Advice Memorandum.

d.   Revenue Ruling.

_____ 4.   Which of the following methods are used to select tax returns for audit? More than one answer may be correct.

a.   Computer-generated formula.

b.   Tip from informant.

c.   Amount of gross income.

d.   Type of income, e.g. cash-oriented business, not wages

_____ 5.   Which type of audit is used most often for individuals who have chiefly wage income, to substantiate items of income or deduction?

a.   Field.

b.   Office.

c.   Home.

d.   Internet.

_____ 6.   An agent may do which of the following when attempting to negotiate a settlement after an audit? More than one answer may be correct. He or she may:

a.   Attempt to settle an unresolved issue, based on the hazards of litigation.

b.   Settle a question of fact.

c.   Request technical advice from the National Office.

d.   Reach an agreement that will be accepted unconditionally by the IRS.

_____ 7.   When signing a closing agreement, the following result(s) occur. More than one answer may be correct.

a.   The taxpayer still may appeal to a higher level of the IRS.

b.   The interest on the assessment stops accruing immediately.

c.   The agreement is binding on both the taxpayer and the IRS.

d.   The tax must be paid, but a suit for refund can be filed in the District Court or the Claims Court.

_____ 8.   When an agreement cannot be reached with an agent, a letter is transmitted, stating that the taxpayer has thirty days to:

a.   File a suit in Tax Court.

b.   Request an administrative appeal.

c.   Pay the tax.

      d.   Find additional facts to support his or her position.

_____ 9.   A statutory notice of deficiency gives the taxpayer ninety days to:
      a.   Pay the tax.
      b.   Request an appeal.
      c.   File a suit in Tax Court.
      d.   File a protest.

_____ 10.   Which of the following requirements of the AICPA applies to CPAs in tax practice? More than one answer may be correct.
      a.   A CPA may not prepare a return using estimates.
      b.   A CPA need not sign a return if he or she did not receive a fee for preparing it.
      c.   A CPA must sign a return that he or she merely has reviewed.
      d.   A CPA need not disclose a position taken that is contrary to a Treasury Interpretation.

_____ 11.   With respect to noncorporate taxpayers, if the interest rate on an overpayment of tax is 10 percent, the rate of interest on an underpayment of tax is:
      a.   9 percent.
      b.   10 percent.
      c.   10.5 percent.
      d.   11 percent.

_____ 12.   With respect to a C corporation that has underpaid its taxes by $200,000, if the interest rate on an overpayment of tax is 10 percent, the rate of interest on the underpayment of tax is:
      a.   10 percent.
      b.   11 percent.
      c.   12 percent.
      d.   13 percent.
      e.   14 percent.

_____ 13.   Tam underpaid $5,000 of her prior-year income taxes; $4,000 of the underpayment was attributable to negligence. Tam's negligence penalty is:
      a. $0.
      b. $200.
      c. $400.
      d. $800.
      e.   None of the above.

Short Answer

1. Generally, only CPAs, Attorneys, and Enrolled Agents are allowed to practice before the IRS. List exceptions to this rule.

2. Distinguish among individual rulings, Revenue Rulings, and Determination Letters.

SOLUTIONS TO CHAPTER 26 QUESTIONS

True or False

1. F   In certain circumstances, such as cases that essentially involve a question of fact, the IRS will not issue a ruling. [IRS Procedure – Letter Rulings p. 26-4]
2. T   Commercial publishers do make available such rulings to the public, though. [IRS Procedure – Letter Rulings p. 26-4]
3. T   Determination Letters address issued covered by existing tax authority.   [IRS Procedure – Other Issuances p. 26-5]
4. F   The rate of interest that is paid by a noncorporate taxpayer on an overpayment is one percentage point less than the rate charged on an underpayment.   [Interest p. 26-12]
5. F   Persons other than CPAs, attorneys and enrolled agents are allowed to practice before the IRS in limited situations.   [The Tax Practitioner p. 26-22]
6. F   Where a taxpayer understates gross receipts by 25% or more, the statute of limitations is extended to six years; however, there is no comparable rule for an overstatement of deductions. [Statutes of Limitations p. 26-31]
7. T   The status of jeopardy might come from a danger that the taxpayer will leave the country imminently. [Assessment and Demand p. 26-5]
8. F   The statute of limitations extends beyond three years in numerous situations including when a fraudulent return, or no return, is filed. [Statutes of Limitations p. 26-31]
9. F   The statute of limitations with respect to bad debt deductions is seven years. [Statutes of Limitations p. 26-31]
10. T   The taxpayer may request a TAM when there is evidence that the tax law is not being administered consistently.   [IRS Procedure – Other Issuances p. 26-5]
11. T   A CPA may do so if it is impractical to obtain exact data. [Statement No. 4: Estimates p. 26-28]
12. T   Not all parties who work on a return, though, have *prepared* the return for this purpose. [Tax Practice p. 26-22]

Fill-in-the-Blanks

1. Statements on Standards for Tax Services [AICPA Statements on Standards for Tax Services p. 26-26]
2. correspondence   [The Audit Process p. 26-7]
3. field   [The Audit Process p. 26-7]
4. protest   [The Taxpayer Appeal Process p. 26-10]
5. Claims, District, Tax   [The Taxpayer Appeal Process p. 26-10]
6. CPA, attorney, enrolled agent   [The Tax Practitioner p. 26-22]
7. amount, ability to pay   [Offers in Compromise and Closing Agreements p. 26-11]
8. 3, 2 [Statutes of Limitations p. 26-20]
9. 100% [Taxpayer Penalties p. 26-13]
10. 45 [Interest p. 26-12]
11. Circular 230   [Tax Practice p. 26-22]
12. statute of limitation   [Statutes of Limitations p. 26-20]

Multiple Choice

1. a, b   TAMs are issued during the audit process. [IRS Procedures – Other

		Issuances p. 26-5]
2.	c, d	PLRs are not issued with respect to hypothetical transactions or to an issue of fact. [IRS Procedure – Letter Rulings p. 26-4]
3.	c	Other items can addressed proposed transactions. [IRS Procedures – Other Issuances p. 26-5]
4.	a, b, c, d	All options are correct. [The Audit Process p. 26-7]
5.	b	Such audits also can be conducted by correspondence. [The Audit Process p. 26-7]
6.	b, c	Agents cannot consider the hazards of litigation, nor can they enact a final settlement. [The audit Process p. 26-7]
7.	d	The closing agreement ends the taxpayer-IRS negotiations. [Offers in Compromise and Closing Agreements p. 26-11]
8.	b	The thirty-day letter is issued upon completion of the revenue agent's report. [The Taxpayer Appeal Process p. 26-10]
9.	c	The notice of deficiency is known as the ninety-day letter. [The Taxpayer Appeal Process p. 26-10]
10.	d	The AICPA Statements on Standards for Tax Services control these activities. [AICPA Statements on Standards for Tax Services p. 26-26]
11.	b	The same rate is used for most under- and overpayments. [Interest p. 26-12]
12.	d	(10% + 1% rate differential + 2% large underpayment penalty). [Interest p. 26-12]
13.	d	The accuracy-related penalty is $800 ($4,000 x 20%). [Taxpayer Penalties p. 26-13]

Short Answer

1.   Pertinent rules include the following.
- A taxpayer always can represent him- or herself.
- Regular full-time employees may represent an employer.
- Corporations may be represented by a bona fide officer.
- A partnership may be represented by any partner.
- Any tax preparer may represent a client at the agent level, but only CPAs, Attorneys, and Enrolled Agents may go beyond this level.
- An individual may represent a member of his or her immediate family if no compensation is received for such services.
- Trusts, receiverships, guardianships, or estates may be represented by their trustees, receivers, guardians, or administrators or executors.

[The Tax Practitioner p. 26-22]

2.   Individual rulings are issued by the National Office and represent a written statement of the position of the Service concerning the tax consequences of actions that are contemplated by a specific taxpayer. Revenue Rulings are official pronouncements of the IRS and are designed to provide interpretation of the tax law to the general public. Determination Letters are issued as an opinion on the classification of a completed transaction.

[IRS Procedure – Letter Rulings p. 26-4]

Chapter 27

The Federal Gift and Estate Taxes

CHAPTER HIGHLIGHTS

The federal estate tax and gift tax compose a unified tax on transfers of property from one taxpayer to another. Although the Code may give one the impression that there are two separate taxes in operation, the transfer tax system actually entails *one tax*, levied on transfers that occur both during the taxpayer's lifetime ("inter vivos" transfers) and at or after his or her death. The unified tax is cumulative in effect, and it uses a progressive rate structure.

The federal gift tax complements the federal estate tax. It is part of the unified transfer tax system that was put into place by the Tax Reform Act of 1976. Because the federal gift tax is imposed upon the taxpayer's right to transfer property for less than full and adequate consideration, it acts as a *backstop* to the estate tax, preserving the integrity of the transfer tax system as a whole.

I.   Formula for the Federal Gift Tax - See Figure 27-1   [The Federal Gift Tax p. 27-10]
     A.   The objective of the federal gift tax formula is to compute a tax on the current year's taxable gifts.
     B.   However, since the transfer tax system applies a unified, cumulative, progressive transfer tax, all prior taxable gifts must enter into the calculation. As is the case with the estate tax formula, the current year's taxable transfers are *put onto stilts*, possibly raising them into a higher gift tax bracket.
     C.   There are several important distinctions between the gift and estate tax formulas. For gift tax purposes, all prior taxable gifts are added into the transfer tax base, whereas, in the estate tax formula, only post-1976 taxable gifts are added back. This is the case even though the Tax Reform Act of 1976 changed radically the concept of the taxable gift.

D. Another important distinction between the gift and estate tax formulas is the credit allowed for taxes attributable to prior taxable gifts.

    1. For estate tax purposes, actual gift tax paid on post-1976 gifts, net of the unified credit allowed in the year of the gift, constitutes the reduction.

    2. For gift tax purposes, however, the reduction is a hypothetical number, i.e., the gift tax that would have been payable, using the unified transfer tax rate schedule that is effective for the current year and before applying the unified transfer tax credit, on all prior years' taxable gifts.

    3. Given that the composition of the tax base differs between the gift and estate taxes, the difference between the two reductions is proper. This difference recognizes that the gift tax base may include taxable gifts made prior to the introduction of the unified transfer tax rate schedule in 1976. To correspond the amount of the *stilts* with the tax thereon, the use of this hypothetical number is necessary.

E. Application of the unified transfer tax credit also differs between the two transfer tax formulas.

    1. For estate tax purposes, the entire credit that is appropriate for the year of death is applied.

    2. For gift tax purposes, only that portion of the current year's credit that has not been exhausted by prior taxable gifts can be applied.

    3. This distinction is necessary because of the use of the hypothetical gift tax reduction, explained above.

F. Persons subject to the tax.

    1. The federal gift tax applies to all transfers by gift of property, wherever located, by individuals who at the time of the gift were citizens or residents of the US.

    2. For nonresident aliens, the gift tax applies only to transfers by gift of property situated within the US.

G. Legislation passed in 2001 imposed a phase-out of the federal estate tax by mid-2010, with the tax reappearing for 2011 and thereafter. There is no gift tax phase-out scheduled.

II. Definition of a Gift   [Transfers Subject to the Gift Tax p. 27-12]

A. To be considered a gift, the transfer must be made for less than *full and adequate consideration*, where the donor retains no right to reclaim or repossess the property (an incomplete transfer). However, there is no requirement that the transfer be made out of love or affection, or with any donative intent.

    1. Transfers to political organizations are exempt from the gift tax.

    2. In addition, very few business transactions are gifts. The Regulations presume that such transfers are at arm's length, i.e., for full consideration. No judgments are made as to the propriety of such business acumen.

    3. The federal gift tax does not apply to tuition payments made to an educational organization on another's behalf. Nor does it apply to amounts paid for medical care on another's behalf.

B. One does not make a gift when he or she names another as the beneficiary of a life insurance policy. The gift of such a policy requires the transfer of all of the *incidents of ownership* for the policy. *Incidents of ownership* include the power to change beneficiaries, to revoke an assignment, to pledge the policy for a loan, or to surrender or cancel the policy.

The gift-tax definition of a gift is much narrower than the income-tax definition, such as that of *Duberstein*. For identifying a gift-tax gift, one simply compares the value of assets received with the value of those given up. If that difference is positive, one is a donee.

C.   When property is purchased by more than one party as equal co-owners, but equal consideration is not given, a gift may result. Exceptions to this rule include:
   1.   A gift via unequal contributions to a joint bank account. In this situation, a gift occurs only in the year, and to the extent, that a co-owner withdraws more from the account than he or she contributed; and
   2.   The same rule applies to co-ownership of US Savings Bonds.
D.   In general, the settlement of marital rights in a divorce proceeding is subject to the gift tax. However, if a final decree of divorce is obtained within **two years after, or one year before**, the exercise of a written agreement between spouses, in settlement of such marital rights, the transfer is exempt from gift tax (IRC §2516). Similarly, *child support* payments are exempt from gift tax.

III.   Deductions and Exclusions   [Deductions p. 27-15]
   A.   Transfers to charitable organizations qualify for the gift tax charitable deduction. No dollar or percentage limitations exist with respect to the gift tax charitable deduction.
   B.   A marital deduction, similar to that for the estate tax, is available for the gift tax.
      1.   There is no dollar or percentage limitation on the amount of the gift tax marital deduction if the donee spouse is a U.S. citizen.
      2.   The deduction also is available for a transfer of community property.
      3.   To qualify for the deduction, the property generally must be of a nature such that it will be included in the donee's gross estate, i.e., unless it is consumed during the survivor's lifetime.
      4.   The first $100,000 of gifts per year to a spouse who is not a U.S. citizen is excluded from the gift tax. However, to the extent that gifts are made in excess of this amount, no marital deduction is permitted.

> **KEY TERMS**
>
> - Estate, gift, generation-skipping tax
> - Donor, donee, decedent, beneficiary, grantor
> - Unified credit, exemption equivalent
> - Joint tenancy, tenancy in common, community property
> - Gift splitting
> - Annual gift tax exclusion
> - Marital, charitable deductions
> - Incidents of ownership

   C.   An annual exclusion of $12,000 per donee is available to reduce the amount of the current year's taxable gift (IRC §2503). This amount is indexed for inflation.
      1.   To qualify for the annual exclusion, the donee must receive a "present interest" in the property transferred, i.e., he or she immediately must receive possession or enjoyment of the property.
      2.   With respect to property transferred to a trust, an annual exclusion is available for each beneficiary of the trust.

3.   Under IRC §2503(c), the donor may create a trust for the benefit of a minor, even though the minor cannot obtain use or enjoyment of the trust property until he or she attains age 21, and still qualify the gift for the annual exclusion. However, certain stringent conditions must be met before this exception will apply.

D.   **Taxable gifts** constitute the amount of gifts given during the year reduced by the annual exclusions and the marital and charitable deductions.

IV.   Transfer Tax and the Unified Transfer Tax Credit   [Role of the Unified Credit p. 27-6]

A.   The **unified credit** varies in amount according to the year of gift or death.   With respect to U.S. citizens and residents, the unified credit results in a $2 million **exemption equivalent** for the estate and generation-skipping taxes, and a $1 million **by-pass amount** for the gift tax.

B.   The exemption equivalent is scheduled to increase several times over the decade as part of the phase-out of the federal estate tax.

V.   Gift-Splitting   [The Election to Split Gifts by Married Persons p. 27-15]

A.   Spouses can elect to treat gifts of either of their separate property to third parties as having come equally from both of them. This gift-splitting election allows for the optimal use of the spouses' unified credits and annual exclusions (IRC §2513).

B.   The gift-splitting election applies to all gifts made by the spouses in the taxable year of the election.

C.   To split gifts, the spouses must be legally married to each other at the time of the gift, and both must be citizens or residents of the U.S. on the date of the gift.

VI.   Formula for the Federal Estate Tax - See Figure 27-2   [The Federal Estate Tax p. 27-19]

A.   Note that the objective of the formula is to compute a tax on the **Taxable Estate**, i.e., the transfer of assets by the decedent at or after his death.

B.   However, to compute this tax using the unified, cumulative, progressive transfer tax system, taxable gifts made after 1976 must enter the calculation. In effect, the Taxable Estate is *put onto stilts*, by adding the post-1976 taxable gifts, so that the Taxable Estate may be put into higher brackets in the progressive transfer tax rate structure than otherwise might be the case.

C.   For purposes of this formula, "Taxable Gifts" has a precise technical definition. See III. D of this outline.

D.   If the decedent paid a gift tax on his lifetime gifts, such taxes are used to reduce the transfer tax payable at death. In effect, this reduction brings the Taxable Estate back off the *stilts* that are used to compute the tax.

E.   Persons subject to the tax.

1.   The federal estate tax is applied to the entire taxable estate of a decedent who, at the time of death, was a US citizen or resident.

2.   For the nonresident alien, the estate tax is imposed only on the value of any of the decedent=s property located within the US.

VII.   Elements of the Gross Estate   [Gross Estate p. 27-19]

A.   Property owned outright by the decedent is included in his or her **gross estate**. There are few exceptions to this definition.

1.   Generally, all personal- and business-use, tangible and intangible property is included, wherever it is situated (IRC §2033).

2.   This property is valued at its fair market value at the date of the decedent's death (or on the alternative valuation date if applicable). Exceptions to this rule exist, however, for certain farm and business property, and to alleviate potential hardships that may occur when a large estate tax is due from an illiquid estate (IRC §§2031, 2032, 2032A).

B.   The gross estate includes proceeds from life insurance policies on the decedent's life, if the policy (1) is payable to, or for the benefit of, the estate; or, (2) was under the control of the decedent before his death, e.g., as to the designation of beneficiaries or the ability to cancel the policy (IRC §2042). This provision includes whole life and term insurance, group life policies, and travel and accident insurance, including those policies provided by an employer.

C.   Policies owned by the decedent, payable upon the death of some other party, are included in the decedent's gross estate, but under §2033, i.e., not under §2042. The amount includible in the gross estate is the replacement value of the policy on the other person's life.

D.   Property owned jointly by the decedent and another party may enter the gross estate (IRC §2040).

1.   One-half of the value of property owned jointly by spouses is included automatically in the gross estate of the first spouse to die, regardless of whether the spouses contributed equally to the original purchase of the asset.

2.   Property held in a joint tenancy with someone other than the decedent's spouse is included fully in the decedent's gross estate.

3.   To the extent, however, that the executor can prove that the co-owner(s) contributed to the original purchase price of the asset, a pro rata exclusion from the gross estate is allowed, equal to:

Surviving Co-owner's Contributions   x   **FMV of Asset**
Total Contributions

4.   Community property, and property held as a tenancy in common, are included in the gross estate, according to the decedent's proportionate ownership rights.

5.   Dower and curtesy interests are included in the gross estate of the first spouse to die (IRC §2034).

E.   If the decedent made a gift of some property during his or her lifetime, but the gift was in some measure *incomplete*, the property is included in the gross estate. Such property is valued in the gross estate at the date of death, and not the date of the original gift! For transfer tax purposes, a gift is *incomplete* if:

1.   the donor-decedent continued to use the property or receive income from the property after the *gift*, or he or she could designate who could use the property or receive the income (IRC §2036); or,

2.   the donor-decedent had the right to cancel the *gift* or to change its terms (IRC §2038).

F.   Survivorship provisions of most pension plans are included in the gross estate. This includes balances in IRA, Keogh, Roth, §401(k), and §403(b) plans. (IRC §2039)

G.   An adjustment is made to the gross estate with respect to taxable gifts made by the decedent **within three years** of his/her death. The gross estate includes:

1.   Gift taxes paid on gifts made within three years of death; and,

2.   The face value of life insurance policies on the decedent, if the decedent

made gifts of such policies within three years of his/her death. This adjustment is in addition to that for certain *incomplete* gifts (See E., above) (IRC §2035). Of course, the estate still claims a credit for the gift taxes paid, even if the taxes are included in the gross estate.

VIII. Death Tax Deductions [Taxable Estate p. 27-28]
    A.   The expenses of administering the estate, including executor's commissions, legal and accounting fees, and certain selling expenses, are allowed as a deduction from the gross estate.
    B.   Other deductions include certain funeral expenses for the decedent; accrued property, gift, and income taxes; casualty or theft losses that occur during the administration of the estate; and, other debts, mortgages, and liabilities of the decedent, for which there was personal liability (IRC §§2053, 2054). If the decedent held non-recourse financing on any property, the asset should be included in the gross estate "net" of the related liability.
    C.   A deduction is allowed for charitable bequests directed by the will, or initiated before death (IRC §2055). The bequest must be mandatory in amount, but a third party can have the power to select the specific charitable beneficiary.
    D.   If the surviving spouse is a U.S. citizen, transfers to the decedent's spouse qualify for the marital deduction.
        1.   There is no dollar limitation on the amount of property transferred for which a marital deduction can be claimed (IRC §2056).
        2.   The property can pass to the surviving spouse as heir of the will, co-owner of jointly held property, or beneficiary of a trust or life insurance policy.
        3.   When the property is subject to a mortgage or other encumbrance, it passes net of the corresponding liability. However, if the executor is required under the terms of the decedent's will or under local law to discharge the mortgage or other encumbrance out of other assets of the estate or to reimburse the surviving spouse, the payment or reimbursement constitutes an additional interest passing to the surviving spouse.
        4.   Generally, however, to claim a marital deduction the property must be of a nature such that it will be included in the survivor's gross estate, if it is not consumed during the survivor's lifetime.
        5.   A *terminable interest* does not qualify for the marital deduction. A marital deduction, however, is allowed for transfers of qualified terminable interest property **(QTIP)**.
        6.   In general, the marital deduction is not allowed for transfers to a spouse that is not a U.S. citizen unless the property transferred satisfies the normal requirements for the martial deduction and passes to a qualified domestic trust **(QDT)**.
    E.   A deduction is allowed for death taxes paid to a state or locality (IRC §2058).

IX. Death Tax Credits [Estate Tax Credits p. 27-34]
    A.   The unified transfer tax credit is applied against the tax on total taxable transfers (IRC §2010).
        1.   The entire amount of the credit is applied, regardless of whether some or all of the credit was used relative to lifetime gift activity of the decedent.
        2.   The credit, however, effectively is used only once, since the tax to which it applies is included in the estate tax formula. The tax on total transfers includes the taxes computed on those gifts (i.e., the "stilts" concept).

B.   To mitigate the possibly harsh effects of multiple death taxation, credits are allowed for foreign death taxes paid, and for federal death taxes paid on property acquired by the decedent shortly before his or her own death (IRC §§2013, 2014).

X.   Generation Skipping Transfer Tax   [The Generation-Skipping Transfer Tax p. 27-37]
A.   The generation skipping transfer tax **(GSTT)** is imposed in situations in which a younger generation is bypassed in favor of a later generation. The tax applies both to the lifetime transfers and to transfers by death.
B.   This tax is imposed at the highest transfer tax rate for the year of the transfer.
C.   In determining the transfers subject to the generation skipping tax, each grantor is entitled to a $2 million exemption.

Exhibit 27-1
TRANSFER TAX FORMULA--TRANSFERS BY GIFT

TOTAL GIFTS to which the gift tax might apply

- GIFT TAX DEDUCTIONS   (charitable and marital deductions)

- <u>ANNUAL EXCLUSIONS</u>

TAXABLE GIFTS MADE THIS YEAR

+ <u>TAXABLE GIFTS MADE IN ALL PRIOR YEARS</u>

<u>TOTAL TAXABLE GIFTS</u>

TAX ON TOTAL TAXABLE GIFTS   (Consult Rate Schedule)

- TAX PAYABLE ON PRIOR GIFTS *

- <u>UNUSED UNIFIED TRANSFER TAX CREDIT</u>

<u>GIFT TAX PAYABLE THIS YEAR</u>

*   **Computed without regard to the unified transfer tax credit at the rates currently in effect, regardless of the actual rate existing at the time of the gift.**

Exhibit 27-2
TRANSFER TAX FORMULA--TRANSFER AT DEATH

GROSS ESTATE

-    **DEDUCTIONS**   **(expenses, indebtedness, taxes, losses, charitable bequests, state death tax, and marital deduction)**

TAXABLE ESTATE

+   **TAXABLE GIFTS**   **made after 1976**

     TAXABLE TRANSFERS   **Consult Rate Schedule**

TENTATIVE TRANSFER TAX

-    **ACTUAL GIFT TAXES PAID**   **on post-1976 gifts**

-    **CREDITS**   **(unified credit, credit for tax on prior transfers, and foreign death tax credit)**

     TRANSFER TAX AT DEATH   **on Taxable Estate**

TEST FOR SELF-EVALUATION - CHAPTER 27

True or False

Indicate which of the following statements are true or false by circling the correct answer.

T   F   1.   The annual federal gift tax exclusion is $12,000 per donor.

T   F   2.   To be exempt from federal gift tax, a property settlement transfer must be included in the divorce decree.

T   F   3.   A gift is a transfer of property that is made out of love or admiration for the donee. A mere transfer of property for less than adequate consideration is not sufficient to constitute a gift.

T   F   4.   For gift tax purposes, the unexhausted unified transfer tax credit is the unified transfer tax credit for the applicable year, less all prior gift taxes paid.

T   F   5.   For gift tax purposes, only the post-1976 taxable gifts are added into the transfer tax base.

T   F   6.   A donor's taxable gifts are equal to the value of the gifts given during the year reduced by the marital and charitable deductions.

T   F   7.   If the decedent's retirement annuity has no survivorship feature, it will be excluded from the gross estate.

T   F   8.   The effect of a disclaimer is to pass the property to someone else.

T   F   9.   All property owned by the decedent as a joint tenant with one other party who is not his or her spouse is included in the gross estate of the first co-owner to die, to the extent of 50 percent of the fair market value of the property.

T   F   10.   The federal gift tax is reduced only by the unexhausted portion of the unified transfer tax credit.

T   F   11.   The generation skipping transfer tax applies only to lifetime transfers.

T   F   12.   To elect gift-splitting, the spouses must be legally married to each other at the end of the tax year.

Fill-in-the-Blanks

Complete the following statements with the appropriate word(s) or amount(s).

1.   Except for gifts of _____ interests, a donor is allowed an annual exclusion of $_____ per donee.

2.   For federal gift tax purposes, a gift is defined as a _____ _____ _____ for less than _____ and _____ _____.

3.   The highest transfer tax rate is _____.

4.   Gift-splitting allows for a more optimal use of both the _____ _____ _____ _____ and the _____ _____ of the electing spouses.

5.   A _____ interest is an unrestricted right to the immediate use, possession, or enjoyment of property or the income therefrom.

6.   Proceeds of a life insurance policy on the decedent will be included in his or her gross estate if he or she possessed _____ _____ _____ over the policy.

7.   To mitigate the possibly harsh effects of multiple transfer taxation, tax credits are allowed for _____ _____, and _____ _____ taxes paid.

8.   Regardless of the type of property involved, any federal gift tax paid on a taxable gift made by the decedent within _____ _____ of his or her death must be included in his gross estate.

9.   The federal death tax applies to every _____ or _____ of the United States, and to property situated in the United States that is owned by others.

10.   For estate tax purposes, the transfer tax base includes both the _____ _____ and any taxable gifts made by the decedent after 19__.

11.   The 2007 unified credit for the estate tax allows an exemption equivalent of _____.

12.   A _____ is a refusal by a person to accept property designated to pass to that person.

Multiple Choice

_____   1.   The donor takes out a life insurance policy on her own life and names Donee to be the beneficiary of the policy. The face amount of the policy is $600,000. Annual premiums total $14,000. The donor pays these premiums for five years. She is still living. What is the total amount of taxable gifts by Donor with respect to the policy over the five years?
        a. $0.
        b. $15,000.
        c. $20,000.
        d. $70,000.
        e. $600,000.

_____ 2.   Donee owns a life insurance policy on Donor's life. Donee is the beneficiary. The face amount of the policy is $600,000. Annual premiums total $14,000. Donor pays these premiums for five years. She is still living. What is the total amount of taxable gifts by Donor with respect to the policy over the five years?
a. $0.
b. $10,000.
c. $20,000.
d. $70,000.
e. $600,000.

_____ 3.   Donor takes out a life insurance policy on her own life and names Donee to be the beneficiary of the policy. The face amount of the policy is $600,000. Annual premiums total $14,000. Donor dies after making five years of premium payments, and Donee receives the face value of the policy. What is the total amount of taxable gifts by Donor with respect to the policy over the five years?

a. $0.
b. $20,000.
c. $70,000.
d. $600,000.
e. $670,000.

_____ 4.   Donor puts $100,000 into a joint savings account in 2006. Donee, the only other (equal) co-owner of the account, puts $19,000 into the account. What is Donor's 2006 taxable gift to Donee?
a. $0.
b. $30,000.
c. $40,000.
d. $100,000.

_____ 5.   Donor puts $100,000 into a joint savings account in 2006. Donee, the only other (equal) co-owner of the account, puts $19,000 into the account. Donee withdraws $35,000 from the account in 2007. Compute Donor's 2007 taxable gift to Donee.
a. $0.
b. $4,000.
c. $16,000.
d. $35,000.

_____ 6.   Maria died in September of Year 1. At the time of her death, she had the following interests in property.

Property	*FMV at Death*
Cash invested in a CD that matures January Year 2.	$115,000
Face amount of life insurance policy on Maria's life purchased by her and given to her brother Tony in Year 0.	$175,000
Apartment house owned jointly with Tony. Maria paid 70% of the original cost and Tony paid the remaining 30%. Tony can prove that he made the 30% contribution to purchase the property.	$300,000
Clothes, jewelry, and furniture.	$90,000

Maria gave Tony $25,000 in cash in August Year 1. No gift tax was due, because of the annual exclusion and the unified credit.

What is Maria's gross estate?
a. $415,000.
b. $440,000.
c. $500,000.
d. $590,000.
e. $680,000.

_____ 7. Maria died in September of Year 1. At the time of her death, she had the following interests in property.

Property	FMV at Death
Cash invested in a CD that matures January Year 2.	$115,000
Face amount of life insurance policy on Maria's life purchased by her and given to her brother Tony in Year 0.	$175,000
Apartment house owned jointly with Tony. Maria paid 70% of the original cost and Tony paid the remaining 30%. Tony can prove that he made the 30% contribution to purchase the property.	$300,000
Clothes, jewelry, and furniture.	$90,000

Maria gave Tony $25,000 in cash in August Year 1. No gift tax was due, because of the annual exclusion and the unified credit. Tony is Maria's husband. Maria's gross estate is:
a. $205,000.
b. $340,000.
c. $415,000.
d. $530,000.
e. $590,000.

_____ 8. Neal died in December Year 1, when he had the following interests in property.

Property	FMV at Death
Face amount of group life insurance policy paid for by employer. Neal had the right to change beneficiaries.	$560,000
Life interest in a trust established by Neal's father; Neal had a special power of appointment.	140,000
Residence owned by Neal and his wife as joint tenants. His wife paid for the home entirely.	220,000
Neal gave his son IBM stock in Year 0, when it was worth $510,000. Neal and his wife did not elect gift-splitting. A $59,500 gift tax was paid.	600,000

What is Neal's gross estate?
a. $670,000.
b. $729,500.
c. $869,500.
d. $1,170,000.

e. $1,270,000.

_____   9.   Neal died in December Year 1, when he had the following interests in property.

Property	FMV at Death
Face amount of group life insurance policy paid for by employer.	
Neal had the right to change beneficiaries.	$560,000
Life interest in a trust established by Neal's father;	
Neal had a special power of appointment.	140,000
Residence owned by Neal and his wife as joint tenants.	
His wife paid for the home entirely.	220,000
Neal gave his son IBM stock in Year 0, when it was worth	
$510,000. Neal and his wife did not elect gift-splitting.	
A $59,500 gift tax was paid.	600,000

Neal's taxable transfers total:
a. $0.
b. $110,000.
c. $1,060,000.
d. $1,070,000.
e. $1,119,500.

_____   10.   The decedent owned land with her brother, as equal joint tenants. The land cost $100,000, and the decedent's brother can prove that he paid $40,000 of this amount. The decedent paid the balance. At her death, the land has a fair market value of $400,000. With respect to the land, decedent's gross estate includes:
a. $100,000.
b. $200,000.
c. $240,000.
d. $400,000.

_____   11.   The decedent owned land with her brother, as equal tenants in common.. The land cost $100,000, and the decedent's brother can prove that he paid $40,000 of this amount. The decedent paid the balance. At her death, the land has a fair market value of $400,000. With respect to the land, decedent's gross estate includes:
a. $100,000.
b. $200,000.
c. $240,000.
d. $400.000.

_____   12.   The decedent owned land with her husband, as equal joint tenants. The land cost $100,000, and the decedent's brother can prove that he paid $40,000 of this amount. The decedent paid the balance. At her death, the land has a fair market value of $400,000. With respect to the land, decedent's gross estate includes:
a. $100,000.
b. $200,000.
c. $240,000.
d. $400.000.

_____   13.   The decedent owned land with her brother, as equal joint tenants. The land cost

$100,000, and the decedent's brother contributed $40,000 of this amount, but the brother has lost the records that prove his $40,000 contribution. The decedent paid the balance. At her death, the land has a fair market value of $400,000. With respect to the land, decedent's gross estate includes:
    a. $200,000.
    b. $240,000.
    c. $280,000.
    d. $400,000.

14. The decedent's will allows the executor to "donate from my estate to Green Bay University, a qualifying charity, an amount not less than $100,000." The executor pays $210,000 to the university. The allowable federal estate tax charitable contribution deduction for this estate is:
    a. $0.
    b. $100,000.
    c. $105,000 (50% limitation).
    d. $210,000.

15. The decedent's wife, pursuant to the will and other proper documents, receives $200,000 life insurance proceeds in which the decedent held the incidents of ownership; real estate worth $315,000; and, the decedent's share of joint tenancy property. The total fair market value of the jointly owned property is $100,000. The decedent's gross estate equals $1,000,000. No other deductions are allowed. The allowable marital deduction is:
    a. $365,000.
    b. $500,000 (50% limitation).
    c. $565,000.
    d. $615,000.
    e. $619,500.

16. The decedent gave to his sister in 2006 a painting worth $70,000. As his unified transfer tax credit had been exhausted, he paid a $22,200 federal gift tax. When the decedent died in 2008, the painting was worth $50,000. With respect to the painting, the decedent's gross estate must include:
    a. $0.
    b. $22,200.
    c. $50,000.
    d. $70,000.

17. The decedent gave to his sister in 2006 a painting worth $70,000. As his unified transfer tax credit had been exhausted, he paid a $22,200 federal gift tax. When the decedent died in 2008, the painting was worth $50,000. With respect to the painting, what is the exemption equivalent for the unified transfer tax credit that will affect the decedent's estate tax return?
    a. $0.
    b. $780,800.
    c. $1 million.
    d. $2 million.

18. Mary made a revocable gift of her home, valued at $400,000, to her son. When Mary died ten years later, the home was worth $700,000. With respect to the home, Mary's gross estate includes:

        a. $0.
        b. $300,000.
        c. $400,000.
        d. $700,000.

_____   19.   Art paid $50,000 of Jim's medical bills and gave him a car valued at $8,000. Jim is Art's brother. What is the amount of Art's taxable gifts for the year?
        a. $0.
        b. $8,000.
        c. $48,000.
        d. $58,000.

Short Answer

1.   Review the estate and gift tax formulas, noting their similarities and differences.

2.   Discuss property that would make good and bad candidates for lifetime gifts.

3.   Discuss tax planning considerations concerning the estate tax marital deduction.

4.   The decedent's gross estate was valued at $1,700,000. Allowable federal estate tax deductions totaled $150,000. The decedent died on 9-10-07. The decedent had given a taxable gift of $550,000 to her brother, on 11-10-93. The gift tax that she paid on this transfer was $18,500. The decedent made no other lifetime gifts. Compute her federal death tax payable. Ignore state death taxes.

5.   Compute how much should be included in the decedent's gross estate for each item below. Each case is independent.

a.   The decedent was a minister. At death, she owned the following.

	Basis	Fair Market Value
Auto, artwork, furniture	$20,000	$12,000
Clothes, kitchenware	1,800	450
Bibles, religious materials	1,000	965

b.   At the date of his death, decedent held $20,000 of promissory notes issued by him to his daughter. In his will, decedent forgives these notes, relieving his daughter of any obligation to make payments thereon.

c.   The decedent's employer provided her with a $50,000 group-term life insurance policy on her life. The decedent paid none of the premiums; her surviving husband received the policy proceeds.

d.   The decedent owned a life insurance policy on her own life. The policy proceeds were $35,000. The decedent gave the policy to her beneficiary-husband five years before her death.

e.   The decedent owned a life insurance policy, proceeds $35,000 on the life of her husband. The cost of a comparable policy was $8,100.

f.   The decedent died intestate. The applicable state statute guarantees that her husband will receive a one-third interest from the $450,000 gross estate, as a curtesy interest.

g.   The decedent's collection included a painting worth $75,000. It was purchased by the decedent's wife from her separate funds after their marriage. The spouses lived in California, a community property state.

h. The decedent owned a painting worth $75,000. It was purchased by the decedent and his wife as joint tenants. The decedent contributed $6,000 of the original $10,000 purchase price.

i. The decedent owned a painting worth $75,000. It was purchased by the decedent and his sister as joint tenants.

j. The decedent transferred an asset worth $10,000 to a trust. He retained an income interest in the trust for eight years after the transfer; the trust corpus was to go to the decedent's grandchild thereafter. The asset was worth $30,000 when the decedent died, five years after the transfer.

SOLUTIONS TO CHAPTER 27 QUESTIONS

True or False

1.   F $12,000 per *donee*. [Annual Exclusion p. 27-14]
2.   F   Property settlements can escape gift tax if the divorce occurs within a prescribed period of time; the settlement, however, is not required to be included in the divorce decree. [Certain Property Settlements p. 27-12]
3.   F   This is the definition of a gift for income tax, but not transfer tax purposes. [General Considerations p. 27-10]
4.   F   It is less all prior gift taxes "deemed" paid. [Computing the Federal Gift Tax p. 27-16]
5.   F   All prior gifts are added back. [Computing the Federal Gift Tax p. 27-16]
6.   F   The value of the gifts also must be reduced by the annual exclusions to arrive at the amount of taxable gifts. [Annual Exclusion p. 27-14]
7.   T   At the date of death, the annuity terminates. [Annuities p. 27-22]
8.   T   The recipient is identified in the will or trust document. [Disclaimers p. 27-13]
9.   F   100% is included, unless a contribution by the other party can be proven. [Joint Interests p. 27-23]
10.   T   The available credit is reduced by gift taxes paid and deemed paid in prior years. [The Deemed-Paid Adjustment p. 27-15]
11.   F   The GSTT applies both to lifetime transfers and transfers by death. [The Generation-Skipping Transfer Tax p. 27-37]
12.   F   The spouses must be legally married to each other at the time of the gift. [Marital Deduction p. 27-29]

Fill-in-the-Blanks

1.   future, $12,000 [Annual Exclusion p. 27-14]
2.   transfer of property, full, adequate consideration [Nature of the Taxes p. 27-2]
3.   45% [Computing the Federal Estate Tax p. 27-33]
4.   unified transfer tax credits, annual exclusions [The Election to Split Gifts by Married Persons p. 27-16]
5.   present [Annual Exclusion p. 27-14]
6.   incidents of ownership [Life Insurance p. 27-26]
7.   federal gift, foreign death [Estate Tax Credits p. 27-34]
8.   three years [Adjustments for Gifts Made Within Three Years of Death p. 27-21]
9.   citizen, resident [Nature of the Taxes p. 27-2]
10.   taxable estate, 1976 [Formula for the Federal Estate Tax p. 27-5]
11. $2 million [Role of the Unified Tax Credit p. 27-6]
12.   disclaimer [Disclaimers p. 27-13]

Multiple Choice

1.   a   Naming another as a beneficiary of a life insurance policy does not constitute a gift. [Incomplete Transfers p. 27-12]
2.   b   5 x ($14,000 - $12,000 annual exclusion). [Life Insurance p. 27-26]
3.   a   The life insurance proceeds constitute a testamentary transfer. [Life Insurance p.

4. a   27-26]
A gift occurs only in the year, and to the extent, that a co-owner withdraws more from the account than he or she contributed. [Joint Interests p. 27-23]

5. b   ($35,000 - $19,000 contribution - $12,000 annual exclusion) [Joint Interests p. 27-23]

6. d   [$115,000 + $175,000 (the life insurance was transferred within three years of death) + $210,000 (70% x $300,000) + $90,000] [Joint Interests p. 27-23]

7. d   [$115,000 + $175,000 + (50% x $300,000) + $90,000] [Joint Interests p. 27-23]

8. b   [$560,000 + (50% x $220,000) + $59,500]   [Joint Interests p. 27-23]

9. e   ($729,500 - $110,000 marital deduction + $500,000 post-1976 taxable gifts) [Formula for the Federal Estate Tax p. 27-5]

10. c   (60% x $400,000). [Joint Interests p. 27-23]

11. b   (50% x $400,000). [Joint Interests p. 27-23]

12. b   (50% x $400,000). [Joint Interests p. 27-23]

13. d   The entire value must be included in the decedent's gross estate. [Joint Interests p. 27-23]

14. a   The amount of a deductible charitable contribution must be specified in the decedent's will. [Transfers to Charity p. 27-29]

15. c   [$200,000 + $315,000 + (50% x $100,000)]. [Marital Deduction p. 27-29]

16. b   Gift taxes paid on gifts made within three years of death are included in the gross estate. [Adjustments for Gifts Made Within Three Years of Death p. 27-21]

17. d   The exemption equivalent for the estate tax currently is $2 million.   [Unified Tax Credit p. 27-34]

18. d   Since the gift was revocable, the FMV at the date of death is included in the gross estate. [Revocable Transfers p. 27-22]

19. a   ($8,000 - annual exclusion) The payment of Jim's medical bills is not subject to the gift tax. [Certain Excluded Transfers p. 27-12]

Short Answer

1. Differences -   Selection of prior taxable gifts, and the tax thereon
                          Treatment of unified credit
    Similarities -   Rate schedule
                          Amount of unified credit, since 7-1-77
                          Charitable and marital deductions
                          Cumulative application

    See Exhibits 27-1 and 27-2.   [Nature of the Taxes p. 27-2]

2. Good candidate -   Non-income producing (except to a low-bracket donee)
                          Depreciable, with a high fair market value, but a low adjusted basis
                          Group-term life insurance
    Bad candidate -   Low basis, high fair market value
                          Installment notes
                          High-income producing (except to a low-bracket donee)

    [The Federal Gift Tax p. 27-10]

3. When both spouses are US citizens, the payment of an immediate federal estate tax is unnecessary, due to the unlimited marital deduction. However, the unified credit of the

first spouse to die should not be wasted.

The present value of the federal death tax, if it is deferred by a large marital deduction, may be very small. However, the value of the asset may grow, due to inflation or appreciation, in the hands of the survivor.

State death taxes may not allow an unlimited martial deduction.

A terminable interest does not qualify for the marital deduction. With the proper election, a marital deduction is allowed for transfers of qualified terminable interest property (QTIP).

[Approaches to the Marital Deduction p. 27-40]

4.
Gross estate	$1,700,000	(already includes the $18,500 gift tax)
Deductions	- 150,000	
Taxable Estate	$1,550,000	
Adjusted Taxable Gifts	+ 550,000	
Taxable Transfers	$2,100,000	

Tentative Transfer Tax	$ 828,800
Gift Tax Paid	- 18,500
Unified Credit	- 780,800
Transfer Tax at Death	$ 29,500

[Computing the Federal Estate Tax p. 27-34]

5.
a.	$13,415	Fair market value.
b.	$20,000	Fair market value.
c.	$50,000	The decedent held the policy's incidents of ownership .
d.	$0	The decedent's spouse owned the policy.
e.	$8,100	IRC §2033.
f.	$450,000	The gross estate includes the curtesy interest.
g.	$37,500	Community property.
h.	$37,500	IRC §2040.
i.	$75,000	Unless the decedent's sister can prove her own contribution to the original purchase price.
j.	$30,000	IRC §2036 (retained life estate).

[Gross Estate p. 27-19]

Chapter 28

Income Taxation of Trusts and Estates

CHAPTER HIGHLIGHTS

Trusts and estates are distinct taxable entities, separate from their beneficiaries, trustees, and grantors. Both of these entities can be useful for estate and gift tax planning purposes. In this chapter, we examine the income tax consequences of creating and operating trusts and estates, as they are presented in Subchapter J of the Code.

I. Definitions [An Overview of Subchapter J p. 28-2]
    A. An estate is a temporary entity, used to collect, preserve, and distribute the assets of the decedent, and satisfy his or her outstanding liabilities. Parties involved include the decedent, his or her beneficiaries, and the executor or administrator of the estate. The term of the estate will be monitored closely by the Internal Revenue Service. The estate is ignored for tax purposes if the Service believes that the existence of the entity has been prolonged unduly. The assets of the probate estate are not identical to the decedent's assets that are subject to the federal estate tax. For instance, some assets included in the gross estate are disposed of outside of the probate estate, e.g., life insurance proceeds and jointly-owned property.
    B. A trust is an entity that protects, conserves, and distributes the assets contributed to it by the grantor, according to the terms of the trust instrument, and satisfies

attendant liabilities. Parties involved include the grantor, the beneficiaries of the trust, and the trustee. Beneficiaries of a trust fall into two categories: those holding an income interest, who are entitled to receive the trust's accounting income during the term of the trust, and those holding a remainder interest, who will receive the trust principal upon termination of the trust. The term of the trust is dictated by the trust agreement. It could be for a fixed number of years, i.e., a term certain, or it could be measured by the lifetime of one or more individuals. The assets of the trust are only those whose titles are transferred by the grantor to the trustee, and any income earned subsequently on the trust principal (or "corpus").

1.   The Code defines a simple trust as one that:
   a.   Is required to distribute its annual accounting income;
   b.   Makes no distributions of corpus during the year; and,
   c.   Has no charitable organizations as beneficiaries.
2.   A complex trust is defined as any trust other than a simple trust. For any given trust, the classification as a simple or complex trust may change from year to year.

II.   Nature of Trust and Estate Taxation [Nature of Trust and Estate Taxation p. 28-6]
   A.   Generally, the entity acts as a conduit of the taxable income that it receives. Thus, to the extent that such income is distributed or deemed distributed by the entity, it is taxable to the

> **KEY TERMS**
> ▶ Income, Remainder interest
> ▶ Distribution deduction
> ▶ Distributable net income
> ▶ First, second-tier distribution
> ▶ Entity accounting income

beneficiary. Taxable income retained by the entity is taxable to the entity itself. Taxable income of the entity is reported on Form 1041, which is due 3 1/2 months after the end of the entity's taxable year. The executor must file a return if the estate has gross income of at least $600 for the year. The trustee must file a Form 1041 if the trust either receives gross income of at least $600 for the year or has any taxable income.
   B.   In any given year, the alternative minimum tax (AMT) may apply to a trust or estate. However, few of these entities generally will incur the tax, unless they are engaged in the active conduct of certain types of businesses.
      1.   In general, derivation of alternative minimum taxable income (AMTI) for a trust or estate follows the rules that apply to individual taxpayers.
      2.   The entity is allowed a $22,500 annual exemption amount which phases out at a rate of one-fourth of the amount by which AMTI exceeds $75,000.
   C.   The entity may elect any tax accounting method that is allowed by the Code for individual taxpayers. An estate may elect to use a fiscal year for tax purposes. However, all trusts, except certain charitable trusts and tax-exempt trusts, must adopt a calendar taxable year.
   D.   An estate is allowed a $600 annual personal exemption. Trusts that are required to distribute their accounting income currently receive a $300 exemption. All other trusts are limited to a $100 annual exemption.

III.   Taxable Income Computation - See Exhibit 28-1 [Taxable Income of Trusts and Estates p. 28-9]
   A.   The entity's accounting (or "state law") income is determined by the trust instrument or will. Where such document is silent, state laws determine whether

an item is to be allocated to the income or remainder beneficiary. For a simple trust, trust accounting income is the amount that is paid or deemed paid to the income beneficiary. As determined below, some or all of this amount is taxable to the recipient. Generally, depreciation expense, capital gains and losses, casualty gains and losses, and one-half of administration expenses are allocated to corpus. Other income items, operating expenses, and the remaining one-half of administration expenses generally are allocated to income. The grantor or decedent can alter these conventions in the trust agreement or will.

B.   Computation Guidelines

1.   Gross income of the entity, as defined in IRC §61, is the starting point for determining the taxable income of the entity. For the most part, this amount is computed as it would be for an individual. For instance, municipal bond interest is exempt from gross income, and the deduction for an entity's net capital losses is limited to $3,000 per year. The gross income of the entity also includes income in respect of a decedent (IRD).

2.   The tax basis for property controlled by the entity is computed as it would be for an individual. Property acquired by the trust or estate from a decedent generally takes a basis equal to the property's fair market value at the date of the decedent's death. Other property acquired by a trust receives a carryover basis from the grantor, as adjusted by §1015 for federal gift taxes paid, and increased by any gain (or decreased by loss) recognized by the grantor upon the transfer.

3.   Generally, no gain or loss is recognized by the entity upon distribution of assets to a beneficiary under the will or trust agreement. However, there are several exceptions to this general rule.

    a.   When property that has appreciated or declined in value in the hands of the entity is distributed in lieu of a specific dollar or asset bequest, gain or loss is recognized to the entity.

    b.   If the fiduciary elects, the trust or estate may recognize any realized gain or loss on a property distribution that is not a specific gift, bequest, or charitable contribution, as if the property had been sold to the beneficiary for its fair market value on the date of distribution.

4.   To the extent that they have been included in gross income, charitable contributions are deductible by the entity without any dollar or percentage limitation. The contribution must be paid in the year that the deduction is claimed, or in the immediately following year. In addition, the contribution must be authorized by the will or trust agreement.

5.   Losses on wash sales or between related parties are disallowed.

6.   The trust or estate applies the 2%-of-AGI floor to many of its §212 expenses. For this purpose, AGI is calculated as the greater of:

    a.   The pertinent-year AGI of the trust grantor, or

    b.   The AGI of the entity, computed as though it were an individual.

7.   To the extent that an expenditure is allocable to tax-exempt income, a deduction is disallowed. Typically, a pro-rata allocation is made, using the income elements of entity accounting income. This limitation most often is applied to administration expenses and charitable contributions.

8.   Trusts and estates are allowed cost recovery deductions. However, such deductions are allocated pro rata to recipients of entity accounting income. Thus, a simple trust, for example, receives no such deduction.

9.   The trust or estate computes its own qualified production activities income

amount. Then each beneficiary receives an allocable share of the income and W-2 wages paid, so that the production activities deduction can be computed at the beneficiary level.

10. IRC §642(g) prohibits the deduction of certain expenditures, e.g., administration expenses, on both the estate tax return and the estate's income tax return. Nonetheless, the executor is permitted to allocate such deductions in an optimal manner. The prohibition against double deductions does not apply to expenses in respect of a decedent.

11. A deduction is allowed to the entity for most distributions made to beneficiaries.

12. A trust or estate is allowed a deduction for casualty or theft losses not covered by insurance or other arrangement.

13. Net operating losses of the entity are subject to carryover provisions, i.e., carry back two years and carry forward twenty years. In the year of the termination of the trust or estate, unused net operating and capital loss carryforwards are "distributed" to the income beneficiaries.

C. The distribution deduction is limited to the lesser of distributable net income (DNI) of the entity (less any net tax-exempt income that is included in distributable net income), or the amount actually distributed to the beneficiaries during the year. Distributable net income equals entity taxable income before the distribution deduction, with the following adjustments:

1. Add back the entity's personal exemption.

2. Add tax-exempt income, net of disallowed deductions attributable to such income.

3. Remove capital transactions of the entity; i.e., subtract net long-term capital gains or add back the net capital loss allocated to corpus.

D. Beneficiaries are taxed on the entity accounting income that they receive, or in the case of a simple trust, the accounting income that they are deemed to have received. However, such taxable income is limited to distributable net income allocable to the beneficiaries.

E. The character of the income received by the beneficiaries (e.g., ordinary income, net long-term capital gain, dividend income, exempt income) retains the proportions found within distributable net income, unless the governing instrument specifically allocates different classes of income, deduction, or credit to different beneficiaries.

F. Where the entity has more than one beneficiary, a further proration is required. The amount and character of distributable net income taxable to the beneficiary is based upon the percentage of entity accounting income received.

G. Allocations of distributable net income by estates and complex trusts are determined under a special rule. DNI is allocated first to "first-tier" beneficiaries, i.e., those that are required by the document. To the extent that the DNI of the entity has not been exhausted by the first-tier distributions, it is allocated to "second-tier" beneficiaries. For this purpose, first-tier distributions are those of current entity accounting income required to be distributed by the trust document. All other proper payments are second-tier distributions. The character of the distributions as first- or second-tier is determined by the trust document.

H. NOLs and net capital losses of a trust or estate do not flow through to the entity's beneficiaries. They are subject to the same carryover rules that apply to an individual. A net taxable loss remaining at the end of the entity's last year of existence is allowed to the beneficiaries as a deduction from AGI on the date when the entity's last tax year ends. Other (capital and NOL) losses flow through at the end of the entity's existence, to the beneficiaries in proportion to the corpus assets that are received.

Typically, the trust document should place lower-income and -wealth beneficiaries, such as the very young, the elderly, and those with mental or physical handicaps, on the first tier, as they are more likely to need the cash from the distribution, and they are likely subject to a lower marginal tax rate. This approach also increases the chances that upper-income and -wealth beneficiaries, now on the second tier, will receive non-taxable distributions of corpus.

J.   Entity credits are apportioned among the trust or estate and its beneficiaries on the basis of the accounting income allocable to each.

Exhibit 28-1
TAXABLE INCOME OF TRUSTS, ESTATES, AND BENEFICIARIES

1.   **Determine Entity Accounting Income**

2.   **Determine Entity Taxable Income Before the Distribution Deduction**

3.   **Compute Distributable Net Income and the Distribution Deduction**

4.   **Compute Entity Taxable Income**
     (Step 2 less the deduction determined in Step 3)

5.   **Allocate Distributable Net Income, and its Character, to the**
     Beneficiaries. Use the Tier system, if necessary.

TEST FOR SELF-EVALUATION - CHAPTER 28

True or False

Indicate which of the following statements are true or false by circling the correct answer.

T   F   1.   Distributable net income does not include net tax-exempt interest.

T   F   2.   The distribution deduction is limited to the distributable net income (DNI) of the entity (less any net tax-exempt income that is included in distributable net income), or the amount distributed during the year.

T   F   3.   Depreciation deductions are allocated to trust beneficiaries on their ratable portion of DNI received.

T   F   4.   If the fiduciary elects, a trust or estate may recognize gain or loss on an in-kind property distribution that is not a specified gift, bequest, or charitable contribution.

T   F   5.   The first step in determining the taxable income of a trust or estate is to compute the entity's distribution deduction.

T   F   6.   A beneficiary must include in his or her taxable income the amount of accounting income actually received during the year.

T   F   7.   Trusts and estates are required to use a calendar tax year.

T   F   8.   If the trustee can determine, within guidelines included in the trust document, the timing of income or corpus distributions, the trust is referred to as a reversionary trust.

T   F   9.   The personal exemption allowed for all complex trusts is $100.

T   F   10.   Estates and complex trusts are not subject to a limitation on the extent of their deductible charitable contributions for a given year.

T   F   11.   The assets of the estate are identical to the decedent's assets that are subject to the federal estate tax.

Fill-in-the-Blanks

Complete the following statements with the appropriate word(s) or amount(s).

1.   The parties to an estate include the _____, his or her beneficiaries, and the _____.

2.   The parties to a trust include the _____, his or her beneficiaries, and the _____.

3.   Trusts and estates are treated as _____ taxable _____, but they are taxed using a modified _____ concept.

4.   A trust consists of its _____ (or principal), and its accumulated or distributed _____.

5.   A(n) _____ will be ignored for tax purposes, if the IRS believes that the existence of the entity has been prolonged unduly.

6.   The annual personal exemption for a trust that is required to distribute its current accounting income is $_____. Other trusts receive a $_____ annual exemption.

7.   Beneficiaries of trusts and estates can hold an _____ interest or a _____ interest.

8.   Where a will or trust instrument is silent, _____ _____ determine(s) whether an item is to be allocated to corpus or the income beneficiary.

9.   DNI equals entity taxable income before the _____ _____, plus the entity's personal exemption, plus net _____ income, and less _____ _____ of the entity.

10.   _____ _____ _____ is the maximum amount taxable to the beneficiaries from estate or trust distributions.

11.   If the grantor of a trust retains the remainder interest, such interest is known as a _____ _____.

12.   A trust must be classified as either a _____ trust or a _____ trust.

Multiple Choice

Choose the best answer for each of the following questions.

_____   1.   The income taxation of fiduciary entities is governed largely by which subchapter of the Internal Revenue Code?
          a.   C.
          b.   J.
          c.   K.
          d.   S.

_____   2.   The Roz trust received taxable income of $20,000 and $10,000 of tax-exempt interest. The trustee paid fiduciary fees of $6,000 and a charitable contribution, as authorized by the trust agreement, of $9,000. Roz is allowed a charitable contribution deduction of:
          a. $0.
          b. $3,000.
          c. $6,000.
          d. $9,000.

_____   3.   The Roz trust received taxable income of $20,000 and $10,000 of tax-exempt interest. The trustee paid fiduciary fees of $6,000 and a charitable contribution, as authorized by the trust agreement, of $9,000. Under the trust agreement, a charitable contribution be paid from taxable income. Roz is allowed a charitable contribution deduction of:

    a. $0.
    b. $3,000.
    c. $6,000.
    d. $9,000.

USE THE FOLLOWING INFORMATION FOR PROBLEMS 4 THROUGH 8

A simple trust has one income beneficiary. Its accounting income is $9,000, including $6,000 taxable interest, $4,000 exempt interest, and $1,000 administration expense. No other trust activities occurred during the year.

4.   The beneficiary received from the trust:
    a. $6,000.
    b. $8,700.
    c. $9,000.
    d. $10,000.

5.   The deduction allowable to the trust for administration expense is:
    a. $0.
    b. $400.
    c. $600.
    d. $1,000.

6.   Distributable net income is:
    a. $6,000.
    b. $7,100.
    c. $9,000.
    d. $10,000.

7.   The trust's deduction for distributions to beneficiaries is:
    a. $5,100.
    b. $5,400.
    c. $5,600.
    d. $7,100.
    e. $9,000.

8.   Taxable income of the trust is:
    a.   ($300).
    b. $0.
    c. $1,000.
    d. $5,000.

USE THE FOLLOWING INFORMATION FOR PROBLEMS 9 THROUGH 16

An estate distributes an asset to its sole income beneficiary. The distribution was not a specific bequest. The basis of the asset to the estate is $1,000, and the asset's fair market value is $5,000. Distributable net income of the estate is $9,500. No other distributions are made, nor was an election made by the fiduciary with respect to this distribution.

9.   The estate's distribution deduction, and the beneficiary's taxable income, from the

distribution is:
a. $1,000.
b. $4,000.
c. $5,000.
d. $9,500.

____ 10. The basis of the asset to the beneficiary after the distribution is:
a. $1,000.
b. $4,000.
c. $5,000.
d. $9,500.

____ 11. Gain recognized to the estate due to the distribution is:
a. $0.
b. $1,600 (after the 60% net long-term capital gain deduction).
c. $4,000.
d. $5,000.

____ 12. An executor elected to recognize gain or loss on the distribution of an asset as if the property had been sold to the beneficiary. The estate's distribution deduction, and the beneficiary's taxable income, from the distribution is:
a. $1,000.
b. $4,000.
c. $5,000.
d. $9,500.

____ 13. If the distribution was made in lieu of a specific bequest of $9,000 cash, the gain recognized to the estate due to the distribution, if the executor did not elect to recognize gain or loss on the distribution is:
a. $0.
b. $1,600 (after the 60% net long-term capital gain deduction).
c. $4,000.
d. $5,000.

____ 14. If the distribution was made in lieu of a specific bequest of $9,000 cash, the gain recognized by the beneficiary due to the distribution, if the executor did not elect to recognize gain or loss on the distribution is:
a. $0.
b. $4,000.
c. $5,000.
d. $9,500.

____ 15. If the fair market value of the property is $500, rather than $5,000, the estate's distribution deduction, and the beneficiary's taxable income, from the distribution is:
a. $ 500.
b. $1,000.
c. $4,000.
d. $5,000.
e. $9,500.

____ 16. If the fair market value of the property was $5,000, but the distributable net income was only $400, the estate's distribution deduction, and the beneficiary's taxable income, from the distribution is:

a. $ 400.
b. $ 500.
c. $1,000.
d. $4,000.
e. $5,000.

17.   Under the terms of the Razz Trust, the trustee has complete discretion as to the timing of the distributions from Razz' current accounting income. The depreciation deduction allowable to Razz in the current year is $120,000 and the trust agreement allocates all depreciation expense to corpus. In the current year, the trustee distributes 25% of trust accounting income to Al and 45% of the trust accounting income to Bo. The trust may claim a depreciation deduction of:

a. $0.
b. $30,000.
c. $36,000.
d. $54,000.
e. $120,000.

18.   Which of the following is the annual maximum amount to be included as gross income by all of the income beneficiaries of the trust or estate?

a.   Fiduciary (accounting) income
b.   Entity taxable income
c.   Adjusted gross income, before the standard deduction
d.   Distributable net income
e.   20% of the entity's gross income

19.   The Edgerton Estate generated Distributable Net Income this year of $100,000, one-half of which was tax-exempt interest, and the balance of which was long-term capital gain. Kyle Edgerton, the sole income beneficiary of the Estate, received a distribution of the entire $150,000 fiduciary income of the entity. How does Kyle account for this distribution?

a. $150,000 ordinary income
b. $75,000 long-term capital gain, $75,000 exempt interest
c. $100,000 ordinary income
d. $66,667 long-term capital gain, $33,333 exempt interest
e. $50,000 long-term capital gain, $50,000 exempt interest

20.   The Eagleton Trust generated Distributable Net Income this year of $100,000, one-third of which was portfolio income, and the balance of which was exempt interest. Under the terms of the trust, Clara Eagleton is to receive an annual income distribution of $40,000. At the discretion of the trustee, additional income distributions can be made to Clara, or to Clark Eagleton III. This year, the trustee's distributions to Clara totaled $70,000. Clark received $30,000. How much of the trust's distributable net income is assigned to Clara?

a. $100,000, under the "majority of income" rule
b. $70,000
c. $50,000
d. $30,000
e. $0

_____ 21. The Eagleton Trust generated Distributable Net Income this year of $100,000, one-third of which was portfolio income, and the balance of which was exempt interest. Under the terms of the trust, Clara Eagleton is to receive an annual income distribution of $40,000. At the discretion of the trustee, additional income distributions can be made to Clara, or to Clark Eagleton III. This year, the trustee's distributions to Clara totaled $70,000. Clark received $60,000. How much of the trust's distributable net income is assigned to Clark?
   a. $100,000, under the "generation-skip" rule
   b. $60,000
   c. $46,154
   d. $40,000
   e. $0

_____ 22. The trustee of the Epsilon Trust distributed an asset to Telly, a qualifying income beneficiary. The asset's basis to the trust was $10,000, and its fair market value on the distribution date was $30,000. Which of the following statements is true?
   a.   Lacking any election by the trustee, Telly's basis in the asset is $10,000
   b.   Lacking any election by the trustee, Telly's basis in the asset is stepped up to $30,000
   c.   Lacking any election by the trustee, the trust recognizes $20,000 gross income on the distribution
   d.   Assuming that the trustee made an election under IRC ' 643(e), the trust is allowed a $10,000 distribution deduction for this transaction
   e.   Assuming that the trustee made an election under IRC ' 643(e), Telly recognizes $20,000 gross income on the distribution

_____ 23. Three weeks after Tina died, her brother Tony properly received Tina's last paycheck from her employer. The gross amount of the check was $2,000, and a $150 deduction for state income taxes was subtracted in computing the net amount of the payment. Which of the following statements is true?
   a.   Tony deducts the $150 on his income tax return for the year; no other deduction is allowed for the taxes
   b.   Tina's executor deducts the $150 on Tina's last income tax return
   c.   The $150 is deductible only on the income tax return of Tina's estate
   d.   The $150 is deductible only in computing Tina's Taxable Estate
   e.   The $150 is deductible both on Tony's income tax return and on Tina's estate tax return.

Short Answer

1.   The Bellow Trust has the following activities during Year 2.

Dividend Income	$100,000
Tax-Exempt Interest Income	15,000
Recognized Long-Term Capital Gain, allocated by the trust agreement to income beneficiaries	25,000
Fiduciary's Fees	10,000
Contribution to Mt. Olive Church, Paid on 8-30-Year3 from Year 2 trust accounting income, as authorized by the trust agreement.	20,000
Deduction for Discretionary Beneficiary Distributions (assumed)	98,214

The trustee could, at her discretion, distribute any amount of the B Trust income or corpus during the term of the trust. Compute Bellow's taxable income.

2.   The Cello Trust, a simple trust, receives the following items.

Taxable Income	$ 30,000
Tax-Exempt Interest	10,000
Long-Term Capital Gain - allocated to corpus	5,000
Fees - allocated to income	4,000

a)   Compute Cello's accounting income.

b)   Compute Cello's taxable income before the distribution deduction.

c)   Calculate Cello's distributable net income and the distribution deduction.

d)   Complete the computation of Cello's taxable income.

3.   The DayGlo trust has net rental income of $40,000. The trust agreement allocates to
      corpus:

                    Net Long-Term Capital Gain $10,000
                    Administration Fees   3,000

      a)   Compute the trust's accounting income, required under the agreement to be
            distributed completely every year.

      b)   Compute the trust's distributable net income.

      c)   Compute the trust's taxable income.

      d)   Compute the taxable amount received by the trust beneficiaries. None of the
            beneficiaries are charitable organizations.

4.   a)   The Elbow Trust has distributable net income of $20,000. The trust agreement requires the full distribution of current accounting income. Capital gains are allocated to the income beneficiaries.

The trust recognizes:	Ordinary Income	$30,000
	Tax-Exempt Income	4,000
	Long-Term Capital Gain	2,000
	Trust Accounting Income	$36,000

Compute the nature and amount of the taxable distributions to equal beneficiaries Ankle and Boot.

b)   The Fallow Trust has Distributable Net Income of $18,000. The trust agreement allows additional payments from income and corpus.

Trust Accounting Income is $30,000. Art is guaranteed a payment of $20,000 per year from the trust. During the year, the trust makes payments of $30,000 to Art, and $10,000 to Babs.

Compute the nature and amount of the taxable distributions to Art and Babs.

c)   Assume that Fallow is subject to the same trust agreement as in problem b) above.

Distributable Net Income is $28,000 and trust accounting income is $30,000. The trust makes payments of $20,000 each to Art and Babs.

Compute the nature and amount of the taxable distributions to Art and Babs.

SOLUTIONS TO CHAPTER 28 QUESTIONS

True or False

1. F   DNI includes tax-exempt interest, reduced for allocable deductible expenses. [Gross Income p. 28-12]
2. T   The deductible portion of DNI is used to compute this amount. [Deduction for Distributions to Beneficiaries p. 28-17]
3. F   Depreciation is allocated based on the distributions of trust accounting income. [Ordinary Deductions p. 28-15]
4. T   This is a key planning opportunity for fiduciaries. [Property Distributions p. 28-12]
5. F   The first step in determining taxable income is to compute the accounting income of the entity. [Entity Accounting Income p. 28-9]
6. F   A beneficiary is taxed only on the amount of DNI that is allocated to him or her. [Taxation of Beneficiaries p. 28-21]
7. F   Estates and certain charitable trusts may elect to use a fiscal year. [Tax Accounting Periods, Methods, and Payments p. 28-7]
8. F   The trust is referred to as a sprinkling trust. [An Overview of Subchapter J p. 28-2]
9. F   A trust that is required to distribute all of its income currently is allowed an exemption of $300. All other trusts are allowed a $100 exemption each. [Tax Rates and Personal Exemption p. 28-7]
10. T   No percentage or dollar limitation applies. [Charitable Contributions p. 28-17]
11. F   Some assets included in the gross estate are disposed of outside of the probate estate. [What is an Estate? p. 28-5]

Fill-in-the-Blanks

1. decedent, executor [What is an Estate? p. 28-5]
2. grantor, trustee [What is a Trust? p. 28-4]
3. separate, entities, conduit [Nature of Trust and Estate Taxation p. 28-6]
4. corpus, income [What is a Trust? p. 28-4]
5. estate [What is an Estate? p. 28-5]
6. 300, 100 [Tax Rates and Personal Exemption p. 28-7]
7. income, remainder [What is a Trust? p. 28-4]
8. state laws [Entity Accounting Income p. 28-9]
9. distribution deduction, tax-exempt, capital transactions [Deduction for Distributions to Beneficiaries p. 28-17]
10. distributable net income [Taxation of Beneficiaries p. 28-21]
11. reversionary interest [What is a Trust? p. 28-4]
12. simple, complex [Other Definitions p. 28-4]

Multiple Choice

1. b   Fiduciary entities are addressed in a separate subchapter of the Code. [An Overview of Subchapter J p. 28-2]
2. c   [$9,000 - 10/30($9,000)]. [Charitable Contributions p. 28-17]
3. d   The DNI from which a gift is paid can be specified in the trust document.

[Charitable Contributions p. 28-17]

4.   c   For a simple trust, trust accounting income is the amount that is paid or deemed paid to the income beneficiary. [Entity Accounting Income p. 28-9]

5.   c   [$1,000 - 4/10($1,000)]   [Ordinary Deductions p. 28-15]

6.   c $5,100 (taxable income before distribution deduction) + $300 personal exemption) + $3,600 (net tax-exempt interest). [Deduction for Distributions to Beneficiaries p. 28-17]

7.   b $9,000 (DNI) - $3,600 (tax-exempt component). [Deduction for Distributions to Beneficiaries p. 28-17]

8.   a $5,100 (taxable income before distribution deduction) - $5,400 (distribution deduction). [Deduction for Distributions to Beneficiaries p. 28-17]

9.   a   These amounts are equal to the basis of the assets to the estate. [Property Distributions p. 28-12]

10.   a   The basis of the assets carries over to the beneficiary. [Property Distributions p. 28-12]

11.   a   Unless the estate makes an election, no gain or loss is recognized on the distribution of the asset. [Property Distributions p. 28-12]

12.   c   Because the election was made, the distribution deduction and taxable income are equal to the FMV of the asset. [Property Distributions p. 28-12]

13.   c   [Property Distributions p. 28-12]

14.   a   [Property Distributions p. 28-12]

15.   a   [Property Distributions p. 28-12]

16.   a   The distribution deduction and the beneficiary's taxable income is limited to DNI. [Property Distributions p. 28-12]

17.   c   Since 30% of accounting income was accumulated by the trust, Razz may claim a $36,000 depreciation deduction ($120,000 X 30%). [Ordinary Deductions p. 28-15]

18.   d   This is a key function of DNI. [Taxation of Beneficiaries p. 28-21]

19.   e   The elements of DNI flow through to the beneficiaries. [Taxation of Beneficiaries p. 28-21]

20.   b   This is a key function of DNI. [Taxation of Beneficiaries p. 28-21]

21.   d   Clara receives $40,000 DNI on the first tier. There is now $60,000 DNI remaining, which is allocated pro rata to the second tier beneficiaries. Clark receives $40,000 DNI ($60,000/$90,000 x $60,000) [Distributions by Estates and Complex Trusts p. 28-22]

22.   a   The basis of the assets carries over to the beneficiary. [Property Distributions p. 28-12]

23.   e   IRD is taxed, and DRD is deductible, on both returns. [Income in Respect of a Decedent p. 28-12]

Short Answer

1.   Gross Taxable Income: Dividends $100,000
                                 NLTCG   + 25,000
                                                        $125,000

      Deductions: Distributions (given) $98,214
                  Fees (125/140 x $10,000)   8,929
                  Charitable Contribution

(125/140 x $20,000)	17,857	
Exemption	100	-125,100
Taxable Income		$ (100)

[Deduction for Distributions to Beneficiaries p. 28-17]

2. a)
Taxable Interest	$ 30,000
Exempt Interest	10,000
Fees	(4,000)

Trust Accounting Income (Simple Trust: This amount must be distributed)	$ 36,000

b)
Taxable Interest	$ 30,000
Long-Term Capital Gain of Corpus	5,000
Exemption	(300)
Fees (30/40 x $4,000)	(3,000)
TI before Distribution Deduction	$ 31,700

c)
TI before Distribution Deduction		$ 31,700
Exemption		+ 300
NLTCG of corpus		- 5,000
Exempt interest	$ 10,000	
Disallowed Expenses (10/40 x $4,000)	- 1,000	+ 9,000
Distributable Net Income		$ 36,000

Distribution Deduction ($36,000 - $9,000 Net Exempt Income)	$ 27,000

d)
TI before Distribution Deduction	$ 31,700
Distribution Deduction	- 27,000
Trust Taxable Income	$ 4,700

[Deduction for Distributions to Beneficiaries p. 28-17]

3. a)
Trust Accounting Income	$ 40,000

b)
Net Rental Income	$ 40,000
Long-Term Capital Gain of Corpus	10,000
Fees	(3,000)
Exemption	(300)
TI before Distribution Deduction	$ 46,700

TI before Distribution Deduction	$ 46,700
Exemption	+ 300
NLTCG of Corpus	- 10,000
Distributable Net Income = Distribution Deduction	$ 37,000

c)   TI before Distribution Deduction $ 46,700
       Distribution Deduction   - 37,000

       Trust Taxable Income $ 9,700

d)   Received by beneficiaries (Trust Accounting Income) $ 40,000
                           Taxable [Limit: DNI] $ 37,000
                           Non-Taxable [PLUG]   3,000

[Deduction for Distributions to Beneficiaries p. 28-17]

4.   a)   All distributions to Ankle and Boot are first-tier distributions. The beneficiaries'
          total taxable income is limited to DNI. The character of the amount received is
          determined by the composition of DNI.

Allocation	*Ankle*	*Boot*
Ordinary Income (30/36 x 1/2 each x $20,000 DNI)	$ 8,333	$8,333
Tax-Exempt (4/36 x 1/2 x DNI)	1,111	1,111
Long-Term Capital Gain (2/36 x 1/2 x DNI)	556	556
Non-Taxable (PLUG)	8,000	8,000
Total Distribution (1/2 of accounting income)	$18,000	$18,000

[Character of Income p. 28-23]

b)   First-tier Distribution to Art, $20,000.
       Second-tier Distribution to Art, $10,000; to Babs, $10,000.

       The beneficiaries' taxable income still is limited to DNI of $18,000. DNI is
       exhausted by required first-tier distribution.

Allocation		*Art*	*Babs*
First-tier	- Taxable	$18,000	
	- Non-Taxable	2,000	
Second-tier	- Non-Taxable	$10,000	$10,000

[Distributions by Estates and Complex Trusts p. 28-22]

c)   The first-tier distribution to Art is still $20,000. However, DNI is not exhausted by
       this distribution. Nevertheless, the beneficiaries' taxable income still is limited to
       DNI of $28,000.

       First-tier Distribution to Art, $20,000.
       Second-tier Distribution to Art, $0; to Babs, $20,000.

Allocation		*Art*	*Babs*
First-tier	- Taxable	$20,000	
Second-tier	- Taxable		$ 8,000
	- Non-Taxable		12,000

[Distributions by Estates and Complex Trusts p. 28-22]

Notes

Notes

Notes

Notes

Notes

Notes

Notes

Notes

Notes

Notes